NEW DEVELOPMENTS IN COMPUTABLE GENERAL EQUILIBRIUM ANALYSIS FOR TRADE POLICY

FRONTIERS OF ECONOMICS AND GLOBALIZATION

7

Series Editors:

HAMID BELADI
University of Texas at San Antonio, USA

E. KWAN CHOI
Iowa State University, USA

FRONTIERS OF ECONOMICS AND GLOBALIZATION VOLUME 7

NEW DEVELOPMENTS IN COMPUTABLE GENERAL EQUILIBRIUM ANALYSIS FOR TRADE POLICY

Edited by

John Gilbert

Department of Economics and Finance,
Jon M. Huntsman School of Business, Utah State University,
Logan, UT, USA

Emerald

United Kingdom – North America – Japan
India – Malaysia – China

Emerald Group Publishing Limited
Howard House, Wagon Lane, Bingley BD16 1WA, UK

First edition 2010

British Library Cataloguing in Publication Data
A catalogue record for this book is available from the British Library

ISBN: 978-0-85724-141-2
ISSN: 1574-8715

ABOUT THE SERIES: FRONTIERS OF ECONOMICS AND GLOBALIZATION

This series is aimed at economists and financial economists worldwide and will provide an in-depth look at current global topics. Each volume in the series will focus on specialized topics for greater understanding of the chosen subject and provide a detailed discussion of emerging issues. The target audiences are professional researchers, graduate students, and policy makers. It will offer cutting-edge views on new horizons and deepen the understanding in these emerging topics.

With contributions from leading researchers, each volume will present a fresh look at the current topics. This series will present primarily original works, and employ references appropriate to the topic being explored.

Each volume will bring a set of highly concentrated articles that will provide in-depth knowledge to a target audience, while the entire series will appeal to a wide audience by providing them with deeper knowledge on a broad set of emerging topics in the global economy.

The *Frontiers of Economics and Globalization* series will publish on topics such as:

- Frontiers of Trade Negotiations
- Frontiers of Derivative Pricing
- Frontiers of International Lending and Debt problems
- Frontiers of Economics Integration
- Frontiers of Trade and Environment
- Frontiers of Foreign Exchange
- Frontiers of International Finance
- Frontiers of Growth of Open Economies
- Frontiers of Futures Pricing
- Frontiers of International Financial Markets
- Frontiers of Investment Banking
- Frontiers of Mergers and Acquisitions
- Frontiers of Government Policy and Regulations
- Frontiers of Multi-Sector Growth Models
- Frontiers of Intellectual Property Rights
- Frontiers of Fragmentations and Outsourcing

Hamid Beladi
E. Kwan Choi
Series Editors

ABOUT THE VOLUME: NEW DEVELOPMENTS IN COMPUTABLE GENERAL EQUILIBRIUM ANALYSIS FOR TRADE POLICY

About the editor

John Gilbert is a professor of economics in the Department of Economics and Finance, Jon M. Huntsman School of Business, at Utah State University. He has worked as a consultant for the World Bank, UNESCAP, ADBI, and the Peterson Institute for International Economics, and has published extensively in the area of trade theory and policy, and on the computable general equilibrium analysis of regional trading arrangements.

About the volume

Computable general equilibrium (CGE) modeling is a well-established method for evaluating changes in economic systems, and has found wide application in the evaluation of international trade policy. This volume contains contributions on both the methodology of CGE and applications of those methods to the analysis of contemporary international trade policy issues. The selected applications cover a diverse range of important trade policy topics, including regional economic integration in Latin America, South and Southeast Asia, and the Pacific Rim, the impact of trade policy changes on poverty and income distribution (with applications to Southeast Asia and South Asia), immigration, liberalization of services, and agricultural trade policy. Major CGE models such as the Michigan model, FTAP, LINKAGE, and GTAP and its extensions are well represented in the applications, along with numerous custom models. CGE methods are advanced by chapters on the econometric estimation of constrained optimization models, new approaches to CGE modeling with heterogeneous firms, and new approaches to modeling a wide range of other trade-related issues including illegal immigration, services, biofuels, and economy–ecology interactions.

Aims and scope of the volume

The volume presents new developments in the methodology and practice of CGE techniques as they apply to recent issues in international trade policy. The chapters contained in the volume are written by leading experts in the field. The volume will be of interest to academic researchers working in trade policy analysis and computable/applied general equilibrium, advanced graduate students in international economics, applied researchers in multilateral organizations, and policymakers who need to work with and interpret the results of CGE analysis.

Acknowledgements

I would like to thank Professors Hamid Beladi and E. Kwan Choi for inviting me to edit this volume, and all of the contributing authors for generously offering their time and expertise for the project.

John Gilbert
Editor

LIST OF CONTRIBUTORS

Drew Behnke	Department of Agricultural and Resource Economics, University of California–Berkeley, Berkeley, CA, USA
Drusilla K. Brown	Department of Economics, Tufts University, Medford, MA, USA
Lorenzo Caliendo	Department of Economics, University of Chicago, Chicago, IL, USA
Arthur J. Caplan	Department of Applied Economics, Utah State University, Logan, UT, USA
Philippa Dee	Crawford School of Economics and Government, Australian National University, Canberra, Australian Capital Territory, Australia
Ndiame Diop	World Bank, Washington, DC, USA
Peter B. Dixon	Centre of Policy Studies, Monash University, Clayton, Australia
David C. Finnoff	Department of Economics and Finance, University of Wyoming, Laramie, WY, USA
Joseph F. Francois	Department of Economics, Johannes Kepler University Linz, Linz, Austria
John Gilbert	Department of Economics and Finance, Utah State University, Logan, UT, USA
Alla Golub	Department of Agricultural Economics and Center for Global Trade Analysis, Purdue University, West Lafayette, IN, USA
Thomas Heckelei	Institute of Agricultural Policy, Market Research and Economic Sociology, University of Bonn, Bonn, Germany
Thomas W. Hertel	Department of Agricultural Economics, and Executive Director, Center for Global Trade Analysis, Purdue University, West Lafayette, IN, USA

Torbjörn Jansson	Agrifood Economics Centre, Swedish University of Agricultural Sciences, Uppsala, Sweden
Shikha Jha	Economics and Research Department, Asian Development Bank, Manila, Philippines
Kozo Kiyota	Faculty of Business Administration, Yokohama National University, Yokohama, Japan
Will Martin	Agriculture and Rural Development, Development Research Group, World Bank, Washington, DC, USA
Reza Oladi	Department of Applied Economics, Utah State University, Logan, UT, USA
Fernando Parro	Department of Economics, University of Chicago, Chicago, IL, ISA
Maureen T. Rimmer	Centre of Policy Studies, Monash University, Clayton, Australia
David Roland-Holst	Department of Agricultural and Resource Economics, University of California–Berkeley, Berkeley, CA, USA
Robert Scollay	Department of Economics, University of Auckland, Auckland, New Zealand
Songsak Sriboonchitta	Faculty of Economics, Chiang-Mai University, Chiang Mai, Thailand
Robert M. Stern	Department of Economics and Ford School of Public Policy, University of Michigan, Ann Arbor, MI, USA
Susan Stone	Development Division, Trade and Agriculture Directorate, Organization for Economic Cooperation and Development, Paris, France
Anna Strutt	Department of Economics, University of Waikato, Hamilton, New Zealand
Farzad Taheripour	Center for Global Trade Analysis, Purdue University, West Lafayette, IN, USA
Wallace E. Tyner	Department of Agricultural Economics, Purdue University, West Lafayette, IN, USA
Fan Zhai	Department of Asset Allocation and Strategic Research, China Investment Corporation, Beijing, People's Republic of China

CONTENTS

INTRODUCTION

John Gilbert

Department of Economics and Finance, Jon M. Huntsman School of Business, Utah State University, Logan, UT 84322-3565, USA
E-mail address: jgilbert@usu.edu

Computable general equilibrium, or CGE, is a well-established numerical simulation technique for evaluating the economy-wide effects of changes in an economic system. It has become very widely used throughout the economics discipline, but is perhaps employed most frequently in the analysis of changes in international trade policy, where changes in tariffs and other taxes are often large and almost always involve multiple sectors and/or regions simultaneously. CGE methods, while certainly not without their limitations, have proved very effective at tracking the myriad of feedback and flow-through effects associated with new regional trading agreements and multilateral trade reforms, and have provided a consistent mechanism of analyzing the effects of changes in trade policy and related areas on a diverse range of economic outcomes.

CGE analysis of international trade and trade policy is an exciting and dynamic field. The purpose of this volume is to present selected new developments in the methodology and practice of CGE as they apply to recent issues in international trade policy. The volume contains 13 chapters, written by some of the leading experts in the area. The chapters will be of interest to academic researchers working in trade policy analysis and computable/applied general equilibrium, advanced graduate students in international economics, applied researchers in multilateral organizations, and policymakers who need to work with and interpret the results of CGE analysis.

Aspects of both the methodology of CGE and applications of those methods to the analysis of contemporary international trade policy issues are covered in the volume. The selected applications deal with a diverse range of important trade policy topics covering numerous regions of the globe, including regional economic integration in Latin America, South and Southeast Asia, and the Pacific Rim, the impact of trade policy changes on poverty and income distribution (with applications to Southeast and South Asia), immigration, services reform, and agricultural trade policy. Major CGE models such the Michigan model of world production and trade, LINKAGE, FTAP, and GTAP and its extensions, are well represented in the applications, along with numerous custom models. CGE methods are advanced by chapters on the econometric estimation of constrained optimization models, new approaches to CGE modeling with heterogeneous firms, and new approaches to modeling a wide range of other trade-related issues including illegal immigration, trade in services, biofuels, and economy–ecology interactions.

The chapters in the volume are loosely arranged by topic area, although there is considerable crossover and complementarity across the works. In this introductory note I provide a very brief overview of the contributions.

Until relatively recently, CGE methods have been seen as an alternative to econometrically estimated simulation models, and in many cases one of the primary advantages of CGE is that it can be executed in situations where data are relatively thin (e.g., in the context of developing economies). As Golub, Hertel, Taheripour, and Tyner note in Chapter 6, however, the line between these two methods has become increasingly blurry with recent advances in structural econometric modeling techniques and the statistical estimation of CGE models. CGE models are essentially very large systems of nonlinear equations, and while the most common approach to parameterization in the CGE literature remains calibration, perhaps combined with separate estimation of key model parameters, recent advances have made estimation of constrained optimization problems a feasible alternative. In Chapter 1 of this volume, Torbjörn Jansson and Thomas Heckelei present some significant advances in this area. Their approach involves a combination of numerical techniques and utilization of out-of-sample information via Bayesian methods. Their proposed framework is suitable for typical empirical problems arising in trade analysis such as the estimation of trade equilibrium models in addition to a much wider class of problems, and they provide a number of demonstrations. The chapter should be of interest not only to those working with CGE trade models, but also to researchers working in numerical simulation much more generally.

The next two chapters in the volume address a common critique of CGE models: that the standard competitive Armington structure used by the most models can sometimes do a relatively poor job at predicting the changes in the trade flows resulting from a given change in trade policy. This line of argument is made most forcefully in a well-known paper by Kehoe (2003) who explored the CGE literature on NAFTA *ex post*. Further analysis along the same lines is provided by DeRosa and Gilbert (2006). In essence, the argument is that while standard structures do a good job of capturing changes in the intensive margin (changes in the quantity of existing trade), they do not capture changes in the extensive margin (entirely new trade). Empirical evidence suggests that the latter may in fact be more important (Kehoe and Ruhl, 2003).

Recent developments in the pure theory of international trade have sought to explain the extensive margin phenomenon by introducing firm heterogeneity. The most well-known examples of what has come to be known as the "new new" trade theory are the works of Eaton and Kortum (2002) and Melitz (2003). Chapters 2 and 3 present new attempts to incorporate firm heterogeneity along these lines into the CGE framework. In Chapter 2, Fan Zhai presents a model based on the Melitz (2003) framework, and examines the relative importance of the intensive and extensive margins in trade expansion following trade liberalization and a reduction in fixed trade costs. His results indicate that the extensive margin accounts for around one-third of the trade growth induced by the reduction in tariff or variable trade costs, and almost 200% in the case of reducing fixed trade costs.

In Chapter 3, Lorenzo Caliendo and Fernando Parro present an application of a heterogeneous firm model to the case of a Uruguay leaving MERCOSUR and forming a free trade agreement with the United States. Their approach, detailed further in Caliendo and Parro (2009), generalizes the Eaton and Kortum (2002) model by adding multiple sectors and countries, and incorporating trade in intermediate goods and the interaction across tradables and nontradables. Their approach has the advantage of relatively low computational and data requirements. In an interesting and timely application given recent US engagement in regional trading arrangements, they show that a free trade agreement with the United States would have positive welfare effects for Uruguay, with most of the gains coming from having access to lower cost intermediate inputs for production. This is a very promising area of future research.

While many CGE studies are concerned with the impacts of liberalization of merchandise trade, there is also a growing recognition that the liberalization of services might be equally or more important. In a very carefully constructed study presented as Chapter 4 of the volume, Philippa Dee and Ndiame Diop apply the FTAP model (an extension of the GTAP model to include a treatment of foreign direct investment) to evaluating the potential impacts of behind the border reforms in the provision of services in the Tunisia. The chapter presents a detailed discussion of the issues relating to measurement of barriers to services, and how appropriate liberalization shocks can be implemented in a CGE framework. Their results suggest that in the case of Tunisia the aggregate gains from liberalizing a subset of services would be roughly equivalent to those associated with fully eliminating barriers to its manufacturing trade, although smaller than those available from their proposed agricultural reform scenarios (involving an agreement with the EU). However, they also find that the adjustment costs associated with services liberalization in this case are considerably smaller than those required under merchandise trade reform scenarios, suggesting that, at least for Tunisia, services reform might be considered "low hanging fruit."

The next chapter deals with an issue that might not traditionally be thought of as the domain of trade policy, but is in fact an issue of efficient movement of factor services across national boundaries. In a highly topical piece, Peter B. Dixon and Maureen T. Rimmer apply the USAGE model of the United States to the question of designing immigration policy, in particular as it relates to "imports" of low-skilled labor. They consider several scenarios, ranging from a reduction in the supply of low-skilled labor induced by tighter border security, to a fully liberalized regime under various assumptions, and complementary tax policies. They find that a tighter-border-security strategy generates a sustained reduction in the economic welfare of US households of 0.55%, equivalent to a permanent annual loss in economic welfare of about $80 billion. By contrast, an optimally chosen liberalization policy would result in substantial economic gains. The sources of the gains are extensively decomposed in the chapter. A technical appendix sets out the details of the modeling of the labor market, and will be a useful reference to practitioners considering expanding the labor-market sides of their modeling efforts.

There is considerable debate on the effects of international trade on the environment, and the next two chapters deal with different aspects of the economy–environment interactions. In Chapter 6, Alla Golub, Thomas W. Hertel, Farzad Taheripour, and Wallace E. Tyner present an extensive survey of recent literature applying CGE methods to the analysis of biofuels policies. As they note, global biofuels production has boomed over the last decade in response to government interventions in various nations, and the complex web of linkages between biofuels and crops, livestock, and energy activities make it an area ripe for the application of general equilibrium methods. The chapter details a series of modifications to the standard CGE framework (the model builds extensively on GTAP-E, the version of GTAP designed to handle energy–environment–economy interactions) to handle biofuels, including a detailed specification of biofuels demand and supply, and demand for biofuels byproducts. Applications to the global biofuels boom, global emissions from land-use change, and the interplay between biofuels and the livestock sectors are discussed extensively, and the chapter concludes with a series of future challenges that remain. As such, the chapter both comprehensively covers the existing work in the area, and sets out a very useful map of where future contributions can be made.

In Chapter 7, David Finnoff and Arthur J. Caplan make another contribution to the trade and environment literature, presenting an interesting example of "bioeconomic" modeling. In their work, a general equilibrium ecosystem model is integrated with a CGE model of the regional and international economies. The ecosystem model is of the Great Salt Lake, and their approach accounts for the basic ecological relationships and human activities that interact within the lake's watershed. It allows the quantification of ecosystem externalities that might occur as a result of changes within the watershed and ecosystem, thereby identifying the degree to which certain species may be threatened. The chapter also demonstrates how international trade might be incorporated into the modeling framework. While the CGE model component in the current iteration of the model is still relatively simple, the approach is quite novel and this is a promising area for future research at the interface between international and environmental economics.

One of the most controversial aspects of international trade liberalization is the potential for adverse impacts on poverty and/or income distribution. The Doha Round of multilateral trade talks provides a recent example, where concerns over rural poverty led to demands by India and China for enhanced safeguards for developing countries in agriculture. In July 2008 the talks collapsed, once again, as negotiators failed to reach agreement on this very issue.

The effects of trade liberalization on poverty and income distribution have been an area of intense recent research in CGE and related areas. A number of applications have been surveyed in Hertel and Reimer (2005), Hertel and Winters (2005), and Gilbert (2008). As Hertel and Reimer (2005) note, CGE techniques have proved to be particularly useful in this area, in particular in combination with microsimulation models. Chapters 8–10 provide different examples of how CGE techniques can be applied to issues of poverty and household income distribution consequences of trade reform.

In Chapter 8, Anna Strutt, Thomas W. Hertel, and Susan Stone consider the implications of trade reform in Southeast Asia (ASEAN) on the economies of the Greater Mekong Subregion (GMS). They use a version of the GTAP model (Hertel, 1997) that has been modified to incorporate poverty impacts (see Hertel *et al.*, 2009). The approach employs a sequential, macro-micro modeling strategy in which results from the global trade model are passed on to a series of microsimulation models. Their results suggest that trade reform (they consider completion of ASEAN, expansion to include Japan, Korea and China, and further expansion to include Australia, New Zealand and India, i.e., ASEAN+3 and ASEAN+6) is likely to bring significant gains to the region in terms of economic welfare. Perhaps more importantly, they show that liberalization will likely lead to significant reductions in poverty in the region, perhaps as many as 320,000 people moved out of extreme poverty, with the largest share of those in Cambodia (one of the poorest countries in the GMS). Their results also suggest that poverty reduction is particularly significant in the agricultural and rural diversified stratum, suggesting a positive impact on rural poverty in the region.

Chapter 9 addresses South Asia, also one of the poorest regions of the world. John Gilbert and Reza Oladi consider the implications of regional trade reform under SAFTA. They take a somewhat different approach, using a model with multiple representative households directly built into the model. This approach has the advantage of directly tracking the household behavior within the model, but the disadvantage (similar to the extensive margin problem) of being unable to track intra-household changes. This is mitigated by a greater number of households, and Gilbert and Oladi directly incorporate information on 43 household archetypes across the countries in the region. Their results suggest that, in contrast to the received wisdom, the distributional impacts of trade reform in South Asia are not likely to be biased against the rural poor in many of the economies. By contrast, in most of the economies the bias is against the urban non-poor, a result with significant political economy implications. Gilbert and Oladi also suggest some directions for future analysis, analyzing the theoretical implications of households with varying ability to respond to changes in factor prices.

In Chapter 10, Shikha Jha, David Roland-Holst, Songsak Sriboonchitta, and Drew Behnke provide another analysis of Southeast Asia, this time with a focus on developing agro-food markets and the emergence of China as a significant destination market for these commodities. They argue that because low-income Southeast Asia is below its agro-food potential, there is a significant opportunity for self-directed poverty reduction through regional agro-food market expansion. The analytical component of the chapter applies a version of the dynamic LINKAGE model developed at the World Bank. Scenarios cover changes in productivity, trade facilitation, and market access measures, and changes in foreign direct investment. Their results suggest that the potential effects of these changes on growth are significant, especially for the poorer economies in the GMS regions, but that they can only be fully realized if the policies are integrated and complementary.

CGE techniques have been very widely used for the *ex-ante* analysis of regional trading agreements, which have proliferated at a terrific rate over the last decade. Surveys of recent CGE literature in this area include Scollay and Gilbert (2000), Gilbert and Wahl (2002), Robinson and Thierfelder (2002), and Lloyd and MacLaren (2004). Several of the preceding chapters have considered the impact of regional trade reform in various contexts, and the next two chapters in the volume make further contributions in this area, focusing on some of the broader regionalism trends and consequences for three major economies in the Asia-Pacific region: the United States, Japan, and China.

In Chapter 11, Drusilla K. Brown, Kozo Kiyota, and Robert M. Stern present an updated version of their work on United States–Japan trade options (Brown, Kiyota and Stern, 2006). Using the Michigan model of world production and trade, the authors evaluate the welfare and sectoral employment consequences of the various free trade agreements negotiated and in process by the two economies. They also benchmark with unilateral and multilateral trade reform alternatives, which are found to be substantially superior in welfare terms, both for the economies under study and for nonmembers. As they note, many of the recent agreements signed by these two economies are of the "hub-and-spoke variety." They argue that the spokes emanate out in different and often overlapping directions, suggesting that the complex web of bilateral FTAs may create significant distortions of the global trading system.

In chapter 12, Robert Scollay and John Gilbert continue in a similar vein. They extend their earlier work on disentangling the many new developments in the Asia-Pacific region (Scollay and Gilbert, 2001). Their chapter focuses on the implications for China and its trading partners of China's participation in regional trading arrangements in the Asia-Pacific region. As they note, while the "trade architecture" that will emerge in the Asia-Pacific remains very uncertain, it is clear that China will play a major role in regional trading developments. Using the GTAP model, they investigate the potential economic effects of several alternative architectures that may emerge in the region, ranging from "ASEAN+3" to a full free trade area of the Asia-Pacific, involving all members of APEC (the FTAAP). Their results suggest that the FTAAP yields a welfare outcome for China that is far superior than that offered by any other scenario. In the absence of the FTAAP, on the other hand, most of China's East Asian partners derive the greatest welfare gain from either an ASEAN+3 arrangement or through expansion to include Australia, New Zealand, and India, indicating that there is some divergence of economic interests between China and its partners in the sequencing of preferential trade liberalization in the region.

References

Brown, D.K., Kiyota, K., Stern, R.M. (2006), Computational analysis of the menu of U.S.-Japan trade policies. *World Economy* 29 (6), 805–855.

Caliendo, L., Parro, F. (2009), Estimates of the trade and welfare effects of NAFTA. University of Chicago Working Paper.

DeRosa, D., Gilbert, J. (2006), Predicting trade expansion under FTAs and multilateral agreements. Peter G. Peterson Institute for International Economics Working Papers Vol. 1, Washington, DC.

Eaton, J., Kortum, S. (2002), Technology, geography and trade. *Econometrica* 70, 1741–1779.

Gilbert, J. (2008), Agricultural trade reform and poverty in the Asia-Pacific: a survey and some new results. *Asia-Pacific Development Journal* 15 (1), 1–34.

Gilbert, J., Wahl, T. (2002), Applied general equilibrium assessments of trade liberalization in China. *World Economy* 25 (5), 697–731.

Hertel, T. W. (Ed.) (1997). *Global Trade Analysis: Modeling and Applications*. Cambridge University Press, Cambridge, UK.

Hertel, T.W., Reimer, J. (2005), Predicting the poverty impacts of trade reform. *Journal of International Trade and Economic Development* 14 (4), 377–405.

Hertel, T.W., Winters, L.A. (2005), Estimating the poverty impacts of a prospective Doha development agenda. *World Economy* 28 (8), 1057–1071.

Hertel, T.W., Keeney, R., Ivanic, M., Winters, L.A. (2009), Why isn't the Doha development agenda more poverty-friendly? *Review of Development Economics* 13 (4), 543–559.

Kehoe, T.J. (2003), An evaluation of the performance of applied general equilibrium models of the impact of NAFTA. Federal Reserve Bank of Minneapolis Research Department Staff Report 320.

Kehoe, T.J., Ruhl, K.J. (2003), How important is the new goods margin in international trade? Federal Reserve Bank of Minneapolis Research Department Staff Report 324.

Lloyd, P.J., MacLaren, D. (2004), Gains and losses from regional trading agreements: a survey. *Economic Record* 80 (251), 445–497.

Melitz, M.J. (2003), The impact of trade on intra-industry reallocations and aggregate industry productivity. *Econometrica* 71 (6), 1695–1725.

Robinson, S., Thierfelder, K. (2002), Trade liberalisation and regional integration: The search for large numbers. *Australian Journal of Agricultural and Resource Economics* 46 (4), 585–604.

Scollay, R., Gilbert, J. (2000), Measuring the gains from APEC trade liberalisation: an overview of CGE assessments. *World Economy* 23 (2), 175–193.

Scollay, R., Gilbert, J. (2001), *New Subregional Trading Arrangements in the Asia-Pacific*. Institute for International Economics, Washington, DC.

In the concluding chapter of the volume, Joseph F. Francois and Will Martin present a comprehensive survey of the issues relating to the measurement of the welfare effects of trade reform in computable general equilibrium models. They argue that standard CGE models understate the potential gains from trade reform for a wide variety of reasons, including poor measurement of barriers to trade, inappropriate aggregation of those barriers, missing process productivity gains and product quality/variety improvements, factor market misspecification, and gains from investment. Their challenging chapter synthesizes many of the issues raised separately in the preceding works in the volume and presents a call to action for those involved in CGE analysis. It should be required reading for all researchers active in the analysis of trade reform using CGE methods.

CHAPTER 1

Estimation of Parameters of Constrained Optimization Models

Torbjörn Jansson[a] and Thomas Heckelei[b]

[a]*Agrifood Economics Centre, Swedish University of Agricultural Sciences, Uppsala, Sweden*
E-mail address: Torbjorn.Jansson@ekon.slu.se
[b]*Institute of Agricultural Policy, Market Research and Economic Sociology, University of Bonn, Bonn, Germany*
E-mail address: thomas.heckelei@ilr.uni-bonn.de

Abstract
Estimating parameters of constrained optimization models in a consistent way requires a different set of methods than what is available in a typical econometric toolkit. We identify three complications likely to arise in this context, and suggest solutions to those complications: (i) the bi-level programming character, (ii) ill-posedness, and (iii) derivation of estimator properties. The solutions suggested involve a combination of numerical techniques and utilization of out-of-sample information through Bayesian techniques. The proposed framework is also suitable for typical empirical problems arising in trade analysis such as the estimation of trade equilibrium models and data balancing exercises.

Keywords: Mathematical programming, econometrics, Bayesian estimation, errors-in-variables, bi-level programming

1. Rationality and the empirical specification of economic models

The idea of optimizing behavior of economic agents has a firm hold of economic thought and is the key ingredient in the works of neoclassical economists such as Alfred Marshall and Paul Samuelson. Some economists have even doubted the possibility of constructing valid economic models without it (Blaug, 1992). Apart from optimization behavior inherent in the neoclassical school of thought, most (all?) definitions of economics also imply the allocation of scarce means among competing ends, for example Robbins (1945, p. 16):

> *Economics is the science which studies human behaviour as a relationship between ends and scarce means which have alternative uses.*

Frontiers of Economics and Globalization
Volume 7 ISSN: 1574-8715
DOI: 10.1108/S1574-8715(2010)0000007004

The strong case for using constrained optimization models in economic analyses stands in some contrast to the econometrics available for quantifying the models. Whereas applied economic models tend to be nonlinear, inequality constrained, and not amenable to repeated experiments, much of the econometric toolkit assumes linear or linearized equations, continuous derivatives, and the possibility to distinguish exogenous or predetermined variables from endogenous ones.

Since the introduction of the concept of Positive Mathematical Programming to a wider audience by Howitt (1995), the gap between normativism and positivism in economics has begun to narrow. Buysse *et al.* (2007) term the emerging strand of literature Econometric Mathematical Programming. This chapter can be considered in that context.

This chapter picks up three problems, described in the next section, that the applied economist is likely to encounter when attempting to estimate parameters of a constrained economic model. The structural model is taken as given, that is the problem of model specification is tacitly omitted.

This setting of constrained optimization models may at first appear narrow for a contribution to a book on trade analysis. However, we develop a Bayesian estimation approach applicable to ill-posed problems and models with complementary slackness conditions as long as sufficient prior information is available. After the development of the approach in the context of optimization models – which are of course also used in trade analysis – we point at alternative applications to equation systems originating from accounting or equilibrium structures. For example, ill-posed data balancing exercises for social accounting matrices such as the one presented in Golan *et al.* (1994) could be useful applications of our Bayesian framework where entries of accounting identities are estimated instead of parameters of optimization models. This estimation approach has already been illustrated by Heckelei *et al.* (2008). Furthermore, the ability to estimate across regime switches is deemed useful not only for inequality constrained optimization models but also in the context of equilibrium models with quantitative restrictions such as tariff rate quotas (TRQs).

After discussing the difficulties associated with the set of estimation problems considered, the text builds upon existing practices of the economic modeling trade to develop solutions. The methods are described in a general way in an attempt to sketch a general estimation framework. In particular, Bayesian econometric tools and terms are employed, but parallels are drawn to other econometric schools. After the theoretical sections on problems and suggested solutions, the concepts introduced are illustrated by a fully elaborated example. Then possibilities to apply the principle approach to other estimation problems in trade analysis are discussed before the final section concludes.

2. *Three problems*

2.1. The economic model

The problem is to estimate the parameter vector $\boldsymbol{\beta}$ of the following general constrained optimization problem:

$$\max_{\mathbf{y}|\mathbf{x},\boldsymbol{\beta}} f(\mathbf{y},\mathbf{x},\boldsymbol{\beta}) : \mathbf{g}(\mathbf{y},\mathbf{x},\boldsymbol{\beta}) \leqslant 0,\ \mathbf{h}(\mathbf{y},\mathbf{x},\boldsymbol{\beta}) = 0 \tag{1}$$

Here, and throughout the text if not stated otherwise, a bold face letter indicates a vector or matrix, whereas scalars are denoted by regular italic letters. The symbols "$\mathbf{y}|\mathbf{x},\boldsymbol{\beta}$" beneath the directive "max" means that the function $f(\mathbf{y},\mathbf{x},\boldsymbol{\beta})$ is being maximized with respect to $\mathbf{y}$ while treating $\mathbf{x}$ and $\boldsymbol{\beta}$ as exogenous. The general problem can have inequality constraints $\mathbf{g}$ as well as equality constraints $\mathbf{h}$. Further notation is introduced along the way.

We constrain the study to cases where f is twice continuously differentiable and the feasible space S defined by the constraints for any $(\mathbf{y},\mathbf{x},\boldsymbol{\beta})$, that is $S(\mathbf{x},\boldsymbol{\beta}) = \{\mathbf{y}\text{: } \mathbf{g}(\mathbf{y},\mathbf{x},\boldsymbol{\beta}) \leqslant 0,\ \mathbf{h}(\mathbf{y},\mathbf{x},\boldsymbol{\beta}) = 0\}$ is compact. Furthermore, all elements of $\mathbf{y}$ and $\mathbf{x}$ are required to be real continuous variables, thus excluding integer programming problems.

2.2. Extremum estimation is a bi-level programming problem

An *extremum estimator* can be defined as one that optimizes an estimation metric or estimation objective function, depending on parameters and data (Mittelhammer *et al.*, 2000). Most estimators used in practice are encompassed in the class of extremum estimators, for example least squares, maximum likelihood, and entropy estimators.

Performing an extremum estimation of the model (1), using the criterion function F (which we assume is to be maximized) implies solving the following optimization problem:

$$\begin{aligned} & \max_{\mathbf{x},\mathbf{y},\boldsymbol{\beta}|\boldsymbol{\gamma}} F(\mathbf{y},\mathbf{x},\boldsymbol{\beta},\boldsymbol{\gamma}) \\ \text{subject to}\quad & \mathbf{G}(\mathbf{y},\mathbf{x},\boldsymbol{\beta},\boldsymbol{\gamma}) \leqslant 0 \\ & \mathbf{H}(\mathbf{y},\mathbf{x},\boldsymbol{\beta},\boldsymbol{\gamma}) = 0 \\ \text{and } \mathbf{y} \text{ solves}\quad & \max_{\mathbf{y}|\mathbf{x},\boldsymbol{\beta}} f(\mathbf{y},\mathbf{x},\boldsymbol{\beta}) \\ \text{subject to}\quad & \mathbf{g}(\mathbf{y},\mathbf{x},\boldsymbol{\beta}) \leqslant 0 \\ & \mathbf{h}(\mathbf{y},\mathbf{x},\boldsymbol{\beta}) = 0 \end{aligned} \tag{2}$$

This problem is a *bi-level programming problem* (BLPP, see Colson *et al.*, 2007, for a recent survey), and it is well known in operations research and game theory, albeit it has also briefly appeared in agricultural economics (e.g. Hazell and Norton, 1986, pp. 139).

The BLPP has two parts. The last three lines of (2) constitute the economic model to estimate and are jointly termed the *lower level problem*,[1] where the agent (in the case of an economic model) is assumed to choose $\mathbf{y}$ as if the parameters $(\mathbf{x},\boldsymbol{\beta})$ are exogenous. On the *upper level* the econometrician chooses values of $(\mathbf{y},\mathbf{x},\boldsymbol{\beta})$ in a way that maximizes the econometric criterion $F(\mathbf{y},\mathbf{x},\boldsymbol{\beta},\gamma)$, subject to (possibly) some inequality constraints $\mathbf{G}$ and equality constraints $\mathbf{H}$, and in particular subject to the constraint that $\mathbf{y}$ is an optimal solution[2] to the lower level problem given $(\mathbf{x},\boldsymbol{\beta})$. The criterion depends on the parameters and variables of the economic model and is conditional on the parameter vector γ containing things that are exogenous in the estimation, like observations and prior information. The inequality and equality constraint vectors $\mathbf{G}$ and $\mathbf{H}$ on the upper level may contain restrictions on the parameters to estimate or definitions of hyperparameters.

There are some benefits to be gained from viewing the estimation problem in the form of a BLPP. Most common econometric problems can be viewed as special cases of (2). For example, assume that the economic model (the lower level problem) is represented by its first-order conditions, which happen to be a single linear equation. There are no restrictions on the parameters, the econometric criterion is to minimize the sum of squared deviations of the variable $\mathbf{y}$ from observed values, treating $\mathbf{x}$ as known with certainty (fixed also in the upper level problem), then an ordinary least squares estimator would result. In a similar manner, it is possible to identify other estimation methods such as maximum likelihood, entropy, or Bayesian estimators as special cases of BLPP.

The BLPP formulation allows using a primal approach to describe the microeconomic problem faced by the agent, and as such many restrictions that generally need to be imposed to ensure the existence of an optimization problem (e.g. the restrictions on cost, profit, indirect utility, or expenditure functions) are automatically satisfied.

The Kuhn–Tucker conditions of inequality constrained optimization models contain complementary slackness conditions. In economic terms, those conditions show up in the form of complementarities between a scarce resource and a shadow price, for example a binding quota and a positive quota rent, a filled TRQ and a high import price, a nonutilized

---

[1] Other authors call the components the *outer and inner* problems, or the *leader* and *follower* problems. We stick here with the terms upper and lower level.

[2] If the lower level problems has many solutions for some $(\mathbf{x},\boldsymbol{\beta})$, then the econometrician may choose the one that yields the best value on the upper level. This is called the optimistic case. In other BLPP applications, such as leader–follower games, there is no reason to believe that the lower level (follower) would select the particular $\mathbf{y}$ that is most beneficial on the upper level (to the leader).

transportation node, and the size of a transportation cost, etc. Unfortunately, those economically meaningful complementarities are causing much headache for the econometrician (as well as for the mathematician, evidenced by several monographs on the subject, e.g. Luo *et al.*, 1996, Bard, 1998, and many other references in Colson *et al.*, 2007), whence only few econometric applications can be found where they are explicitly considered.

One strand of literature initiated by Wales and Woodland (1983) and applied and further developed by, for example, Lee and Pitt (1986), Phaneuf *et al.* (2000), Golan *et al.* (2001), and Yue and Beghin (2009) estimates demand based on random utility functions where the complementary slackness conditions connected with the choice of the consumer to consume a good or not (nonnegativity conditions) are explicitly considered. In that strand of literature, it is generally referred to as the Kuhn–Tucker approach. However, the binding status of the complementary slackness conditions in these models is predetermined by the observed (measured) choice of the consumer, and thus the difficulty of endogenously estimating the switching regime is avoided altogether. In contrast, Jansson and Heckelei (2009) estimate a Takayama–Judge-style spatial price equilibrium model endogenously determining the utilization of each trade link, the associated trade cost, and the price difference between the nodes, using bi-level programming techniques. Finally, the BLPP is somewhat akin to the Tobit model as suggested by Ransom (1985) and to the limited-dependent-variable estimation technique, as shown by Ransom (1987) in using that technique to endogenously estimate the labor participation decision in households of married couples.

A simple example is useful to illustrate the key difficulties that are involved in BLPP. Consider an economic model of a small country importing a single homogeneous good subject to a TRQ with zero in-quota tariffs. Denote the price of the good by p, the quantity imported by q, and the quota by TRQ. The Kuhn–Tucker necessary conditions for an optimal solution for some utility maximizing consumer problem will contain the following complementary slackness condition: As long as $0<q<Q$, the tariff applied is zero and the price equal to the world market price p_w. Imports in excess of the quota are subject to a tariff, raising the price to the "most favored nation" (MFN) level p_{mfn}. The situation is illustrated graphically in Figure 1(a).

Assume that observations on imports and prices are subject to random errors and that we obtain one observation $A = (q_o,p_o)$, with, say, $q_o<$TRQ and $p_w \leqslant p_o \leqslant p_{mfn}$. This is illustrated in Figure 1(b). Assuming that the parameters TRQ, p_w, and p_{mfn} are known with certainty, the econometric problem is to determine the true price and quantity, which must be a point along the piecewise linear graph $p(q)$. The concentric ellipses represent level curves of some estimation metric (in this case to minimize). Clearly, point C is the point on $p(q)$ that touches the lowest level curve.

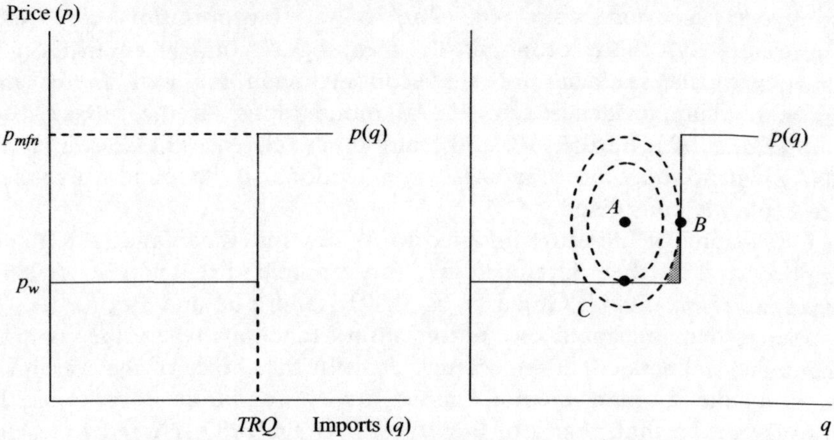

***Fig. 1. Illustration of nonconvexities in the bi-level estimation program, by the example of imports* q *under a tariff rate quota (TRQ). Point* A *is the observed quantity and price, the points* B *and* C *are locally and globally optimal estimates of "true"* p *and* q.**

However, point B is a local minimum, implying that all feasible solutions to the lower level problem, points on $p(q)$, in the neighborhood of B are worse in terms of the estimation criterion (the upper level problem). Furthermore, to travel along $p(q)$ from B to the global optimum C, the gray shaded corner must be passed, where ordinary derivative dp/dq is not defined. That is where the corresponding complementary slackness condition or switching regime switches from, in words, "import quota slack zero, quota rent positive" to "quota rent zero, import quota slack positive."

This simple example should be sufficient to illustrate that in general, BLPP is a nonconvex problem (with potentially many local optima) with discontinuous derivatives. Those properties make the numerical solution hard and render the derivation of estimator properties difficult also in cases where the error distributions are known. Nevertheless, one should be aware of the following points:

1. Not considering switching regimes is a specification error, likely to produce biased estimates.
2. Numerical techniques for solving BLPPs exist and are continuously further developed, perhaps soon to form part of standard mathematical modeling software (see e.g. Ferris *et al.*, 2005).
3. With ever increasing computing power, numerical derivation of estimator properties, such as MC integration, becomes cheaper.

As is evident in the example with a TRQ trading scheme in Figure 1, exact knowledge of either imports or prices would determine the binding status of the corresponding complementary slackness condition and reduce the complexity of the estimation. In applied models, that is rarely the case, because of measurement errors on **x** as well as on **y**, a circumstance that places the typical estimation in the class of errors-in-variables (EIV) models, to be further elaborated on later in the text.

2.3. Ill-posedness

Statistical inference is a problem of inversion, where the function to invert is the one mapping true parameters to observed outcomes. An inversion problem can be ill-posed in several ways. Jaynes (1984) mentions the following variants of ill-posedness: An *underdetermined* problem does not contain enough information to uniquely identify a solution, whereas in an *overdetermined* one no solution exists. The solution to an ill-posed problem may be *unstable* or so *difficult to obtain* that solution trials with real data are useless. But Jaynes (1984, p. 151) claims that "In biology, econometrics, geophysical exploration, medical diagnosis and synthesis of electrical filters or optical systems, a truly well-posed problem is virtually unknown."

In the context of estimations of economic optimization models, there are several reasons why ill-posedness is common. We identify three main reasons:

1. *Economics is a nonexperimental science.* In most cases, it is not possible to perform controlled repeated experiments. Repeated measurements tend to pertain to either different agents or different points in time, and unless restrictive parameter constraints are imposed across agents or time, the lack of repeated measurements in a controlled environment leads to ill-posedness. "On those stepping into rivers the same, other and other waters flow."
2. *EIV.* Economic models typically contain several different kinds of variables, such as quantities and prices, which are not experimentally controlled but need to be observed and are subject to measurement errors. Even if the Kuhn–Tucker first-order conditions for a model may be solved for, say, demanded quantities as a function of prices, the "explanatory" variables (i.e. the prices) are also likely to be subject to stochastic errors. It is well known (e.g. Carroll *et al.*, 1995) that neglect of errors in explanatory variables results in biased estimates. Estimation of an EIV model requires information about the ratio of variances among different sets of variables, without which the problem is underdetermined and thus ill-posed.
3. *Complexity of the subject matter (reality).* A model that is deemed by the researcher to be sufficiently sophisticated to form an appropriate representation of reality tends to contain too many parameters to be identifiable.

We will address the problem of ill-posedness in a Bayesian context.

2.4. Derivation of estimator properties

There are a few results that apply to the class of extremum estimators. Newey and McFadden (1994) give sufficient conditions for consistency and asymptotic normality of extremum estimators. A problem in this context is, however, that in the general case the set of optimal solutions to the lower level problem constraining the parameter space for the estimation criterion is nonconvex as laid out earlier. Therefore, the sufficient conditions for consistency are not satisfied and then also not the sufficient conditions for normality. The failure to satisfy these sufficient conditions in turn means that the conditions for the use of inference tools for extremum estimators such as Lagrange multiplier tests and confidence regions are also not satisfied (e.g. Mittelhammer *et al.*, 2000, p. 144).

In practice, the lack of standard econometric tools is unfortunate, because without information about the distribution of derived estimates, it is not possible to perform hypothesis testing or to derive confidence regions for model results of the final model. Information about the variance of parameters would provide valuable input into systematic sensitivity analyses. In the wake of general asymptotic results for the class of BLPP, numerical (Monte Carlo) methods have to be relied upon.

3. *A Bayesian approach*

The previous section outlined three types of serious problems likely to pertain to the estimation of applied economic models, namely (i) the bi-level programming character, (ii) the ill-posedness, and (iii) the lack of off-the-shelf methods for deriving certain estimator properties for inference. In this section, we formulate a Bayesian framework capable of handling the latter two problems while acknowledging the difficulties caused by (i).

3.1. Ill-posed inverse problems

Ill-posed inverse problems is a subject area that attracted considerable attention in the 1980s. O'Sullivan (1986) surveys and classifies ill-posed inverse problems and points to the interrelations between different methods for resolving ill-posedness and in particular maximum entropy (ME) and Bayesian methods. Interestingly, he points out that "It can be shown that the optimal inversion algorithms are methods of regularization procedures, but to completely specify these algorithms the signal to noise ratio must be supplied." The method of regularization (MOR) class of algorithms contains, in addition to ME and many Bayesian estimators also methods such as the Stein, Ridge (Hoerl and Kennard, 1970), and maximum penalized likelihood (Silverman, 1982) estimators.

The scientific debate sometimes gives the impression that proponents of different statistical methods think their particular approach the Philosopher's Stone of resolving ill-posedness, see for example the short note by Titterington (1984) in *Nature* with reply by Skilling in the same issue, and the quotation by Titterington (1985, p. 164) that "Gull and Skilling (1983) claim a unique position for the maximum entropy method as 'the only consistent regularisation technique for images', by trying to relate it to Jaynes's (1978) Principle of Maximum Entroy. This author, however, cannot but regard it merely as one of the wide class of minimum penalized distance prescriptions" [capitalizations and misspelling original].

Yet the overall consensus seems to be that the different MOR methods are interrelated and that they are amenable to a Bayesian interpretation. For instance, Titterington (1985) establishes that the maximum penalized likelihood estimator is an MOR estimator and equivalent to a particular Bayesian estimator, Denzau *et al.* (1989) use Bayesian reasoning to derive a cross-entropy estimator of proportions, George (1986) shows how Stein-like estimators arise naturally out of Bayes rule applied to mixture priors, and Hoerl and Kennard (1970 p. 64) find that "each ridge estimate can be considered as the posterior mean based on giving the regresssion coefficients, $\boldsymbol{\beta}$, a prior normal distribution," thus suggesting a Bayesian interpretation also of the ridge estimator.

The doyen of ME econometrics Jaynes (1984) himself advocates using prior information to resolve ill-posedness and prescribes that each inverse problem is scrutinized and an appropriate prior derived on a case by case basis. In the two examples that he provides, he derives one purely Bayesian estimator with uninformative priors and one ME estimator.

We apply a Bayesian perspective, because (i) in our opinion it makes the inclusion of prior information to resolve ill-posedness transparent and straightforward, (ii) by suitable re-interpretation of the terms, other estimators are subsumed as special cases, and (iii) Bayes rule appears to be making full use of the available information (Zellner, 1988; Clarke, 1996).

3.2. A Bayesian point estimator

Returning to the general model given in (1), we now formulate a stochastic model and an estimation that is motivated by a Bayesian argument and put in the form of a BLPP (2).

To be explicit, we start by assuming an additive error model relating measurements $\mathbf{Y}$ and $\mathbf{X}$ to the true $\mathbf{y}$ and $\mathbf{x}$:

$$\begin{aligned} \mathbf{Y} &= \mathbf{y} + \mathbf{e} \\ \mathbf{X} &= \mathbf{x} + \mathbf{u} \end{aligned} \tag{3}$$

and complete the stochastic model by requiring that $\mathbf{x}$ and $\mathbf{y}$ satisfy

(i) the Kuhn–Tucker first-order conditions, i.e. $(\mathbf{x},\mathbf{y})$ is an optimal solution to the lower level problem for some parameter matrix $\boldsymbol{\beta}$ and dual vector $\boldsymbol{\lambda}$, and

(ii) the parameter restrictions **G** and **H** of the upper level of (2) for the given upper level parameters γ.

The way the BLPP (2) was defined, $[\mathbf{Y}\ \mathbf{X}]'$ is part of the upper level parameter vector γ, and the error model (3) is part of the equality constraint set **H**. To be able to express the sampling model compactly in what follows, we define the set $\Omega(\gamma)$ as the set of parameters satisfying (i) and (ii) above as

$$\Omega(\gamma) = \left\{ (\mathbf{e},\mathbf{u},\mathbf{y},\mathbf{x},\boldsymbol{\lambda},\boldsymbol{\beta}) : \begin{array}{c} \mathbf{y},\boldsymbol{\lambda} \text{ solve (1) for } \mathbf{e},\mathbf{u},\mathbf{x},\boldsymbol{\beta} \\ \mathbf{G}(\mathbf{y},\mathbf{x},\boldsymbol{\beta},\gamma) \leqslant 0 \\ \mathbf{H}(\mathbf{y},\mathbf{x},\boldsymbol{\beta},\gamma) = 0 \end{array} \right\} \tag{4}$$

The formulation above implies a degenerate density function returning a constant density value for any $(\mathbf{e},\mathbf{u},\mathbf{y},\mathbf{x},\boldsymbol{\lambda},\boldsymbol{\beta}) \in \Omega(\gamma)$, and else zero. That does in turn imply the following likelihood function:

$$L(\mathbf{e},\mathbf{u},\mathbf{y},\mathbf{x},\boldsymbol{\lambda},\boldsymbol{\beta}|\gamma) = \{1 \text{ if } (\mathbf{e},\mathbf{u},\mathbf{y},\mathbf{x},\boldsymbol{\lambda},\boldsymbol{\beta}) \in \Omega(\gamma) \text{ and } 0 \text{ otherwise}\}$$

The likelihood function thus defined generally associates a continuum of parameters to any given γ (recall that γ entails the observations **Y**, **X**) and is therefore by itself not sufficient for deriving point estimates. This is a manifestation of the problem of ill-posedness referred to above. To resolve ill-posedness, prior information needs to be introduced. Expressing the joint prior information as a density function $\pi(\mathbf{e},\mathbf{u},\mathbf{y},\mathbf{x},\boldsymbol{\lambda},\boldsymbol{\beta})$, we use Bayes rule to derive the posterior density function

$$p(\mathbf{e},\mathbf{u},\mathbf{y},\mathbf{x},\boldsymbol{\lambda},\boldsymbol{\beta}|\gamma) \propto L(\mathbf{e},\mathbf{u},\mathbf{y},\mathbf{x},\boldsymbol{\lambda},\boldsymbol{\beta}|\gamma)\pi(\mathbf{e},\mathbf{u},\mathbf{y},\mathbf{x},\boldsymbol{\lambda},\boldsymbol{\beta}) \tag{5}$$

This posterior can be used in inference about the parameters. In particular, consider the posterior mode estimator defined as the parameter vector(s) for which the posterior density reaches its maximum value.[3]

Since the likelihood function means, in words, "using only parameters that solve the lower level problem and satisfy the upper level constraints in (2)," finding the posterior mode is equivalent to maximizing the prior density function subject to the constraint that the solution satisfies the Kuhn–Tucker conditions of the economic model plus the constraint vectors **G** and **H**. Hence, the posterior mode estimator belongs to the class of extremum estimators, and if the Kuhn–Tucker conditions contain complementary slackness conditions, the estimator will be difficult to find numerically, as explained earlier.

---

[3] Also the posterior mean can be computed, as discussed later in the text. In some instances, the mean is defined even though no (unique) mode exists, for example with uniform priors.

In our view, the estimation approach outlined above has the advantage that it (i) directly estimates the structural equations of the model, thus ensuring transportability[4] of the estimates, (ii) allowing the transparent incorporation of priors to resolve problems with ill-posedness or improve estimates with out-of-sample information, while maintaining a coherent theoretical framework. The posterior density function can be used to derive other estimates than the posterior mode, as is discussed later in text.

In many applications, no informative priors will be available for some of the parameters and no particular upper level constraints apart from the additive error model apply. In such cases, (5) can be simplified. Consider for instance the case in which no prior is available for **y**, **x**, $\boldsymbol{\beta}$, and $\boldsymbol{\lambda}$, and the errors **e** and **u** come from iid normal distributions with zero means, $e_i \sim N(0,\sigma_e)$ and $u_i \sim N(0,\sigma_u)$ for all $i = 1, \ldots, n$, where σ_e and σ_u are the standard deviations of the errors. We may then use the error model (3) to substitute in $\mathbf{Y}-\mathbf{e}$ and $\mathbf{X}-\mathbf{u}$ for **y** and **x**, respectively, and formulate the posterior mode estimator as (taking logs of the prior and dropping constant terms) as

$$\begin{aligned}\hat{\boldsymbol{\beta}} &= \arg\ \max p(\boldsymbol{\beta}|\mathbf{Y},\mathbf{X},\sigma_e,\sigma_u) \\ &= \min_{\mathbf{e},\mathbf{u},\boldsymbol{\beta}} \frac{1}{\sigma_e^2}\mathbf{e}'\mathbf{e} + \frac{1}{\sigma_u^2}\mathbf{u}'\mathbf{u} \\ &\quad \text{subject to } (\mathbf{e},\mathbf{u},\boldsymbol{\lambda}_g,\boldsymbol{\lambda}_h,\hat{\boldsymbol{\beta}}) \in \Omega(\mathbf{Y},\mathbf{X},\boldsymbol{\sigma}_e,\boldsymbol{\sigma}_u) \text{ for some } \boldsymbol{\lambda}_g,\boldsymbol{\lambda}_h\end{aligned}$$

where $\boldsymbol{\lambda}_h$ and $\boldsymbol{\lambda}_g$ are the dual vectors associated with the constraints **h** and **g**. This is thus a constrained weighted least squares estimation.

3.3. Solving the bi-level program

In the previous section, the posterior mode estimator was formulated without explicit consideration of the bi-level programming character of the problem, which was hidden in the formulation of Ω. If the inner problem is represented by its Kuhn–Tucker conditions, the Bayesian posterior mode estimator becomes

$$\max_{\mathbf{x},\boldsymbol{\psi}|\Theta} \quad \pi(\mathbf{e},\mathbf{u},\mathbf{y},\mathbf{x},\boldsymbol{\gamma},\boldsymbol{\beta}) \tag{6}$$

$$\text{subject to} \quad \mathbf{G}(\mathbf{e},\mathbf{u},\mathbf{y},\mathbf{x},\lambda,\boldsymbol{\beta},\boldsymbol{\gamma}) \leqslant 0 \tag{7}$$

$$\mathbf{H}(\mathbf{e},\mathbf{u},\mathbf{y},\mathbf{x},\boldsymbol{\lambda},\boldsymbol{\beta},\boldsymbol{\gamma}) = 0 \tag{8}$$

$$\nabla_y' f(\mathbf{y},\mathbf{x},\boldsymbol{\beta}) - \nabla_y' \mathbf{g}(\mathbf{y},\mathbf{x},\boldsymbol{\beta})\boldsymbol{\lambda}_g' - \nabla_y' \mathbf{h}(\mathbf{y},\mathbf{x},\boldsymbol{\beta})\boldsymbol{\lambda}_h' = 0 \tag{9}$$

---

[4] By transportability we mean that the estimating equations are equivalent to the model in which the parameters are to be used. Transportability is by no means automatically ensured when estimates are produced in one econometric model and used in another.

$$\mathbf{g}(\mathbf{y}, \mathbf{x}, \boldsymbol{\beta}) \leqslant 0 \perp \boldsymbol{\lambda}_g \geq 0 \tag{10}$$

$$\mathbf{h}(\mathbf{y}, \mathbf{x}, \boldsymbol{\beta}) = 0 \tag{11}$$

Equation (9) is the first-order condition for the lower level problem, where ∇_y means the first derivatives (Jacobian) with respect to y. Equation (10) is the complementary slackness conditions, where the operator $\mathbf{a} \leqslant 0 \perp \mathbf{b} \geq 0$ is shorthand for writing "$\mathbf{a} \leqslant 0$, $\mathbf{b} \geqslant 0$, and $\mathbf{a}'\mathbf{b} = 0$". Together, (9)–(11) form the Kuhn-Tucker conditions of the lower level problem.

As pointed out earlier, the BLPP is difficult to solve due to the presence of (10). This is neither the right place nor the right authors to comprehensively discuss solution methods for BLPPs. The survey of Colson *et al.* (2007) contains references to works of many authors. In addition, a few hands-on suggestions are provided, derived from the results in Jansson and Heckelei (2009). In our experience, at least one of the three following approaches seems to work.

First, new mathematical software specifically developed for solving BLPP emerges. For example, consider the solver GAMS/NLPEC (Ferris *et al.*, 2005 and GAMS, 2010a) developed for the software package GAMS (GAMS, 2010b), which solves MPEC[5] through iterative reformulation of the complementarity constraints.

Second, the BLPP can be considered a global optimization problem and solved with existing techniques for that class. For instance, on the basis of Fortuny-Amat and McCarl (1981), (6)–(11) can be reformulated as a mixed integer problem by replacing (10) with the five new conditions

$$\mathbf{g}(\mathbf{y}, \mathbf{x}, \boldsymbol{\beta}) \leqslant 0$$

$$\mathbf{g}(\mathbf{y}, \mathbf{x}, \boldsymbol{\beta}) \geq -M\mathbf{v}$$

$$\boldsymbol{\lambda}_g \geq 0$$

$$\boldsymbol{\lambda}_g \leqslant M(1 - \mathbf{v})$$

$$\mathbf{v} \in \{0, 1\}^n$$

where $\mathbf{v}$ is a vector of binary variables of the same dimension as the vector of inequalities $\mathbf{g}$ and, M a sufficiently large scalar. This turns the BLPP into a Mixed Integer Program (MIP) that can be solved by for example branch-and-bound (BB) techniques. The reader should be able to verify that setting each element of $\mathbf{v}$ to either 1 or 0 is equivalent to (10) if M is sufficiently large. This reformulation, which is called "big-M" after the big scalar M, was tried in Jansson (2007) and found to be very slow when the

[5] MPEC: Mathematical Programs with Equilibrium Constraints. A class of programming models with mixed complementarity conditions in the constraints, subsuming BLPP as a special case.

dimension n increased, but to be able to accurately find the global optimum in repeated experiments with smaller models.

Finally, the iterative smooth reformulations and solution by constrained optimization suggested by Ferris *et al.* (2005) can be implemented directly. In particular, Jansson and Heckelei (2009) report good results from a penalty function formulation where (10) is replaced by the much simpler conditions

$$\mathbf{g}(\mathbf{y}, \mathbf{x}, \boldsymbol{\beta}) \leqslant 0$$

$$\boldsymbol{\lambda}_g \geq 0$$

and the objective function augmented with a function penalizing violations of the complementarity slackness. One candidate is to augment (6) to

$$\pi(\mathbf{e}, \mathbf{u}, \mathbf{y}, \mathbf{x}, \boldsymbol{\lambda}, \boldsymbol{\beta}) - \mu\boldsymbol{\lambda}'_g[-\mathbf{g}(\mathbf{y}, \mathbf{x}, \boldsymbol{\beta})]$$

where μ is a positive scalar that initially is set to zero, thus fully relaxing the complementary slackness conditions, and iteratively increased, each time solving the constrained optimization model using the previous solution as starting values until the *complementarity gap* $\boldsymbol{\lambda}'_g[-\mathbf{g}(\mathbf{y},\mathbf{x},\boldsymbol{\beta})]$ equals zero. Beware, however, that this is by no means guaranteed to find the global optimum, but that in our experience, several starting values and step sizes for μ must be tried and the resulting objective values compared in order to find an algorithm that works well for each particular problem.

3.4 Estimator properties

The estimator described in the previous section chooses the posterior mode as a point estimate. In addition to the mode, the researcher is likely to be interested in other properties of the posterior density such as mean, variance, and credible regions[6] for the point estimates.

All these posterior characteristics are integrals of the posterior density function. In the general case, the posterior density does not belong to any standard family of distributions, so analytical solutions for its integrals – if at all available – will need to be derived for each particular case. "Ordinary" Monte Carlo integration, that is repeatedly drawing from the posterior and numerically approximating the desired integral may not be possible due to the inability to generate random draws from the posterior.

However, the form of the posterior is fairly straightforward, as it is (proportional to) the product of the joint prior and an indicator function, that is a truncated density. Therefore, it is not difficult to compute the

[6] A credible region is the Bayesian concept that most closely corresponds to a confidence interval, albeit its interpretation is different.

density value of any given draw. This fact suggests the use of some algorithm that neither requires drawing from the posterior nor being able to compute any of its integrals analytically. Two candidates are the *Metropolis-Hastings Markov Chain Monte Carlo sampling* (M-H MCMC, see e.g. Chib and Greenberg, 1996) and *importance sampling* (Geweke, 1989). Here, an importance sampling algorithm is developed. We note, however, that M-H MCMC may be more efficient in many cases.

Letting g denote some function of interest – not to be confused with the inequality constraint of the lower level problem – we wish to compute the integral

$$E[g(\theta)] = \frac{\int_\Omega g(\theta)p(\theta)\,\mathrm{d}\theta}{\int_\Omega p(\theta)\,\mathrm{d}\theta}$$

In "ordinary" Monte Carlo integration, this expression is numerically approximated by producing n random draws from the posterior p and computing the average, or

$$n^{-1}\sum_{i=1}^{n} g(\theta_i) \rightarrow E[g(\theta)]$$

For situations such as ours, when drawing directly from the posterior is not feasible, we may instead draw from another density function $I(\boldsymbol{\theta})$, called the importance sampling density, and computing the weighted average

$$\frac{\sum_{i=1}^{n} g(\boldsymbol{\theta}_i)w(\boldsymbol{\theta}_i)}{\sum_{i=1}^{n} w(\boldsymbol{\theta}_i)} \rightarrow E[g(\boldsymbol{\theta})], \quad \text{where } w(\boldsymbol{\theta}_i) = \frac{p^*(\boldsymbol{\theta}_i)}{I(\boldsymbol{\theta}_i)} \tag{12}$$

and $p^*(\boldsymbol{\theta}_i)$ is a function that is proportional to the posterior density function. A natural choice for p^* is the product of likelihood and prior, leaving out the normalizing constant. This does not change the relative weighting and therefore not the value of the approximated integral. Geweke (1989) gives four conditions for almost sure convergence:

1. The product of the prior density, $\pi(\boldsymbol{\theta})$, and the likelihood function, $L(\boldsymbol{\theta})$, is proportional to a proper probability density function defined on Ω.
2. $\{\boldsymbol{\theta}_i\}_{i=1}^{\infty}$ is a sequence of iid random vectors, the common distribution having a probability density function $I(\boldsymbol{\theta})$.
3. The support of $I(\boldsymbol{\theta})$ includes Ω.
4. $E[g(\boldsymbol{\theta})]$ exists and is finite.

Conditions 1 and 4 are satisfied by the definition in (5) and by assumption, respectively. Satisfying conditions 2 and 3 is also not difficult with an appropriate random number generator sampling from a density with sufficiently large support. More difficult is to choose an appropriate importance sampling density $I(\boldsymbol{\theta})$ to render the convergence quick enough. For this $I(\boldsymbol{\theta})$ should be as similar to the posterior as possible, in particular as regards behavior in the tails. The intuitive reason for that is that if the tails behave differently, then we will occasionally draw a $\boldsymbol{\theta}_i$ that results in a ratio $p^*(\boldsymbol{\theta}_i)/I(\boldsymbol{\theta}_i)$ that is very large, negatively influencing the convergence of (12).

Given that the joint prior density is simple enough to draw from, one may consider the following Monte Carlo integration technique:

Algorithm 1.

1. Draw a vector $\boldsymbol{\theta}_r \equiv (\mathbf{e}_r, \mathbf{u}_r, \mathbf{y}_r, \mathbf{x}_r, \boldsymbol{\lambda}_r, \boldsymbol{\beta}_r)$ from the joint prior density function, that is use $I(\boldsymbol{\theta}_r) \equiv \pi(\mathbf{e}_r, \mathbf{u}_r, \mathbf{y}_r, \mathbf{x}_r, \boldsymbol{\lambda}_r, \boldsymbol{\beta}_r)$.
2. Evaluate the likelihood function, that is $L(\boldsymbol{\theta}_r|\gamma) = \{1 \text{ if } \boldsymbol{\theta}_r \in \Omega(\gamma), \text{ else } 0\}$. If the result is zero, then the weight is also zero (since the prior density factors cancel out in the definition of the importance weights), else it is 1.
3. Repeat steps 1 and 2 until the sample is large enough to evaluate the integral numerically. Geweke (1989) provides a method for determining what a sufficiently large sample size is.

Unfortunately, step 2 will result in zero almost for every draw, so the approach is useless in practice. The reason is that the likelihood function $L(\boldsymbol{\theta}_r|\gamma)$ is zero for almost all values of the parameters for the given observations. Intuitively, it is very unlikely that a random draw will produce parameters and error terms that exactly satisfy the Kuhn–Tucker conditions and the upper level constraints. Consider then the algorithm adjusted in the following way.

Algorithm 2.

1. Draw $\mathbf{u}_r$ and $\boldsymbol{\beta}_r$ from the prior density function. If the prior was uninformative, as might often be the case for $\boldsymbol{\beta}$, then $\boldsymbol{\beta}_r$ must be drawn from some other distribution, since drawing from uniform $(-\infty, \infty)$ is not possible. A workable solution is to select from a distribution with infinite support and mode $\boldsymbol{\beta}_{\text{hpd}}$, that is the estimated posterior mode of $\boldsymbol{\beta}$.
2. Compute $\mathbf{e}_r$ by first computing $\mathbf{x}_r = \mathbf{X} - \mathbf{u}_r$, solving the lower level problem for $\mathbf{y}_r$ and $\boldsymbol{\lambda}_r$, and computing the implied error $\mathbf{e}_r = \mathbf{Y} - \mathbf{y}_r$.
3. Repeat step 1 and 2 m times. This takes us one step further than algorithm 1, because we have now obtained a sample of $\boldsymbol{\theta}$ such that each $\boldsymbol{\theta}_r \in \Omega(\gamma)$.
4. Compute *importance weights* for $w(\boldsymbol{\theta}_r)$ using the definition above. Note that if the sampling density used was $\pi(\mathbf{u}_r, \boldsymbol{\beta}_r)$ (the remaining parameters were derived using a one to one mapping), then the importance weights, after canceling factors, are simply $\pi(\mathbf{e}_r)$, because only outcomes with a likelihood value of "1" were selected.
5. Compute Monte Carlo integrals as described earlier.

4. Demonstration of the concepts

This section demonstrates the estimation framework outlined earlier by an elaborated example, where all the steps from stochastic model formulation over posterior mode estimation through bi-level programming to the numerical computation of integrals such as posterior mean, variance, and credible sets of the posterior density are worked out in full.

To present all concepts involved yet keeping notation to a minimum, a wholly synthetic example is used. The advantage is that it is possible to obtain an example that exhibits all the difficulties described earlier while not involving any of the complications inevitably associated with a real application. The disadvantage is of course that the problem can be perceived as somewhat abstract. After the synthetic example has been worked out in full, this section is concluded with a discussion of how the method can be applied to selected real-world cases.

4.1. A synthetic economic model

Consider the following constrained economic optimization model

$$\begin{aligned} &\max_{y|x} y \\ \text{subject to}\quad & g_1(y|x,\beta_{11},\beta_{12}) = y - \beta_{11} - \beta_{12}x \leqslant 0 \\ & g_2(y|x,\beta_{21},\beta_{22}) = y - \beta_{21} - \beta_{22}x \leqslant 0 \end{aligned} \tag{13}$$

For concreteness, think of this as a firm producing a single output y subject to two linear inequality constraints depending on a single endowment x. We are interested in estimating the parameter matrix $\boldsymbol{\beta}$.

4.2. Stochastic model

Both the output y and the endowment x can be measured, but are subject to additive measurement errors. There are n observations of X and Y for different firms, stored in vectors $\mathbf{X}$ and $\mathbf{Y}$. We use upper case letters for observations and bold face letters to denote vectors or matrices. The error model for the entire sample then becomes

$$\mathbf{X} = \mathbf{x} + \mathbf{u} \tag{14}$$

$$\mathbf{Y} = \mathbf{y} + \mathbf{e} \tag{15}$$

All firms are assumed to have the same $\boldsymbol{\beta}$ but different $\mathbf{x}$ and $\mathbf{y}$. No “optimization error” is involved, so that $\mathbf{x}$, $\mathbf{y}$ exactly satisfy the Kuhn–Tucker conditions of the economic model (13) for some $\boldsymbol{\beta}$ and dual vector $\boldsymbol{\lambda} = [\boldsymbol{\lambda}_1\ \boldsymbol{\lambda}_2]$ associated with the two constraints (and all of these for each firm $i = 1, \ldots, n$). For simplicity we write $(\mathbf{x},\mathbf{y},\mathbf{u},\mathbf{e},\boldsymbol{\beta},\boldsymbol{\lambda}) \in \Omega(\mathbf{X},\mathbf{Y})$

when we mean that values of **x**, **y**, **λ**, **u**, **e**, and **β** satisfy both the stochastic model for the observations (**X**,**Y**) and the Kuhn–Tucker conditions of the economic model, or

$$\Omega(\mathbf{X},\mathbf{Y}) = \left\{ (\mathbf{x},\mathbf{y},\mathbf{u},\mathbf{e},\boldsymbol{\lambda},\boldsymbol{\beta}) : \begin{bmatrix} \mathbf{X} = \mathbf{x} + \mathbf{u} \\ \mathbf{Y} = \mathbf{y} + \mathbf{e} \\ \mathbf{1} - \boldsymbol{\lambda}_1 - \boldsymbol{\lambda}_2 = 0 \\ \mathbf{y} - \beta_{11} - \beta_{12}\mathbf{x} \leqslant 0 \perp \boldsymbol{\lambda}_1 \\ \mathbf{y} - \beta_{21} - \beta_{22}\mathbf{x} \leqslant 0 \perp \boldsymbol{\lambda}_2 \end{bmatrix} \right\}$$

A set of $n = 25$ observations were generated for the stochastic model described here. The sample was generated by assuming true $(\beta_{11}, \beta_{12}, \beta_{21}, \beta_{22}) = (0, 1, 1, -1)$ and using a pseudo random number generator to draw true x_i and errors u_i and e_i, $n = 25$ times. True x_i were drawn from uniform [0.3,0.9], e_i and u_i were both drawn from $N(0,\sigma_e)$ and $N(0,\sigma_u)$ with $\sigma_u = \sigma_u = 0.05$. The model was solved for the true y_i for each $i = 1, \ldots, n$, and the drawn errors were added to obtain the "observations." The resulting **x**, **y**, **X**, and **Y**, rounded off to five decimal places, are shown in Table 1.

Table 1. Synthetic sample for the demonstrative example model, rounded off to five decimal places

Observations	x	y	X	Y
1	0.62140	0.37860	0.59649	0.38334
2	0.50713	0.49287	0.50364	0.53540
3	0.50927	0.49073	0.49180	0.52329
4	0.35506	0.35506	0.41847	0.38338
5	0.81216	0.18784	0.80002	0.08587
6	0.64107	0.35893	0.66436	0.34373
7	0.49594	0.49594	0.47396	0.54909
8	0.48144	0.48144	0.51836	0.51284
9	0.46550	0.46550	0.48496	0.47516
10	0.34101	0.34101	0.36484	0.32570
11	0.64708	0.35292	0.67186	0.28920
12	0.76019	0.23981	0.83067	0.22753
13	0.34687	0.34687	0.29827	0.26192
14	0.52728	0.47272	0.45394	0.41315
15	0.32393	0.32393	0.26688	0.21522
16	0.66713	0.33287	0.68001	0.39094
17	0.88171	0.11829	0.87202	0.21630
18	0.58081	0.41919	0.57889	0.40774
19	0.54943	0.45057	0.44161	0.41716
20	0.46568	0.46568	0.49402	0.54412
21	0.47800	0.47800	0.49395	0.42157
22	0.31604	0.31604	0.31283	0.36823
23	0.64850	0.35150	0.63971	0.33300
24	0.54714	0.45286	0.71661	0.46741
25	0.65187	0.34813	0.61899	0.25762

4.3. Likelihood function

The error model does not specify the distribution of the error terms any further than them being additive. Therefore, the likelihood function is degenerate, taking the value "1" if the data and model constraints are satisfied and else "0," or formally

$$L(\mathbf{x},\mathbf{y},\mathbf{u},\mathbf{e},\boldsymbol{\lambda},\boldsymbol{\beta}|\mathbf{X},\mathbf{Y}) = \begin{Bmatrix} 1: & (\mathbf{x},\mathbf{y},\mathbf{u},\mathbf{e},\boldsymbol{\beta},\boldsymbol{\lambda}) \in \Omega(\mathbf{X},\mathbf{Y}) \\ 0: & \text{else} \end{Bmatrix}$$

This likelihood function is not by itself sufficient for identifying the parameters for any sample size, since there is not yet any information about the relative importance of errors on x and y. Lack of identification in the absence of relative variances is a known feature of measurement error models (see e.g. Carroll *et al.*, 1995). So far, the estimation problem is ill-posed even if there are more observations than parameters $\boldsymbol{\beta}$ of the model. The reason is that with the current model, the "true $\mathbf{x}$" is also a parameter, and so each new observation introduces an additional parameter to estimate. Thus, the $\mathbf{x}$ are akin to the incidental parameters of Neyman and Scott (1948).

4.4. Prior information

To resolve the ill-posedness, one could specify the distribution of the measurement errors. For independently distributed errors with zero mean, it would be sufficient to know the ratio of the variances. We assume here that we have a little more information (perhaps from previous studies) that can be expressed as

$$[u_i \quad e_i] \sim N\left(0, \begin{bmatrix} \sigma_x^2 & 0 \\ 0 & \sigma_y^2 \end{bmatrix}\right) \quad \text{for } i = 1,\ldots,n, \text{ and}$$

$$E[u_i u_j] = E[e_i e_j] = 0 \text{ for } i \neq j$$

where σ_x^2 and σ_y^2 are known positive constants.

Furthermore, we know that the first linear inequality in (13) has a positive slope, whereas the second has a negative slope, that is $\beta_{12} \geq 0$, $\beta_{22} \leqslant 0$. Apart from this, any combination of values of the remaining parameters $\mathbf{x}$, $\mathbf{y}$, $\boldsymbol{\beta}$, and $\boldsymbol{\lambda}$ is a-priori assumed to have equal probability, that is we assign an improper uninformative prior $\pi(\mathbf{x},\mathbf{y},\boldsymbol{\beta},\boldsymbol{\lambda}) = c$ for some positive constant c (say 1) to any combination where $\beta_{12} \geq 0$, $\beta_{22} \leqslant 0$, and zero else. We are aware that the prior on $(\mathbf{u},\mathbf{e})$ directly implies a corresponding distribution of $(\mathbf{x},\mathbf{y})$ [see Equations (14), (15)]. However, this relationship is taken care of by the likelihood function. In fact, since we have no informative priors on $\mathbf{x}$ and $\mathbf{y}$, they can be substituted out from the definition of Ω by replacing $\mathbf{x}$ by $\mathbf{X}-\mathbf{u}$ and $\mathbf{y}$ by $\mathbf{Y}-\mathbf{e}$, which reduces notation in what follows. As other implied distributions follow from more complicated model relations and cannot be easily derived "a-priori" (e.g. for $\boldsymbol{\beta}$ and $\boldsymbol{\lambda}$ in this case), it seems useful to keep this clear distinction between prior and model based likelihood.

4.5. Posterior density function

Using Bayes's rule, we define the joint posterior density function of all parameters as

$$p(\mathbf{u},\mathbf{e},\boldsymbol{\beta},\boldsymbol{\lambda}|\mathbf{X},\mathbf{Y}) \propto L(\mathbf{u},\mathbf{e},\boldsymbol{\beta},\boldsymbol{\lambda}|\mathbf{X},\mathbf{Y})\pi(\mathbf{u},\mathbf{e})\pi(\boldsymbol{\beta},\boldsymbol{\lambda})$$
$$= \prod_{i=1}^{n} I_{\Omega(\mathbf{X},\mathbf{Y})}(\mathbf{u},\mathbf{e},\boldsymbol{\beta},\boldsymbol{\lambda}) f(u_i|0,\sigma_u) f(e_i|0,\sigma_e) c I_{[0,\infty)\times(-\infty,0]}(\beta_{12},\beta_{22})$$

where $I_{\mathrm{A}}(\cdot)$ is the indicator function taking value "1" if the arguments are in the interval defined by the subscript and "0" otherwise, $f(v|\mu,\sigma)$ is the normal density function with mean μ and standard deviation σ.

4.6. Posterior mode estimator

The posterior mode estimator is defined as the argument maximizing $p(\mathbf{u},\mathbf{e},\boldsymbol{\beta},\boldsymbol{\lambda}|\mathbf{X},\mathbf{Y})$. Taking the logarithm of the objective function turns the product into a sum and allows ignoring the constant multipliers of the normal density function and the normalization required to obtain a proper posterior. The indicator function can be replaced by the restrictions to be satisfied for $(\mathbf{u},\mathbf{e},\boldsymbol{\beta},\boldsymbol{\lambda})\in\Omega(\mathbf{X},\mathbf{Y})$. We then obtain the following constrained optimization problem, where the complementary slackness conditions have been written out in full:

$$\max_{x,y,u,e,\lambda_1,\lambda_2,\beta|X,Y} \sum_{i=1}^{n} \left(\frac{-u_i^2}{\sigma_x^2} + \frac{-e_i^2}{\sigma_y^2} \right)$$
$$\begin{aligned}
\text{subject to}\quad & X_i = x_i + u_i \\
& Y_i = y_i + e_i \\
& 1 - \lambda_1 = \lambda_2 = 0 \\
& y_i - \beta_{11} = \beta_{12}x \leqslant 0 \\
& y_i - \beta_{21} = \beta_{22}x \leqslant 0 \\
& \lambda_1 \geq 0 \\
& \lambda_2 \geq 0 \\
& \beta_{12} \geq 0 \\
& \beta_{22} \leqslant 0 \\
& (y_i - \beta_{11} - \beta_{12}x)\lambda_1 = 0 \\
& (y_i - \beta_{21} - \beta_{22}x)\lambda_2 = 0
\end{aligned} \tag{16}$$

4.7. A bi-level programming solution

For the incumbent problem, both iterative smooth approximations and a BB algorithm were tried. The former turned out to be much faster, but its performance was strongly depending on the starting values and tuning of the smoothing parameter. The BB algorithm took longer to compute,[7] but produced higher values of the estimation criterion.[8] Since descriptions of BB are available in textbooks on numerical methods, we only briefly sketch the principles of the algorithm here.

To implement the BB in our case, the BLPP is rewritten as a mixed integer problem using the "big-M" formulation with *binary variables* determining the binding status of the complementary slackness conditions as described earlier. By systematically fixing the relaxed variables to 0 or 1, a tree with *all* potential solutions can be constructed. The tree contains a large number of distinct solutions (2^{25}, since there is one binary variable in each of 25 observations) and solving them all is generally intractable.

With BB, the number of potential solutions to analyze can generally be strongly reduced. BB starts at the "root node" of the tree, where all but one binary variable are *relaxed*, meaning that they are allowed to take on fractional values, effectively removing the corresponding complementary slackness conditions. BB then navigates the tree using the principles of *branching* and *bounding*.

Branching means that once a relaxed problem has been solved, and the solution still contains fractional variables, then one of the fractional variables is selected for the next branching of the tree. Since the objective value cannot be improved by fixing one variable, the relaxed solution provides an upper bound for the objective value of all binary solutions on the current branch. Therefore, a whole branch can be *cut* (bounded) if the upper bound of a relaxed problem is lower than the best integer solution already found. By consistently navigating down the branch with the highest bound, the vast majority of all potential solutions can generally be cut away from the tree.

The algorithm as outlined earlier and the data given in Table 1 finished after 1439 iterations, which is considerably less than the 2^{25} combinations of 25 binary variables. The best objective value found was −19.76172, where the first inequality was binding for the observations $i = 1, 5, 6, 8, 11,$ 12, 16, 17, 18, 20, 23, 24, 25, and for the remaining observations the second

---

[7] The BB algorithm was implemented in the programming language GAMS and ran for 10 min on an ordinary lap top computer. It should not be excluded that speed gains could be realized by an improved implementation of the algorithm.

[8] For a small program with only four binary variables where the global optimum was known by complete enumeration, the BB algorithm accurately found the optimal solution.

Table 2. Characteristics of the posterior distribution of β

$\boldsymbol{\beta}$	Mode	Mean	Standard deviation
β_{11}	−0.138	−0.031	0.077
β_{12}	1.316	1.103	0.158
β_{21}	1.128	0.911	0.158
β_{22}	−1.175	−0.814	0.221

inequality was binding. The estimated posterior modes are displayed in Table 2.

4.8. Importance sampling for mean and variance

An importance sampling algorithm along the lines of algorithm 2 can be implemented as follows:

1. For the rth draw, draw $\mathbf{u}_r$ from $N(0,\sigma_u)$, and $\boldsymbol{\beta}_r$ from $N(\boldsymbol{\beta}_{\text{hpd}},I)$, where $\boldsymbol{\beta}_{\text{hpd}}$ are the posterior mode estimates obtained in the previous section and I a four-by-four diagonal matrix of "1." The standard deviation of 1 for the sampling distribution of $\boldsymbol{\beta}$ was chosen based on the consideration that the estimated $\boldsymbol{\beta}$ were of magnitude 1 and that the slope coefficients β_{12} and β_{22} were bounded away from zero, so the standard deviation of 1 should, given the three-sigma-rule concentrate the sample where the true values are expected to be found. Repeat the sample if $\beta_{12}<0$ or $\beta_{22}>0$, since such betas have a probability of zero and would result in zero importance weights anyway.
2. Compute $\mathbf{x}_r = \mathbf{X}-\mathbf{u}_r$, and solve (13) to obtain $\mathbf{y}_r$. Compute $\mathbf{e}_r = \mathbf{Y}-\mathbf{y}_r$.
3. Compute $w_r = \prod_{i=1}^{n} f(e_r|0,\sigma_e)/\prod_{j=1}^{2}\prod_{k=1}^{2} f(\beta_{jk}|\hat{\beta}_{jk},0.5)$, where $f(z|\mu,\sigma)$ is the normal density function of z given mean μ and standard deviation σ, and $\hat{\beta}_{jk}$ is the posterior mode estimate of β_{jk}.
4. Repeat steps (1)–(3) until a sufficiently large sample has been obtained. We sampled $R = 100\,000$ times.
5. Compute the estimate of the posterior mean as $\hat{\boldsymbol{\beta}} = \hat{E}(\boldsymbol{\beta}|\mathbf{X},\mathbf{Y}) = \sum_{r=1}^{R} w_r\boldsymbol{\beta}_r/\sum_{r=1}^{R} w_r$ and the estimate of the posterior variance as $\hat{E}[(\boldsymbol{\beta}-\hat{\boldsymbol{\beta}})^2|\mathbf{X},\mathbf{Y}] = \sum_{r=1}^{R} w_r(\boldsymbol{\beta}_r-\hat{\boldsymbol{\beta}})/\sum_{r=1}^{R} w_r$.

The algorithm was implemented in GAMS and importance weights below machine precision obtained in step (3) were discarded and re-sampled. The built-in random number generators were used in step (1). Since the draws were made in batches of 10 000, the target 100 000 draws was not hit exactly, but instead 100 242 nonzero weights were obtained. The resulting estimates of mean and standard deviation of $\boldsymbol{\beta}$ are also shown in Table 2.

4.9. Other applications

The estimation framework described in this chapter can be applied to a wide variety of models where any of the three problems discussed in Section 2 are present. Real world examples with relevance to trade analysis would include the estimation of import demand and quota rents in models with TRQs or the balancing of social accounting matrices (Golan *et al.*, 1994; Heckelei *et al.*, 2008). Estimation procedures for the TRQ example can be outlined as follows.

For a country importing a single commodity under a TRQ, the import price p_d equals the CIF price (the border price including Cost, Insurance and Freight) p_w plus in- or out-of-quota tariffs (t_{in},t_{out}) plus any quota rent ρ. As is common in trade analysis, we formulate the mixed complementarity problem (MCP) directly, without specifying primal optimization models. As indicated above, and illustrated in Figure 1, the MCP formulation leads to the same kind of numerical problems that are involved in the BLPP. The economic model to estimate is specified by the following equation system.

Import demand function:

$$p_d = \beta_{d1} + \beta_{d2}(q_{in} + q_{out}) \tag{17}$$

Export supply function:

$$p_w = \beta_{w1} + \beta_{w2}(q_n + q_{out}) \tag{18}$$

Zero arbitrage condition:

$$p_d = \rho_w + t_{in} + \rho \tag{19}$$

Complementary slackness conditions:

$$q_{in} \leqslant \text{TRQ} \perp \rho \geq 0 \tag{20}$$

$$\rho \leqslant t_{out} - t_{in} \perp q_{out} \geq 0 \tag{21}$$

q_{in}, q_{out}, p_d, p_w, and ρ are variables of the equilibrium problem, and the tariffs t_{out} and t_{in} are known parameters. q_{in}, q_{out} denote the within- and out of quota exports, respectively, where it is tacitly assumed that q_{in} will always be positive. p_d and p_w are (domestic) import price and (world) export price, respectively, and they are linear functions of the total traded volume, governed by the parameter matrix $\boldsymbol{\beta}$, which is to be estimated. For a small country, β_{w2} is fixed *a priori* to zero. As before, the perpendicular operator $a \leqslant b \perp c \leqslant d$ means that at least one of the inequalities holds with equality, or $(a-b)(c-d) = 0$, implying that if the quota rent $\rho > 0$, then $q_{in} = \text{TRQ}$, and if $q_{out} > 0$ then $\rho = t_{out} - t_{in}$ etc.

Observations, denoted by upper case letters, with additive disturbances e and u are available for prices and quantities, giving the following error model:

$$Q_{ik} = q_{ik} + e_{ik} \quad \text{for } i = \{\text{“in”}, \text{“out”}\} \tag{22}$$

$$P_{ik} = p_{ik} + u_{ik} \quad \text{for } j = \{\text{“d”}, \text{“w”}\} \tag{23}$$

where $k = 1, \ldots, K$ is the set of repeated observations.

As before, we define the set $\Omega(\mathbf{Q},\mathbf{P},\mathbf{t})$ as the set of parameters (including true prices, quantities and quota rent) that satisfy the model Equations (17–21) and error model (22 and 23) at the observed quantities, prices and tariffs. The likelihood function for the parameters given K observations $\mathbf{Q}$ and $\mathbf{P}$, if q_{in} is everywhere replaced by $Q_{\text{in}}-e_{\text{in}}$ and similar for the other observable model variables, is defined as

$$L(\boldsymbol{\beta}, \rho, \mathbf{e}, \mathbf{u}|\mathbf{Q}, \mathbf{P}, \mathbf{t}) \equiv \{1 \text{ if } (\boldsymbol{\beta}, \rho, \mathbf{e}, \mathbf{u}) \in \Omega(\mathbf{Q}, \mathbf{P}, \mathbf{t}), \ \ 0 \text{ otherwise}\}$$

For reasons discussed in Section 2, prior information is required to obtain point estimates for $\boldsymbol{\beta}$. Denote the prior distribution of all parameters by $\pi(\boldsymbol{\beta},\rho,\mathbf{e},\mathbf{u})$. The posterior density is then

$$p(\boldsymbol{\beta}, \rho, \mathbf{e}, \mathbf{u}|\mathbf{Q}, \mathbf{P}, \mathbf{t}) \propto L(\boldsymbol{\beta}, \rho, \mathbf{e}, \mathbf{u}|\mathbf{Q}, \mathbf{P}, \mathbf{t})\pi(\boldsymbol{\beta}, \rho, \mathbf{e}, \mathbf{u}) \tag{24}$$

If the prior distribution is sufficiently informative, a posterior mode estimator can be obtained by solving the problem

$$\max_{\boldsymbol{\beta},\rho,\mathbf{e},\mathbf{u}} \pi(\boldsymbol{\beta}, \rho, \mathbf{e}, \mathbf{u}) : (\boldsymbol{\beta}, \rho, \mathbf{e}, \mathbf{u}) \in \Omega(\mathbf{Q}, \mathbf{P}, \mathbf{t}) \tag{25}$$

The problem (25) requires using any of the BLPP[9] techniques described earlier, because of the complementary slackness conditions hiding in the definition of Ω.

Means, variances, and other inferences can be computed by applying numerical integration methods such as importance sampling or M-H MCMC to the posterior density function (24).

5. *Conclusion*

This chapter introduced a general Bayesian estimation approach of (inequality) constrained optimization models with errors in variables. The suggested procedure is able to address three methodological problems in this context: (1) solving the implied bi-level programming set-up with complementarity restrictions, (2) ill-posedness of the errors in variables formulation, and (3) the general failure of classical inference techniques.

---

[9] The problem (25) is in fact an MPEC, which is closely related to BLPP. See e.g. Luo et al. (1996).

Maximizing the prior density of unknown parameters subject to the economic model represented by its optimality conditions provides the posterior mode. The mode is used to define an appropriate sampling density that – combined with solving the economic model – generates outcomes from an importance function. A sufficient number of draws allows to numerically integrate the posterior distribution and thereby provides statistical inference measures on model parameters. The full approach is demonstrated with a one variable, two constraints model.

The outlined technique allows estimating complex models with discontinuities and/or errors in variables relevant for trade analysis. This extends well beyond the estimation of explicit optimization models. The economic model in the form of the optimality conditions can be easily replaced by equations characterizing market equilibriums or by accounting constraints. The set-up for the estimation of a country's trade equilibrium with a TRQ has been illustrated as another example for a model combining discontinuities and EIV. Considerably simpler is the application in the context of a data balancing exercise, for example to derive a Social Accounting Matrix based on incomplete and uncertain information. Here, only the EIV characteristic applies reflecting incomplete and uncertain information on coefficients as well as row and column aggregates.

Even though the reader may also come up with possibilities for conceptual improvements, we currently see the main need for improving simplicity and speed of application. As far as we know, until now no generally reliable algorithm solving a large variety of bi-level programming models is available. More robust algorithms or at least a set of rules on which algorithm works best for a certain class of models would be very helpful. Furthermore, the chosen importance sampling scheme shows slow convergence and Markov Chain Monte Carlo techniques might help to derive posterior measures of equal precision in shorter time.

References

Bard, J. (1998), *Practical Bilevel Optimization*. Kluwer Academic Publishers, Dordrecht.

Blaug, M. (1992), *The Methodology of Economics, or How Economists Explain*, second ed. Cambridge University Press, Cambridge, reprinted in 1997.

Buysse, J., Van Huylenbroeck, G., Lauwers, L. (2007), Normative, positive and econometric mathematical programming as tools for incorporation of multifunctionality in agricultural policy modelling. *Agriculture, Ecosystems and Environment* 120, 70–81.

Carroll, R., Ruppert, D., Stefanski, L. (1995), *Measurement Error in Nonlinear Models*. Chapman and Hall, Suffolk, Great Britain.

Chib, S., Greenberg, E. (1996), Markov chain Monte Carlo simulation methods in econometrics. *Econometric Theory* 12 (3), 409–431.

Clarke, B. (1996), Information optimality and Bayesian modelling. *Journal of Econometrics* 138, 405–429.

Colson, B., Marcotte, P., Savard, G. (2007), An overview of bilevel optimization. *Annals of Operations Research* 153, 235–256.

Denzau, A.T., Gibbons, P.C., Greenberg, E. (1989), Bayesian estimation of proportions with a cross-entropy prior. *Communications in Statistics – Theory and Methods* 18 (5), 1843–1861.

Ferris, M.C., Dirkse, S.P., Meeraus, A. (2005), Mathematical programs with equilibrium constraints: automatic reformulation and solution via constrained optimization. In: Kehoe, T.J., Srinivasan, T.N., Whalley, J. (Eds.), *Frontiers in Applied General Equilibrium Modelling: In Honour of Herbert Scarf*. Cambridge University Press, Cambridge, UK.

Fortuny-Amat, J., McCarl, B. (1981), A representation and economic interpretation of a two-level programming problem. *The Journal of the Operational Research Society* 32 (9), 783–792.

GAMS. (2010a), NLPEC solver manual. Available at http://www.gams.com/dd/docs/solvers/nlpec.pdf (accessed February 2010).

GAMS. (2010b), GAMS – A user's guide. GAMS Development Corporation, Washington, DC, USA. Available at http://www.gams.com/dd/docs/bigdocs/GAMSUsersGuide.pdf (accessed July 2010).

George, E.I. (1986), Minimax multiple shrinkage estimation. *The Annals of Statistics* 14 (1), 188–205.

Geweke, J. (1989), Bayesian inference in econometric models using Monte Carlo integration. *Econometrica* 51 (6), 1317–1339.

Golan, A., Judge, G., Robinson, S. (1994), Recovering information from incomplete or partial multisectoral economic data. *The Review of Economics and Statistics* 76 (3), 541–549.

Golan, A., Perloff, J.M., Shen, E.Z. (2001), Estimating a demand system with nonnegativity constraints: Mexican meat demand. *Review of Economics and Statistics* 83 (3), 541–550.

Hazell, P., Norton, R. (1986), *Mathematical Programming for Economic Analysis in Agriculture*. MacMillan, New York.

Heckelei, T., Mittelhammer, R., Jansson, T. (2008), A Bayesian alternative to generalized cross entropy solutions for underdetermined econometric models. Food and Resource Economics Discussion Paper 2008(2), University of Bonn.

Hoerl, A.E., Kennard, R.W. (1970), Ridge regression: biased estimation for nonorthogonal problems. *Technometrics* 12 (1), 55–67.

Howitt, R.E. (1995), Positive mathematical programming. *American Journal of Agricultural Economics* 77, 329–342.

Jansson, T. (2007), Econometric specification of constrained optimization models. Dissertations, Universität Bonn.

Jansson, T., Heckelei, T. (2009), A new estimator for trade costs and its small sample properties. *Economic Modelling* 26, 489–498.

Jaynes, E.T. (1984), Prior information and ambiguity in inverse problems. *SIAM-AMS Proceedings* 14, 151–166.

Lee, L., Pitt, M. (1986), Microeconomic demand systems with binding nonnegativity constraints: the dual approach. *Econometrica* 54, 1237–1242.

Luo, Z., Pang, J., Ralph, D. (1996), *Mathematical Programs with Equilibrium Constraints*. Cambridge University Press, Cambridge, UK.

Mittelhammer, R., Judge, G., Miller, D. (2000), *Econometric Foundations*. Cambridge University Press, New York.

Newey, W.K., McFadden, D. (1994), Large sample estimation and hypothesis testing. In: *Handbook of Econometrics*, vol. 4. Elsevier, Amsterdam, pp. 2111–2145.

Neyman, J., Scott, E. (1948), Consistent estimation from partially consistent observations. *Econometrica* 16, 1–32.

O'Sullivan, F. (1986), A statistical perspective on ill-posed inverse problems. *Statistical Science* 1 (4), 502–527.

Phaneuf, D.J., Kling, C.L., Herriges, J.A. (2000), Estimation and welfare calculations in a generalized corner solution model with an application to recreation demand. *Review of Economics and Statistics* 82, 83–92.

Ransom, M. (1985), A comment on consumer demand systems with binding nonnegativity constraints. Working Paper No. 192, Industrial relations section, Princeton University.

Ransom, M.R. (1987), The labor supply of married men-a switching regressions model. *Journal of Labor Economics* 5, 63–75.

Robbins, L. (1945), *An Essay on the Nature and Significance of Economic Science*. Macmillan, London.

Silverman, B.W. (1982), On the estimation of a probability density function by maximum penalized likelihood. *The Annals of Statistics* 19 (3), 795–810.

Titterington, D.M. (1984), The maximum entropy method for data analysis. *Nature* 312, 381–382.

Titterington, D.M. (1985), Common structure of smoothing techniques in statistics. *International Statistical Review* 53 (2), 141–170.

Wales, T.J., Woodland, A.D. (1983), Estimation of consumer demand systems with binding nonnegativity constraints. *Journal of Econometrics* 21, 263–285.

Yue, C., Beghin, J.C. (2009), Tariff equivalent and forgone trade effects of prohibitive technical barriers to trade. *American Journal of Agricultural Economics* 91 (4), 930–941.

Zellner, A. (1988), Optimal information processing and Bayes's theorem. *The American Statistician* 42 (4), 278–284.

CHAPTER 2

Trade Liberalization and the Extensive Margin of Trade in a CGE Model with Heterogeneous Firms

Fan Zhai

Department of Asset Allocation and Strategic Research, China Investment Corporation, People's Republic of China
E-mail address: zhaifan@china-inv.cn

Abstract
This chapter presents a global computable general equilibrium model with firm heterogeneity based on the Melitz (2003) framework and examines the relative importance of the intensive and extensive margins in the trade expansion following trade liberalization. Using a set of plausible parameters values suggested by empirical studies and calibrating the model to the recent Global Trade Analysis Project (GTAP) global database, our illustrative simulations indicate that the extensive margin accounts for around one-third of the trade growth induced by a reduction in tariffs or variable trade costs. In the case of reducing fixed trade costs, the extensive margin contributes almost 200 percent of the trade expansion, with the intensive margin contributing negatively to trade growth.

Keywords: Trade liberalization, extensive margin, CGE model

1. Introduction

Recent empirical research has revealed the importance of the extensive margin for international trade. Larger countries trade not only larger volumes but also a wider variety of goods. Hummels and Klenow (2005) find that the extensive margin accounts for 60 percent of the increase of exports of larger economies and about one-third of that of the same countries. Eaton *et al.* (2004) examine firm-level export data of French firms and conclude that the number of exporting firms, rather than the amount exported by each firm, determines the variation across destinations. The extensive margin is also a crucial force behind trade expansion following liberalization. Kehoe and Ruhl (2003) find that trade in goods

Frontiers of Economics and Globalization
Volume 7 ISSN: 1574-8715
DOI: 10.1108/S1574-8715(2010)0000007005

that were not traded earlier shows substantial growth following a decrease in trade barriers. A set of goods that accounted for only 10 percent of trade before the liberalization may come to account for 40 percent following it.

Traditional computable general equilibrium (CGE) models are based on the Armington assumption of national product differentiation (Armington, 1969). Under this assumption, each country produces a single variety in each category of goods, so there is no extensive margin. The differences in trade volume across countries are fully accounted for by the quantities of each good exported, that is, the intensive margin. Given the absence of the extensive margin, traditional CGE models fail to capture the rapid trade expansion following trade liberalization. Moreover, these models often underestimate the welfare effect of trade liberalization due to the absence of variety effects as well as the strong adverse terms-of-trade effects associated with intensive export growth (Zhai, 2008).

On the basis of recent developments in heterogeneous firm trade theory, some attempts have been made to explicitly introduce the extensive margin into CGE models (see Balistreri *et al.*, 2007; Zhai, 2008; Kancs, 2010). Following the Melitz (2003) model that incorporates firm productivity heterogeneity into the Krugman (1979) monopolistic competition framework, this new generation of CGE models emphasize the interaction of trade costs and productivity differences across firms operating in imperfectly competitive industries. The existence of fixed trade costs induces only the most productive firms to export. When trade costs decrease, new firms with lower productivity enter the export markets in response to the potential higher profits. By contrast, the least productive non-exporting firms are forced to exit because of the increased import competition in domestic markets. This selection mechanism of firms to export leads to the extensive margin of trade adjustment. Simulations using heterogeneous firm CGE models have found larger trade and welfare gains from trade liberalization (Zhai, 2008; Kancs, 2010).

Building on previous work of Zhai (2008), this chapter explores in depth the extensive margin in a global CGE model with heterogeneous firms. It investigates the quantitative significance of the extensive margin following trade liberalization in an empirically calibrated CGE model. The remainder of the chapter is organized as follows: the next section presents the specification of the firm heterogeneity CGE model. Section 3 examines the trade adjustment at the extensive and intensive margins in the wake of cutting three types of trade barriers: tariffs, variable trade costs, and fixed trade costs. The final section offers conclusions.

2. *The CGE model*

Following the spirit of Melitz (2003) and Chaney (2008), the CGE model used in this chapter assumes firm level heterogeneity in productivity.

It features three sectors (primary, manufacturing, and services) and five regions (the United States, European Union, Japan, China, and rest of the world). In the primary sector of each region, there is a representative firm that operates under constant returns to scale technology, and the Armington assumption is applied to model international trade. Manufacturing and services sectors produce differentiated products. Each of these two sectors is populated by a continuum of firms differentiated by the varieties they produce and their productivity. Firms face fixed production costs, resulting in increasing returns to scale of production. As in Chaney (2008), there are no entry costs to the domestic market and the number of potential entrants is fixed in each sector. On the demand side, the agents are assumed to have Dixit–Stiglitz preferences over the continuum of varieties. As each firm is a monopolist for the variety it produces, it sets the price of its product at a constant markup over its marginal cost.

There are also fixed costs and variable costs associated with exporting activities. A firm enters export markets if and only if the net profits generated from its exports to a given country are sufficient to cover the fixed exporting costs. The zero cutoff profit conditions in domestic and exporting markets define the productivity thresholds for a firm's entry into the domestic and export markets, and in turn determine the equilibrium distribution of non-exporting firms and exporting firms, as well as their average productivities. Typically, the combination of fixed export costs and variable export costs ensures that the exporting productivity threshold is higher than that for production for the domestic market, that is, only a small fraction of firms with high productivity engage in export markets. These exporting firms supply both the domestic and export markets.

2.1. Demand

In each region of the model, the representative consumer receives income from the supply of production factors to the firms, dividends from the firms, and lump-sum transfers from the government. The consumer allocates their disposable income among the consumer goods and savings using an extended linear expenditure system, which is derived from maximizing a Stone–Geary utility function.[1] The consumption/saving decision is completely static. Savings enter the utility function as a "good," and its price is set as equal to the average price of consumer goods.

Investment demand and government consumption are specified as a Leontief function. I assume that in each sector s, a composite good Q_s is used for household consumption, investment, government consumption,

[1] The modeling of household behavior follows the LINKAGE model. See van der Mensbrugghe (2005).

and intermediate input. The composite good is a Constant Elasticity of Substitution (CES) aggregation of domestic goods and imports:

$$Q_j^s = \left[\sum_{i \in R} (\alpha_{ij}^s)^{1/\sigma^s} (Z_{ij}^s)^{(\sigma^s - 1)/\sigma^s} \right]^{\sigma^s/(\sigma^s - 1)} \tag{1}$$

where Z_{ij}^s is the quantity of good s produced in region i sold in the market of region j. R denotes the set of regions. The dual price index of composite good s, P_j^s, is defined over the aggregate prices of each supplier, P_{rij}^s

$$P_j^s = \left[\sum_{i \in R} \alpha_{ij}^s \left(\frac{\varepsilon_j}{\varepsilon_i} P_{rij}^s \right)^{1-\sigma^s} \right]^{1/(1-\sigma^s)} \tag{2}$$

where ε_i is the exchange rate expressed as units of region i's currency per US dollar. The demand function generated from (1) is:

$$\frac{Z_{ij}^s}{Q_j^s} = \alpha_{ij}^s \left(\frac{P_j^s}{P_{rij}^s} \frac{\varepsilon_i}{\varepsilon_j} \right)^{\sigma^s} \tag{3}$$

In the primary sector, I follow the standard Armington assumption of national production differentiation, thus σ^s represents the substitution elasticity of good s among different regions in these sectors. The Armington share parameters α_{ij}^s in these sectors reflect the preferences of consumers' bias for home or other regions' products. In the manufacturing and services sectors, σ^s represents the substitution elasticity among varieties of each firm and the Armington share parameters α_{ij}^s always equal one, meaning that the pattern of bilateral trade flows in these sectors are totally determined by the relative prices of the aggregated varieties from each region, P_{rij}^s. In these two sectors, Z_{ij}^s is the CES aggregate of the individual varieties that are produced in country i and sold in region j, that is, the standard Dixit–Stiglitz preference is assumed:

$$Z_{ij}^s = \left[\int_{\varphi \in \Omega_{ij}^s} q(\varphi)^{(\sigma^s - 1)/\sigma^s} \, \mathrm{d}\varphi \right]^{\sigma^s/(\sigma^s - 1)} \tag{4}$$

where Ω_{ij}^s is the set of varieties that are produced in country i and sold in region j. Ω_{ij}^s is endogenously determined in equilibrium. The dual price index of the aggregate varieties, P_{rij}^s, is defined over the prices of each good, p_φ,

$$P_{rij}^s = \left[\int_{\varphi \in \Omega_{ij}^s} p(\varphi)^{1-\sigma} \, \mathrm{d}\varphi \right]^{1/(1-\sigma)} \tag{5}$$

And the demand for each variety is:

$$q(\varphi) = Z\left[\frac{P_r}{p(\varphi)}\right]^{\sigma} \tag{6}$$

2.2. Production and trade

2.2.1. Factor markets

There are four primary factors: capital, skilled labor, unskilled labor, and land/natural resources for the primary sector. It is assumed that factor endowments are fully employed. Capital and labor are fully mobile across sectors. All primary factors are immobile across regions.

2.2.2. Production technology

Production is modeled using a nesting of CES functions. At the top level, the output X^s is produced as a combination of aggregate intermediate demand and value added. At the second level, aggregate intermediate demand is split into each commodity according to Leontief technology. Value added is produced by a capital–land bundle and aggregate labor. Finally, at the bottom level, aggregate labor is decomposed into unskilled and skilled labor, and the capital–land bundle is decomposed into capital and land/natural resources (for the primary sector). At each level of production, there is a unit cost function that is dual to the CES aggregator function and demand functions for corresponding inputs. The top-level unit cost function defines the marginal cost of sectoral output, C^s.

2.2.3. Firm heterogeneity

In sectors with heterogeneous firms, firms are assumed to get productivity draws φ from a Pareto distribution with lower bound $\varphi_{\min}$ and shape parameter $\gamma > \sigma - 1$.[2] Without a loss of generality, the units of quantity can be chosen so that the low bound parameter $\varphi_{\min}$ equals unity. Then the density function $g(\varphi)$ and the cumulative distribution function $G(\varphi)$ are

$$g(\varphi) = \gamma\varphi^{-\gamma-1}, \quad 1 - G(\varphi) = \varphi^{-\gamma}, \quad \varphi \in [1, \infty) \tag{7}$$

where γ is an inverse measure of firm heterogeneity. The higher γ, the more homogeneous the firms are. The total mass of entrants in sector s of region i, N_i^s, is assumed to be fixed.

Firms are price setters. The model assumes "large group" monopolistic competition under an arbitrarily large number of firms, such that the elasticity of demand for each firm's output is the substitution elasticity

---

[2] The assumption $\gamma > \sigma - 1$ ensures that the size distribution of firms has a finite mean.

among varieties, σ^s. The optimal pricing rule for a firm is to charge a constant markup over the marginal cost:

$$p_{ij}^s(\varphi) = \frac{\sigma^s}{\sigma^s - 1}\frac{(1 + t_{ij}^s)\tau_{ij}^s C_i^s}{\varphi} \tag{8}$$

where t_{ij}^s is the tariff rate, and τ_{ij}^s is iceberg-type variable trade costs whereby only a fraction $1/\tau_{ij}$ of each unit of good shipped from country i to j ($\tau_{ij} = 1$ for $i = j$) arrives. And the value of sales of individual firm is:

$$\begin{aligned} q_{ij}^s(\varphi)p_{ij}^s(\varphi) &= P_j^s Q_j^s \left(\frac{\varepsilon_i}{\varepsilon_j}\right)^{\sigma^s}\left(\frac{P_j^s}{p_{ij}^s(\varphi)}\right)^{\sigma^s - 1} \\ &= Q_j^s\left(P_j^s\frac{\varepsilon_i}{\varepsilon_j}\right)^{\sigma^s}\left(\frac{\sigma^s - 1}{\sigma^s}\frac{\varphi}{(1 + t_{ij}^s)\tau_{ij}^s C_i^s}\right)^{\sigma^s - 1} \end{aligned} \tag{9}$$

In addition to variable costs C^s, firms in the manufactures and services sectors face fixed costs for their production and exports. The fixed inputs of these firms are a fixed combination of capital (f_{Kij}^s), labor (f_{Lij}^s), and intermediate inputs (f_{Xij}^{ts}). Therefore, the expenditure of fixed costs, F_{ij}, is defined as:

$$F_{ij}^s = W_i f_{Lij}^s + R_i f_{Kij}^s + \sum_t P_i^t f_{Xij}^{ts} \tag{10}$$

where W_i, R_i, and P_i^t are the wage rate, rental rate of capital, and price of good t, respectively. The fixed costs are assumed to be same for all firms.

The profits obtained by firm φ in country i from selling in the domestic market (π_{ii}) and exporting to country j (π_{ij}) are given by:

$$\begin{aligned} \pi_{ij}^s(\varphi) &= \frac{q_{ij}^s(\varphi)p_{ij}^s(\varphi)}{(1 + t_{ij}^s)} - c(q_{ij}^s(\varphi), \varphi) - F_{ij}^s \\ &= \frac{(P_j^s\varepsilon_i/\varepsilon_j)^{\sigma^s} Q_j^s}{(1 + t_{ij}^s)\sigma^s}\left(\frac{\sigma^s - 1}{\sigma^s}\frac{\varphi}{(1 + t_{ij}^s)\tau_{ij}^s C_i^s}\right)^{\sigma - 1} - F_{ij}^s \end{aligned} \tag{11}$$

After drawing their productivity, firms will decide whether to produce and to export. A firm will not produce if its expected profits are nonpositive. Thus, any firm whose productivity is lower than a threshold φ^* will choose to exit without even starting production. Similarly, a firm will choose to export to a given country if and only if the net profits generated by the exports are sufficient to cover the fixed exporting costs. The condition defining the threshold is the zero cutoff profit condition:

$$\varphi_{ij}^{s*} = \frac{\sigma^s\tau_{ij}^s C_i^s}{\sigma^s - 1}\left(\frac{P_j^s}{1 + t_{ij}^s}\frac{\varepsilon_i}{\varepsilon_j}\right)^{\sigma^s/(1 - \sigma^s)}\left(\frac{F_{ij}^s\sigma^s}{Q_j^s}\right)^{1/(\sigma^s - 1)} \tag{12}$$

where φ_{ii}^* is the productivity threshold for production and φ_{ij}^* is the productivity threshold for the least productive firm in country i able to export to country j. Firms with productivity levels between φ_{ii}^* and the lowest exporting productivity threshold ($\min \varphi_{ij}^*$, $j \in R$, $j \neq i$) only produce for their domestic markets. The other firms vary in their exporting partners, depending on their productivity levels and the threshold φ_{ij}^* in specific exporting market.

In equilibrium, the weighted average productivity level of the producing firms in country i as well as that for exporting firms, $\tilde{\varphi}_{ij}^s$, is defined as a function of the cutoff levels, φ_{ij}^*:

$$\begin{aligned}\tilde{\varphi}_{ij}^s(\varphi_{ij}^{s*}) &= \left[\frac{1}{1-G(\varphi_{ij}^{s*})}\int_{\varphi_{ij}^{s*}}^{\infty}\varphi^{\sigma^s-1}g(\varphi)\,d\varphi\right]^{1/(\sigma^s-1)}\\ &= \varphi_{ij}^{s*}\left(\frac{\gamma_i^s}{\gamma_i^s-\sigma^s+1}\right)^{1/(\sigma^s-1)}\end{aligned} \tag{13}$$

where the weights reflect the relative output shares of firms with different productivity levels. Then the variety adjusted aggregate prices of domestic sale and exports can be expressed as:

$$P_{r\;ij}^s = \frac{\sigma^s}{\sigma^s-1}\frac{(1+t_{ij}^s)\tau_{ij}^s C_i^s}{\tilde{\varphi}_{ij}^s}[N_i^s(1-G(\varphi_{ij}^{s*}))]^{1/(1-\sigma^s)} \tag{14}$$

where $N_i^s(1-G(\varphi_{ij}^{s*}))$ represents the total mass of firms in sector s and region i that sell in market j.

2.3. Equilibrium and closure

The equilibrium of the good markets requires that the output, X_i^s, equal the sum of the demand from each markets, that is:

$$X_i^s = \begin{cases}\sum_{j\in R}\frac{Z_{ij}^s}{\tau_{ij}^s}, & \text{for primary sector}\\ \sum_{j\in R}[N_i^s(1-G(\varphi_{ij}^{s*}))]^{1/(1-\sigma^s)}\frac{Z_{ij}^s}{\tau_{ij}^s\tilde{\varphi}_{ij}^s}, & \text{for manufactures and services sectors}\end{cases} \tag{15}$$

Note that for sectors with heterogeneous firms, demand is adjusted by the Dixit–Stiglitz variety effects and the average productivity.

There are three closure rules: the net government balance, investment-savings, and trade balance. I assume that changes in the government budget are automatically compensated by changes in marginal income tax rates. Government expenditures are exogenous in real terms.

Domestic investment is equal to the sum of domestic saving resources, that is, household saving, government saving, and net foreign saving. As government saving is exogenous, changes in investment are determined by changes in the levels of household saving and foreign saving.

The final closure rule concerns the current account balance. In each region, either the foreign saving or the real exchange rate can be fixed, whereas the other is allowed to adjust, providing alternative closure rules. When foreign saving is set exogenously, the GDP (at factor cost) price deflator in each region is fixed and the equilibrium is achieved by changing the exchange rate across regions. Alternatively, both the GDP price deflator and the exchange rate in each region are fixed, and foreign saving is endogenous (subject to the constraint of the global balance) to maintain the trade balance.

2.4. Calibration

The model is calibrated to the GTAP global database (version 7.0). Some key firm-level parameters are set based mainly on a review of the relevant literature. The markup ratios are 30 percent for the manufacturing sector and 35 percent for the services sector. The choices of markup ratios, together with the optimal pricing rule for monopolistic firms, imply that the substitution elasticity between varieties is 4.3 for manufacturing sectors and 3.9 for services sector. The shape parameters of the Pareto distribution are calibrated to match the profit ratio in total markup, which is estimated to be 66.7 percent based on French firm data by Eaton *et al.* (2007). Assuming that all regions have access to same technology, the marginal costs C are set equal to unity in all regions for the calibration.

I assume the mass of potential entrants in each sector, N_i^s, is proportional to the sectoral output. As fixed production costs, fixed exporting costs and variable trade costs are not available, they are calibrated to the base year's bilateral trade flows. In the CGE model, the bilateral trade flows are determined by the following gravity equation:

$$P_{rij}^s Z_{ij}^s = \left(P_j^s \frac{\varepsilon_i}{\varepsilon_j}\right)^{\sigma^s} Q_j^s N_i^s (\varphi_{ij}^{s*})^{-\gamma_i^s+\sigma^s-1} \left(\frac{\sigma^s(1+t_{ij}^s)\tau_{ij}^s C_i^s}{\sigma^s - 1}\right)^{1-\sigma^s} \frac{\gamma_i^s}{\gamma_i^s - \sigma^s + 1} \tag{16}$$

Hummels and Klenow (2005) find that extensive margin accounts for 60 percent of the difference in export values across regions. On the basis of their empirical finding and (16), we have:

$$\left(\frac{P^s_{r\,ij}Z^s_{ij}}{P^s_{r\,jj}Z^s_{jj}}\right)^{(1-0.6)} = \frac{\int_{\varphi^{s*}_{ij}}^{\infty}(p_{ij}(\varphi)q_{ij}(\varphi))g(\varphi)\,\mathrm{d}\varphi}{\int_{\varphi^{s*}_{ij}}^{\infty}(p_{jj}(\varphi)q_{jj}(\varphi))g(\varphi)\,\mathrm{d}\varphi} = \frac{\varepsilon_i^{\sigma^s}((1+t^s_{ij})\tau^s_{ij}C^s_i)^{1-\sigma^s}\gamma^s_i(\gamma^s_j-\sigma^s+1)}{\varepsilon_j^{\sigma^s}(\tau^s_{jj}C^s_j)^{1-\sigma^s}\gamma^s_j(\gamma^s_i-\sigma^s+1)} \tag{17}$$

Assuming that domestic trade incurs no iceberg costs, that is, τ_{ii} equals 1, the variable trade costs, τ_{ij}, can be calculated from (16) using the base year trade flows and domestic sales data. I also assume that 80 percent of entrants produce and sell in the domestic market. Then the shares of firms selling in each market and their respective productivity thresholds can be derived from (15) and (7). Finally, (15) can be rewritten as

$$P^s_{r\,ij}Z^s_{ij} = N^s_i(1-G(\varphi^{s*}_{ij}))(F^s_{ij}(1+t_{ij})\sigma^s)\frac{\gamma^s_i}{\gamma^s_i-\sigma^s+1} \tag{18}$$

from which the fixed costs can be solved.

3. *Extensive and intensive margins of trade*

The changes in aggregate trade flows can be decomposed into two margins. The intensive margin refers to how much the volume of existing export varieties change. The extensive margin refers to how much new varieties are exported. Figure 1 illustrates the two margins when there is a

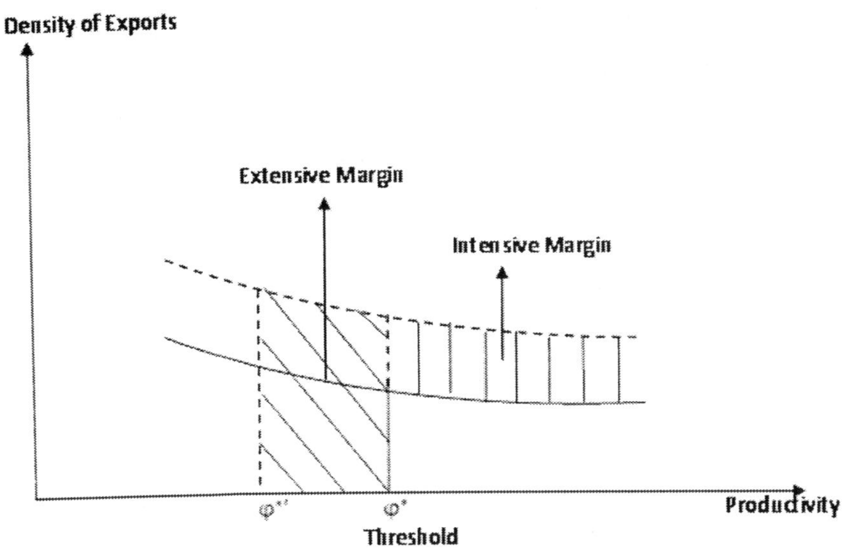

Fig. 1. The intensive and extensive margins of exports.

shock which leads to lower productivity threshold and larger exports per firm. For aggregate exports, $P^s_{rij}Z^s_{ij} = \int_{\varphi^{s*}_{ij}}^{\infty} p(\varphi)q(\varphi)g(\varphi)\,\mathrm{d}\varphi$, the two margins can be expressed as

$$\Delta(P^s_{rij}Z^s_{ij}) \underbrace{\int_{\varphi^{s*}_{ij}}^{\infty} \Delta(p(\varphi)q(\varphi))g(\varphi)\,\mathrm{d}\varphi}_{\text{intensive margin}} - \underbrace{p(\varphi^{s*}_{ij})q(\varphi^{s*}_{ij})g(v)\Delta(\varphi^{s*}_{ij})}_{\text{extensive margin}} \tag{19}$$

Chaney (2008) derived the elasticities of the extensive and intensive margins to trade costs in Melitz model. Following his approach and using the definition of equilibrium individual exports from Equation (9) and the definition of equilibrium productivity threshold from Equation (12), we obtain the elasticities of each margin to variable trade costs, fixed trade costs, tariffs, and the exchange rate as follows:

$$-\frac{\mathrm{d}\ln(P^s_{rij}Z^s_{ij})}{\mathrm{d}\ln\tau^s_{ij}} = \underbrace{\sigma^s - 1}_{\text{intensive margin}} + \underbrace{\gamma^s_i - \sigma^s + 1}_{\text{extensive margin}} = \gamma^s_i \tag{20}$$

$$-\frac{\mathrm{d}\ln(P^s_{rij}Z^s_{ij})}{\mathrm{d}\ln F^s_{ij}} = \underbrace{0}_{\text{intensive margin}} + \underbrace{\frac{\gamma^s_i}{\sigma^s - 1} - 1}_{\text{extensive margin}} = \frac{\gamma^s_i}{\sigma^s - 1} - 1 \tag{21}$$

$$\begin{aligned}-\frac{\mathrm{d}\ln(P^s_{rij}Z^s_{ij})}{\mathrm{d}\ln t^s_{ij}} &= \underbrace{(\sigma^s - 1)\frac{t^s_{ij}}{1 + t^s_{ij}}}_{\text{intensive margin}} + \underbrace{\frac{\sigma^s}{\sigma^s - 1}(\gamma^s_i - \sigma^s + 1)\frac{t^s_{ij}}{1 + t^s_{ij}}}_{\text{extensive margin}} \\ &= \left(\frac{\sigma^s\gamma^s_i}{\sigma^s - 1} - 1\right)\frac{t^s_{ij}}{1 + t^s_{ij}}\end{aligned} \tag{22}$$

$$-\frac{\mathrm{d}\ln(P^s_{rij}Z^s_{ij})}{\mathrm{d}\ln\varepsilon_i} = \underbrace{-\sigma^s}_{\text{intensive margin}} - \underbrace{\frac{\sigma^s}{\sigma^s - 1}(\gamma^s_i - \sigma^s + 1)}_{\text{extensive margin}} = \frac{\sigma^s\gamma^s_i}{1 - \sigma^s} \tag{23}$$

Equations (20)–(23) suggest that there is adjustment at the extensive margin for changes in all the three types of trade barriers and exchange rate. However, the intensive margin moves in response to changes of variable trade costs, tariffs, and exchange rate, but not for fixed trade costs. Quantitatively, the trade elasticity is larger relative to the exchange rate and variable costs, but smaller to tariffs and fixed trade costs. Table 1 presents the values of these elasticities under the specific parameter choices of our CGE model.

The derivation of elasticities in (20)–(23) implicitly assumes that the changes in trade barriers and exchange rate have no significant impact on the aggregate demand, $P^s_jQ^s_j$, and aggregate price P^s_j in importing country *j*. If country *i* is large or several exporting countries are involved in

Table 1. Elasticities of trade margins to various trade barriers, exchange rate, and domestic demand in CGE model

	Manufacturing sector ($\sigma = 4.3$, $\gamma = 5.0$)			Services sector ($\sigma = 3.9$, $\gamma = 4.3$)		
	Intensive margin	Extensive margin	Total	Intensive margin	Extensive margin	Total
Variable costs (τ)	3.3	1.7	5.0	2.9	1.4	4.3
Fixed costs (F)	0.0	0.5	0.5	0.0	0.5	0.5
Tariffs (t)	$3.3t/(1+t)$	$2.2t/(1+t)$	$5.5t/(1+t)$	$2.9t/(1+t)$	$1.9t/(1+t)$	$4.8t/(1+t)$
Exchange rate (ε)	−4.3	−2.2	−6.5	−3.9	−1.9	−5.8
Value of domestic demand (PQ)	1.0	0.5	1.5	1.0	0.5	1.5
Aggregate price (P)	3.3	1.7	5.0	2.9	1.4	4.3

the reduction of trade barriers, the aggregate demand and price in importing country will be impacted. The elasticities of the extensive and intensive margins to the demand and price in importing countries are as follows:

$$-\frac{d\ \ln(P^s_{rij}Z^s_{ij})}{d\ \ln(P^s_jQ^s_j)} = \underbrace{1}_{\text{intensive margin}} + \underbrace{\frac{\gamma^s_i - \sigma^s + 1}{\sigma^s - 1}}_{\text{extensive margin}} = \frac{\gamma^s_i}{\sigma^s - 1} \tag{24}$$

$$-\frac{d\ \ln(P^s_{rij}Z^s_{ij})}{d\ \ln\ P^s_j} = \underbrace{\sigma^s - 1}_{\text{intensive margin}} + \underbrace{\gamma^s_i - \sigma^s + 1}_{\text{extensive margin}} = \gamma^s_i \tag{25}$$

Equation (24) suggests that trade would grow faster than income ($\gamma > \sigma - 1$). With the specific parameter choices in our model, intensive margin contributes two-thirds of the trade adjustment induced by the changes in aggregate demand or aggregate price of importing countries (Table 1).

To quantitatively explore the different margins of trade, I run three unilateral liberalization simulations under which the tariff, variable trade costs, and fixed trade costs for China's manufacturing imports are cut by 10 percent, respectively. Table 2 reports the trade effects from these simulations. It shows that 10 percent cuts in China's manufacturing tariff and in variable trade costs for China's manufacturing imports result in a 2–3 percent expansion in its manufacturing imports. The effects of reducing variable trade costs are much bigger in comparison with tariff and fixed trade costs, with a 10 percent reduction in variable trade costs for China's manufacturing imports leading to around 25 percent increase in its manufacturing imports. The intensive margin contributes two-thirds of the trade expansions under the scenarios of tariff cut and variable trade cost reduction. In the case of reducing fixed trade costs, the intensive margin

Table 2. Effects of China's manufacturing trade liberalization on its manufacturing imports (%)

Imports from:	United States	EU	Japan	Rest of the world
Tariff cut	1.9	2.9	2.2	1.7
Intensive margin	1.2	1.9	1.5	1.1
Extensive margin	0.6	1.0	0.7	0.6
Reduce variable trade costs	25.4	24.7	23.5	23.9
Intensive margin	16.9	16.5	15.6	15.8
Extensive margin	8.5	8.3	7.9	8.1
Reduce fixed trade costs	2.4	2.4	2.3	2.3
Intensive margin	−2.2	−2.2	−2.3	−2.3
Extensive margin	4.6	4.6	4.5	4.6

Table 3. Effects of China's manufacturing trade liberalization on exchange rate and manufacturing demand and price (%)

	Tariff cut	Reduce variable trade costs	Reduce fixed trade costs
Exchange rate (ε)[a]			
China	0.0	−2.9	−0.2
United States	0.0	0.0	0.0
EU	0.0	−0.1	0.0
Japan	0.0	−0.3	0.0
Rest of the world	0.0	−0.4	0.0
Manufacturing demand (PQ)			
China	−0.4	−7.6	−0.7
United States	0.0	−0.2	0.0
EU	0.0	−0.2	0.0
Japan	0.0	−0.3	0.0
Rest of the world	0.0	−0.2	0.0
Aggregate manufacturing price (*P*)			
China	−0.4	−7.3	−0.7
United States	0.0	−0.1	0.0
EU	0.0	−0.1	0.0
Japan	0.0	−0.3	0.0
Rest of the world	0.0	−0.4	0.0

[a]Indicates depreciation.

makes negative contributions to trade expansion, offsetting around half of the import growth at the extensive margin.

Because of the impacts on aggregate manufacturing demand and price as well as on the exchange rate resulting from lowering trade barriers, the general equilibrium effects on trade are smaller than that suggested by the trade elasticities reported in Table 1. Table 3 reports the changes in exchange rates and in manufacturing demand and price. The reduction of

Table 4. Effects of China's manufacturing trade liberalization on number of firms (%)

	Tariff cut	Reduce variable trade costs	Reduce fixed trade costs
Number of manufacturing firms exporting to China			
United States	1.9	25.5	13.8
EU	2.9	24.8	13.7
Japan	2.2	23.7	13.6
Rest of the world	1.7	24.3	13.7
Number of China's domestic manufacturing firm	−0.6	−10.5	−1.0

import barriers lowers the domestic market prices and the demand (in value term) of manufacturing goods in China, which in turn dampens its direct stimulating effects on imports. In the scenarios of reducing variable and fixed trade costs, the China's currency appreciates slightly against other regions' currencies, providing some further stimulus to the imports. Combining these related elements together, the model simulations suggest that trade effects induced by cutting trade barriers are roughly 50 percent lower than that calculated directly from the elasticities reported in Table 1.

The extensive margin comes from the engagement of new firms into exporting markets. Table 4 reports changes of firm numbers in manufacturing sector under the three trade liberalization simulations. As a result of the 10 percent reduction in China's manufacturing tariff, the number of manufacturing firms exporting to China increases by 1.7–2.9 percent in the United States, European Union, Japan, and rest of the world. In the scenarios of reducing variable trade costs and fixed trade costs, the expansion of exporting firms increases to around 14 percent and 24 percent, respectively. However, the extensive margins of trade expansion are much smaller than the increases of exporting firms, on account of the small size of new entrants into the export market. In face of the competition from cheaper imports, China's manufacturing sector experiences decreases in the number of domestic producing firms, which shrinks by 0.6 percent in the case of tariff cut and 10.5 percent in the case of variable trade costs reduction.

4. Concluding comments

The importance of the extensive margin of trade has been well documented in recent theoretical and empirical literature, but has not been widely appreciated in the area of applied trade policy models. This chapter tries to bridge this gap by examining the relative contributions of the intensive and extensive margins to the trade expansion following trade liberalization in a global CGE model with heterogeneous firms. Using a set of plausible parameters values suggested by empirical studies and calibrating the model, the recent GTAP global database, our simulations indicate that the extensive margin accounts for around one-third of the trade growth induced by the reduction in tariff or variable trade costs. In the case of reducing fixed trade costs, the extensive margin contributes almost 200 percent of the trade expansion. To better compare the numerical predictions from the CGE model with the empirical evidences, future effort needs to be devoted to empirical estimation of the fixed trade costs and their roles played in recent global trade liberalization.

References

Armington, P.S. (1969), A theory of demand for products distinguished by place of production. *IMF Staff Paper* 16 (1), 159–178.

Balistreri, E.J., Hillberry, R.H., Rutherford, T.F. (2007), Structural estimation and solution of international trade models with heterogeneous firms. Mimeo, Colorado School of Mines.

Chaney, T. (2008), Distorted gravity: the intensive margin and extensive margins of international trade. *American Economic Review* 98 (4), 1707–1721.

Eaton, J., Kortum, S., Kramarz, F. (2004), Dissecting trade: Firms, industries, and export destinations. *American Economic Review* 94 (2), 150–154.

Eaton, J., Kortum, S., Kramarz, F. (2007), An anatomy of international trade: evidence from French firms. Unpublished Mimeo.

Hummels, D., Klenow, P.J. (2005), The variety and quality of a nation's exports. *American Economic Review* 95 (3), 704–723.

Kancs, D.A. (2010), Variety gains of trade integration in a heterogeneous firm model. LICOS Discussion Paper Series No. 258/2010, LICOS Centre for Institutions and Economic Performance, Katholieke Universiteit Leuven.

Kehoe, T.J., Ruhl, K.J. (2003), How important is the new goods margin in international trade? Staff Report 324, Federal Reserve Bank of Minneapolis.

Krugman, P. (1979), Increasing returns, monopolistic competition and international trade. *Journal of International Economics* 9, 469–479.

Melitz, M.J. (2003), The impact of trade on intra-industry reallocations and aggregate industry productivity. *Econometrica* 71 (6), 1695–1725.

van der Mensbrugghe, D. (2005), LINKAGE technical reference document. Mimeo, Economic Policy and Prospects Group, The World Bank, Washington, DC.

Zhai, F. (2008), Armington meets Melitz: introducing firm heterogeneity in a global CGE model of trade. *Journal of Economic Integration* 23 (3), 575–604.

CHAPTER 3

Welfare Gains from Changing Partners in a Trade Bloc: The Case of MERCOSUR

Lorenzo Caliendo and Fernando Parro

Department of Economics, University of Chicago, Chicago, IL, USA
E-mail address: lcaliend@uchicago.edu; fparro@uchicago.edu

Abstract
This chapter applies the new heterogeneous firm CGE model of Caliendo and Parro (2009) to determine what the Ricardian gains are from changing partners for members of a trade bloc. We focus on the MERCOSUR case, using a model with 48 sectors and 5 countries. Motivated by recent policy discussions, we quantify Uruguay's trade and welfare effects from signing a Free Trade Agreement with the United States and leaving MERCOSUR. We find positive welfare effects for Uruguay from bilaterally reducing tariffs with the United States. Most of the gains come from having access to lower-cost intermediate inputs for production. We then consider the policy experiment of bilaterally eliminating tariffs between all members of MERCOSUR and the United States. We find that Uruguay has the largest gains, while Argentina and Brazil do not benefit much. This chapter also illustrates how new models are a promising tool for the analysis of trade.

Keywords: Gains from trade, trade policy, intermediate goods, MERCOSUR

1. Introduction

This chapter uses the heterogeneous firm, multicountry–multisector quantitative general equilibrium model described by Caliendo and Parro (2009) for trade policy analysis in order to determine what the Ricardian welfare gains are from changing partners for members of a trade bloc. Consider a group of countries that form a customs union. These countries enjoy free trade in goods among members and will apply a common external tariff to nonmember countries. Suppose now that a large developed country that does not belong to the trade bloc offers to sign a Free Trade Agreement (FTA) with one of the member countries. Should the country not sign the agreement? Should the country sign the agreement and therefore leave the bloc? Should the bloc sign the agreement? These are some of the questions that will be addressed here.

Frontiers of Economics and Globalization
Volume 7 ISSN: 1574-8715
DOI: 10.1108/S1574-8715(2010)0000007006

We focus on the case of the Mercado Comun del Sur (henceforth MERCOSUR). MERCOSUR is a customs union formed by four countries: Argentina, Brazil, Uruguay, and Paraguay. In the year 2006, Uruguay faced the decision of whether or not to sign an FTA with the United States. This presented an evident trade-off for Uruguay. On the one side, the United States would lower the tariffs it applied to Uruguay. On the other side, Uruguay would have to leave MERCOSUR, and therefore Argentina, Brazil, and Paraguay would increase the tariffs they applied to Uruguay to the external common tariff level.[1] However, since Uruguay would not belong to MERCOSUR anymore, it would have the option of modifying the tariff policy it applied to the rest of the world (ROW). In this chapter we show how to apply the quantitative model developed in Caliendo and Parro (2009) to quantify and decompose the welfare effects for Uruguay of leaving MERCOSUR and signing an FTA with the United States. We also use the model to quantify the trade and welfare effects of other counterfactual scenarios such as MERCOSUR, as a bloc, signing an FTA with the United States.

More generally, the empirical application presented in this chapter sheds light on the welfare effects of customs unions. Viner (1950) was the first to address theoretically the issue of welfare gains of customs unions, introducing the concepts of trade creation and trade diversion. Bhagwati *et al.* (1999) present a synthesis of theoretical research on this topic since Viner's work. Empirical literature on the welfare effects of customs unions and regional trade agreements is much more scarce. Magee (2008) studied the intrabloc and extrabloc trade effects of different customs unions, regional trade agreements and FTAs using a dynamic gravity equation controlling for country pair, importer-year, and exporter-year fixed effects. He found that customs unions generate the largest long-run increase in intrabloc trade on average. Preferential trading arrangements, on the other hand, lead to much smaller increases in trade flows. Ghosh and Yamarik (2004) studied the intrabloc trade effect of 12 regional trade agreements, concluding that they have increased intrabloc trade. Yeats (1998) concludes that MERCOSUR trade flows have not changed according the comparative advantages of its members. Most of the empirical literature uses a gravity-type model to evaluate the *ex-post* trade effects of different trade agreements. The model developed by Caliendo and Parro (2009) allows quantification of *ex-ante* welfare effects. This chapter provides an example of an *ex-ante* evaluation of trade policy questions.

The most popular tools for trade policy evaluation are the computable general equilibrium (CGE/AGE) models. These are multisector general equilibrium models and can be employed to evaluate *ex-ante* changes in

[1] MERCOSUR rules establish a common external tariff and the adoption of a common trade policy in relation to nonmember countries. An FTA between the United States and Uruguay would violate this rule; thus, Uruguay would have to leave the customs union.

trade policy. Examples of these models are the Michigan Brown–Deardorff–Stern model and the Purdue GTAP model (see Hertel, 1997).[2] We contribute to this area of research by providing a new model for tariff policy evaluation that uses the new trade literature on heterogeneous firms.

The chapter is organized as follows: Section 2 describes the Caliendo and Parro (2009) model, and Section 3 briefly describes the history and characteristics of MERCOSUR. The data used to perform the empirical exercises are described in Section 4, and Section 5 explains the empirical exercises we perform and shows the results. Finally, Section 6 presents the main conclusions.

2. *A quantitative model for trade policy analysis*

Caliendo and Parro (2009) are the first to develop a multisector and multicountry Ricardian model for counterfactual trade policy analysis. They generalize Eaton and Kortum's (2002) Ricardian model by adding multiple sectors and countries and incorporating trade in intermediate goods and the interaction across tradable and nontradable sectors observed in the input–output (I–O) tables. Some of the key advantages of their approach are that it brings new insights on the effects of tariff changes (from the microfounded Ricardian explanation of the reasons why heterogeneous firms trade in the model), there are low computational requirements to solve for the equilibrium variables and a low data requirement to evaluate the general equilibrium effects of tariff policy (only one elasticity has to be estimated) and it is an open-source and flexible tool to evaluate any type of tariff concessions. In this section we briefly describe the production structure of the model. For a more detailed description of the structure of the model and the way to solve for the equilibrium, we refer the reader to Caliendo and Parro (2009).

The model is a general equilibrium model with multiple countries. Each country has multiple sectors. Within each sector, intermediate goods are produced using labor and a composite intermediate good. The composite intermediate good can be thought of as an aggregate (bundle) of intermediate inputs. Sectors are interconnected according to the input–output structure of the economy. Therefore, a composite intermediate good of a given sector can be used to produce intermediate goods not only in its own sector but also in every other sector. For instance, machinery is used to produce not only machinery but also cars, textiles, etc. Also, each composite good is used to produce not only intermediate goods but also final goods. Similar to the models of Eaton and Kortum (2002) and

[2] Gilbert and Wahl (2002), and the works cited therein, present a description of the basic structure of CGE models.

Alvarez and Lucas (2007), intermediate goods within each sector are produced with a stochastic efficiency level coming from a Frechet distribution. Making the model more general than those in Eaton and Kortum (2002) and Alvarez and Lucas (2007), this probabilistic distribution is assumed to be sector specific. Households derive utility from consuming final goods and income is given by labor income, lump-sum transfers from the government due to tariff revenues, and income coming from the country-level trade deficit.

There are two types of sectors: tradable and nontradable. Within each tradable sector, intermediate goods are also tradable. Each tradable good is subject to two types of trade costs: an iceberg-type cost as in Dornbush *et al.* (1977), and an ad valorem flat-rate tariff applied over unit prices. The model allows for endogenous sectoral trade deficit, but deficits at the country level are exogenous.

Figure 1 considers an example of a two-tradable-sectors economy. $Q_n^j(i)$ is the production of intermediate variety i in sector j and country n. The primary input in the economy is labor (L_n) and this is used in both sectors (arrows going into the production of varieties). In order to produce this variety, producers demand labor (L_n^j) and composite intermediate goods (q_n^j) from both sectors. Intermediate varieties can be exported or sold locally. Intermediate varieties either from these local producers or imported from another country are the only input for the production

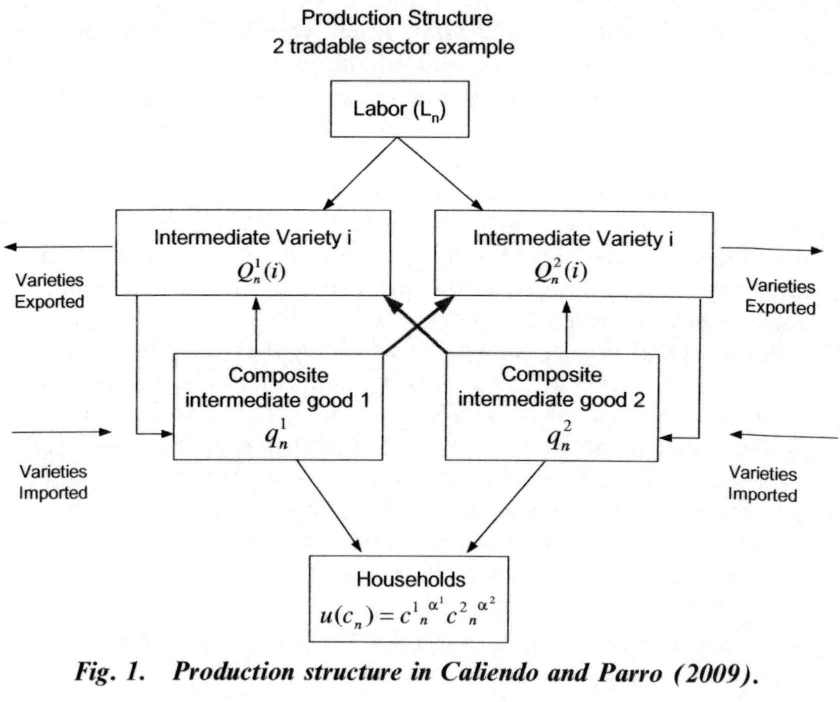

Fig. 1. Production structure in Caliendo and Parro (2009).

of the composite intermediate goods in this economy, as represented in the figure. Producers of the composite intermediate goods will demand intermediate varieties from the lowest-cost supplier in the world (subject to trade costs), which in some cases could be local. Households derive utility from the consumption of final goods that are produced with composite intermediates and no value added.

Changes in trade policy have general equilibrium effects in this economy. For instance, if the cost of importing intermediate varieties into sector 1 increases, this will affect the input cost of the production of the composite intermediate goods in sector 1. These goods are inputs for the production of final goods and intermediate varieties in sector 2 (I–O tables will determine how important this interconnection is); therefore, this cost increase will impact the price of final goods and intermediate varieties in other sectors. Some of these goods will lose their cost advantage and stop exporting to the ROW. This will also impact the price of the composite intermediate good in sector 2. Note that in an integrated world, these changes in prices also affect prices in other countries. If exported intermediate varieties increase in price, this will affect the cost of production of goods in all countries that import them. Note that in this model changes in trade policy have effects on the intensive as well as the extensive margin. Changes in trade policy can not only increase or reduce the amount of goods imported from abroad (intensive margin) but also change the lowest-cost supplier of particular goods (change in the extensive margin). All of these channels are contemplated in this model.

Using the case of MERCOSUR, which is described in the next section, we will present several policy experiments as an example of the applicability of the model.

3. *MERCOSUR: characteristics and trade policy*

3.1. Historical background

In 1960, Argentina, Brazil, Chile, Mexico, Paraguay, Peru, and Uruguay (joined by Colombia and Ecuador one year later) signed the Treaty of Montevideo, which created the "Asociación Latinoamericana de Libre Comercio" (ALALC, Latin-American Association of Free Trade) with a strong commitment between the members to create a Free Trade Area of the South within a time frame of 12 years. This time frame was later extended to the year 1980, but, given the national policies that each member implemented during the 1970s, which gave more preference to national development projects, and the political and military instability of the countries as well as the economic and political rivalry that arose between Argentina and Brazil, the ALALC lacked support to achieve its original goals. That is why after two decades of existence, the ALALC was abolished and a second Treaty of Montevideo was signed. In this treaty the "Asociación Latinoamericana de Integración" (ALADI, Latin-American Integration Association) was created, which had the same goals as ALALC, but without imposing any concrete compromise between the members to create a free trade area.

In the middle of the 1980s Argentina was returning to a democratic political system, and surprisingly, in 1985, after years of political and economic confrontation, the new presidents of Argentina and Brazil signed the "Declaración de Iguazú" (Declaration of Iguazú), in which they manifested their will to accelerate the process of bilateral integration. This was formally established in 1986 when the "Programa de Integración y Cooperación Económica Argentina–Brazil" (PICE, Argentina–Brazil Economic and Integration Cooperation Program) was signed. It consisted of 24 protocols involving topics from capital goods to economic and social planning. This was a real success for both economies, as manifested by the increasing flow of trade between them, which fomented in 1988 a new treaty of integration, cooperation, and development that fixed a time frame of 10 years to eliminate all barriers of trade between the two countries. Finally, in 1990 both countries signed the Buenos Aires Act, in which they compromised to reach a bilateral integration by December 31, 1994. Paraguay and Uruguay, both countries geographically situated between Argentina and Brazil, felt the need to be incorporated in this integration (following a domino effect, we believe). The initial step their government took was to hold a meeting with the presidents of Argentina and Brazil in order to express their will to create a multilateral agreement among the four countries.

The 26 of March of 1991, with the treaty of Asuncion, Argentina, Brazil, Paraguay, and Uruguay, formalized the creation of a common market between the countries, as it is wrote in the article 1 of the treaty, involving the free flow of capital goods, services, and productive factors by eliminating all tariffs between members and imposing a unique external tariff. They also compromised to coordinate their macroeconomic policies involving international trade, agriculture, industry, currency, transportation, and communications in order to ensure adequate conditions for competitiveness between the members. So far, more than 10 years later, MERCOSUR has only achieved the creation of a customs union with some exceptions. This is a real example of the difficulty involved in the creation of a customs union. We will try to describe briefly the process that was necessary to unify the common external tariffs and eliminate the interregional tariffs.

3.2. Interregional tariffs

In the treaty of Asuncion, articles 5 and 6 established the procedure by which the interregional tariffs of the members must be reduced. It was a progressive, linear, and automatic method starting in 1991 in order to reach the zero tariffs level by January 1, 1995. The first reduction was in the amount of 47% and in each consecutive semester there was a further reduction of 7%. In order to adjust to the process of integration and minimize the possible negative effects of changing the production structure of the economy, each country was allowed to present a list of exceptions to the tariff reduction. Argentina presented a list with 394 items, Brazil had 324, Paraguay 439, and Uruguay 960. These lists had to be reduced each year by 20% for Argentina and Brazil, and by 10% for the first two years and then 20% in each subsequent year for Paraguay and Uruguay. In the year 1995, the interregional tariffs were to drop to zero for most of the items, leaving each country with a small list of exceptions. Some of the items that are on the list of exceptions are autos and auto parts, sugar, telecommunication equipment, and electronics; these exceptions have created some debate between Argentina and Brazil. This has occurred because most of these sectors or items have had very different tariff treatment by the two countries in the past. For example, Argentina has in the last decades been reducing the tariffs applied to the electronics sector in order to catch up with new technologies; Brazil, on the other hand, has protected its national sector. In this case, Argentina could expect that as a result of the customs union trade could divert from the ROW's superior and lower-cost technology to Brazil's inferior and higher-cost technology. This problem is also directly related to the external tariffs of the union, as we will see in the next section.

3.3. Common external tariff

Changes in the welfare effects over the members of a customs union are very sensitive to the vector of common external tariffs that is implemented. Kemp and Wan (1976) showed that if the members of the customs union optimally established the level of the tariff vector, then the resulting outcome is that no member is worse off than before, even when one is better off than before. However, in practice it is very difficult to implement that optimal vector.

The common external tariff in MERCOSUR has been applied since 1995 to more than 80% of imported items, ranging in value from 0% to 20% and with 11 different levels. As in the case of the interregional tariff, each country has its own list of exceptions to the common external tariff. In the Protocol of Ouro Preto (1995), it was established that the products in the list should reach their "normal tariff level" in the year 2001 for Brazil and Argentina, and in the year 2006 for Uruguay and Paraguay. This implied an absolute convergence of the external tariffs for the two largest members of the union only 10 years after the treaty of Asuncion, a complete success. But in 1997, Brazil and Argentina suggested that the

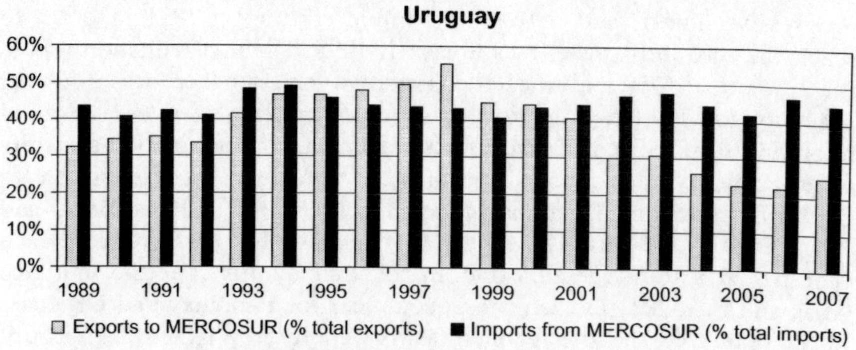

Fig. 2. Intra-MERCOSUR exports and imports of Uruguay.

external tariffs were transitory readjusted by a magnitude of 3%, which implied a 25% increment in the average tariff of 14%, until the year 2001. Then, because of the economic crises that affected MERCOSUR, especially its two larger members (Brazil's crisis began in 1998, and Argentina's in 2001), the convergence was further delayed by the readjustment of the external tariffs to 1997 levels. By the end of 2003 the tariffs ranged between 0% and 20% again. Also, there has been a readjustment of the target dates for the convergence of the products on the list of exceptions for Argentina and Brazil.

Some of the items that were included in the exceptions list have been a source of debate because of the different tariff structure that each country had with extrazone countries. Electronics and telecommunication equipment had an average tariff rate of 35% in Brazil, while in the rest of the member countries they had a very low or no tariff. After long negotiations a consensus has been reached to apply an external tariff of around 16% to these products. By the year 2006, all members had to adjust and converge to this level.

These and some further issues, such as the redistribution of tariff revenues and tariffs on capital goods, are among the problems that the members of MERCOSUR must solve in order to continue with the process of complete integration.

3.4. Has MERCOSUR increased trade among members?

In this section we document the evolution of trade flows for MERCOSUR members. Figures 2–4 show each country's annual percentage of total exports to and imports from other MERCOSUR members between 1989 and 2007.[3]

[3] We excluded Paraguay from this analysis and from the policy experiments described in the following text because of data constraints.

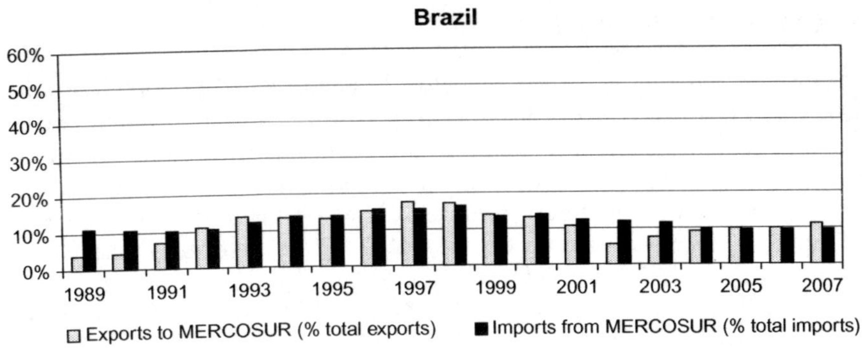

Fig. 3. Intra-MERCOSUR exports and imports of Brazil.

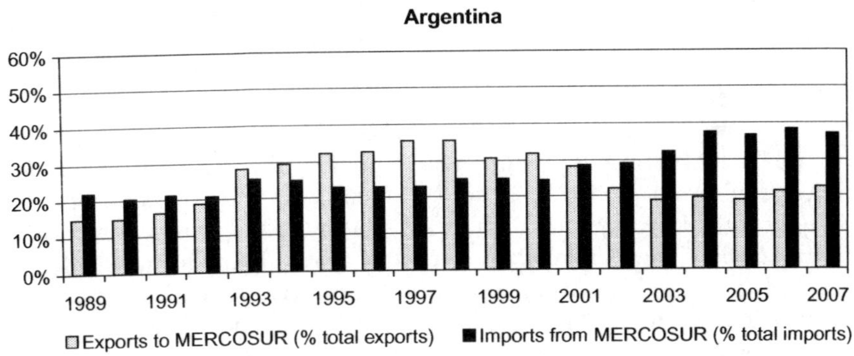

Fig. 4. Intra-MERCOSUR exports and imports of Argentina.

As we can see from these figures, in general there has not been a substantial increase in the magnitude of trade within the MERCOSUR bloc. First, we do not observe a jump in trade flows among the members when MERCOSUR was created in 1994. Second, we find that, in general, exports to other MERCOSUR countries make up less than 25% of total exports for each member (less than 15% for Brazil) and imports from other members make up less than 40% of the total (less than 10% for Brazil). Moreover, with the exception of Argentina's imports from MERCOSUR, trade flows among members are lower than when the bloc was created.

The figures suggest that there has not been a substantial increase in intrabloc trade since the creation of MERCOSUR. This observation raises the question of what the welfare effects would be if its members left the bloc and signed an FTA with a large economy such as the United States. The next section describes the empirical counterfactual that we perform to consider this question.

4. *Quantitative exercise: data*

One of the advantages of the model in Caliendo and Parro (2009) is the low amount of data needed in order to perform any type of policy experiment. The data needed are sectoral data on bilateral trade flows, import tariffs, value added, share of value added in gross production, share of intermediate inputs in final production, and estimates of the dispersion of productivity. We use data for Argentina, Brazil, Uruguay, the United States, and the ROW for 2006 for 48 two-digit ISIC rev 3 sectors.

Trade flow data are from the UN COMTRADE dataset. Commodities are classified according to the Harmonized System 2002 (HS-02). We use a concordance table to classify the commodities according the ISIC rev 3 classification, which is how the production data are defined. Tariff data are from UNCTAD-TRAINS. Commodities are also classified according to the HS-02; thus, we proceed in the same way as with trade flows to concord data to ISIC rev 3. External common tariffs are from the Ministry of Economics of Uruguay. Value added is obtained from the OECD and national agencies' I–O tables. We construct the ROW using I–O tables for 34 countries.[4] In cases where no I–O table was available for 2006, we used a table from a previous year, updating the value added to 2006 using values from the UN Industry National Accounts dataset at the most disaggregated level we found. Share of value added in gross production is from the OECD and national agencies' I–O tables. The value for the ROW is simply the weighted average of the 34 countries we included. Share of intermediate inputs in final production is also obtained from the OECD and national agencies' I–O tables. The values for the ROW are constructed as a weighted average of 22 OECD countries that have I–O tables available for a common year. The sectoral dispersion of productivity was obtained from Caliendo and Parro (2009).

We use these data to calibrate the model to the year 2006 and perform the policy exercises described below.[5]

5. *Quantitative exercise: counterfactual scenarios and results*

We now turn to the computational quantitative exercise where we focus on four policy experiments: Counterfactual scenario 1 examines a situation in which Uruguay leaves MERCOSUR and therefore faces the external common tariff applied by Argentina and Brazil. Counterfactual scenario 2

---

[4] These countries are Australia, Austria, Belgium, Canada, Chile, China, Czech Republic, Denmark, Finland, France, Germany, Greece, Hong Kong, Hungary, India, Indonesia, Ireland, Israel, Italy, Japan, Mexico, Netherlands, New Zealand, Norway, Poland, Portugal, Russia, Slovakia, South Africa, Spain, Sweden, Switzerland, Turkey, and the UK.

[5] See Caliendo and Parro (2009) for details on the calibration.

Table 1. Current scenario

Importer/ exporter	Uruguay	Argentina	Brazil	United States	Rest of the world
Uruguay		0	0	ECT^j	ECT^j
Argentina	0		0	ECT^j	ECT^j
Brazil	0	0		ECT^j	ECT^j
United States	$tariff^j_{US,UY}$	$tariff^j_{US,ARG}$	$tariff^j_{US,BRA}$		$tariff^j_{US,ROW}$
Rest of the world	$tariff^j_{ROW,UY}$	$tariff^j_{ROW,ARG}$	$tariff^j_{ROW,BRA}$	$tariff^j_{ROW,US}$	

Notes: This table describes the tariff structure presented by MERCOSUR countries. $tariff^j_{i,n}$ represents tariffs applied by country *i* to country *n* in sector *j*; ECT^j is the external common tariff applied by MERCOSUR members in sector *j*; and ARG, BRA, UY, US, and ROW are Argentina, Brazil, Uruguay, the United States, and the Rest of the World, respectively.

considers the case in which Uruguay and the United States sign an FTA. Counterfactual scenario 3 is the case in which Uruguay unilaterally reduces the tariffs it applies to the ROW; and finally, counterfactual scenario 4 tries to capture the effects of Uruguay signing FTAs with countries in the ROW. We caution the reader on the way the results of the policy experiments should be interpreted. The model will consider how variables are affected by only a change in the tariff vector. Other policy variables such as changes in nontariff barriers, quotas, and capital restrictions will not be analyzed here. We do believe that these other variables are important and that they play an important role in the process of liberalization. However, we want to focus on one channel: the effect of only tariffs on the allocation of resources in a heterogeneous firm model.

Consider the case in which Uruguay leaves MERCOSUR. As a consequence, Argentina and Brazil impose the external common tariff on all goods imported from Uruguay. In this first scenario, we assume that there is no other change in the system. Table 1 summarizes the current scenario and Table 2 this first counterfactual scenario.

The first two columns of Table 3 present the changes in welfare and real wages under counterfactual scenario 1. Since Uruguay leaves MERCOSUR, Argentina and Brazil impose the external common tariff level to Uruguay. As a consequence, welfare and real wages decrease by 1.8% in Uruguay. The change in tariff revenue is negligible for Argentina and Brazil, and therefore there is no significant change in the equilibrium wages and prices for these countries. We then consider what the welfare effects are of Uruguay signing an FTA with the United States – counterfactual scenario 2. The FTA between Uruguay and the United States would most likely take the form of other FTAs that the United States has signed with other Latin American countries, such as Chile. Even though tariffs are not reduced to zero immediately, tariffs drop quickly over time and reach values of zero in a short period. We model a possible

Table 2. Counterfactual scenario 1

Importer/ exporter	Uruguay	Argentina	Brazil	United States	Rest of the world
Uruguay		0	0	ECT^j	ECT^j
Argentina	ECT^j		0	ECT^j	ECT^j
Brazil	ECT^j	0		ECT^j	ECT^j
United States	$tariff^j_{US,UY}$	$tariff^j_{US,ARG}$	$tariff^j_{US,BRA}$		$tariff^j_{US,ROW}$
Rest of the world	$tariff^j_{ROW,UY}$	$tariff^j_{ROW,ARG}$	$tariff^j_{ROW,BRA}$	$tariff^j_{ROW,US}$	

Notes: This table describes the tariff structure for counterfactual scenario 1. $tariff^j_{i,n}$ represents tariffs applied by country *i* to country *n* in sector *j*; ECT^j is the external common tariff applied by MERCOSUR members in sector *j*; and ARG, BRA, UY, US, and ROW are Argentina, Brazil, Uruguay, the United States, and the Rest of the World, respectively.

Table 3. Changes in welfare and real wages in four counterfactual scenarios

	Simulated values example							
	Scenario 1: Uruguay leaves MERCOSUR		Scenario 2: Scenario 1+FTA with United States		Scenario 3: Scenario 2+zero tariff with ROW		Scenario 4: Scenario 3+FTA with ROW	
	ΔWelfare (%)	ΔReal wages (%)	ΔWelfare (%)	ΔReal wages (%)	ΔWelfare (%)	ΔReal wages (%)	ΔWelfare (%)	ΔReal wages (%)
Uruguay	−1.8336	−1.8475	4.9984	5.2550	4.9387	5.9237	6.6467	7.6907
Argentina	−0.0031	−0.0147	0.1047	0.0855	−0.0285	−0.0374	−0.0073	−0.0177
Brazil	0.0161	0.0086	0.0483	0.0390	−0.0051	−0.0109	0.0012	−0.0049
United States	0.0003	0.0004	−0.0053	−0.0057	−0.0083	−0.0091	−0.0044	−0.0048
Rest of the world	0.0005	0.0005	−0.0032	−0.0030	0.0006	0.0006	−0.0018	−0.0013

Notes: This table presents the welfare results of the four counterfactual experiments considered. Scenario 1 is the case in which Uruguay leaves MERCOSUR. Scenario 2 is the case in which Uruguay signs an FTA with the United States. Scenario 3 is the case in which Uruguay signs an FTA with the United States and unilaterally reduces its tariffs to the rest of the world. Scenario 4 is the case in which Uruguay signs FTAs with the United States and with the rest of the world. All the results are percentage changes from the initial condition.

FTA by reducing tariffs between the United States and Uruguay to zero. One way to interpret the findings of the exercise is to consider the medium-run effects from the FTA and not the immediate short-run effects. Table 3 (scenario 2) presents the results. The benefits to Uruguay of signing an FTA with the United States more than compensate for the welfare losses from leaving MERCOSUR (compare the results from scenarios 1 and 2). As a consequence, welfare increases by 5% and real wages by 5.3%.

Having access to cheaper and more efficient intermediate inputs from the United States produces an increase in welfare even after the reduction in tariff revenues from dropping tariffs to the United States. The increase in real wages is explained by two effects. On the one hand, the aggregate price index of the economy falls due to imports of cheaper intermediate inputs from the United States.

On the other hand, nominal wages go up from the increase in the demand for labor from producers of final and intermediate goods. Producers with a comparative advantage will export more as a consequence of the reductions in cost (thanks to cheaper intermediate inputs) and the increase in the demand for their goods from the larger U.S. market. The computational exercise shows that there is also a small increase in welfare for Argentina in this scenario. The reason is that Uruguay is now a more efficient producer in certain sectors. Therefore, Argentina can have access to cheaper intermediate inputs from Uruguay as a consequence of the FTA. This happens in sectors in which Argentina was already importing intermediate goods from Uruguay. The conclusion of the exercise is that there are positive Ricardian gains for Uruguay from signing an FTA with the United States.

We now consider another trade policy experiment. Suppose that Uruguay is considering signing an FTA with several other countries. The logic behind this exercise is that once Uruguay decides not to be a member of the MERCOSUR trading bloc anymore, it can apply any tariff concession it wants to the ROW. We consider first the case in which Uruguay applies zero tariffs to the ROW – that is, the case where Uruguay follows a unilateral liberalization process, counterfactual scenario 3. Table 3 (scenario 3) presents the results. Uruguay's real wages increase by 5.9% and its welfare increases by a lower amount, 4.9%. In this case there is a larger decrease in tariff revenues, which explains the difference between the two measures. Notice that in this case welfare in Argentina is not affected. This is because the gains from having access to cheaper intermediate goods are countered by the loss from the fact that now Argentina cannot be the most efficient producer for Uruguay in some sectors.

Now we analyze counterfactual scenario 4, in which Uruguay leaves MERCOSUR, signs an FTA with the United States, and also starts signing other FTAs with important economies in addition to following a unilateral liberalization process. This has been the integration strategy of other developing countries such as Chile. The difference from scenario 3 is that the ROW also decreases tariffs applied to Uruguay to the zero level. Scenario 4 in Table 3 shows the results of this policy experiment. Uruguay's welfare increases by 6.6% and its real wages by 7.7%. Therefore, this integration strategy enhances welfare the most for Uruguay.

To further understand these results, we now evaluate the role of trade in intermediate inputs. In Table 4 we repeat the four counterfactual exercises described above for the case in which only final goods are traded.

Table 4. Welfare gains for Uruguay in a model without trade in intermediate goods

	Simulated values example			
	Scenario 1 (%)	Scenario 2 (%)	Scenario 3 (%)	Scenario 4 (%)
Uruguay	−1.0261	2.8105	2.9577	3.8899
Argentina	0.0060	0.0235	−0.0317	−0.0276
Brazil	0.0114	0.0173	−0.0070	−0.0059
United States	0.0003	0.0024	0.0015	0.0011
Rest of the world	0.0002	−0.0030	−0.0015	−0.0018

Notes: This table presents the welfare results of the four counterfactual experiments considered. Scenario 1 is the case in which Uruguay leaves MERCOSUR. Scenario 2 is the case in which Uruguay signs an FTA with the United States. Scenario 3 is the case in which Uruguay signs an FTA with the United States and unilaterally reduces its tariffs to the rest of the world. Scenario 4 is the case in which Uruguay signs FTAs with the United States and with the rest of the world. All the results are percentage changes from the initial condition.

In scenario 1, when Uruguay leaves MERCOSUR, welfare decreases by 1% instead of 1.8%. Since there is no trade in intermediate goods in the model, there is less trade overall. The changes in relative prices due to the increase in tariffs will only have an effect on final consumption and not on the production of goods, as was the case before. Therefore, this model predicts a lower welfare loss compared to the model in which intermediate inputs are traded.

When Uruguay starts signing FTAs, the welfare effects are almost half of those predicted by models with trade in intermediate inputs. Therefore, intermediate goods magnify the welfare gains from trade liberalization. The intuitive explanation is that having access to cheaper intermediate goods not only increases real income in Uruguay (through the effect of a reduction in prices), but also provides another channel through which firms can produce more efficiently and gain comparative advantage (through the effect of cheaper and more efficient inputs). Therefore, the key insight is that in a model with trade in intermediate inputs, tariff reductions have both a production as well as a consumption effect. However, in a model with no trade in intermediate inputs, there are only consumption gains from reductions in tariffs.

In Caliendo and Parro (2009) we show that sectoral linkages also help to spread the gains from tariff reductions. The reason is that tariff reductions not only affect the sector to which the tariff is targeted, but also indirectly affect all the sectors in the economy that are related to that particular sector. Therefore, there can be a propagation as well as an amplification effect of changes in tariffs.

Table 5 shows the welfare effects under the above four scenarios when we shut down the sectoral links through the I–O table. Again, under

Table 5.* *Welfare gains for Uruguay in a model without sectoral interconnections

	Simulated values example			
	Scenario 1 (%)	Scenario 2 (%)	Scenario 3 (%)	Scenario 4 (%)
Uruguay	−1.0875	2.9098	2.9802	3.9373
Argentina	0.0055	0.0281	−0.0336	−0.0284
Brazil	0.0128	0.0208	−0.0068	−0.0052
United States	0.0004	0.0023	0.0015	0.0011
Rest of the world	0.0002	−0.0032	−0.0015	−0.0018

Notes: This table presents the welfare results of the four counterfactual experiments considered. Scenario 1 is the case in which Uruguay leaves MERCOSUR. Scenario 2 is the case in which Uruguay signs an FTA with the United States. Scenario 3 is the case in which Uruguay signs an FTA with the United States and unilaterally reduces its tariffs to the rest of the world. Scenario 4 is the case in which Uruguay signs FTAs with the United States and with the rest of the world. All the results are percentage changes from the initial condition.

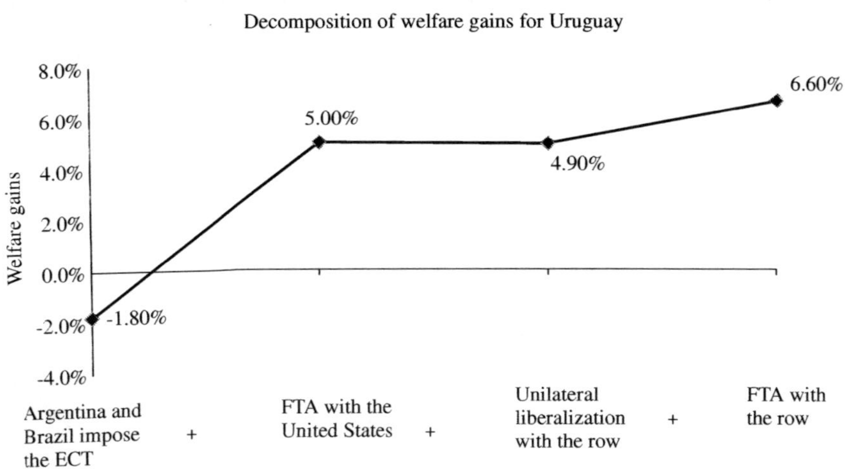

Fig. 5. ***Welfare effects in counterfactual scenarios 1–4. All the results are percentage changes from the initial condition.***

scenario 1, welfare losses are lower for Uruguay because when Argentina and Brazil impose the external common tariff the magnifying effect is absent. When Uruguay signs an FTA with the United States and the ROW (scenarios 2–4) welfare gains are almost 50% lower if we do not consider the input–output interconnections.

Figure 5 presents a summary of the welfare gains for Uruguay under different integration strategies. We can see that the optimal integration strategy for Uruguay is to leave MERCOSUR and sign FTAs with the United States and every other important economy in the world.

This strategy yields welfare gains of 6.6%, which are far larger than the losses due to the increase in tariffs by Argentina and Brazil. We can also see in the figure that the FTA with the United States makes the highest contribution to these gains.

We now focus on the trade effects of these integration strategies. Figure 6 shows Uruguay's total trade with MERCOSUR, the United States, and the ROW in the current scenario and in the four policy experiments. When Uruguay leaves MERCOSUR and Argentina and Brazil impose the external common tariff (scenario 1), trade with MERCOSUR decreases from 35.4% to 29.6% of total trade. On the other hand, trade with the United States increases from 8.9% to 10.1% of total trade, and with the ROW from 55.7% to 60.3%. Using scenario 1 as a baseline, if Uruguay also signs an FTA with the United States (scenario 2), we observe a big increase in trade with the United States, while trade with MERCOSUR decreases to 24.5% of total trade and trade with the ROW decreases to 46.9%. If Uruguay unilaterally lowers its tariffs applied to the ROW, trade with the ROW increases to 54.5% of total trade while trade with MERCOSUR decreases to 16.1%. Finally, the results show that if Uruguay follows the most welfare-enhancing integration strategy, leaving MERCOSUR and signing FTAs with the United States and with the ROW, trade with MERCOSUR represents

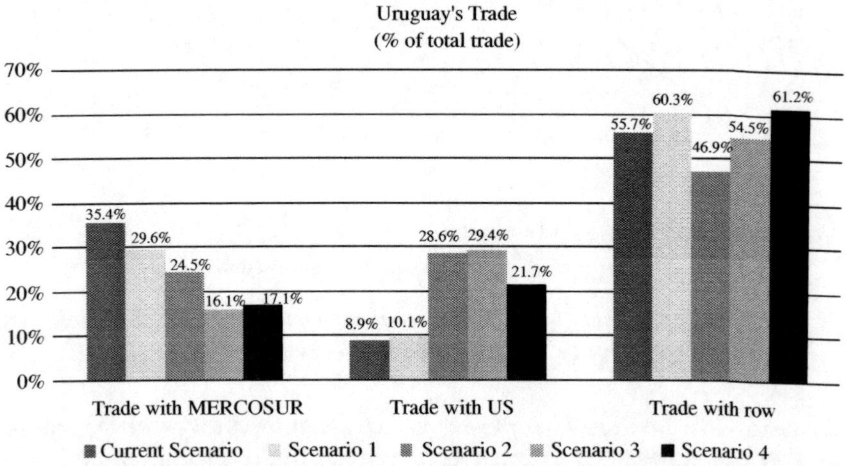

Fig. 6. Trade effects for Uruguay in counterfactual scenarios 1–4. Scenario 1 is the case in which Uruguay leaves MERCOSUR. Scenario 2 is the case in which Uruguay signs an FTA with the United States. Scenario 3 is the case in which Uruguay signs an FTA with the United States and unilaterally reduces its tariffs to the ROW. Scenario 4 is the case in which Uruguay signs FTAs with the United States and with the ROW. All the results are percentage changes from the initial condition.

Table 6. Welfare gains for MERCOSUR from signing an FTA with the United States

	Simulated values example	
	ΔWelfare (%)	ΔReal wages (%)
Uruguay	5.5760	5.8359
Argentina	−0.0215	0.2794
Brazil	−0.9564	−0.6702
United States	0.2060	0.2358
Rest of the world	−0.0395	−0.0383

Note: Simulated values are percentage changes from the initial condition.

only 17.1% of total trade, almost a half of trade in the current scenario, while trade with the United States makes up 21.7%, almost three times as much as in the current situation. Uruguay's trade with the ROW is 61.2% of total trade.

We now focus on a different type of policy experiment: what are the trade and welfare effects of MERCOSUR, as a bloc, signing an FTA with the United States? The idea is to use the model to evaluate whether a bilateral trade liberalization between all members of MERCOSUR and the United States is beneficial or not. Recall that we are only evaluating the static gains from tariff elimination.

Table 6 presents the results. The results indicate that Uruguay is the country with the most favorable effects from signing the FTA, with an increase in welfare of 5.6%, followed by the United States. Argentina and Brazil experience a reduction in welfare, while real wages increase in all countries except Brazil. There are several reasons for this result. On one hand, after the FTA is active, both Argentina and Brazil face competition from lower-cost suppliers of intermediate inputs from the United States. The simulated results show that both countries reduce their intratrade dependence. Argentina reduces its exports to Brazil of goods in which it had a comparative advantage, while Brazil reduces its exports to Argentina of goods in which it had a comparative advantage. Both of them start importing more from the United States. On the other hand, having access to lower-cost intermediate inputs allows Argentina and Brazil to increase their exports to the United States, Uruguay, and the ROW of goods in which they continue to have a comparative advantage.

Figure 7 presents the trade effects of an FTA between MERCOSUR and the United States. We can see that intrabloc trade decreases from 15.1% to 13.3% of total trade. As we mentioned before, this is mostly due to the reduction in trade between Brazil and Argentina. Trade between MERCOSUR members and the United States increases from 16.0% to 24.8% of total trade. Trade between MERCOSUR members and the

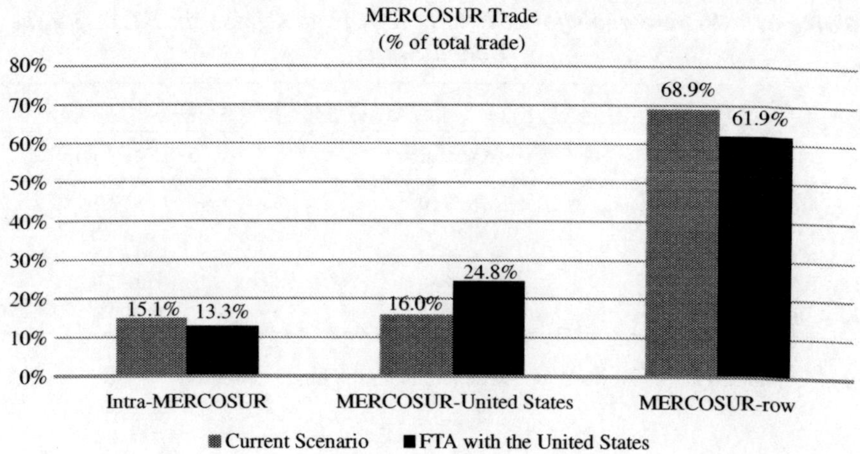

Fig. 7. Trade effects for MERCOSUR of signing an FTA with the United States.

ROW decreases from 68.9% to 61.9% of total trade. This decrease is due to the reduction in total imports from the ROW. Both Brazil and Argentina experience an increment in total exports to the ROW in this scenario.

6. Summary and conclusion

This chapter applies a new heterogeneous firm, multicountry–multisector quantitative general equilibrium model for trade policy analysis to determine what the Ricardian welfare gains are from changing partners for members of a trade bloc. The policy experiment considered for the empirical application is the MERCOSUR case. We start by quantifying the welfare effects for Uruguay from leaving MERCOSUR and adopting different integration strategies with the world economy. Through the lens of this Ricardian model, we find that the most welfare-enhancing integration strategy for Uruguay is to sign FTAs with all important economies in the world. Most of the benefits are due to the standard Ricardian gains from trade, allowing Uruguay to reallocate resources to sectors in which it has a comparative advantage. In this case welfare increases by 6.6% and real wages by 7.7%. Almost half of these gains are due to new access to cheaper intermediate inputs. These counterfactual exercises provide evidence on the welfare costs of custom unions compared with free trade integration. Our results also indicate an important decline in trade with the other MERCOSUR members and an increase in trade with the United States and the ROW if Uruguay opens up to free trade.

When we compare the welfare effects of MERCOSUR signing an FTA with the United States, the results indicate that Uruguay has the largest gains, while Argentina and Brazil do not benefit much. The analysis reveals that most of the trade between Brazil and Argentina is in industries in which they do not have a comparative advantage. After reducing tariffs, both economies experience a reduction in trade with each other, an increase in imports of intermediate inputs from the United States and an expansion in exports to countries outside MERCOSUR. One of the reasons for this result is that tariffs applied from the United States to Argentina and Brazil are substantially lower than the ones applied by these countries to the United States (except on agricultural products). Therefore, after signing an FTA, Argentina and Brazil do not increase their total exports to the United States much. Moreover, Argentina and Brazil experience a reduction in total expenditure due to the large reduction in tariff revenue. Both these effects make Argentina and Brazil not gain as much as Uruguay from the reduction in tariffs as a consequence of signing the FTA. The results from our analysis should be interpreted with caution since we are only quantifying the gains from tariff changes. A more comprehensive analysis should also consider the effects of changes in nontariff barriers, foreign direct investment, and technological transfers, which are also key elements of any type of trade agreement. Nevertheless, the results illustrate how new models are a promising tool for the analysis of trade policy. More work needs to be done in this direction.

Acknowledgments

We are grateful for the comments of Fernando Alvarez, Veronica Guerrieri, Samuel Kortum, Robert Lucas, Brent Neiman, Ralph Ossa, Rob Scollay, Robert Shimer, Nancy Stokey and seminar participants at the University of Chicago Capital Theory Working Group and International Economics Working Group, the University of Auckland and the Central Bank of Uruguay. Caliendo acknowledges the support of the Tinker Field Research Grant from the Center for Latin American Studies, Division of Social Sciences and Humanities at the University of Chicago. We also thank Cecilia Duran from the Ministry of Economics of Uruguay and Gerardo Licandro from the Central Bank of Uruguay for guiding us to the data. All errors are our own.

References

Alvarez, F., Lucas, R.E. (2007), General equilibrium analysis of the Eaton–Kortum model of international trade. *Journal of Monetary Economics* 54, 726–768.

Bhagwati, J., Krishna, P., Panagariya, A. (Eds.) (1999). *Trading Blocs: Alternative Approaches to Analyzing Preferential Trade Agreements.* The MIT Press, Cambridge, MA.

Caliendo, L., Parro, F. (2009), Estimates of the trade and welfare effects of NAFTA. Working Paper, The University of Chicago.

Dornbush, R., Fisher, S., Samuelson, P. (1977), Comparative advantage, trade and payments in a Ricardian model with a continuum of goods. *American Economic Review* 67, 823–839.

Eaton, J., Kortum, S. (2002), Technology, geography and trade. *Econometrica* 70, 1741–1779.

Ghosh, S., Yamarik, S. (2004), Does trade creation measure up? A reexamination of the effects of regional trading arrangements. *Economic Letters* 82, 213–219.

Gilbert, J., Wahl, T. (2002), Applied general equilibrium assessments of trade liberalization in China. *World Economy* 25 (5), 697–731.

Hertel, T.W. (1997), *Global Trade Analysis: Modeling and Applications.* Cambridge University Press, New York.

Kemp, M., Wan, H. (1976), An elementary proposition concerning the formation of customs unions. *Journal of International Economics* 1, 95–97.

Magee, C. (2008), New measures of trade creation and trade diversion. *Journal of International Economics* 74, 349–362.

Viner, J. (1950), *The Customs Union Issue*. Carnegie Endowment for International Peace, New York.

Yeats, A. (1998), Does MERCOSUR's trade performance raise concerns about the effects of regional trade arrangements? *The World Bank Economic Review* 12, 1–28.

CHAPTER 4

The Economy-Wide Effects of Further Trade Reforms in Tunisia's Services Sectors

Philippa Dee[a] and Ndiame Diop[b]

[a]*Crawford School of Economics and Government, The Australian National University, Canberra, Australian Capital Territory, Australia*
E-mail address: philippa.dee@anu.edu.au
[b]*The World Bank, Washington, DC, USA*
E-mail address: ndiop@worldbank.org

Abstract
The purpose of this chapter is to benchmark Tunisia against other emerging economies in terms of the regulatory barriers affecting particular services sectors and to assess the economy-wide effects of further liberalizing these services trade restrictions, compared with reducing the dispersion in barriers to its merchandise trade. On the basis of a rather restricted sample of services sectors, partial regulatory reform would yield gains roughly equivalent to full unilateral reform of manufacturing tariffs, but roughly one-tenth the gains from full bilateral reform of border protection in agriculture with the European Union. The adjustment costs associated with these services trade reforms would be minimal. The chapter identifies the reasons why the gains from these services reforms are relatively small and argues that a wider set of reforms could provide win-win outcomes and even fewer adjustment costs. By contrast, the gains in agriculture and manufacturing tend to come at the expense of domestic output in the reforming sectors – the gains are greater, but so too are the adjustment costs.

Keywords: Services trade liberalization, regulatory restrictions, regulatory reform

JEL classifications: F13, F15

1. Introduction

Tunisia has been one of the best performers in the Middle East and North Africa region since the mid-1990s, when it accelerated market-oriented reforms. Economic growth reached an average 5 percent in 1996–2007,

Frontiers of Economics and Globalization
Volume 7 ISSN: 1574-8715
DOI: 10.1108/S1574-8715(2010)0000007007

despite many external shocks. As a result, the poverty incidence dropped to about 7 percent in 2007 (World Bank Global Poverty numbers 2008). Nevertheless, because of its strong trade ties with Europe, Tunisia's real sector was affected by the global financial crisis through Europe's 2009 recession. As a result of a sharp decline in exports (−12 percent in real terms), GDP growth was only half of what was predicted (3 percent against an expected 6 percent).

Tunisia's global integration policies can be traced back to 1971, when the country decided to create an offshore sector to reduce the anti-export bias inherent in the heavy protection of the economy. The offshore sector provided generous fiscal and financial incentives to exporters and triggered a rapid rise in foreign direct investment (FDI) and the birth of a large labor-intensive textile industry integrated vertically with the European Union's (EU's) production networks. This heterodox trade policy stance – similar to the ones also applied at different points in time by Japan, Korea, Malaysia, and Mauritius – led to the first wave of diversification away from hydrocarbons. However, overall productivity growth was heavily constrained by the high level of protection of the economy.

A decisive step toward liberalizing trade occurred in the middle of the 1990s. As part of the Tunisia–EU Association Agreement (AA), trade protection vis-à-vis the EU was scheduled for gradual and systematic dismantling, starting in 1996. As a result, tariffs on industrial goods imported from the EU (the source of 65 percent of Tunisia's imports) went from about 100 percent in 1996 to 0 percent in January 2008. World Bank (2008) shows that Tunisia's industrial sectors that are highly integrated to the global market have been able to attract investment, converge to EU's labor productivity standards, and boost job creation. In sharp contrast, in the services sector where many entry and competition barriers remain, convergence to EU labor productivity standards is slow.

Tunisia is now preparing to embark on bolder services liberalization. The sector currently provides 59 percent of GDP and absorbs 55 percent of employment. So far, the country has no free trade agreement (FTA) that includes services. Its multilateral liberalization of services under Word Trade Organization's (WTO's) General Agreement on Trade in Services (GATS) has been very limited. Tunisia included only three sectors (tourism, telecommunications, and financial services) in its GATS Uruguay Round commitments. Although some of its sectors not included are quite open (e.g., maritime transport), entry into many other services sectors is restricted. Under the Uruguay Round, Tunisia bound without limitation many cross-border (mode 1) transactions (e.g., in the financial sector), but in reality, those GATS measures overlap with strict foreign exchange controls, making them partly ineffective. Apart from the financing of current operations, opportunities for cross-border (mode 1) trade are sharply restricted, and foreign competition is mostly possible through commercial presence (mode 3) or through the presence of natural persons (mode 4). But the measures affecting the presence of natural persons (mode 4) remain unbound, with the exception of wholly exporting enterprises that can recruit up to four executives and managers of foreign nationality.

It is not clear whether Tunisia will significantly increase its commitments at the end of the ongoing Doha Round. In its *conditional* Doha offer of 2005, Tunisia maintained some restrictive horizontal commitments. For instance, freedom of investment would be guaranteed only to "wholly exporting" firms and a nationality condition would be attached to the exercise of commercial activities (whole and retail trade) in Tunisia. In terms of sectoral coverage, five sectors were included in the conditional offer (out of 11 possible): telecommunications, environmental services, financial services, health services, tourism, and travel.[1] In a recent unilateral move, however, a new global telecom license (fixed, mobile, and VSAT) has been granted to a new operator that started operations in April 2010.

Tunisia started a process of negotiations for a services trade agreement with the EU in March 2006 in the Euro-Med context. Discussions on the general provisions of the agreements have started. These will be followed by bilateral negotiations on market access commitments. For Tunisia, mode 4 (temporary movement of professional services providers) and mode 2 in the area of health services represent two big areas of interest. These negotiations are crucial to secure better market access for its services providers to Europe, which would require a relaxing of restrictions in obtaining visas and mutual recognition agreements for diplomas and professional qualifications with some EU countries.

To our knowledge, the only quantitative analysis of the impact of services trade liberalization for Tunisia is Konan and Maskus (2006). An earlier quantitative analysis of potential impacts of Tunisia–EU AA by Brown *et al.* (1997) did not include services sectors. Konan and Maskus used a computable general equilibrium model with multiple products, services, and trading partners and found that reducing services barriers would generate relatively large welfare gains and low adjustment costs. However, their benchmark data and Social Accounting Matrix are dated 1995, which no longer reflect the current situation. Moreover, a strong assumption made in their paper is that barriers to FDI were half rent-creating and half cost-escalating. As is well known, the results of reform simulations are very sensitive to those assumptions. In this chapter, the treatment of barriers is based on empirical evidence, where available, rather than assumption.

---

[1] Environment services relate to the management of solid waste, dangerous waste, and sanitation. Foreign firms can enter the market but face a majority holding restriction (they can own up to 49 percent of the capital), and they should agree to transfer technologies, recruit local staff, and train staff locally. In the health sector, establishment is free without limit imposed on the capital for a list of medical fields where Tunisia has an export potential.

The purpose of this chapter is to (i) benchmark Tunisia against other emerging economies in terms of the regulatory barriers affecting its services trade; (ii) assess the economy-wide effects of further liberalizing services trade restrictions in particular sectors, either regionally or unilaterally; (iii) compare this with the effects of further liberalizing Tunisia's agricultural and manufacturing trade in the context of its AA with the EU; and (iv) also contrast this with the effects of bringing its MFN tariff rates on manufacturing goods closer to EU preferential rates. These comparisons give important insights into Tunisia's trade policy priorities over the next few years.

2. *Methodological approach to measure services trade barriers*

Barriers in services trade vary by sector, and a sector-by-sector analysis is needed to identify policy restrictions to entry and competition in services. The analytical framework that has been used to measure services trade barriers comprises three stages.

The *first stage* is to collect qualitative information about regulatory restrictions affecting services delivery and to convert it into a quantitative index (or indexes), using weights that reflect the relative severity of the different restrictions. Sometimes the weights are based on a priori judgments drawn from detailed knowledge of the industry concerned. Sometimes the weights are derived using statistical techniques, giving greatest weight to restrictions that have the greatest variability within the sample. Studies along these lines include the OECD studies of product market regulation (OECD, 2005a, 2005b; Conway *et al.*, 2005), Findlay and Warren (2000); Kalirajan (2000); Kalirajan *et al.* (2000); Nguyen-Hong (2000); Doove *et al.* (2001); Copenhagen Economics (2005) and OECD (2005c).

Since services trade barriers typically operate behind the border, the *second stage* is to quantify the effects of these indexes of services trade barriers on some behind-the-border measure of economic performance – often prices or price-cost margins, but sometimes quantities or costs – while controlling for all the other factors that affect economic performance in that market. These econometric results are used to construct the counterfactual – what economic performance would be in the absence of the services trade restrictions, holding all other factors constant.

This does not give a "tariff equivalent," because the "tariff equivalent" concept assumes (a) that services are traded primarily cross-border, whereas most are traded behind the border by the movement of people or capital, and (b) that domestic and foreign services are perfect substitutes, whereas most are highly differentiated to particular users. Instead, the counterfactual comparison gives a behind-the-border "tax equivalent," if the restrictions have raised price-cost margins, or a behind-the-border "productivity equivalent," if the restrictions have raised real resource costs. Econometric studies along these lines include Findlay and Warren (2000), Gonenc and Nicoletti (2000), Steiner (2000), Kalirajan (2000), Nguyen-Hong (2000), Barth *et al.* (2004), Clark *et al.* (2004), and OECD (2005c).

In the *third stage*, the "tax equivalents" or "productivity equivalents" are entered into a computable general equilibrium model, which is then used to project the direct and indirect effects of services trade liberalization for each sector and for the economy as a whole. Examples include Dee and Hanslow (2001), Dee *et al.* (2003), OECD (2004), and Copenhagen Economics (2005).

This study benchmarks Tunisia against a range of other emerging countries using index measures of services trade barriers derived from the first stage. The index measures are somewhat arbitrary – it is the econometrics in the second stage that establishes the true economic significance of the barriers. However, the index measures bear a monotonic relationship to the tax or productivity equivalent measures, and there are more of the former available than the latter. So for benchmarking purposes, the arbitrariness of the index measures is not a drawback.

3. *Benchmarking Tunisia on services restrictiveness*

This section benchmarks Tunisia against emerging and high-income countries for which restrictiveness indices, calculated consistently, exist. We consider seven key services sectors – postal services, telecommunications, air passenger transport, the accounting, legal and engineering professions, and banking. Tourism and maritime services sectors, two important sectors in Tunisia, are not covered because they are traditionally open to trade and investment with no significant barriers. One important sector not included is distribution. Entry into the distribution sector is strictly regulated, and trading activities, including wholesale distribution and retail trading services, are reserved for enterprises in which Tunisians hold a majority interest. Table 1 shows the importance of the different services sectors in Tunisia's economy (where the professional services are included in "other business services" and banking is included in "other financial services").

As noted, one rich source of index measures is the OECD studies of product market regulation (OECD 2005a, 2005b). Figures 1–6 show how Tunisia compares against the worst performing developed and emerging countries in the OECD sample in six key services sectors of interest. The scoring is based on answers to the questions shown in Tables 2–6. The OECD questionnaires collect and score information about a range of regulatory restrictions, but do not distinguish whether the restrictions only affect foreign operators or also affect domestic players.

Table 1. Sectoral value added in Tunisia

	Millions of US dollars	Percentage of total
Agriculture, other primary, and food	3281	20.1
Other manufacturing	2111	12.9
Electricity	344	2.1
Gas and water	126	0.8
Construction	975	6.0
Trade	2744	16.8
Other transport	1194	7.3
Air transport	382	2.3
Communications	778	4.8
Other financial services	557	3.4
Insurance	67	0.4
Other business services	680	4.2
Other services	3098	19.0
Total	16336	100.0

Source: FTAP model database, based on the GTAP version 6 database (Hertel, 1997).

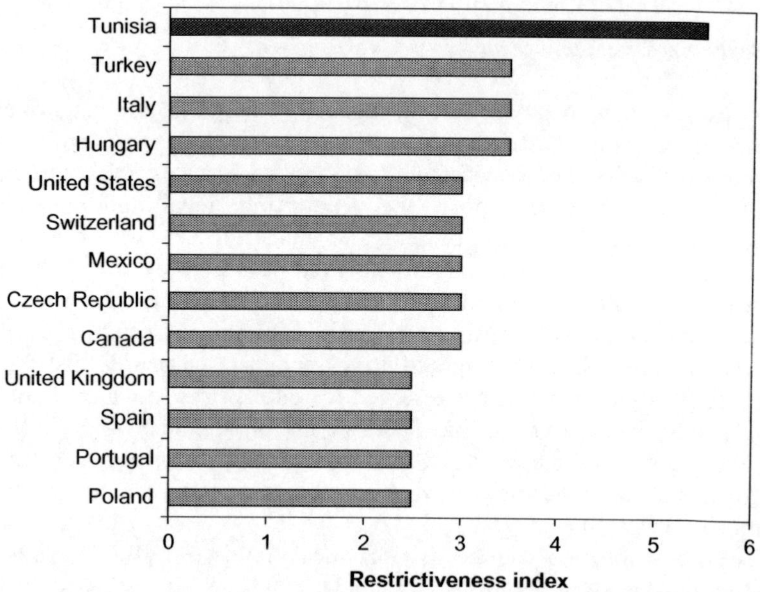

Fig. 1. OECD index of regulatory restrictions in postal services. Sources: Based on 2003 data from OECD indicators in energy, transport and communications (ETCR) (www.oecd.org/eco/structural/regreform); OECD (2005b).

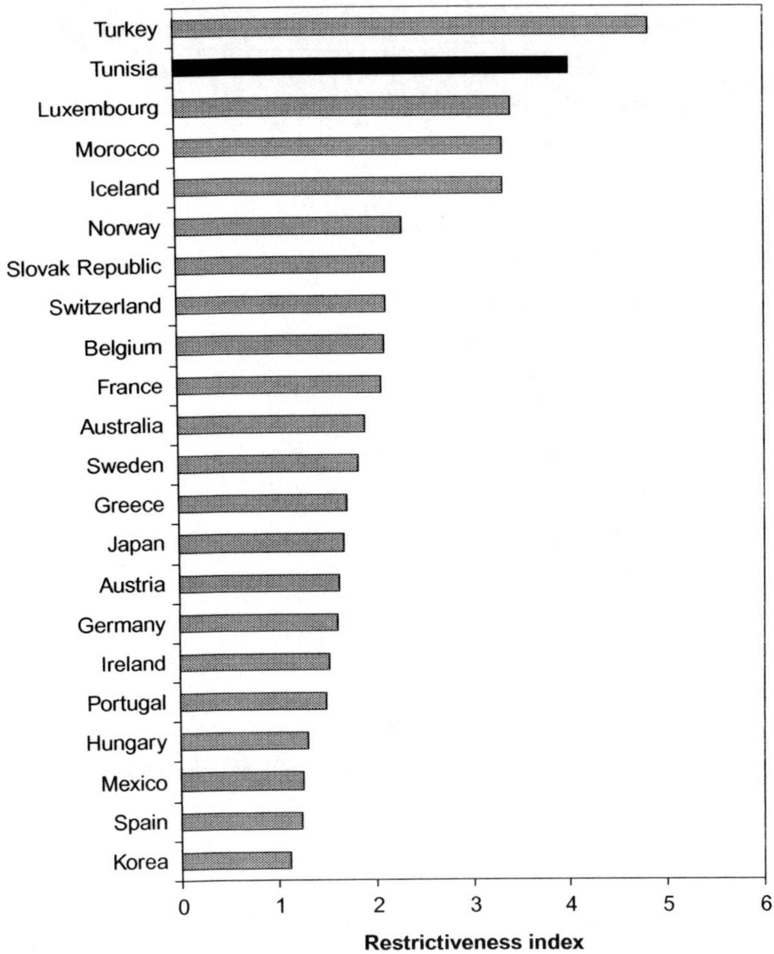

Fig. 2. OECD index of regulatory restrictions in telecommunications services. Sources: Based on 2003 data from OECD indicators in energy, transport and communications (ETCR) (www.oecd.org/eco/structural/regreform); OECD (2005b).

Tunisia scores particularly poorly in postal services because it is one of the few countries in the world to retain restrictions on courier services – private operators are required to operate in partnership with Rapid Poste. Tunisia's restrictions are second only to Turkey's in telecommunications, largely because it still has a monopoly in fixed line telecommunications and a duopoly in mobile telephony. Its restrictions in air passenger transport are second only to Hungary, because Tunisia has not entered into an open skies agreement with the United States or regionally, because

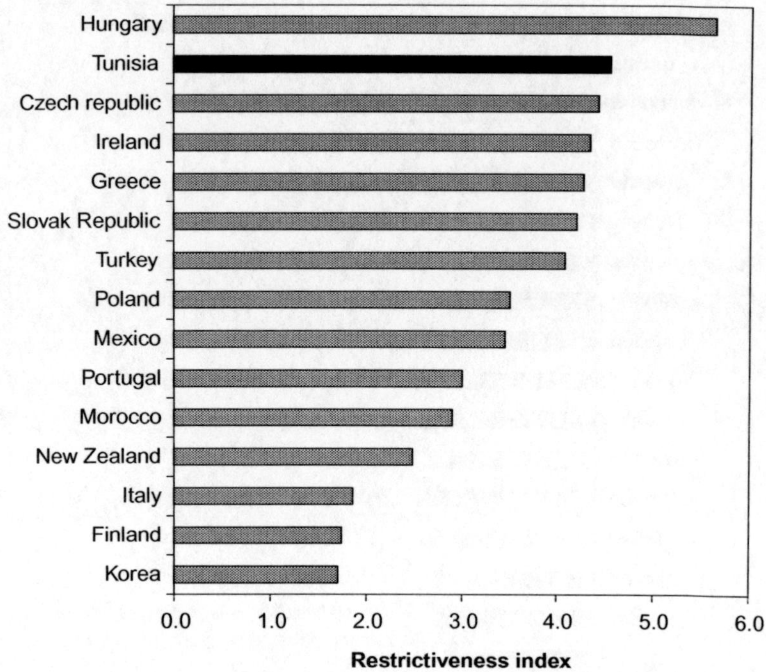

Fig. 3. OECD index of regulatory restrictions in air passenger transport. Sources: Based on 2003 data from OECD indicators in energy, transport and communications (ETCR) (www.oecd.org/eco/structural/regreform); OECD (2005b).

the rates are regulated for domestic aviation, and because the government still retains majority ownership in the largest carrier.

Tunisia also scores relatively poorly in legal and accounting services. Here the OECD questionnaires are largely restricted to measures that are nondiscriminatory – for example, exclusive licensing and restrictions on fees, advertising, and the legal form of business. Tunisia's range of regulations, particularly on fees, make it second only to Turkey and Italy in restricting competition in accounting, and second only to Greece and Turkey in restricting competition in law. What the OECD index fails to indicate is the strength of Tunisia's discriminatory restrictions in these professions – foreign firms cannot practice law, but can only provide legal consulting services, and accounting firms must be 100 percent locally owned.

Only in engineering services does Tunisia receive a relatively liberal score. Tunisia has been trying to encourage FDI and accordingly provides a relatively unrestrictive regulatory regime for both the domestic and the foreign engineers required for large projects.

The index measures of regulatory restrictions in banking services originate from one of a series of studies carried out by the Australian

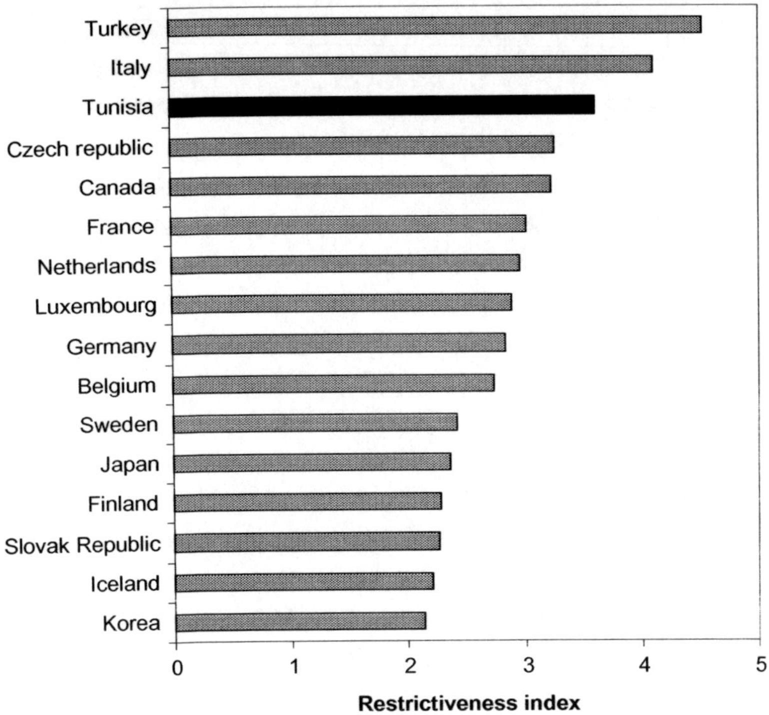

***Fig. 4.* OECD index of regulatory restrictions in accounting services. Sources: Based on 2003 data from OECD indicators of regulatory conditions in the professional services (www.oecd.org/eco/structural/regreform); OECD (2005a).**

Productivity Commission (McGuire and Schuele, 2000). Figure 7 shows how Tunisia compares against the worst performing developed and developing countries for which recent banking estimates are available. The scoring is based on the template shown in Table 7.

These index measures in banking explicitly distinguish between regulations that affect only foreign banks (the foreign index), and those that affect domestic and foreign banks equally (the domestic index). Thus the difference between the domestic and the foreign index measures the pure margin of discrimination against foreign banks.

Tunisia's banking restrictions against foreign banks are not as severe as those in Malaysia, China, Vietnam, and Brazil. But they are marginally worse than those in Morocco and significantly worse than those in South Eastern Europe. Tunisia's score reflects in part the restrictions on both lending and raising funds that are faced by foreign banks. Tunisia also maintains nondiscriminatory restrictions, including the authorization process that is required of both domestic and foreign banks.

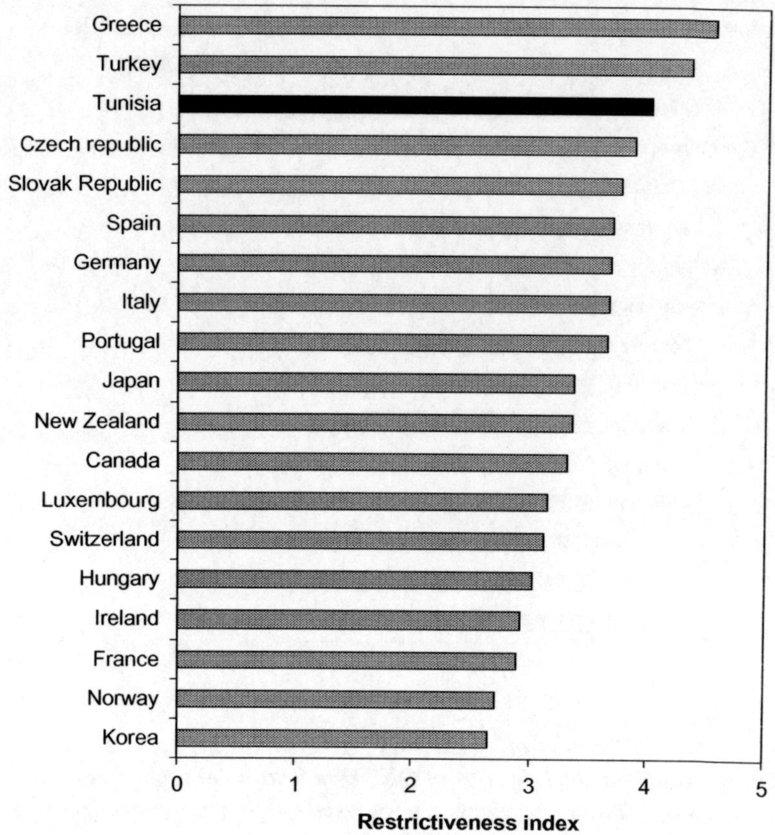

Fig. 5. OECD index of regulatory restrictions in legal services. Sources: Based on 2003 data from OECD indicators of regulatory conditions in the professional services (www.oecd.org/eco/structural/regreform); OECD (2005a).

4. Reform options

4.1. Reform strategies

It appears that the regulatory restrictions affecting Tunisia's services sector are generally relatively severe, compared with those in comparable emerging economies. Liberalizing these restrictions could help to harness the export potential of its emerging services such as ICT-enabled services and the professions, allowing Tunisia to be better positioned as a location for the outsourcing of the back-office functions of European companies. Greater use of business-to-business (B2B) ecommerce within Tunisia could also improve the competitiveness of Tunisia's own manufacturing and services sectors. Finally, liberalizing the restrictions in key backbone

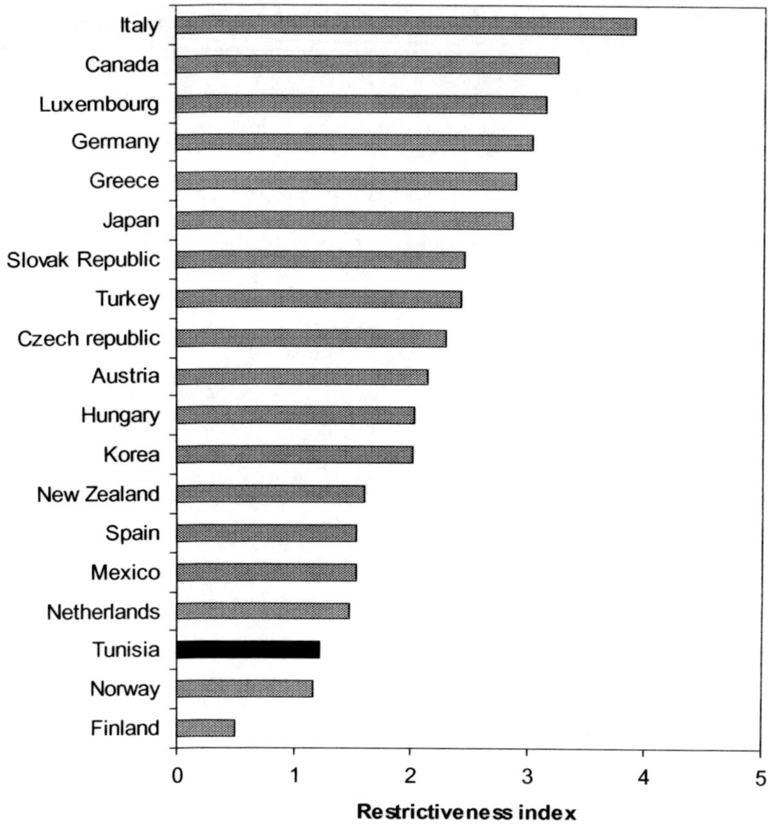

Fig. 6. OECD index of regulatory restrictions in engineering services. Sources: Based on 2003 data from OECD indicators of regulatory conditions in the professional services (www.oecd.org/eco/structural/regreform); OECD (2005a).

services such as banking, telecommunications, and air passenger transport could boost competition and investment in these sectors, for further gains to the economy as a whole.

Given Tunisia's relatively uncompetitive position in services relative to other emerging economies, there is little reason for Tunisia to wait for other countries to reciprocate in liberalizing their services. France, its key client economy within Europe, is already significantly more liberal than Tunisia. And Tunisia lags behind many of the emerging countries that would compete with it for outsourced services. For the professions, banking and telecommunications, it would make sense for Tunisia to liberalize unilaterally, although there is also scope for reform on a bilateral basis in the professions.

Air passenger transport is another matter. International air flights require international cooperation to provide the necessary infrastructure

Table 2. OECD regulatory questionnaire for postal services

Weights by theme	Question weights	Score	Question
1/2			***Entry regulation***
	1/3		*Do national, state, or provincial laws or other regulations restrict the number of competitors allowed to operate a business in at least some markets in the sector: national post – basic letter services?*
		6	Yes, in all markets
		3	Yes, in some markets
		0	No, free entry in all markets
	1/3		*Do national, state, or provincial laws or other regulations restrict the number of competitors allowed to operate a business in at least some markets in the sector: national post – basic parcel services?*
		6	Yes, in all markets
		3	Yes, in some markets
		0	No, free entry in all markets
	1/3		*Do national, state, or provincial laws or other regulations restrict the number of competitors allowed to operate a business in at least some markets in the sector: courier activities other than national post?*
		6	Yes
		0	No
1/2			***Public ownership***
	1/3		*What percentage of shares in the largest firm in the sector: national post – basic letter services are owned by the government?*
		6	100%
		3	Between 0% and 100%
		0	None
	1/3		*What percentage of shares in the largest firm in the sector: national post – basic parcel services are owned by the government?*
		6	100%
		3	Between 0% and 100%
		0	None
	1/3		*What is the extent of public ownership in the courier activities (other than national post) sector?*
		6	Government controls all dominant firms in the sector
		3	Government controls at least 1 firm, but other firms operate as well
		0	No government involvement in the sector

Sources: Based on OECD indicators in ETCR (www.oecd.org/eco/structural/regreform); OECD (2005b).

Table 3. OECD regulatory questionnaire for telecommunications services

Weights by theme	Question weights[a]	Score	Question
1/3			***Entry regulation***
	$w^t(1-w^m)$		*What are the legal conditions of entry into the trunk telephony market?*
		6	Franchised to 1 firm
		3	Franchised to 2 or more firms
		0	Free entry
	$(1-w^t)(1-w^m)$		*What are the legal conditions of entry into the international market?*
		6	Franchised to 1 firm
		3	Franchised to 2 or more firms
		0	Free entry
	w^m		*What are the legal conditions of entry into the mobile market?*
		6	Franchised to 1 firm
		3	Franchised to 2 or more firms
		0	Free entry
1/3			***Public ownership***
	$(1-w^m)$		*What percentage of shares in the public telecommunications operator is owned by the government?*
		(% government ownership/100) × 6	
	w^m		*What percentage of shares in the largest firm in the mobile telecommunications market is owned by the government?*
		(% government ownership/100) × 6	
1/3			***Market structure***
	$w^t(1-w^m)$		*What is the market share of new entrants in the trunk telephony market?*
		6 normalized market share[b]	
	$(1-w^t)(1-w^m)$		*What is the market share of new entrants in the international telephony market?*
		6 normalized market share[b]	
	w^m		*What is the market share of new entrants in the mobile telephony market?*
		6 normalized market share[b]	

Sources: Based on OECD indicators in ETCR (www.oecd.org/eco/structural/regreform); OECD (2005b).

[a]The weight w^m is the OECD-wide revenue share from mobile telephony in total revenue from trunk, international, and mobile. The weight w^t is the OECD-wide revenue share of trunk in total revenue from trunk and international telephony.

[b]The market share of new entrants has been normalized to be between 0 and 6 with 6 being the smallest market share over all countries and 0 being the largest.

Table 4. OECD regulatory questionnaire for air passenger transport

Weights by theme	Question weights[a]	Score	Question
1/2			***Entry regulation***
	(1/2)w		*Does your country have an open skies agreement with the United States?*
		6	No
		0	Yes
	(1/2)w		*Is your country participating in a regional agreement?*
		6	No
		0	Yes
	$(1-w)$		*Is the domestic aviation market in your country fully liberalized? That is, there are no restrictions on the number of (domestic) airlines that are allowed to operate on domestic routes?*
		6	No
		0	Yes
1/2			***Public ownership***
	1		*What percentage of shares in the largest carrier (domestic and international traffic combined) is owned by national, state, or provincial authorities?*
		(% of shares owned by government/100) × 6	

Sources: Based on OECD indicators in ETCR (www.oecd.org/eco/structural/regreform); OECD (2005b).

[a]The weight w is the average share of international traffic in total traffic (measured in '000 revenue passenger kilometres) for each country.

and air traffic rights. If Tunisia were to liberalize, while its partners continued to restrict entry, capacity, and air fares, this could lead to adverse outcomes for Tunisia's aviation industry, without providing benefits to its consumers. A more sensible first step would be a bilateral "open skies" agreement with the EU. This would not provide the maximum opportunity for Tunisia to optimize its own international air services network and hence achieve the full cost savings available from reaping network economies. This would likely require open skies agreements with Tunisia's Arab League partners as well. However, an open skies agreement with the EU would open those bilateral routes up to low-cost carriers, putting competitive pressure on air fares on those routes.

4.2. First-round impacts on sectoral prices

In *telecommunications*, Tunisia could lift the numerical restrictions on the number of carriers in both fixed and mobile telephony, to increase the

Table 5. OECD questionnaire for entry regulation in the professions[a]

Weights by theme	Question weights	Score	Question
2/5			***Licensing***
	1		*How many services does the profession have an exclusive or shared exclusive right to provide?*
		6	More than 3
		4.5	3
		3	2
		1.5	1
		0	0
2/5			***Education requirements (only applies if licensing not 0)***
	1/3		*What is the duration of special education/university/other higher degree?*
		Equals number of years of education (maximum of 6)	
	1/3		*What is the duration of compulsory practice necessary to become a full member of the profession?*
		Equals number of years of compulsory practice (maximum of 6)	
	1/3		*Are there professional exams that must be passed to become a full member of the profession?*
		6	Yes
		0	No
1/5			***Quotas and economic needs tests***
	1		*Is the number of foreign professionals/firms permitted to practice restricted by quotas or economic needs tests?*
		6	Yes
		0	No

Sources: Based on OECD indicators of regulatory conditions in the professional services (www.oecd.org/eco/structural/regreform); OECD (2005a).
[a]The indicator for each profession is calculated as the simple average of the indicators of entry (Table 5) and conduct (Table 6) regulation.

general contestability of the market. It could also lift the foreign ownership limits on competitive carriers, to attract further FDI. This would likely have two types of effects.

First, the greater market contestability and foreign competition would squeeze price-cost margins within telecommunications. This effect has been quantified in second-stage econometric work by Warren (2000), as summarized in Dee (2005). The top portion of Table 8 shows that Tunisia's general restrictions on competition could currently be inflating the prices of domestically owned telecommunications services by 6.8 percent, whereas the additional restrictions on foreign ownership mean that the prices from foreign suppliers could be inflated by 15.5 percent. Were Tunisia to remove

Table 6. OECD questionnaire for conduct regulation in the professions[a]

Weights by theme	Question weights	Score	Question
0.38			***Regulations on prices and fees***
	1		*Are the fees or prices that a profession charges regulated in any way (by government or self-regulated)?*
		6	Minimum prices on all services
		5	Minimum prices on some services
		4	Maximum prices on all services
		3	Maximum prices on some services
		2	Nonbinding recommended prices on all services
		1	Nonbinding recommended prices on some services
		0	No regulation
0.23			***Regulations on advertising***
	1		*Is advertising and marketing by the profession regulated in any way?*
		6	Advertising is prohibited
		3	Advertising is regulated
		0	No specific regulations
0.19			***Regulations on form of business***
	1		*Is the legal form of business restricted to a particular type?*
		6	Sole practitioner only
		5	Incorporation forbidden
		2	Partnership and some incorporation allowed
		0	No restrictions
0.19			***Quotas and economic needs tests***
	1		*Is cooperation between professionals restricted?*
		6	Generally forbidden
		4.5	Only allowed with comparable professions
		3	Generally allowed
		0	All forms allowed

Sources: Based on OECD indicators of regulatory conditions in the professional services (www.oecd.org/eco/structural/regreform); OECD (2005a).

[a]The indicator for each profession is calculated as the simple average of the indicators of entry (Table 5) and conduct (Table 6) regulation.

these restrictions, price-cost margins would be squeezed, and prices would be lower accordingly (middle portion of Table 8).

In *banking*, Tunisia could remove the discretion associated with the granting of new bank licenses (domestic and foreign). It could also lift the restrictions faced by foreign banks in lending and raising funds domestically. These moves would squeeze price-cost margins in banking, an effect that has been quantified in second-stage econometrics by Kalirajan *et al.* (2000), as summarized in Dee (2005). The results suggest

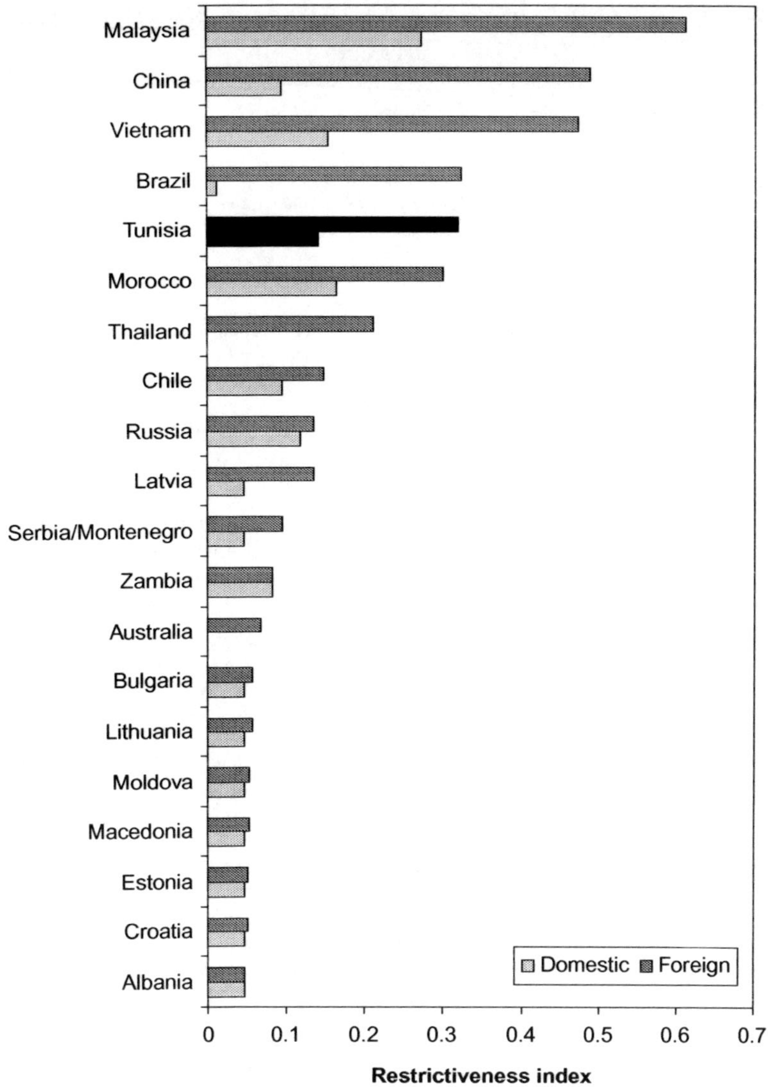

Fig. 7. Productivity Commission index of regulatory restrictions in banking services. Sources: Based on Dee (2005); McGuire and Schuele (2000).

that the removal of authorization could reduce the price impact of services trade restrictions on domestic banks from an estimated 7.5 percent to 4.9 percent (Table 8). This, together with the removal of the restrictions on foreign bank lending and raising funds, could reduce the price impact of services trade restrictions on foreign banks from 17.5 percent to 6.8 percent (Table 8).

Table 7. Productivity Commission template for restrictions in banking services

Weight-foreign index	Weight-domestic index	Score	Restriction
			Restrictions on commercial presence
0.1900	0.1900		Licensing
		1.00	Issues no new banking licenses
		0.75	Issues up to 3 new banking licenses with only prudential restrictions
		0.50	Issues up to 6 new banking licenses with only prudential restrictions
		0.25	Issues up to 10 new banking licenses with only prudential restrictions
		0.00	Issues new banking licenses with only prudential restrictions
0.1900	0.1900		Direct investment
			The score will be inversely proportional to maximum equity participation permitted in an existing domestic bank. For example, ownership to a maximum of 49% of a bank would receive a score of 0.51.
0.0950	0		No new licenses and JV arrangements
		1.00	Issues no new banking licenses and no entry is allowed through a joint venture with a domestic bank
		0.50	Bank entry is only through a joint venture with a domestic bank
		0.00	No requirement for a bank to enter through a joint venture with a domestic bank
0.0190	0		Movement of people-permanent
		1.00	No entry of executives, senior managers, or specialists
		0.80	Executives, specialists, and/or senior managers can stay a period of up to 1 year
		0.60	Executives, specialists, and/or senior managers can stay a period of up to 2 years
		0.40	Executives, specialists, and/or senior managers can stay a period of up to 3 years
		0.20	Executives, specialists, and/or senior managers can stay a period of up to 4 years
		0.00	Executives, specialists, and/or senior managers can stay a period of more than 5 years
			Other restrictions
0.1425	0.1425		Raising funds by banks
		1.00	Banks are unable to raise funds from domestic sources
		0.75	Banks are restricted from raising funds from domestic capital markets
		0.50	Banks are restricted in accepting deposits from the public or face interest rate controls
		0.00	Banks can raise funds from any source with only prudential restrictions

Table 7. *(Continued)*

Weight-foreign index	Weight-domestic index	Score	Restriction
			Lending funds by banks
0.1425	0.1425	1.00	Banks are not permitted to lend to domestic clients
		0.75	Banks are restricted to specified lending size or lending to Government projects
		0.5	Banks are restricted in providing certain lending services such as leasing, credit cards, and consumer finance
		0.25	Banks are directed to lend to certain sectors such as housing and small business
		0.00	Banks can lend to any source with only prudential restrictions
0.0950	0.0950		Other business of banks – insurance and securities services
		1.00	Banks can only provide banking services
		0.50	Banks can provide banking services plus one other line of business – insurance or securities services
		0.00	Banks have no restrictions on conducting other lines of business
0.0475	0.0475		Expanding operations – street branches, offices, and ATMs
		1.00	One banking outlet with no new banking outlets permitted
		0.75	Number of bank outlets is limited in number and location
		0.25	Expansion of banking outlets is subject to nonprudential regulatory approval
		0.00	No restrictions on banks expanding operations
0.0095	0		Movement of people – temporary
		1.00	No temporary entry of executives, senior managers, and/or specialists
		0.75	Temporary entry of executives, senior managers, and/or specialists up to 30 days
		0.50	Temporary entry of executives, senior managers, and/or specialists up to 60 days
		0.25	Temporary entry of executives, senior managers, and/or specialists up to 90 days
		0.00	Temporary entry of executives, senior managers, and/or specialists over 90 days
0[a]	0		Movement of people – Board of Directors
		1.00	Board cannot comprise of foreigners
		0.00	No restrictions on the composition of the board of directors
			The score is inversely related to the percentage of the board that can comprise foreigners. For example, if 20% of a BOD can comprise foreigners, they would receive a score of 0.80.
0.9310	0.8075		Total

Source: Dee (2005) based on McGuire and Schuele (2000).
[a]Weight was 0.019 in McGuire and Schuele (2000).

Table 8. Direct price impacts of Tunisia's regulatory restrictions in selected services (percentage)

Sector	Direct price impact		
	Through markups on		Through costs
	Output	*Exports to Tunisia*	
Currently			
Telecommunications			
Domestic providers[a]	6.8		
Foreign providers[a]	15.5		
Banking			
Domestic providers	7.5		
Foreign providers	17.5		
Professional services			
Domestic providers[b]			6.0
Foreign providers[b]	19.1	19.1	
After unilateral reform			
Telecommunications			
Domestic providers[a]	0.0		
Foreign providers[a]	0.0		
Banking			
Domestic providers	4.9		
Foreign providers	6.8		
Professional services			
Domestic providers[b]			6.0
Foreign providers[b]	11.9	11.9	
After further bilateral reform			
Professional services			
Domestic providers[b]			6.0
Foreign providers[b]	6.4	6.4	

Sources: Dee (2005), based on Warren (2000), Kalirajan *et al.* (2000), and Nguyen-Hong (2000).
[a]Simple average of price impacts for fixed line and cellular services.
[b]Simple average of estimates for legal, accounting, and engineering services.

In the *professions*, Tunisia could unilaterally get rid of the nationality requirement affecting law, accounting, and engineering. The corresponding requirement in law and accounting for partners to be local could also be relaxed, with partners only required to be locally licensed. This reform would reduce the price impact of services trade restrictions from an estimated 19.1 percent to 11.9 percent for foreign services suppliers. And this would affect not just those wanting to establish a permanent commercial presence in Tunisia but also those wanting to supply these services through ecommerce or through the temporary movement of individual professionals (Table 8, first and second columns, based on econometric work by Nguyen-Hong, 2000).

A further potential reform would be for Tunisia to seek bilateral concessions in the context of its AA with the EU, to facilitate the outsourcing of back-office accounting and legal services to Tunisia, especially from France. Accordingly, Tunisia could allow up to 50 percent EU ownership of local accounting or law firms, to allow those companies some management control over the local firms undertaking the outsourcing activities. And it could seek a mutual recognition agreement with France, allowing French recognition of local Tunisian professional qualifications for the purposes of undertaking the back-office activities, in exchange for the recognition of French qualifications in Tunisia. This latter move could further reduce the price impact of remaining restrictions on the supply of foreign professional services in Tunisia to 6.4 percent (bottom portion of Table 8), with a corresponding improvement in the competitiveness of Tunisian suppliers into the EU market.

It is assumed here that in return for these unilateral and bilateral reforms, the EU would agree to remove its discriminatory restrictions on a preferential basis – not just granting Tunisian professionals mutual recognition, but also relaxing the investment restrictions, nationality requirements, hiring, and other restrictions that apply in at least some professions, as they affect Tunisian suppliers. This would reduce the average price impact of remaining restrictions on the supply of Tunisia professional services into Europe from 9.5 percent to an estimated 5 percent (not shown in Table 8).

Finally, the econometric work on which these estimates are based suggests that the unilateral and bilateral reductions in discrimination against foreign professionals would reduce prices by reducing price-cost margins. This is in contrast with the removal of nondiscriminatory restrictions on both domestic and foreign professionals, which could reduce prices by reducing real resource costs.

As noted, in *air passenger transport*, Tunisia could seek an open skies agreement with the EU. The likely effects of this have been quantified in second-stage econometric work by Gonenc and Nicoletti (2000) and Doove *et al.* (2001). For the purposes of this chapter, that work has been updated using more recent information about the content of air services agreements from International Civil Aviation Organization (ICAO) (2004). The price impact of Tunisia's current air services agreements with the EU has been quantified at 15.4 percent. This would drop to zero in a bilateral basis under an open skies agreement (Table 9). As noted earlier, this price reduction is likely to come about through a reduction in price-costs margins rather than through a reduction in resource costs. Cost savings from achieving greater network economies would probably require a more extensive series of open skies agreements.

Furthermore, it is assumed that the open skies agreement extends to freight as well as passenger traffic. A freight agreement is likely to be less contentious and could achieve similar benefits. Accordingly, the

Table 9. Direct price impacts of bilateral air service agreements (percentage)

Destination countries	Origin countries			
	Tunisia	EU	GAFTA	Rest of world
Currently				
Tunisia	Na	15.4	15.9	14.2
EU	15.4	0	12.3	16.9
GAFTA	15.5	12.3	15.9	14.9
Rest of world	14.2	18.2	14.9	18.3
After Tunisian open skies agreement with EU				
Tunisia	Na	0	15.9	14.2
EU	0	0	12.3	16.9
GAFTA	15.5	12.3	15.9	14.9
Rest of world	14.2	18.2	14.9	18.3

Sources: Updated from Dee (2005) and based on Doove *et al.* (2001).

aforementioned estimated reduction in price-cost margins is applied to exports of the entire air transport industry, covering both freight and passengers.

5. *The economy-wide effects of services trade liberalization in Tunisia*

5.1. Modeling framework

The effects of these reform initiatives have been projected using the FTAP model of the world economy, which was developed by Dee and Hanslow (2001), is documented fully in Hanslow *et al.*, 1999, and is available for download at http://www.crawford.anu.edu.au/staff/pdee.php. The FTAP model is a computable general equilibrium model incorporating services delivered through FDI. It differs in turn from GTAP (Hertel, 1997), the "plain vanilla" model from which it was derived, in three important respects.

First, because many services are delivered primarily through commercial presence, the modeling framework includes FDI as a mode of services trade delivery and covers separately the production and trading activity of foreign multinationals. In other words, GTAP, the conventional multi-country model, is split out by ownership as well as location. In the current version of FTAP, the foreign ownership shares for Tunisia were obtained from survey data provided by Tunisia's Institut National de la Statisique (INS). The relative size of the Tunisian communications industry was also adjusted upwards, compared with that in the original GTAP database (version 6), based on value-added shares provided by INS.

Second, by virtue of foreign ownership, at least some of the profits of foreign multinationals will be repatriated back to the home countries. Thus the profit streams in the conventional multi-country model have to be reallocated from the host to the home country, after provision is made for them to be taxed in either the home or the host country. This reallocation leads to a distinction between GDP – the income *generated* in a region – and GNP – the income *received by residents* of a region. The latter forms the basis of (although is not identical to) the welfare measure in FTAP. The information on profit repatriation comes from the Balance of Payments Statistics of the International Monetary Fund (IMF).

Finally, not all profits of foreign multinationals need be repatriated to the home country. Some may be reinvested in the host country. To account for this phenomenon, and to allow for the effect that regulatory reform may have on both domestic and foreign direct investment more generally, the model makes provision for savings and capital accumulation. This is particularly important, since some regulatory barriers are aimed directly at limiting foreign equity participation. It is therefore important to capture how regulatory reform will affect not just foreign ownership *shares* but also the *total amount* of productivity capacity available to an economy. National savings rates are derived from the macroeconomic data in the International Financial Statistics and Balance of Payments Statistics of the IMF. Government savings rates are derived from the Government Finance Statistics of the IMF. Household savings rates are calculated as a residual.

The FTAP model also differs from GTAP in other respects. In particular, it allows for firm-level product differentiation, economies of scale, and large-group monopolistic competition. This is also important, since services tend to be highly specialized, being tailored to the needs of individual customers. In the current version, economies of scale are assumed to be regional for services and global for all other sectors (Dee, 2003).

The version used here contains four regions – Tunisia, the EU, the GAFTA countries, and the rest of the world. It contains 30 sectors, including 11 in the services sector (Table 10). Note that tourism is included in the model as a sales activity rather than a separate productive industry. This means that sales to foreign tourists are recorded among the exports of the industries producing goods that foreign tourists buy (air passenger transport, and so on), whereas sales to domestic tourists are recorded among the sales to household consumption of those industries.

The model provides a long-run snapshot of how different each economy would look about 10 years after the introduction of the reforms, compared to the situation at that same point in time if the reforms had not taken place. During the 10-year adjustment period, many other changes would affect each economy, but they are not taken into account in the current analysis. For this reason, the results should not be interpreted as indicating

Table 10. Sectoral aggregation of the FTAP model

Sectors in the FTAP model	Corresponding GTAP sectors
Live animals, products	Cattle, sheep goats, horses, animal products not elsewhere classified (nec), meat, meat products nec
Dairy products	Raw milk, dairy products
Coffee, etc., sugar, cut flowers	Sugar cane, crops nec, sugar
Fruit and vegetables	Vegetables
Cereals	Paddy rice, wheat, cereal grains, processed rice
Oil seeds and fats	Oil seeds, vegetable oils
Beverages and tobacco	Beverages and tobacco
Other agricultural products	Plant-based fibers, wool, silk-worm cocoons, forestry, food products nec
Fish and products	Fishing
Mineral products	Coal, oil, gas, minerals nec
Metals, products	Ferrous metals, metals nec, metal products
Chemical, etc.	Petroleum, coal products, chemical, rubber, plastic products, mineral products nec
Leather products	Leather products
Wood products, pulp, paper	Wood products, paper products, publishing
Textiles and apparel	Textiles, wearing apparel
Transport equipment	Motor vehicles and parts, transport equipment nec
Other machinery and equipment	Machinery and equipment nec
Electrical machinery	Electronic equipment
Other manufacturing	Manufactures nec
Electricity	Electricity
Gas and water	Gas manufacture, distribution, water
Construction	Construction
Trade	Trade
Other transport	Sea transport, transport nec
Air transport	Air transport
Communications	Communication
Other financial services	Financial services nec
Insurance	Insurance
Other business services	Business services nec
Other services	Recreation and other services, public admin, defence, health, education, ownership of dwellings

Source: Based on GTAP version 6 database.

the likely changes that would occur *over time* in each economy – this would require all changes, not just those in regulatory trade barriers, to be taken into account.

The distinction is important to keep in mind. Sometimes, to aid fluency, the results are couched as if key indicators "rise" or "fall." This does not mean that the indicators would be higher or lower than they are now. It means that at some future time, they would be higher or lower than they would be otherwise. In both cases, in a growing economy, they could be higher than they are now.

5.2. Results

The effects of the aforementioned Tunisian services trade liberalization scenarios on economic well-being in each region are shown in Table 11. The effects on Tunisia are not large – gains in economic well-being of around US $77 million per year after 10 years (in an economy with GDP of about US $20 billion per year in the model's initial database, which is mostly calibrated to 2001). The economy is also projected to be slightly larger, with real GDP being 0.29 percent larger than otherwise.

These projected macroeconomic effects are driven by the changes to consumer prices (from domestic and import sources), producer prices (of both Tunisian-owned and EU-owned firms), and real resource costs (for both Tunisian-owned and EU-owned firms) that are shown in Table 12. This pattern of projected price changes largely reflects the pattern of first-round effects shown in Tables 8 and 9.

The reason that the welfare gains are small is that most of the reforms are targeted at restrictions that have inflated price-cost margins, rather than real resource costs. The distinction is crucial for economic well-being. The prices of services have been inflated, not because the real resource cost of producing them has been inflated, but because incumbent firms have been able to earn economic rents – akin to a tax, but with the revenue flowing to the incumbents rather than to government. Liberalization of these barriers yields "triangle gains" in producer and consumer surplus associated with improvements in allocative efficiency, but also has

Table 11. ***Welfare implications of Tunisian unilateral and bilateral services trade reform initiatives ($US million)***

Reform scenario	Welfare in			
	Tunisia	EU	GAFTA	Rest of world
Unilateral telecommunications reforms	21	−13	0	−1
Increased B2B ecommerce	31	4	1	0
Unilateral banking reforms	3	−2	0	0
Unilateral and bilateral reforms in the professions	17	2	0	−5
Open skies agreement with the EU	4	14	−2	−37
Total[a]	77	4	−1	−42
Full reform in these sectors	175	−18	−2	−42

Source: FTAP model projections.
[a]Individual entries may not add to total because of interaction effects.

Table 12. Implications of Tunisian unilateral and bilateral services trade reform initiatives for consumer and producer prices and real resource costs in Tunisia (percentage deviation from baseline)

	Consumer prices		Producer prices[a]		Real resource costs[a]	
	Domestic goods	Imports	Tunisian owned	EU owned	Tunisian owned	EU owned
Electricity	0.4	0.0	0.4	0.0	0.4	0.0
Gas and water	0.3	0.0	0.3	0.0	0.3	0.0
Construction	0.3	0.0	0.3	0.3	0.3	0.3
Trade	−0.2	0.0	−0.2	−0.2	−0.2	−0.2
Other transport	0.4	0.0	0.4	0.4	0.4	0.4
Air transport	5.1	−8.1	5.1	5.0	5.1	5.0
Communications	−4.8	0.0	−4.5	−5.3	2.0	9.3
Other financial services	−1.2	0.0	−1.1	−1.7	1.3	8.1
Insurance	0.1	0.0	0.1	0.1	0.1	0.1
Other business services	−0.5	−8.4	−0.4	−1.8	−0.4	9.9
Other services	0.8	0.0	0.8	0.8	0.8	0.8

Source: FTAP model projections.
[a]Producer prices are inclusive of rents from services trade barriers, whereas real resource costs are not.

redistributive effects associated with the elimination of rents to incumbents. The net result is a large transfer from incumbent producers to consumers and other using industries and a relatively small gain to the economy as a whole.

This is in contrast to the situation when services trade restrictions increase the real resource cost of doing business. Liberalization is then equivalent to a productivity improvement (saving in real resources) and yields "roughly rectangle" gains associated with a downward shift in supply curves. This can increase returns for the incumbent service providers, as well as lowering costs for users elsewhere in the economy. The net result is a relatively large gain to the economy as a whole.

Whether barriers create rents or add to resource costs is under-researched currently. In some cases, the empirical evidence from the second stage econometrics is suggestive, but not conclusive. In other cases, a price impact is estimated, and then it is simply asserted whether the effect operates through price-cost margins or through real resource costs. For example, it was simply assumed in the Konan and Maskus (2006) study of Tunisia that barriers were half rent-creating and half cost-escalating.

However, theory can provide some guidance. Rents are likely to be created by quantitative and other barriers that limit entry (or exit, though this is far less common). Some red-tape measures may add to resource costs. There are also many ways in which rents can be dissipated or capitalized. So, regulatory barriers that may once have been rent-creating for the initial incumbent can become cost-escalating for subsequent incumbents. For example, Kalirajan (2000) provides indirect evidence that some of the zoning and other restrictions common in the wholesale and retail sector create rents that are subsequently capitalized into the price of commercial land.

The limited empirical evidence tends to accord with this intuition. In banking and telecommunications, where explicit barriers to entry are rife, barriers appear to create rents. In distribution services, where indirect trade restrictions also apply, barriers appear to increase costs. In air passenger transport and the professions, barriers can potentially have both effects (Gregan and Johnson, 1999; Kalirajan *et al.*, 2000; Kalirajan, 2000; Nguyen-Hong, 2000; Copenhagen Economics, 2005; OECD, 2005c). And theoretical arguments suggest that barriers in maritime and electricity generation primarily affect costs (Steiner, 2000; Clark *et al.*, 2004).

The aforementioned reform scenarios were concentrated in sectors where barriers appear to create rents. In addition, the reform measures were largely aimed at removing discrimination against foreign suppliers. This is no coincidence. When regulatory restrictions are targeted only at foreign suppliers, they tend to be explicit quantity controls, since this is the most feasible way of imposing discrimination.

The welfare gains modeled here are significantly smaller than those in the Konan and Maskus (2006) study of the impact of services liberalization in Tunisia. As noted, those authors simply assumed that barriers to FDI were half rent-creating and half cost-escalating. On the basis of this assumption, their projected gains in economic well-being from services trade liberalization were about 4 percent. By contrast, when they assumed the barriers to be entirely rent-creating, their projected gains in economic well-being fell to 0.33 percent, close to that projected here (see their Table 4). In the current study, the treatment of barriers is based on available empirical evidence, where available, rather than assumption.

Another reason for the gains in the Konan and Maskus (2006) to be slightly bigger is that they implicitly assumed that the services of domestic and foreign-owned firms in Tunisia were perfect substitutes (they did not explicitly identify the proportion of each industry that was foreign-owned, but assumed that the reduction in barriers to foreign investment would affect the prices of all firms in Tunisia, not just the foreign-owned firms). By contrast, the FTAP model assumes that the services of domestic and foreign-owned firms are close but imperfect substitutes. This also reduces the gains from reform slightly, but this is of second-order importance, compared to the different treatment of the barriers themselves (as the Konan and Maskus sensitivity analysis shows).

If Tunisia were to also contemplate domestic regulatory reform initiatives aimed at the nondiscriminatory restrictions in sectors such as ports, electricity generation, and wholesale and retail trade, where the empirical evidence suggests that restrictions raise real resource costs, this could provide much larger gains to the economy as a whole.

This can be demonstrated in a small way by considering the gains to the Tunisian economy from full rather than partial reform in the four chosen sectors. Here, full reform is defined to mean that all the discriminatory *and* nondiscriminatory restrictions in telecommunications, banking, and professional services are eliminated entirely, whereas air passenger transport is liberalized on a bilateral basis with the EU. So importantly, full reform would include reform of the nondiscriminatory restrictions in the professions that appear to raise real resource costs (see the last column of Table 8). The welfare gains to the Tunisian economy from full reform are projected to be US $175 million per year after 10 years (last row of Table 11), compared to US $77 million per year from partial reform. And fully 80 percent of the difference is accounted for by lower resource costs in the professions.

The point is also demonstrated by studies that have looked at the impact of more widespread reforms in services, including reform of the nondiscriminatory restrictions in wholesale and retail trade, electricity generation, and ports, where costs have been raised. These studies suggest that reform of the nondiscriminatory restrictions can yield between 75 and 90 percent of the total gains from reform (e.g., OECD, 2004). These results suggest that if Tunisia were to contemplate broader domestic regulatory reform initiatives aimed at nondiscriminatory restrictions in these other sectors, the gains could be several orders of magnitude greater than those projected here.

There are still some useful insights from the narrower set of reforms. Because the Tunisian reforms are mostly behind the border (with the main exception of the open skies agreement in air passenger transport, which is in any event bilateral), the gains to other regions from so-called free-riding are minimal. This has been observed in other studies of services trade reform. In the current case, the EU is in fact projected to lose slightly in welfare terms from unilateral reform of Tunisia's telecommunications and banking sectors. The EU is an important source of Tunisia's foreign investment in these sectors, so is adversely affected to a small degree by the loss of rents of its foreign multinationals in Tunisia. In other studies, trading partner countries can be slightly adversely affected by unilateral reforms, especially those that reduce costs in the reforming country. This is because such reforms improve the international competitiveness of the reforming country, so partners suffer a small terms of trade loss.

But reversing the argument, it means that Tunisia also has little to gain from behind-the-border reform in other countries. This is an additional reason why Tunisia should not wait for services trade reform initiatives to be reciprocated, except in sectors such as air passenger transport where unilateral action would clearly be unwise.

The reforms also have implications for the ownership structure of Tunisian industries. Surprisingly, even though many of the reforms remove discrimination against foreign suppliers, the projections do not suggest that domestically owned services suppliers would be significantly smaller than otherwise (Table 13). Only in the professions (the model's "other business services" sector) are domestically owned firms projected to be smaller than otherwise – by less than 1 percent, a result that could be easily absorbed by normal economic growth. In banking (the model's "other financial services" sector) and communications, the domestically

Table 13. Implications of Tunisian unilateral and bilateral services trade reform initiatives for sectoral output in Tunisia (percentage deviation from baseline)

Sector	Tunisian firms owned by		
	Tunisia	EU	Rest of world
Live animals, products	−0.4	0.0	0.0
Dairy products	0.2	0.0	0.0
Coffee, etc., sugar, cut flowers	−0.6	−0.5	−0.5
Fruits and vegetables	−0.5	−0.4	−0.4
Cereals	−1.3	−1.2	−1.2
Oil seeds and fats	−0.9	0.0	0.0
Beverages and tobacco	−0.3	−0.2	−0.2
Other agricultural products	−1.3	−1.2	−1.2
Fish and products	0.0	0.0	0.0
Mineral products	−0.1	−0.1	−0.1
Metals, products	−1.3	−1.2	−1.2
Chemical, etc.	−0.9	−0.9	−0.9
Leather products	−0.8	−0.7	−0.7
Wood products, pulp, paper	−0.5	−0.4	−0.4
Textiles and apparel	−1.0	−0.9	−0.9
Transport equipment	−0.7	−0.6	−0.6
Other machinery and equipment	1.3	1.4	1.4
Electrical machinery	−0.8	−0.8	−0.8
Other manufacturing	−0.7	−0.6	−0.6
Electricity	−0.3	0.0	0.0
Gas and water	−0.5	0.0	0.0
Construction	0.1	0.2	0.2
Trade	0.3	0.4	0.5
Other transport	−1.1	−1.0	0.0
Air transport	16.1	16.6	16.6
Communications	1.2	10.4	10.4
Other financial services	0.5	7.0	7.0
Insurance	0.4	0.5	0.5
Other business services	−0.7	14.9	7.8
Other services	−1.4	−1.3	−1.3

Source: FTAP model projections.

owned firms are projected to benefit from the removal of some of the discrimination against foreign firms.

One important reason for this is that domestically owned and foreign firms in these sectors have been modeled as providing closely, but not perfectly, substitutable services. In many services sectors, local firms in fact have local advantages that allow them to thrive alongside foreign providers.

Another reason is that, as in most other countries, the most intensive users of services are other services sectors, not agriculture or manufacturing. For example, there are typically more telephones in office buildings than in factories. So the sectors to benefit most from services sector reform are the services sectors themselves – not just banking and telecommunications but also construction, trade, and insurance. Most sectors in agriculture and manufacturing are projected to be slightly smaller than otherwise as a result of the services sector reforms. This is because there is assumed to be the same amount of skilled and unskilled labor available to the economy, whether or not the reforms take place. So if the reforms encourage some sectors to be larger than otherwise, then at least some other sectors need to be smaller than otherwise. But overall, the services sector reforms are good for the Tunisian labor market – real wages are projected to be 1.4 percent higher than otherwise as a result of the reforms.

Table 14 confirms a significant boost in exports from the services sectors undergoing reform – by about 30 percent in air passenger transport (including increased exports to foreign tourists), 50–70 percent in communications, 10–20 percent in banking, and 30–50 percent in professional services. Again, the export performance comes not only from the foreign-owned services suppliers in these industries but also from Tunisian-owned firms and contributes to a 0.9 percent increase in total export volumes. The services exports shown in Table 14 are those recorded in traditional balance of payments statistics – predominantly exports delivered through cross-border trade and consumption abroad (e.g., sales of services to foreign tourists). The growth in the output of foreign-owned firms in Tunisia (Table 13), and the corresponding increases in their sales to other firms in Tunisia, represents an increase in Tunisian imports of services delivered through commercial presence. But Table 14 confirms that those same foreign-owned firms contribute significantly to increases in services exports delivered through other modes.

In summary, the services sector reforms examined here could provide small but useful benefits to the Tunisian economy. The economy is projected to be slightly bigger than otherwise, slightly more services intensive than otherwise, with a slightly bigger proportion of foreign ownership than otherwise, and with a greater export intensity than otherwise (Table 15), providing a projected slight improvement in economic well-being.

Note that the representation of the Tunisian economy in the benchmark equilibrium in Table 15 is after the injection into the FTAP model's

Table 14. Implications of Tunisian unilateral and bilateral services trade reform initiatives for sectoral export volumes from Tunisia (percentage deviation from baseline)

Sector	Exports from Tunisian firms owned by		
	Tunisia	EU	Rest of world
Live animals, products	−5.6	0.0	0.0
Dairy products	−1.3	0.0	0.0
Coffee, etc., sugar, cut flowers	−1.5	−1.5	−1.5
Fruits and vegetables	−3.9	−3.8	−3.8
Cereals	−2.6	−2.5	−2.5
Oil seeds and fats	−0.9	0.0	0.0
Beverages and tobacco	−4.4	−4.3	−4.3
Other agricultural products	−1.7	−1.6	−1.6
Fish and products	−2.3	−2.2	−2.2
Mineral products	−0.1	0.0	0.0
Metals, products	−1.8	−1.7	−1.7
Chemical, etc.	−1.2	−1.1	−1.1
Leather products	−1.0	−0.9	−0.9
Wood products, pulp, paper	−1.2	−1.1	−1.1
Textiles and apparel	−1.0	−0.9	−0.9
Transport equipment	−1.1	−1.0	−1.0
Other machinery and equipment	1.3	1.4	1.4
Electrical machinery	−1.2	−1.2	−1.2
Other manufacturing	−1.1	−1.0	−1.0
Electricity	−3.9	0.0	0.0
Gas and water	−3.4	0.0	0.0
Construction	−3.3	−3.2	−3.2
Trade	2.3	2.4	2.4
Other transport	−2.7	−2.6	0.0
Air transport	28.3	28.8	28.8
Communications	58.6	73.1	73.2
Other financial services	11.7	18.9	18.9
Insurance	−0.9	−0.8	−0.8
Other business services	29.1	49.4	40.1
Other services	−8.1	−8.0	−8.0

Source: FTAP model projections.

database of the estimated initial barriers to services trade in each region (carried out using the GTAP model's "altertax" procedure adapted to the FTAP model – see Malcolm, 1998, for details), and after an increase in the relative size of the Tunisian communications industry, to better match national data (carried out by a taste shift in favor of communications). The benchmark equilibrium matches neither national data nor the GTAP model database exactly.

A further policy question is how the benefits from services sector reforms would compare to those from further reform of agriculture and manufacturing. This is the topic of the next section.

Table 15. Structure of the Tunisian economy before and after unilateral and bilateral services trade reforms

	In benchmark equilibrium	After reforms
Output ($US million)	37758	37811
Services share (%)	48.4	48.7
Value added at factor cost ($US million)	16335	16600
Services share (%)	67.0	67.5
Intermediate usage ($US million)	20439	20347
Services share (%)	34.0	33.9
Household consumption ($US million)	11611	11693
Services share (%)	37.8	37.8
Investment ($US million)	5402	5421
Services share (%)	59.0	59.0
Government consumption ($US million)	3006	3027
Services share (%)	100.0	100.00
Imports cif ($US million)	10355	10438
Services share	10.6	10.9
Exports fob ($US million)	8976	9052
Services share (%)	25.0	26.2
Export share of output (%)	23.8	23.9
Foreign ownership share of output (%)	15.37	15.40

Source: FTAP model database and projections.

6. The economy-wide effects of further liberalizing agriculture and manufacturing

In 2005, the tariff assistance provided to Tunisia's agricultural and manufacturing sectors was both high and variable. Detailed data for 2005 (summarized in WTO, 2005) show that tariffs on agricultural products were in the 20–90 percent range, whereas MFN tariffs on manufactures were mostly 20–30 percent (Table 16). Thus, the protection in agriculture was much higher than in manufacturing. Both were higher than the tax equivalents of the regulatory restrictions in the particular services sectors considered earlier. However, they would not necessarily be of less economic significance than cost-raising restrictions elsewhere in services.

Tunisia has been in the process of phasing out its tariffs on manufactured imports from the EU, so that in 2005 tariffs on manufactures from this source were less than 10 percent (Table 16). This is an additional source of variability in Tunisia's protection structure.

Table 16. Tunisia's tariff structure, 2005

Sector	EU preferential tariff (%)	MFN tariff (%)	Imports 2004 ($US $ million)
Live animals, products	91.8	91.8	40.5
Dairy products	94.2	95.3	42.2
Coffee, etc., sugar, cut flowers	66.1	70.3	188.5
Fruits and vegetables	94.6	96.8	61.7
Cereals	45.1	45.3	342.3
Oil seeds and fats	38.0	42.6	309.9
Beverages and tobacco	23.9	31.3	70.7
Other agricultural products	21.8	28.0	126.8
Fish and products	40.0	40.1	28.7
Mineral products	5.3	25.6	584.8
Metals, products	4.0	20.4	1051.1
Chemical, etc.	2.1	15.5	1371.4
Leather products	7.6	32.8	270.1
Wood products, pulp, paper	8.2	31.6	426.2
Textiles and apparel	9.1	31.1	2464.8
Transport equipment	4.1	18.3	924.4
Other machinery and equipment	2.7	12.5	1474.5
Electrical machinery	5.1	24.0	1448.7
Other manufacturing	4.2	23.7	396.8

Source: WTO (2005).

Once account is taken of tariff rate quotas and the *ad valorem* equivalent of specific tariffs, Tunisia's protection structure may be even more variable. Such protection estimates are available from the GTAP model database for the year 2001 and are shown in Table 17. The estimates for manufactures from this source are very roughly the same as those for 2005 from the WTO (note that the GTAP version 6 database incorporates trade-weighted applied preferential tariff rates). The estimates for agriculture are more variable than from the WTO, reflecting in part the incidence of tariff rate quotas and specific tariffs in this sector.

Tunisia has also signed a trade agreement with GAFTA countries and has been reducing its formal tariffs from this source. But reports are that any reduction in tariffs on imports from GAFTA has been countered by an increase in administrative barriers, with no real increase in market access. So the extent of true protection from GAFTA imports now is probably the same as that shown in Table 17 for 2001. It generally lies somewhere between that for the EU and that for other countries.

The policy dilemma facing Tunisia is that the further reductions in its tariffs on imports from EU, while reducing the average level of protection, may greatly increase the dispersion in protection – both the dispersion between agriculture and manufacturing, and the dispersion between different country sources of manufactured goods. Since the welfare

Table 17. Estimates of the tariff equivalents of* ad valorem *and specific tariffs and tariff rate quotas on Tunisian imports, 2001 (percentage)

Sector	Imports from EU	Imports from GAFTA	Imports from rest of world
Live animals, products	87.9	18.8	75.4
Dairy products	60.7	9.2	108.3
Coffee, etc., sugar, cut flowers	78.6	20.9	21.2
Fruits and vegetables	74.0	67.0	85.1
Cereals	87.7	15.4	56.6
Oil seeds and fats	14.7	114.1	21.8
Beverages and tobacco	32.5	17.2	34.8
Other agricultural products	28.4	12.4	45.9
Fish and products	41.4	20.4	27.0
Mineral products	7.2	6.0	16.4
Metals, products	9.3	16.7	27.0
Chemical, etc.	6.0	7.9	25.9
Leather products	14.5	21.0	38.1
Wood products, pulp, paper	16.8	14.6	25.6
Textiles and apparel	18.0	9.0	32.6
Transport equipment	7.5	13.4	19.5
Other machinery and equipment	7.9	7.4	18.2
Electrical machinery	4.8	12.4	20.3
Other manufacturing	21.7	19.3	34.0

Source: GTAP version 6 database.

damage done by import protection comes from the dispersion as well as the average level, Tunisia's current policy course may not yield benefits unless the question of dispersion is also addressed.

The extent of this policy dilemma is now examined empirically. For this purpose, the structure of protection from the GTAP version 6 database is used, since although it slightly overstates the current tariffs on manufactures from the EU, it picks up the incidence of tariff rate quotas and specific tariffs in agriculture, as well as the likely real structure of protection against imports from GAFTA countries.

6.1. Reform scenarios

One way that Tunisia could address the issue of dispersion in protection is by including agriculture in its bilateral reductions in protection with the EU – currently agriculture is largely omitted by both sides. This forms the basis of one reform scenario – Tunisia eliminates its border protection (import barriers and export subsidies) on agricultural goods from the EU and the EU reciprocates.

Tunisian agricultural producers could have difficulty taking full advantage of this market access, without improvements in the quality of the exportables they produce.

"The cases of citrus and olive oil illustrate how potential is not being realized. The key issue is quality. Supply chains must be responsive to consumers' specific demands. But to get premium oranges and oil onto the market, farmers need first-rate technical and marketing support from research, extension and producers' organizations. And Government interventions, in the form of fixed retail margins and the Office des Huiles' control over quotas and testing, are interposed between the producer and consumer. The result is that Tunisian oranges and olive oil command low prices and EU quota is left unused. Conversely, when Government has made partial reforms, such as the removal of the ONH's olive oil export monopoly, the private sector has responded" (World Bank, 2006, pp. 6–7).

Improving the quality of agricultural exportables would require not just technical solutions (research, extension) but also domestic regulatory reforms to remove government controls over quality control and wholesale and retail distribution networks, allowing Tunisian producers' direct access to their customers in Europe. The benefits of a 10 percent productivity improvement in Tunisia's agricultural exportables (fruit and vegetables, oil seeds and fats, other agricultural products) are also examined here, although the broader benefits of reform in wholesale and retail distribution, which could help bring it about, are not included.

Another way in which Tunisia could address the issue of dispersion in protection is by accompanying the elimination of the remaining tariffs on manufactures from Europe with a concomitant reduction in applied tariffs on imports from other sources. Tariffs on imports from the EU have been eliminated in recent years – Tunisia could also consider reducing its tariffs on imports from all other sources by 25 percent.

6.2. Results

The effects of these reform scenarios in Tunisian agriculture and manufacturing are shown in Table 18. As expected, the results confirm that there are significant gains from reforming border protection in Tunisian agriculture. Current protection levels are so high that any form of liberalization yields gains, even if it is on a preferential basis with the EU. This alone is projected to improve economic well-being in Tunisia by US $114 million per year after about 10 years.

Unlike in services, there are also significant gains in other countries reciprocating. Tunisia would gain US $295 million per year after about 10 years if the EU were to drop its border protection (import tariffs and quotas and export subsidies) against Tunisian agriculture. Productivity

Table 18. Welfare implications of Tunisian reform of agricultural and manufacturing protection (US $ million)

Reform scenario	Welfare in			
	Tunisia	EU	GAFTA	Rest of world
Tunisia removes border protection on agriculture from the EU	114	63	13	−52
EU reciprocates	295	−70	−1	3
10% productivity improvement in Tunisia's agricultural exportables	258	58	12	5
Subtotal[a]	*733*	*183*	*23*	*−61*
Tunisia eliminates remaining tariffs on manufactures from EU	−184	417	−3	−133
Tunisia lowers tariffs on manufactures from other sources by 25%	74	−38	3	65
Subtotal[a]	*−104*	*388*	*−1*	*−93*
Total[a]	641	570	22	−153
Full unilateral liberalization in manufacturing	65	203	6	210

Source: FTAP model projections.
[a]Individual entries may not add to total because of interaction effects.

improvements in Tunisian agriculture are probably a precondition for these gains to be realized. But a 10 percent productivity improvement in agricultural exportables would by itself provide US $258 million per year in gains. The combined package of agricultural reforms would provide total gains of US $733 million per year after about 10 years (equivalent to almost 4 percent of GDP). Real GDP itself would be 4.6 percent higher than otherwise.

The results confirm, however, that manufacturing tariffs against EU imports in 2005 were sufficiently low, relative to protection elsewhere, that the welfare cost of exacerbating the dispersion in protection would dominate – phasing out the remaining tariffs against EU manufactures would mean economic well-being was US $184 million per year lower than otherwise, after about 10 years. This adverse effect could be partially offset by reducing tariffs on imports from all other sources by 25 percent. By itself, this would provide gains of US $74 million per year. The combined package of reforms to manufacturing tariffs would yield a net loss of US $104 million per year.

But the structure of protection in Tunisia in 2005 was so variable that perhaps the only strategy in manufacturing to guarantee an overall net gain would be an across-the-board-approach – full liberalization of protection on imports from all sources, both EU and otherwise. In the bottom line of Table 18, this is shown to produce net gains of US $65 million per year, after about 10 years.

So it appears that on the basis of a rather restricted sample of services sectors, partial regulatory reform in those sectors would yield gains roughly equivalent to full unilateral reform of manufacturing tariffs, but roughly one-tenth the gains from full bilateral reform of border protection in agriculture with the EU.

Unlike in services, however, the gains in agriculture and manufacturing tend to come at the expense of domestic output in the reforming sectors – the gains are greater, but so too are the adjustment costs.

In agriculture, the biggest loser in output terms would be Tunisia's highly protected cereals industry, which is projected to be about 40 percent smaller than otherwise after about 10 years as a result of the agricultural reforms. This would be consistent with the economy as a whole growing by 5 percent a year over that period, but the cereals industry remaining stagnant. Thus if the agricultural reforms took place in an environment where general economic growth was greater than 5 percent a year, the cereals industry might have to contract in *relative* terms in response to the reforms, but it would not have to contract in *absolute* terms.

The adjustment pressures would not be as great in manufacturing as in agriculture, because the initial levels of assistance are not as great. The worst affected sectors – wood and paper products, metals and products, and transport equipment – would be smaller than otherwise by 10 percent or less after about 10 years as a result of eliminating the remaining tariffs on EU imports and cutting tariffs on imports from other sources by 25 percent. Adjustment of this magnitude could be absorbed with underlying economic growth rates of just 1 percent a year.

In summary, the protection afforded Tunisia's agricultural and manufacturing sectors is both high and variable. Expanding the scope of bilateral liberalization with the EU to include agricultural products would yield significant gains to Tunisia. In manufacturing, there is now an urgent need to address the increasing dispersion of assistance created by the gap between tariffs on imports from the EU and imports from other sources. Accompanying the elimination of the remaining tariffs on EU products with a reduction in tariff rates from other sources appears to be a precondition for further economic gains. These expanded reforms in agriculture and manufacturing will create adjustment pressures, but especially in manufacturing, they are of a scope to be easily absorbed with normal rates of underlying economic growth.

7. *Concluding comments*

This chapter has examined the possible effects of services trade initiatives that could improve Tunisia's competitiveness relative to comparable emerging economies, particularly in European markets. Tunisia's ongoing discussions with the EU in a Euro-Med context could provide a possible forum for these next steps. The chapter considers seven key services sectors – postal services, telecommunications, air passenger transport, the accounting, legal and engineering professions, and banking. Tourism and maritime services, which are important to the Tunisian economy, are not covered because they are traditionally open to trade and investment with no significant barriers.

The possible first-round impacts of services trade initiatives in these sectors have been determined using econometric work that has quantified the effects of regulatory restrictions on economic performance in the sectors, while controlling for all other factors that affect that economic performance. The economy-wide effects of the services trade initiatives have then been projected using a computable general equilibrium model that includes FDI as an important mode of services trade delivery and covers separately the production and trading activity of foreign multinationals.

On the basis of this restricted sample of services sectors, partial regulatory reform would yield gains roughly equivalent to full unilateral reform of manufacturing tariffs, but roughly one-tenth the gains from full bilateral reform in border protection in agriculture with the EU. The adjustment costs associated with these services trade reforms are minimal. Even though many of the reforms remove discrimination against foreign suppliers, the projections do not suggest that domestically owned services suppliers would be significantly smaller than otherwise. In many services sectors, local firms in fact have local and/or niche market advantages that allow them to thrive alongside foreign providers. The model makes provision for this differentiation.

One reason that the projected gains from services trade reform are relatively small is that most of the reforms are targeted at restrictions that have inflated price-cost margins rather than real resource costs. Liberalization therefore induces a relatively large transfer from incumbent producers to consumers, and a relatively small net gain to the economy as a whole. Nevertheless, whether barriers create rents or add to resource costs is under-researched currently. In the past, the issue has tended to be resolved by assertion, and sensitivity analysis has merely confirmed the importance of the assertion. Ideally, the econometric work that quantifies the first-round effects of regulatory restrictions should use a sufficiently rich set of performance measures to shed empirical light on the issue (Dee, 2005).

Another reason that the projected gains from services trade reform are relatively small is that, as noted, the services trade reforms are largely aimed at removing discrimination against foreign suppliers. Dee (2007) provides a number of reasons why in practice, formal services trade negotiations tend to focus on this dimension of liberalization. But those regulatory restrictions that are targeted only at foreign suppliers tend to be explicit quantity controls, since this is the most feasible way of imposing discrimination. Quantity controls in turn are the restrictions most likely to inflate price-cost margins rather than raise real resource costs.

Studies that have looked at the impact of more widespread reforms in services, including reform of nondiscriminatory restrictions that tend to raise real resource costs, suggest that these can yield more than three-quarters of the overall gain from services trade reform. If Tunisia were to contemplate wider reforms, including in areas such as wholesale and retail trade, electricity generation and ports, the gains could be several orders of magnitude greater than those projected here. To the extent that the wider reforms targeted nondiscriminatory restrictions, they could further benefit locally owned new entrants. To the extent that they targeted restrictions at raised real resource costs, they could even benefit incumbent suppliers. A wider set of reforms could therefore provide win-win outcomes and even fewer adjustment problems than projected here.

Relative to the selected services trade reforms considered here, reducing the dispersion in to Tunisia's barriers to its merchandise trade would yield at least as big a gain. This could be achieved either by including agriculture in the bilateral liberalization occurring with the EU or by accompanying the current elimination of tariffs against EU manufactures with a reduction in tariffs against imports from other sources. Unlike in services, however, the gains in agriculture and manufacturing would tend to come at the expense of domestic output in the reforming sectors – the gains are greater, but so too are the adjustment costs.

References

Barth, J., Caprio, G., Levine, R. (2004), Bank regulation and supervision: what works best? *Journal of Financial Intermediation* 13, 205–248.

Brown, D., Deardorff, A.V., Stern, R.M. (1997), Some economic effects of the free trade agreement between Tunisia and the European Union. In: Galal, A., Hoekman, B. (Eds.), *Regional Partners in Global Markets: Limits and Possibilities of the Euro-Med Agreements*. Centre for Economic Policy Research, London, pp. 71–97.

Clark, X., Dollar, D., Micco, A. (2004), Port efficiency, maritime transport costs, and bilateral trade. *Journal of Development Economics* 75, 417–450.

Conway, P., Janod, V., Nicoletti, G. (2005), Product market regulation in OECD countries: 1998 to 2003. ECO/WKP(2005)6, OECD, Paris.

Copenhagen Economics (2005), *Economic Assessment of the Barriers to the Internal Market for Services*. Copenhagen Economics, Copenhagen.

Dee, P. (2003), Modelling the policy issues in services trade. *Économie Internationale* (94–95), 283–300.

Dee, P. (2005), A compendium of barriers to services trade. Prepared for World Bank, available at http://www.crawford.anu.edu.au/pdf/Combined_report.pdf

Dee, P. (2007), East Asian economic integration and its impact on future growth. *The World Economy* 30 (3), 405–423.

Dee, P., Hanslow, K. (2001), Multilateral liberalization of services trade. In: Stern, R. (Ed.), *Services in the International Economy*. University of Michigan Press, Ann Arbor, pp. 117–139.

Dee, P., Hanslow, K., Phamduc, T. (2003), Measuring the cost of barriers to trade in services. In: Ito, T., Krueger, A. (Eds.), *Services Trade in the Asia-Pacific Region, NBER-East Asia Seminar on Economics*, Vol. 11. University of Chicago Press, Chicago, pp. 11–43.

Doove, S., Gabbitas, O., Nguyen-Hong, D., Owen, J. (2001), Price effects of regulation: international air passenger transport, telecommunications and electricity supply. Productivity Commission Staff Research Paper, Ausinfo, Canberra.

Findlay, C., Warren, T. (Eds.) (2000). *Impediments to Trade in Services: Measurement and Policy Implications*. Routledge, London and New York.

Gonenc, R., Nicoletti, G. (2000), Regulation, market structure and performance in air passenger transport. Working Paper No. 254, ECO/WKP(2000)27, Economics Department, OECD, Paris, August 3.

Gregan, T., Johnson, M. (1999), Impacts of Competition enhancing air services agreements: a network modelling approach. Productivity Commission Staff Research Paper, Ausinfo, Canberra, July.

Hanslow, K., Phamduc, T., Verikios, G. (1999), The structure of the FTAP model. Research Memorandum. Productivity Commission, Canberra, December, available from http://www.pc.gov.au/research/rm/ftap/index.html

Hertel, T. (1997), *Global Trade Analysis: Modelling and Applications*. Cambridge University Press, Cambridge.

ICAO (International Civil Aviation Organization) (2004), Database of the world's air services agreements, Doc 9511, 2004 edition, CD-Rom.

Kalirajan, K. (2000), Restrictions on trade in distribution services. Productivity Commission Staff Research Paper, Ausinfo, Canberra.

Kalirajan, K., McGuire, G., Nguyen-Hong, D., Schuele, M. (2000), The price impact of restrictions on banking services. In: Findlay, C., Warren, T. (Eds.), *Impediments to Trade in Services: Measurement and Policy Implications*. Routledge, London and New York, pp. 215–230.

Konan, D., Maskus, K. (2006), Quantifying the impact of services liberalization in a developing economy. *Journal of Development Economics* 81 (1), 142–162.

Malcolm, G. (1998), Adjusting tax rates in the GTAP data base. GTAP Technical Paper No. 12, Purdue University, West Lafayatte, IN.

McGuire, G., Schuele, M. (2000), Restrictiveness of international trade in banking services. In: Findlay, C., Warren, T. (Eds.), *Impediments to Trade in Services, Measurement and Policy Implications*. Routledge, London and New York, pp. 201–214.

Nguyen-Hong, D. (2000), Restrictions on trade in professional services. Productivity Commission Staff Research Paper, Ausinfo, Canberra.

OECD (2004), The economy-wide effects of services trade barriers in selected developing countries. TD/TC/WP(2004)42, OECD, Paris.

OECD (2005a), Indicators of regulatory conditions in the professional services, December 2, 2005, available at http://www.oecd.org/document/24/0,2340,en_2649_37421_35858776_1_1_1_37421,00.html

OECD (2005b), Indicators of regulatory conditions in seven non-manufacturing sectors, December 2, 2005, available at http://www.oecd.org/document/32/0,2340,en_2649_37421_35791136_1_1_1_37421,00.html

OECD (2005c), Modal estimates of services barriers. TD/TC/WP(2005)36, OECD, Paris.

Steiner, F. (2000), Regulation, industry structure and performance in the electricity supply industry. Working Paper No. 238, ECO/WKP(2000)11, Economics Department, OECD, Paris, April 12.

Warren, T. (2000), The impact on output of impediments to trade and investment in telecommunications services. In: Findlay, C., Warren, T. (Eds.), *Impediments to Trade in Services: Measurement and Policy Implications*. Routledge, London and New York, pp. 85–100.

World Bank (2006), Tunisia agricultural policy review. Report No. 35239-TN, Washington, DC.

World Bank (2008), *Tunisia Global Integration: A New Generation of Reforms to Support Employment*. World Bank, Washington, DC.

WTO (Word Trade Organization) (2005), Trade policy review. Report by Secretariat, Tunisia, WT/TPR/S/152, WTO, Geneva.

CHAPTER 5

U.S. Imports of Low-Skilled Labor: Restrict or Liberalize?☆

Peter B. Dixon[a] and Maureen T. Rimmer[b]

[a]*Centre of Policy Studies, Monash University, Clayton, Australia*
E-mail address: peter.dixon@buseco.monash.edu.au
[b]*Centre of Policy Studies, Monash University, Clayton, Australia*
E-mail address: maureen.rimmer@buseco.monash.edu.au

Abstract
We use simulations from a detailed dynamic computable general equilibrium (CGE) model to study three broad policies toward illegal workers in U.S. employment: supply restriction (tighter border security), demand restriction (prosecution of employers), and legalization through a guest-worker program with a visa tax. From the point of view of the welfare of legal residents, the results strongly favor the third option. In our welfare analysis, we use a six-part decomposition. This identifies effects on the occupational mix of legal employment as a major factor. Throughout the chapter, model results are explained through arguments and diagrams that will be familiar to economists, particularly those working in trade. No familiarity with the underlying CGE model is assumed. Technical details on our labor market assumptions are given in the Appendix.

Keywords: Illegal immigration, dynamic modeling, U.S. immigration policy

☆The work reported here is part of a broader project concerned with the creation and application of USAGE (U.S. Applied General Equilibrium), a detailed policy-relevant model of the U.S. economy. Contributions to the USAGE project have been made by the U.S. International Trade Commission; the U.S. Departments of Agriculture, Commerce and Homeland Security; and the Centre of Policy Studies at Monash University. Since its inception in 2001, the USAGE project has been guided and inspired by Bob Koopman, director of the Office of Economics at the U.S. International Trade Commission. Bryan Roberts of Homeland Security has been the driving force behind the application of USAGE to immigration issues. The present study was suggested to us by Dan Griswold of the Cato Institute who organized the publication of a nontechnical version (Dixon and Rimmer, 2009).

Frontiers of Economics and Globalization
Volume 7 ISSN: 1574-8715
DOI: 10.1108/S1574-8715(2010)0000007008

1. Introduction

The United States is a major importer of low-skilled labor, much of which is illegal. In 2005 there were 7.3 million illegal immigrants[1] (about 5 per cent of total employment) working in the United States, mainly in low-skilled occupations.

The aim of this chapter is to explain the implications for the U.S. economy of different policies on illegal labor. In working out these implications, we need to process data on the number of illegal immigrants, their skill mix, their wage rates, the taxes they pay, and the public expenditures made on their behalf. We need to combine these data with the data on the structure of the U.S economy and the skill mix of U.S. workers. In drawing conclusions from the data, we need to make assumptions about demands for and supplies of illegal immigrants and growth prospects for the U.S. economy. Dynamic computable general equilibrium (CGE) modeling offers the best prospect for handling this load. Here we apply such a model, USAGE.[2]

Readers will not be required to understand the USAGE model. In the absence of the model, we would not have been able to think of all the effects identified in this chapter, let alone quantify them. However, once the results are revealed by the model, they can be understood and explained through familiar economic mechanisms supplemented by back-of-the-envelope calculations. By providing such explanations, we hope to give readers the opportunity to assess our results in terms of both the plausibility of the underlying theory and the reliability of the data. In our view, any result that cannot be elucidated in this way is highly suspect and probably should be ignored.

The only point about USAGE that readers need to understand from the outset is that a simulation of the effects of a policy shock requires two runs of the model: a business-as-usual run and a policy run. The business-as-usual run is intended to be a plausible forecast, whereas the policy run generates deviations away from the forecast caused by the policy under consideration. For this chapter, the policies encapsulate different approaches to illegal immigration. For the most part, we report percentage deviations in variables (such as wage rates and employment) away from their business-as-usual paths caused by the policy. Altogether we conduct

[1] see Van Hook *et al.*, 2005.

[2] The USAGE model is a detailed, dynamic economy-wide model of the United States created at the Centre of Policy Studies in collaboration with the U.S. International Trade Commission. The theoretical structure of USAGE is similar to that of the MONASH model of Australia (Dixon and Rimmer, 2002). USAGE has been used in several applications by U.S. Government Departments, see for example, USITC (2004, 2007, 2009), Osborne (2007), and Fox *et al.* (2008). Previous USAGE-based studies of immigration include Dixon and Rimmer (2009) and Dixon *et al.* (2010).

six USAGE simulations, each with the same business-as-usual run but with a different policy runs.

The chapter is organized as follows. Section 2 specifies the six simulations and gives an overview of key results. Section 3 describes the business-as-usual run. Then Section 4 explains the results from the first simulation in detail, concentrating particularly on the implications for the economic welfare of U.S. households. Results from the other five simulations are explained in Section 5. Concluding remarks are presented in Section 6. Technical details of the USAGE labor-market specification are in the Appendix.

Before getting started we address some terminological issues. The chapter is about policies concerning unauthorized or illegal immigrants. Some of the policies that we consider authorize these people to work in the United States on a limited tenure. Thus it would be confusing to continue to refer to them as illegal. Under such policies, we would expect most illegal immigrants to transform into what we refer to as guest workers.

Another terminological issue is what we mean by U.S. households. We use this expression to cover everyone in the United States excluding illegal immigrants and guest workers. Similarly we use the expression U.S. workers to cover everyone in the workforce except illegal immigrants and guest workers.

2. *Description of simulations and key results*

2.1. Description

The first simulation gives the effects of a restrictive policy toward illegal immigrants. Simulations 2–6 give the effects, under various assumptions, of liberalizing policies where illegal immigrants are transformed into guest workers.

Simulation 1: tighter border security. This simulation computes the effects on the U.S. economy of reduced supply of illegal immigrants induced by a policy of tighter border security.[3] The policy change can be thought of as an increase in the difficulties faced by smugglers in organizing illegal border crossings. This could be expected to increase smugglers' fees. In the simulation, the policy is equivalent to an increase in these fees from their present level of about $4,000 per illegal immigrant to about $9,000. As can be seen from row 9 of Table 1, this reduces supply of

[3] Another approach to reduce illegal employment is to reduce demand through prosecution of employers. Dixon *et al.* (2010) compare the supply-side approach described here with a demand-side approach and conclude that the effects are quite similar.

Table 1. Long-run (2019) percentage effects on welfare of U.S. households (excludes guest workers & illegal immigrants)

	Reduced entry through:	Liberalized entry with:				
	Tighter border security	No change in characteristics of immigrants	Increased substitutability	Increased substitutability and productivity	Increased substitutability and productivity plus employment-neutralizing visa charge	Increased substitutability and productivity plus optimal visa charge
Simulation:	(1)	(2)	(3)	(4)	(5)	(6)
1. Direct effect (F1)	−0.29	0.31	0.27	0.57	0.80	0.75
2. Occupation-mix effect (F2)	−0.31	0.32	0.41	0.73	0.15	0.48
3. Capital effect (F3)	−0.24	0.26	0.28	0.49	0.24	0.39
4. U.S.-employment effect (F4)	−0.11	0.11	0.11	0.26	0.02	0.16
5. Public-expenditure effect (F5)	0.17	−0.19	−0.23	−0.32	0.00	−0.17
6. Macro-price effect (F6)	0.23	−0.24	−0.28	−0.55	−0.06	−0.34
Welfare (real GNP of U.S. households)	*−0.55*	*0.57*	*0.56*	*1.19*	*1.15*	*1.27*
Employment and wage rates of guest workers or illegal immigrants						
7. Real cost to employers, per person	9.2	−7.7	−4.8	1.3	13.0	6.0
8. Real post-tax wage rate, people	9.2	−7.7	−4.8	1.3	−21.6	−8.7
9. Employment, people	−28.6	32.0	38.7	53.2	0.0	29.3
10. Real cost to employers, effective units	9.2	−7.7	−4.8	−11.4	−1.1	−7.3
11. Employment, effective units	−28.6	32.0	38.7	75.1	14.3	47.8
12. Real post-tax wage, effective units	9.2	−7.7	−4.8	−11.4	−31.4	−20.1

illegal immigrants sufficiently to cut their employment in the long run by 28.6 per cent.

Simulation 2: liberalized entry with no change in characteristics. This simulation is the opposite of simulation 1. We consider a policy in which illegal immigration is largely replaced by a program of entry permits. Under such a program, employers in the United States would be able to offer jobs on a temporary basis to people outside the United States. Such a policy change would largely eliminate smuggler fees, thereby inducing an increase in the supply of what we now refer to as guest workers. In simulation 2 the shift that we impose on the immigration supply function to the United States is the same as that in simulation 1 but with opposite sign. An important assumption in simulation 2 is that the workforce characteristics (e.g., productivity) of guest workers are the same as those of the illegal immigrants considered in simulation 1.

Simulation 3: liberalized entry with increased substitutability. Our view is that legality is an important characteristic to employers. Many employers who do not currently use illegal immigrants may require considerable reductions in illegal/legal wage ratios to tempt them to switch to illegal workers. This suggests that illegal immigrants in a given occupational category (e.g., janitors) are currently only moderately substitutable for U.S. workers. We assume a substitution elasticity of 5. With a legalization program, we would expect substitutability to increase. In simulation 3 we investigate the implications of this possibility. We assume that the liberalization program introduced in simulation 2 is accompanied by a sharp increase in substitutability: rather than an elasticity of substitution of 5, we assume that the elasticity of substitution between guest workers and U.S workers moves up to 10.

Simulation 4: liberalized entry with increased substitutability and increased productivity. Rates of pay for illegal immigrants in a given occupation are below those for U.S. workers. We interpret this as meaning that illegal immigrants have relatively low productivity. This could reflect lack of reliability (the possibility that they will suddenly become unavailable). It could also reflect lack of skill, with employers being unwilling to provide training for transient workers of uncertain tenure. With legalization giving more reliability and permanency to their employment, we would expect the productivity of guest workers to gradually move toward that of legal immigrants in similar occupations. We impose this in simulation 4 by assuming that the transition of an illegal immigrant to a guest worker is accompanied by a 12.5 per cent increase in productivity.

Simulation 5: liberalized entry with increased substitutability, increased productivity, and an employment-neutralizing visa charge. With legalization, it would be possible for the government to raise revenue and to influence the number of guest workers through the use of a visa tax or charge for entry permits. In simulation 5 we add this feature to simulation 4. The rate of visa tax is chosen so that in the long run the employment of guest workers is at the same level as that of illegal immigrants in the business-as-usual forecast. In other word, the negative effect of the visa tax on employment of guest workers just offsets the positive effects of the elimination of smugglers fees and of the increases in substitutability and productivity.

Simulation 6: liberalized entry with increased substitutability, increased productivity, and an optimal visa charge. This simulation is the same as simulation 5 except that the visa tax is set at the level that maximizes the long-run welfare benefit to U.S. households.

In all the simulations, we assume that the policies are implemented over the period 2006–2009. Although it might be more natural to look at policies implemented at a future date, we choose 2006 as a starting point because our main data on illegal immigration is for 2005. Section 4 reports some results of the immediate effects of changes in immigration policy. However, our emphasis is on results for 2019, 10 years out from the policy shocks. We interpret these 10-year results as long-run or sustainable effects.

2.2. Overview of principal results

The principal long-run results from the six simulations are in Table 1. The row in italics reports effects on the economic welfare of U.S. households (people apart from the illegal immigrants and guest workers). We measure the effect of a change in immigration policy on the welfare of U.S. households by the deviation in 2019 in real GNP of U.S. households. We measure GNP of U.S. households by GNP (that is GDP less net income flowing to foreign investors) minus post-tax income accruing to illegal immigrant or guest workers. To convert to *real* GNP for U.S. households, we deflate by a weighted average of the price indexes for private and public consumption. In our simulations we assume that percentage deviations in private consumption by U.S. households and public consumption on their behalf are the same as the percentage deviations in real GNP for U.S. households. Consequently deviations in consumption by U.S. households also indicate deviations in welfare.

Under the tighter-border-security strategy assumed in simulation 1, real GNP of U.S. households (and their private and public consumption) is

0.55 per cent lower in 2019 than it would be without the policy change. We take this to mean that the policy in simulation 1 generates a sustained reduction in the economic welfare of U.S. households of 0.55 per cent. For readers who prefer to think in terms of current (2009) dollars, this is equivalent to a permanent annual loss in economic welfare of about $80 billion.

As will be explained in more detail in Sections 4 and 5, there are six factors that contribute to the long-run effect of a change in immigration policy on the welfare of U.S. households. The rest of this section briefly describes these factors in the context of simulation 1 and then overviews their operation in the other simulations.

F1: The direct effect. The first factor is the change in GDP *directly* attributable to the change in employment of guest workers or illegal immigrants less the change in the cost to the economy of employing them. This cost is measured by their wages less the taxes they pay in the United States. The direct effect in simulation 1 is negative, contributing −0.29 per cent (row 1, column 1, Table 1) to sustained long-run welfare of U.S. households. The main reason for the negative effect is that restricting the supply of illegal immigrants increases the wage rates of those that remain in the United States. This can be seen in row 8 of Table 1, which indicates that the policy of tighter border security in simulation 1 increases the post-tax wage rate of illegal immigrants by 9.2 per cent.

F2: Occupation-mix effect. Illegal immigrants take jobs mainly in low-skilled, low-paid occupations. Restricting illegal immigration opens up employment opportunities for U.S. workers in these occupations. At the same time, it makes the economy smaller thereby reducing employment opportunities for U.S. workers in high-skilled, high-paid occupations. Eventually the occupational mix of U.S. workers shifts in way that reduces their overall productivity. In simulation 1, this effect contributes −0.31 per cent to sustained long-run welfare of U.S. households. The occupation-mix effect will be a familiar phenomenon to students of the history of U.S. immigration. As described by Griswold (2002, p. 13), the inflow of low-skilled immigrants early in the 20th century induced native-born U.S. residents to complete their education and enhance their skills. In our terms, this was a positive occupation-mix effect.

F3: Capital effect. If a change in immigration policy had no effect on U.S. savings *up to* 2019, then it would have no effect on U.S. ownership of capital *in* 2019. In this case, if a change in immigration policy led to a reduction in the stock of capital in the United States, then it would lead to a corresponding reduction in the stock of foreign-owned capital, with little effect on capital income accruing to U.S. households. Nevertheless, they would suffer a welfare loss because the U.S. treasury would lose taxes paid by foreign owners of U.S. capital. Through the direct effect and other negative effects in Table 1, the tighter-border-security policy in simulation 1 reduces saving by U.S. households throughout the simulation period. Thus, in the policy run, U.S. households own less U.S. capital in 2019 than they had in the business-as-usual forecast and lose the full income of this lost capital. As explained in Section 4.1, the policy in simulation 1 causes a long-run reduction in U.S. capital stock of 1.7 per cent. This is split approximately evenly between reductions in foreign-owned and U.S.-owned capital. Taking account of the tax effects of the loss of foreign-owned capital and the full-income effects of the loss of U.S.-owned capital, we find that the 1.7 per cent reduction in capital contributes −0.24 per cent to sustained long-run welfare of U.S. households.

F4: U.S.-employment effect. In our simulations, we assume that changes in policies toward illegal immigrants do not affect the supply of U.S. labor. Nevertheless, these policies can have permanent long-run effects on aggregate employment of U.S. workers. This is because equilibrium unemployment rates are higher for low-skilled occupations than for high-skilled occupations. Consequently, aggregate employment of U.S. workers is reduced when the mix of their employment shifts toward low-skilled occupations. Changes in aggregate employment of U.S. workers impose changes in their income and welfare beyond those quantified in F2. Changes in immigration policy also have transitory effects on aggregate employment of U.S. workers: it takes some time for wage rates to adjust to eliminate gaps between demand for and supply of labor. In our simulations, transitory effects can cause small deviations in the employment of U.S. workers from their fully adjusted levels even as far out as 10 years from the policy change. In simulation 1, the permanent equilibrium employment effects and small transitory effects of tighter border security cause a reduction in U.S. employment in 2019 that contributes −0.11 per cent to the welfare of U.S. households. Despite the transitory nature of some of this effect, we will count it all as a contribution to sustained long-run welfare of U.S. households.

F5: Public-expenditure effect. With a reduction in the number of illegal immigrants working in the United States, the public sector would cut its expenditures, particularly on elementary education, emergency health care, and correctional services. This would allow either cuts in taxes or increased provision of public services to U.S. households. In simulation 1, this effect contributes 0.17 per cent to sustained long-run welfare of U.S. households. It should be noted that F5 encompasses only public-sector expenditures and does not take account of taxes paid by illegal immigrants. These taxes are accounted for in F1 where we compute the direct contribution of illegal immigrants to GDP net of their *post-tax* wages.

F6: Macro-price effect. An advantage to the United States of a smaller economy is that it would supply less exports and demand less imports. Because foreign-demand curves for U.S. exports slope down and supply curves for U.S. imports slope up, a cut in trade volumes improves the terms of trade, that is, it raises the price of exports relative to the price of imports. This enables U.S. households to transform whatever they produce with their capital and labor into a greater volume of consumption: they need to give up less exports to obtain any given volume of imports. More technically, an improvement in the terms of trade increases the real GNP or welfare of U.S. households by increasing the price of U.S. output relative to the price of U.S. consumption. In simulation 1, the reduction in illegal employment generates a terms-of-trade improvement that contributes 0.23 per cent to sustained long-run welfare of U.S. households.

The results in Table 1 for simulations 2–6 can be understood by reference to those for simulation 1. Here we give a broad-brush description. More details can be found in Section 5.

Simulation 2 is similar to simulation 1 except that the results have opposite sign. The minor differences from simple sign reversal are discussed in Section 5. The elimination of smugglers' fees in simulation 2 means that more immigrants (now as guest workers rather than as illegals) are willing to come to the United States at a lower wage. This produces positive results for factors F1–F4 but negative results for factors F5 and F6. One way to think about factor F1 is that legalization transforms what was formerly smugglers' fee into a benefit for U.S. households through lower costs of using immigrant labor.

From the point of view of the welfare effect on U.S. households, the move from simulation 2 to simulation 3 introduces two almost offsetting forces. On the one hand, as substitutability increases, more guest workers are hired. The increase in guest-worker employment in simulation 3 is 38.7 per cent compared with 32.0 per cent in simulation 2 (row 9). This explains the expansion in factors F2–F6 as we go from simulation 2 to simulation 3. On the other hand, increased substitutability limits the fall in the wage rate of guest workers. In simulation 3, the cost of employing these people falls by only 4.8 per cent compared with a fall of 7.7 per cent in simulation 2 (row 7), reducing the direct effect from 0.31 per cent in simulation 2 to 0.27 per cent in simulation 3.

Simulation 4 shows that the productivity of guest workers is a major determinant of their welfare effect on U.S. households. In moving from simulation 3 to simulation 4, we assume that legalization increases the productivity of guest workers to match that of legal immigrants.

Specifically we assume that each guest worker produces 12.5 per cent more effective labor. This raises the wages of guest workers, increasing their supply to the United States. In combination, the productivity and supply effects mean that the increase in employment of *effective* units of guest workers (row 11) is almost twice as large in simulation 4 as in simulation 3: 75.1 per cent (made up of the increase in the number of guest workers, 53.2 per cent, inflated by the increase in their productivity, 12.5 per cent[4]), compared with 38.7 per cent. With approximately twice the increase in effective labor input from guest workers, simulation 4 gives results for factors F1–F4 and F6 that are approximately twice as large as in simulation 3. However, the negative contribution from F5 in simulation 4 is considerably less than double that in simulation 3, helping to explain the more than doubling of the welfare benefit for U.S. households as we go from simulation 3 to simulation 4 (1.19 per cent compared with 0.56 per cent). The change in the public-expenditure effect (F5) between these simulations depends on the change in the number of guest workers, not in the number of effective units.

Simulation 5 introduces a visa tax on guest workers. This is set so that the number of guest workers in 2019 in the policy run is 12.4 million, the same as the number of illegal workers in the business-as-usual forecast (Section 3). The appropriate tax turns out to be 31 per cent of the cost of employing a guest worker (includes the visa tax). Why is the U.S. government able to impose such a tax without driving the supply of and demand for guest workers below the business-as-usual forecast? The answer is that the tax absorbs what were formerly smugglers' fees as well as the productivity increase generated by legalization. Together, these two factors represent about 31 per cent of what legalized guest workers can produce. Comparing simulation 5 with simulation 4, we see that the visa tax has a slight negative effect on long-run welfare of U.S. households (reducing the gain from 1.19 per cent to 1.15 per cent). Capturing the guest workers' productivity increase through the treasury has a strongly positive direct effect on U.S. welfare: by bearing down on guest worker post-tax wage rates, it increases F1 from 0.57 in simulation 4 to 0.80 in simulation 5. However, this gain is offset by the movements in the other factors (F2–F6) that are sharply reduced by the cut in the number of guest workers (no increase rather than an increase in 53.2 per cent).

In simulation 6 we set the visa tax at 14 per cent of the cost of employing a guest worker. We found after a little experimenting that this rate generated the maximum welfare gain for U.S. households (1.27 per cent) by striking the optimal balance between the positive effect of capturing part of the productivity increase of guest workers and the negative effect of limiting the number of guest workers.

---

[4] The increase in effective units is calculated as 100*[1.532/(1−0.125)]−1.

3. *Business-as-usual forecast*

This section provides some details of the business-as-usual run that underlies the six simulations. For understanding the simulation results for the effects of different immigration policies, the most important aspects of the business-as-usual run are those concerning the number of illegal immigrants and their share in the aggregate wagebill.

In creating the business-as-usual forecast, we recognized that employment of illegal immigrants was growing by about 5.5 per cent in 2005, with a net inflow of about 400,000 contributing to a stock of 7.3 million. In the absence of fresh U.S. policy initiatives, growth in net inflow of illegal immigrants is likely to be moderate because population growth in the main source country, Mexico, is slowing (Hanson and McIntosh, 2007). We assume an average annual growth in net inflow of only 1 per cent to 2019. Under this assumption, growth in the employment of illegal immigrants slows but nevertheless averages 3.8 per cent for the period. As shown in Figure 1, this means that employment of illegal immigrants in the business-as-usual forecast grows from 7.3 million in 2005 to 12.4 million in 2019.

Other features of our business-as-usual forecast are that average annual growth rates between 2005 and 2019 will be 3.0 per cent for real GDP, 3.2 per cent for real private consumption, 4.0 per cent for real investment, 2.0 per cent for real public consumption, 6.0 and 5.6 per cent for real exports and imports, and 1.0 per cent for employment of U.S. workers. All these forecasts are middle of the road and imply that the current global slowdown will be short-lived. Our conclusions about immigration policy are not sensitive to reasonable variations in these macro forecasts.

With employment of U.S. workers growing at only 1.0 per cent a year and that of illegal immigrants growing at 3.8 per cent a year, the share of

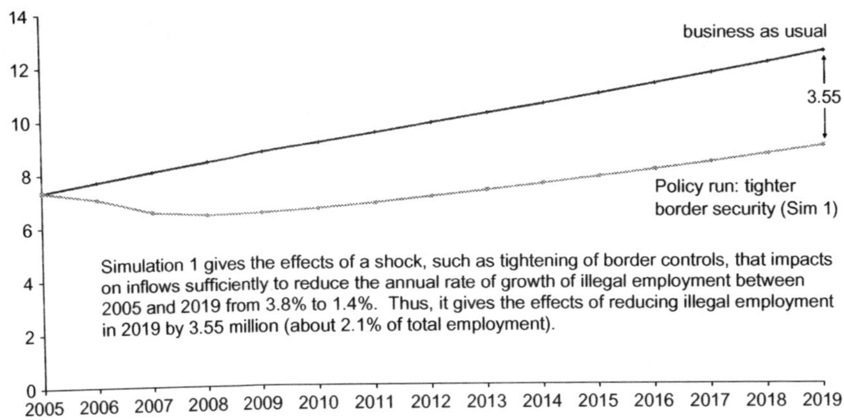

Fig. 1. Employment of illegal immigrants (millions) in the business-as-usual forecast and the simulation 1 policy run.

illegal immigrants in total employment increases from 4.98 per cent in 2005 to 7.17 per cent in 2019. Because illegal immigrants have low-paid jobs, their share in the total wagebill is less than their employment share. In the business-as-usual forecast, their wagebill share goes from 2.69 per cent in 2005 to 3.64 per cent in 2019.

4. Restricting the supply of illegal labor by tighter border security: Simulation 1[5]

This section provides an in-depth explanation of the results from simulation 1. It fills in the missing details from the overview in Section 2 and acts as a reference point for the detailed explanations of simulations 2–6 given in Section 5. As can be seen from Figure 1, the shocks in the simulation 1 policy run reduce illegal employment in 2019 by 3.55 million (= 12.4−8.9) or 28.6 per cent. The focus of our analysis is the effects of this 3.55 million cut in illegal employment, not the exact nature of the supply-reducing shocks that cause it.

4.1. Macroeconomic effects of reducing the supply of illegal immigrants

Figure 2 shows that the supply-reducing policy causes a long-run (2019) reduction in total jobs of 2.2 per cent. This mainly reflects the reduction of 3.55 million in the number of illegal jobs: 3.55 million is 2.1 per cent of the total jobs in 2019 in the business-as-usual forecast. There is also a small loss of legal jobs (Section 4.3).

Loss of jobs is not necessarily a good measure of loss of labor input. This is because different jobs have different levels of productivity, broadly reflected by different wage rates. Thus, if the economy loses a low-paid job, then the reduction in labor input is less than when the economy loses a high-paid job. Because the lost jobs in simulation 1 are mainly for low-paid workers, the reduction in labor input in 2019 is less than 2.2 per cent. We might expect the percentage loss in labor input to be 1.04 per cent: 28.6 per cent (the reduction in illegal employment) of 3.64 per cent (the illegal share in the business-as-usual forecast of the total wagebill for 2019). However, restriction of illegal employment shifts the occupational mix of remaining employment toward low-paid occupations, expanding the loss in labor input in 2019 to about 1.6 per cent. The implications of this shift in occupational mix for the welfare of U.S. households are discussed in Section 4.4.

The long-run percentage reduction (1.7 per cent) in U.S. capital stock (equipment, buildings, roads, and other structures) approximately matches that of labor input. Consistent with economic theory, our simulations

---

[5] This simulation is also described in Dixon *et al.* (2010).

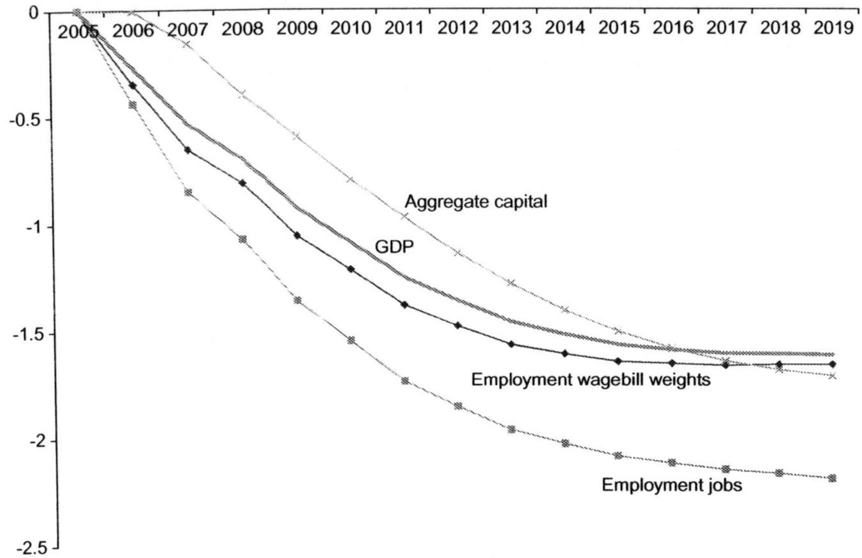

Fig. 2. GDP, employment and capital with tighter border security, simulation 1 (percentage deviations from business-as-usual).

imply that changes in immigration policy do not have a noticeable long-run effect on the amount of capital used per unit of labor input.[6] With 1.6 per cent less input of labor and 1.7 per cent less input of capital, the economy produces around 1.6 per cent less goods and services, that is, GDP is reduced by about 1.6 per cent.

Figure 3 shows how the reduction in GDP is distributed between expenditure components. As can be seen from the figure, the long-run percentage effects on these components are all negative and range around that for GDP.

Public consumption falls relative to private consumption because consumption of public goods by illegal immigrants is high relative to their consumption of private goods. In the business-as-usual forecast for 2019, illegal immigrants account for 3.7 per cent of public consumption but only 2.4 per cent of private consumption.[7] Thus, reduction in the number of illegal immigrants reduces public consumption relative to private consumption.

Both private and public consumption rise relative to GDP in the long run, that is, the policy in simulation 1, allows the United States to increase its consumption (C+G) relative to its production (GDP). This is because the policy increases the prices of goods and services produced by the United States relative to prices of the goods and services consumed by the

---

[6] We assume that immigration policy does not change either technologies or long-run rates of return, implying that it has little effect on the K/L ratio.

[7] Details of these estimates are available in Dixon *et al.* (2009).

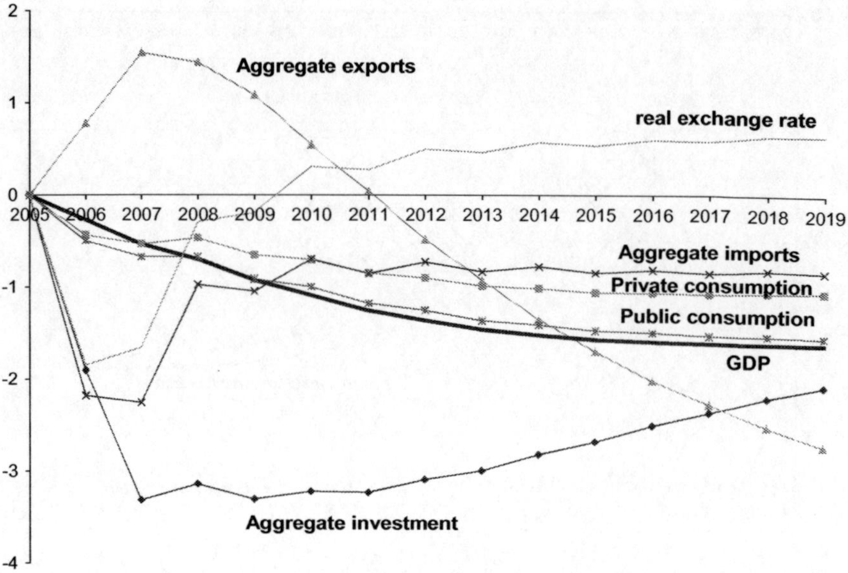

Fig. 3. Expenditure aggregates with tighter border security, simulation 1 (percentage deviations from business-as-usual).

United States. It does this by increasing the terms of trade: the price of exports divided by the price of imports. This is a benefit from having a 1.6 per cent smaller economy that demands less imports (thereby lowering their price) and supplies less exports (thereby raising their price).

Another implication of the improvement in the terms of trade is a long-run real appreciation. This means that the U.S. exchange rate increases by a greater percentage than can be accounted for by differences between the U.S. rate of inflation and the rates of inflation of its trading partners. In other words, the terms-of-trade improvement reduces U.S. international competitiveness. As can be seen in Figure 3, this leaves the long-run deviation in imports above that of GDP and the long-run deviation in exports below that of GDP. Nevertheless there is no deterioration in the trade balance: the improvement in the terms of trade means that the United States can pay for any volume of imports with less exports.

The 2019 deviation in investment is below that of GDP. Investment provides the change in capital stock each year. In the very long run, a change in immigration policy will have little identifiable effect on the growth rate of capital relative to that of GDP and therefore on the ratio of investment to GDP. As can be seen in Figure 2, the deviation line for capital is still falling slightly in 2019 indicating that the capital stock has not fully adjusted to the 1.6 per cent reduction in labor input. With capital still adjusting downwards in 2019, the investment to GDP ratio is still below its eventual long-run level.

The short-run results in Figure 3 are dominated by the need for the economy to adjust in the policy run to a lower capital stock than it had in the business-as-usual forecast. In the short run, the policy causes a relatively sharp reduction in investment. With the U.S. investment at the margin being financed mainly by foreigners, a reduction in investment weakens demand for the U.S. dollar. Consequently, a reduction in investment weakens the U.S. exchange rate. This temporarily stimulates exports and inhibits imports. As the downward adjustment in the capital stock is completed, investment recovers, causing the real exchange rate to rise, exports to fall and imports to rise. As already mentioned, this process is not quite completed by 2019.

4.2. Industry effects of reducing the supply of illegal immigrants

In popular discussions, it is often asserted that some U.S. industries rely on illegal labor to such an extent that they would not be able to survive without it. This position is not supported by simulation 1. Table 2 shows that the long-run effects on industry outputs of tighter border security are not very pronounced. The percentage deviations in industry outputs from a policy that restricts the supply of illegal employment by 28.6 per cent lie in the range −2.97 to 1.68. The variations within this narrow range are explained mainly by macroeconomic effects.

Simulation 1 gives a positive long-run deviation in the real exchange rate (Figure 3). Consequently, in Table 2, trade-exposed industries (e.g., agriculture, apparel, textiles, and export tourism) show output deviations in 2019 that are more negative than that for GDP. The long-run output deviation in Construction is also slightly more negative than that of GDP, in line with the long-run investment deviation (Figure 3). Non-trade-exposed consumption-oriented industries, mainly services, have output deviations that are less negative than that for GDP. This is explained by the long-run increase in the ratio of private and public consumption to GDP (Figure 3). Foreign vacation is an outlier in Table 2. Its strongly positive output result reflects long-run exchange-rate-induced substitution of foreign vacations for domestic vacations.

The results for an industry's output and labor input in Table 2 are not closely linked to the industry's use of illegal labor. Column (2) shows the illegal labor share of industry costs in 2005. The correlation coefficient between the output results in column (3) and the share data in column (2) is −0.20, whereas that between the labor input results in column (4) and the data in column (2) is −0.25.[8] It is true that industries relying relatively heavily on illegal immigrants incur cost increases when the supply of this

---

[8] We compute Pearson product-moment correlation coefficients leaving out industries 33–36 that do not employ labor.

Table 2. Data for 2005 on labor costs as percentages of industry costs and deviation results for 2019 in simulation 1(tighter border security)

Industry	Percentage shares in costs, 2005		Simulation 1: per cent deviations in 2019		
	Legal	Illegal	Output	Labor input	Jobs
	(1)	(2)	(3)	(4)	(5)
1 Agriculture	14.18	0.59	−2.10	−2.17	−3.26
2 Ground maintenance	50.44	4.08	−1.71	−2.19	−3.70
3 Mining	23.51	0.55	−2.18	−2.23	−2.61
4 Construction	45.99	4.51	−2.14	−2.12	−3.30
5 Dairy and sugar manufacturing	10.88	0.76	−1.57	−1.60	−2.62
6 Other food manufacturing	15.43	1.39	−1.81	−1.94	−3.18
7 Tobacco products	16.20	0.89	−1.54	−1.61	−2.58
8 Apparel	14.12	1.34	−1.95	−2.00	−3.32
9 Textiles	21.90	1.50	−2.38	−2.69	−3.67
10 Wood and furniture	28.26	1.82	−2.71	−2.72	−3.57
11 Paper and publishing	32.07	0.76	−2.10	−2.11	−2.58
12 Chemicals	20.71	0.53	−2.02	−3.71	−4.22
13 Petroleum products	4.38	0.10	−1.53	−1.04	−1.43
14 Footwear	20.05	1.45	−2.14	−2.18	−3.17
15 Metal products	26.87	1.00	−2.87	−2.94	−3.52
16 Machinery	31.61	0.76	−2.97	−3.01	−3.43
17 Computers	7.33	0.07	−1.69	−1.62	−1.84
18 Electrical machinery	21.40	0.49	−2.63	−2.71	−3.15
19 Motor vehicles	16.59	0.71	−2.60	−2.61	−3.25
20 Transport equipment	27.79	0.60	−2.25	−2.23	−2.64
21 Manufacturing nec	30.82	1.08	−2.54	−2.61	−3.21
22 Communication	17.77	0.15	−1.52	−1.50	−1.63
23 Utilities	9.87	0.27	−1.19	−0.94	−1.38
24 Wholesale and retail	45.76	1.17	−1.54	−1.51	−2.01
25 Housing services	10.26	0.15	−1.68	−1.54	−1.92
26 Business and financial services	52.78	0.29	−1.65	−1.62	−1.73
27 Medical services	60.52	0.45	−1.05	−0.90	−1.15
28 Education	51.15	0.24	−1.58	−1.50	−1.64
29 Social services	57.24	0.79	−1.17	−1.16	−1.57
30 Government Enterprise	32.92	0.32	−1.24	−1.26	−1.49
31 Other private services	53.11	1.98	−1.63	−1.68	−2.48
32 Government services	53.33	0.36	−1.54	−1.52	−1.72
33 Vacation[a]	0	0	−1.48	–	–
34 Foreign vacation[a]	0	0	1.68	–	–
35 Export tourism[a]	0	0	−2.64	–	–
36 Other nonresident[a]	0	0	−1.46	–	–
37 Transport margins	32.00	0.89	−1.93	−1.95	−2.43
38 Auto rental	24.12	0.84	−1.70	−1.69	−2.28
Total	37.31	1.00		−1.66	−2.19

[a]In USAGE, the vacation industry is a collection of inputs such as hotels and airline travel that are used by U.S. residents when they take a vacation in the U.S. Foreign vacation is a collection of inputs such as airline travel and shopping in foreign countries that are used by U.S. residents when they take a vacation outside the U.S. Export tourism is a collection of inputs used by foreign tourists when they take a vacation in the U.S. Other nonresident is a collection of inputs purchased in the U.S. by diplomats, World Bank officials etc. None of these artificial industries employs people directly.

type of labor is restricted. Consequently, these industries suffer adverse substitution effects as the prices of their products rise relative to those of other industries. These effects are included in USAGE simulations, but are weak. Illegal-labor cost shares are small, the largest being 4.51 per cent for Construction. As we saw in Table 1, real wage rates for illegal workers in simulation 1 increase on average by 9.2 per cent. Those of competing legal workers increase by considerably less (column 3, Table 3). These wage increases are not sufficient to generate significant substitution effects because they do not induce significant changes in relative prices.

The correlation coefficient between the jobs results in column (5) of Table 2 and the share data in column (2) is −0.52. The larger absolute size of this coefficient reflects replacement of illegal labor with legal labor in industries that currently rely relatively heavily on illegal labor. As mentioned in Section 2, illegal workers in any occupation receive lower wages than legal workers in the same occupation, and we interpret this as meaning they are less productive.[9] Consequently, when we simulate the effects of restricting the supply of illegal workers, we find that job numbers fall relatively sharply in those industries in which there is a significant replacement of low-productivity illegal workers with higher-productivity legal workers.

4.3. Occupation and wage effects

Column (1) of Table 3 shows the share of illegal immigrants in the wagebill of each U.S. occupation. The occupational classification was chosen to give maximum detail on employment of illegal immigrants. About 90 per cent of their employment is in the first 49 occupations. The last occupation, services other, accounts for about 60 per cent of employment in the United States but only 10 per cent of illegal employment. Columns (2) and (3) show the long-run effects of the supply-restriction policy on employment and real wage rates of U.S. workers by occupation.

In broad terms, the employment results in Table 3 show a long-run transfer of U.S. workers from services other, an amalgam of predominantly high-skilled, high-paid jobs to the occupations that currently employ large numbers of illegal immigrants. These latter occupations are mainly low-skilled, low-paid jobs. The correlation coefficient between the deviations in jobs for U.S. workers (column 2) and illegal shares (column 1) is close to 1. In occupations vacated by illegal immigrants, U.S. workers not only gain jobs but also benefit from significant wage increases.

---

[9] In the database for the initial year, 2005, we set wage rates for legal and illegal immigrants in any occupation at 0.9 and 0.8 times those of native workers. Support for the 0.9 is provided by Rector and Kim (2007, Table 2, p. 11). The 0.8 is an assumption.

Table 3. Occupational data for 2005 and simulation 1 deviation results for 2019

	Illegal immigrants:	% deviation in 2019	
	% of labor costs in 2005	Legal jobs	Legal real wage
	(1)	(2)	(3)
1 Cooks	15.6	4.20	1.89
2 Grounds maintenance	24.8	7.45	3.19
3 House keeping and cleaning	22.0	6.56	2.82
4 Janitor and building cleaner	10.4	2.31	1.19
5 Misc. agriculture worker	34.3	10.70	4.55
6 Construction laborer	23.9	7.10	3.16
7 Transport packer	24.6	7.37	3.19
8 Carpenter	15.1	3.90	1.92
9 Transport laborer	7.2	1.09	0.71
10 Cashier	4.7	0.31	0.43
11 Food serving	6.4	0.88	0.62
12 Transport driver	4.0	−0.09	0.25
13 Waiter	5.7	0.64	0.53
14 Production, miscellaneous assistant	8.3	1.07	0.72
15 Food preparation worker	13.3	3.42	1.61
16 Painter	24.9	7.46	3.31
17 Dishwasher	22.7	6.83	2.86
18 Construction, helper	24.8	7.42	3.30
19 Retail sales	2.4	−0.50	0.11
20 Production, helper	20.4	5.54	2.52
21 Packing machine operator	23.6	6.88	3.01
22 Butchers	21.0	6.20	2.74
23 Stock clerk	4.6	0.26	0.40
24 Child care	5.2	0.56	0.51
25 Miscellaneous food preparator	14.5	3.80	1.74
26 Dry wall installer	35.8	11.43	4.87
27 Nursing	2.8	−0.01	0.29
28 Industrial truck operation	8.5	1.47	0.87
29 Transport, cleaners	15.8	4.24	1.93
30 Automotive repairs	6.3	0.88	0.64
31 Sewing Machine operator	18.8	4.95	2.39
32 Concrete mason	22.6	6.61	3.00
33 Roofers	28.2	8.64	3.78
34 Plumbers	7.1	1.07	0.80
35 Personal care	5.7	0.91	0.66
36 Shipping clerk	5.2	0.35	0.43
37 Brick mason	22.5	6.56	2.97
38 Carpet installer	21.4	6.21	2.82
39 Laundry	15.5	4.22	1.93
40 Other production workers	9.1	1.57	0.91
41 Maintenance and repairs	2.2	−0.71	−0.01
42 Repair, helper	16.8	4.56	2.09
43 Welder	6.2	0.31	0.41
44 Supervisor, food preparatory	3.4	−0.20	0.22

Table 3. (*Continued*)

	Illegal immigrants:	% deviation in 2019	
	% of labor costs in 2005	Legal jobs	Legal real wage
	(1)	(2)	(3)
45 Construction supervisors	3.4	−0.27	0.27
46 Farm-food-clean, other	6.1	0.61	0.53
47 Construction, other	5.5	0.38	0.49
48 Production, other	4.6	−0.11	0.21
49 Transport, other	3.2	−0.40	0.13
50 Services, other	0.4	−1.27	−0.13
Total	2.6	−0.16	−0.46

The correlation coefficient between the employment and wage results in columns (2) and (3) is also close to 1.

The long-run shift in occupational mix shown in column (2) of Table 3 does not imply that existing U.S. workers change their occupations. For each occupation, restricting the supply of illegal workers presents U.S. workers with opportunities to replace illegal workers. On the other hand, the economy is smaller, generating a negative effect on employment opportunities for U.S. workers. The positive replacement effect dominates in the low-paid occupations that currently employ large numbers of illegal immigrants. The negative effect of a smaller economy dominates in high-paid occupations that currently employ few illegal immigrants. Thus, there is an increase in vacancies in low-paid occupations relative to high-paid occupations, allowing low-paid occupations to absorb an increased proportion of new entrants to the workforce and unemployed workers.

Another way of understanding the change in the occupation mix of U.S. workers is to recognize that the labor market involves job shortages. At any time, not everyone looking for a job in a given occupation can find a job in that occupation. So people settle for second best. The college graduate who wants to be an economist settles for a job as an administrative officer. The high-school graduate who wants to be a police officer settles for a job in private security. The unemployed person who wants to be a chef settles for a job as a short-order cook, and so on. It is this shuffling process that explains how a reduction in supply of illegal immigrants reduces the skill composition of employment of U.S. workers.[10]

While restriction of illegal immigration would increase employment and wages for U.S. workers in many occupations, the overall effect would be

[10] The Appendix contains additional technical information on our modeling of the labor market.

negative. Columns (2) and (3) in Table 3 show reductions in aggregate employment of U.S. workers and their average real wage rate of 0.16 and 0.46 per cent.

It is not surprising that the aggregate employment effect is small (−0.16 per cent): in the absence of supply shocks to the U.S. workforce, restricting illegal immigration can have no more than a minor effect on aggregate long-run employment of U.S. workers. But why is the effect negative? The decrease in employment of U.S. workers arises from the occupational shift in the composition of their employment toward low-skilled occupations. These occupations have relatively high equilibrium rates of unemployment, which we have assumed are unaffected by immigration policy. It is sometimes asserted that cuts in employment of illegal immigrants would reduce unemployment rates of low-skilled U.S. workers. Although our modeling suggests that there would be increases in the number of jobs for U.S. workers in low-skilled occupations, this does not mean that unemployment rates in these occupations would fall. In fact, with cuts in illegal immigration, low-skilled U.S. workers might find themselves under increased pressure from higher-skilled workers who can no longer find vacancies in higher-skilled occupations.

Column (3) of Table 3 shows that restriction of illegal immigration increases wage rates for U.S. workers in all occupations except services other in which the wage rate is reduced by only 0.13 per cent. However, the average hourly wage rate of U.S. workers is reduced by 0.46 per cent, reflecting the shift in the occupational composition of their employment to low-paid jobs.

4.4. Effects on the welfare of U.S. households

Table 1 shows that the long-run effect on the welfare of U.S. households of the supply-restriction policy in simulation 1 is −0.55 per cent. The aim of this subsection is to go further than the largely qualitative explanation given in Section 2 by providing more quantitative justifications. We do this through the six factors described in Section 2.

F1: Direct effect. In Figure 4, DD is the demand curve for illegal immigrants in 2019, drawn as a function of their pre-income-tax wage rate. In simulation 1, the pre-income-tax wage rate is the cost to employers of illegal immigrants. SS and S′S′ are the supply curves for illegal immigrants in the business-as-usual and policy runs. Both relate supply to pre-income-tax wage rates and are drawn on the assumption that the income tax rate applying to illegal immigrants is held constant.

The numbers in Figure 4 refer to simulation results for 2019. In the business-as-usual run for 2019, the pre-tax wage rate for illegal workers is \$1, rising to \$1.092 in the policy run (row 7, Table 1). The U.S. wagebill in the business-as-usual forecast for 2019 is \$17,900 billion. As mentioned in

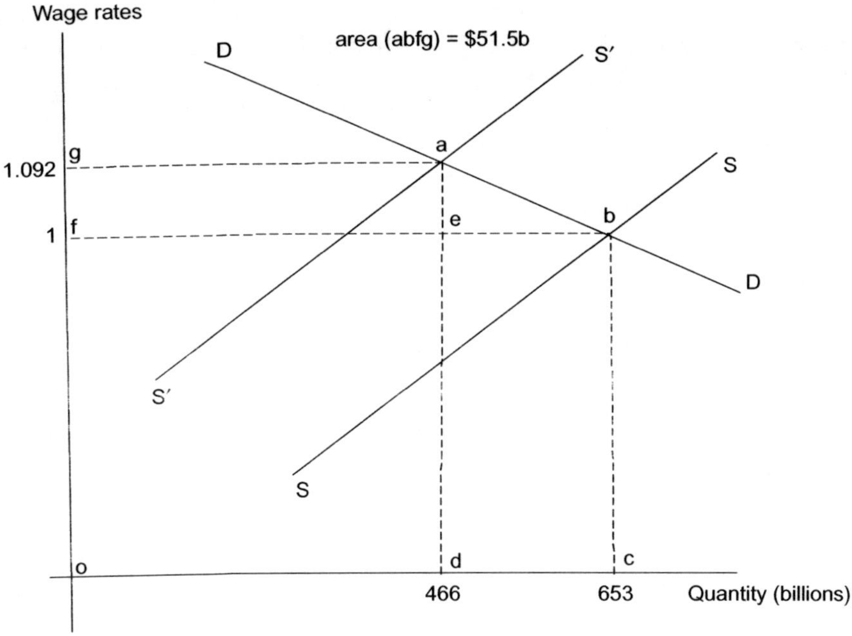

Fig. 4. Demand for and supply of illegal immigrants in 2019, simulation 1.

Section 3, the share of illegal immigrants in the total wagebill is 3.64 per cent. Thus, with the wage rate at $1, business-as-usual employment of illegal immigrants in 2019 is 653 billion units (= 0.0364*17,900b). In the policy run, the quantity of illegal immigrant employment is 28.6 per cent lower, 466 billion units.

To a first approximation, the loss in output (represented by GDP) from reducing illegal employment is the change in the area under the demand curve, area(abcd). The change in the total cost to employers of illegal immigrants is area(gado), the cost with the policy in place, minus area(fbco), the cost in the business-as-usual forecast. This can be represented as area(gaef), the increase in costs associated with the increase in the illegal immigrant wage rate, minus area(ebcd), the reduction in costs associated with employment of less illegal immigrants.

Ignoring taxes, the analysis so far suggests that the direct effect of cutting illegal employment (the change in GDP less the change in the costs of employing illegal workers) is a loss represented by area(abfg). As indicated in Figure 4, this area is worth $51.5 billion.

Taxes complicate the situation in two ways. First, the change in the area under the demand curve is an underestimate of the loss in GDP because indirect taxes mean that pre-tax wage rates are less than the marginal product of workers. Second, illegal immigrants pay income taxes.

Consequently, area(ebcd) overstates the saving to the U.S. economy associated with paying wages to 28.6 per cent less illegal immigrants and area(gaef) overstates the cost to the U.S. economy of paying higher wage rates to illegal immigrants who remain in employment. Adjusting for taxes takes our final estimate of the direct effect to a loss of $77.3 billion in 2019, which is 0.29 per cent of the business-as-usual GNP of U.S. households (row 1, column 1, Table 1).

F2: Occupation-mix effect. As explained in Section 4.3, restricting the supply of illegal immigrants changes the occupational mix of employment of U.S. workers, reducing their average hourly wage rate by 0.46 per cent (Table 3). In 2019 this costs legal residents $80.3 billion, calculated as the wage effect times the business-as-usual wagebill of U.S. workers [0.0046*(1−0.0364)*17900]. Translating this cost into an effect on welfare gives the F2 result for simulation 1 in Table 1, −0.31 per cent.

F3: Capital effect. Simulation 1 shows a −1.7 per cent long-run deviation in capital (Figure 2). With returns to capital being 26 per cent of GDP, the 1.7 per cent reduction in capital causes a reduction in GDP of 0.44 per cent (= 1.7*0.26). Not all of this loss in GDP is a loss in welfare for U.S. households. As explained in Section 2, the welfare effect for U.S. households is the U.S.-owned part of the lost capital income plus just the tax component of the foreign-owned part. In simulation 1, the U.S.-owned share of the reduction in capital is about 40 per cent. Taking this into account and allowing for tax effects on foreign-owned capital, we find that the reduction in GDP of 0.44 per cent translates into a long-run welfare loss of 0.24 per cent.

F4: U.S.-employment effect. The tighter-border-security policy reduces U.S. employment by 0.16 per cent (Table 3). In the business-as-usual forecast, the wagebill for U.S. workers in 2019 is $17,250 billion [= (1−0.0364)*17,900]. Thus the reduction in employment costs U.S. workers $27.6 billion (= 17,250*0.0016). The cost to U.S. households is slightly greater than this because, with a reduction in U.S. employment, there is a reduction in the collection of indirect taxes. Taking this into account expands the loss in U.S. income to $28.8 billion. Expressed as a percentage of GNP for U.S. households in 2019, this gives a welfare loss of 0.11 per cent.

F5: Public-expenditure effect. For public consumption, we assume that expenditure per capita on both legal residents and illegal immigrants is proportional to private consumption per capita by legal residents. The factor of proportionality for illegal immigrants is set at 0.49 times the value applying to legal residents.[11] Thus we assume: that as legal residents become richer they demand more services from the public sector; that illegal immigrants cannot be prevented from enjoying improvements in public amenities made available for legal residents: but that not all government services available to legal residents are available to illegal immigrants.

In the business-as-usual forecast for 2019, the share of illegal immigrants in the workforce is to 7.17 per cent (Section 3). We assume that this is also their share in the population and that the 0.49 ratio for public expenditure is maintained. Thus in the business-as-usual forecast for 2019, the share of illegal immigrants in public expenditure is 3.65 per cent [= 100*0.49*0.0717/(0.49*0.0717 + 1 – 0.0717)].

Public consumption in 2019 in the business-as-usual forecast is $4,222.8 billion. With a 28.6 per cent reduction in illegal immigrants, the public sector reduces its expenditure in 2019 on their behalf by $44.1 billion, calculated as 28.6 per cent of 3.65 per cent of $4,222.8 billion. As shown in Table 1, this is a welfare gain to U.S. households of 0.17 per cent.

F6: Macro-price effects. The cut in illegal immigration in simulation 1 reduces the price index for private and public consumption relative to that for GDP in 2019 by 0.23 per cent. This increases the consuming power of the GNP of U.S. households or their welfare by 0.23 per cent. The main reason for the relative decline in the price of consumption is the improvement in the terms of trade, discussed in Section 2. A terms-of-trade improvement generally reduces the price index for gross national expenditure (GNE, private and public consumption plus investment) relative to that for GDP because GNE includes imports but not exports, whereas GDP includes exports but not imports. In simulation 1, the reduction in the price of consumption relative to the price of GDP is accentuated by movements in the component prices in GNE. The price of consumption falls relative to the price of GNE because the price of the other component of GNE, investment, is elevated due to heavy representation of illegal immigrants in the construction industry.

5. *Liberalizing through a guest-worker program: Simulations 2–6*

This section fills in the missing details from Section 2 on the results in Table 1 for simulations 2–6.

---

[11] The main sources for this estimate are Rector and Kim (2007) and Strayhorn (2006).

5.1. Simulation 2: Liberalized entry with no change in characteristics

The results in simulation 2 are close to an exact reversal of those in simulation 1. The most interesting difference from exact reversal is for the direct effect. As illustrated in Figure 5, the wage reduction in simulation 2 applies to more workers than the wage increase in simulation 1. This suggests that the direct effect should be noticeably larger in absolute size in simulation 2 than in simulation 1. However, the slight nonlinearity of the demand curve (DD) for illegal immigrants or guest workers means that the wage reduction in simulation 2 is slightly smaller in absolute size that the wage increase in simulation 1 (7.7 per cent down compared with 9.2 per cent up). This acts in the opposite direction, leaving the direct effect in simulation 2 only slightly larger in absolute size than that in simulation 1 (0.31 per cent compared with −0.29 per cent).

5.2. Simulation 3: Liberalized entry with increased substitutability

In the policy run of simulation 3, the demand curve for guest workers is flatter than in simulation 2 (Figure 6). This explains why the wage reduction for guest workers is smaller in simulation 3 than in simulation 2 (4.8 per cent compared with 7.7 per cent, Table 1). On the contrary, the

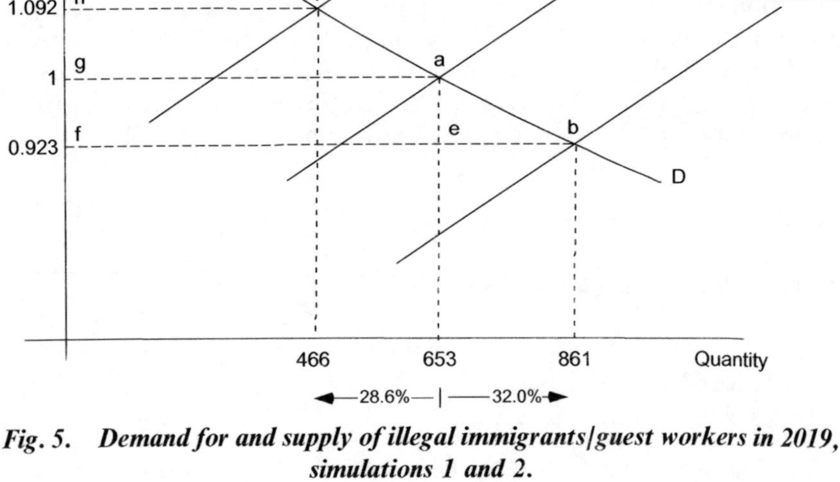

Fig. 5. Demand for and supply of illegal immigrants/guest workers in 2019, simulations 1 and 2.

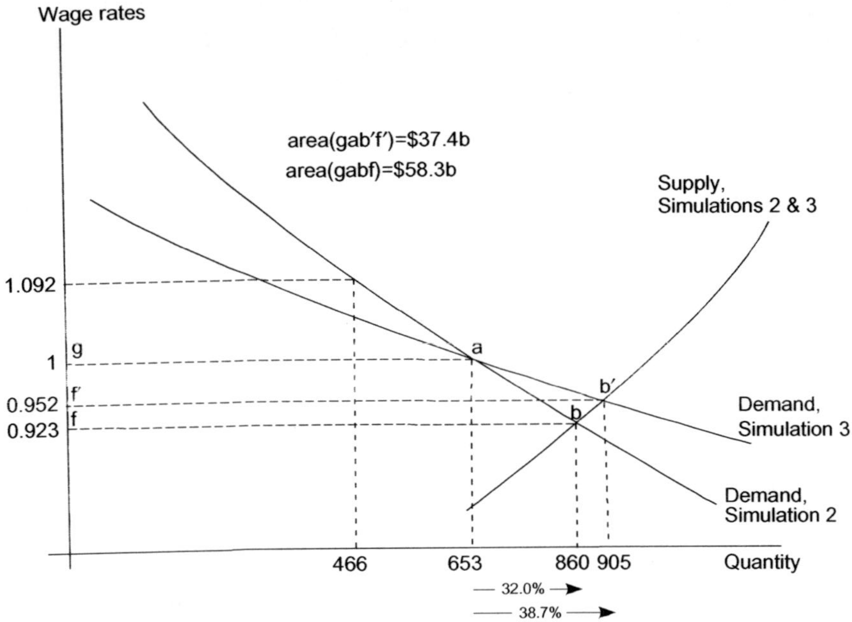

Fig. 6. ***Demand for and supply of guest workers in 2019, simulations 2 and 3.***

increase in employment of guest workers is larger (38.7 per cent compared with 32.0 per cent). The wage effect dominates: area(gab′f′) is smaller than area(gabf), leaving the direct effect in simulation 3 smaller than that in simulation 2.[12] The other five contributing factors to welfare are larger in absolute size in simulation 3 than in simulation 2, reflecting the increased number of guest workers. Overall, the total for the six factors in simulation 3 is about the same as that in simulation 2 (0.56 per cent compared with 0.57 per cent), indicating that the substitution assumption is not a major determinant of the welfare result.

5.3. Simulation 4: Liberalized entry with increased substitutability and increased productivity

Figure 7 presents demand and supply curves for effective units of guest workers as functions of wage rates for effective units. In simulation 3, the number of effective units and the wage per effective unit are simply the number of guest workers and their wage per person. In simulation 4, the number of effective units is the number of guest workers inflated by

[12] The two areas indicated in Figure 6 are not strictly proportional to the direct effect. The USAGE computation of the direct effect takes account of taxes that are not included in the figure.

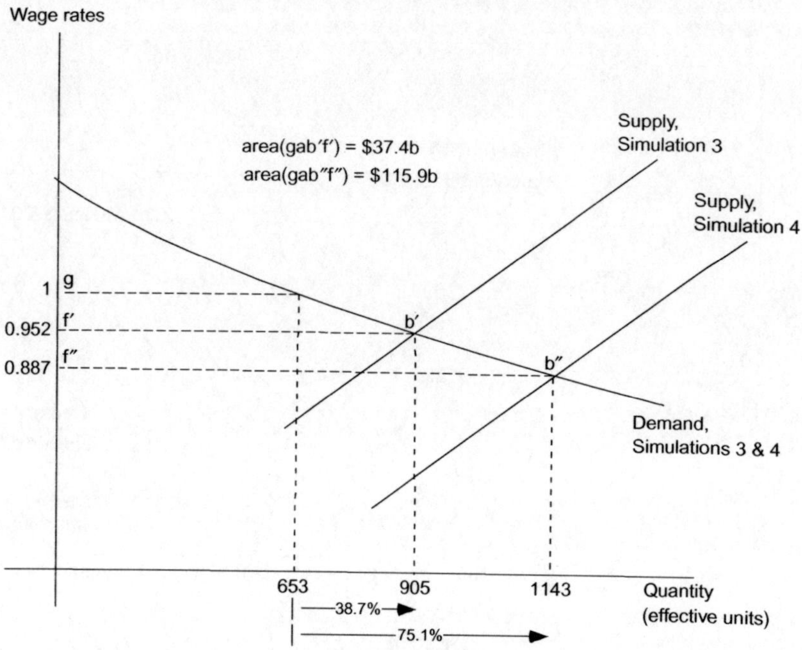

Fig. 7. Demand for and supply of effective units of guest workers in 2019, simulations 3 and 4.

12.5 per cent (divided by 1–0.125), and the wage per effective unit is the wage per guest worker deflated by 12.5 per cent (multiplied by 1–0.125). The productivity increase in simulation 4 does not move the demand curve for effective units. However, as indicated in Figure 7, it moves the supply curve to the right. The supply curve moves because at any given wage for effective units, the wage for people in simulation 4 is 12.5 per cent higher than it was in simulation 3. This generates supply from more people (a 53.2 per cent increase relative to business as usual in simulation 4 compared with a 38.7 per cent increase in simulation 3), and each person supplies more effective units. With the supply curve for effective units of guest workers moving strongly to the right, Figure 7 indicates a large increase in the direct effect: area(gab″f″) is more than twice as large as area(gab′f′).[13]

In the move from simulation 3 to simulation 4, most of the other welfare effects expand broadly in line with the expansion in the quantity of effective units of guest workers. The exception is the public expenditure effect (F5), which depends on the number of people rather than on

[13] Again we note that tax effects mean that welfare areas in our demand and supply diagrams are not strictly proportional to the direct effect as computed in USAGE.

effective units. As already noted in Section 2, the subdued response of F5 to the increase in the number of effective units of guest workers accentuates the welfare gain in simulation 4 compared with simulation 3.

5.4. Simulations 5 and 6: Liberalized entry with increased substitutability, increased productivity and visa charges

In the policy runs of simulations 5 and 6, the demand and supply curves for effective units of guest workers are in the same positions that they had in the policy run of simulation 4. As illustrated in Figure 8, the visa taxes in simulations 5 and 6 (represented by heights rs and uw) restrict the increases in employment of effective units (beyond that in the business-as-usual run) to 14.3 and 47.8 per cent. In terms of Figure 8, the welfare gain from the policy in simulation 5 with unchanged numbers of illegal workers is area (garsv), which amounts to $230.1 billion. With the optimal visa tax, in simulation 6, the welfare gain indicated in Figure 8 is area (gauwz), which amounts to $162.6 billion. Figure 8 leaves out income tax and indirect tax effects taken into account in the USAGE computations of direct effects. Nevertheless, the figure correctly indicates that imposition of the optimal visa tax gives a smaller direct effect than imposition of the

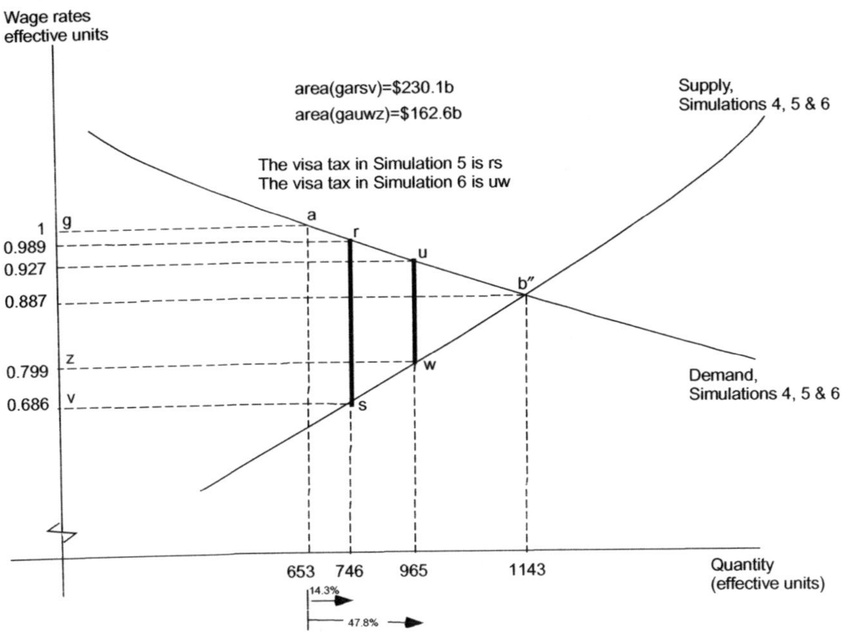

Fig. 8. ***Demand for and supply of effective units of guest workers in 2019, simulations 5 and 6.***

employment-neutral visa tax (0.75 per cent in simulation 6 compared with 0.80 per cent in simulation 5, Table 1).

As well as the direct effect (F1), the public-expenditure and macro-price effects (F5 and F6) are less favorable (more unfavorable) in simulation 6 than in simulation 5. The public-expenditure effect in simulation 5 is zero because the liberalization policy in this simulation leaves the number of guest workers unchanged from the number of illegal workers in the business-as-usual forecast. In simulation 6 the number of guest workers is 29.3 per cent greater than the number of illegal workers in the business-as-usual forecast, generating a public-expenditure effect of −0.17 per cent. In simulation 5, the policy has relatively little effect on the size of the economy and consequently on the level of exports and the terms of trade. This leaves the welfare loss from the macro-price effect considerably smaller in simulation 5 than in simulation 6.

The deteriorations in F1, F5, and F6 as we go from simulation 5 to simulation 6 are outweighed by the improvements in F2, F3, and F4. The increase in the occupation-mix effect (F2) is particularly pronounced (0.48 per cent compared with 0.15 per cent). This effect moves in line with the increase in the number of effective units of guest workers.

6. Concluding remarks

We present two sets of conclusions. The first covers what our modeling suggests about the effects of U.S. policies toward illegal immigration. The second covers some methodological issues.

6.1. Policy approaches to illegal immigration

Getting the policy right on illegal immigration is important for the welfare of U.S. households. Our simulations show that the difference between the long-run welfare effects for U.S. households of the worst and best policies that we considered is about $260 billion a year (2009 dollars). This is the welfare gap between the tighter-border-security policy in simulation 1 (a welfare loss of 0.55 per cent) and the liberalized policy with optimal visa charge in simulation 6 (a welfare gain of 1.27 per cent).

The major ingredient in good policy is legalization. This would eliminate smugglers fees and allow immigrants (now guest workers rather than illegals) to have higher productivity. Elimination of smugglers fees would lower the wage required to attract immigrants and increases in their productivity would raise the value of immigrant labor relative to this wage. Both these effects of legalization raise the value of immigrant labor relative to the cost of employing it. Our simulations show that this creates a considerable surplus that can be enjoyed by U.S. households.

Would legalization lead to an unmanageable influx of guest workers? We don't think so.[14] In any case, under a program of legal guest workers, numbers could be controlled through the imposition of visa taxes. Our simulations suggest that a visa tax levied on employers at about 31 per cent of the cost of employing a guest worker would keep the number of guest workers on about the same path as illegal immigrants in the business-as-usual forecast. Why 31 per cent? This is approximately the value of smugglers fees plus the value of the productivity increase that we think would follow from legalization.

The simulations show that the optimal visa tax is about 14 per cent. This would allow the number of guest workers to grow beyond the number of illegals in the business-as-usual forecast. A visa tax of 14 per cent strikes the optimal balance between the advantage of capturing surplus value from guest workers and the disadvantage of limiting their numbers. By using a 31 per cent visa tax to hold back the number of guest workers, U.S. households forego too much of the potentially available movement up the occupational ladder, that is they lose too much occupation-mix effect.

While 14 per cent is the optimal rate for the visa tax, the simulations indicate that the welfare penalty for adopting different rates is not very high. The welfare gain moves from 1.19 per cent in simulation 4 with no visa tax to 1.27 per cent in simulation 6 with the optimal visa tax of 14 per cent and back to 1.15 per cent with the employment-neutral visa tax of 31 per cent. The major benefit to U.S. households in these three simulations is from legalization and associated productivity increase. The visa tax is a useful instrument for fine tuning numbers of guest workers but not a major determinant of welfare.

While the modeling reported in this chapter identifies and quantifies many interesting effects, there is clearly room for improvement. For example, we could refine the calculation of the public-expenditure effect. Currently we have assumed that pubic expenditure per head on guest workers is the same as that on illegal workers. If the guest-worker program involved just workers and not their families, then guest workers might cost the public purse less per head than illegals. Another obvious improvement that could be undertaken in future work is the introduction of the implementation costs of policies. The present analysis omits these costs. Legalization would not eliminate the need for tight border security. However, we doubt that it would significantly increase the costs of border security. Internally, the trade off would be administration of a visa tax program against a program of internal enforcement. Remembering that the welfare difference between policies can be as high as $260 billion a

---

[14] For a description of the effects of the 1965 liberalization of U.S. immigration policy, see Griswold (2002, p. 4).

year, it seems unlikely that explicit recognition of implementation costs would challenge our conclusion in favor of liberalization.

6.2. Methodological issues

Trade theory gives us a framework for looking at the issues discussed in this chapter. We can think of low-skilled immigrant labor as an import to the United States currently subject to stringent quantitative restrictions and large-scale smuggling. A guest-worker program with a visa tax can be thought of as replacement of quantitative restrictions with a tariff. Because smuggling is expensive, a suitably chosen tariff can be used to eliminate smuggling while leaving imports unchanged. With tariff revenue replacing smuggling fees, the government of the importing country benefits at the expense of the smugglers. If the tariff (visa tax) is set sufficiently low, then imports will increase with resulting efficiency gains that can be illustrated by producer-surplus diagrams (our effect F1). On the contrary, increased imports for a large country such as the United States generate negative terms-of-trade effects (F6). Another negative effect is increased public administration costs. In the case of commodity imports, these costs include security and health inspections. The analogous cost for imports of low-skilled labor is the public-expenditure effect (F5) covering such services as emergency hospital treatment. Increased imports may also cause a deterioration in income distribution by decreasing the price of the scarce factor in the United States, low-skilled labor, relative to the price of the abundant factor, high-skilled labor (Table 3).

By using a large-scale, dynamic, CGE model, we can not only quantify effects from elementary trade theory but also identify and quantify other effects. In this chapter, we have found that increased imports can alter the long-run composition of the importing country's factor endowment and the intensity with which this endowment is used. If the United States were to import more low-skilled labor, then the composition of the United States' own labor endowment would transform over time toward high skills [the occupation-mix effect (F2)] and levels of unemployment would be reduced (F4). We would also expect the quantity of U.S. capital to increase. This has welfare implications through taxes (F3).

Along with the advantages of large-scale CGE modeling, there are disadvantages. As Rauscher (1999) puts it:

> *To many economists, computable general equilibrium (CGE) models are a bit dubious. They are huge, they are complex, and they appear to be large black boxes that produce results that cannot be traced to an accessibly small set of simple assumptions or axioms.*

Both the creation and application of large-scale CGE models require detailed theoretical specifications, many pages of computer code and years of work on industry, trade, and occupational data. It is not practical for consumers of analyses from these models to be familiar with all their aspects. In this chapter we have tried to open the "black box" by explaining the results through familiar economic mechanisms and back-of-the-envelope calculations. By doing so we hope to give readers a framework for understanding and assessing our results and for anticipating the effects of variations in assumptions and data input.

Appendix: the USAGE labor-market extension for the study of illegal immigration

A1. Introduction

The six key ingredients in the labor-market specification in USAGE are (1) the division of the workforce into categories at start of each year reflecting workforce functions in the previous year; (2) the identification of workforce activities, that is what people do during the year; (3) the determination of labor supply from each category to each activity; (4) the determination of demand for labor in employment activities; (5) the specification of wage adjustment processes reflecting demand and supply; and (6) the determination of everyone's activity, who gets the jobs and what happens to those who don't?

A broad picture of the specification is given in Figure A1. We divide the workforce at the start of year t into categories. These categories reflect the activities that people undertook in year $t-1$, with the main activities being employment in occupations. The number of people in a given category that undertake a particular activity in year t is determined mainly by the category's supply to that activity, relative to supply from people in other categories, and by demand for the services of that activity.

Table A1 lists the equations explained in this appendix that form the labor-market module of the version of USAGE used in our studies of illegal immigration.

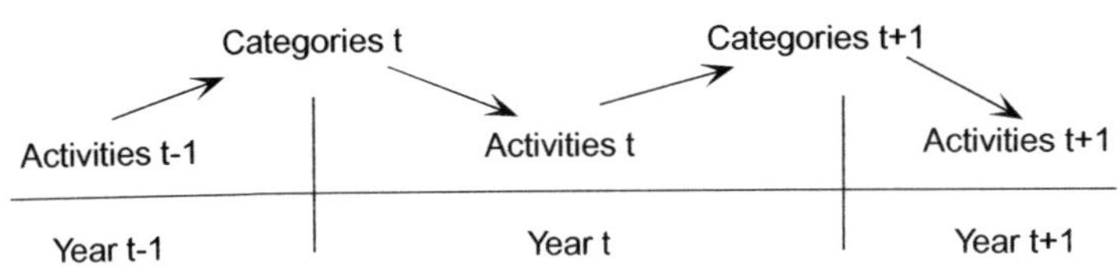

Fig. A1. Labor–market dynamics in USAGE.

Table A1. USAGE representation of the labor market

Numbers in each category at the beginning of year t

$$\mathrm{CAT}_t(b,s,\ell) = \sum_{ss\in \text{Legal status}} \mathrm{ACT}_{t-1}(b,ss,\ell)\,T(b,ss,\ell,s)$$
for all b, s and $\ell \neq \text{New}$ (A.1)

$$\mathrm{CAT}_t(b,s,\text{ New}) = \text{exogenous} \quad \text{for all } b \text{ and } s. \tag{A.2}$$

Planned labor supply

$$L_t(c;a) = \mathrm{CAT}_t(c)\left\{\frac{B_t(c;a)\mathrm{ATW}_t(a)^{\eta}}{\sum_q [B_t(c;q)\mathrm{ATW}_t(q)]^{\eta}}\right\}$$
for all categories c and activities a (A.8)

$$L_t(a) = \sum_c L_t(c;a) \quad \text{for all activities } a. \tag{A.9}$$

Demand for labor and employment in the U.S.

$$D_t^1(j) = f_j^1(\mathrm{BTW}_t^1(j); K_t(j); A_t(j)) \quad \text{for all U.S. industries } j \tag{A.11}$$

$$\mathrm{BTW}_t^1(j) = g_j^1(\mathrm{BTW}_t(b,s,o)\ \forall\, b,s, \text{ and U.S. occupations } o)$$
for all U.S. industries j (A.12)

$$D_t(b,s,o,j) = D_t^1(j)\, h_{b,s,o,j}(\mathrm{BTW}_t(bb,ss,oo)\ \forall\, bb, ss, \text{ and U.S. occupations } oo)$$
for all $b, s,$ and U.S. occupations and industries o and j (A.17)

$$D_t(b,s,o) = \sum_j D_t(b,s,o,j) \quad \text{for all } b, s, \text{ and U.S. occupations } o. \tag{A.18}$$

$$E_t(b,s,o) = D_t(b,s,o) \quad \text{for all } b, s, \text{ and U.S. occupations } o. \tag{A.19}$$

Relationship between after-tax and before-tax wage rates

$$\mathrm{ATW}_t(b,s,o) = \mathrm{BTW}_t(b,s,o)[1 - T_t(b,s)]$$
for all b, s and U.S. occupations o (A.20)

$$\mathrm{ATW}_t(b,s,u) = \mathrm{BTW}_t^{\mathrm{ave}}(b,s)F_t(b,s)$$
for all $b, s,$ and unemployment functions u (A.21)

Wage adjustment

$$\frac{\mathrm{ATW}_t(b,s,o)}{\mathrm{ATW}_t^{\mathrm{base}}(b,s,o)} - \frac{\mathrm{ATW}_{t-1}(b,s,o)}{\mathrm{ATW}_{t-1}^{\mathrm{base}}(b,s,o)} = \alpha\left[\frac{D_t(b,s,o)}{D_t^{\mathrm{base}}(b,s,o)} - \frac{L_t(b,s,o)}{L_t^{\mathrm{base}}(b,s,o)}\right],$$
for all (b, s) and all U.S. occupations o (A.22)

Table A1. (Continued)

Vacancies and movements into employment activities

$$V_t(a) = E_t(a) - H_t[a;a]$$

for all U.S. employment activities a (A.23)

$$H_t(c;a) = V_t(a)\left[\frac{L_t(c;a)}{\sum_{s\neq a} L_t(s;a)}\right],$$

for all categories $c \neq a$ and all U.S. employment activities a. (A.24)

$$H_t(c;c) = \mathrm{CAT}_t(c) - \sum_{a\neq c} H_t(c;a),$$

for all employment categories c (including Mexico) (A.25)

Movements into unemployment and Mexican activities

$$H_t(c;u) = \begin{cases} L_c(c;u) + \mu(c)\mathrm{CAT}_t(c) & \text{for short-run unemployment activities } u \\ 0 & \text{for long-run unemployment activities } u \end{cases}$$

for all U.S. employment categories c, (A.26)

$$H_t(c;u) = \begin{cases} 0 & \text{for short-run unemployment activities } u \\ \mathrm{CAT}_t(c) - \sum_{a\in \text{employment activ}} H_t(c;a) & \text{for long-run unemployment activities } u \end{cases}$$

for all U.S. unemployment categories c and all unemployment activities u (A.27)

$$H_t(c;u) = \begin{cases} \mathrm{CAT}_t(c) - \sum_{a\in \text{U.S. employ activ}} H_t(c;a) & \text{for } c \text{ not foreign, illegal and for short-run unemploy activ } u \\ \mathrm{CAT}_t(c) - \sum_{a\in \text{U.S. employ activ}} H_t(c;a) & \text{for } c \text{ foreign, illegal and for Mexican activities } u \\ 0 & \text{otherwise} \end{cases}$$

for all New categories c and all unemployment or Mexican activities u (A.28)

$$H_t(c;u) = \begin{cases} L_t(c;u) & \text{for } c \text{ non-Mexican} \\ \mathrm{CAT}_t(c) - \sum_{a\in \text{U.S. employ activ}} H_t(c;a) & \text{for } c \text{ Mexican} \end{cases}$$

for all non-New categories c and for Mexican activities u (A.29)

$$\sum_c H_t(c;a) = E_t(a),$$

for all U.S. unemployment activities and Mexican activities a (A.30)

Table A1. (Continued)

Notation

$CAT_t(b, s, \ell)$ is the number of people in the extended workforce at the start of year t who are from birthplace b, have legal status s and who performed workforce function ℓ in year $t-1$.

$CAT_t(b, s, \text{New})$ is the number of people at the start of year t who are from birthplace b, have legal status s and were not in the extended workforce in year $t-1$.

$ACT_{t-1}(bb, ss, \ell)$ is the number of people in activity (bb, ss, ℓ) in year $t-1$.

$T(b, ss, \ell, s)$ is the proportion of people in activity (b, ss, ℓ) in year $t-1$ who are allocated to category (b, s, ℓ) at the start of year t.

$L_t(c;a)$ is the labor supply that people in category c make to activity a. Both c and a are (b,s,ℓ) triples.

$L_t(a)$ is total labor supply to activity a.

$L_t^{\text{base}}(a)$ is the base or forecast value of $L_t(a)$.

α is a positive parameter.

$ATW_t(a)$ is the real after-tax wage rate of labor in activity a (for nonemployment activities it is a social security payment or other support).

$ATW_t^{\text{base}}(a)$ is the base or forecast value of $ATW_t(a)$.

η is a parameter reflecting the ease with which people feel that they can shift between activities.

$B_t(c;a)$ is a variable reflecting the preference of people in category c for earning money in activity a in year t.

$K_t(j)$ is industry j's capital stock at the start of year t.

$BTW_t^1(j)$ is the overall real before-tax wage rate to industry j.

$A_t(j)$ is a vector of variables that influence industry j's demand for labor.

$D_t^1(j)$ is labor input to industry j.

$BTW_t(b, s, o)$ is the real before-tax wage rate of workers of birthplace b, legal status s, and U.S. occupation o.

$D_t(b, s, o, j)$ is j's input of labor of birthplace b, legal status s, and U.S. occupation o.

$D_t(b, s, o)$ is aggregate demand for (b, s, o) labor.

$D_t^{\text{base}}(b, s, o)$ is the base or forecast value of $D_t(b, s, o)$.

$E_t(b, s, o)$ is employment of (b, s, o) labor.

$T_t(b, s)$ is the payroll and income-tax rate applying to all (b, s) workers in the United States.

$BTW_t^{\text{ave}}(b, s)$ is the average real before-tax wage rate of (b, s) workers in the United States.

$F_t(b, s)$ is the fraction of $BTW_t^{\text{ave}}(b, s)$ that (b, s) people receive in unemployment activities from social security payments or other support.

$V_t(a)$ is vacancies in activity a.

$H_t[c;a]$ is the flow of people from category c to activity a.

$\mu(c)$ is the fraction of people of category c people who become involuntarily unemployed.

A2. Workforce, categories, functions, and activities

We adopt two concepts of workforce: the U.S. workforce and the extended workforce. The U.S. workforce is everyone of working age in the United States excluding people in full-time education and those who are ruled out of work by disabilities. Under this definition, the U.S. workforce includes discouraged workers and other people who are not actively seeking employment. The extended workforce is the U.S. workforce plus potential foreign illegal immigrants working outside the United States. For convenience we refer to these potential foreign illegal immigrants as working in Mexico.

At the beginning of each year, we allocate people in the extended workforce to categories according to their birthplace, legal status, and recent labor market function. We allow for two birthplaces, domestic[15] and foreign, and two legal statuses, legal and illegal.[16] A person's recent workforce function refers to what he or she did in the labor market in the previous year, year $t-1$. The functions we identify are:

- employed in occupation *m*, where *m* is one of the 50 U.S. occupations (Table 3);
- short-run unemployed in the United States, that is unemployed for a substantial amount of year $t-1$ but not unemployed in year $t-2$;
- long-run unemployed in the United States, that is unemployed for a substantial amount of year $t-1$ and also of year $t-2$;
- living in the United States but not in the workforce;[17]
- employed in the single Mexican occupation recognized in USAGE;
- living in Mexico but not in the workforce.[18]

A final concept that we need to explain before setting out the algebra of the labor-market specification is activity. Activities are defined by birthplace, legal status, and workforce function in the current year. Examples of activities in year *t* are working in the United States as a domestic-legal construction laborer; working in the United States as a foreign-illegal cook; and experiencing short-run unemployment in the United States as a foreign-legal resident. Another activity is working as a foreign illegal in Mexico. As already mentioned, we do not wish to imply that Mexicans are working illegally in Mexico. As we will see, Mexican workers in Mexico will be modeled as potential workers in foreign illegal activities in the United States.

The link (the upward-sloping arrows in Figure A1) between the number of people in different activities in year $t-1$ and the number

---

15 By domestic we mean people born in the United States or people who entered the United States as dependents of legal residents of the United States.

16 All people with birthplace "domestic" have the status "legal." Some foreign residents of the United States are legal, whereas others are illegal. We classify all workers in Mexico as illegal. This of course does not mean that Mexicans are working illegally in Mexico. It means that from the point of view of the United States, Mexican workers in Mexico are potential foreign illegal immigrants.

17 This is the workforce function of those U.S. residents who are new entrants to the workforce at the start of year *t*.

18 This is the workforce function of new entrants to the workforce in Mexico.

of people in each category at the start of year t is specified by the equations:

$$\mathrm{CAT}_t(b,s,\ell) = \sum_{ss \in \text{legal status}} \mathrm{ACT}_{t-1}(b,ss,\ell)T(b,ss,\ell,s) \tag{A.1}$$

for all b, s, and non-new functions, that is, $\ell \neq \text{New}$

$$\mathrm{CAT}_t(b,s,\text{New}) = \text{exogenous} \quad \text{for all } b \text{ and } s. \tag{A.2}$$

In these equations,

$\mathrm{CAT}_t(b, s, \ell)$ is the number of people at the start of year t who are from birthplace b, have legal status s and who performed workforce function ℓ in year $t-1$.

$\mathrm{CAT}_t(b, s, \text{New})$ is the number of people at the start of year t who are from birthplace b, have legal status s and were not in the extended workforce in year $t-1$, that is the number of new (b,s) entrants to the extended workforce. As indicated in (A.2), the numbers of people in "New" categories are set exogenously, reflecting demographic factors.

$\mathrm{ACT}_{t-1}(bb, ss, \ell)$ is the number of people in activity (bb, ss, ℓ) in year $t-1$, that is, the number of people who, in year $t-1$, belonged to birthplace bb, had legal status ss and labor-force function ℓ.

$T(b, ss, \ell, s)$ is the proportion of people in activity (b, ss, ℓ) in year $t-1$ who are allocated to category (b, s, ℓ) at the start of year t; we assume that people never change their birthplace.[19]

In the simulations reported in Sections 4 and 5, we set

$$T(b,ss,\ell,s) = \begin{cases} 0.99 & \text{for all } \ell \text{ and } b, \text{ and for all } s, ss \text{ such that } s = ss \\ 0.00 & \text{otherwise} \end{cases} \tag{A.3}$$

Under (A.3), we assume that no one changes legal status and that 1 per cent of people in every activity in year $t-1$ drop out of the extended workforce at the beginning of year t, through either retirement or death. More sophisticated transition assumptions are possible.

A3. Labor supply from each category to each activity

USAGE specifies labor supply from people in each category to each activity. Through these specifications, we ensure that people in a category with birthplace b and legal status s make offers only to activities with these characteristics. Thus, people in the category domestic-legal

[19] Consistent with the definition of a category, only people from activities with workforce function ℓ in year $t-1$ are allocated to categories with workforce function ℓ at the start of year t.

construction laborer can offer only to activities with the domestic and legal characteristics. Most of these people offer to the activity domestic-legal construction laborer, that is, they offer to continue their employment of last year. However, some will offer to change occupation in response to changes in relative wages and a few will offer to unemployment. Some people in the category foreign-illegal Mexico will offer to foreign-illegal occupations in the United States, that is, they will seek to enter the United States as illegal immigrants, and some people in foreign-illegal categories operating in the United States will make offers to the activity foreign-illegal Mexico, that is, they will offer to return home. In making these decisions, people in these foreign-illegal categories compare wages in Mexico with wages for foreign-illegal occupations in the United States.

In developing the labor-supply functions for USAGE, we assume that at the beginning of year t, people in category c [where c is a (birthplace, legal status, labor-market function) triple] decide their offers to activity a [where a is also a (b, s, ℓ) triple] for the year by solving a problem of the form:

$$\text{choose } L_t(c;a) \quad \text{for all activities } a] \tag{A.4}$$

$$\text{to maximize } U_c[\text{ATW}_t(a)\ L_t(c;a) \quad \forall \text{ activities } a] \tag{A.5}$$

$$\text{subject to} \sum_a L_t(c;a) = \text{CAT}_t(c) \tag{A.6}$$

where

$L_t(c;a)$ is the labor supply that people in category c make to activity a;
$\text{CAT}_t(c)$ is the number of people in category c;
$\text{ATW}_t(a)$ is the real after-tax wage rate of labor in activity a (for nonemployment activities, that is, short- and long-run unemployment, $\text{ATW}_t(a)$ can be thought of as a social security payment or other support); and
U_c is a homothetic function with the usual properties of utility functions (positive first derivatives and quasi-concavity).

In (A.4), (A.5) and (A.6), people in category c treat dollars earned in different activities as imperfect substitutes. This is a convenient and flexible specification through which we can allow labor supplies to shift between activities in response to changes in after-tax rewards. By specifying a separate utility function for each c, we can ensure that each category makes supplies to activities that are compatible with the category's birthplace, legal status, and occupational characteristics.

In the applications presented in Sections 4 and 5, U_c has the CES form:

$$U_c\left\{\sum_a [B_t(c;a)\text{ATW}_t(a)L_t(c;a)]^{\eta/(1+\eta)}\right\}^{(1+\eta)/\eta}. \tag{A.7}$$

where

η is a parameter reflecting the ease with which people feel that they can shift between activities; and

$B_t(c;a)$ is a variable reflecting the preference of people in category c for earning money in activity a in year t.

The $B_t(c;a)$'s play two roles in our analysis. The first is through their initial settings, that is, the values assigned to them in our base-year data (2004 in the applications in this chapter).

- By setting $B_{2004}(c;a)$ at 0, if the birthplace and legal characteristics of c differ from those of a, we ensure that people in categories with birthplace b and legal status s offer labor only to (b, s) activities.
- By setting $B_{2004}(c;a)$ at relatively high values when c and a agree in their (b, s) characteristics and have a functional characteristic referring to the same occupation, we ensure that most people employed in year $t-1$ in occupation m (including the Mexican occupation) offer to continue to work in m in year t.
- By setting $B_{2004}(c;a)$ at suitably chosen positive values when c and a agree in their (b, s) characteristics but have functional characteristics referring to different occupations, we ensure that people make offers to work in occupations compatible with their skills.
- By setting $B_{2004}(c;a)$ at 0 where the functional characteristic of c is either short-run or long-run unemployment and the functional characteristic of a is short-run unemployment, we ensure that no one can stay in short-run unemployment in successive years or move from long-run unemployment back to short-run unemployment.
- By setting $B_{2004}(c;a)$ at a moderately large value where c and a agree in their (b, s) characteristics and c has the functional characteristic of short-run unemployment and a has the functional characteristic long-run unemployment, we introduce a mild discouraged-worker effect for people suffering short-run unemployment.
- By setting $B_{2004}(c;a)$ at a larger value where c and a agree in their (b, s) characteristics and where c and a both have the functional characteristic of long-run unemployment, we introduce a stronger discouraged-worker effect for the long-run unemployed.

The second role of the $B_t(c;a)$'s is to carry shocks in policy runs. In Section 4 we represent the impact of tighter border security by reductions in the $B_t(c;a)$'s where c and a both have the (b,s) characteristics foreign illegal and c has the functional characteristic of either Mexico or New and a has the functional characteristic of a U.S. occupation. Increases in these $B_t(c;a)$'s are used in Section 5 to represent the elimination of smugglers fees and other costs of illegal entry.

Under (A.7), problem (A.5)–(A.6) generates labor-supply functions of the form:

$$L_t(c;a) = \text{CAT}_t(c)\left\{\frac{B_t(c;a)\text{ATW}_t(a)^{\eta}}{\sum_q [B_t(c;a)\text{ATW}_t(q)]^{\eta}}\right\}. \tag{A.8}$$

Total supply of labor to activity a is obtained as

$$L_t(a) = \sum_c L_t(c;a) \quad \text{for all activities } a. \tag{A.9}$$

In the simulations in Sections 4 and 5 we set η in (A.8) at 2. For understanding what this means, it is useful to express (A.8) in percentage change form as:

$$\ell_t(c;a) = \text{cat}_t(c) + \eta * (\text{atw}_t(a) - \text{atw}_t^{\text{ave}}(c)) + \eta * (b_t(c;a) - b_t^{\text{ave}}(c)). \tag{A.10}$$

In (A.10), the lowercase symbols $\ell_t(c;a)$, $\text{cat}_t(c)$, $\text{atw}_t(a)$, and $b_t(c;a)$ are percentage changes in the variables denoted by the corresponding uppercase symbols, and $\text{atw}_t^{\text{ave}}(c)$ and $b_t^{\text{ave}}(c)$ are weighted averages of the $\text{atw}_t(q)$s and $b_t(c;q)$s with the weights reflecting the share of activity q in the offers from people in category c. Thus (A.10) implies that people in category c will switch their offers toward activity a if the wage rate in activity a rises relative to an average of the wage rates across all the activities in which category-c people could participate. With η set at 2, we assume that the number of people who wish to change jobs, in particular the number of people who wish to move from Mexico to U.S. occupations, is quite sensitive to changes in relative wage rates. However, an increase in $\text{ATW}_t(a)$ does not have much affect on $L_t(a;a)$. This is because the bulk of offers from people in category a are to activity a, so that $\text{atw}_t(a) - \text{atw}_t^{\text{ave}}(a)$ is always close to 0. The major part of the supply of labor to any work activity a is from incumbents [i.e., $L_t(a;a)$ is a very large fraction of $L_t(a)$]. Thus, even with η as high as 2, the elasticity of supply of labor to activity a with respect to the wage rate in a is relatively low. Dixon *et al.* (2010) provide analysis of the sensitivity of results from simulation 1 to variations in η.

A4. Demand for labor in the United States

The labor input, $D_t^1(j)$, to U.S. industry j in year t is specified in USAGE along conventional CGE lines as a function of the industry's capital stock, $K_t(j)$; the overall real before-tax wage rate to the industry, $\text{BTW}_t^1(j)$; and other variables, $A_t(j)$, that influence industry j's demand for labor, including technology and commodity prices:

$$D_t^1(j) = f_j^1(\text{BTW}_t^1; K_t(j); A_t(j)). \tag{A.11}$$

The overall real wage rate to industry j is determined as a suitable average of the real wage rates applying to the types of labor that the industry employs:

$$\mathrm{BTW}_t^1(j) = g_j^1(\mathrm{BTW}_t(b, s, o))$$
$$\text{for all } b, s, \text{ and U.S. occupations } o, \qquad \text{(A.12)}$$

where

$\mathrm{BTW}_t(b, s, o)$ is the real before-tax wage rate of workers of birthplace b, legal status s, and U.S. occupation o.

Within industry j's labor input, the demand for labor by birthplace, legal status, and occupation is determined by a nested CES cost minimization problem. The nesting and the substitution elasticities are indicated in Figure A2. As discussed at the end of this section, we assume that there are low substitution possibilities between occupations such as Cooks, Grounds maintenance workers, etc. (substitution elasticity of 0.35) but high substitution possibilities between legal and illegal workers of the same

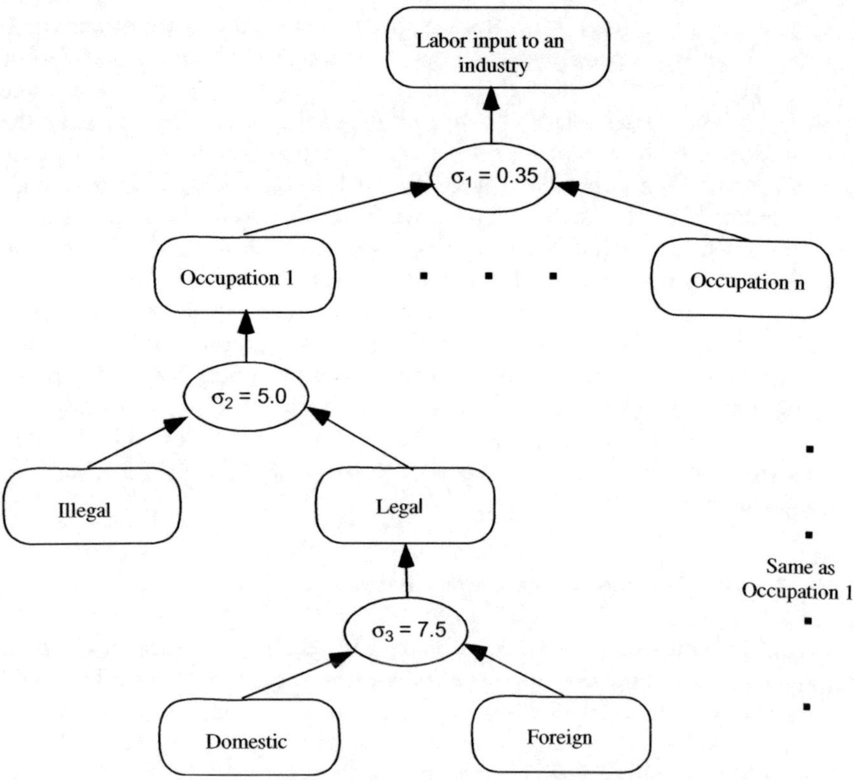

Fig. A2. Nesting assumptions in the creation of the labor input to each industry.

occupation (substitution elasticity of 5) and between domestic and foreign legal workers of the same occupation (substitution elasticity of 7.5).

In algebraic terms, we assume that industry j satisfies its labor requirements by choosing:

$D_t(b, s, o, j)$, j's input of labor of birthplace b, legal status s, and U.S. occupation o,
$D_t^3(s, o, j)$, j's input of labor of legal status s and U.S. occupation o, defined as a CES aggregate over b of (b, s, o, j) inputs, and
$D_t^2(o, j)$, j's input of labor of U.S. occupation o, defined as a CES aggregate over s of (s, o, j) inputs,

$$\text{to minimize} \sum_{b,s,o} \text{BTW}_t(b,s,o) D_t(b,s,o,j) \quad \text{(A.13)}$$

$$\text{subject to } D_t^1(j) = CES_o^j[D_t^2(o,j)] \quad \text{(A.14)}$$

$$D_t^2(o,j) = \text{CES}_s^j[D_t^3(s,o,j)] \quad \text{for all U.S. occupations } o, \quad \text{(A.15)}$$

$$\text{and } D_t^3(s,o,j) = \text{CES}_b^j[D_t(b,s,o,j)] \quad \text{(A.16)}$$

for all U.S. occupations o and legal status s.[20]

The CES functions in (A.14)–(A.16) incorporate the elasticities shown in Figure A2 and are calibrated to reflect data on the occupational, birthplace, and legal status of workers in U.S. industries.[21]

From problem (A.13)–(A.16) we obtain demand functions of the form

$$D_t(b,s,o,j) = D_t^1(j) h_{b,s,o,j}(\text{BTW}_t(bb,ss,oo)\ \forall\ bb, ss, \text{ and U.S. occupations } oo) \quad \text{for all } b, s, \text{ and U.S. occupations and industries } o \text{ and } j. \quad \text{(A.17)}$$

These can be aggregated across industries to determine aggregate demand for (b, s) workers in U.S. occupation o as

$$D_t(b,s,o) = \sum_j D_t(b,s,o,j) \quad \text{for all } b, s, \text{ and U.S. occupations } o. \quad \text{(A.18)}$$

---

20 As shown in Figure A2, there is no level 3 CES nest when s = illegal (only foreigners can provide illegal labor). However, it is unnecessarily clumsy to include this detail in the algebraic overview of our theory. We can simply assume that industries use tiny amounts of domestic illegal labor.

21 The Bureau of Labor Statistics (2006) gives detailed data on employment and wage rates by occupation and industry. These were processed into USAGE categories by Dixon and Rimmer (2006). The birthplace and legal status dimensions were added by using Van Hook *et al.* (2005) and by assuming that wage rates for legal and illegal migrants in any occupation are 0.9 and 0.8 times those of native workers.

We assume that employment of (b, s) workers in U.S. occupation o, $E_t(b, s, o)$, is determined by demand:

$$E_t(b,s,o) = D_t(b,s,o) \quad \text{for all } b,s, \text{ and U.S. occupations } o. \qquad (A.19)$$

A4.1. Discussion of demand-side substitution elasticities. The value, 0.35, adopted for the occupation-occupation substitution elasticity is a rather old Australian estimate (see Higgs *et al.*, 1981). Fortunately, substitution between occupations is not important for the results in this chapter. Our choice of 7.5 for the domestic/foreign substitution elasticity is suggested by the econometric work of Ottaviano and Peri (2006). We set the substitution elasticity between legal and illegal workers in the same occupation at a somewhat lower value, namely 5, because, from the point of view of employers, legality is likely to be an important characteristic. For many employers who do not currently use illegals, it may require a considerable reduction in the wage of illegals relative to that of legals to tempt them to switch to a given number of illegals.

A5. Relationship between after-tax and before-tax wage rates in the United States

As can be seen from the previous sections, after-tax wage rates are important in motivating labor supply, whereas before-tax wage rates motivate demand. To relate after-tax wage rates to before-tax wage rates, we include in USAGE:

$$\text{ATW}_t(b,s,o) = \text{BTW}_t(b,s,o)[1 - T_t(b,s)]$$
$$\text{for all } b,s, \text{ and U.S. occupations } o \qquad (A.20)$$

$$\text{ATW}_t(b,s,u) = \text{BTW}_t^{\text{ave}}(b,s)F_t(b,s)$$
$$\text{for all } b,s, \text{ and unemployment functions } u. \qquad (A.21)$$

In these equations,

$T_t(b, s)$ is the payroll and income-tax rate applying to all (b, s) workers in the United States;

$\text{BTW}_t^{\text{ave}}(b,s)$ is the average real before-tax wage rate of (b, s) workers in the United States; and

$F_t(b, s)$ is the fraction of $\text{BTW}_t^{\text{ave}}(b,s)$ that (b, s) people receive in unemployment activities from social security payments or other support. In the simulations described in this chapter we assume that the $F_t(b, s)$'s are unaffected by changes in immigration policies, that is, we assume that percentage movements in unemployment benefits match those in average before-tax wage rates.

In simulations 5 and 6 the visa tax is introduced through shocks to $T_t(b, s)$ for $b =$ foreign and $s =$ illegal.

A6. Wage adjustment

In policy runs, we assume that wage rates adjust according to the equation:

$$\frac{\mathrm{ATW}_t(b,s,o)}{\mathrm{ATW}_t^{\mathrm{base}}(b,s,o)} - \frac{\mathrm{ATW}_{t-1}(b,s,o)}{\mathrm{ATW}_{t-1}^{\mathrm{base}}(b,s,o)} = \alpha\left[\frac{D_t(b,s,o)}{D_t^{\mathrm{base}}(b,s,o)} - \frac{L_t(b,s,o)}{L_t^{\mathrm{base}}(b,s,o)}\right],$$

for all (b, s) and all U.S. occupations o (A.22)

where the superscript "base" refers to values in the basecase forecast and α is a positive parameter.

This equation implies that if a policy causes the market for (b, s, o) employment in year t to be tighter than it was in the basecase forecast (i.e., if the policy causes a larger percentage deviation in demand than supply), then there will be an increase between years $t-1$ and t in the deviation in (b, s, o)'s real after-tax wage rate. In other words, in periods in which a policy has elevated demand relative to supply, real wages will grow relative to their basecase values.

Our assumed wage-adjustment process is compatible with a search model (see for example, Böhringer *et al.*, 2005) in which reductions in labor supply, and resulting reductions in the unemployment rate, generate decreases in the value of having a job relative to the value of not having a job, thereby emboldening workers to demand higher wage rates. It is also compatible with efficiency-wage theory (see for example, Layard *et al.*, 1994, pp. 33–45). Under this theory, employers offer wage rates that optimize worker effort per dollar of wage cost. The theory suggests that the effort-optimizing wage rate rises when there is a decrease in labor supply and a consequent temporary decrease in unemployment.

In the context of USAGE, we can think of Equation (A.22) as having the role of determining after-tax wage rates for occupations in the United States. Then at given tax rates, Equations (A.20) and (A.21) determine before-tax wage rates for these occupations and for unemployment. The only other wage rate in our model is the after-tax wage rate in Mexico. We set this exogenously.

A7. The determination of everyone's activity: who gets the jobs and what happens to those who don't?

Under (A.22), markets for U.S. occupations do not clear. Consequently, we need to specify which offers of employment are accepted and what activities are undertaken by those whose offers of employment are not accepted. In terms of Figure A1, we need to specify the downward sloping arrows.

In linking categories at the start of year t to activities in year t, we specify an equation for the flow from each category c to each activity a, $H_t(c;a)$.

Flows from all categories to employment in U.S. occupations (area 1 in Figure A3). We start by defining vacancies in U.S. employment activity a in year t as employment, $E_t(a)$, less the number of jobs filled in the activity by people in category a, that is vacancies in a are jobs less those filled by incumbents:

$$V_t(a) = E_t(a) - H_t[a; a] \quad \text{for all U.S. employment activities } a \tag{A.23}$$

where

$V_t(a)$ is vacancies and
$H_t[a;a]$ is employment of people in category a in activity a.

The flow of people from category c to U.S. employment activity a, $a \neq c$, is modeled as being proportional to the vacancies in a and to the share of category c in the supply of labor to activity a from people outside category a. Thus, if people in category c account for 10 per cent of the

Activities / Categories	Employment in U.S. occupation	Unemployed in U.S.	Employed in Mexico
Employment in U.S. occupation	1	2	5
Unemployed in U.S.	1	3	5
Employed in Mexico	1	zero	5
New entrant	1	4	4

***Fig. A3.** Specifying the flows from categories to activities.*

people outside category a who want jobs in employment activity a, then people in category c fill 10 per cent of the vacancies in a. That is,

$$H_t(c;a) = V_t(a)\left[\frac{L_t(c;a)}{\sum_{s\neq a} L_t(s;a)}\right],$$

for all categories $c \neq a$ and all U.S. employment activities a. (A.24)

In (A.24), we assume that there is always competition for jobs, that is we assume that the number of people from outside category a who plan to work in employment activity a, $\Sigma_{s\neq a}L_t(s;a)$, is greater or equal to the number of vacancies [$V_t(a)$] in a.[22] This ensures that $H_t(c;a)$ is less than or equal to $L_t(c;a)$ for all categories $c\neq a$ and all U.S. employment activities a.

A familiar idea in labor economics is that unemployed people, especially long-term unemployed people, have a lower probability of filling vacancies than employed people wanting to move. This idea could be handled in (A.24) by attaching weights to the L's appearing on the RHS. We achieve a similar effect by assuming that the unemployed, especially the long-term unemployed, make comparatively weak offers to employment. [Recall the last two dot points in our discussion of the $B_t(c;a)$'s.] That is, $\Sigma_{a\in \text{U.S. employ activ}} L_t(c;a)/\text{CAT}_t(c)$ is low for people in unemployment categories c.

The number of incumbents in employment category c who remain in activity c [$H_t(c;c)$] is defined as the number of people in category c less the number who move out of activity c:

$$H_t(c;c) = \text{CAT}_t(c) - \sum_{a\neq c} H_t(c;a),$$

for all employment categories c (including Mexico) (A.25)

With [$H_t(c;a)$] being less than or equal to [$L_t(c;a)$] for $a\neq c$, [$H_t(c;c)$] is greater than or equal to [$L_t(c;c)$]. People in employment category c who planned to work in activity $a\neq c$ but who are unable to move to a due to insufficient vacancies simply remain in c.

Flows from all U.S. employment categories to U.S. unemployment activities (area 2 in Figure A3). People in U.S. employment category at the start of year t cannot move to a long-run unemployment activity. If they move into unemployment, it must be to short-run unemployment. The number of people who make the move to short-run unemployment is the sum of two parts: voluntary moves, $L_t(c;u)$, and involuntary moves. We model involuntary moves from U.S. employment category c as a fraction, $\mu(c)$,

---

22 While this condition is not guaranteed by the equations in Table A1, it was in fact satisfied in the applications reported in Sections 4 and 5.

of the number of people in the category:

$$H_t(c;u) = \begin{cases} L_c(c;u) + \mu(c) * \text{CAT}_t(c) & \text{for short-run unemployment activities } u \\ 0 & \text{for long-run unemployment activities } u \end{cases}$$

$$\text{for all U.S. employment categories } c, \tag{A.26}$$

Normally, $\mu(c)$ is exogenous. However, it is possible that (A.26) in conjunction with (A.24) will give values for $H_t(c;c)$ in (A.25) that exceed $E_t(c)$. In this case, $V_t(c)$ would be negative. We avoid this situation by treating $\mu(c)$ as an endogenous variable. If $V_t(c)$ is greater than zero, then $\mu(c)$ equals an exogenously given minimum value determined by the rate at which individuals are dismissed because of their performance or other factors unrelated to overall demand for people in activity c. Alternatively, $\mu(c)$ moves sufficiently above its minimal value to ensure that $V_t(c)$ equals zero. When $\mu(c)$ is above its minimum value, then there are involuntary flows from employment category c to unemployment caused by overall shortage of jobs.

Flows from U.S. unemployment categories to U.S. unemployment activities (area 3 in Figure A3). Next we deal with flows between unemployment categories and unemployment activities. We ensure that short-term unemployed people who fail to obtain a job flow to long-term unemployment and that long-term unemployed people who fail to obtain a job remain in long-term unemployment:

$$H_t(c;u) = \begin{cases} 0 & \text{for short-run unemployment activities } u \\ \text{CAT}_t(c) - \sum_{a \in \text{employment activ}} H_t(c;a) & \text{for long-run unemployment activities } u \end{cases}$$

$$\text{for all U.S. unemployment categories } c \text{ and all unemployment activities } u. \tag{A.27}$$

Flows from New categories to U.S. unemployment activities or to Mexico (area 4 in Figure A3). New legal entrants (either domestic or foreign) who fail to get a U.S. job are allocated to a short-run unemployment activity. New illegal entrants who fail to get a U.S. job are allocated to employment in Mexico. These allocations are specified by:

$$H_t(c;u) = \begin{cases} \text{CAT}_t(c) - \sum_{a \in \text{U.S. employ activ}} H_t(c;a) & \text{for } c \text{ not foreign, illegal and} \\ & \text{for short-run unemploy} \\ & \text{activities } u \\ \text{CAT}_t(c) - \sum_{a \in \text{U.S. employ activ}} H_t(c;a) & \text{for } c \text{ foreign, illegal and} \\ & \text{for Mexican activities } u \\ 0 & \text{otherwise} \end{cases}$$

for all New categories c and all unemployment or Mexican activities u. (A.28)

Flows from non-New categories to Mexico (area 5 in Figure A3). We assume that flows to Mexico from non-Mexican, non-New categories are voluntary. This means that foreign illegal workers in the United States can go home if they want to. Finally, the flow from the category of working in Mexico to the activity of working in Mexico is determined as the number of people in the category less the number that obtain jobs in the United States. Thus we have:

$$H_t(c;u) = \begin{cases} L_t(c;u) & \text{for } c \text{ non-Mexican} \\ \text{CAT}_t(c) - \sum_{a \in \text{employ activ}} H_t(c;a) & \text{for } c \text{ Mexican} \end{cases}$$

for all non-New categories c and for Mexican activities u (A.29)

Completing the link from categories to activities. To complete the link from categories at the start of year t to activities in year t we include the equation:

$$\sum_c H_t(c;a) = E_t(a),$$

for all U.S. unemployment activities and Mexican activities a (A.30)

A similar equation is not required for U.S. employment activities. Such an equation is implied by (A.23) and (A.24).

References

Böhringer, C., Boeters, S., Fiel, M. (2005), Taxation and unemployment: an applied general equilibrium approach for Germany. *Economic Modelling* 22, 81–108.

Bureau of Labor Statistics. (2006), *Special purpose files – national employment matrix files*. Available at http://www.bls.gov/emp/empocc2.htm

Dixon, P.B., Rimmer, M.T. (2002), *Dynamic General Equilibrium Modelling for Forecasting and Policy: A Practical Guide and Documentation of MONASH*. CEA 256. North-Holland Publishing Company, pp. xiv+338.

Dixon, P.B., Rimmer, M.T. (2006), Employment by occupation and industry, 2004 and 2014: technical documentation. Centre of Policy Studies, Monash University, May, p. 34. Available at http://www.monash.edu.au/policy/ftp/techusage1.pdf

Dixon, P.B., Rimmer, M.T. (2009), Restriction or legalization? Measuring the economic benefit of immigration reform. *Trade Policy Analysis* 40, Cato Institute, Washington, DC, p. 24. Available at http://www.freetrade.org/node/949

Dixon, P.B., Johnson, M., Rimmer, M.T. (2009), Reducing illegal immigrants in the U.S.: a dynamic CGE analysis. CoPS/Impact Working Paper G-183. Available at http://www.monash.edu.au/policy/ftp/workpapr/g-183.pdf

Dixon, P.B., Johnson, M., Rimmer, M.T. (2010), Economy-wide effects of reducing illegal immigrants in U.S. employment. *Contemporary Economic Policy*, DOI: 10.1111/j.1465-7287.2010.00208.x forthcoming.

Fox, A., Powers, W., Winston, A. (2008), Textile and apparel barriers and rules of origin: what's left to gain after the agreement on textiles and clothing? *Journal of Economic Integration* 23 (3), 656–684.

Griswold, D.T. (2002), Willing workers: fixing the problem of illegal Mexican migration to the United States. *Trade Policy Analysis* 19, Cato Institute, Washington DC, p. 24. Available at http://www.cato.org/pub_display.php?pub_id=3638

Hanson, G.H., McIntosh, C. (2007), The great Mexican emigration. NBER Working Paper 13675, National Bureau of Economic Research, Cambridge, MA, December, p. 55. Available at http://www.nber.org/papers/w13675.pdf

Higgs, P.J., Parham, D., Parmenter, B.R. (1981), Occupational wage relativities and labour-labour substitution in the Australian economy: applications of the ORANI model. IMPACT Project Working Paper No. OP-30, August, p. 45. Available from the Centre of Policy Studies, Monash University, Clayton, 3800, Australia.

Layard, R., Nickell, S., Jackman, R. (1994), *Employment Crisis*. Oxford University Press, Oxford, UK.

Osborne, S. (2007), Energy in 2020: assessing the economic effects of Commercialization of cellulosic ethanol. *U.S. Department of Commerce, International Trade Administration*, p. 20. Available at www.trade.gov/media/publications/pdf/cellulosic2007.pdf

Ottaviano, G.I.P., Peri, G. (2006), Rethinking the effects of immigration on wages. NBER Working Paper 12497, National Bureau of Economic Research, Cambridge, MA, March, p. 53. Available at http://www.nber.org/papers/w12497

Rauscher, M. (1999), Book review of Global Trade Analysis: Modeling and Applications, edited by T.W. Hertel. *The Economic Journal* 109 (459), F799–F800.

Rector, R., Kim, C. (2007), The fiscal cost of low-skill immigrants to the U.S. Taxpayer. Heritage Special Report SR-14, The Heritage Foundation, Washington, DC, May, p. 70. Available at http://www.heritage.org/Research/Immigration/sr14.cfm

Strayhorn, C.K. (2006), Undocumented immigrants in Texas: a financial analysis of the impact to the state budget and economy. Special Report, Office of the Comptroller of Texas, December, p. 22.

United States International Trade Commission. (2004, 2007, 2009), The economic effects of significant U.S. import restraints: fourth, fifth and sixth updates. Investigation No. 332–325, Publications 3701, 3906 & 4094.

Van Hook, J., Bean, F.D., Passel, J. (2005), Unauthorized migrants living in the United States: a mid-decade portrait. Pew Hispanic Center, September, p. 43. Available at http://www.migrationinformation.org/feature/display.cfm?ID=329

CHAPTER 6

Modeling Biofuels Policies in General Equilibrium: Insights, Pitfalls, and Opportunities

Alla Golub, Thomas W. Hertel, Farzad Taheripour and Wallace E. Tyner

Department of Agricultural Economics, Center for Global Trade Analysis, Purdue University, 403W. State Street, West Lafayette, IN 47907, USA
E-mail address: golub@purdue.edu; hertel@purdue.edu; tfarzad@purdue.edu; wtyner@purdue.edu

Abstract
Over the past decade, biofuels production in the European Union and the United States has boomed – much of this due to government mandates and subsidies. The United States has now surpassed Brazil as the world's leading producer of ethanol. The economic and environmental impact of these biofuel programs has become an important question of public policy. Due to the complex intersectoral linkages between biofuels and crops, livestock as well as energy activities, CGE modeling has become an important tool for their analysis. This chapter reviews recent developments in this area of economic analysis and suggests directions for future research.

Keywords: Biofuels, economic analysis, general equilibrium, renewable fuel standard, land use

1. Motivation

1.1. Why is it important to provide quantitative analyses of biofuels?

Ethanol has been produced for fuel in the United States for over 30 years. The industry launch was initiated by a subsidy of 40 cents/gallon provided in the Energy Policy Act of 1978. Between 1978 and today, the ethanol subsidy has ranged between 40 and 60 cents/gallon. The federal subsidy in 2010 for corn ethanol is 45 cents/gallon. The subsidy has always been a fixed amount that is invariant with oil or corn prices (Tyner and Quear, 2006).

Frontiers of Economics and Globalization
Volume 7 ISSN: 1574-8715
DOI: 10.1108/S1574-8715(2010)0000007009

In addition to the federal blending credit subsidy, there are also some other federal and state subsidies. Many states have complicated combinations of state subsidies, renewable fuel standards, producer incentives, etc. For example, the current Minnesota producer tax credit is 20 cents/gallon. (Schumacher, 2006). In fact, Koplow (2006) calculates the total ethanol subsidy in 2006 to range between $1.05 and $1.38 per gallon or between $1.42 and $1.87 of gasoline equivalent. Many would regard these figures as being high, but they do demonstrate that the ethanol industry has been one with substantial subsidies.

In addition to these state and federal subsidies, there is also a tariff on imported ethanol of 54 cents/gallon plus 2.5% of the import value (Tyner, 2008b). This tariff was originally designed to offset the ethanol subsidy that applies to both domestic and imported ethanol. Congress wanted to subsidize domestic ethanol and not imported ethanol, so the import barrier was created. No doubt, this import protection has prevented lower-cost foreign ethanol from entering in the volumes that might be possible without the tariff.

In 1990, the Clean Air Act was passed, which required vendors of gasoline to have a minimum oxygen percentage in their product. Adding oxygen enables the fuel to burn cleaner, so a cleaner environment became another important justification for ethanol subsidies. By requiring the oil industry to meet an oxygen percentage standard instead of a direct clean air standard, the policy favored additives like ethanol that contain a high percentage of oxygen by weight. However, methyl tertiary butyl ether (MTBE), a competitor for oxygenation, was generally cheaper than ethanol and was produced by the oil industry, so it continued to be the favored way of meeting the oxygen requirements.

Crude oil price as measured by composite U.S. refinery acquisition cost (IEA, 2009) in nominal terms has ranged between $10 and $30 per barrel between 1983 and 2003, except for a couple of short-term spikes. Thus, for most of the period we have had a fixed ethanol subsidy, while the crude oil price has been around $20 per barrel. That subsidy together with oil in the $10 to $30 range was sufficient to permit growth in ethanol production from about 430 million gallons in 1984 to about 3.4 billion gallons in 2004 (Tyner, 2007). In other words, production grew 149 million gallons/year. In 2004, the crude oil price began its steep climb to around $70 per barrel, and in 2008 topped $140 per barrel. This rapid increase in the crude price while the ethanol subsidy remained fixed led to a tremendous boom in construction of ethanol plants. In addition, MTBE was found in many local water sources, and it is highly toxic. In the 1990s, states began to ban MTBE, and the ban was complete in May of 2006. Thus, ethanol became the primary oxygenate and octane enhancer for gasoline (Tyner, 2008a; Hertel *et al.*, 2010b).

In 2007, Congress passed the Energy Independence and Security Act (U.S. Congress, 2007). That legislation substantially increased the

Renewable Fuel Standard (RFS) from 7.5 billion gallons to 36 billion gallons total, which must be achieved by 2022. Of the 36 billion gallons total, 15 billion can be corn-based ethanol, which must be attained by 2015. On an energy equivalent basis, the 36 billion gallons amounts to about 15% of projected U.S. liquid fuel consumption in 2022.

By 2009 U.S. corn ethanol production had increased to about 10.5 billion gallons. But capacity had grown to about 12.4 billion gallons. During 2008–2009, there was at times over 2 billion gallons of capacity shut down because of adverse economic conditions (high corn price and low ethanol and gasoline prices).

Perhaps the biggest barrier facing the biofuels industry in the United States today is the blend wall (Taheripour and Tyner, 2008). In the United States, ethanol blends at present are limited to 10% for standard vehicles. There is a second blend called E85, which is up to 85% ethanol, but can only be used in flexible-fuel vehicles (FFVs) designed to accommodate the higher ethanol blends. The E85 market in the United States is miniscule, so most ethanol is marketed through the E10 channel. The U.S. total gasoline-type fuel consumption is about 140 billion gallons/year. If every drop of gasoline could be blended with ethanol, the maximum ethanol consumption at the 10% blend limit would be 14 billion gallons. However, for infrastructure and environmental reasons, ethanol cannot be blended at the maximum level in every region and throughout the year. Our estimate is that the effective maximum blending level is about 9% or about 12.5 billion gallons. The United States already has this level of ethanol production capacity, so the industry has hit the blend wall. EPA has indicated it will rule on the request to increase the blending limit in the summer of 2010. If the limit is not increased, the ethanol industry cannot grow at all, and the 15-billion gallon RFS will not be attained. If it is increased to 15%, then the effective blend wall becomes about 19 billion gallons. In that case corn ethanol can meet its RFS level, but there will be little room under the blend wall for cellulose-based biofuels.

The European Union also has ambitious biofuel mandates and significant production levels at present. The EU target is 10% of liquid fuels on an energy basis from renewable resources by 2020. This target is part of a broader goal of 20% of total energy consumption from renewable sources by 2020. The EU is producing and consuming both ethanol from sugar and wheat and biodiesel from oilseeds, primarily rapeseed. Biodiesel is by far the largest share of renewable liquid fuels in the EU as the automobile fleet utilizes a much higher fraction diesel than in the United States. The EU target has detailed sustainability criteria including greenhouse gas (GHG) emissions reductions targets. Indirect land use change (iLUC) must be considered in measuring GHG impacts as in the United States.

The other leading biofuel producer is Brazil. Over the past three decades Brazil has been the leading global producer of sugarcane, the primary input for ethanol in the country (Zuurbier and van de Vooren, 2008).

Ethanol production took off in the 1970s when oil prices skyrocketed and sugar prices had experienced a sharp decline and the Brazilian government created a program in order to promote growth within the ethanol industry. In the 1980s, oil prices began to decline following the second oil crisis, and Latin America began experiencing financial difficulties and hyperinflation (Martines-Filho *et al.*, 2006). In the mid-1990s ethanol prices were deregulated and the industry began to flourish once again. In 2002, the first FFVs were introduced by Ford (Sandlow, 2006). In early 2008, ethanol consumption exceeded gasoline consumption for the first time. Also, in that year, the United States surpassed Brazil to become the leading ethanol producer in the world.

Many other nations are also experimenting with biofuels and have biofuels targets in place, including Argentina, Canada, China, Colombia, India, Indonesia, Peru, the Philippines, and Thailand. All in all, the biofuel industry has developed a very significant global presence, with subsidies, tariffs, quantitative restrictions all in operation. What is the welfare cost of these policies? What is the distribution of costs and benefits from the policies across sectors and across countries? What are the environmental impacts of these policies? How much do they affect the global demand for petroleum, and hence oil prices? Are they likely to lead to increased or decreased commodity market price volatility? All of these are important questions that need to be addressed. The next section of this chapter explains why applied general equilibrium analysis is the preferred vehicle for such analysis.

1.2. Why CGE analysis?

In principle, if the biofuels sector is a small portion of the total economy, it would seem that partial equilibrium analysis of the sector should be sufficient. These policies are unlikely to significantly affect economy-wide wages and national spending. However, as one looks more closely at the issue it becomes difficult to ascertain where to draw the line between the modeled sectors and the rest of the economy. Take for example the feedstock used to produce ethanol. Since corn comprises such an important share of total ethanol costs, their production must be explicitly modeled. As the ethanol industry expands, a key issue is how fast corn prices will rise. Ultimately, these rising feedstock costs are what choke off ethanol expansion.

Of course how much corn prices rise depends on the availability of land. In the United States, the first impact of increased corn production has been to divert acreage from competing crops – shifting, for example, from corn–soybean rotations to continuous corn production. Modeling these other crops is important since reductions in U.S. soybean production translate into increases in soybean production overseas. And this increased production has been the subject of considerable policy debate (Searchinger *et al.*, 2008a, 2008b). Does it lead to increased deforestation and hence GHG emissions? Part of the problem in the early days of U.S. biofuel policy formation was that more comprehensive models were not used in the environmental assessment of the U.S. ethanol program. Initial estimates of the GHG emissions impacts of ethanol were based solely on commodity-specific, partial equilibrium analysis. These studies (e.g., Farrell *et al.*, 2006) highlighted the GHG emissions reductions likely to ensue if ethanol produced from corn were used to replace petroleum in the liquid fuel economy. It was on this basis that the U.S. renewable fuel mandate for corn ethanol was proposed, assuming that it would benefit the environment, while reducing dependence on imported oil and boosting farm incomes. Only when more comprehensive economic modeling was undertaken did the phenomenon of indirect land use (to be further discussed in the following text) enter the debate. This turned out to reverse the conclusions. Therefore, it is clearly important to include the competing land-using activities in any biofuels policy model – specifically livestock pasture and forestry. At this point we have argued in favor of expanding the partial equilibrium model beyond the ethanol sector to include agricultural cropping, livestock production, and forestry (Figure 1).

But there are further important linkages that must also be taken into account in order to obtain an accurate assessment of biofuels policies. Turning to the demand side, we note that the demand for ethanol in the United States depends critically on the overall demand for liquid fuels in transportation. As noted previously, once ethanol use reaches 10% of fuel demand, the blend wall becomes binding. So it is important to model aggregate liquid fuel demand explicitly, as biofuels policy affects fuel prices

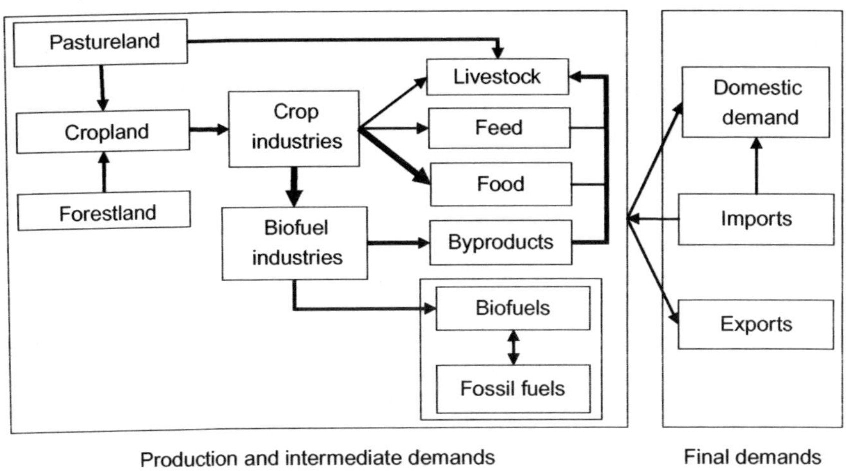

Fig. 1. ***Key economic linkages between biofuels and other sectors of the economy.***

and fuel prices affect aggregate demand. This involves following what happens to petroleum prices, which are expected to fall under significant biofuel developments, as petroleum is displaced in the fuel mix. Adding energy markets significantly expands the scope of the model.

However, this is not the end of the story when it comes to expanding the model. In the case of ethanol, about 16.5% of industry revenue comes from by-products (dried distillers' grains with solubles, or DDGS) Taheripour *et al.* (2010). This figure is even larger in the case of biodiesel processing. DDGS substitutes for corn in livestock feeding (Figure 1). In effect, the process of ethanol production does not fully exhaust the feed value of the corn. So if one wants an accurate picture of the impact of ethanol production on global land use, for example, it is critical to take into account the role of by-products in filling part of the niche vacated by the corn being diverted from the livestock sector to energy production. This entails developing a proper model of the livestock feeding decision. In short, if one were to take a partial equilibrium approach to the problem, it would be hard to know where to draw the line on which components of the economy to model and which to ignore. In the end, it is easier to take a general equilibrium approach in order to ensure that nothing important has been missed.

An additional dimension of this strategic modeling decision has to do with the trade-off between econometric and CGE/simulation modeling of biofuels. With recent advances in structural econometric modeling and statistical estimation of CGE models, the line between these two methodologies has blurred somewhat. However, the fact remains that in order to undertake effective econometric estimation of key economic parameters, it is necessary to have a reasonably long time series of data for estimation of the biofuel supply and demand relationships. However, in most parts of the world, the biofuel boom is a relatively recent phenomenon and estimation of the key parameters is simply not a realistic option. This is another factor favoring the use of CGE analysis for biofuels.

2. *Modeling framework*

2.1. Key elements of the GTAP model for biofuel analysis

The Global Trade Analysis Project (GTAP) (Hertel, 1997) model is widely used for global economy wide analysis of trade, energy, and environmental issues. The great strength of the standard GTAP model is the fact that it is well documented, publicly available, and readily modified. In this chapter we focus on a variant of the standard GTAP model nick-named GTAP-BIO (Birur *et al.*, 2008). GTAP-BIO is modification of the GTAP-E model (Burniaux and Truong, 2002; McDougall and Golub, 2007) designed for the energy–economy–environment–trade linkages analysis. With respect to biofuels, the most important feature of GTAP-E is energy substitution – a key factor for environmental policy analysis, which is absent from the standard GTAP model.

Birur *et al.* (2008) modify the GTAP-E model to incorporate both the Leontief demand for ethanol as a fuel oxygenator as well as the potential for ethanol and other biofuels to substitute for petroleum products as an energy source. We adopt this specification. Furthermore, we draw on the revised set of parameters proposed by Beckman *et al.* (2010), who undertake a historical validation exercise and find that the energy demand elasticities in the standard GTAP-E model were far too elastic. Here, we focus on several key elements of the GTAP-BIO model that are important for the subsequent applications considered. These model features include the specification of bilateral trade, the determination of land cover changes in response to increased biofuel feedstock production, and the response of crop yields – both at the intensive and extensive margins – to higher prices induced by biofuel policies.

2.1.1. Bilateral trade specification

Increasing production of biofuels from crops results in price increases for feedstocks and related crops, sending the signal to producers to expand the area under cultivation. While most of this increased area will likely come from other crops, eventually some is expected to come from the conversion of pastureland and forests, which in turn results in increased GHG emissions. The extent of such land cover conversion and the carbon intensity of the land cover that is converted to crops depend critically on the country/agro-ecological zone (AEZ) where this conversion occurs. Accordingly, the specification of international trade in the economic model is critical. There are two different views on how patterns of trade in commodity markets affect the crop replacement: "Armington" and integrated world market (IWM) for agricultural commodities. And these two approaches give rise to quite different predictions about the location of land cover change.

Under the Armington approach to import demand, utilized in the GTAP model, products are differentiated by national origin. This introduces a strong element of economic geography into the analysis. In the GTAP trade specification, agents first decide on the sourcing of their imports, and then, on the basis of the resulting composite import price, they determine the optimal mix of imported and domestic goods. In the case of increased production of biodiesel in the EU, the Armington model tends to predict that a majority of the cropland conversion will arise domestically, within the EU, followed by its dominant export competitors and import suppliers. This makes intuitive sense. However, the downside of this modeling approach is that price differences are allowed to persist over time for products that many would consider to be relatively homogeneous.

The main alternative to the Armington view is that of IWMs, which postulates a single global market for agricultural commodities and a single market clearing price. This is the modeling approach utilized in the study by Searchinger *et al.* (2008a). Under this view of the world, land cover change in response to an EU or U.S. biofuels program is equally likely to take place anywhere in the world where the product is currently produced, *ceteris paribus*. As a result, that study predicted significant land cover change in India – a country that trades relatively little in agricultural commodities. (Of course, other considerations enter into the determination of land cover change in both modeling frameworks, including the supply responsiveness of crops in each region.)

The trade specification not only determines what regions and ecosystem types the additional cropland comes from, but also affects the size of the net global cropland requirement, depending on relative yields in the different regions. Consider the case of U.S. corn production for ethanol. U.S. yields are among the highest in the world. When one hectare of corn grown for food is displaced by one hectare of corn for fuel in the United States, more than one hectare in the rest of the world will be needed to cover the shortage of corn for food. As we move from the Armington to the integrated world market assumption, the shock originated in the United States is more easily transmitted through the global economy and the production change in the rest of the world is greater. Because U.S. corn yields are higher than corn yields in other regions of the world, the net global land requirement under integrated world market will be higher than under Armington assumption. In summary, the trade specification selected for biofuels analysis will have an important impact in determining how "green" the biofuel is determined to be.

Ultimately, it is an empirical question as to which trade specification is more appropriate for a particular biofuels scenario. Villoria and Hertel (2009) formulate an econometric model that permits them to test these competing hypotheses. Their model seeks to predict the pattern of global cover change, as reported by the FAO, in response to U.S. coarse grains prices, among other things. In the IWM formulation of the model, U.S. export prices are a significant explanatory variable in this land cover change equation. However, when geographic variables (e.g., measures of export competition in third markets) are permitted to enter the model, the world price effect is no longer significant. Thus, they reject the IWM hypothesis in favor of the Armington model.

However, this finding is not definitive, and it does not apply to all markets. Since the analysis is done at the level of coarse grains, it could be argued that the Armington effect is being picked up due to differences in product composition. It would be good to test this hypothesis at the level of a more narrowly defined commodity (e.g., corn). Even if the IWM hypothesis is rejected for corn, it may still be valid for other feedstocks (e.g., sugar or oilseeds). This is fundamentally an empirical question that should ideally be tested in the case of each biofuel feedstock.

Finally, there is the question of length of run. While these geography effects surface in annual time series data, do they persist over a period of 10 years? Some evidence on this matter may be gleaned from a cross-sectional approach to the estimation of trade share equations, as in Hertel *et al.* (2007). Those authors estimate the responsiveness of import trade shares to bilateral variations in international trade and transport costs. They obtain highly significant estimates of the associated Armington parameters, ranging from 30 for natural gas (essentially confirming the IWM hypothesis) to 2.6 for the heterogeneous category of "other crops." In the work discussed below, on the basis of the GTAP model, we utilize Hertel *et al.* (2007) econometric estimates of the Armington parameters.

2.1.2. Land use component

When modeling competition for land, it is important to recognize that land is a heterogeneous endowment. Following the pioneering work of Darwin *et al.* (1995), this heterogeneity can be reflected in a CGE model via the introduction of AEZs (Lee *et al.*, 2005). In each region of GTAP-BIO, there may be as many as 18 AEZs that differ along two dimensions: growing period (six categories of 60-day growing period intervals) and climatic zones (three categories: tropical, temperate, and boreal). Building on the work of the FAO and IIASA (2000), the length of growing period depends on temperature, precipitation, soil characteristics, and topography. The suitability of each AEZ for production of alternative crops and livestock is based on currently observed practices, so that the competition for land within a given AEZ across uses is constrained to include activities that have been observed to take place in that AEZ. The different AEZs then enter as inputs into a national production function for each land-using sector (e.g., wheat). With a sufficiently high elasticity of substitution in use, the returns to land across AEZs, but within a given use, will move closely together as would be expected in the case of a homogeneous product produced in 18 different regions of the country (Hertel *et al.*, 2009).

However, even after introducing AEZs, further adjustments are required to reflect observed behavior in land use. Empirical evidence on land rental differentials suggests that land does not move freely between alternative uses. There are many other factors, beyond agronomic factors, that limit land mobility within an AEZ. These include costs of conversion, managerial inertia, unmeasured benefits from crop rotation, among others. Therefore, in the model, such movement is constrained by a constant elasticity of transformation (CET) frontier. Thus, within an AEZ/region in the model, the returns to land in different uses are allowed to differ. A nested CET structure of land supply is implemented

(Ahammad and Mi, 2005) whereby the rent-maximizing land owner first decides on the allocation of land among three economic uses/broad land cover types, that is, forest, cropland, and grazing land, based on relative returns to land. The land owner then decides on the allocation of land between various crops, again based on relative returns in crop sectors.

A CET parameter governs the ease of land mobility across uses within each AEZ. The parameter in the cropland, grazing, and forestland nest determines the ease with which land is transformed across the three economic uses (e.g., from pastureland to cropland). Similarly, the CET parameter in the crop nest determines the ease to transformation of land from one cropping activity to another (e.g., oilseeds to corn). The absolute value of the CET parameter represents the *upper bound* (the case of an infinitesimal share for that use) on the elasticity of supply to a given use of land in response to a change in its rental rate. The more dominant a given use in total land revenue, the smaller is its own-price elasticity of acreage supply. The lower bound on this supply elasticity is zero (if all land in an AEZ is devoted to crops, then there is no scope for cropland to expand within the AEZ). Therefore, the actual supply elasticity is dependent on the relative importance (measured by land rents share) of a given land use in the overall market for land and is therefore endogenous. The CET parameters among the three land cover types and among crops are set according to the recommendations in Ahmed *et al.* (2008), based on earlier econometric investigations by Lubowski (2002).

While the CET function is a popular device in CGE models and permits these models to be calibrated to estimated land supply elasticities, it has some significant drawbacks. As with the constant elasticity of substitution (CES)/Armington specification, it allows significant differences in returns to land in the same AEZ to persist over time. One might expect that such differences might result in more conversion over time, and indeed Ahmed *et al.* (2008) suggest raising the absolute value of this parameter as the time frame for analysis lengthens.

Another important limitation of the CET function is that the fundamental constraint in the CET production possibility frontier for land in a given AEZ is *not* expressed in terms of physical hectares, but rather in terms of *effective* hectares – that is productivity-weighted hectares. "… this creates a rift between the physical world and the economic model which can pose problems when attempting to relate model results back to the physical environment" (Golub *et al.*, 2009). To estimate LUCs measured in physical hectares, GTAP-BIO incorporates a new structure that translates changes in effective hectares to physical hectares. This is done by incorporating an additional constraint into the model that requires physical hectares employed in cropping (all crops together), grazing, and forestry to add up (i.e., remain unchanging). Satisfaction of this additional equation is permitted via introduction of an endogenous variable that adjusts AEZ-wide economic productivity to reflect the changing mix of cropping, grazing, and forestry activities. Thus, if relatively low productivity pastureland (productivity is inferred from the observed level of land rents per hectare) is converted to cropping, the average productivity of cropland is expected to fall, as the new land is less productive than the existing cropland. In addition, we expect the average productivity of the pastureland to fall, as the best pastureland is converted to crops. Overall, in this case, the productivity of the AEZ would need to fall in order to continue to satisfy the adding up constraint for physical hectares.

Such productivity adjustments can have a significant impact on the results, and since they are largely driven by differences in per hectare land rents, there is some concern that these may not be accurate in some cases. This is particularly true in the case of the lower-level CET nest where land cover is determined. The GTAP-AEZ database shows very large differences in per hectare land rents; yet we believe that, with some investments, the converted pastureland or forestland might be nearly as productive as current cropland. For this reason, we have modified this lower-level land productivity story by specifying a model parameter, the value of which can be set exogenously, and which determines how many additional hectares of marginal lands are required to make up for one hectare of average cropland. In the specification used below, we will assume that it takes three additional hectares of pastureland and forestland to produce the same amount as two hectares of displaced current croplands. This assumption determines the extensive margin of cropland expansion under biofuels, as will be discussed in the next section.

2.1.3. Changes in yield

Yield changes in the wake of a biofuels program are central in the analysis with GTAP-BIO. Here, there is both an intensive (higher yields on existing lands in response to higher prices) and an extensive margin (lower yields on new lands in response to cropland expansion). They work in opposite directions, but which one dominates in which AEZs, and then on a global basis, is an empirical question.

Yield intensification: As feedstock prices rise, with land in relatively inelastic supply, producers have an incentive to increase use of nonland inputs to boost production per unit of land. This change in yield, which is endogenous to the increases in demand for biofuels, must be modeled as such in order to properly estimate the change in land area due to biofuels production. The strength of this response is governed by the potential for substitution among inputs in the CES production function. In contrast to standard GTAP model (Hertel, 1997), where value added and intermediate inputs are used in fixed proportion, crop production functions of GTAP-BIO are not Leontief in intermediate inputs, since increased application of fertilizer, pesticides, and other purchased inputs can be an important avenue for boosting yields in response to higher commodity prices.

Keeney and Hertel (2009) review the literature on yield response to corn prices and find evidence that this price response has been diminishing in recent years. They focus on the more recent studies and take a simple average of these estimates in order to obtain an elasticity of yield to corn price of 0.25. This suggests that a permanent increase of 10% in crop price, *relative to variable input prices*, would result in roughly a 2.5% rise in yields. If the long-run price of the crop were to double, from $2 per bushel to $4 per bushel, and the price of land substituting inputs increased by 50%, then the output–input price ratio would rise by 33.33% and the expected yield increase would be $0.25 \times 33.33\% = 8.33\%$. In current applications of GTAP-BIO, the same long-run elasticity is adopted for all crops and all regions. In the future, as more data from different countries and for different crops become available, crop- and region-specific estimates will be incorporated and this is likely to be important for the results on global LUC.[1]

Yield extensification: As identified by Searchinger *et al.* (2008a), we expect there to be an offsetting effect on yields, as cropland cover is extended beyond current levels. We define the extensive margin as the change in crop yields when land employed in other uses (other crops, pasture, or forest) is converted to grow crops in question. There are two important contributors to yield extensification in the model. Taking corn as an example – first, there is the change in corn yields as corn replaces other crops on existing cropland (e.g., shifting from a corn–soybean rotation to continuous corn). This effect is estimated by referring to the differential in net returns to land in existing uses. If U.S. corn production expands onto lower productivity land, then average corn yields will fall. If EU oilseeds production expands into higher productivity lands, then average oilseeds yield will increase. (Recall the discussion of the CET land supply functions above.) The second extensive margin measures the change in average crop yields as cropland area is expanded into pastureland, and possibly forestland. In the absence of strong empirical evidence, we simply assumed a value of 0.66 in our earlier work, as per the discussion above. This suggests that it takes three additional hectares of marginal cropland to offset the impact of diverting two hectares of current (average) cropland to biofuels production. In a recent work Tyner *et al.* (2010) have estimated regional land conversion factors at the AEZ level using a terrestrial ecosystem model (TEM). These land conversion factors measure productivity of existing cropland versus new cropland. Future econometric work aimed at estimating this parameter more precisely is a high priority, and we discuss below the impact of systematic sensitivity analysis on this parameter.

---

[1] Keeney and Hertel (AAEA presentation in 2009) explore the implications of systematic differences between developing and developed country yield response for indirect land use change from biofuel production in the United States.

2.2. Extensions to the GTAP model for biofuel analysis

Thus far, we have discussed features of the model and parameter settings that, while important for biofuel analysis, are not specific to biofuels. We now turn to those features of GTAP-BIO that are specific to biofuels. We begin with those designed to appropriately characterize the demand for biofuel, and then turn to the supply side.

2.2.1. Modeling demand for biofuels

Ethanol plays two roles in fuel use. As noted in the introduction to this chapter, until recently in the United States, the main role of ethanol was as a fuel additive – aimed at allowing the fuel to burn cleaner, thereby meeting air quality standards. This type of demand is best treated as a Leontief-derived demand by the petroleum refining sector. As the aggregate demand for liquid fuels expands, so too does the additive demand for ethanol. There is no price responsiveness to this demand. Indeed, until 2006 when this demand was satiated, ethanol was priced at a premium over petroleum, despite its inferior energy content.

The second type of ethanol demand is based on its energy content. Once the additive demand is satiated, further ethanol expansion lowers, the price of ethanol as it must now compete with petroleum, at the margin, on an energy basis. This derived demand is very sensitive to price. At high oil prices, there is great potential for ethanol use – provided the blend wall is not binding. Once the blend wall is reached, this derived demand becomes wholly inelastic. As noted in the introduction, U.S. ethanol consumption is virtually "at the blend wall" at present, sharply altering the demand for ethanol until such time as the blend wall is adjusted (e.g., to 12% or 15% – this is a regulatory decision) or until such time as the fleet of FFVs and E-85 service stations expands markedly.

The situation is clearly different with biodiesel, which is not subject to these constraints and which can be blended freely with diesel fuel. In this case, it is just the energy substitution margin that matters. The structure of household demand for private goods including biofuels is shown in Figure 2.

2.2.2. Modeling the supply of biofuels

Three new sectors have been introduced into GTAP-BIO in order to properly handle the supply side of the biofuel markets. The first sector represents grain-based ethanol (mainly corn ethanol for the United States and wheat ethanol for EU region). The second sector represents sugarcane-based ethanol (mainly produced in Brazil) and finally the third sector produces biodiesel from vegetable oil. Taheripour *et al.* (2007) have introduced these sectors in the standard GTAP database to support this modeling framework. A key feature of these biofuel sectors is that they typically produce by-products. In some cases, sale of these by-products

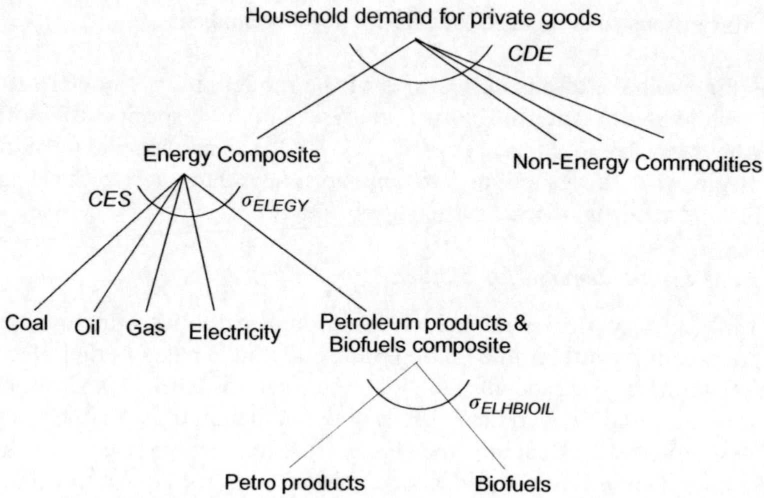

Fig. 2. Structure of consumption side of the GTAP-BIO model (Birur et al., 2008).

represents a very important revenue source for the industry, so explicit modeling of the by-product market and price determination is necessary in order to provide an appropriate estimate of revenue for the industry.

In the case of grain-based ethanol, it is produced in conjunction with various distillers' grains products, mainly DDGS. Producing biodiesel from vegetable oil also increases the supplies of oilseed meals (Vegetable Oils By-Products (VOBP)) that are joint products obtained from production of vegetable oils from oilseeds. In general, DDGS and oilseed meals are valuable inputs for the livestock industry.

An important outcome of this joint production process in the biofuel industry is that when biofuel production is encouraged, for example, due to government subsidies or positive oil price shocks, the production of these by-products also increases and as a result their prices fall relative to other animal feed ingredients. This encourages livestock producers to use more biofuel by-products in their production processes and avoid high-cost crops. Another important aspect of biofuel by-products is that they help mitigate the environmental consequences of expansion by the biofuel industry. For example, DDGS substitutes for both corn and soybean meal in livestock rations but mainly for corn. This ultimately reduces the land use consequences of biofuel production and eases the demand for chemical inputs, such as fertilizers and pesticides, in crop production. Hence, it is crucial for biofuel analyses to introduce production and consumption of DDGS and oilseed by-products into the modeling framework.

The standard GTAP framework does not permit multiproduct sectors. Therefore, Taheripour *et al.* (2010) have modified the model to handle joint production. Three new equations are required. The first refers to the percentage change in the index of activity level in the industries with joint products (grain-based ethanol and crude vegetable oil industries), qz_j. The second determines the percentage change in unit return to activity in each industry, pz_j. The model endogenously determines the activity level variables according to the following zero-profit condition:

$$pz_j = \sum_i \theta_{ij} pf_{ij} \quad \text{for } j = \text{EthanolC, Cveg\_Oil} \tag{1}$$

In this equation θ_{ij} and pf_{ij} represent, respectively, the share of input i in total costs of producing commodity j and the percentage change in price of input i paid by sector j, respectively. The change in return to activities in the two industries is simply a composite price index, comprising prices of the main and by-products according to the following equations:

$$pz_j = \sum \Omega_{kj} . ps_{kj} \quad \begin{array}{l} \text{for } j = \text{EthanolC and } k = \text{ethanol 1, DDGS,} \\ \text{for } j = \text{Cveg\_oil and } k = \text{Cveg\_Oil 1, VOBP.} \end{array} \tag{2}$$

Here, Ω_{kj} is the revenue share of the kth product in total revenues of sector j.

Output levels for the industry are a function of activity level and relative prices, where $\sigma_j^T \leq 0$ represents the CET parameter between the main and by-products in industry j:

$$qo_{kj} = qz_j + \sigma_j^T (pz_j - ps_{kj}) \quad \begin{array}{l} \text{for } j = \text{EthanolC and } k = \text{ethanol 1, DDGS,} \\ \text{for } j = \text{Cveg\_Oil and } k = \text{Cveg\_Oil 1, VOBP.} \end{array} \tag{3}$$

Finally, we modify the derived demand functions for inputs into the grain-based ethanol and crude vegetable oil industries by replacing the indices of outputs with the indices of sector activity levels:

$$qf_{ij} = qz_j + \sigma_j (pz_j - pf_{ij}).$$

This completes the supply side modifications in the model to handle by-products.

2.2.3. Modeling the demand for biofuel by-products

Several successive efforts to introduce consumption of DDGS and oilseed meals into the GTAP modeling framework have been undertaken. Taheripour *et al.* (2009) represent the latest modifications in this area. This chapter uses a three-level nesting structure for the demand for animal feedstuffs in the livestock industry. Figure 3 depicts this nesting structure composite. At the lowest level, DDGS and coarse grains are combined to create a feedstuff energy composite. At this level oilseeds and oilseed meals

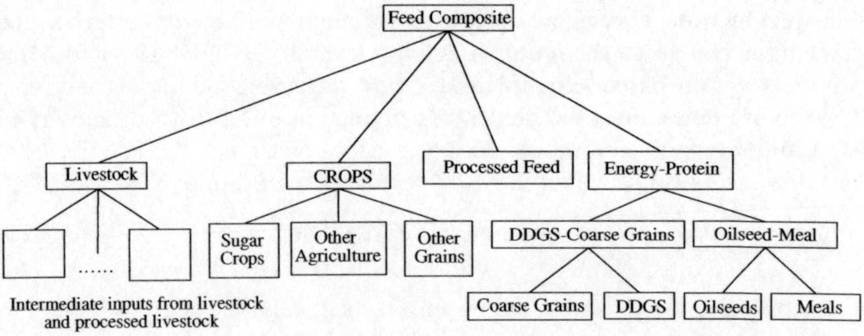

Fig. 3. Structure of nested demand for feed in livestock industry.

are combined to create a protein feedstuff as well. At a higher level the protein and energy feed ingredients are combined. At this level other crop-based feedstuffs are also introduced. The livestock industry receives some feedstuff inputs from processing sectors as well, and these materials are bundled together at the second level too. Finally, all feed ingredients are combined to create a feed composite. Taheripour *et al.* (2009) assigned elasticities of substitution to the different components of the demand for feed in order to permit replication of changes in the prices of DDGS and meals in the United States and EU during the time period of 2001–2006. In addition, those authors did several experimental simulations and sensitivity tests to reach the desired displacement ratios between DDGS, grains, oilseeds, and oilseed meals according to the literature in this area.

3. *Selected applications*

3.1. Historical analysis of the biofuels boom

One of the first applications undertaken with the biofuels model was a historical validation exercise. Since this is a global general equilibrium model, there are many different variables upon which we could focus our attention. However, we believe the most important of these is the *share of total liquid fuels provided by biofuels*. Indeed many of the biofuel mandates are expressed in terms of such a share, so being able to track this over the 2001–2006 period is quite important. Hertel *et al.* (2010b) note that the U.S. share tripled from 2001 to 2006, rising from less than 0.6% to more than 1.8%. Most of this increase came in the form of domestically produced, corn-based ethanol, but a seventh of the total came in the form of imports of sugarcane-based ethanol; finally, a very small amount came from biodiesel. In the EU, the share of biofuels in total liquid fuel consumption rose more than sixfold over this period, from 0.2% to 1.23%, with the majority being delivered as biodiesel.

According to Hertel *et al.* (2010b), the major drivers of this growth in biofuels have been petroleum prices, biofuel subsidies, and the ban on competing fuel additives in the United States. They illustrate the roles of these different forces using the following partial equilibrium expression for the change in ethanol output, qo^*:

$$qo^* = \frac{\varepsilon_S[(1-\alpha)ai - \varepsilon_D(p+s)]}{\varepsilon_S - \varepsilon_D} \tag{4}$$

Here the key drivers of ethanol output change are as follows: ai is the percentage change in the input–output ratio prescribing additive use in gasoline (this rises under the MTBE oxygenator ban discussed in the introduction); p, the percentage change in the price of composite liquid fuels; and s, the percentage change in the power of the *ad valorem*-equivalent subsidy on ethanol production (i.e., s is one plus the subsidy rate). The parameters in this equation are as follows: $\varepsilon_D = -\alpha\sigma$ is the composite price elasticity of demand for ethanol (the product of the share of ethanol going to the price-sensitive (energy-substitution) side of the market, α, and the elasticity of substitution in use between ethanol, biodiesel, and petroleum, σ); $\varepsilon_s = v_c\theta_c^{-1}$ is the price elasticity of supply for ethanol, which is determined by the product of the own-price elasticity of supply of corn, v_c, and the inverse of the share of costs of corn in ethanol production, θ_c^{-1}.

From Equation (4), the authors obtain some useful insights into the impact of these drivers on the growth in biofuels output. First of all, the contribution of changes in the additive requirements of gasoline to total ethanol output depends on the change in the input–output ratio, ai, as well as the initial share of total sales going to this market segment. The price-sensitive portion of the market depends on what happens to the price of energy in general, p, and the power of the subsidy, s. When the change in the latter is expressed as the change in the power of the *ad valorem* subsidy equivalent (as is the case here), these two effects are additive. Their combined significance depends on the share of the total market for ethanol that is price sensitive (α) and the ease of substitution between ethanol and other fuels (σ). Furthermore, we see from Equation (4) that feedstock supply response is also important. If the total availability of feedstock (corn) is fixed ($v_c = 0$), then $qo^* = 0$. Furthermore, as v_c rises and the share of corn in overall ethanol costs falls ($\theta_c \to 0$), $v_c\theta_c^{-1} = \varepsilon_s$ rises, thereby boosting supply.

Given estimates of the other parameters and shocks in Equation (4), the authors choose σ to replicate the historically observed value of qo. The main drivers of the biofuel boom during 2001–2006 as offered by Birur *et al.* (2008) are the increase in crude oil price, which rises by 136% (from \$25 per barrel to \$60), the increase in additive demand for ethanol in the United States which rises by 49%, a subsidy of \$0.51 per gallon of ethanol and $1 per gallon of biodiesel in the United States, and tax credit of $1 per gallon of ethanol and $1.9 per gallon of biodiesel in the EU.

The estimated elasticities of substitution between biofuels and petroleum products (σ) are as follows: Brazil = 1.35, EU = 1.65, and USA = 3.95. The authors note that the relatively low elasticity in Brazil reflects the fact that ethanol already commands a large share of that market, and large percentage changes become more difficult as ethanol becomes more dominant. The estimated elasticity of substitution in the United States is high, relative to Europe, particularly in light of the fact that the EU renewable fuel share grew by a much larger percentage over this period. However, the latter growth is well explained by the significant subsidies implicit in the fuel tax exemptions in France and Germany. In addition, in the base period (2001), the share of U.S. ethanol going to the price inelastic additive market was quite high (about 75%). This requires the elasticity of substitution in the price-sensitive part of the market to be higher. Finally, the economic "power" of the U.S. ethanol subsidy has been diminishing as the prices of gasoline and ethanol rise. For all these reasons, a large elasticity of substitution is required to explain the growth in the renewable fuel share in the United States.

Given these estimates of the elasticity of substitution between biofuels and other energy products, the authors are able to decompose the impact of the main drivers of renewable fuel output growth in the EU and U.S. markets over the 2001–2006 period. Of the total change in ethanol growth in the United States (133.5%), 64% of the total figure is attributed to the MTBE ban, 93% is attributed to the rise in petroleum prices, −23% is due to the diminishing relative importance of the $.51 per gallon blenders' subsidy. In the case of EU biodiesel growth over this period (341%), the most important driver is the fuel tax exemptions (202%) since the *ad valorem* equivalent of the power of the EU subsidy on biodiesel rose by 81.2% over this period. This is followed by the contribution of higher oil prices (140%).

3.2. Global GHG emissions from land use change

Probably the most controversial feature of biofuels in the past decade has been the impacts on global land use and associated "indirect" GHG emissions. This has been the subject of legislation in the EU (EC Directive 2009/29/EC), the United States (the National Renewable Fuel Standard program as mandated in the Energy Independence and Security Act of 2007: EISA), and California (California Air Resource Board Low Carbon Fuel Standard: CARB-LCFS adopted in April 2009). In all of these regulations, biofuels' environmental impact measures include estimates of emissions due to (i) feedstock production, (ii) fuel production (e.g., corn to ethanol), and (iii) global iLUCs triggered by expanded biofuels production. The first two components, emissions from feedstock and fuel production, are usually calculated using a life cycle model (e.g., GREET (Wang, 2005)). The third, iLUC component requires estimation with a global economic model that links global production, consumption and trade, and energy, biofuel, and agricultural markets within and across regions. The total emissions are then compared to a life cycle emission for gasoline to evaluate whether biofuels contribute to GHG reductions in transportation.

In this section we focus on two GTAP-BIO applications, Hertel *et al.* (2010a) and Tyner *et al.* (2009), investigating environmental impacts of U.S. corn ethanol. Both analyses combine economic modeling results with assumptions about the carbon fluxes (emission factors) from land cover changes. While the CGE models used in the two studies are very similar[2] (both based on the GTAP-BIO model of Birur *et al.*, 2008), the experimental design and assumptions behind calculation of emission factors are different, resulting in different GHG emissions per unit of ethanol produced.

Hertel *et al.* (2010a) focus on the so-called market-mediated changes in global land use in response to the expansion of U.S.-grown corn for ethanol. They model expansion of U.S. maize ethanol use from 2001 levels to the 2015 mandated level of 15 billion gallons/year by forcing 13.75 billion gallons of additional ethanol production with the increased costs passed forward to consumers in the form of higher fuel prices. It is important to emphasize that the task in Hertel *et al.* (2010a) is to estimate the independent effect of the increase in corn ethanol production, and not to predict total land use change (or its GHG discharge) caused by the many other factors that affect land use. It may be, for example, that technological change will increase maize yields so much that, even as biofuel production expands over some future period, total maize acreage actually falls over the same period of time. But that is not the point of this study, which seeks instead to assess by how much more land use would have fallen without the biofuel increase. This comparative static analysis has the great advantage of simplicity and transparency. It also facilitates relatively detailed analysis of the impacts of biofuels on global markets. An alternative approach, used, for example, by the EPA in its analysis for the renewable fuel standard (USEPA, 2009), involves projecting changes over time with and without a given quantity of biofuels production. This has the great advantage of being more appealing to decision makers who are not accustomed to thinking in terms of comparative statics. The drawback is that often much more effort is devoted to construction of the

[2] Regional and sectoral aggregations of the version 6 of GTAP database are different in two studies. While both use 18 regions, there are differences in how African and Asian countries are aggregated.

baseline, thereby shortchanging the time and resources available for analysis of the actual biofuels impacts.

On the basis of the estimates of Hertel *et al.* (2010a), the naïve estimate of the global land requirements needed to achieve the 15 billion gallon mandated level of corn ethanol production in the United States is about 15 million ha.[3] This gross land requirement is reduced to 4.2 million ha due to number of market-mediated effects that include availability of coproducts, the reduction in food consumption due to higher prices, and increased yields due to higher prices. This figure is further reduced to 3.8 million ha once the growth in baseline yields is taken into account.[4]

The first panel of Figure 4 summarizes the continental pattern of land conversion induced by increased ethanol production. In the majority of AEZs, cropland increases at the expense of both pasture and forestry. However, some of this decrease in forestry is compensated for elsewhere in AEZs where both forestry and cropland increase at the expense of pasture. Most cropland conversion arises within the United States, followed by its dominant export competitors and trading partners. This geographic approach to trade is supported by the recent econometric work of Villoria and Hertel (2009). Compared to study by Searchinger *et al.* (2008a) where IWM hypothesis is employed, this study finds far less conversion in some of the large, but relatively closed, agricultural economies such as India.

To examine the global warming implications of these land conversions, Hertel *et al.* (2010a) developed an emission factor for each type of transition predicted, in each region: forest-to-crop, pasture-to-crop, and pasture-to-forest. The emissions factors are based on the model developed by Searchinger *et al.* (2008a), which in turn relies on data compiled by the Woods Hole Research Institute (see Searchinger *et al.*, 2008b, for the model details). The emission factors account for changes in above- and below-ground carbon stocks, as well as changes in 30-year carbon sequestration by ecosystems actively gaining carbon. Hertel *et al.* (2010a) modified the calculation of emission factors to include small replacement cropping system carbon storage, assumption of 10% of forest biomass sequestered in timber products or charcoal in soil upon forest clearance, and exclusion of non-CO_2 emissions in the calculation. These assumptions

[3] If corn ethanol yield is 2.6 gallons/bushels, baseline coarse grains yield is 335 bushels/ha and additional ethanol volume is 13.75 billion gallons, then gross area required is about 15 million ha.

[4] With time and improved technologies, we expect the efficiency of ethanol conversion as well as corn yields to increase, both of which will reduce the land requirements for ethanol. While ethanol conversion efficiency has not changed significantly since the base period (2001) for the Hertel *et al.* (2010a) analysis, USDA reports that corn yields had risen by 9.3% by 2007. This has a direct impact on the amount of land required to fulfill a given level of ethanol mandate – reducing the land use requirement by a factor of 8.5% in the United States and globally.

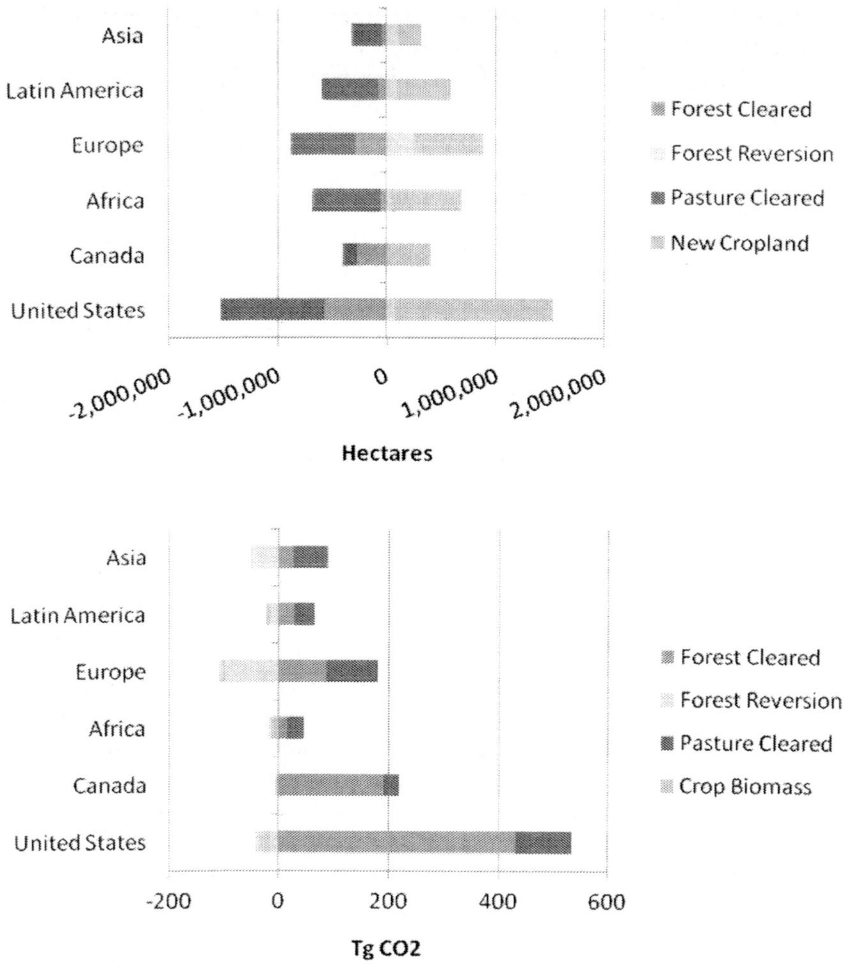

Fig. 4. Global land conversion and associated GHG emissions due to increased maize ethanol production of 50.15 Gl/year at 2007 yields in the United States, by region. Source: Hertel et al. (2010a).

result in slightly lower emission factors than shown in Searchinger *et al.* (2008a).[5]

Applying the emission factors to land conversions predicted by GTAP, Hertel *et al.* (2010a) found 870 Tg of CO_2 emissions, or 800 g/MJ of increased annual ethanol production. The second panel of Figure 4 shows emissions by region and conversion type. The largest shares of emissions

[5] For more information on emission factors used in the study, see Hertel *et al.* (2010a) and the supplementary online material at https://www.gtap.agecon.purdue.edu/resources/res_display.asp?RecordID=3160.

occur in the United States and Canada, where a greater proportion of the forest is expected to be cleared for crops.

To calculate iLUC emissions per mega joule (MJ), it is necessary to make an assumption about length of biofuel production period. If production continues for 30 years, then using straight-line amortization results in iLUC emissions of 27 g CO_2 per MJ, roughly one-fourth the value estimated by Searchinger *et al.* (2008a). It is important to note that assumptions about timing and the length of biofuel production period are very important in this analysis (see O'Hare *et al.*, 2009). Assuming 20 years instead of 30 years of production increases emissions per mega joule value implied by 800 g initial discharge by 50%, from 27 to 40 g CO_2/MJ.

Adding 27 g CO_2 per MJ iLUC emissions to 65 g CO_2 per MJ direct emissions from typical U.S. corn ethanol production (emissions during cultivation and industrial processing of ethanol) "... would nearly eliminate carbon benefit of this biofuel relative to typical gasoline (94 to 96 g/MJ; Farrell *et al.*, 2006; Wang *et al.*, 2007)" (Hertel *et al.*, 2010a).

Tyner *et al.* (2009) evaluate carbon emissions due to the global land use changes induced by US. corn ethanol production. Their analysis of land use changes is also based on GTAP-BIO model, but employs different experimental design and assumptions about carbon fluxes. Those authors start from version 6 of the GTAP database representing global economy in 2001 and update the data to 2006. It is important to understand how the database is updated and what exogenous variables are shocked. To update the database, Tyner *et al.* (2009) follow the approach outlined in Hertel *et al.* (2010b). Instead of shocking all the exogenous variables in the economy, only those variables are shocked that are important in determining *structure* of biofuel economy. Under this approach, the information requirements for historical 2001–2006 simulation are greatly reduced. In the historical simulation, the focus is only on those elements of the history that are critical in shaping structure of biofuel economy as it changed from 2001 to 2006: rise in petroleum prices, the replacement of MTBE by ethanol as gasoline additive, and the subsidies to the ethanol and biodiesel industries in the United States and the European Union. Because changes in other exogenous variables are not targeted (e.g., population, labor, trade policies, technological change, and/or income growth), the update from 2001 to 2006 is in terms of *shares* of renewable fuels in total liquid fuel consumption. Thus, this historical simulation replicates historical changes in shares, but not in quantities of biofuels in 2006, and the resulting quantity of biofuels produced are smaller than actually observed in 2006 (3 billion gallons vs. 7 billion gallons).

Starting from the updated database, several simulations are conducted: from 3 to 7 billion gallons, and then from 7 to 15 billion gallons by increment of 2 billion gallons. Cumulative simulation result indicates that an increase in U.S. corn ethanol production from 2001 to mandated 15 billion gallons requires additional 3.55 Mha of cropland globally at 2001 yields. This requirement is smaller than 4.2 Mha (at 2001 yield) reported in Hertel *et al.* (2010a), which is due to the different simulation design. Tyner *et al.* (2009) find that net land required for production of extra 1000 gallons of ethanol rises (and hence carbon emissions) as we move to higher levels of ethanol production. For example, moving from 3 to 7 billion gallons requires 0.25 ha per 1000 gallons. While obtaining 2 billion gallons of corn ethanol after 13 billion gallons already produced requires 0.31 billion gallons per 1000 gallons, similar to per 1000 gallons land requirement reported in Hertel *et al.* (2010a) when large increment is modeled in one step from 2001 to 2015 mandated level.

Tyner *et al.* (2009) utilize two different sets of emission factors. The first set of emission factors is calculated on the basis of the model developed by Searchinger *et al.* (2008a), similar to Hertel *et al.* (2010a), but with different assumptions. For example, Tyner *et al.* (2009) do not take into account carbon storage in replacement cropping systems and assume that 75% of the carbon stored in the forest type vegetation will be released into the atmosphere at the time of land conversion and that 25% are stored in buildings, furniture, etc., while Hertel *et al.* assume a 90%/10% analogous split. As a result, emission factors used in the two studies differ. Because of the differences in emission factors and simulation design, in Tyner *et al.* (2009) the one time discharge from land use change due to increase in corn ethanol production to 15 billion gallons is 766 Tg vs. 870 Tg of CO_2, below 870 Tg of CO_2 reported in Hertel *et al.* (2010a).

The second set of emissions factors reported in Tyner *et al.* (2009) is calculated on the basis of the IPCC land and land cover carbon profiles. The IPCC data set provides data at a global scale with no geographic distribution. IPCC factors are much larger than the corresponding regional factors derived from the Woods Hole data set, and result in 2489 Tg of CO_2 emissions.

Finally, Tyner *et al.* (2009) sum emissions due to production and consumption of ethanol with obtained emissions from land use changes to compare life cycle GHG discharges from ethanol (pure ethanol fuel, or E100) with conventional gasoline using emissions per mile metric. With Woods Hole emission factors, average total GHGs emissions due to production and consumption of E100 (including land use emissions) are about 96% of those for gasoline. With the IPCC carbon profile, emissions released due to production and consumption of E100 per mile are 66.2% more than the conventional gasoline emissions per mile. The overall conclusion from Tyner *et al.* (2009) does not depart from Hertel *et al.* (2010a); unless corn is grown for fuel for 100 years; there is no environmental benefit in producing U.S. corn ethanol to displace gasoline.

3.3. Interplay between biofuels and the livestock sectors

A very important, yet under-researched aspect of the biofuel impacts is the interplay between the livestock and biofuels industries. Taheripour *et al.* (2009) analyze these linkages in considerable detail for the case of biofuel mandates in the United States and the EU. The most obvious consequence of large-scale biofuel production for the livestock industry is higher crop prices, which increase input costs. Biofuel production also raises returns to cropland, which, in turn, encourages conversion of some pastureland to crops, thereby further increasing production costs for ruminant livestock. On the other hand, biofuels are produced in conjunction with valuable by-products that can be used in the livestock industry as animal feeds and can substitute for the higher priced crops in animal rations. This serves to dampen the cost increases confronting livestock producers.

However, not all livestock industries are well placed to capitalize on the increased availability of biofuel by-products. Ruminants (dairy and beef) are better able to make use of DDGS in their feed rations and are therefore better positioned to gain from increased DDGS availability – particularly when compared to other livestock sectors that may not be able to adjust their feed rations as readily to take advantage of the increased supply of DDGS. As noted previously, biofuel by-products represent an important component of biofuel industry revenues. If the livestock industry could not absorb these by-products, their prices would fall sharply, thereby limiting expansion of the biofuel industry. In addition, both industries compete for crop feedstocks. The interactions between these industries become even more complicated when we take into account other economy-wide linkages with energy and agricultural markets.

Taheripour *et al.* (2009) find that, due to the U.S. and EU biofuel mandates, the overall global volume of livestock and processing livestock industries is expected to fall by about $3.7 billion (Figure 5). About 61.7% of this reduction is estimated to take place within non–biofuel-producing regions. The United States show only a minor reduction ($0.9 billion) in its livestock and processed livestock products, while the EU also experiences a slight increase. In general, the livestock industries of the United States and EU do not suffer significantly from biofuel mandates, which is rather surprising. However, closer investigation by those authors reveals that this muted impact is due to their ability to make use of biofuel by-products to ameliorate the cost consequences of higher crop prices. This stands in sharp contrast to the livestock industries of other regions (including Brazil) that do not have the same access to biofuel by-products. Here production falls by much more than in the EU and the United States (Figure 5). This is due to a combination of factors. In Brazil, the other major biofuel-producing region, the sugarcane by-product is not a feedstuff, rather it is used to power the sugarcane processing facilities. One might expect that international trade would distribute the by-products to the global livestock

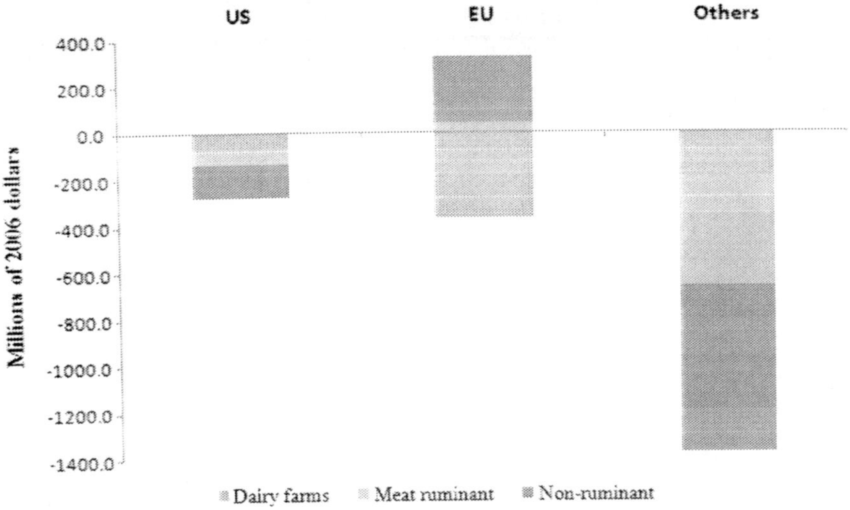

Fig. 5. ***Changes in global livestock outputs due to the EU and U.S. 2015 biofuel mandates. Source: Taheripour et al. (2009).***

industry. However, the geography of global trade is such that the greatest benefits from the increased by-product availability remain in the producing region.

Figure 5 shows the impacts of biofuel mandates on the outputs (in $US millions at constant prices) of dairy farms, meat ruminant, and nonruminant activities by region. As shown in this figure the outputs of these industries fall in all regions except for the EU. The outputs of the meat ruminant and nonruminant activities of the EU slightly grow due to biofuel mandates. At the global level the nonruminant sector will experience the greatest output volume reduction among all livestock sectors.

Taheripour *et al.* (2009) also find that the impact mandate varies significantly across livestock subsectors due to differential potentials for absorbing the by-products. Their results show that the mandates will significantly reduce the cost share of coarse grains in feed rations in the United States and EU and will raise shares of DDGS and oilseed meals across all livestock industries (see panels A, B, and C of Figure 6). The ruminant meat industry benefits more from the expansion of DDGS than other livestock activities as shown in Figure 6. One can see a similar pattern of by-product use in the EU.

Several papers indicate that dairy and ruminant industries are in better positions to use more DDGS in their feed rations compared to nonruminant industry (e.g., Arora *et al.*, 2008). This suggests that they could take advantage of these by-products and move away from using expensive corn in their feed rations in the presence of corn ethanol production. A large expansion in corn ethanol production in the United

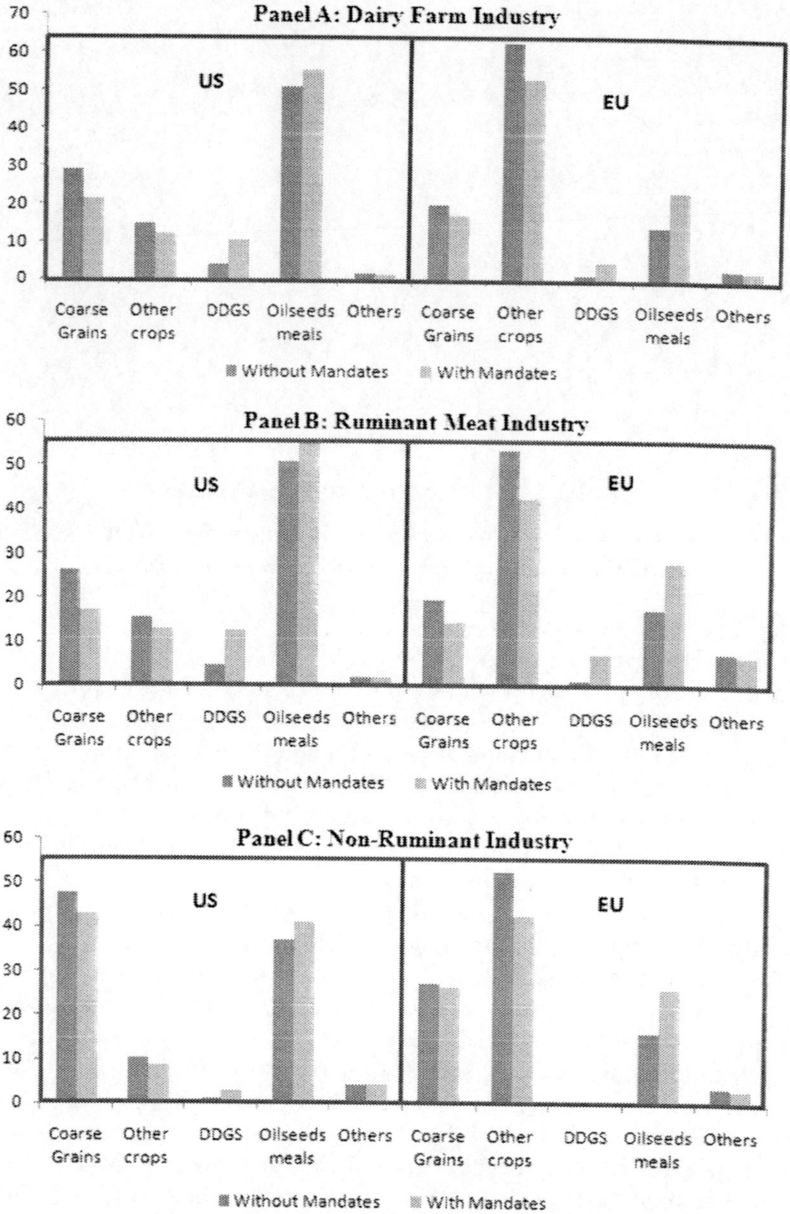

Fig. 6. Shares of coarse grains, DDGS, and oilseeds meals in total costs of animal feed rations without and with the EU and U.S. 2015 biofuel mandates (figures represent cost shares calculated at constant 2006 prices). Source: Taheripour et al. (2009).

States increases significantly the supply of DDGS (6.5 lb DDGS are produced per gallon of ethanol). Other factors being equal, this reduces the price of DDGS versus corn. Since ruminants species (say dairy and cattle beef in the United States) can digest DDGS better than nonruminants, dairy and meat ruminant producers will add more DDGS in their animal rations. This increases share of DDGS and decreases share of corn in feed costs of these industries, as shown in Figure 6. This helps dairy and beef cattle producers to partially offset adverse cost impacts of higher corn prices. However, nonruminant producers are more limited in their substitution possibilities; hence, they suffer more than other livestock producers and therefore curb their production more, as shown in Figure 5.

3.4. How robust are these findings? Sensitivity analysis of biofuel impacts

With the increased use of CGE models for policy analysis, decision makers have begun to insist more on formal sensitivity analysis of results with respect to parametric uncertainty. In their analysis of the global land use impacts of biofuels, Keeney and Hertel undertake a comprehensive sensitivity analysis. Hertel *et al.* (2010a) also provide a complete sensitivity analysis with respect to the GHG emissions impacts of the U.S. corn ethanol program. We draw on both of these studies here.

Keeney and Hertel (2009) specify uncertainty in key model parameters as follows. The CET transformation parameters describing land supply are drawn from Lubowski *et al.* (2006) and Ahmed *et al.* (2008) and these are judged to range over the interval [−0.03, −0.19] with mean −0.11. Keeney and Hertel (2009) use this same range (±80% of the point estimate) to define the distribution for acreage response across crops, implying an interval of [−0.10, −0.90] about the −0.5 point estimate. For nonland factor supplies, the authors maintain the ratio of labor and capital supply elasticities in their base model and consider a distribution symmetric about the base assumption of a common multiplicative factor, λ, which equals 1.0 in the base case. A reasonable lower bound for this value is assumed to be zero, indicative of the short run when factors are immobile between agriculture and nonagriculture sectors. With this lower bound assumption, a symmetric treatment for the upper bound implies an interval for λ of [0.00, 2.00] and hence a labor and capital supply elasticity range of [0.00, 1.40] and [0.00, 2.00], respectively. As previously discussed, the substitution component of the yield elasticity is derived from the literature estimates for corn with a range of [0.00, 0.50] surrounding the 0.25 point estimate for the long-run yield response to price. The trade elasticities are drawn from Hertel *et al.* (2007), each of which is estimated with a standard error. The authors only conduct sensitivity on the trade elasticities for crop sectors and draw directly from the point estimates and standard errors provided by those authors.

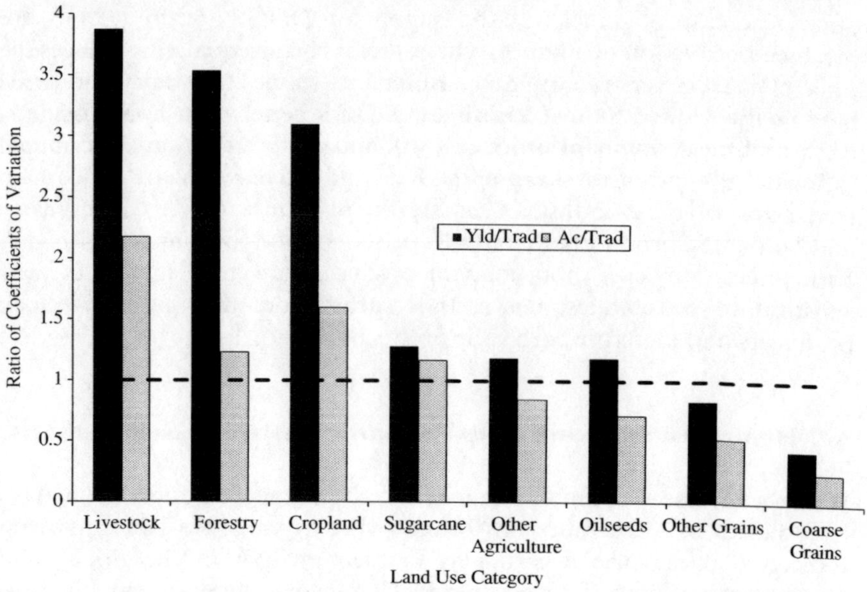

Fig. 7. The relative importance of supply response versus bilateral trade response assumptions in uncertainty about land use changes. Source: Keeney and Hertel (2009). Notes: Systematic sensitivity analysis for yield response includes factor supply and substitution parameters. Acreage response includes both levels of land allocation). Bilateral trade response includes all trade elasticities for commodities featured in this figure using the confidence intervals from Hertel et al. (2007).

We focus here on Keeney and Hertel's analysis of the sensitivity of land cover change results with respect to variation in one set of parameters at a time. Their key findings are summarized in Figure 7 by focusing on the relative coefficients of variation (CVs) for land use change associated with the three major sources of model uncertainty. Since the CV reports the ratio of the standard deviation to the mean of the variable, a high CV reflects a large degree of uncertainty in the land use change results. By reporting the CVs in Figure 7 in ratios, we can readily see which sources of parameter uncertainty are most influential in driving the land cover change results.

Turning to the details of Figure 7, we have two sets of bars. Each measures the CV of one source of uncertainty, relative to the base uncertainty that is driven by uncertainty in the trade elasticities. Specifically, the darker columns in this figure show the ratio of CVs deriving from yield uncertainty versus uncertainty in trade elasticities, while the lighter columns report the ratio of CVs stemming from acreage response versus trade elasticities. Upon studying this figure, we see that for broad categories of forestry, livestock, and crops it is the case that the yield response determinants dominate the uncertainty in predicted changes in land use, with CVs much larger than those from the acreage and trade elasticity assumptions. For land use changes within the agricultural sector, we find that in general the trade elasticities, yield, and acreage assumptions all make comparable contributions to uncertainty in model predictions, with the exception of the other grains and coarse grains sectors where uncertainty in trade elasticities dominate (i.e., the height of the vertical bars is considerably below the dashed line at a value of one). The assumed ease with which adjustment of export and import levels of these crop commodities occurs, in particular in the case of coarse grains (where the U.S. demand shock initially acts), represents a critically important assumption when predicting the global land use change following the mandated increase in biofuel production.

Naturally in policy analyses where a particular estimate, say the grams of CO_2 equivalent GHG emissions per mega joule of biofuel produced, is of critical importance, one wants to establish a comprehensive confidence interval on the findings. This was the task of Hertel *et al.* (2010a) who sought to estimate the GHG emissions from indirect land use change associated with corn ethanol for purposes of establishing the California LCFS. As with Keeney and Hertel, those authors specified distributions on their parameters. However, in addition to uncertainty in the economic behavioral parameters, those authors included uncertainty in the physical GHG emissions factors associated with land use change as well. The authors then sampled from these distributions following the Gaussian quadrature (GQ) approach to estimate means and standard deviations of model results (DeVuyst and Preckel, 1997; Pearson and Arndt, 2000). For large models, the GQ method is more tractable than a full Monte Carlo analysis.[6] Hertel *et al.* (2010a) found the CV with global iLUC (global additional cropland) to be 0.37. The CV associated with global emissions from land use change is 0.46, with a mean value of 27 g/MJ of corn ethanol produced annually. The associated 95% confidence interval, which ranges from 2 to 52 g/MJ suggests considerable uncertainty in this key value. It also suggests that zero emissions from land use change are also a very unlikely outcome.

4. Conclusions and future challenges

The application of CGE analysis to biofuels has been a boom industry in the past few years – fueled by the need to provide solid quantitative analysis of a rapidly growing industry that has been the recipient of numerous government subsidies, mandates, and regulations. The use of

---

[6] This model solves in approximately 12 min. A Monte Carlo analysis using just 1000 simulations would take more than 8 days.

one of the variants of the GTAP model described in this chapter in the formulation of California's LCFS raised this type of CGE analysis to a new level of scrutiny and criticism. As a result, the use of CGE models in this area has become rather sophisticated, with numerous special features aimed at addressing previous limitations. This chapter has reviewed the motivation for the use of CGE models for biofuel analysis, as well as the key conceptual issues that have arisen in the course of this work.

As with much of such policy modeling, this work has highlighted the need for improved parameter estimates. The very wide, 95% confidence interval on the CARB-LCFS emission estimates reported in this study shows the need for additional econometric work to narrow the underlying parameter distributions – both for the economic parameters and for the physical GHG emissions parameters. Areas of particular concern include the land supply functions and the feedstuff demand elasticities – both of which have spotty econometric underpinnings, but have proven crucial to our findings. Also, the yield response to price – both the intensive and extensive margins – needs more work. The latter, in particular, has received almost no attention in the literature.

Additional econometric work aimed at discriminating between competing models of key components of the analytical framework is also important. We find that the international trade specification makes a big difference in the global location of additional production in the wake of a national biofuels program. Depending on the location of production, the total amount of area converted as well as the GHG emissions per hectare converted can vary greatly. And this global distribution of production depends on the assumptions made about the role of geography in international trade.

One of the most pervasive challenges over the course of the research experience documented here involves bridging the economic and physical worlds, which come together in the context of biofuel analysis. Since the ultimate objective of much of this work has been to produce an estimate of physical emissions per unit of physical energy, the base economic data and parameters need to bear a close relationship to the underlying physical data. This is rather different from the usual requirements of CGE analysis, where the focal point is economic welfare or aggregate output and employment changes, measured in dollars terms or as price or quantity index changes. In order to meet this objective in future work, several key links between the economic and physical data should be improved. First, there is the matter of the matching quantities with values of crops produced as reported from international statistical resources (e.g., FAO and IEA). It is also important to match quantities of oilseeds produced, traded, and crushed along with produced and traded vegetable oil and oilseed meals all across the world with their corresponding values in GTAP. An important and crucial key link in analyzing land use impacts of biofuel production is the link between value added of land in livestock and forest industries with contribution of physical land to the physical outputs of these industries.

As one looks ahead, one of the most significant challenges facing those seeking to undertake CGE analysis of biofuels relates to the modeling of the so-called second-generation biofuels. These include ethanol or hydrocarbons produced from agricultural residues, municipal wastes, or dedicated energy crops such as miscanthus, switchgrass, and poplar.

In the United States, the part of the biofuels mandate that can be filled with corn is essentially complete, so the future growth will be mainly from these cellulosic materials. The U.S. mandate is for 20 billion gallons ethanol equivalent (roughly 13.6 billion gallons gasoline equivalent) of advanced biofuels by 2022. The mandate for advance biofuels began in 2010 at a level of 100 million gallons, but EPA was forced to waive all but 6.5 million gallons of that mandate because the plants to produce cellulosic biofuels have not been developed.

There are three main sources of uncertainty that inhibit private sector investment in cellulosic biofuels: market, technology, and government policy. Most technology developers believe their technology could be viable without government subsidies if crude oil were $120 per barrel. However, crude oil is far from $120, and investors are not willing to invest in a technology that requires $120 crude oil to be viable. Even though technology developers may believe they can be competitive with $120 oil, no commercial plants have been built, so there still remains huge technology uncertainty. In addition to market and technology uncertainty, we also have government policy uncertainty. For example, the U.S. subsidy on corn ethanol is set to expire in 2010, and the cellulose biofuel subsidy in 2012. Even if the subsidies are renewed this year, they will likely be renewed for five years – not long enough to pay off a $400 million cellulosic biofuel plant. The RFS is also uncertain. Right now, it is the only assurance of a market for second-generation biofuels, but as we have seen from the U.S. experience in 2010, the RFS can be waived. There is similar government policy uncertainty in the EU. While the EU mandates technically are just that, in reality, they are more like targets that can be relaxed or even ignored.

Given these huge uncertainties, it is not surprising that the needed investments in second-generation biofuels have not yet materialized. However, the slowdown gives us the needed time to prepare economic, environmental, and policy analyses for these second-generation biofuels. That is the future direction for research in this arena. In addition to the food/fuel, GHG, and other environmental issues, we will face in this new analysis the question of water constraints. To what extent will production of these feedstocks face binding water constraints?

In summary, while CGE analyses of the impacts of biofuels on the economy and the environment have made great strides over the past few years, there is much yet to be done if economic analysis is to meet the needs of policy makers interested in designing policies related to renewable energy, climate change mitigation, and energy security.

Acknowledgments

The authors acknowledge support for this work from Argonne National Labs, the Energy Bio-science Institute at the University of California, the Office of Transportation and Air Quality of the U.S. Environmental Protection Agency, and the U.S. Department of Energy.

References

Ahammad, H., Mi, R. (2005), Land use change modeling in GTEM: accounting for forest sinks. Australian Bureau of Agricultural and Resource Economics, Presented at EMF 22: Climate Change Control Scenarios, Stanford University, California, 25–27 May 2005.

Ahmed, A.S., Hertel, T.W., Lubowski, R. (2008), Calibration of a land cover supply function using transition probabilities. GTAP Research Memorandum No. 12, Center for Global Trade Analysis, Purdue University.

Arora, S., Wu, M., Wand, M. (2008), *Updated of Distiller Grains Displacement Rations for Corn Ethanol Life-Cycle Analysis*. Center for Transportation Research, Energy System Division, Argonne National Laboratory, Argonne, IL, USA.

Beckman, J., Hertel, T.W., Tyner, W.E. (2010), Validating energy-oriented CGE models. GTAP Working Paper No. 54, Center for Global Trade Analysis, Purdue University, West Lafayette, IN, USA. Available at https://www.gtap.agecon.purdue.edu/resources/res_display.asp?RecordID=2954

Birur, D., Hertel, T., Tyner, W. (2008), Impact of biofuel production on world agricultural markets: a computable general equilibrium analysis. GTAP Working Paper No. 53, Center for Global Trade Analysis, Purdue University, West Lafayette, IN, USA.

Burniaux, J., Truong, T. (2002), GTAP-E: an energy-environmental version of the GTAP model. GTAP Technical Paper No. 16, Center for Global Trade Analysis, Purdue University, West Lafayette, IN.

California Air Resource Board (2009), *Low Carbon Fuel Standard*. Available at http://www.arb.ca.gov/fuels/lcfs/lcfs.htm

Darwin, R., Tsigas, M., Lewandrowski, J., Raneses, A. (1995), World agriculture and climate change: economic adaptations. Agricultural Economic Report No. 703, Economic Research Service, US Department of Agriculture, Washington, DC.

DeVuyst, E.A., Preckel, P.V. (1997), Sensitivity analysis revisited: a quadrature based approach. *Journal of Policy Modeling* 19, 175–185.

EC Directive 2009/29/EC. Available at http://eur-lex.europa.eu/LexUriServ/LexUriServ.do?uri=OJ:L:2009:140:0063:0087:en:PDF

FAO and IIASA (2000), Global agro-ecological zones – 2000. Food and Agriculture Organization (FAO) of the United Nations, Rome, Italy, and International Institute for Applied Systems Analysis (IIASA), Laxenburg, Austria.

Farrell, A.E., Plevin, R.J., Turner, B.T., Jones, A.D., O'Hare, M., Kammen, D.M. (2006), Ethanol can contribute to energy and environmental goals. *Science* 311, 506–508.

Golub, A., Hertel, T., Sohngen, B. (2009), Land use modelling in recursively-dynamic GTAP framework. In: Hertel, T., Rose, S., Tol, R. (Eds.), *Economic Analysis of Land Use in Global Climate Change Policy*. Routledge, University of Stirling, UK.

Hertel, T.W. (1997), *Global Trade Analysis, Modeling and Applications*. Cambridge University Press, Cambridge, UK.

Hertel, T.W., Hummels, D., Ivanic, M., Keeney, R. (2007), How confident can we be of CGE-based assessments of free trade agreements? *Economic Modeling* 24, 611–635.

Hertel, T., Lee, H.-L., Rose, S., Sohngen, B. (2009), Modeling land-use related greenhouse gas sources and sinks and their mitigation potential. In: Hertel, T., Rose, S., Tol, R. (Eds.), *Economic Analysis of Land Use in Global Climate Change Policy*. Routledge, University of Stirling, UK.

Hertel, T.W., Golub, A.A., Jones, A.D., O'Hare, M., Plevin, R.J., Kammen, D.M. (2010a), Global land use and greenhouse gas emissions impacts of U.S. maize ethanol: estimating market-mediated responses. *BioScience* 60 (3), 223–231.

Hertel, T.W., Tyner, W.E., Birur, D.K. (2010b), The global impacts of biofuel mandates. *The Energy Journal* 31 (1), 75–100.

IEA (2009), IEA energy statistics [cited May 27, 2009]; Available at http://www.iea.org/Textbase/stats/prodresult.asp?PRODUCT=Balances

Keeney, R., Hertel, T. (2009), Indirect land use impacts of US biofuels policies: the importance of acreage, yield and bilateral trade responses. *American Journal of Agricultural Economics* 91, 895–909.

Koplow, D. (2006), *Biofuels – At What Cost? Government Support for Ethanol and Biodiesel in the United States*. International Institute for Sustainable Development, Geneva, Switzerland.

Lee, H.-L., Hertel, T.W., Sohngen, B., Ramankutty, N. (2005), Towards and integrated land use data base for assessing the potential for greenhouse gas mitigation. GTAP Technical Paper No. 25, Center for Global Trade Analysis, Purdue University. Available at https://www.gtap.agecon.purdue.edu/resources/res_display.asp?RecordID=1900

Lubowski, R.N. (2002), Determinants of land-use transitions in the United States: econometric analysis of changes among the major land-use categories. PhD Dissertation, Harvard University, Cambridge, MA.

Lubowski, R., Plantinga, A., Stavins, R. (2006), Land-use change and carbon sinks: econometric estimation of the carbon sequestration supply function. *Journal of Environmental Economics and Management* 51, 135–152.

Martines-Filho, J., Burnquist, H.L., Vian, C.E.F. (2006), Bioenergy and the rise of sugarcane-based ethanol in Brazil. *Choices Magazine* 21 (2), 91–96.

McDougall, R., Golub, A. (2007), GTAP-E release 6: a revised energy-environmental version of the GTAP model. GTAP Research Memorandum No. 15, Center for Global Trade Analysis, Purdue University, West Lafayette, IN, USA.

O'Hare, M., Plevin, R.J., Marin, J.I., Jones, A.D., Kendall, A., Hopson, E. (2009), Proper accounting for time increases crop-based biofuels' greenhouse gas deficit versus petroleum. *Environmental Research Letters* 4, 024001, doi:10.1088/1748-9326/4/2/024001.

Pearson, K., Arndt, C. (2000), Implementing systematic sensitivity analysis using GEMPACK. GTAP. Center for Global Trade Analysis, Purdue University, Technical Paper No. 3.

Sandlow, D. (2006), Ethanol: lessons from Brazil. *Aspen Institute: A High Growth Strategy for Ethanol.* Available at http://www.brookings.edu/views/articles/fellows/sandalow_20060522.pdf

Schumacher, J. (2006), *Oilseed, Biodiesel and Ethanol Subsidies & Renewable Energy Mandates: US Federal & Selected State Initiatives.* Montana State University-Extension, Bozeman, MT, USA.

Searchinger, T., Heimlich, R., Houghton, R.A., Dong, F., Elobeid, A., Fabiosa, J., Tokgoz, S., Hayes, D., Yu, T.-H. (2008a), Use of US croplands for biofuels increases greenhouse gases through emissions from land use change. *Science* 319, 1238–1240.

Searchinger, T., Heimlich, R., Houghton, R.A., Dong, F., Elobeid, A., Fabiosa, J., Tokgoz, S., Hayes, D., Yu, T.-H. (2008b), Supporting online materials for: use of US croplands for biofuels increases greenhouse gases through emissions from land use change. *Science* 1151861.

Taheripour, F., Tyner, W.E. (2008), Ethanol policy analysis – what have we learned so far? *Choices* 23 (3), 6–11.

Taheripour, F., Birur, D., Hertel, T., Tyner, W. (2007), Introducing liquid biofuel into the GTAP database. GTAP Research Memorandum No. 11, Center for Global Trade Analysis, Purdue University, West Lafayette, IN, USA.

Taheripour, F., Hertel, T., Tyner, W. (2009), Implications of the biofuels boom for the global livestock industry: a computable general equilibrium analysis. An earlier version used for the background paper for the 2009 *State of Food and Agriculture (SOFA) From the Food and Agriculture Organization of the UN (FAO)*. A revised version is also presented at *2009 Applied and Agricultural Economics Association* meeting in Milwaukee Wisconsin, Center for Global Trade Analysis, Purdue University.

Taheripour, F., Hertel, T.W., Tyner, W.E., Beckman, J.F., Birur, D.K. (2010), Biofuels and their by-products: global economic and environmental implications. *Biomass and Bioenergy* 34 (3), 278–289.

Tyner, W.E. (2007), Policy alternatives for the future biofuels industry. *Journal of Agricultural and Food Industrial Organization* 5 (2), Article 2. DOI: 10.2202/1542-0485.1189. Available at: http://www.bepress.com/jafio/vol5/iss2/art2

Tyner, W.E. (2008a), The global impacts of US and EU biofuels policies. In: Zuurbier, P., van de Vooren, J. (Eds.), *Sugarcane Ethanol: Contributions to Climate Change Mitigation and the Environment*. Wageningen Academic Publishers, Wageningen, Netherlands, pp. 181–197.

Tyner, W.E. (2008b), The US ethanol and biofuels boom: its origins, current status, and future prospects. *BioScience* 58 (7), 646–653.

Tyner, W.E., Quear, J. (2006), Comparison of a fixed and variable corn ethanol subsidy. *Choices* 21 (3), 199–202.

Tyner, W., Taheripour, F., Baldos, U. (2009), *Land Use Changes Carbon Emissions due to US Ethanol Production*. Department of Agricultural Economics, Purdue University, West Lafayette, IN, USA.

Tyner, W., Taheripour, F., Zhuang, Q., Birur, D., Baldos, U. (2010), *Land Use Changes and Consequent CO_2 Emissions due to US Corn Ethanol Production: A Comprehensive Analysis*. Department of Agricultural Economics, Purdue University, West Lafayette, IN, USA.

U.S. Congress (2007), Energy Independence and Security Act of 2007. In: *H.R. 6, 110 Congress, 1st session.*

USEPA (2009), *Renewable Fuel Standard*. Available at http://www.epa.gov/otaq/fuels/renewablefuels/index.htm

Villoria, N., Hertel, T. (2009), The role of geography in determining the global land use impacts of biofuels. Paper presented at the 12th Annual Conference on Global Trade Analysis, Santiago, Chile. Available at https://www.gtap.agecon.purdue.edu/resources/res_display.asp?RecordID = 3049

Wang, M. (2005), Updated energy and greenhouse gas emission results of fuel ethanol. Presented on the 15th International Symposium on Alcohol Fuels, September 26–28, 2005, San Diego, CA, USA.

Wang, M., Wu, M., Huo, H. (2007), Life-cycle energy and greenhouse gas emission impacts of different corn ethanol plant types. *Environmental Research Letters* 2, 13.

Zuurbier, P., van de Vooren, J. (Eds.) (2008). *Sugarcane Ethanol: Contributions to Climate Change Mitigation and the Environment*. Wageningen Academic Publishers, Wageningen, the Netherlands.

CHAPTER 7

Bioeconomics and International Trade: The Case of the Great Salt Lake, Utah

David C. Finnoff[a] and Arthur J. Caplan[b]

[a]*Department of Economics and Finance, University of Wyoming, Laramie, WY, USA*
E-mail address: finoff@uwyo.edu
[b]*Department of Applied Economics, Utah State University, Logan, UT, USA*
E-mail address: arthur.caplan@usu.edu

Abstract
We present a computable general equilibrium model of the interface between the Great Salt Lake (GSL) ecosystem and both the international and regional economy that impacts the ecosystem. International trade is accounted for in the simplest of terms, involving the export of each of the ecosystem's main commodities and importation of a composite good, as well as equilibrium balances in the savings-investment and current accounts. With respect to the ecosystem, the model treats the various representative species as net energy maximizers and bases population dynamics on the period-by-period sizes of surplus net energy. Energy markets – where predators and prey exchange biomass – determine equilibrium energy prices. With respect to the regional economy, we model five production sectors (at the aggregate industry level) – brine cyst harvesters, the mineral-extraction industry, agriculture, recreation, and a composite-good industry – as well as the household sector. By performing dynamic simulations of the joint ecosystem–regional economy model, we isolate the effects of period-by-period stochastic changes in salinity levels and an initial shock to species-population levels on the ecological and economic variables of the model.

JEL classifications: C68, D58, Q57

Keywords: Net energy, biomass demand and supply, regional economy, Great Salt Lake

1. Introduction

Management of the Great Salt Lake (GSL) watershed has evolved sporadically during the past 150 years – from a state provision in 1850

Frontiers of Economics and Globalization
Volume 7 ISSN: 1574-8715
DOI: 10.1108/S1574-8715(2010)0000007010

appropriating two islands in the lake for herding purposes, to a state-sponsored study in 1958 focusing solely on the need for extensive diking to control the lake's intermittent flood levels, to a plan published by the Utah Department of Natural Resources (DNR) in 2000 promoting *inter alia* the maintenance of the lake and its marshes as a critical waterfowl flyway system (DNR, 2000 and Adler, 1999). As Adler (1999) points out, this planning process is perhaps best described as a slow evolution toward a broadly focused, multiple-use plan that nevertheless lacks sufficient research and monitoring, has often been institutionally disjointed, and is inappropriately tethered to the lake's official meander line rather than its watershed. Echoing this sentiment, the DNR (2000, p. 48) has noted that "managers [of the GSL] do not fully understand how reductions in inflows and other water and land uses [within the watershed] will affect population dynamics and species interactions." How these effects in turn feedback through the regional and international economies is even less understood.

This chapter demonstrates a new integrated ecological/economic, or bioeconomic, model of the GSL watershed that (a) accounts for the basic ecological relationships and human activities that interact within the lake's watershed, (b) enables the measurement of ecosystem externalities that might occur as a result of "shocks" within the watershed and ecosystem, thereby identifying the degree to which certain species may be threatened, and (c) demonstrates how international trade might be incorporated into the modeling framework. In other words, the chapter demonstrates one approach that the DNR might use to help it understand the interrelationships between human activity and biological interactions within the GSL watershed and how these interrelationships impact the vulnerability of any given species. The model, patterned closely after Finnoff and Tschirhart (2003, 2004) (henceforth FT), is based on individual species behavior directing aggregate outcomes in a multiple species food web. In effect, a general equilibrium ecosystem model (GEEM) is combined with a computable general equilibrium (CGE) model of the regional and international economies, providing a tight integration of the GSL's ecology and economy.

Our model extends FT in three important respects. First, it incorporates stochastic ecological parameters such as the salinity and nitrogen balances of the lake at any given point in time. Second, unlike FT's application to a marine ecosystem, the application here is to an inland water body where water in- and outflows are crucial to the health of the ecosystem and economy. The model is therefore an initial attempt at capturing the multidimensional effects of human intervention in an ecosystem, rather than solely through the harvesting of a focal species as in the case of a marine environment. Third, commercial harvesting of the focal species – brine shrimp – is not of the species itself, but rather of its eggs, and the eggs are a relatively high-valued export commodity. Thus, harvesting impacts the species' population dynamics in a unique way, which has been heretofore unexplored in the literature.

We find evidence that the GSL ecosystem is stable at current levels of human intervention and at the current level of government regulation of the brine shrimp industry. However, our results illustrate the extent to which unintended ecological and economic consequences may occur as humans intentionally interact with the ecosystem. We demonstrate these consequences through a simple simulation exercise that is initiated by a series of one-time species-population shocks to the ecosystem in concert with period-by-period stochastic shocks to the lake's salinity and nitrogen balances. The primary goal of this exercise is to demonstrate how the model can be used for management purposes, to better understand the specific ways in which water- and land-use changes within the watershed affect population dynamics and species interactions within the GSL ecosystem. The model also provides a rudimentary example of how international trade can be incorporated into the overall modeling framework.

The next section describes the GSL ecosystem and presents the simple ecology underlying the GEEM submodel. Here, we discuss not only the basic food web within which the various species interact but also the constrained optimization problems solved by each species on an individual basis. Section 3 describes the CGE regional economy submodel and the mechanisms through which humans impact the GSL. In this section, we portray the household- and industry-level optimization problems that motivate these impacts. Section 4 presents results from a simple dynamic simulation of the joint GEEM–CGE bioeconomic model in which the various species encounter alternate 10% positive and negative one-time population shocks. Lake salinity and nitrogen balances are assumed to encounter periodic random shocks drawn from a normal distribution. Section 5 concludes with a summary of our findings and a discussion of future research avenues. The specific parameter values and functional forms used to calibrate our bioeconomic model to the steady-state equilibrium are provided in a Technical Appendix.

2. *The Great Salt Lake ecosystem*

Figure 1 displays a map of the GSL. The ecosystem is estimated to be 3,011 square miles in area, approximately half of which is encompassed by the lake's meander line, whereas the land area that actually contributes water to the lake (i.e., its watershed) is an estimated 22,000 square miles (Adler, 1999; Aldrich and Paul, 2002). In size, therefore, the GSL is the largest saline and terminal lake in North America and the fourth largest in the world (Arnow and Stephens, 1990; Adler, 1999). The lake is located within five Utah counties, and three-quarters of the state's wetlands are located along its shores (Adler, 1999). More than 50% of the state's

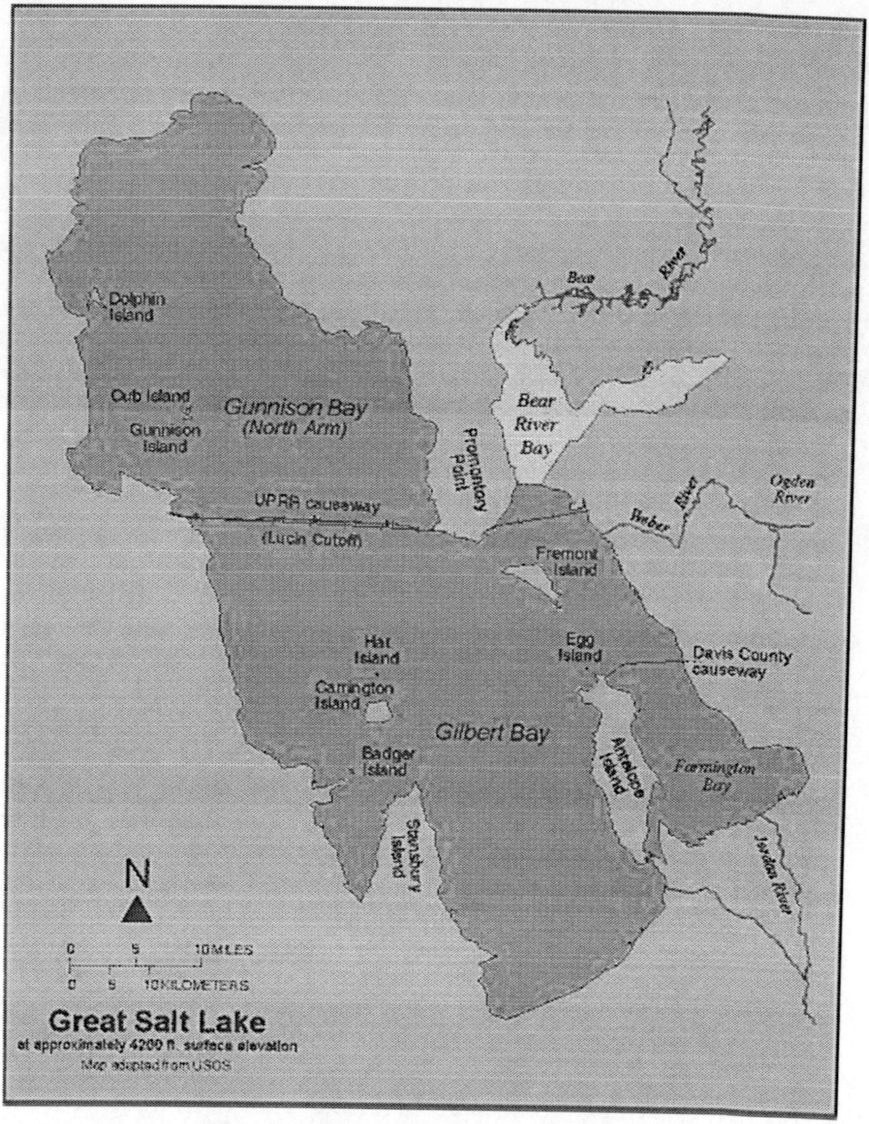

Fig. 1. Map of the Great Salt Lake.

1.8 million people live within 20 miles of its meander line and adjacent wetlands (DNR, 2000).

Approximately 66% of total inflow to the lake is in the form of surface water; the three largest sources being the Bear, Weber, and Jordan Rivers. These rivers flow into the southern arm of the lake (primarily Gilbert Bay), but incoming freshwater is prevented from mixing with the lake's northern arm (Gunnison Bay) due to a massive east–west railroad causeway constructed in 1902. As a result, only the southern arm maintains a salinity balance conducive to brine shrimp (the focal species) reproduction. Along with mineral extraction (primarily salt and magnesium), wildlife viewing, and waterfowl hunting, the brine shrimp industry accounts for a predominant share of the lake's economic value.

There is an extensive literature on the GSL's unique biology and limnology. Aside from gleaning what statistics are available from this literature for model-calibration purposes, three universally acknowledged characteristics of the GSL have guided the formulation of our bioeconomic model. First, while the diversity of species in the lake itself is considered quite low, its biological productivity is extremely high. In other words, the GSL's food web is simple and capable of supporting dense species populations. Second, the reproductive capability of the brine shrimp is highly sensitive to the lake's salinity and nitrogen balances. These balances are in turn sensitive to anthropogenic activity within the lake's boundaries itself (e.g., through mineral extraction) as well as within the watershed (e.g., through agricultural production and urbanization). Thus, the brine shrimp population contends not only with these indirect impacts but also with the direct impacts of commercial harvesting and predation by waterfowl and shorebirds. Third, the GSL ecosystem is considered a critical waterfowl flyway system, reflected by its designation as one of 19 habitat sites in the Western Shorebird Reserve Network (Adler, 1999). An estimated 5 to 10 million waterfowl and shorebirds (representing 257 different species) annually utilize the ecosystem's resources for migration and nesting purposes. As a result, wildlife viewing is emerging as one of the GSL's most lucrative industries.

Figure 2 presents a schematic of the ecosystem's basic food web, based primarily on a synthesis of Gliwicz, *et al.* (1995), Wurtsbaugh (1995), Belovsky (1996), Belovsky and Mellison (1997 and 1998), Stephens (1997a,

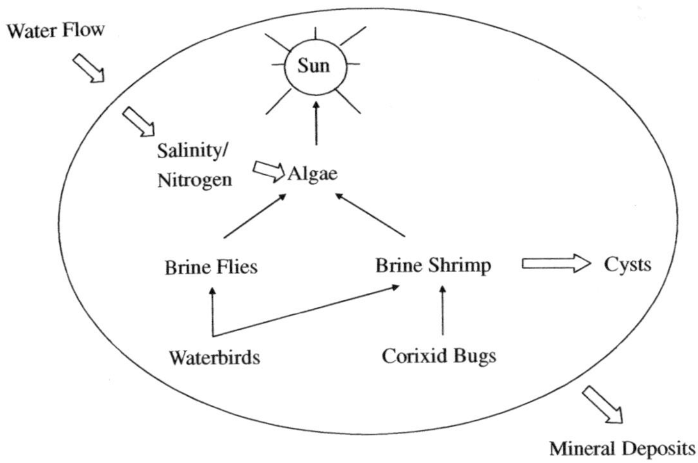

Fig. 2. The Great Salt Lake ecosystem.

1997b, 1999), Belovsky, *et al.* (1999), DNR (2000), and Stephens and Birdsey (2002). As with all ecosystems, the sun is the primary energy source. Green algae (*Dunaliella*) obtain energy (and thus biomass) from the sun and are regulated primarily by the inflow of fresh water and nutrient loadings, which determine the lake's nitrogen and salinity balances. The growth in green algae is believed to be parabolic with respect to salinity level and increasing with respect to the nitrogen balance.

Both brine flies (*Ephydra cinerea*) and brine shrimp (*Artemia fransiscana*) prey on algae and in turn are preyed upon by waterfowl and shorebirds (designated simply as waterbirds). Corixid bugs (*Trichocorixa verticalis*) also prey on the brine shrimp. Most importantly from an economic standpoint, the brine shrimp produce hard-cased eggs, or cysts, that overwinter to produce the next generation of shrimp. Cysts are harvested in the fall (under relatively strict governmental regulation) and sold primarily as high-grade prawn feed to large-scale operations in Southeast Asia and Latin America (Isaacson *et al.*, 2002). Estimated market value of the GSL cysts averaged approximately \$30 million from 1992 to 1997 and has fluctuated between \$75 million and \$150 million since then (Isaacson *et al.*, 2002; *The Salt Lake Tribune*, 2003).

The GSL is similarly rich in mineral deposits, particularly salt and magnesium chloride. Approximately 3 million tons of mineral products are extracted from the lake annually by six companies, averaging roughly \$220 to \$300 million in aggregate market value (Adler, 1999; DNR, 2000; Isaacson *et al.*, 2002). Mineral production at its current level results in 95,000–180,000 acre feet of water diverted per year, although if used to their fullest extent, perfected water rights would allow approximately 360,000 acre feet diverted per year (DNR, 2000).

As in FT, our analysis of the GSL ecosystem occurs at the micro level – individual organism behavior drives ecosystem behavior. The analysis exploits three themes fundamental to economics – rational behavior, efficiency, and equilibrium. Simultaneous solutions for equilibrium "energy prices" and biomass quantities evolve in "energy markets" as a result of the predator–prey interactions between representative "demanders" for and "suppliers" of biomass. Representative organisms are assumed to maximize their energy flow subject to limiting resources, respiration requirements, predator–prey relationships, etc. Maximization yields the organism biomass demands for and supplies to other organisms in the food web. In a general equilibrium, demands and supplies are equal at the species' level. In an economic system, long-run general equilibrium is obtained through entry and exit of firms as they respond to changes in profits. Analogously, long-run general equilibrium is obtained in the ecosystem when species populations are adjusted upward (downward) in response to positive (negative) surplus net energies at the species level. To facilitate our discussion of the GSL food web, we assign numbers to each species included in Figure 2 (including the sun) according to Table 1.

Table 1. Species identification

Species number	Species name
0	Sun
1	Algae
2	Brine shrimp
3	Cysts
4	Brine flies
5	Waterbirds
6	Corixids

As mentioned earlier, each representative organism of a given species i ($i = 1,\ldots,6$, $i \neq 3$) is a net energy maximizer, where net energy is defined as the difference between energy inflows and outflows. Consider, for example, an adult brine shrimp's net energy maximization problem,

$$\max_{\{x_{21}\}} R_2 = (e_1 - e_{21})x_{21} - e_2[(1 + t_{25}e_{52})y_{25}(x_{21}) + (1 + t_{26}e_{62})y_{26}(x_{21})] - f_2(x_{21}) - \beta_2 \quad (1)$$

where R_2 is a brine shrimp's net energy measured in power units (e.g., watts or kilocalories) per unit of time, constant e_i is the energy embodied in a unit of species i's biomass (kilocalories/kilogram), and variable e_{ji} is the energy (kilocalories/kilogram) that a member of species j must expend to locate, capture, and handle a unit of species i's biomass (i.e., it is the given energy price species j "pays" for preying on a unit of species i's biomass, $j > i$). For example, e_{21} is the energy a shrimp expends in preying on a unit of algae, e_{52} is the energy a waterbird expends in preying on a biomass unit of shrimp, etc. Within the ecosystem energy prices are endogenous, determined by demand and supply interactions explained below.

Variable x_{21} is the biomass (in kilograms/time) transferred to, or demanded by, a shrimp from algae and variable y_{ij} is the biomass transferred from, or supplied by, a member of species i to the population of species j. For example, y_{25} is the biomass supplied by a shrimp to the waterbird population and y_{26} is the biomass supplied by a shrimp to corixid bugs. Note that y_{25} and y_{26} are strictly increasing, concave functions of x_{21}, implying that as a brine shrimp demands more algae biomass, it in turn supplies more of its biomass to its predators.

Variable f_2 represents the respiratory energy expended by a shrimp in reproduction, defecation, defense of territory, etc. Since f_2 depends on energy intake, it too is a strictly increasing, concave function of x_{21}. On the contrary, β_2 is a shrimp's constant rate of basal metabolism, which is independent of energy intake. Finally, constant t_{ij} is a "tax rate" on each member of species i to account for the energy it expends to avoid being captured by members of species j, for example, t_{25} is a shrimp's tax rate for avoiding waterbirds and t_{26} is its tax rate for avoiding corixid bugs.

In the case of brine shrimp, this energy disbursement would be due to schooling effort, etc. Note that the total tax paid by a member of species i is assumed to increase in the effort expended by members of species j to capture it. For example, as waterbirds expend more effort to capture a given supply of shrimp the per-unit energy price of shrimp (e_{52}) increases, thus increasing the tax paid by any given shrimp (in terms of a greater amount of energy that the shrimp expends avoiding capture).

To summarize Equation (1), the first term $[(e_1-e_{21})x_{21}]$ represents a shrimp's energy intake, whereas the sum of the last three terms $\{e_1[(1+t_{25}e_{52})y_{25}(x_{21})+(1+t_{26}e_{62})y_{26}(x_{21})],\ f_2(x_{21}),$ and $\beta_2\}$ represent energy outflow. The R functions for each representative species are similarly described in Table 2. Note that for algae we assume the salinity and nitrogen balances (represented by the cumulative variable S_a and measured as a deviation from the steady-state level) directly affects variable respiration f_1. This seems to reflect general findings in Wurtsbaugh and Berry (1990), Rushforth and Felix (1982), Stephens and Gillespie (1976), and Van Auken and McNulty (1973).

In solving its net energy maximization problem (as in Equation (1)), each organism sets the marginal energy received from preying on a lower species equal to the sum of (a) the marginal energy lost from being preyed upon by a higher species and (b) marginal respiration. The resulting first-order conditions can be solved for the vector of six equilibrium demands $\mathbf{x_{ji}}$, where each x_{ji} is a function of *inter alia* the entire vector of energy prices $\mathbf{e_{ji}}$. These demand expressions may then be substituted into their corresponding y_{ij} supply functions to obtain a vector of traditional supplies as functions of $\mathbf{e_{ji}}$.

Table 2. Species' net energy functions

Species number	Net energies (R_i)
1	$R_1=(e_0-e_{10})x_{10}-e_1[(1+t_{12}e_{21})y_{12}x_{10}+(1+t_{14}e_{41})y_{14}x_{10}]-f_1(x_{10},S_a)-\beta_1$
2	$R_2=(e_1-e_{21})x_{21}-e_2[(1+t_{25}e_{52})y_{25}x_{21}+(1+t_{26}e_{62})y_{26}x_{21}]$ $-f_2(x_{21})-\beta_2$
3	N/A[a]
4	$R_4=(e_1-e_{41})x_{41}-e_4(1+t_{45}e_{54})y_{45}x_{41}-f_4(x_{41})-\beta_4$
5	$R_5=(e_2-e_{52})x_{52}+(e_4-e_{54})x_{54}-f_5(x_{52},x_{54})-\beta_5$
6	$R_5=(e_2-e_{62})x_{62}-f_6(x_{62})-\beta_6$

[a]Because brine shrimp cysts are in egg form, they are assumed completely constrained in net energy production.

A short-run equilibrium (within a reproductive period) emerges satisfying two properties. First, aggregate demand and supply are equated in each of six biomass markets (i.e., between each predator–prey pair), resulting in species biomass levels that are consistent with their corresponding market-clearing energy prices. For example, in the brine shrimp-algae biomass market the market-equilibrium condition is expressed as $N_{2}x_{21} = N_{1}y_{12}$, where N_1 and N_2 represent algae and brine shrimp population levels, respectively. In this case, $N_{2}x_{21}$ represents brine shrimp aggregate demand for algae biomass and $N_{1}y_{12}$ represents algae aggregate supply of biomass to brine shrimp. The resulting algae biomass level consumed by brine shrimp is consistent with the equilibrium energy price e_{21}. Second, each species population is constant. A representative organism and its species may have nonzero net energy at its maximum; however, a nonzero net energy leads to population changes in the long run (across reproductive periods). Positive (negative) net energy implies greater (lesser) fitness, thus inducing a population increase (decrease). Populations adjust toward a long-run equilibrium in which all individuals have zero net energy, and the short-run equilibrium conditions hold (analogous to a competitive economy where the number of firms in an industry changes in accordance with positive or negative profits).

The bioeconomic model ultimately captures this population adjustment through an equation relating next period's population to this period's population of species i. To begin, consider how population changes for a top predator such as waterbirds. In the steady state, it must be the case that births equal deaths. If s_5 is the lifespan of a representative waterbird, then the total number of waterbird births and deaths must be N_5/s_5, with per-capita steady-state birth and death rates of $1/s_5$. Letting the representative waterbird's maximized net energy be given by $R_5(x_{52}, x_{54}; \mathbf{N^t}) = R_5^*$, where (a) x_{52} and x_{54} are optimum biomass demands as functions of equilibrium energy prices e_{52} and e_{54} and (b) $\mathbf{N^t}$ is a vector of all species' populations, it must be the case that $R_5^* = 0$ in the steady state.

Reproduction requires energy, which is subsumed in the functional form of f_5. Let v_5^{ss} be a waterbird's steady-state variable respiration and $\rho_5 v_5^{ss}$ be the proportion of this variable respiration devoted to reproduction. Thus, in a steady state, the energy given by $\rho_5 v_5^{ss}$ over all members of the waterbird species yields the number of births that exactly offset deaths, that is, Births = Deaths $\Rightarrow N_5^t(\rho_5 v_5^{ss}) = N_5^t/s_5$, where $\rho_5 = 1/(v_5^{ss} s_5)$ converts reproductive energy into individuals. If the waterbird species is not in the steady state, then $R_5^* \neq 0$ and an individual's variable respiration is v_5. Assuming that the proportion of R_5^* available for reproduction is the same as that from v_5, the total energy now available for reproduction is $\rho_5(R_5^* + v_5)$. Further assuming that reproduction is linear in available energy, it follows from $N_5^t(\rho_5 v_5^{ss}) = N_5^t/s_5$ that $\rho_5(R_5^* + v_5)$ yields a per-capita birth rate of $(R_5^* + v_5)/(s_5 v_5^{ss})$. Finally, assuming that the death rate is independent of energy available for reproduction, the waterbird population adjustment equation may be written as,

$$N_5^{t+1} = N_5^t + \frac{N_5^t}{s_5}\left(\frac{R_5^* + v_5}{v_5^{ss}} - 1\right). \tag{2}$$

Note that (2) reduces to $N_5^{t+1} = N_5^t$ in the steady state and that $R_5^* > (<)0$ is sufficient for the waterbird population to increase (decrease), that is, $N_5^{t+1} > (<) N_5^t$, when $v_5 > (<) v_5^{ss}$. Furthermore, because biomass demands depend on the period-t populations of each species, the population adjustment for species i indirectly depends on the populations of all other species.

If the species is not a top predator and is prey for another species, then in the steady state, births equal the sum of deaths and individuals lost to predation. Using brine flies as an example, recall that each individual fly loses $y_{45}(x_{41})$ in biomass per period to waterbirds. The summation of all individual losses to predation yields total brine-fly biomass lost to predation, and total biomass divided by an individual brine fly's weight, w_4, in turn yields the number of individuals lost to predation, that is, $N_4^t y_{45}(x_{41})/w_4$. Therefore, the steady-state number of births (from respiration energy) equals the sum of deaths from predation and natural mortality net of losses to predation, that is, $N_4^t \rho_4 v_4^{ss} = N_4^t[(y_{45}x_{41}^{ss}/w_4)(1 - 1/s_4) + 1/s_4]$, resulting in $\rho_4 = \{[(y_{45}x_{41}^{ss}/w_4)(1 - 1/s_4) + 1/s_4]\}/v_4^{ss}$. Again, assuming that equal proportions of R_4^* and f_4 are available for reproduction, the non-steady-state population-update equation for brine flies becomes,

$$N_4^{t+1} = N_4^t\left(1 + \left\{\frac{[(y_{45}x_{41}/w_4)(1 - 1/s_4) + 1/s_4]}{v_4^{ss}}\right\}(R_4^* + v_4),\right.$$
$$\left. - \left[\left(\frac{y_{45}x_{41}}{w_4}\right)\left(1 - \frac{1}{s_4}\right) + \frac{1}{s_4}\right]\right) \tag{3}$$

where in the steady state (3) reduces to $N_4^{t+1} = N_4^t$. The population-updating equations for each representative species are provided in Table 3.

The brine shrimp and cyst population-updating equations require further discussion. The cyst population in period $t+1$, that is, N_3^{t+1}, equals period-t brine shrimp births (the first term in the cyst's population-updating equation) net of the period-t cyst harvest, H_3^t (discussed further in Section 3). This updating equation abstracts from two facets of brine shrimp and cyst population dynamics. First, two to three generations of brine shrimp are typically reproduced by ovoviviparity in a single season (from spring to mid-summer) before the reproduction of a single generation of cysts by oviparity at the end of the season (late summer to late fall). We have avoided modeling the process of ovoviviparity reproduction, as this would unnecessarily complicate the model. Second, a fraction of unharvested cysts do not survive the winter to hatch into next

Table 3. Species' population-updating equations

Species number	Population-updating equations
1	$N_1^{t+1} = N_1^t\left(1+\left\{\frac{[(y_{12}x_{10}^{ss}/w_1)(1-1/s_1)+1/s_1]}{v_1^{ss}}\right\}(R_1^*+v_1) - \left[\left(\frac{y_{14}x_{10}}{w_1}\right)\left(1-\frac{1}{s_1}\right)+\frac{1}{s_1}\right]\right)$
2	$N_2^{t+1} = N_2^{ss} + N_3^{t+1}$
3	$N_3^{t+1} = N_2^t\left\{\frac{[[(y_{25}x_{52}^{ss}+y_{25}x_{52}^{ss})/w_2](1-1/s_2)+1/s_2]}{v_2^{ss}}\right\}(R_2^*+v_2) - H_3^t$
4	$N_4^{t+1} = N_4^t\left(1+\left\{\frac{[(y_{45}x_{41}^{ss}/w_4)(1-1/s_4)+1/s_4]}{v_4^{ss}}\right\}(R_4^*+v_4) - \left[\left(\frac{y_{45}x_{41}}{w_4}\right)\left(\frac{1-1}{s_4}\right)+\frac{1}{s_4}\right]\right)$
5	$N_5^{t+1} = N_5^t + \frac{N_5^t}{s_5}\left(\frac{R_5^*+v_5}{v_5^{ss}}-1\right)$
6	$N_6^{t+1} = N_6^t + \frac{N_6^t}{s_6}\left(\frac{R_6^*+v_6}{v_6^{ss}}-1\right)$

season's first generation of brine shrimp due *inter alia* to being washed up on shore and desiccating. However, scant empirical information about the overwintering process is presently available, thus precluding us from explicitly accounting for overwintering survivability in our cyst population-updating equation. With respect to the brine shrimp population-updating equation, we assume that period $t+1$'s population, that is, N_2^{t+1}, is the sum of N_3^{t+1} and the brine shrimp steady-state population, N_2^{ss}. This is an "accounting convention" that maintains a consistency between our estimate of the steady-state population and subsequent populations that arise in future periods through model simulation.

3. *The GSL regional and international economies*

Our CGE model of the GSL regional and international economies closely follows the approach laid out in FT. The FT approach is "myopically dynamic" in that it consists of a sequence of static optimizations resulting in a dynamic equilibrium where the sequences are linked through the evolution of factor stocks and household saving. Households are intertemporal utility maximizers making savings decisions (for the purpose of future consumption) based on myopic expectations about future prices. Current consumption is over regionally produced goods and imports of a composite good (discussed later), given prices. The savings process consists of households instantaneously purchasing investment goods with their savings to augment their capital endowments for future periods. Balanced growth is assumed to occur when the capital stock and labor force grow at the same rate. Finally, incomes are endogenously derived from (a) the sale/rental to firms of the household's (homogeneous and perfectly mobile) labor, land, and capital endowments (the latter being partially determined by savings) and (b) government revenue obtained through the sale of water rights to the mineral extraction and agricultural industries and certificates of registration (CORs) to the brine shrimp industry (discussed later). The resulting household product demands and factor supplies satisfy the neoclassical tenants of nonnegativity, continuity, and dependence solely on relative prices.

Production in the regional economy occurs at a high level of aggregation in five (single-product) production sectors: the brine shrimp fishery, recreation/wildlife viewing, a composite good, and the mineral extraction and agricultural sectors. Individual firms, for simplicity aggregated at the industry level, are myopic, static profit maximizers operating under constant returns-to-scale technology and given prices. They purchase labor and capital from households to produce differentiated output that is allocated between domestic and export markets given endogenous domestic and export prices and Armington (1969) imperfect substitution possibilities between the two markets. In addition to labor and capital, agricultural and mineral extraction firms purchase water allocations determined by the DNR, agricultural firms also purchase land from households, and cyst-harvesting firms purchase CORs (i.e., quotas) from the DNR. Although each sector engages in production for both domestic and export markets, only the composite good sector is assumed to compete with an imperfectly substitutable import, which is resold to the households. Similar to the households, firms' factor demands and output supplies satisfy the neoclassical tenants of equality between output prices and unit costs and between given factor prices and marginal value products.

The economic system is in general equilibrium when all individuals of all sectors optimize, there exists a set of prices and output levels consistent with zero profits for all firms, and all markets clear. Given the set of market-clearing prices, consumer expenditure exhausts current disposable income to maintain Walras Law, and trade balances in the current account. The final requirement of the static single-period economic model is that it replicates an assumed equilibrium benchmark dataset through model parameterization known as calibration. When the parameterized model is run with the benchmark dataset, a general equilibrium for the economy is obtained. The benchmark dataset is presented in the Technical Appendix.

3.1. The brine shrimp fishery

The brine shrimp fishery is modeled as a single, vertically integrated industry, assumed to encapsulate cyst harvesting, processing, and marketing. As the fishery is heavily regulated by the DNR, we derive a "regulated open-access equilibrium" following FT. The regulatory instrument is total allowable catch (TAC). Given its TAC, the fishery makes a three-tiered decision each period concerning (a) the amounts of labor, L_f, and capital, K_f, to demand from the household sector to harvest cysts at level Q_f, (b) the proportion of Q_f that is exported (e.g., to fisheries markets located in south Asia), and (c) the amount of investment (I_f) to "supply" to the domestic household sector. We assume a Cobb–Douglas production function for Q_f according to

$$Q_f = d_f L_f^{a_f} K_f^{b_f} N_3^{c_f} \tag{4}$$

where parameters a_f, b_f, and c_f are each less than 1 and $a_f + b_f + c_f = 1$, d_f is a Hicks-neutral technology parameter, and N_3 is the cyst population as defined earlier. Given economy-wide wage (w) and rental (r) rates, the cost-minimizing ratio of L_f and K_f is therefore obtained from

$$\frac{w}{r} = \frac{a_f K_f}{b_f L_f}. \tag{5}$$

The fishery also abides by the following conditions:

$$Q_f = \mathrm{TAC}(N_3) = q_f^d(p_f^d, p_f^e) + q_f^e(p_f^d, p_f^e) \tag{6a}$$

$$I_f = a_f^I Q_f \tag{6b}$$

$$P_f Q_f = wL_f + rK_f + \mathrm{COR} \tag{6c}$$

where a_f^I is a (given) proportionality factor equal to the ratio of the steady-state levels of I_f and domestic quantity of cysts supplied (q_f^d), q_f^e is quantity of cysts exported, p_f^d and p_f^e are the respective per-unit prices of q_f^d and q_f^e, P_f is the composite price of p_f^d and p_f^e, and COR is the fixed certificate-of-registration cost. Equation (6a) states that the cyst harvest (a) equals the TAC for each period, which is ultimately a function of the cyst population in that period, and (b) is divided between the domestic and export markets. This division of Q_f between q_f^d and q_f^e is determined by a (constrained) revenue maximization problem based on the Armington (1969) assumption of imperfect substitutability, which, similar to (5), defines the optimal ratio of q_f^d and q_f^e as a ratio of p_f^d and p_f^e. Equation (6b) states that the effective proportion of the industry "supplied" to households in the form of investment (which in turn adds to the value of the household sector's capital endowment) is a constant proportion of Q_f, and (6c) is a zero-profit condition.

3.2. The mineral extraction sector

Similar to the brine shrimp fishery, we assume a Cobb–Douglas production function for the total quantity of minerals extracted, Q_m, according to

$$Q_m = d_m L_m^{a_m} K_m^{b_m} W_m^{c_m}, \tag{7}$$

where parameters a_m, b_m, c_m, and d_m and variables L_m and K_m are defined analogously to the brine shrimp fishery's, the optimal ratio of L_m and K_m is determined analogously to (5), and W_m is a fixed water allocation determined by the DNR. The mineral extraction sector likewise abides by equations analogous to (6a)–(6c), obviously without a regulatory limit such as the TAC in (6a) and with $P_W W_m$ replacing COR in (6c), where the per-unit price of water P_W is set equal to zero.

3.3. The agricultural sector

Similar to the mineral extraction sector, we assume a Cobb–Douglas production function for the total quantity of agricultural goods produced, Q_a, according to

$$Q_a = d_a L_a^{a_a} K_a^{b_a} W_a^{c_a} T_a^{g_a}, \tag{8}$$

where parameters a_a, b_a, c_a, and d_a and variables L_a, K_a, and W_a are defined analogously to the mineral extraction industry's. The variable T_a is the amount of land devoted to agricultural production, with parameter $g_a > 0$ such that $a_a + b_a + c_a + g_a = 1$. Because T_a is effectively a choice variable of the industry, the optimal ratios of L_a, K_a, and T_a require the simultaneous solution of two conditions – one analogous to (5) and the other

$$\frac{P_T}{r} = \frac{g_a K_a}{b_a T_a} \tag{9}$$

where P_T is the per-unit price of land.

The agricultural sector likewise abides by equations analogous to (6a)–(6c), again without a regulatory limit such as TAC in (6a) and with $P_W W_a$ replacing COR in (6c), where again the per-unit price of water P_W is set equal to zero. Also, the total cost of land, that is, $P_T T_a$, is included on the right-hand side of analogous (6c).

3.4. The recreation/wildlife-viewing sector

Similar to the previous sectors, we assume a Cobb–Douglas production function for the total quantity of recreation and wildlife viewing, Q_R, according to

$$Q_R = d_R L_R^{a_R} K_R^{b_R} N_5^{c_R}, \tag{10}$$

where parameters a_R, b_R, c_R, and d_R and variables L_R and K_R, are defined analogously to the brine shrimp fishery's. An analogous Equation (5) determines the cost-minimizing ratio of L_R and K_R and analogous Equations (6a)–(6c), obviously without a regulatory limit such as TAC in (6a) and without a fixed cost such as COR in (6c), are also satisfied.

3.5. The composite good sector

The composite good sector is modeled slightly differently from the previous sectors, due in part to the role of imports in this sector. Following FT, we assume that importation of the composite good is the residual difference between what domestic households demand overall and what is produced by the domestic composite good sector. Thus, the domestic composite good sector effectively imports the foreign-produced composite good for resale to households at zero cost and mark-up. Similar to the other sectors, the composite good sector abides by conditions analogous to (6a) for determining the proportions of domestic production allocated to the domestic and export markets, (6b) for determining the proportion of domestic production supplied to households in the form of investment, and (6c) for zero profits.

We assume a constant-elasticity-of-substitution (CES) cost function to ultimately determine the total quantity of the domestically produced composite good, Q_C, according to

$$\mathrm{TC}_c = \frac{Q_C}{\phi_C}\left[\delta_C w^{1-\sigma_C} + (1-\delta_C) r^{1-\sigma_C}\right]^{1/(1-\sigma_C)} \tag{11}$$

where TC_C is total cost of production, ϕ_C is an efficiency parameter, $0<\delta_C<1$ is a distribution parameter, and σ_C is the partial elasticity of substitution. Application of Shepard's Lemma to (11) results in the sector factor demand functions for labor (L_C) and capital (K_C), respectively,

$$L_C = \left(\frac{Q_C}{\phi_C}\right)^{1-\sigma_C}\left[\mathrm{TC}_C\left(\frac{\delta_C}{w}\right)\right]^{\sigma_C} \tag{12a}$$

$$K_C = \left(\frac{Q_C}{\phi_C}\right)^{1-\sigma_C}\left[\mathrm{TC}_C\left(\frac{1-\delta_C}{r}\right)\right]^{\sigma_C}. \tag{12b}$$

Rather than derive Q_C from the (dual) production function associated with (11), we obtain its value directly from the household sector's utility-maximization problem, to which we now turn.

3.6. The household sector

The household sector consumes goods from the five producing sectors and saves for future consumption. Following FT, the sector derives gross income (Y) from the sale/rental of its current labor and capital endowment (described further in Section 3.7). Given Y, household behavior is modeled according to a tri-level nesting structure. In the top nest, an allocation is made between aggregate consumption today (C_T) and composite future consumption (C_F) given composite prices P_{C_T} and P_{C_F}, respectively. In terms of household inter-temporal behavior, C_F is funded through the stock of household savings (S), costing, or valued at, P_S per unit. Savings decisions are based on expected increments to a stream of consumption in future periods (e.g., C_1, C_2, …), with C_F being a composite measure. Consumer expectations of future consumption are assumed to be myopic, in that current prices,P_{C_T}, are expected to remain constant in all future periods, that is, from the household's standpoint $P_{C_T} = P_{C_F}$ in each period. $P_S S$ is used to purchase investment goods I [e.g., I_f in (6b) from the brine shrimp fishery], which add to the stock of household capital to be used for future consumption.

The transformation of household savings into capital services is governed by the identity $P_S S = r\gamma S$, where γ is the initial real rate of return associated with the benchmark value of r (i.e., the proportion of savings translated into capital services in future periods). Household income derived from capital services (i.e., $r\gamma S$) in turn allows future consumption according to the identity $P_{C_T} C_F = r\gamma S$. Manipulation of this expression equates the value of savings to the present value of expected future consumption, that is,

$$P_S S = \frac{P_S P_{C_T}}{r\gamma} C_F. \tag{13}$$

Therefore, the household's top-nest utility-maximization problem in any given period is

$$\max_{\{C_T, C_F, S\}} U_{\text{TN}} = \left[\alpha_{\text{TN}}^{1/\sigma_{\text{TN}}} C_T^{(\sigma_{\text{TN}}-1)/\sigma_{\text{TN}}} + (1-\alpha_{\text{TN}})^{1/\sigma_{\text{TN}}} C_F^{(\sigma_{\text{TN}}-1)/\sigma_{\text{TN}}}\right]^{\sigma_{\text{TN}}/(\sigma_{\text{TN}}-1)} \tag{14}$$

subject to

$$Y = P_{C_T} C_T + \frac{P_S P_{C_T}}{r\gamma} C_F \tag{15a}$$

$$P_{C_T} = \left[(1 - \beta_{\mathrm{TN}})\bar{P}^{1-\upsilon_{\mathrm{TN}}} + \beta_{\mathrm{TN}} P_R^{1-\upsilon_{\mathrm{TN}}}\right]^{1/(1-\upsilon_{\mathrm{TN}})} \tag{15b}$$

where $0 < \alpha_{\mathrm{TN}} < 1$ and $0 < \beta_{\mathrm{TN}} < 1$ are distribution parameters; σ_{TN} and ν_{TN} are partial elasticities of substitution; $\bar{P}$ is a per-unit composite price of the mineral extraction, agricultural, and composite goods; and P_R is the per-unit price of the recreation/wildlife-viewing good. Equation (14) indicates that utility in the top nest is determined by a CES function defined over current and future composite consumption. Equation (15a) is the household budget constraint and (15b) indicates that P_{C_T} is a CES weighted average of (a) a composite price of the mineral extraction, agricultural, and composite goods and (b) the price of the recreation/wildlife-viewing good.

From this problem, the first-order optimality condition is obtained for the stock of household savings

$$S = \frac{(1 - \alpha_{\mathrm{TN}})Y}{P_S^{\sigma_{\mathrm{TN}}}(P_{C_T}/r\gamma)^{\sigma_{\mathrm{TN}}-1}\left[\alpha_{\mathrm{TN}} P_{C_T}^{1-\sigma_{\mathrm{TN}}} + (1 - \alpha_{\mathrm{TN}})(P_S P_{C_T}/r\gamma)^{1-\sigma_{\mathrm{TN}}}\right]}. \tag{16}$$

In the second nest, income for current consumption (C_T) is divided between expenditures on recreation (X_R) at price P_R and the composite consumption commodity ($\bar{X}$) that encompasses the mineral extraction, agricultural, and composite goods at price $\bar{P}$. Similar to its top nest problem, the household sector's second-nest utility-maximization problem is

$$\max_{\{X_R, \bar{X}\}} U_{\mathrm{SN}} = \left[\alpha_{\mathrm{SN}}^{1/\sigma_{\mathrm{SN}}} X_R^{(\sigma_{\mathrm{SN}}-1)/\sigma_{\mathrm{SN}}} + (1 - \alpha_{\mathrm{SN}})^{1/\sigma_{\mathrm{SN}}} \bar{X}^{(\sigma_{\mathrm{SN}}-1)/\sigma_{\mathrm{SN}}}\right]^{\sigma_{\mathrm{SN}}/(\sigma_{\mathrm{SN}}-1)} \tag{17}$$

subject to

$$Y - P_s S = \bar{P}\bar{X} + P_R X_R \tag{18}$$

where $0 < \alpha_{\mathrm{SN}} < 1$ is a distribution parameter and σ_{SN} is a partial elasticity of substitution. The respective first-order optimality conditions for the recreation/wildlife-viewing and composite consumption commodities are

$$X_R = \frac{\alpha_{\mathrm{SN}}(Y - P_S S)}{P_R^{\sigma_{\mathrm{SN}}}[\alpha_{\mathrm{SN}} P_R^{1-\sigma_{\mathrm{SN}}} + (1 - \alpha_{\mathrm{SN}})\bar{P}^{1-\sigma_{\mathrm{SN}}}]} \tag{19a}$$

$$\bar{X} = \frac{(1 - \alpha_{\mathrm{SN}})(Y - P_S S)}{\bar{P}^{\sigma_{\mathrm{SN}}}[\alpha_{\mathrm{SN}} P_R^{1-\sigma_{\mathrm{SN}}} + (1 - \alpha_{\mathrm{SN}})\bar{P}^{1-\sigma_{\mathrm{SN}}}]}. \tag{19b}$$

Finally, in the third nest, income is divided between expenditures on the mineral extraction (X_m), agricultural (X_a), and composite (X_c) goods at prices P_m, P_a, and P_c, respectively. Following Ballard *et al.* (1985), the household sector's third-nest subutility-maximization problem is

$$\max_{\{X_m,X_a,X_c\}} \bar{X} = X_m^{\lambda_m} X_a^{\lambda_a} X_c^{\lambda_c} \tag{20}$$

subject to

$$Y - P_S S - P_R X_R = P_m X_m + P_a X_a + P_c X_c \tag{21}$$

where λ_i, $i = m$, a, c are the Cobb–Douglas expenditure shares. The respective first-order optimality conditions for this problem are

$$X_i = \frac{\lambda_i (Y - P_S S - P_R X_R)}{P_i}, \quad i = m, a, c. \tag{22}$$

Combining Equations (20)–(22) results in the following definition of $\bar{P}$,

$$\bar{P} = \prod_i \left(\frac{p_i}{\lambda_i}\right)^{\lambda_i}, \quad i = m, a, c. \tag{23}$$

As Ballard *et al.* (1985) point out, an especially convenient property of this kind of Cobb–Douglas price index is that the composite price can be calculated without knowing X_i, $i = m$, a, c, thus simplifying our calculations considerably.

3.7. The market-clearing and endowment-updating equations

We begin this section by defining the composite price indices for each of the production sectors, reflecting the fact that the indices are weighted averages of domestic and foreign prices. In the composite good sector, the domestic price faced by households (P_c) is

$$P_c = \frac{p_c^d q_c^d + p_c^{\mathrm{IM}} q_c^{\mathrm{IM}}}{q_c^d + q_c^{\mathrm{IM}}} \tag{24}$$

where p_c^d and p_c^{IM} are the domestically determined and exogenous import prices, respectively, and q_c^d and q_c^{IM} are corresponding quantities. As shown in FT, the prices p_c^d and p_c^{IM} are taken by the household sector in a CES cost-minimization problem that determines its optimal mix of the domestically produced and imported composite goods according to

$$\frac{q_c^d}{q_c^{\mathrm{IM}}} = \left[\frac{p_c^{\mathrm{IM}}}{p_c^d}\left(\frac{1-\delta^c}{\delta^c}\right)\right]^{\sigma^c} \tag{25}$$

where δ^c is a distributional share parameter in a CES transformation function and σ^c is an associated elasticity of transformation between domestically produced and imported composite goods.

The domestic prices faced by each production sector (and, except for the composite good, by the household sector) are

$$P_i = \frac{p_i^d q_i^d + p_i^e q_i^e}{Q_i} \quad i = f,\ m,\ a,\ R, \tag{26a}$$

$$P_c' = \frac{(p_c^d q_c^d + p_c^e q_c^e)}{Q_c}. \tag{26b}$$

where, again, $Q_i = q_i^d + q_i^e$, $i = f, m, a, R, c$ and the remaining variables were defined previously in this section. The domestic market-clearing conditions are,

$$q_i^d = I_i + X_i, \quad i = f,\ m,\ a,\ R,\ c, \tag{27}$$

which are used to determine X_i, $i = f, m, a, R, c$.

In terms of the household sector's income balance, the following condition holds by definition

$$Y = w\sum_i L_i + r\sum_i K_i + P_T T_a + P_W \sum_j W_j + \mathrm{COR}, \quad i = f,\ m,\ a,\ R,\ c, \quad j = m,\ a. \tag{28}$$

and with respect to the economy's balance of payments, we have the identity

$$P_S S - \sum_i p_i^d I_i = p_c^{\mathrm{IM}} q_c^{\mathrm{IM}} - \sum_i p_i^e q_i^e, \quad i = f,\ m,\ a,\ R,\ c, \tag{29}$$

where the left-hand side represents the savings-investment balance and the right-hand side represents the current-account balance.

Finally, household endowments of capital, labor, land, and water are updated per period according to the following series of equations

$$\sum_i K_i^{t+1} = \sum_i K_i^t + \gamma S^t, \quad i = f,\ m,\ a,\ R,\ c \tag{30a}$$

$$\sum_i L_i^{t+1} = (1+n)\sum_i L_i^t, \quad i = f,\ m,\ a,\ R,\ c, \tag{30b}$$

$$\sum_j W_j^{t+1} = \sum_j W_j^t, \quad j = m,\ a \tag{30c}$$

$$T_a^{t+1} = T_a^t. \tag{30d}$$

Equation (30a) states that the capital endowment in period $t+1$ equals the capital endowment in period t plus the (real) growth in period t's "stock" of savings, where again γ represents the proportion of savings translated into capital services. Equation (30b) states that the labor endowment in period $t+1$ equals the labor endowment in period t plus the growth in labor at the rate n. Rate $n = \gamma S^{\mathrm{ss}} / \sum_i K_i^{\mathrm{ss}}$, $i = f, m, a, R, c$, that is, the rate at which labor would have to grow in the steady state to ensure that the capital–labor ratio remains constant, where the superscript ss indicates a steady-state level.

4. Simulation results

Our simulation results are based on initial one-time shocks to the species' steady-state population levels. Specifically, we shock the populations of algae, brine flies, and corixid bugs downward by 10% each and simultaneously shock the populations of brine shrimp and waterbirds upward by 10% each. These arbitrary shocks are merely to demonstrate how the bioeconomic model updates these population levels, as well as the remaining ecological and economic variables, over time (for the next 100 periods). In addition to these one-time shocks, recall that the salinity level is also being "hit" with period-by-period random shocks (see the Technical Appendix for further details).

Figures 3 and 4 present the simulation results for the algae and brine cyst populations. Beginning with the algae population note that following the population shocks, algae density [the smooth, dark (variable) line without (with) random salinity shocks] returns rather smoothly to a steady state after approximately 10 periods. This steady state is significantly beneath the predicted steady state without human interventions (lightest line at the top of the diagram). For this exercise, ecological and economic steady states were determined in isolation from one another, although the data used to calibrate the model is drawn from a point in time where the

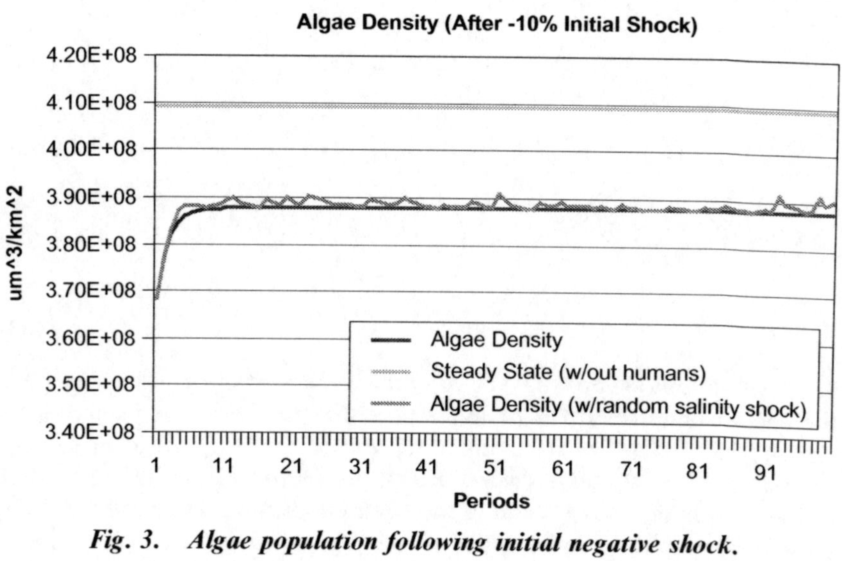

Fig. 3. Algae population following initial negative shock.

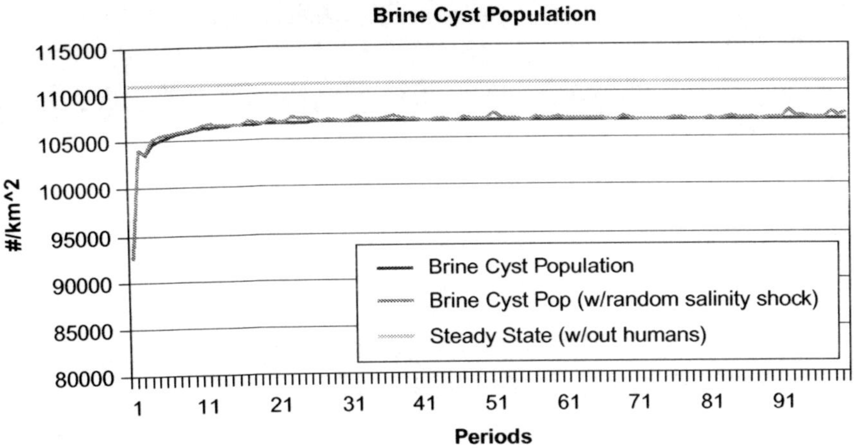

Fig. 4. ***Brine cyst population following initial population shocks.***

two submodels are obviously interacting. Thus, the distance between the steady-state and the simulation lines can also be interpreted as the model's degree of error in calibrating the joint model to an overall steady state. In our future work, where we calibrate the model using more actual data, we expect this error to shrink. In the meantime, the steady state established by the blue/pink line is a better approximation to the actual joint steady state of the GSL and the regional economy.

A similar smooth transition to the steady state for the brine cyst population is depicted in Figure 4. Note, however, that the transition occurs more rapidly, after approximately five years. This result is driven by the fact that as the algae population falls and the brine shrimp population increases, the brine shrimp must compete for a diminished food source that now carries with it an increased energy price. The representative brine shrimp "responds" to this higher energy price by reducing the variable respiration available for reproduction and devoting more energy to searching for algae biomass. As a result, not only does the representative brine shrimp reduce its production of brine cysts, but the brine shrimp population itself shrinks relatively quickly back to its steady-state level. These two reactions lead to a decrease in the brine cyst population, but as the brine shrimp population quickly recovers, so too does the cyst population.

With respect to the path of the regional economy, Figures 5 and 6 present the transition paths for the brine shrimp fishery capital stock and household demand for recreation/wildlife-viewing. In Figure 5, the brine shrimp fishery responds to the initial positive (negative) shock to the brine shrimp (algae) population (which translates into an initial decrease in the cyst population) by decreasing its capital stock. This implies an initial shift of investment out of the brine shrimp industry. However, following the

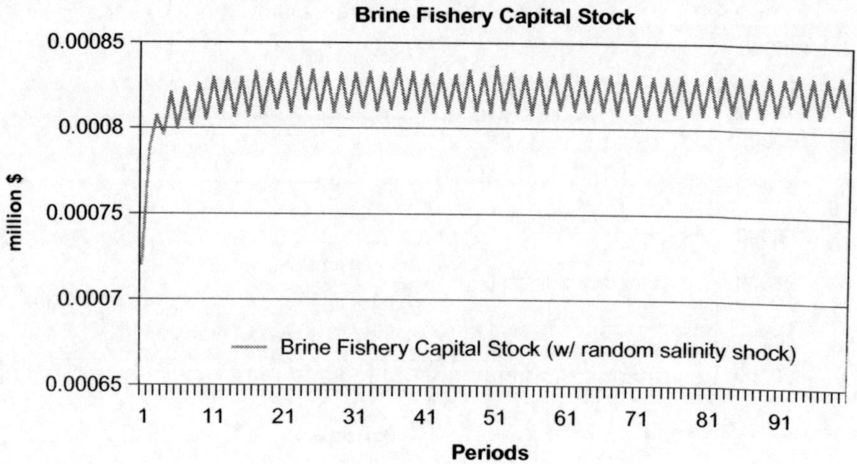

Fig. 5. The brine shrimp fishery capital stock following the initial population shocks.

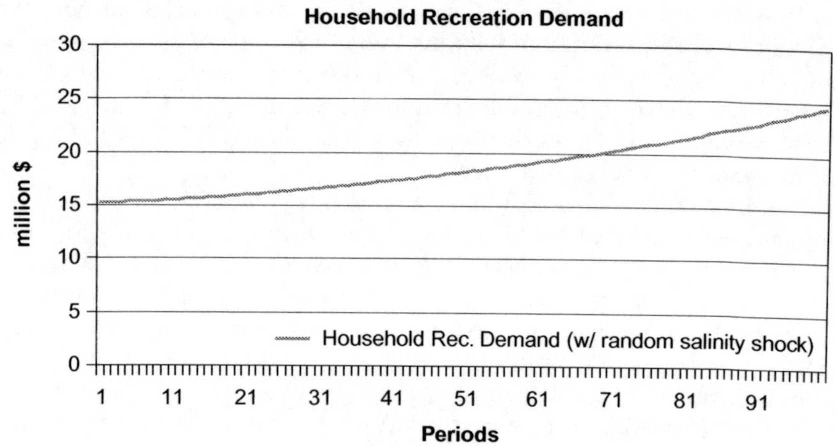

Fig. 6. Household recreation/wildlife-viewing demand following the initial population shocks.

recovery of the cyst population to its steady-state level, the capital stock returns to its steady-state level rather quickly. Also evidenced in Figure 5 is the slight oscillation of the capital stock around its steady-state value over time, which similarly mirrors the slight oscillations evident in the cyst and brine shrimp populations over time as well.

With respect to household demand for recreation/wildlife-viewing, we note that the household sector's demand rises steadily over time from its steady-state value of $16 million per period. Two forces account for this steady increase in demand. First, the initial increase in the waterbird population provides an initial *ceteris paribus* positive shock to the household sector's utility. Given that recreation/wildlife-viewing is a normal good, this provides a *ceteris paribus* boost to household demand. Furthermore, since it is assumed that labor supply increases at a constant rate of return (n), household sector income increases overtime as well. This increase has a multiplier effect on income, since savings increases with income, enabling a higher level of future consumption of all commodities.

5. *Conclusions*

This chapter demonstrates a new technique for modeling the "bioeconomics" of a watershed, in particular the GSL watershed located in north-central Utah. The bioeconomic model accounts for the basic ecological relationships and human activities that interact within the lake's watershed and enables the measurement of ecosystem externalities that might occur as a result of "shocks" within the watershed and ecosystem, thereby identifying the degree to which certain species may be threatened. Since the regional and international economies are premised on a household sector utility-maximization problem, the model is ultimately capable of estimating compensating-variation welfare measures for threatened species that account for the full breadth of interdependencies that exist within the watershed, as well as possible effects on international trade patterns involving the ecosystem's main exportable commodities.

This capability should prove useful to regulatory authorities such as the Utah Department of Natural Resources in helping its scientists and policy makers better understand the interrelationships that exist between human activity and biological interactions within the GSL watershed and how these interrelationships impact the vulnerability of any given species. Of course, to be truly effective in guiding public policies concerning the GSL ecosystem, the bioeconomic model will ultimately need to be linked with models of the watershed's hydrology and regional economy, particularly that of the Wasatch Front. In addition, much of the ecological data that are currently used to calibrate the model's steady state need to be updated. These "needs" form the basis of future research avenues; avenues that will enable regional planners to better forecast the effects of economic growth on the GSL ecosystem and to weigh the benefits and costs associated with various aspects of this growth.

Finally, with respect to better assessing the potential ecosystem and regional-economic impacts of international trade in this type of bioeconomic model, it is important to explicitly account for the role played by different international trade policies. Example trade-policy questions that might be answered through a more advanced version of our bioeconomic model include (1) what are the ecological consequences of trade liberalization, (2) what are the ecological effects of a reduction in agricultural subsidies as a result of on-going trade talks in the World Trade Organization, (3) how might international market structure for the export of key species, such as the Asian market for GSL brine shrimp, influence the ecosystem, and (4) how might commercial policies of the importing countries influence the ecosystem's equilibrium? These are the types of questions that can conceivably be answered in the context of next-generation bioeconomic models.

Acknowledgments

The authors thank the Utah Agricultural Experiment Station for the multiyear funding used to complete this project. We also thank participants at the 2004 Utah State University Spring Runoff Conference and at the 2005 W1133 annual meeting in Salt Lake City for their insightful comments.

Technical Appendix

We begin with the specific functional forms used for the species' biomass-supply functions appearing in Tables 2 and 3 and the variable-respiration functions appearing in Table 2. The first column in Table A1 presents the functional forms for supply functions y_{12}, y_{14}, y_{25}, y_{26}, and y_{45}, respectively, whereas the second column presents the variable-respiration functions f_1, f_2, f_4, f_5, and f_6. Specific values for the parameters, $\delta_{ij}^{\mathrm{GSL}}, \alpha_{ij}^{\mathrm{GSL}}, \gamma_i^{\mathrm{GSL}}, r_i^{\mathrm{GSL}}$, and r_{ji}^{GSL} are provided in Table A2.

The variable-respiration functions for algae and waterbirds requires further explanation. For algae, $S_a^{\mathrm{ss}} = 1$ is the steady-state level of salinity and $S_a = s_m + s_a$ is the salinity level in any given time period, where $s_m = [W_m/(W_m + W_a)] + \varepsilon_m$ and $s_a = [W_a/(W_m + W_a)] + \varepsilon_a$ and ε_m and ε_a are independently distributed normal with means 0 and standard deviations equal to 0.1. In other words, the overall salinity level as it impacts algae respiration is a sum of the salinity effects from the mineral extraction and agricultural sectors, where the salinity effects are in turn weighted averages of the water used in the respective sectors

Table A1. Species' biomass-supply and variable-respiration functions

$\delta_{12}^{\mathrm{GSL}} x_{10}^{\alpha_{12}^{\mathrm{GSL}}}$	$r_1^{\mathrm{GSL}}[(S_a - S_a^{\mathrm{ss}})^2 + 1]x_{10}^{\gamma_1^{\mathrm{GSL}}}$
$\delta_{14}^{\mathrm{GSL}} x_{10}^{\alpha_{14}^{\mathrm{GSL}}}$	$r_2^{\mathrm{GSL}} x_{21}^{\gamma_2^{\mathrm{GSL}}}$
$\delta_{25}^{\mathrm{GSL}} x_{21}^{\alpha_{25}^{\mathrm{GSL}}}$	$r_4^{\mathrm{GSL}} x_{41}^{\gamma_4^{\mathrm{GSL}}}$
$\delta_{26}^{\mathrm{GSL}} x_{21}^{\alpha_{26}^{\mathrm{GSL}}}$	$r_5^{\mathrm{GSL}}(x_{52} + x_{54}) + 0.5r_5^{\mathrm{GSL}}(r_{54}^{\mathrm{GSL}} x_{52}x_{54} + x_{52}^{\gamma_5^{\mathrm{GSL}}} + r_{54}^{\mathrm{GSL}} x_{54}^{\gamma_5^{\mathrm{GSL}}})$
$\delta_{45}^{\mathrm{GSL}} x_{41}^{\alpha_{45}^{\mathrm{GSL}}}$	$r_6^{\mathrm{GSL}} x_{62}^{\gamma_6^{\mathrm{GSL}}}$

Table A2. Ecological parameter and steady-state variable values

Embodied energies	Taxes	r parameters*
$e_0 = 1500$	$t_{12} = 0.0000688$	$r_1^{GSL} = 3989$
$e_1 = 1300$	$t_{14} = 0.0000131$	$r_2^{GSL} = 932$
$e_2 = 1000$	$t_{45} = 0.0115926$	$r_4^{GSL} = 1018$
$e_4 = 500$	$t_{26} = 0.0004738$	$r_5^{GSL} = 186$
	$t_{25} = 0.0090030$	$r_{54}^{GSL} = 0.018$
		$r_6^{GSL} = 2399$

Species populations	Alpha parameters	Beta parameters*
$N_1 = 409{,}139{,}538$	$\alpha_{12}^{GSL} = \alpha_{14}^{GSL} = \alpha_{25}^{GSL} = \alpha_{26}^{GSL} = \alpha_{45}^{GSL} = 0.5$	$\beta_1 = 1.381$
$N_2 = 386{,}392$		$\beta_2 = 86.111$
$N_4 = 200{,}000$		$\beta_4 = 53.478$
$N_5 = 200$		$\beta_5 = 47175.134$
$N_6 = 100{,}000$		$\beta_6 = 3.460$

Biomass demands	Delta parameters*	Species life spans
$x_{10} = 0.007$	$\delta_{12}^{GSL} = 0.0074$	$s_1 = s_2 = s_4 = s_6 = 5$
$x_{21} = 0.656$	$\delta_{14}^{GSL} = 0.0023$	$s_5 = 15$
$x_{41} = 0.401$		
$x_{52} = 156$	$\delta_{25}^{GSL} = 0.1000$	
$x_{54} = 104$	$\delta_{26}^{GSL} = 0.0053$	
$x_{62} = 0.016$		
$A = N_{1 \times 10}$	$\delta_{45}^{GSL} = 0.1647$	

Biomass energy prices	Gamma parameters	Species weights
$e_{10} = 0.09N_1^{0.4}$	$\gamma_1^{GSL} = \gamma_2^{GSL} = \gamma_4^{GSL} = \gamma_5^{GSL} = \gamma_6^{GSL} = 1.3$	$w_1 = 0.007$
$e_{21} = 0.09e_1$		$w_2 = 0.776$
$e_{41} = 0.15e_1$		$w_4 = 0.887$
$e_{52} = 0.09e_2$		
$e_{54} = 0.09e_4$		
$e_{62} = 0.09e_2$		

plus independent stochastic shocks that follow mean-zero normal distributions. For waterbirds, variable respiration is a polynomial function that accounts for available prey-substitution possibilities between brine shrimp and brine flies.

Table A2 contains the parameter values and steady-state values of the model's ecological variables. The superscript * indicates that the parameter or variable value is determined as an outcome of the calibration process. As mentioned in the text, those values not determined as an outcome of the calibration process were obtained from the ecological literature cited throughout Section 2.

With respect to the regional economy, we first account for the functional forms expressed in (6a) for each production sector. Following FT, these functional forms are presented as the first-order conditions that determine sector-level exports through constrained maximization of sector-level CES revenue functions

$$\frac{q_i^d}{q_i^e} = \left[\frac{(1-\delta_i)p_i^e}{\delta_i p_i^d}\right]^{\sigma_i} \qquad i = f,\ m,\ a,\ R,\ c. \tag{A1}$$

There is no corresponding first-order condition determining the importation of the composite good since it is assumed that imports are the residual of the household sector's overall demand in excess of domestic production.

We next create a per-sector aggregated social accounting matrix based on data obtained from IMPLAN, thus ensuring cross-sector account balances. Table A3 contains the parameter values and steady-state values of the model's economic variables, presented by sector. Note that all noncomposite output and input prices are normalized to 1 in the steady state (except for $\gamma = 0.04$ and $P_W = 0$), implying that the physical quantities are also the dollar values in the steady state. The superscript* indicates that the parameter or variable value is determined as an outcome of the calibration process.

Table A3. Economic parameter and steady-state variable values

Brine shrimp	Mineral extraction	Agriculture	Composite	Recreation	Household
$q_f^d = 0.5$	$q_m^d = 5.1$	$q_a^d = 87.5$	$q_c^d = 370.9$	$q_R^d = 16$	$C_T = 456$
$q_f^e = 9.5$	$q_m^e = 94.9$	$q_a^e = 62.5$	$q_c^e = 10$	$q_R^e = 4$	$C_F = 24$
$I_f = 0.5$	$I_m = 5$	$I_a = 7.5$	$q_c^{IM} = 180.9$	$I_R = 1$	$S = 24$
$a_f^I = 0.05^*$	$a_m^I = 0.05^*$	$a_a^I = 0.05^*$	$I_c = 10$	$a_R^I = 0.05^*$	$Y = 480$
$L_f = 4.96$	$L_m = 45$	$L_a = 40$	$a_c^I = 0.05^*$	$L_R = 10$	$\beta_{TN} = \alpha_{SN} = 0.035^*$
$K_f = 4.96$	$K_m = 50$	$K_a = 40$	$L_c = 100$	$K_R = 10$	$\nu_{TN} = \sigma_{SN} = 0.867$
$a_f = b_f = 0.375^*$	$W_m = 5$	$W_a = 10$	$K_c = 100$	$a_R = 0.375^*$	$\alpha_{TN} = 0.731^*$
$c_f = 0.25$	$a_m = 0.337^*$	$T_a = 60$	$N_c = 2^*$	$b_R = 0.375^*$	$\sigma_{TN} = 1.6$
$d_f = 0.121^*$	$b_m = 0.375^*$	$\mathrm{a}_a = 0.2^*$	$\delta_c = 0.5^*$	$c_R = 0.25$	$\lambda_m = 0.0002^*$
$\delta_f = 0.258^*$	$c_m = 0.25$	$\mathrm{b}_a = 0.2^*$	$\sigma_c = 0.867^*$	$d_R = 0.945^*$	$\lambda_a = 0.181^*$
$\sigma_f = 2.79$	$d_m = 4.268^*$	$c_a = 0.25$	$\delta_c = 0.785^*$	$\delta_R = 0.622^*$	$\lambda_c = 0.818^*$
$COR = 0.08$	$\delta_m = 0.26^*$	$\mathrm{d}_a = 5.647^*$	$\sigma_c = 2.79$	$\sigma_R = 2.79$	
$\mathrm{TAC} = 0.0000001 N_3^{ss}$	$\sigma_m = 2.79$	$\mathrm{g}_a = 0.3^*$	$\delta^c = 0.488^*$		
		$\delta_a = 0.522^*$	$\sigma^c = 2.12$		
		$\sigma_a = 3.9$			

References

Adler, R.W. (1999), Toward comprehensive watershed-based restoration and protection for Great Salt Lake. *Utah Law Review* 1999 (1), 99–204.

Aldrich, T.W., Paul, D.S. (2002), Avian ecology of Great Salt Lake. In: Gywnn, J.W. (Ed.), *Great Salt Lake: An Overview of Change*. Utah Department of Natural Resources, Salt Lake City, pp. 343–373.

Armington, P. (1969), A theory of demand for products distinguished by place of production. *IMF Staff Papers* 16, 159–178.

Arnow, T., Stephens, D. (1990), Hydrologic characteristics of the Great Salt Lake, Utah: 1847–1986. U.S. Geological Survey Water-Supply Paper No. 2332.

Ballard, C.L., Fullerton, D., Shoven, J.B., Whalley, J. (1985), *A General Equilibrium Model for Tax Policy Evaluation*. The University of Chicago Press, Chicago.

Belovsky, G.E. (1996), Brine shrimp population dynamics and sustainable harvesting in the Great Salt Lake, Utah. 1996 Progress Report to the Utah Division of Wildlife Resources, Salt Lake City, Utah.

Belovsky, G.E., Kilham, S., Larson, C., Mellison, C. (1999), Brine shrimp population dynamics and sustainable harvesting in the Great Salt Lake, Utah. 1999 Progress Report to the Utah Division of Wildlife Resources, Salt Lake City, Utah.

Belovsky, G.E., Mellison, C. (1997), Brine shrimp population dynamics and sustainable harvesting in the Great Salt Lake, Utah. 1997 Progress Report to the Utah Division of Wildlife Resources, Salt Lake City, Utah.

Finnoff, D., Tschirhart, J. (2004), A multiple species bioeconomic computable general equilibrium model. Unpublished manuscript.

Finnoff, D., Tschirhart, J. (2003), Protecting an endangered species while harvesting its prey. *Land Economics* 79 (2), 160–180.

Gliwicz, Z.M., Wurtsbaugh, W.A., Ward, A. (1995), Brine shrimp ecology in the Great Salt Lake, Utah, June 1994-May 1995. Department of Fisheries and Wildlife and Ecology Center, Utah State University, Utah.

Isaacson, A.E., Hachman, F.C., Robson, R.T. (2002), The economics of Great Salt Lake. In: Gywnn, J.W. (Ed.), *Great Salt Lake: An Overview of Change*. Utah Department of Natural Resources, Salt Lake City, pp. 187–199.

Rushforth, S.R., Felix, E.A. (1982), Biotic adjustments to changing salinities in the Great Salt Lake, Utah, USA. *Microbial Ecology* 8, 157–161.

Stephens, D.W., Gillespie, D.M. (1976), Phytoplankton production in the Great Salt Lake, Utah, and a laboratory study of algal response to enrichment. *Limnology and Oceanography* 21 (1), 74–87.

Stephens, D.W., Birdsey, P.W., Jr. (2002), Population dynamics of the brine shrimp, *Artemia franciscana*, in Great Salt Lake and regulation of commercial shrimp harvesting. In: Gywnn, J.W. (Ed.), *Great Salt Lake: An Overview of Change*. Utah Department of Natural Resources, Salt Lake City, pp. 327–335.

Stephens, D.W. (1997a), Brine shrimp ecology in the Great Salt Lake, Utah, July 1996-June 1997. Progress Report in Cooperation with the Utah Division of Wildlife Resources, U.S. Geological Survey, Salt Lake City, Utah.

Stephens, D.W. (1997b), Brine shrimp ecology in the Great Salt Lake, Utah, August 1995-June 1996. Administrative Report in Cooperation with the Utah Division of Wildlife Resources.

Stephens, D.W. (1999), Brine shrimp ecology in the Great Salt Lake, Utah, July 1997-June 1998. Progress Report in Cooperation with the Utah Division of Wildlife Resources.

The Salt Lake Tribune, (2003), Salt Lake's shrimp haul hits record volume but catch quality leaves lots to be desired. *The Salt Lake Tribune*, February 20, p. B1.

Utah Department of Natural Resources (DNR) (2000), Great Salt Lake comprehensive management plan resource document. Report prepared by the Great Salt Lake Planning Team.

Van Auken, O.W., McNulty, I.B. (1973), The effect of environmental factors on the growth of a halophylic species of algae. *The Biological Bulletin* 145, 210–222.

Wurtsbaugh, W.A., Berry, T.S. (1990), Cascading effects of decreased salinity on the plankton, chemistry and physics of the Great Salt Lake (Utah). *Canadian Journal of Fisheries and Aquatic Sciences* 47, 100–109.

Wurtsbaugh, W.A. (1995), Brine shrimp ecology in the Great Salt Lake, Utah. Performance Report to the Utah Division of Wildlife Resources, Salt Lake City, Utah.

CHAPTER 8

Exploring Poverty Impacts of ASEAN Trade Liberalization for Cambodia, Lao PDR, Thailand and Vietnam

Anna Strutt[a], Thomas W. Hertel[b] and Susan Stone[c]

[a]*Department of Economics, University of Waikato, Hamilton, New Zealand*
E-mail address: astrutt@waikato.ac.nz
[b]*Department of Agricultural Economics and Center for Global Trade Analysis, Purdue University, West Lafayette, IN, USA*
E-mail address: hertel@purdue.edu
[c]*Development Division, Trade and Agriculture Directorate, Organization for Economic Cooperation and Development, Paris, France*
E-mail address: susan.stone@oecd.org

Abstract
This chapter uses a global trade model, supplemented with household survey data, to explore the potential impact of ASEAN trade liberalization on poverty in Cambodia, Lao PDR, Thailand, and Vietnam. Our tentative results suggest that ASEAN liberalization is likely to bring substantial gains to the region and lead to significant reductions in poverty. In a simulation of full removal of intra-ASEAN tariffs, we find 320,000 people are moved out of extreme poverty, with a further 1.4 million lifted above the \$2 per day poverty line. Poverty reductions are particularly significant in the case of agricultural and rural diversified households and for Cambodia. Under broader ASEAN+3 and ASEAN+6 liberalizations, we find a similar pattern of poverty reduction and the overall reduction in poverty is much higher.

Keywords: Trade liberalization, ASEAN, CGE modeling, poverty

1. Introduction

International trade liberalization has been shown to have a potentially important role to play in economic growth and poverty alleviation (McCulloch *et al.*, 2001). In this chapter, we use a global model to explore the impact of various liberalization scenarios for the Association of

Frontiers of Economics and Globalization
Volume 7 ISSN: 1574-8715
DOI: 10.1108/S1574-8715(2010)0000007011

Southeast Asian Nations (ASEAN).[1] We supplement the global model with household survey data, which allows us to focus on potential poverty impacts in four relatively low-income ASEAN countries: Cambodia, Lao PDR, Thailand, and Vietnam.

We begin with a description of the four economies on which we focus, before detailing the global trade model and database used. This includes discussion of initial levels of intra-ASEAN trade and the tariff structure in the region, along with a detailed explanation of how poverty is modeled. We then turn to explore the potential impacts of eliminating intraregional tariffs under three alternative ASEAN liberalization scenarios, including analysis of potential poverty impacts for Cambodia, Lao PDR, Thailand, and Vietnam. The chapter ends with some observations on the implications and limitations of this work.

2. *Overview of Cambodia, Lao PDR, Thailand, and Vietnam*

The four economies on which we focus fall within the Greater Mekong Subregion (GMS).[2] While the GMS is relatively poor, some rapid economic development has been achieved and it remains a region with enormous potential (Strutt and Stone, 2009). Table 1 presents selected summary indicators for Cambodia, Lao PDR, Thailand and Vietnam.

Table 1. Selected aggregate indicators, 2008

	Population (million)	GDP (US$ billion)	GDP per capita (current US$)	Poverty[a] (% of population)	Agriculture (% GDP)[b]	Rural population (% of total)
Cambodia	14.7	9.6	651.3	40.2	31.9	78.4
Lao PDR	6.2	5.2	837.3	44.0	39.9	69.1
Thailand	67.4	260.7	3,868.6	2.0	11.8	66.7
Vietnam	86.2	90.7	1,052.1	21.4	20.3	72.2

Source: World Bank (2010).
[a]Poverty headcount at the $1.25 level (PPP): 2002 data for Lao PDR; 2004 data for Cambodia and Thailand; 2006 data for Vietnam.
[b]2007 data.

[1] ASEAN member countries are Brunei Darussalam, Cambodia, Indonesia, Lao PDR, Malaysia, Myanmar, Philippines, Singapore, Thailand, and Vietnam.
[2] The GMS also includes Myanmar, along with Yunnan Province and Guangxi Zhuang Autonomous Region of China. See www.adb.org/GMS/default.asp for details. However, in the current study, we do not have data to support an assessment of poverty implications for these other GMS economies.

The economies are fairly diverse, with population ranging in size from just over 6 million people in Lao PDR to over 86 million in Vietnam. The economies also vary significantly in size, with the GDP of Lao PDR currently around US$5.2 billion, while Thailand's GDP is over 50 times as large, at US$261 billion. GDP per capita in 2008 ranged from under US$840 in Cambodia and Lao PDR to almost US$3900 in Thailand. While there is diversity among the four countries, they remain relatively poor, categorized as low-income by the World Bank, with the exception of Thailand, which is currently classified as low-middle-income.

When examining poverty in the region, there are many dimensions to consider and a range of different measures could be used (e.g. McCulloch *et al.*, 2001). For example, the most recently available poverty data reported in Table 1 indicates that over 40% of the populations of Cambodia and Lao PDR fall below the World Bank's $1.25 per day poverty line, while for Vietnam it is over 20%. Each of the economies continues to rely relatively heavily on the agriculture sector, particularly the lower-income countries. For Cambodia, agriculture contributes almost 32% of GDP, while for Lao PDR, it contributes almost 40%. The final column of Table 1 indicates that the populations remain predominantly rural, with the rural population remaining more than 66% of the total population for each of the countries. Given the predominantly rural nature of poverty in these countries, addressing rural poverty remains a key concern throughout the region (Strutt and Lim, 2005).

The GMS as a whole has seen increasing integration on a number of levels. For example, significant efforts have been made to improve infrastructure and trade facilitation in the region (Strutt *et al.*, 2008; Stone *et al.*, 2010). Each country in the region is also party to a range of international trade agreements, with the most notable agreement impacting all of the economies being ASEAN (Strutt and Stone, 2009). ASEAN member countries have agreed to implement the ASEAN Economic Community (AEC), which aims to "transform ASEAN into a single market and production base" (ASEAN, 2008). The ASEAN Free Trade Area (AFTA) was introduced in 1992 and aims to eliminate import duties according to an agreed schedule.[3] The six original signatories (Brunei Darussalam, Indonesia, Malaysia, Philippines, Singapore, and Thailand) were expected to eliminate tariffs by 2010 and the four newer members (Cambodia, Laos, Myanmar, and Vietnam) by 2015, effectively leaving ASEAN a tariff-free area (Kawai and Wignaraja, 2007). In addition to the AFTA agreement to liberalize trade, ASEAN has also formed agreements with a number of other countries, as summarized in Table 2. While these agreements are currently at varying stages of implementation (ADB, 2010;

---

[3] The schedule allows more flexibility for certain sensitive products and for the newer member economies of Cambodia, Lao PDR, Myanmar, and Vietnam.

Table 2. ASEAN agreements at various stages of negotiation and enforcement

Agreement	Status
ASEAN Free Trade Area	In force since 1993
ASEAN–Australia–New Zealand Free Trade Agreement (AANZFTA)	In force since 2010
ASEAN–China Comprehensive Economic Cooperation Agreement (ACFTA)	In force since 2005
ASEAN–Japan Comprehensive Economic Partnership (AJCEPA)	In force since 2008
ASEAN–Korea Comprehensive Economic Cooperation Agreement (AKFTA)	In force since 2007
ASEAN–India Framework Agreement on Comprehensive Economic Cooperation (ASEAN–India FA)	In force since 2004
ASEAN–European Union Free Trade Agreement (ASEAN–EU)	Under negotiation since 2007
East Asia Free Trade Area (ASEAN+3)	Proposed/under consultation and study
Comprehensive Economic Partnership for East Asia (CEPA/ASEAN+6)	Proposed/under consultation and study

Sources: UNESCAP (2010) and ADB (2010).

UNESCAP, 2010), there is clear potential for future expansion of the ASEAN free trade area.

As an exploration into the impacts of various ASEAN liberalization options, we focus in this chapter on fairly simple scenarios of full tariff removal in ASEAN, ASEAN+3, and ASEAN+6.[4] Table 2 shows that ASEAN already has some kind of economic cooperation or partnership agreement in place with each country in these groupings. Thus, the simulations of tariff elimination in the ASEAN and wider region are designed to generate useful insights for a regional integration process already underway.

3. Modeling framework and data

We undertake economic modeling of ASEAN liberalization using an adaptation of the Global Trade Analysis Project (GTAP) model[5] that has been modified to incorporate poverty impacts (Hertel *et al.*, 2009; Stone *et al.*, 2010). Our primary data source is the GTAP version 7 database (Narayanan and Walmsley, 2008), augmented with household survey data

[4] ASEAN+3 covers the 10 ASEAN members plus China, Japan, and Korea while ASEAN+6 also includes Australia, New Zealand, and India in the grouping.
[5] See www.gtap.agecon.purdue.edu for detailed information.

for Cambodia, Lao PDR, Thailand, and Vietnam. In this section, we first overview the GTAP model and key aspects of the trade database that are relevant to Cambodia, Lao PDR, Thailand, and Vietnam. We then detail the modifications and additional data used to augment the model in an effort to more fully analyze poverty impacts in Cambodia, Lao PDR, Thailand, and Vietnam.

3.1. The GTAP model and database

The GTAP model captures interactions between regions and sectors within a consistent framework. The version we use retains many standard features of the GTAP model, with the behavior of private individuals, firms, and governments, along with responses to changing resource and market conditions modeled (Hertel, 1997). As is typical with CGE models, consumers maximize welfare, subject to their budget limitations, while firms maximize profits using the limited resources available in the economy. Primary factors of production are combined with intermediate inputs, including imports, to produce final output. Armington elasticities allow differentiation between imports from different countries. We retain the simple, yet empirically robust, assumptions of constant returns to scale and perfect competition, with Section 3.2 describing modifications we make to the model to shed new light on the distributional poverty consequences of ASEAN trade liberalization. When the impact of ASEAN liberalization is simulated, prices and quantities of marketed commodities, along with impacts on incomes and poverty, are endogenously determined within the model.[6]

The database we use is GTAP version 7, covering 113 countries/regions and 57 sectors, with a base year of 2004 (Narayanan and Walmsley, 2008). The full database is aggregated in a way that maintains as full coverage as possible of ASEAN and associated countries,[7] with relatively heavy disaggregation of sectors of key importance to trade and poverty. We model 20 regions and 26 commodities; however, these are generally aggregated for clarity in our analysis of results. We eliminate remaining Agreement on Textiles and Clothing (ATC) quotas to create a baseline from which our simulations are undertaken, since these should have been abolished independently of ASEAN liberalization.[8]

---

[6] The model is solved using GEMPACK software (Harrison and Pearson, 1996), using the RunGTAP interface.

[7] Since Brunei Darussalam is not available in this global database, we exclude it from our analysis of ASEAN.

[8] For further analysis of the ATC quotas that may remain for China, see Whalley (2008).

3.1.1. Intraregional trade and protection

The level of trade between Cambodia, Lao PDR, Thailand, and Vietnam and ASEAN varies a great deal, depending on the countries and commodities under consideration. Table 3 shows the level of intraregional trade, as estimated in the baseline data. The country with the highest level of intra-ASEAN exports in the database is Lao PDR, with 28% of total

Table 3. Exports to ASEAN relative to total exports for Lao PDR, Cambodia, Thailand, and Vietnam, 2004

	ASEAN (%)	ASEAN+3 (%)	ASEAN+6 (%)	World (US$ million)
Cambodia				
Crops	72	74	75	30
Livestock, fish, and forestry	29	44	46	24
Processed foods	10	15	16	100
Textiles, apparel, and leather	3	11	11	2,316
Other manufactures	51	70	71	395
Services	4	16	18	990
Total	9	19	20	3,856
Lao PDR				
Crops	40	45	45	33
Livestock, fish, and forestry	75	91	91	37
Processed foods	15	25	27	18
Textiles, apparel, and leather	2	3	4	164
Other manufactures	67	71	72	189
Services	4	12	15	198
Total	28	34	35	639
Thailand				
Crops	14	54	55	1,812
Livestock, fish, and forestry	20	41	44	301
Processed foods	15	40	43	11,947
Textiles, apparel, and leather	11	30	33	8,402
Other manufactures	19	50	54	82,034
Services	3	15	18	15,716
Total	16	43	47	120,212
Vietnam				
Crops	6	18	25	1,633
Livestock, fish, and forestry	9	43	47	326
Processed foods	13	43	46	3,734
Textiles, apparel, and leather	2	17	18	9,283
Other manufactures	21	59	68	13,046
Services	6	25	28	3,482
Total	12	38	43	31,504

Source: Authors' calculations based on the GTAP version 7 database.

exports going to other ASEAN countries. For Thailand, Vietnam, and Cambodia, between 9 and 16% of exports are intra-ASEAN. Turning to intraregional trade in ASEAN+3 and ASEAN+6, the share for these countries increases significantly. We find that more than one third of exports stay within the broader ASEAN+3 and ASEAN+6 markets, with the exception of Cambodia where intra-ASEAN+6 exports are only 20% of total exports.

Examining the variation in the importance of intraregional exports by sector (Table 3), we find that a relatively high proportion of agricultural exports tend to remain within the region. Labor-intensive textiles, apparel, and leather products, conversely, tend to be exported outside the region. Indeed, one reason for Cambodia's relatively low reliance on intraregional trade is that the majority of exports from this sector, which comprise more than 60% of Cambodia's total exports, go to Europe. Other manufactured products tend to remain largely within the region, no doubt in part due to the dominance of intermediate inputs in this sector and the role these inputs play in regional production chains (Ando and Kimura, 2005).

Table 4 provides an overview of the trade-weighted average tariffs imposed by Cambodia, Lao PDR, Thailand, and Vietnam, while Table 5 indicates the average tariffs faced by each country. These tariffs vary significantly by country and broad sector grouping. However, each of the four countries tends to impose higher tariffs than they face within the region, implying substantial potential gains from lowering their own tariffs. The highest tariffs Cambodia, Lao PDR, Thailand, and Vietnam face for intraregional exports are on crops and processed foods, suggesting that these sectors may experience particularly significant benefits when tariffs within the region are eliminated (Table 5).

3.2. Analysis of poverty impacts[9]

Trade liberalization will not have uniform impacts on diverse population segments. In particular, the poor may well experience quite different effects than the national average, due in part to differences in earnings and spending profiles. For example, we have shown above that crops tend to be highly protected and this sector typically makes up a higher share of both income and expenditure among the poor than for the population as a whole. Therefore, we might expect liberalization of this sector to have a disproportionate impact on the poor. To assess diverse effects and poverty impacts, a general equilibrium approach is desirable. This approach allows us to simultaneously track and measure changes in both income and expenditures from the trade liberalization scenarios modeled. We augment the GTAP database with household survey data from the region, in order

[9] This section draws heavily on Stone *et al.* (2010).

Table 4. Average trade-weighted tariffs applied by Cambodia, Lao PDR, Thailand, and Vietnam (%)

	ASEAN	ASEAN+3	ASEAN+6	World
Cambodia				
Crops	9.2	10.0	10.4	9.6
Livestock, fish, and forestry	14.8	14.8	14.8	14.1
Processed foods	20.0	20.6	20.8	20.3
Textiles, apparel, and leather	15.6	13.4	13.4	14.4
Other manufactures	13.8	13.9	13.9	14.5
Services	0.0	0.0	0.0	0.0
Total	15.1	14.4	14.4	13.7
Lao PDR				
Crops	28.2	28.2	28.2	26.0
Livestock, fish, and forestry	8.5	8.5	8.5	8.4
Processed foods	18.9	19.0	19.0	18.7
Textiles, apparel, and leather	6.6	6.9	7.0	7.0
Other manufactures	8.9	9.9	9.8	9.4
Services	0.1	0.0	0.0	0.2
Total	10.9	11.3	11.2	10.1
Thailand				
Crops	20.6	28.0	22.5	23.3
Livestock, fish, and forestry	2.6	4.7	4.7	5.8
Processed foods	34.6	37.2	30.5	33.0
Textiles, apparel, and leather	10.6	19.7	18.3	18.6
Other manufactures	3.2	9.0	8.8	7.6
Services	0.0	0.0	0.0	0.0
Total	4.0	9.4	9.2	7.9
Vietnam				
Crops	6.1	17.2	13.2	11.2
Livestock, fish, and forestry	1.3	2.4	2.7	3.3
Processed foods	28.2	30.1	24.2	26.4
Textiles, apparel, and leather	7.0	28.2	27.8	28.2
Other manufactures	7.9	10.4	10.2	9.0
Services	0.0	0.0	0.0	0.0
Total	9.0	13.2	12.7	11.1

Source: Authors' calculations based on the GTAP version 7 database.

to permit a more nuanced analysis of the poverty impacts of trade liberalization for Cambodia, Lao PDR, Thailand, and Vietnam.

There are many alternative approaches to estimating the change in poverty headcount due to trade reforms (Winters *et al.*, 2004; Hertel and Reimer, 2005; Hertel and Winters, 2006). The approach here builds on that outlined in Hertel *et al.* (2009), and begins with a consumer demand system and the associated utility function. The *poverty level of utility* is identified

Table 5. Average trade-weighted tariffs faced by Cambodia, Lao PDR, Thailand, and Vietnam (%)

	ASEAN	ASEAN+3	ASEAN+6	World
Cambodia				
Crops	27.3	27.1	26.8	21.3
Livestock, fish, and forestry	1.9	5.1	4.9	2.5
Processed foods	25.4	19.3	17.5	8.2
Textiles, apparel, and leather	0.9	1.0	1.4	3.8
Other manufactures	1.4	1.6	1.6	1.4
Services	0.0	0.0	0.0	0.0
Total	3.8	2.5	2.5	2.9
Lao PDR				
Crops	26.2	25.3	25.1	12.4
Livestock, fish, and forestry	3.3	2.7	2.7	3.0
Processed foods	27.4	21.5	19.9	11.7
Textiles, apparel, and leather	9.0	5.4	5.8	0.6
Other manufactures	3.1	3.1	3.1	2.4
Services	0.0	0.0	0.0	0.0
Total	5.2	4.7	4.6	2.1
Thailand				
Crops	6.5	13.2	13.3	12.5
Livestock, fish, and forestry	1.7	4.9	4.9	4.4
Processed foods	11.7	26.4	24.9	21.0
Textiles, apparel, and leather	4.2	7.2	7.7	9.6
Other manufactures	2.9	3.3	3.5	3.3
Services	0.0	0.0	0.0	0.0
Total	3.8	5.8	5.8	5.4
Vietnam				
Crops	6.9	62.2	53.1	16.8
Livestock, fish, and forestry	1.9	4.6	4.3	8.5
Processed foods	19.0	14.3	13.7	11.6
Textiles, apparel, and leather	4.4	9.0	9.3	9.7
Other manufactures	1.7	1.5	1.5	1.9
Services	0.1	1.0	1.1	0.4
Total	4.3	5.8	5.6	6.0

Source: Authors' calculations using the GTAP version 7 database.

on the basis of international poverty levels (using the World Bank's $1 and $2 per day poverty lines).[10] Evaluation of poverty changes thus amounts to calculating the percentage of the population below this poverty level of utility.

[10] The World Bank has released a new measure of poverty on the basis of purchasing power parity and a $1.25 per day poverty line, which falls between our $1 and $2 measures. For more details on these changes see http://go.worldbank.org/C9GR27WRJ0.

We make use of Rimmer and Powell's (1996) AIDADS demand system to represent consumption in the neighborhood of the poverty line. AIDADS is particularly useful for poverty analysis as it devotes two-thirds of its parameters to consumption behavior in the neighborhood of the poverty line (Cranfield *et al.*, 2006). Estimation of this demand system is undertaken using the per capita consumption data set offered by GTAP version 7, with the parameter estimates then calibrated to reproduce base year per capita demands in each country.[11] From there, per capita income is shocked back to the international poverty line in order to identify the poverty level of utility and to estimate consumption quantities at the poverty line.

A key finding in the work of Hertel *et al.* (2004) is the importance of stratifying households by primary source of income. For example, some rural households in developing countries may rely on the farm enterprise for virtually all of their income, while other households may receive nearly all their income from wage labor. We find that national poverty tends to be concentrated in agriculture-specialized households in the poorest countries in our sample. In these cases, the poor are more likely to benefit from farm price increases. In other countries, the national poverty headcount is dominated by wage earners who will be more susceptible to food price rises. To delineate the patterns of earnings specialization, we follow Hertel *et al.* (2004) and identify five household groups that rely almost exclusively (95% or more) on one source of income: agricultural self-employment, nonagricultural self-employment, rural wage labor, urban wage labor, or transfer payments. The remaining households are grouped into rural and urban diversified strata, giving seven strata.[12]

Given our interest in comparing results across countries, we take a simplified approach to poverty analysis in the individual countries, focusing solely on the poverty headcount – at both the $1 and $2 per day levels. We do so by employing a survey-based highly disaggregated poverty elasticity analysis. In particular, we adopt from Hertel *et al.* (2009) the following equation for predicting the percentage change in poverty headcount, $\hat{H}_r$, in the four countries under study:

$$\hat{H}_r = -\sum_s \beta_{rs}\varepsilon_{rs}\sum_j \alpha^p_{rsj}\left(\hat{W}_{rj} - \hat{C}^p_r\right) \quad (1)$$

The term in parentheses on the right-hand side of Equation (1) reports the change in the after-tax wage rate for endowment j in region r, $\hat{W}_{rj}$,

[11] These were estimated using a prerelease of the database with 96 countries available.

[12] A clear limitation of this approach stems from the rigidity of a given households' classification by earnings specialization. Some households may be induced to change their specialization or diversify in response to changing relative factor returns. We believe that the relatively broad definition of strata circumvents this problem for the majority of households in the face of modest earnings changes.

relative to the change in the cost of living at the poverty line, $\hat{C}_r^p$. This real earnings term is premultiplied by several important parameters. The first of these is the share of earnings type j in total income of households in the neighborhood of the poverty line in stratum s of region r, α_{rsj}^p. This translates a change in, for example, the wage of unskilled labor, into a change in total household income. If wages rise by 10% and thus is 95% of household income for households in the neighborhood of the poverty line in the rural wage earner stratum, then income is predicted to rise by $0.95 \times 10\% = 9.5\%$. By definition, the earnings shares sum to 1: $\sum_j \alpha_{rsj} = 1$, and summing over the share-weighted change in factor returns yields the total income change for households in the neighborhood of the poverty line for a given stratum/region combination.

This change in income is, in turn, multiplied by the estimated elasticity of the stratum-specific poverty headcount with respect to income, ε_{rs}. In order to turn these stratum changes into the estimated percentage change in national poverty headcount, they must be weighted by each stratum's share in national poverty:

$$\beta_{rs} = \frac{(\mathrm{POP}_{rs} \cdot H_{rs})/\mathrm{POP}_r}{H_r} = \frac{\mathrm{POP}_{rs} \cdot H_{rs}}{\sum_k (\mathrm{POP}_{rk} \cdot H_{rk})}$$

Summing across strata, we obtain the national poverty headcount reported in Equation (1).

3.2.1. Integrating poverty into the model

To model poverty impacts within the GTAP framework, we introduce factor market segmentation, which is important in countries where the rural sector remains a dominant source of poverty (Keeney and Hertel, 2005).[13] Thus, farm/nonfarm mobility is restricted in our model by specifying a constant elasticity of transformation (CET) function that limits the mobility of labor and capital between the farm and nonfarm sectors. This allows farm and nonfarm factor returns to diverge, and this becomes a key driver for our distributional analysis.[14] In order to parameterize these CET factor mobility functions, we draw on the OECD's (2001) survey of agricultural factor markets. We assume a constant aggregate level of land, labor, and capital employment, reflecting the belief that the aggregate supply of factors is not overly affected in the medium run by the trade liberalization scenarios presented here.

---

[13] As shown in Table 1, the majority of the population in the GMS are to be found in rural areas.

[14] Our analysis takes place in a comparative static framework and focuses on medium-run outcomes. In this instance, restricting mobility of certain factors is not unrealistic and better reflects the lag in the adjustment process to economic opportunities often found in developing countries.

Implementation of Equation (1) requires us to map factor earnings in the general equilibrium model to household income sources from the survey data. Agricultural labor and capital receive the corresponding farm factor returns from the general equilibrium model, as do nonagricultural labor and capital. Wage labor for diversified households reported in the surveys presents a problem because information is lacking to allocate it between agricultural versus nonagricultural activities. We simply assign to it the composite wage for labor determined by the CET endowment function. Finally, transfer payments are indexed by the growth rate in net national income.

3.2.2. Data and elasticities

While conceptually simple, this approach to poverty analysis is actually quite data intensive. By utilizing estimates from household surveys for Lao PDR and Cambodia (Komoto and Stone, 2009), coupled with previously processed estimates for Vietnam and Thailand (Hertel *et al.*, 2004), we were able to integrate the poverty module described above into our general equilibrium model and examine the results for these four ASEAN countries.

Table 6 reports the estimated earnings shares in the neighborhood of the $1 per day poverty line for each endowment type in the four countries, α^{p}_{rsj}. Endowments are disaggregated into 10 categories, including agricultural land, self-employed agricultural labor (both unskilled and skilled), self-employed nonagricultural labor (both unskilled and skilled), wage labor (both unskilled and skilled), agricultural capital, nonagricultural capital, and transfer payments. The most difficult part of estimating these earnings shares derives from the need to impute returns to factors of production when the source of income is self-employment. This is achieved by assigning the average earned wage for a similar class of workers (ideally, same sex and age, same skill level, same sector, same region) from the household survey data to the self-employed household members. The residual earnings are assigned to capital in the case of nonagricultural income and shared between capital and land in the case of farming.[15]

From the entries in Table 6, we can see a number of important points. First, in the case of the agricultural stratum, where households earn more than 95% of their income from agricultural self-employment, the bulk of their income is imputed unskilled agricultural labor income. This implies that the poor are poor in part because they do not control a lot of productive assets. Returns to land and capital play a larger role in Cambodia, with very little residual remaining after wage imputation in Vietnam. With the exception of Thailand, nonagricultural, self-employed

[15] To split nonwage income between capital and land, we use the factor payment shares from the GTAP database, which are based on econometric studies of cost shares in agriculture.

Table 6. Household earnings shares, by endowment type, stratum, and country: $1 per day (%)

	Agriculture	Nonagriculture	Urban labor	Rural labor	Transfers	Urban diversified	Rural diversified
Cambodia							
Land	16.0	1.8	1.0	1.2	2.2	4.4	5.1
Agricultural unskilled labor	72.5	0.0	0.0	0.0	0.0	19.1	26.7
Agricultural skilled labor	0.0	0.0	0.0	0.0	0.0	0.0	0.0
Nonagricultural unskilled	3.5	84.6	0.0	0.0	0.0	19.5	19.3
Nonagricultural skilled	0.0	0.0	0.0	0.0	0.0	6.6	4.8
Wage labor unskilled	3.3	0.0	46.4	50.3	0.0	20.2	17.2
Wage labor skilled	0.0	0.0	51.5	45.9	0.0	17.6	18.2
Agricultural capital	2.2	0.2	0.1	0.2	0.3	0.6	0.7
Nonagricultural Capital	1.3	11.7	0.0	1.0	0.0	3.9	3.0
Transfers	1.2	1.7	0.9	1.4	97.5	8.0	5.0
Total	100.0	100.0	100.0	100.0	100.0	100.0	100.0
Lao PDR							
Land	9.4	0.0	0.0	0.0	0.1	2.4	3.6
Agricultural unskilled labor	57.8	1.0	0.0	0.0	0.0	15.8	21.0
Agricultural skilled labor	23.1	0.0	0.0	0.0	0.0	9.4	11.5
Nonagricultural unskilled	1.6	31.8	0.0	0.0	0.0	15.6	14.2
Nonagricultural skilled	0.0	33.0	0.0	0.0	0.0	14.5	11.0
Wage labor unskilled	1.9	1.8	50.7	39.4	0.0	12.5	9.0
Wage labor skilled	2.0	0.0	49.3	60.6	0.0	14.5	13.8
Agricultural capital	1.3	0.0	0.0	0.0	0.0	0.3	0.5
Nonagricultural capital	1.8	32.4	0.0	0.0	0.0	8.4	9.6
Transfers	1.1	0.0	0.0	0.0	99.9	6.7	5.9
Total	100.0	100.0	100.0	100.0	100.0	100.0	100.0

Table 6. (*Continued*)

	Agriculture	Nonagriculture	Urban labor	Rural labor	Transfers	Urban diversified	Rural diversified
Thailand							
Land	8.2	0.0	0.1	0.0	0.1	1.9	4.1
Agricultural unskilled labor	79.6	0.0	0.1	0.1	0.1	24.0	20.8
Agricultural skilled labor	7.4	0.0	0.0	0.0	0.0	4.1	2.6
Nonagricultural unskilled	0.0	90.8	0.0	0.0	0.0	3.8	3.1
Nonagricultural skilled	0.0	6.2	0.0	0.0	0.0	0.4	0.7
Wage labor unskilled	0.3	0.4	98.0	97.8	0.7	28.1	23.6
Wage labor skilled	0.1	0.1	1.5	1.5	0.1	5.2	7.1
Agricultural capital	4.0	0.0	0.0	0.0	0.0	0.9	2.0
Nonagricultural capital	0.0	2.3	0.0	0.0	0.0	1.3	1.5
Transfers	0.5	0.2	0.3	0.5	98.9	30.5	34.6
Total	100.0	100.0	100.0	100.0	100.0	100.0	100.0
Vietnam							
Land	3.1	0.0	0.0	0.0	0.0	3.8	1.0
Agricultural unskilled labor	95.6	0.2	0.0	0.0	0.0	43.1	8.6
Agricultural skilled labor	0.0	0.0	0.0	0.0	0.0	0.0	0.0
Nonagricultural unskilled	0.0	57.9	0.0	0.8	0.0	11.3	13.7
Nonagricultural skilled	0.0	0.9	0.0	0.0	0.0	0.0	0.0
Wage labor unskilled	0.0	0.0	98.7	78.8	0.0	1.9	0.0
Wage labor skilled	0.0	0.0	0.0	18.3	0.0	0.0	0.0
Agricultural capital	1.4	0.0	0.0	0.0	0.0	1.7	0.4
Nonagricultural capital	0.0	39.9	1.0	1.6	0.0	24.2	55.2
Transfers	0.0	1.1	0.3	0.5	100.0	14.0	21.0
Total	100.0	100.0	100.0	100.0	100.0	100.0	100.0

households (column 2) in the neighborhood of the poverty line appear to get more of their income from nonlabor income. This is particularly true in Vietnam, where this figure reaches 40%.

Turning to the wage labor households (columns 3 and 4), we see that the share of income coming from skilled labor is relatively high for Cambodia and Lao PDR, the poorest of the four economies. The rural and urban diversified households are just that – highly diversified. This diversified group earns income from agricultural activities, as well as nonfarm activities; it receives transfer payments (quite significant in the case of Thailand) and also receives income from capital (particularly in the case of Vietnam).

As we have seen from Equation (1), the earnings shares translate wage changes into income changes, but it is the poverty elasticities, ε_{rs}, that translate the latter into poverty changes, by stratum. Table 7 reports these stratum-specific poverty elasticities for the four focus countries in this study. These so-called arc elasticities are obtained by examining the change in income as we move across the stratum deciles surrounding the poverty line. As these are expressed in elasticity form, we expect these elasticities to diminish as the total poverty headcount in the stratum rises (i.e., it is harder to reduce poverty by 1% when it represents 28% of the population, as in Lao PDR, as opposed to less than 2% in Thailand). This observation is confirmed by the values reported in Table 7. At the $1 per day level, the poverty elasticities are under 1.0 in all cases in Cambodia and Lao PDR, while they are above 2.0 for all strata in Thailand. The poverty elasticity is nearly 9 in the rural labor stratum of Vietnam, where there are many

Table 7. Poverty elasticity, by stratum and region

	Cambodia	Lao PDR	Thailand	Vietnam
$1 per day stratum				
Agriculture	0.64	0.58	2.30	0.48
Nonagriculture	0.71	0.46	2.42	1.12
Urban labor	0.62	0.59	2.98	2.81
Rural labor	0.54	0.62	2.45	8.98
Transfers	0.33	0.18	2.78	0.84
Urban diversified	0.68	0.70	2.42	0.86
Rural diversified	0.65	0.72	2.60	1.01
$2 per day stratum				
Agriculture	0.42	0.44	1.07	0.47
Nonagriculture	0.57	0.43	2.32	0.73
Urban labor	0.48	0.52	2.83	5.81
Rural labor	0.45	0.34	1.69	2.35
Transfers	0.21	0.14	0.63	0.14
Urban diversified	0.55	0.54	1.47	1.26
Rural diversified	0.49	0.55	1.01	0.77

Table 8. Share of national poverty by stratum (%)

	Cambodia	Lao PDR	Thailand	Vietnam
$1 per day stratum				
Agriculture	39.3	77.0	6.3	38.9
Nonagriculture	3.2	4.0	1.9	1.1
Urban labor	2.0	1.3	0.4	1.1
Rural labor	2.1	0.3	5.6	1.1
Transfers	1.1	0.8	11.4	10.0
Urban diversified	6.3	5.4	6.6	3.3
Rural diversified	46.1	11.2	67.8	44.4
Total	100.0	100.0	100.0	100.0
$2 per day stratum				
Agriculture	32.0	69.3	7.0	24.5
Nonagriculture	5.1	3.2	3.5	1.4
Urban labor	1.9	1.6	1.8	1.2
Rural labor	1.9	0.3	9.5	1.2
Transfers	0.6	0.3	8.3	2.7
Urban diversified	8.8	7.3	8.8	9.8
Rural diversified	49.8	18.0	61.0	59.3
Total	100.0	100.0	100.0	100.0

households clustered around the poverty line, and the poverty headcount is relatively low (see below). We observe the poverty elasticities diminishing as we move from $1 to $2 per day as there are simply more households below the poverty line.

Table 8 reports the share of national poverty in each of these strata, β_{rs}. From this table we again observe that poverty is predominantly a rural phenomenon, with the bulk of the poor concentrated either in the agricultural specialized (Lao PDR) or the rural diversified stratum (Thailand) or both (Cambodia and Vietnam).

Looking at poverty from the expenditure side, Table 9 shows the average expenditure share, at producer prices, on the 10 broad commodity aggregates in our consumer demand system, at both poverty lines. Food clearly dominates the budgets of the poorest ($1 per day) households in all four countries – but particularly for Cambodia and Lao PDR. Therefore, the cost of living at the $1 per day poverty line will be very sensitive to the price of foodstuffs. When income rises to the $2 per day level, the share of crop products in total expenditure declines by nearly half in Cambodia and Vietnam, while at the same time, the share of total expenditure devoted to manufactures and services, including housing and education, rises sharply.

With this information in hand, we can turn to evaluate the impact of ASEAN liberalization on poverty in Cambodia, Lao PDR, Thailand, and Vietnam.

Table 9. Average budget share at the poverty line

	Cambodia	Lao PDR	Thailand	Vietnam
$1 per day category				
Crops	45.7	40.2	28.7	31.4
Meat and fish	2.3	3.9	3.7	7.7
Other foods	28.5	31.5	19.6	22.9
Textiles and apparels	5.0	3.0	8.4	7.6
Utilities	0.5	1.5	2.2	3.6
Wholesale and retail trade	2.6	3.2	7.1	1.3
Manufactures	8.4	4.8	11.5	12.7
Transport and communication	1.3	4.0	10.0	3.3
Business services	0.6	0.2	1.0	2.5
Housing and education	5.1	7.7	7.9	7.0
Total	100.0	100.0	100.0	100.0
$2 per day category				
Crops	23.1	33.0	17.1	16.6
Meat and fish	9.4	5.5	5.3	12.8
Other foods	22.4	32.6	14.4	16.9
Textiles and apparels	5.8	2.5	10.0	9.2
Utilities	2.0	2.1	3.1	6.0
Wholesale and retail trade	6.1	4.1	9.8	1.1
Manufactures	11.4	4.0	13.8	16.9
Transport and communication	5.3	5.8	14.2	5.5
Business services	1.1	0.1	1.6	4.6
Housing and education	13.5	10.3	10.7	10.3
Total	100.0	100.0	100.0	100.0

4. *Potential impacts of ASEAN trade liberalization*

We explore three simulations involving ASEAN trade liberalization to examine potential impacts on poverty in Cambodia, Lao PDR, Thailand, and Vietnam. In particular, we model the impacts of full liberalization of tariffs in ASEAN, ASEAN+3, and ASEAN+6, as described in Section 2. While this set of simulations does not fully capture details of the different time paths of liberalization, we believe it provides insights into the potential impacts of these kinds of agreements on poverty in the region. We begin with an overview of results, followed by analysis of the poverty implications.

4.1. Overall impacts of ASEAN liberalization

Table 10 reports summary results from the three liberalization scenarios for each of the countries under study, as well as the broader ASEAN grouping. The overall impact on welfare and real GDP for the liberalizing region is invariably positive. Welfare, as measured using equivalent

Table 10. Aggregate impacts of ASEAN liberalization scenarios, from 2004 baseline

Indicator	Scenario	Cambodia	Lao PDR	Thailand	Vietnam	ASEAN
EV (US$ million)	ASEAN	139	−4	527	−101	1,847
	ASEAN+3	127	−11	3,746	579	6,806
	ASEAN+6	130	−12	3,661	539	7,822
Real GDP (%)	ASEAN	0.25	0.16	−0.01	−0.12	0.04
	ASEAN+3	0.57	0.37	0.59	1.32	0.36
	ASEAN+6	0.61	0.37	0.61	1.36	0.38
Real exports (%)	ASEAN	6.84	8.71	−0.22	2.16	0.71
	ASEAN+3	8.28	9.67	−2.6	12.56	2.16
	ASEAN+6	8.38	9.62	−2.33	13.14	2.28

variation (EV), increases by US$1.85 billion for ASEAN under the first scenario, by US$6.8 billion under the second, and by US$7.8 billion under the third and most extensive liberalization. The variation in results at the individual country level is, in part, due to the adverse terms of trade impacts on Lao PDR and Vietnam,[16] which give rise to a slight reduction in aggregate welfare under some of the liberalization scenarios.

Turning to impacts on real GDP, we find that most outcomes are significant and positive. However, we note small declines in our results under the first scenario for Thailand and Vietnam. These relatively minor declines stem from the fact that the level of removed distortions in the first ASEAN liberalization is not sufficient to substantially increase real output. However, in the broader liberalizations, we find that each of the four countries experiences substantial increases in real output, despite aggregate factor employment being fixed in our closure, with the broader liberalizations having particularly beneficial impacts on the larger economies of Thailand and Vietnam. Overall, real GDP in ASEAN increases by 0.04% under ASEAN liberalization and by almost 0.4% under the broader ASEAN+3 and ASEAN+6 liberalizations.

The final three rows of Table 10 show the impact of each scenario on real exports. With the exception of Thailand, these are positive and of a significant size. In particular, we find that Cambodian and Lao PDR exports increase by more than 6.8% in all scenarios, despite the fact that both these economies have smaller intraregional trade shares than Thailand and Vietnam (Table 3). These results are discussed in further

[16] This is due mainly to a decline in regional export prices for some products from Lao PDR and Vietnam. In the case of Lao PDR, this is particularly driven by the export prices of textiles, wearing apparel, petroleum, and other manufactures. For Vietnam, it is other foods, electronics, other manufactured products, and transportation export prices that tend to drive this result.

detail below. For Vietnam, the first scenario leads to a 2% increase in exports, while the broader liberalizations drive export increases in excess of 12.5%. While small reductions in total exports are indicated for Thailand, these do not translate into overall output declines. Indeed, under the broader ASEAN+3 and ASEAN+6 scenarios, Thailand's real GDP increases by approximately 0.6%, implying that the reduction in exports is more than offset by increased sales of output to the domestic economy.

4.1.1. Sectoral impacts of ASEAN liberalization

Turning to a more detailed examination of impacts on exports (Table 11). we find for Cambodia and Lao PDR that exports of crops within the region explain much of the increase in regional exports. The initial average tariff faced by this sector was relatively high, at more than 25% for Cambodian and Lao exports to the ASEAN groupings (Table 5). For Cambodia, it is growth of other crops to Malaysia that dominate, due to the elimination of a 400% tariff on this sector. For Lao PDR, exports of crops to Thailand increase substantially when the 47% tariff on imports of fruit and vegetables and the 27% tariff on other crops are removed. For Thailand, exports of processed foods grow particularly strongly, especially in the more extensive liberalization scenarios. Again, this is due to the relatively high initial tariffs faced by Thailand for this sector. As indicated in Table 5, tariffs faced on Thai exports of processed foods are higher than any of those faced by any other sector, at almost 12% within ASEAN and more than 24% to the ASEAN+3 and ASEAN+6 regions. The reason for the particularly strong growth under the second and third scenarios is that exports of processed foods to Japan grow rapidly when this market opens up. For Vietnam, the most striking increase is in the value of exports of textiles, apparel, and clothing in the ASEAN+3 and ASEAN+6 liberalizations. This sector faced relatively high initial tariffs of 9% or more in the initial database and export growth is particularly strong when Japan reduces its tariffs in these sectors. Vietnam's expansion in these labor-intensive sectors appears to come partly at the expense of Thailand, where exports decrease.

Just as the variation in the level of trade barriers affected the change in real exports, so too will it impact changes sector outputs. Table 12 shows the percentage changes in output in the aggregated sectors for each economy under review. For Cambodia, the crops sector is the clear winner across all three scenarios, while Lao PDR experiences smaller but significant increases in the textiles, wearing apparel, and leather sector. For Thailand it is the processed food sector output that tends to grow most, while for Vietnam it is the textile, apparel, and leather sectors that expand most dramatically, particularly under the more expansive ASEAN+3 and ASEAN+6 scenarios.

Table 11. Impact of ASEAN liberalization scenarios on real exports to ASEAN groupings and the world, from 2004 baseline (US$ m)

	ASEAN		ASEAN+3		ASEAN+6	
	ASEAN	World	ASEAN+3	World	ASEAN+6	World
Cambodia						
Crops	184	177	188	182	190	184
Livestock, fish, and forestry	−1	−1	1	0	1	0
Processed foods	19	−14	15	−19	14	−18
Textiles, apparel, and leather	8	55	−36	157	−32	153
Other manufactures	15	32	−2	12	0	12
Services	−1	−39	−6	−72	−5	−68
Total	224	208	160	260	168	262
Lao PDR						
Crops	20	15	22	17	22	16
Livestock, fish, and forestry	2	2	4	4	4	4
Processed foods	6	5	8	7	8	7
Textiles, apparel, and leather	3	16	0	15	0	14
Other manufactures	5	14	−1	9	−1	9
Services	1	6	3	12	4	12
Total	36	57	36	63	36	62
Thailand						
Crops	2	−33	205	−57	214	−23
Livestock, fish, and forestry	4	−2	−7	−43	−5	−35
Processed foods	631	532	4,084	2,580	3,642	2,283
Textiles, apparel, and leather	234	−145	95	−1,106	83	−1,138
Other manufactures	2,103	79	2,480	−1,217	3,216	−506
Services	−23	−688	−454	−3,282	−549	−3,356
Total	2,950	−258	6,403	−3,125	6,601	−2,774
Vietnam						
Crops	26	−37	856	410	875	423
Livestock, fish, and forestry	2	7	12	−1	14	6
Processed foods	293	312	315	−86	287	−50
Textiles, apparel, and leather	77	54	1,798	4,576	1,910	4,630
Other manufactures	347	332	168	−295	224	−200
Services	−2	0	−214	−514	−221	−519
Total	743	668	2,935	4,090	3,089	4,291

The aggregate and sectoral impacts described above have important implications for factor returns, household incomes, and poverty levels throughout the region. It is to these that we now turn.

4.1.2. Impacts on poverty in Cambodia, Lao PDR, Thailand, and Vietnam

We begin with a discussion of the poverty driver of real earnings changes (Table 13). These real earnings changes suggest that, in most cases, factor

Table 12.* *Impact of ASEAN liberalization scenarios on real output from 2004 baseline (%)

Region	Sector	ASEAN	ASEAN+3	ASEAN+6
Cambodia	Crops	13.8	13.8	13.9
	Livestock, fish, and forestry	−10.7	−11.6	−11.8
	Processed foods	−18.9	−19.8	−20.1
	Textiles, apparel, and leather	0.4	3.3	3.0
	Other manufactures	−6.5	−9.5	−9.6
	Services	0.8	0.0	0.1
Lao PDR	Crops	1.1	1.4	1.4
	Livestock, fish, and forestry	−1.2	−1.6	−1.5
	Processed foods	−3.5	−3.1	−3.2
	Textiles, apparel, and leather	5.7	4.3	4.1
	Other manufactures	1.7	0.0	0.0
	Services	1.3	1.6	1.7
Thailand	Crops	−0.2	1.8	1.8
	Livestock, fish, and forestry	0.1	−1.1	−3.0
	Processed foods	0.6	6.0	4.3
	Textiles, apparel, and leather	−1.6	−12.6	−13.0
	Other manufactures	−0.1	−2.5	−2.0
	Services	0.4	3.3	3.3
Vietnam	Crops	0.7	4.2	4.3
	Livestock, fish, and forestry	−0.5	−3.3	−3.2
	Processed foods	0.3	−5.8	−6.0
	Textiles, apparel, and leather	−0.1	27.8	27.9
	Other manufactures	0.7	−3.8	−3.6
	Services	1.4	3.8	3.8

earnings rise relative to the cost of living at the poverty line. The notable exception is Cambodia, where real earnings fall for nonagricultural and waged workers, along with nonagricultural capital and transfers. A key driver of these declines is the manufacturing and processed foods sectors, which generally experience output reductions (Table 12), contributing to lower factor returns for nonagricultural workers and capital. At the same time, however, Cambodia experiences a large expansion of the cropping sector, which drives a substantial increase in real land earnings and returns to both skilled and unskilled agricultural workers. For Lao PDR, Thailand, and Vietnam all real factor returns increase, with the exception of some small reductions in real transfers. For Lao PDR, agricultural returns increase particularly strongly due to the expansion of the cropping sector; however, returns increase across other sectors also due to gains in the manufacturing sectors from reform (Table 12). For Thailand and Vietnam, real factor returns increase across the board, with the

Table 13. Deflated endowment price changes at the $1 per day level (%)

	Cambodia	Lao PDR	Thailand	Vietnam
ASEAN				
Land	54.4	5.0	0.3	3.4
Unskilled agricultural	19.9	4.0	1.0	3.3
Skilled agricultural	13.9	3.6	0.9	2.9
Unskilled nonagricultural	−8.4	2.3	1.8	3.2
Skilled nonagricultural	−11.0	2.3	1.5	2.5
Unskilled waged	−1.1	3.0	1.6	3.2
Skilled waged	−10.7	2.3	1.5	2.5
Agricultural capital	14.2	3.4	1.0	3.2
Nonagricultural capital	−10.9	1.7	1.8	3.1
Transfers	−7.9	−0.6	1.0	−0.1
ASEAN+3				
Land	55.9	6.7	9.5	20.6
Unskilled agricultural	21.1	4.7	7.7	14.5
Skilled agricultural	14.7	4.2	6.9	12.3
Unskilled nonagricultural	−6.9	1.5	6.0	8.6
Skilled nonagricultural	−10.3	1.7	4.7	5.3
Unskilled waged	0.3	2.9	6.2	9.5
Skilled waged	−10.0	1.8	4.7	5.4
Agricultural capital	15.1	3.7	7.5	13.8
Nonagricultural capital	−9.9	0.7	5.9	8.1
Transfers	−8.4	−1.2	3.1	−0.8
ASEAN+6				
Land	56.9	6.3	7.8	18.5
Unskilled agricultural	21.4	4.6	7.1	14.0
Skilled agricultural	14.9	4.1	6.4	11.9
Unskilled nonagricultural	−6.9	1.6	6.7	9.4
Skilled nonagricultural	−10.4	1.9	5.4	6.1
Unskilled waged	0.3	2.9	6.7	10.1
Skilled waged	−10.1	1.9	5.4	6.1
Agricultural capital	15.4	3.7	7.0	13.5
Nonagricultural capital	−9.9	0.9	6.7	9.0
Transfers	−8.5	−1.2	3.5	−0.5

most striking increases resulting when ASEAN liberalization expands to ASEAN+3 and ASEAN+6.[17]

Applying the stratum-specific poverty elasticities to the real earnings changes (Table 13) gives the percentage changes in poverty headcount by stratum (Table 14). Total poverty is reduced for each country under every scenario, with more ambitious regional liberalization tending to lead to the largest poverty reductions. However, within this overall poverty decline,

[17] We do not present a table of results for real factor returns relative to the cost of living at the $2 per day level. The results are consistent with those reported in Table 13, differing only by differences in the relative cost of living at the two poverty lines.

Table 14. Change in poverty headcount, by stratum and country, $1 per day (%)

	Cambodia	Lao PDR	Thailand	Vietnam
ASEAN				
Agriculture	−10.8	−2.0	−2.7	−1.3
Nonagriculture	18.4	−0.9	−2.5	−1.0
Urban labor	12.0	−1.4	−3.1	−3.5
Rural labor	10.1	−1.5	−2.6	−9.7
Transfers	5.8	0.2	−1.3	1.9
Urban diversified	7.6	−1.6	−2.2	−1.2
Rural diversified	5.0	−1.7	−2.3	−0.4
Total	−0.4	−1.9	−2.2	−0.7
ASEAN+3				
Agriculture	−11.4	−2.3	−16.3	−6.2
Nonagriculture	17.1	−0.5	−11.5	−6.3
Urban labor	11.2	−1.2	−15.1	−18.2
Rural labor	9.4	−1.2	−12.5	−43.9
Transfers	6.1	0.3	−7.0	2.5
Urban diversified	6.8	−1.5	−11.8	−6.9
Rural diversified	4.3	−1.7	−12.3	−4.6
Total	−1.0	−2.1	−11.9	−5.2
ASEAN+6				
Agriculture	−11.6	−2.3	−15.1	−6.0
Nonagriculture	17.2	−0.6	−12.8	−7.1
Urban labor	11.2	−1.3	−16.2	−19.5
Rural labor	9.4	−1.3	−13.5	−46.7
Transfers	6.1	0.3	−7.8	2.2
Urban diversified	6.8	−1.5	−12.0	−7.0
Rural diversified	4.2	−1.7	−12.5	−5.1
Total	−1.1	−2.0	−12.2	−5.4

there is much variation by stratum, particularly in the case of Cambodia, where most of the reduction in poverty at the $1 per day level is agricultural, as follows from the discussion above.

For Lao PDR it is the agricultural stratum, along with the urban and rural diversified strata, that tends to experience the greatest reduction in poverty. This reflects the increases in crops and manufacturing sector output experienced by Lao PDR. There is relatively little change in poverty in transfer-dependent households in Lao PDR, which follows from relatively low poverty elasticities reported in Table 7, suggesting a low density of the transfer-dependent households around the poverty line. Thailand experiences larger declines in poverty, especially under the ASEAN+3 and ASEAN+6 scenarios. As discussed above, this is a reflection of the relatively large poverty elasticities reported for Thailand, across the various strata (Table 7). Finally, in the case of Vietnam, it is rural labor that experiences the greatest percentage reduction in poverty.

Table 15. Reduction in poverty headcount by stratum and country under ASEAN liberalization (thousand people)

	Cambodia	Lao PDR	Thailand	Vietnam	Total
$1 per day stratum					
Agriculture	220.2	26.8	1.5	7.5	256.0
Nonagriculture	−9.8	0.6	0.9	0.5	−7.8
Urban labor	−3.8	0.3	0.2	1.2	−2.1
Rural labor	−3.1	0.1	2.5	3.9	3.4
Transfers	−1.2	0.0	3.6	−0.1	2.3
Urban diversified	−0.8	1.6	2.2	1.0	4.0
Rural diversified	27.2	3.5	23.6	13.6	67.9
Total	228.6	32.9	34.6	27.5	323.6
$2 per day stratum					
Agriculture	401.0	52.1	8.9	79.4	541.4
Nonagriculture	−8.0	1.3	19.8	6.5	19.7
Urban labor	0.7	1.0	11.4	41.7	54.8
Rural labor	2.3	0.1	36.1	18.0	56.5
Transfers	−0.2	0.0	6.6	0.0	6.3
Urban diversified	28.1	4.7	23.3	74.2	130.3
Rural diversified	218.1	12.5	110.4	265.6	606.6
Total	641.9	71.7	216.5	485.4	1,415.6

This is notable and follows from the very large poverty elasticity for this stratum (Table 7).[18]

We use these percentage changes to calculate the absolute number of individuals lifted out of poverty, at both poverty levels, for each of the three scenarios (Tables 15–17). We find that in the first ASEAN liberalization scenario (Table 15), for Cambodia, Lao PDR, Thailand, and Vietnam combined, more than 320,000 people are moved out of extreme poverty, with 1.4 million being lifted above the $2 per day poverty line. The largest share of the extreme poverty alleviation is in Cambodia, contributing over 70% to the total poverty reduction at the $1 per day level and 45% at the $2 per day level. This reflects Cambodia's large share in $1 per day poverty in the region. On the other hand, Vietnam becomes much more important when considering the $2 per day poverty reduction in the region, as it dominates the poverty headcount at this higher level of income. At the stratum level, across the region, the bulk of the poverty

[18] Again, we do not report percentage change results for each country and scenario at the $2 per day poverty level. Results at this poverty level tend to follow a similar pattern; however, the different poverty elasticities reported in Table 7 do give rise to some differences in the relative magnitude of changes in poverty for each stratum. For example, rural labor poverty in Vietnam declines by a much smaller percentage at the $2 per day level than at the $1 per day level as the poverty elasticity is much lower.

Table 16. Reduction in poverty headcount by stratum and country under ASEAN+3 liberalization (thousand people)

	Cambodia	Lao PDR	Thailand	Vietnam	Total
$1 per day stratum					
Agriculture	230.5	31.4	11.3	30.9	304.0
Nonagriculture	−7.9	0.4	2.9	1.2	−3.4
Urban labor	−3.1	0.3	0.7	3.3	1.2
Rural labor	−2.5	0.1	9.0	8.6	15.1
Transfers	−1.4	0.0	11.0	−0.8	8.8
Urban diversified	1.4	1.4	9.5	3.3	15.7
Rural diversified	42.6	3.4	101.5	36.9	184.3
Total	259.7	36.9	145.7	83.3	525.7
$2 per day stratum					
Agriculture	414.2	62.3	86.1	392.4	955.0
Nonagriculture	−3.3	0.9	72.8	19.9	90.3
Urban labor	1.9	0.9	46.7	110.4	159.9
Rural labor	3.5	0.1	151.3	55.2	210.1
Transfers	−0.3	0.0	26.9	0.7	27.3
Urban diversified	33.8	4.3	117.8	258.8	414.8
Rural diversified	248.3	12.7	565.5	953.4	1,779.9
Total	698.2	81.1	1,067.0	1,790.9	3,637.3

Table 17. Reduction in poverty headcount by stratum and country under ASEAN+6 liberalization (thousand people)

	Cambodia	Lao PDR	Thailand	Vietnam	Total
$1 per day stratum					
Agriculture	233.5	30.4	10.4	29.8	304.1
Nonagriculture	−8.0	0.5	3.2	1.3	−3.1
Urban labor	−3.1	0.3	0.8	3.4	1.4
Rural labor	−2.5	0.1	9.6	9.0	16.2
Transfers	−1.4	0.0	12.0	−0.5	10.1
Urban diversified	1.6	1.4	9.6	3.4	16.0
Rural diversified	43.8	3.4	103.1	39.8	190.1
Total	263.9	36.0	148.6	86.3	534.9
$2 per day stratum					
Agriculture	419.5	60.1	78.2	369.4	927.1
Nonagriculture	−3.3	1.0	78.4	21.1	97.2
Urban labor	1.9	0.9	48.8	114.5	166.2
Rural labor	3.6	0.1	158.3	57.0	219.0
Transfers	−0.3	0.0	28.2	0.8	28.7
Urban diversified	34.4	4.4	118.5	263.1	420.4
Rural diversified	252.2	12.6	568.1	968.2	1,801.1
Total	708.2	79.0	1,078.3	1,794.1	3,659.6

reduction comes in the rural areas, with agricultural and rural diversified households accounting for most of the poverty reduction at both poverty levels. This suggests that ASEAN trade liberalization is likely to bring important benefits to the rural poor in the region, a key policy concern as noted in Section 2.

For the more expansive ASEAN+3 and ASEAN+6 liberalization scenarios (Tables 16 and 17, respectively), the total reduction in poverty headcount is likely to be even higher – more than 525,000 at the $1 per day level and more than 3.6 million people moving out of poverty at the $2 per day level. For these liberalizations, again it is the poverty reduction for the agricultural stratum at the $1 per day level, and the fall in rural diversified poverty at the $2 per day level that are particularly significant contributors to overall poverty reduction.

5. *Concluding comments*

This chapter has utilized newly available databases and techniques to explore the impact of trade liberalization on poverty for Cambodia, Lao PDR, Thailand, and Vietnam. Our exploratory effort to quantify some of the potential poverty impacts of ASEAN liberalization suggests that it is likely to bring significant gains to the region in terms of economic welfare, real output, and real exports. More importantly, given the focus of the current study, we show that liberalization will likely lead to significant reductions in poverty in the region. In the case of a full removal of ASEAN tariffs, we find 320,000 people are moved out of extreme poverty, and a further 1.4 million being lifted above the $2 per day poverty line. The largest share of the extreme poverty alleviation is in Cambodia, one of the poorest countries in the region. Furthermore, poverty reduction is particularly significant in the agricultural and rural diversified strata, suggesting that ASEAN liberalization may lead to significant and positive impacts on rural poverty in the region, a key policy concern of governments. Under broader ASEAN+3 and ASEAN+6 liberalizations, we find a similar pattern of poverty reduction, but the overall reduction in poverty is much higher.

Trade liberalization will impact the patterns of economic activity and poverty, with results in this chapter indicating substantial potential benefits. Countries need broad-based and sustainable growth, otherwise there will be limited opportunities for those who work and little to redistribute to those who cannot. While our analysis has not focused on economic growth *per se* (we have kept capital and labor endowments fixed), we have shown that openness to international trade may play an important role in poverty reduction. Thus, expansion of trade opportunities, along with other micro and macro policies that encourage productivity and innovation, can be a key contributor to poverty alleviation. While carefully implemented trade liberalization has the potential to contribute significantly to "pro-poor" outcomes (Winters *et al.*, 2004), structural adjustment may be disruptive, and it is appropriate to note that a range of compensatory and complementary policies will need to accompany trade reform to minimize adverse effects and maximize the gains that the poor are able to realize (Winters *et al.*, 2004; Strutt and Lim, 2005).

There are of course many limitations to this kind of study and general limitations with using CGE models are well documented in the literature. For some of the countries we focus on in the current study, data issues may be a particular concern, including the problems of matching domestic data to international frameworks and also unrecorded border trade.[19] The results we present here are determined by the databases used, the model assumptions and the specific scenarios explored; additional information and research are needed before definitive policy conclusions can be reached. Nonetheless, we believe that the analytical approach presented in this chapter can help contribute to improved understanding of some of the potential poverty impacts of trade reform in Asia.

References

ADB. (2010), *Asia Regional Integration Center (ARIC) FTA Database.* Asian Development Bank (ADB), Manila, Philippines.

Ando, M., Kimura, F. (2005). The formation of international production and distribution networks in East Asia. In: Ito, T., Rose, A.K., (Eds.), *International Trade in East Asia.* NBER-East Asian Seminar on Economics Vol. 14. The University of Chicago Press, Chicago, pp. 177–216.

ASEAN (2008), *ASEAN Economic Community Blueprint.* ASEAN Secretariat, Jakarta.

Athukurola, P. (2007), *Trade Performance of GMS Countries: Trends, Patterns and Policy Options.* Asian Development Bank, Manila, Philippines.

Cranfield, J.A.L., Preckel, P.V., Hertel, T.W. (2006), *Poverty Analysis Using an International Cross-Country Demand System.* Centre for Global Trade Analysis, Purdue University, West Lafayette, IN.

Harrison, J.W., Pearson, K.R. (1996), Computing solutions for large general equilibrium models using GEMPACK. *Computational Economics* 9 (2), 83–127.

Hertel, T. W. (Ed.) (1997). *Global Trade Analysis: Modeling and Applications.* Cambridge University Press, Cambridge and New York.

---

19 Informal trade appears to account for a significant share of cross-border trade in the GMS region, perhaps in the order of 20% to 30% of trade (Athukurola, 2007).

Hertel, T.W., Ivanic, M., Preckel, P.V., Cranfield, J.A.L. (2004), The earnings effects of multilateral trade liberalization: implications for poverty. *World Bank Economic Review* 18, 205–236.

Hertel, T.W., Keeney, R., Ivanic, M., Winters, L.A. (2009), Why isn't the Doha development agenda more poverty-friendly? *Review of Development Economics* 13 (4), 543–559.

Hertel, T.W., Reimer, J.J. (2005), Predicting the poverty impacts of trade reform. *Journal of International Trade and Economic Development* 14, 377–405.

Hertel, T.W., Winters, L.A. (2006), *Poverty and the WTO: Impacts of the Doha Development Agenda*. World Bank and Palgrave, Washington, DC.

Kawai, M., Wignaraja, G. (2007), ASEAN+3 or ASEAN+6: which way forward? ADBI Discussion Paper No. 77, Asian Development Bank Institute, Tokyo.

Keeney, R., Hertel, T.W. (2005), *GTAP-AGR: A Framework for Assessing the Implications of Multilateral Changes in Agricultural Policies*. Centre for Global Trade Analysis, Purdue University, West Lafayette, IN.

Komoto, G., Stone, S. (2009). Determining poverty impacts on Lao People's Democratic Republic and Cambodia: reconciling household and GTAP Data. ADBI Working Paper No. 141, Asian Development Bank Institute, Tokyo.

McCulloch, N.L., Winters, L.A., Cirera, X. (2001), *Trade Liberalization and Poverty: A Handbook*. Centre for Economic Policy Research, London.

Narayanan, B. G., Walmsley, T. L. (Eds.) (2008). *Global Trade, Assistance, and Production: The GTAP 7 Data Base*. Centre for Global Trade Analysis, Purdue University, West Lafayette, IN.

OECD (2001), *Market Effects of Crop Support Measures*. Organization for Economic Cooperation and Development (OECD), Paris.

Rimmer, M., Powell, A. (1996), An implicitly additive demand system. *Applied Economics* 28, 1613–1622.

Stone, S., Strutt, A., Hertel, T.W. (2010), Assessing socioeconomic impacts of transport infrastructure projects in the Greater Mekong Subregion. Asian Development Bank Institute Working Paper No. 234.

Strutt, A., Lim, S.A.L. (2005), Trade liberalization and poverty alleviation in the Greater Mekong Subregion. *Journal of Greater Mekong Subregion Development Studies* 2 (1), 1–20.

Strutt, A., Stone, S. (2009), Quantifying the effects of trade liberalization in the Greater Mekong Subregion. *Review of Development and Cooperation* 3 (1), 103–116.

Strutt, A., Stone, S., Minor, P. (2008), Trade facilitation in the Greater Mekong Subregion: impacts of reducing the time to trade. *Journal of Greater Mekong Subregion Development Studies* 4, 1–20.

UNESCAP. (2010), *Trade Agreements Database*. United Nations ESCAP, Bangkok.

Whalley, J. (2008), Post-multifibre arrangement adjustments and China: after all, the emperor is wearing no new clothes? *ARTNeT Policy Brief* 14, 1–4.

Winters, L.A., McCulloch, N., McKay, A. (2004), Trade liberalization and poverty: the evidence so far. *Journal of Economic Literature* 27, 481–506.

World Bank (2010), *World Development Indicators*. World Bank, Washington DC, Available at http://databank.worldbank.org. Retrieved on 8 April.

CHAPTER 9

Regional Trade Reform under SAFTA and Income Distribution in South Asia

John Gilbert[a] and Reza Oladi[b]

[a]*Department of Economics and Finance, Jon M. Huntsman School of Business, Utah State University, Logan, UT 84322-3565, USA*
E-mail address: jgilbert@usu.edu
[b]*Department of Applied Economics, Utah State University, Logan, UT 84322-3530, USA*
E-mail address: reza.oladi@usu.edu

Abstract
South Asia is one of the world's poorest regions. In this chapter we use a representative household model of South Asia to explore the potential impacts of regional trade liberalization under the auspices of SAFTA on both the distribution of economic gains across the countries of South Asia, and across various groups within South Asia. We also discuss the underlying theory of a potential extension to our approach.

Keywords: SAFTA, income distribution, CGE

1. Introduction

The issues surrounding the potential for adverse trade impacts on food security and poverty have been a major area of contention in both multilateral and regional trade negotiations. Hence, it is important to evaluate the likely costs and benefits of regional trade liberalization in terms of not only aggregate measures such economic welfare, but also social measures such as income distribution, especially for the developing economies. This provides policymakers with information on not only the overall costs/benefits, but also the areas where complementary policy interventions may be required.

There has been significant recent interest in using computable general equilibrium (CGE) methods for analyzing the relationship between trade reform and income distribution/poverty. Hertel and Reimer (2005) and Hertel and Winters (2005) survey recent CGE attempts to assess the poverty impact of trade liberalization, while studies applying to countries in the Asia-Pacific region are surveyed in Gilbert (2008). With respect to

Frontiers of Economics and Globalization
Volume 7 ISSN: 1574-8715
DOI: 10.1108/S1574-8715(2010)0000007012

South-Asia, recent work by Pradhan and Sahoo (2006), Gilbert (2007), Panda and Ganesh-Kumar (2008) and Polaski *et al.* (2008) considers India, while results for Bangladesh are available from Annabi *et al.* (2006) and Raihan (2008). Naranpanawa (2005) considers Sri Lanka. Ahmed and O'Donoghue (2008) have a model of Pakistan that can generate information on poverty, although they apply it to macroeconomic shocks rather than trade reform.

Most of these studies use single-economy models, sometimes in combination with a global model such as the Global Trade Analysis Project (GTAP) or LINKAGE, to analyze the socioeconomic impacts of policy changes on a single economy in the region. Gilbert (2008) differs in that it attempts to deal with household income distribution issues in the context of the whole region simultaneously, using a disaggregated CGE model. Since the regional trade reforms involve multiple sectors and regions, an approach that captures potential feedback effects across a region has some advantages. This is particularly important in the case of South Asia, where economic relations with India are a dominant factor in the outcomes for other smaller economies. Hence, a model of the effects of regional trade reform on Sri Lanka in isolation, for example, may be seriously misleading if the indirect effects felt via reform's impact on India are not taken into account.

In this chapter we use a CGE model of South Asia to analyze the economic impact of the South Asian Free Trade Agreement (SAFTA) on the economies of South Asia. The model is similar in structure to that used in Gilbert (2008). But, whereas that model used the GTAP version 6 database with a base year of 2001, this study uses the GTAP7 database with a base year of 2004. The model has also been extended to include Pakistan. The model features multiple (between 5 and 19) households in each of the economies of the region.

The structure of the chapter is as follows. In Section 2 we review the existing CGE studies of trade reform in South Asia. In Section 3 we review the policy background and use trade indices to evaluate the current trading environment in the region. The next section describes the structure of the model we have used, data sources, and experimental design. In Section 5 we present our results and discussion. In Section 6 we discuss the underlying theory of a potential extension. Concluding comments follow.

2. *Literature review*

The linkages between trade reform and poverty, and developing ways to quantitatively assess those linkages have been the subject of intense recent research. Hertel and Reimer (2005) and Hertel and Winters (2005) have reviewed *ex ante* studies and provide a method of classification by simulation type: partial equilibrium models, CGE models, and micro/macro simulation models that combine (not always with feedback) macrolevel simulation with microlevel household models. They conclude that CGE techniques and micro/macro methods have the best potential for fully evaluating the complex web of determinants of changes in poverty *ex ante*.

Within the recent CGE literature, there are a range of ways of addressing poverty impacts of trade reform. Aggregate results at the regional level, such as impacts on prices of staples or returns to unskilled labor, may be combined with ad hoc observations on potential effects on poverty. Other studies take results from a global model with a single representative household and pass them through a submodel to determine the poverty impact. Another approach is to build more sophisticated submodels of household behavior or to incorporate income distribution at the household level directly within a regional CGE model. Several studies of this type can be seen in Hertel and Winters (2006) and OECD (2006).

The most straightforward method for dealing with income distribution and poverty impacts in a CGE framework is to abandon the single representative consumer approach and to incorporate multiple representative household groups into the model. This allows the model to track intergroup income changes directly, but leaves the issue of intragroup income changes external to the model. The greater the number of the household groups, the better the model will be able to capture the pattern of income changes. Recent efforts typically feature between 5 and 10 household categories, though a few have many more.

Several recent CGE studies have used the multiple-household approach to analyze the consequences of trade reform in South Asia. These studies have tended to use single-economy models for the distribution analysis, often in combination with a global model used for estimating world price impacts of the proposed scenarios. There are a number of studies of India.[1] Gilbert (2007) considers the impact of the current proposed modalities for reform in agriculture only under Doha at the household level for India, in addition to more comprehensive agricultural reform. The study uses the GTAP model to estimate the world market effects. The global results are then input into a single-economy CGE model of India, which is a competitive CGE of the Armington variety. Under the Doha scenarios, the welfare of the poorest households (agricultural labor and other rural labor) falls, while the welfare of the richest group (urban self-employed) rises, in both the short and long run. The income of rural self-employed (land owners) also rises under the Doha scenarios, suggesting that ownership of land and capital helps to insulate this group from the terms of trade shifts. The result is similar to that of Annabi *et al.* (2006) for Bangladesh. Under comprehensive reform the aggregate welfare gains

[1] This survey draws on the working paper by Gilbert and Banik (2010), which presents a greatly extended version.

are several orders of magnitude larger, and all households except the rural self-employed rise, suggesting that India's land owning class is able to benefit from rising world prices under Doha reform when India does not engage in significant reforms of its own, but faces considerable falls in income if domestic prices are allowed to fall. Pradhan and Sahoo (2006) use a similar CGE structure in their analysis of potential trade reform scenarios for India and reach similar conclusions.

Panda and Ganesh-Kumar (2008) consider the issue of food security with changes in trade policy. Their modeling approach is very similar to that used in Gilbert (2007), with the exception that they use the MIRAGE model developed by IFPRI as the source of their global price changes rather than GTAP. They consider a Doha scenario, and find that all households experience a rise in welfare, and a decline in poverty. Their conclusions are based on a ex-post assessment of the household consumption patterns that drive the CGE model. Finally, Polaski *et al.* (2008) use a single-economy CGE of India, based on a very detailed social accounting matrix (SAM) for 1998–1999. They consider the impact of price changes in agricultural commodities, and find that a decrease in the price of rice could have a significant negative impact on Indian poverty levels.

Results for Bangladesh are available from Annabi *et al.* (2006) and Raihan (2008). Annabi *et al.* (2006) use the GTAP model to estimate the overall effect of trade reform under the Doha proposals (both agriculture and nonagriculture) at the world level, and then input the world market effects into a single-economy CGE model for Bangladesh. The single-country model is used to generate detailed results at the household level. In addition to the Doha agenda, the study also considers the potential impact of a more comprehensive global reform, and of unilateral reform by Bangladesh. The results indicate aggregate welfare losses for Bangladesh under the Doha scenarios, along with small increases in the headcount ratio (diminishing somewhat but remaining negative in the long run). The negative aggregate welfare effect is driven by adverse terms of trade movements. These remain even in a scenario with complete liberalization in the rest of the world (ROW). Raihan (2008) argues that the effects of unilateral reform in the aggregate are positive but small, suggesting that the export bias of the current regime is minimal. Unfortunately, the chapter does not directly discuss poverty or income distribution impacts.

Two studies are available for Nepal, Cockburn (2002) and Acharya and Cohen (2008). Cockburn (2002) constructs a CGE model of Nepal that explicitly models all households from a nationally representative household survey. The model is an archetype competitive CGE, but with a high degree of household disaggregation. The base year of the model is 1986, and the model incorporates 15 production activities. They consider a trade liberalization scenario and find that urban poverty falls and rural poverty increases as initial tariffs were highest for agriculture. Impacts increase with income level, resulting in rising income inequality. Acharya and

Cohen (2008) consider unilateral trade reform. They conclude that the results are not conclusively pro-poor in that one of the richer household groups benefits most, while the benefit to the poorest household group is only modest. Therefore, they suggest that complementary policies are required to make trade liberalization pro-poor in Nepal.

Sri Lanka has been the focus of several CGE studies, many surveyed by Dasanayake (2000).[2] The most recent study is by Naranpanawa (2005), which considers a manufactured good trade liberalization scenario, and finds that the potential benefits accruing to low-income rural groups are low relative to other groups in the in the model, a fact attributed to a reduction in transfers following falls in government revenue. Long-run liberalization reduces absolute poverty in all groups, with manufacturing reform being more pro-poor than agricultural reform, but may increase relative poverty.

Pakistan has also been the subject of several recent CGE studies. Ahmed and O'Donoghue (2008) use a single-economy CGE to examine various macroeconomic shocks. The CGE model is combined with a microsimulation model to generate poverty information. Prices, wages, and aggregate employment variables from the CGE model are used as input to a microsimulation model that generates changes in individual wages, self-employment incomes, and employment status. Among the most important results, they find that external oil price shocks have the highest potential to impact the socioeconomy. Poverty increases when the overall import price increases, but inequality is most adversely impacted by a rise in the import price of petroleum.

There are few studies that attempt to deal with household income distribution issues in the context of the whole region simultaneously, using a disaggregated CGE model. Khan (2008) presents very preliminary results for a prototype model for South Asia. The model is an interesting approach, incorporating several nonstandard features, including technological dualism and rural–urban migration of the Harris–Todaro type. However, it has been calibrated to a single country (India) at present. Hence, the results are relevant for other countries in the region only by extension in the models' current form, although the approach might be usefully adapted to other countries. Gilbert (2008) uses the same basic model as presented here, but with fewer countries and an older dataset, to examine SAFTA. In terms of the overall policy message, the results of this study confirm those of earlier work by Bandara and Yu (2003) in that the overall welfare effects of trade reform under the auspices of SAFTA are likely to be small.

---

[2] This study also briefly reviews some of the earlier CGE studies of India, Bangladesh, and Nepal.

Table 1. Intra-South Asian trade shares 2001–2007

Region	2001	2002	2003	2004	2005	2006	2007
South Asia as destination							
Bangladesh	8.9	9.7	11.3	9.4	9.7	8.3	10.5
India	2.7	2.8	3.3	2.7	2.6	2.4	2.0
Sri Lanka	7.8	10.4	12.7	14.3	15.1	17.7	19.1
Pakistan	2.8	2.8	2.6	3.3	3.5	4.3	4.3
South Asia	3.7	3.9	4.6	3.9	3.7	3.6	3.9
South Asia as source							
Bangladesh	0.9	0.9	1.2	0.9	0.6	0.5	0.6
India	1.8	2.0	2.3	1.9	1.8	1.8	1.6
Sri Lanka	0.6	0.7	0.8	0.8	0.9	0.7	1.2
Pakistan	0.3	0.3	0.3	0.4	0.4	0.6	0.5
South Asia	3.7	3.9	4.6	3.9	3.7	3.6	3.9

Source: COMTRADE.

3. South Asian trade and poverty patterns

SAFTA will require that the developing economies of South Asia reduce their tariffs to a maximum of 20% initially, followed by annual cuts to zero over a 5-year period for developing economies and an 8-year period for LDCs.[3] To assess the potential impact of closer trading relations between the economies of SAFTA, we begin with an evaluation of the current trade and protection pattern, along with the poverty profiles, using simple descriptive statistics.[4]

Regional trade shares are presented in Table 1.[5] The first set of numbers (South Asia as destination) shows the percentage of South Asian economy exports that are directed to other economies in South Asia. The second set (South Asia as source) shows the percentage of exports from South Asian economies that are directed to the individual economies of South Asia. For most economies within South Asia, the regional market is only a small proportion of their external trade. While intraregional trade has grown in importance over recent years for some economies (Sri Lanka and Pakistan), it has remained stagnant for others. Overall, the intraregional trade share for South Asia is at a low level relative to other regions.

---

[3] Bandara and Yu (2003) provide a detailed description of the evolution of economic integration in the region.

[4] This section draws extensively on the analysis in Gilbert (2008), with updated data. Details on the indices can be found in Mikic and Gilbert (2009).

[5] Our calculations are based on COMTRADE data from 2001 to 2007. Calculations are based on reporter data, but where this information is missing we have reconstructed the relevant flows using the mirror data from partners.

Table 2. Intra-South Asian trade intensity 2001–2007

Region	2001	2002	2003	2004	2005	2006	2007
South Asia as destination							
Bangladesh	8.7	8.9	9.3	7.5	6.9	5.9	6.2
India	2.6	2.5	2.7	2.2	1.8	1.7	1.3
Sri Lanka	7.6	9.5	10.5	11.5	10.8	12.6	11.6
Pakistan	2.8	2.5	2.2	2.7	2.5	3.1	3.0
South Asia	4.0	3.9	4.2	3.5	2.9	2.8	2.2

Source: COMTRADE.

Table 3. Intra-South Asian trade complementarity 2001–2007

Region	2001	2002	2003	2004	2005	2006	2007
South Asia as destination							
Bangladesh	46.0	52.8	49.5	48.2	44.9	44.5	47.3
India	42.0	43.7	44.5	47.8	49.7	54.4	56.9
Sri Lanka	50.2	50.8	51.8	52.3	53.9	57.5	57.8
Pakistan	41.0	43.1	43.4	47.6	47.7	50.2	52.3
South Asia	49.9	52.1	52.7	55.0	54.3	58.9	59.8
South Asia as source							
Bangladesh	5.9	7.2	7.0	8.8	6.4	6.2	10.2
India	58.2	56.5	57.8	59.5	59.2	63.9	64.5
Sri Lanka	19.5	23.7	20.4	21.0	24.0	23.7	25.0
Pakistan	18.4	18.4	18.8	20.7	21.8	21.7	23.1
South Asia	49.9	52.1	52.7	55.0	54.3	58.9	59.8

Source: COMTRADE.

The trade intensity index gives an indication of the degree to which a particular trade linkage is stronger than might be expected given the size of the economies in world trade. The index is presented in Table 2. Values greater than 1 indicate an "intense" trading relationship. Viewed this way, the trading relationships in the region appear somewhat stronger, and the heavy reliance of the smaller economies in the region on the larger economies is revealed clearly.

Turning to the sectoral trade profiles, the complementarity index measures the overlap between the export profile of one region and the import profile of another.[6] The index is often used *ex ante* to evaluate the potential for mutually beneficial interindustry trade. The results are presented in Table 3. A value of 100 indicates a perfect match of the trade profiles, while an index of 0 indicates no overlap. Overall, it seems that the

[6] We have calculated the index using COMTRADE data using HS1996 two-digit classifications.

Table 4. Intra-South Asian export similarity 2001–2007

Region	2001	2002	2003	2004	2005	2006	2007
South Asia as destination							
Bangladesh	36.8	33.9	31.6	31.6	29.2	28.4	30.3
India	82.6	85.0	84.3	84.2	85.1	85.3	87.2
Sri Lanka	51.6	49.1	44.6	42.4	43.8	44.7	42.6
Pakistan	54.0	52.2	52.4	48.7	51.5	50.4	49.0

Source: COMTRADE.

Table 5. Trade-weighted average applied tariffs in 2007

	World	Bangladesh	Sri Lanka	India	Nepal	Pakistan
Bangladesh	11.3	–	17.3	10.8	4.4	15.1
Sri Lanka	6.6	6.5	–	6.1	8.6	2.0
India	10.4	17.8	21.3	–	19.2	23.1
Nepal	13.1	8.7	11.6	13.6	–	8.6
Pakistan	11.9	6.6	4.4	8.4	8.7	–

Source: TRAINS.

degree of complementarity has been increasing over the period, although it remains at a relatively low level.

The export similarity profiles are presented in Table 4. These are constructed in the same way as the complementarity index, and a value of 100 indicates that the two groups share identical export profiles, while an index of 0 indicates that the two groups compete in entirely separate markets. The calculations compare each country with South Asia as a whole. Hence, the figures for India are inflated by its dominant role in the group.[7] Nonetheless, for Sri Lanka and Pakistan, the similarity indices remain high. In other words, the countries of South Asia have a revealed comparative advantage in similar products. The values of the index are declining over time, however. In conjunction with the increase in complementarity, this perhaps suggests production shifts gradually aligning.

Table 5 describes the state of protection in the countries of interest, using the bilateral applied tariff (trade weighted). Substantial progress has been made in lowering the average level of protection in the South Asian economies over the past decade, but applied tariffs remain moderately high on average, with a tendency toward high agricultural protection, especially in India. However, there is also a substantial degree of binding

[7] A country's export similarity with itself is, by definition, 100%.

Table 6. Poverty profiles of South Asian economies

	Year	Headcount (%)	Poverty gap (%)	Squared poverty gap (%)	Gini (%)
$1 per day					
Bangladesh	2005	35.3	7.9	2.4	33.2
India – rural	2005	40.2	9.4	3.1	30.5
India – urban	2005	19.6	4.2	1.3	37.6
Nepal	2004	24.7	5.6	1.7	47.3
Pakistan	2005	9.0	1.4	0.4	31.2
Sri Lanka	2002	5.8	0.7	0.1	40.2
$2 per day					
Bangladesh	2005	81.5	35.6	18.5	33.2
India – rural	2005	87.7	39.8	21.0	30.5
India – urban	2005	61.5	23.1	11.1	37.6
Nepal	2004	64.8	26.4	13.2	47.3
Pakistan	2005	59.5	18.3	7.4	31.2
Sri Lanka	2002	41.5	12.1	4.6	40.2

Source: World Bank (2007).

overhang, especially in Bangladesh, but also in India and Sri Lanka. Overall, the protection levels in the South Asia suggest that there is significant potential for efficiency gains from trade reform.

Finally, Table 6 reviews the poverty/income distribution statistics in the region. These have been drawn from World Bank (2007), and we have extracted the latest available year for each economy in South Asia for which data are available. The figures reflect South Asia's status as one of the world's poorest regions. While the headcount ratio in India has been falling since 1996, and poverty depth and severity has also fallen over the period, the proportion of population in poverty in India remains high, and there is also considerable variation in poverty levels between urban and rural populations. In Bangladesh the poverty headcount is even higher, at 35%, while it is 25% in Nepal. In Pakistan and Sri Lanka, the rates are much lower at 9% and 6%, respectively. Nonetheless, poverty remains an issue, at the $2 per day level the corresponding rates are 60% and 41%. Two other measures are provided in Table 6, both of which attempt to address the issue of poverty depth. The poverty gap measure is the mean distance below the poverty line as a proportion of the poverty line. The squared poverty gap weights individual poverty gaps by the gaps themselves, and provides a measure of inequality among the poor. The areas with the greatest poverty depth are again Bangladesh, rural India, and Nepal. Finally, the Gini coefficient is a common measure of overall income inequality, with the greatest levels of inequality in Nepal and Sri Lanka.

4. Methodology

To analyze the effect of these proposals on the economies of South Asia, we use a custom-built CGE model of the region, with subeconomy models for key countries, programmed using the GAMS system. This section outlines key characteristics of the model structure and experimental design. The model covers India, Bangladesh, Sri Lanka, Pakistan, and rest of South Asia, as well as an incompletely modeled ROW region. Overall, the structure of the model that we built for this study is similar in many respects to GTAP and other global models. Hence, we keep our description brief.

4.1. Model

The model identifies 16 production sectors. Each sector produces a joint product for domestic and foreign markets, with the allocation between the two based on a constant elasticity of transformation (CET) function. The production functions are nested constant elasticity of substitution (CES) functions with intermediate goods used in fixed proportions and all primary factors in variable proportions with a common elasticity. Intermediate inputs are composites of imported goods and domestic production, with proportions that are variable and specified independently by industry.

Competitive conditions hold, so firms pay market prices for all inputs, and make zero (economic) profit. Primary endowments are fixed, and may be treated as specific or mobile. The dataset contains five primary factors. In the default medium run closure, we treat all factors except natural resources as mobile across economic activities.

The model identifies several consumption activities, the government, investment, and multiple consumer households. The number of consumer households varies by region depending on available data, with between 4 and 19 categories in the various regions. Final consumption of each household is modeled using Stone–Geary utility functions, which generate linear expenditure systems (LES) characterizing demand for each household category. Changes in household welfare are measured by equivalent variation (EV).[8] The parameters of the functions vary by household to capture differences in consumption patterns. The quantity of government consumption and investment is held constant in the default closure. All agents consume composites of imported goods and domestic production, with proportions that are variable and specified independently by agent

[8] EV is the monetary value of the increment in income that would have to be given to (or taken away from) a household at today's prices to make them as well off today as they would be under the proposed policy change.

(sometimes called the SALTER specification). On the income side, factors are owned in varying proportions by the households, and we maintain fixed proportions in household savings, taxation, and government transfers.

The exportable goods produced by domestic firms are allocated over destination regions using a second-level CET function; hence, the aggregate exportable goods are a composite of exports to the various regions (the elasticity on both CET functions is set such that export destinations are very close to being perfectly substitutable, with elasticities of 20 and 40 at the lower and upper levels, respectively). Similarly, on the import side, the imports of each country are a CES composite of regional imports (i.e., a second-level Armington function). Unlike at the first level, this function is common across all agents in the domestic economy. Demand for regional exports is derived from the Armington import structure for all regions that are explicitly modeled. For regions that are not explicitly modeled, here the ROW region, we reduce the computational complexity of the model by using constant elasticity of demand functions to represent demand responses. The prices of imports from the ROW region are fixed.

An international transportation sector accounts for the difference between the FOB price of exports and the CIF price of imports. Transportation margins vary by commodity along all international routes. Unlike in the GTAP model, because of our focus on a single, relatively small (in global terms) region, we fix the price of international transportation services.

The price normalization and closure rules are similar to those used in many single-country models. The current account balance is fixed and the nominal exchange rate is allowed to vary to maintain balance within each country. The numeraire in each country is the consumer price index. We must also define a numeraire region for which the nominal exchange rate is fixed, which in this model is the ROW region.

The model includes a full range of distortions in the form of taxes and subsidies on economic activities at all levels to ensure that the second-best implications of the policy scenarios are adequately accounted for.

4.2. Data

The CGE model requires appropriate data in the form of a SAM for each country, trade flow matrices, and estimates of the model parameters and their distributions.[9] These have been compiled from various sources and reconciled prior to model implementation.

---

[9] The SAM is an account of all of the flows between economic agents at a point in time.

The base data on trade, production, aggregate consumption and employment, are extracted from the GTAP7 database. GTAP7 uses 2004 as its base year. Information on sources of household income (ownership of primary factors and transfers/taxes) and variation in consumption patterns across households is obtained from Pradhan and Sahoo (2006) for India, Fontana and Wobst (2001) for Bangladesh, Naranpanawa (2005) for Sri Lanka, and Roland-Holst (2008) for Pakistan.[10] The household categories used in the model are listed in Table 7. The information in each study was aggregated/disaggregated and rebalanced where necessary to match the dimensions of our model and to be consistent with the aggregate GTAP7 household consumption data.[11]

Model elasticity parameters are obtained from the existing estimates in GTAP7. Armington elasticities have recently been estimated by Hertel *et al.* (2007). Base substitution elasticities in production are also obtained from GTAP7.

4.3. Experimental design

The model is quite general in purpose, and can in principle be useful to examine a variety of developments in South Asia. We consider a regional economic integration scenario representing SAFTA, which involves the removal of only internal tariffs in the region. The simulation is run as a comparative static, so the results should be interpreted as representing how the economic system would have appeared in the base year had the proposed changes been implemented and the economic system given sufficient time to adjust to the new equilibrium. As noted above, the factor market closure allows all factors except natural resources to be mobile across economic activities, implying that the simulations are medium run in nature.

Sensitivity analysis is implemented within the simulations by using an unconditional approach adopted in Gilbert and Wahl (2003). This approach improves the policy value of the simulations by highlighting results that are unlikely to be robust, and providing an estimate of the

[10] A newer SAM from Saluja and Yadav (2006) has a base year of 2003–2004, and has 73 productive sectors and 10 household categories, defined by expenditure level. We may update the model to include information from this SAM at a later date.

[11] The procedure we used was to first split the factor income proportions across skilled and unskilled labor using the aggregate level of factor use in GTAP7 and the allocation of labor to agricultural/nonagricultural activities. Once this mapping was complete we were able to construct household incomes consistent with the GTAP7 data. These generally matched the proportions in the original data quite closely. We then matched the consumption categories to GTAP categories, and used the overall GTAP consumption proportions to split the individual household proportions where necessary. Finally, we used the RAS method to ensure that the household consumption shares were consistent with the household incomes and total expenditures in GTAP7. This process was undertaken for each country in the model.

***Table 7.* Household categories in the model by region**

Category	Pakistan	Bangladesh	India	Sri Lanka
H1	Large farm – Sindh	Agricultural landless	Rural self-employed agricultural	Urban low income
H2	Large farm – Punjab	Agricultural marginal land	Rural agricultural labor	Rural low income
H3	Large farm – other	Agricultural small land	Rural nonagricultural labor	Estate low income
H4	Medium farm – Sindh	Agricultural large land	Other rural	Urban high income
H5	Medium farm – Punjab	Non-agricultural poor	Urban agricultural	Rural high income
H6	Medium farm – other	Non-agricultural rich	Urban self-employed nonagricultural	
H7	Small farm – Sindh	Urban illiterate	Urban salaried	
H8	Small farm – Punjab	Urban low educated	Urban casual labor	
H9	Small farm – other	Urban medium educated	Other urban	
H10	Landless farm – Sindh	Urban highly educated		
H11	Landless farm – Punjab			
H12	Landless farm – other			
H13	Rural landless – Sindh			
H14	Rural landless – Punjab			
H15	Rural landless – other			
H16	Rural nonpoor			
H17	Rural nonfarm poor			
H18	Urban nonpoor			
H19	Urban poor			

Source: Pradhan and Sahoo (2006), Fontana and Wobst (2001), Naranpanawa (2005), and Roland-Holst (2008).

range of potential outcomes rather than a point estimate. To undertake the analysis, key parameters (the trade elasticities) are treated as normally and independently distributed random variables.[12] Each simulation is run as a Monte Carlo experiment, with a series of pseudorandom parameter values chosen from the underlying distributions. With a large number of iterations (we have used 1000) of the simulation, we can approximate the mean predictions of the variables of interest, along with indicators of their susceptibility to parametric uncertainty (the standard deviations), and the accuracy of the simulation procedure (the standard errors). This general technique is valid for any type of model structure and the computational complexity does not increase with the number of parameters that are allowed to vary. It is, however, computationally expensive. Variance reduction techniques can therefore be usefully applied here. The two techniques that we use are running alternative simulations using common random numbers and adopting antithetic variates in the sampling. The former ensures that the same pseudorandom numbers are drawn for alternative simulations, and therefore that alternatives can be compared without the risk of a skewed draw. Antithetic variates use the mean of symmetric draws from the underlying distribution as the estimator for mean predictions. Since most of the variables of interest vary monotonically with the elasticities that we treat as random variables, this technique dramatically reduces the standard errors in our preliminary tests (i.e., improves the accuracy of the mean estimates). In simulations with 1000 draws the standard errors were roughly halved relative to 2000 fully random draws, a reduction that would require quadrupling the number of iterations under fully random draws. That is, simulations using 1000 antithetic variates generate a level of accuracy equivalent to 8000 fully random draws.

5. *Results and discussion*

The preliminary results of our analysis are presented in Table 8, which covers economic welfare effects by household and country, and Table 9, which presents information on production shifts. First, consider the impact of the trade reforms on overall economic welfare. The results of our simulations, using the household EV measure, are presented in the third row from the bottom of Table 8, labeled "total." This type of estimate of the benefit/cost of the proposed change is sometimes called a "one-off" gain/loss. However, this is somewhat misleading since the changes are permanent. Rather we can think of this (roughly) as a permanent

[12] We have followed Gilbert and Wahl (2003) and used a uniform margin, here a default standard deviation of 7.5% of the mean value from GTAP7, implying that almost all variation will occur within 25% of the mean.

Table 8. Household welfare impact of trade reform (US$ millions, EV)

	Pakistan	Bangladesh	India	Sri Lanka	Rest of South Asia
H1	4.6	3.5	*−68.1*	24.3	
H2	14.6	41.1	31.7	*−8.3*	
H3	2.5	*4.1*	30.6	10.8	
H4	14.2	−50.7	45.2	71.2	
H5	40.2	26.0	2.6	51.5	
H6	15.0	*1.6*	69.7		
H7	12.3	−17.7	144.2		
H8	52.1	8.2	15.3		
H9	8.6	−155.1	19.1		
H10	4.3	−138.8			
H11	5.2				
H12	1.6				
H13	0.4				
H14	*0.5*				
H15	*0.0*				
H16	12.5				
H17	1.9				
H18	−46.4				
H19	4.5				
Total	148.6	−277.8	290.2	149.5	205.7
Cumulative	7428.9	−13889.6	14508.9	7477.2	10283.0
Cumulative as % of GDP	7.8	−24.8	2.3	37.2	74.0

Table 9. Sectoral impact of trade reform (% change in production)

	Pakistan	Bangladesh	India	Sri Lanka	Rest of South Asia
Food grains	*−0.2*	0.0	0.0	−0.9	0.6
Other agriculture	0.3	−0.9	*0.0*	0.3	6.3
Forestry and fisheries	−0.1	−0.6	−0.1	0.3	2.4
Coal, oil, gas, and other minerals	−0.8	−2.4	−0.2	11.1	−5.7
Processed rice	−1.7	0.0	0.0	0.4	−1.2
Other food	2.0	−0.7	−0.8	3.9	25.6
Textiles	*0.1*	3.9	0.9	−3.5	*0.8*
Wearing apparel	−3.7	15.3	*−0.1*	−11.0	−12.0
Leather	−3.8	8.3	−1.0	−2.5	−20.3
Wood products	−0.6	−1.4	0.2	7.8	*−1.5*
Chemicals, rubber	−0.9	−0.4	0.4	1.1	15.6
Metals and minerals	−0.6	−3.0	*−0.1*	30.1	30.5
Metal products	−10.3	−5.0	0.3	16.1	−2.3
Heavy manufactures	−1.3	−1.7	0.2	14.6	−15.7
Manufactures NEC	−2.2	−2.9	−0.5	−13.5	−3.2
Services	−0.1	−0.5	0.0	−0.6	−1.4

increment to household incomes, at constant prices. In terms of a true "one-off" measure of the benefit/cost, we need to discount the permanent income stream measured by the EV. If the discount rate is assumed to be a standard 2%, then the total estimated benefit is 50 times the annual increment, and this is the row labeled "cumulative." We can think of this as the total benefit of the reduction in trade barriers.[13] The projected benefits of SAFTA are positive for all economies except Bangladesh. India is the biggest winner, followed by the aggregate "rest of South Asia" (Nepal, Maldives, and others). These results are consistent with those in Gilbert (2008), and all are robust to underlying parameter uncertainty.

In terms of relative benefits, we can evaluate the estimated welfare impact relative to a baseline metric, most commonly the initial GDP. The final row of Table 8 expresses the cumulative gain as a proportion of GDP. Viewed from this perspective, by far the biggest beneficiary of trade reforms under SAFTA is for the rest of South Asia region, by a substantial margin. Rest of South Asia is followed by Sri Lanka, with the gains to India from SAFTA being quite small when expressed as a percent of GDP. The large gains to the rest of South Asia reflect significant improvements in market access to its dominant trading partner, India.

On the surface it appears that the simulation results would support (at least in terms of overall efficiency) a regional trade reform process through SAFTA, although as might be expected given the similarity of the export profiles as discussed above, the gains from SAFTA are also modest.

Before turning to the estimated impact on household welfare, it is useful to review the household categories in the model, as presented in Table 7. In the Sri Lankan data, we have five household groups, broken down by location and income level into rural–urban and high-income/low-income groupings. The data for India, Pakistan, and Bangladesh are grouped by archetype.

In India, group H2 (rural agricultural labor) is the poorest group, by a substantial margin, followed by H4 (other rural) and H3 (rural nonagricultural labor). The richest groups are H6 (urban self-employed) and H7 (urban salaried). The households differ substantially in their ownership of productive factors, with the richest rural group (H1, rural self-employed) being substantial owners of land and capital. On the other hand, the poorer households, especially H2, receive income almost

[13] For a variety of reasons, this estimate is likely to be very much a lower bound, since the comparative static simulation technique used here does not capture any potential dynamic accumulation effects (i.e., some proportion of the increment to income may be invested, leading to a multiplier effect), and the competitive model used does not account for potential scale effects.

exclusively from selling their own labor (a large fraction of which is unskilled). Comparing the poorest two groups (H2 and H4) with the richest two (H6 and H7), we observe significant differences in spending patterns also, although the differences are not as great as in ownership of productive resources. In particular, the two poorest groups spend nearly 2.5 times as much of their income on basic food items (in particular processed rice), as the two richest groups. In textiles the pattern is less dramatic, but the poor groups spend about 30% more than the rich groups.

In Bangladesh, the poorest groups are H1 and H2, rural groups with only limited or no holdings of land. They are followed by H7, H3, and to a lesser extent H8, that is, the urban illiterate and poorly educated, and rural households with small land holdings. The richest groups, by a substantial margin, are urban households with high or medium education (H9 and H10). The factor allocation pattern is similar to India, with the lower income groups having a much higher dependence on unskilled labor. Consumption differences are also similar, with the poorest households devoting more than double the proportion of their budget to processed rice than the richest households.

In the Pakistan data, as with Sri Lanka, we have a combined archetype and income-level classification. The data are very detailed, with a concentration on rural households. Households are grouped into multiple farm sizes on the basis of land holdings, and three regions. Also identified are the rural rich, and urban poor/rich. In total, our model tracks changes in the behavior of 43 household groups in the region.

The decomposition of the total welfare impacts on the various household groups is summarized in Table 8. The values in italics are not robust to changes in the underlying parameters of the model, that is, we cannot be sure of the sign of the change. Other values are robust given the assumptions on the parameter distributions.[14]

The results for Pakistan indicate that all households except one are estimated to gain (with a couple not robust). The losing household is the urban rich. The overall impact is positive, and the policy is likely to be pro-poor. For Bangladesh, again the groups that do not gain by reform are the urban rich (H9 and H10). These results are interesting given the debate, which has focused on negative impacts on the rural poor. At least for these three economies, trade reform does not hurt the rural poor as feared, but rather the urban rich. Of course, from a political economy perspective, this could be highly problematic.

---

[14] Roughly, a result can be considered robust to the assumed underlying parametric uncertainty if it retains the same sign within two standard deviations of the mean.

In India also there is a highly skewed income distribution effect, with group H1 being a serious loser from trade reform under SAFTA (although the result is not very robust). The H1 group represents rural landowners. On the whole, this groups is not really poor, so the policies are again not hurting the rural poor (groups H2, H3, and H4), but rather the rural rich. Again, this might have significant political economy implications.

The only result that is consistent with the conventional wisdom is for Sri Lanka, where the model projects a reduction in household incomes only for group H2, the rural poor. All other households gain. The result is not robust in the SAFTA scenario. Nonetheless, this is a concern. It suggests that the impact of trade reform in Sri Lanka may hit the poorest groups in society relatively hard. Since the overall gains are positive, a redistribution makes it feasible to make all groups better off, in principle.

Overall then, the impacts of the changes at the household level exhibit more variation than the aggregate results. While the trade policy scenarios considered here appear to be pro-poor in an absolute sense in some cases, there is little doubt that some household groups would be hard hit by trade liberalization under SAFTA. In most cases, it is relatively advantaged groups that are hurt by reforms, not the rural poor. Our calculations are based on assumption of invariant transfers, taxes, and factor ownership, but in principle these can be changed if the political will exists.

In addition to overall welfare effects, and their distribution across various groups in the societies in question, CGE simulation also generates sectoral information. Of particular interest are changes in the production structure, both because they indicate which sectors are most likely to be impacted by the proposed policy and because they provide an indication of the potential degree of structural adjustment required. Estimates of the sectoral production changes are presented in Table 9. Again, results that are not considered robust under our sensitivity analysis are highlighted in italics.

Overall, the biggest adjustments are expected in the rest of South Asia region, under both scenarios, with large expansions in chemicals and metal production, smaller expansions in textiles, and declines in agriculture textiles and heavy manufactures. The pattern is similar in Sri Lanka, while the production shifts in India are all very small, suggesting little adjustment difficulty.

6. *A future extension*

One assumption of this type of representative household model is that labor can move freely across economic activities. However, this assumption may be misleading. Indeed, it seems that labor owned by poorer households would be less mobile, and ideally we would like to take this into account. While a number of CGE models incorporate imperfect labor mobility at the factor level (e.g., GTAP and Gilbert and Wahl, 2003), they feature single-representative households. To understand the implications of imperfect labor mobility for household welfare responses to trade reform, we need to first develop a framework for exploring the impact on factor incomes. We conclude this chapter with some theoretical considerations.

Consider a simple two-sector general equilibrium model along the lines of Casas (1984). Let the two sectors be X and Y and the two factors be capital and labor (K and L). K is mobile across activities, while L is mobile but sluggish, resulting in a differential wage at equilibrium. All other neoclassical assumptions apply. The production specification is thus rather standard; the zero profit conditions for firms are expressed in terms of the unit cost functions c_j as:

$$c_X(w_X, r) = p \tag{1}$$

$$c_Y(w_Y, r) = 1 \tag{2}$$

where w_j is the price of labor in industry j and r in the price of capital. We have chosen the price of Y as the numeraire. Full employment of factors of production implies that

$$a_{LX}X + a_{LY}Y = L \tag{3}$$

$$a_{KX}X + a_{KY}Y = K \tag{4}$$

where a_{ij} is the optimal unit demand for factor i in industry j, obtained by the derivative properties of the unit cost functions. Now suppose that the economy contains multiple household units that own the factors of production in varying proportions. Let the set of households be denoted $\mathbf{H}$ with elements indexed by h. Suppose that each household's relative allocation of labor across industries is a function of the relative wages such that

$$\frac{w_X}{w_Y} = \psi_h\left(\frac{L_X^h}{L_Y^h}\right)$$

where $\psi'_h > 0$, and L_j^h is the amount of household h's labor employed in industry j. We can think of these expressions as relative labor supply functions. Since labor is homogeneous, by summing across households we obtain the following aggregate function:

$$\frac{w_X}{w_Y} = \psi\left(\frac{a_{LX}X}{a_{LY}Y}\right) = \sum_{\forall h \in \mathbf{H}} \psi_h\left(\frac{L_X^h}{L_Y^h}\right) \tag{5}$$

where we have made use of the fact that total labor supplies of households to each industry equal industry demands at equilibrium.

Now, differentiating the system holding endowments constant and utilizing the well-known solutions for the optimal unit demands (see Jones, 1965) we obtain the following system of equations of change:

$$\theta_{LX}\hat{w}_X + \theta_{KX}\hat{r} = \hat{p} \tag{6}$$

$$\theta_{LY}\hat{w}_Y + \theta_{KY}\hat{r} = 0 \tag{7}$$

$$\lambda_{LX}\hat{X} + \lambda_{LY}\hat{Y} = \delta_{LX}(\hat{w}_X - \hat{r}) + \delta_{LY}(\hat{w}_Y - \hat{r}) \tag{8}$$

$$\lambda_{KX}\hat{X} + \lambda_{KY}\hat{Y} = -\delta_{KX}(\hat{w}_X - \hat{r}) - \delta_{KY}(\hat{w}_Y - \hat{r}) \tag{9}$$

$$\varepsilon(\hat{w}_X - \hat{w}_Y) = (\hat{X} - \hat{Y}) + \sigma[\theta_{KY}(\hat{w}_Y - \hat{r}) - \theta_{KX}(\hat{w}_X - \hat{r})] \tag{10}$$

where a circumflex denotes a proportional change, θ_{ij} is the cost share of factor i in sector j, λ_{ij} is the proportion of factor i utilized in sector j, σ is the elasticity of substitution between K and L, which we have assumed to be constant across the sectors for simplicity, $\delta_{ij} = \lambda_{ij}\theta_{kj}\sigma(k \neq i)$, and $\varepsilon > 0$ is the aggregate elasticity of labor mobility (defined as the proportional change in the ratio of labor allocations per proportional change in the wage ratio).

In this model factor prices are not independent of production levels; hence, we must solve the full system simultaneously. To proceed, we use (6) and (7) to eliminate $\hat{w}_X$ and $\hat{w}_Y$, respectively. The remaining equations can then be expressed in matrix form as

$$\begin{bmatrix} \lambda_{LX} & \lambda_{LY} & \Delta \\ \lambda_{KX} & \lambda_{KY} & -\sigma \\ -1 & 1 & (\varepsilon - \sigma)|\theta|(\theta_{LX}\theta_{LY})^{-1} \end{bmatrix} \begin{bmatrix} \hat{X} \\ \hat{Y} \\ \hat{r} \end{bmatrix} = \begin{bmatrix} \delta_{LX}\theta_{LX}^{-1} \\ -\lambda_{KX}\sigma \\ \theta_{LX}^{-1}(\theta_{KX}\sigma - \varepsilon) \end{bmatrix} \hat{p} \tag{11}$$

where $\Delta = \delta_{LX}\theta_{LX}^{-1} + \delta_{LY}\theta_{LY}^{-1}$ and $|\theta| = \theta_{LX}\theta_{KY} - \theta_{KX}\theta_{LY}$. Solving for $\hat{r}$ we obtain

$$\hat{r} = \frac{\theta_{LX}^{-1}(|\lambda|(\theta_{KX}\sigma - \varepsilon) - \delta_{LX}) - \lambda_{KX}\sigma}{|\lambda||\theta|(\varepsilon - \sigma)(\theta_{LX}\theta_{LY})^{-1} - (\sigma + \Delta)}\hat{p} \tag{12}$$

where $|\lambda| = \lambda_{LX}\lambda_{KY} - \lambda_{LY}\lambda_{KX}$. We can then solve for the changes in wages using (6) and (7):

$$\hat{w}_X = \left[\frac{1}{\theta_{LX}} - \frac{\theta_{KX}}{\theta_{LX}} \frac{\theta_{LX}^{-1}(|\lambda|(\theta_{KX}\sigma - \varepsilon) - \delta_{LX}) - \lambda_{KX}\sigma}{|\lambda||\theta|(\varepsilon - \sigma)(\theta_{LX}\theta_{LY})^{-1} - (\sigma + \Delta)}\right]\hat{p} \tag{13}$$

$$\hat{w}_Y = -\frac{\theta_{KY}}{\theta_{LY}}\frac{\theta_{LX}^{-1}(|\lambda|(\theta_{KX}\sigma-\varepsilon)-\delta_{LX})-\lambda_{KX}\sigma}{|\lambda||\theta|(\varepsilon-\sigma)(\theta_{LX}\theta_{LY})^{-1}-(\sigma+\Delta)}\hat{p} \tag{14}$$

Expressions (12)–(14) characterize the factor income response to changes in domestic prices. Suppose that X is capital-intensive, implying that both$|\lambda|<0$ and$|\theta|<0$. Then it follows from (12) that $\hat{r}>0$ for $\hat{p}>0$. In the limit, as $\varepsilon\to\infty$, Equation (12) reduces to the familiar $-\theta_{LY}\hat{p}/|\theta|$ Similarly, it is easily established that in the limit we have $\hat{w}_Y=\hat{w}_X<0$ for $\hat{p}>0$. However, when labor mobility is restricted, $\hat{w}_Y$ and $\hat{w}_X$ will diverge. When labor is fully immobilized, we have $\hat{w}_X>0$ and $\hat{w}_Y<0$ for $\hat{p}>0$, as in the specific factors model. Generally, then the consequence of imperfect labor mobility is a divergence in the factor price response to trade liberalization.

Now, to see how imperfect labor mobility impacts household welfare, we need to develop expressions for the changes in welfare of individual household groups and correctly map these onto changes in factor incomes and transfers. We start with the familiar balance of trade condition:

$$C_Y + p^*C_X = Y + p^*X$$

where C_j denotes aggregate consumption of good j, and p^* is the world relative price of X. This can be rewritten in terms of domestic prices as

$$C_Y + pC_X = Y + pX + (p-p^*)(C_X - X)$$

where the second term on the right-hand side is tariff revenue. By rewriting GDP on the right-hand side in terms of expenditures on factors, this becomes

$$C_Y + pC_X = w_X a_{LX}X + w_Y a_{LY}Y + rK + (p-p^*)(C_X - X)$$

This expression in turn is amenable to a breakdown across households as follows:

$$C_Y^h + pC_X^h = \phi_{LX}^h w_X a_{LX}X + \phi_{LY}^h w_Y a_{LY}Y + \phi_K^h rK + \phi_t^h(p-p^*)(C_X - X) \quad \forall h\in\mathbf{H} \tag{15}$$

where C_j^h is consumption of good j by household h, ϕ_{Lj}^h is the ownership share of household h in labor employed in industry j (i.e., L_j^h/L_j), ϕ_K^h is the capital ownership share of household h, and ϕ_t^h is the proportion of tariff revenue that is transferred back to household h. Summing across all households, of course, yields the original identity. Totally differentiating (15) yields the following:

$$\begin{aligned} \mathrm{d}\Omega^h = {} & \phi^h_{LX} w_X \lambda_{LX} L\left(\hat{X} + \hat{w}_X + \hat{a}_{LX} + \hat{\phi}^h_{LX}\right) \\ & + \phi^h_{LY} w_Y \lambda_{LY} L\left(\hat{Y} + \hat{w}_Y + \hat{a}_{LY} + \hat{\phi}^h_{LY}\right) \\ & + \phi^h_t [(C_X - X)(\mathrm{d}p - \mathrm{d}p^*) + (p - p^*)(\mathrm{d}C_X - \mathrm{d}X)] \\ & + \phi^h_K r K \hat{r} - p C^h_X \hat{p} \end{aligned} \quad \forall h \in \mathbf{H} \qquad (16)$$

where $\mathrm{d}\Omega^h = \mathrm{d}C^h_Y + p\mathrm{d}C^h_X$ is the change in household consumption at constant prices, our measure of welfare. The expression can ultimately be reduced to terms depending on the trade elasticities and the change in the tariff schedule, but the above breakdown is sufficient for our purposes.

In the usual case (i.e., assuming that the Metzler paradox does not hold at our initial point), a reduction in the tariff will correspond to $\hat{p} < 0$. The third term in (16) captures shifts in the value of capital. With X being capital-intensive, the sign of this term is negative, as established by (12). The fourth term represents the effect of the reform on tariff revenue. This has two components, a volume of trade effect, which is positive, and a terms-of-trade effect, which is negative. The overall impact will depend on which effect dominates. For tariffs that are relatively low (below optimal levels), the terms-of-trade effect will dominate, and this term will be negative. The last term shows the importance of consumption patterns; households that consume relatively large quantities of the protected good will benefit disproportionately from its liberalization.

The first two terms are of primary interest in explaining the impact of labor immobility. They show that imperfect factor mobility will affect households differentially on the basis of both their ownership of labor and the employment pattern in general. If labor is perfectly mobile, then the pattern of employment is of little consequence. The initial wage must be the same across activities, and will rise in response to the liberalization, given the factor intensity assumptions. Households with large ownership shares of labor will benefit, irrespective of where it is initially employed.

What if households vary in terms of their ability to move across activities? If at least one household is unconstrained, and if that household is a large enough owner of labor to be able to absorb the required changes, then again the pattern of initial employment will not matter, it is of little consequence exactly who moves in this context. But, if the overall level of mobility is low across all households, or if the most mobile households do not own enough labor to absorb the shock, the initial distribution of labor takes on new significance, since the impact on wages in different activities will have to differ, resulting in differential household impacts.

This analysis suggests that when attempting to introduce imperfect labor mobility into representative household type models, we will need to think carefully about the mobility levels of different groups, and not just the initial factor ownership pattern, but also the initial employment pattern. This is an interesting area for future applied work.

7. Concluding comments

In this chapter, we have used descriptive statistics and computable general equilibrium methods to assess the potential impact of trade reform under SAFTA on the economies of South Asia. Our model differs from others in the literature in that it isolates household level impacts for a diverse range of household groups across the region. The preliminary results suggest that, in contrast to the received wisdom, the distributional impacts of trade reform in South Asia are not likely to be biased against the rural poor in many of the economies. By contrast, in most of the economies the bias is against the urban nonpoor. We have also proposed that imperfect mobility of labor may be a significant issue, and explored the theoretical implications.

References

Acharya, S., Cohen, S. (2008), Trade liberalisation and household welfare in Nepal. *Journal of Policy Modeling* 30 (6), 1057–1060.

Ahmed, V., O'Donoghue, C. (2008), Welfare impact of external balance in Pakistan: CGE-microsimulation analysis. Paper presented at the 11th Annual Conference on Global Economic Analysis, Helsinki, Finland.

Annabi, N., Khondker, B., Raihan, S., Cockburn, J., Decaluwe, B. (2006), Implications of WTO agreements and unilateral trade policy reforms for poverty in Bangladesh: short vs. long run impacts. In: Hertel, T., Winters, L.A. (Eds.), *Poverty Impacts of a WTO Agreement*. World Bank, Washington, DC.

Bandara, J.S., Yu, W. (2003), How desirable is the South Asian free trade area? A quantitative economic assessment. *World Economy* 26 (9), 1293–1323.

Casas, F.R. (1984), Imperfect factor mobility: a generalization and synthesis of two-sector models of international trade. *Canadian Journal of Economics* 17, 747–761.

Cockburn, J. (2002), Trade liberalisation and poverty in Nepal: a computable general equilibrium micro simulation analysis. CSAE WPS/2002-11.

Dasanayake, S.W.S.B. (2000), *A Literature Survey of Macro Econometric and CGE Models in Sri Lanka*. Institute of Policy Studies, Colombo.

Fontana, M., Wobst, P. (2001), A gendered 1993–94 social accounting matrix for Bangladesh. TMD Discussion Paper No. 74, International Food Policy Research Institute.

Gilbert, J. (2007), *Agricultural Trade Reform under Doha and Poverty in India*. UNESCAP, Bangkok.

Gilbert, J. (2008), Trade policy, poverty, and income distribution in CGE models: an application to SAFTA. In: *Emerging Trade Issues for Policymakers in Developing Countries in Asia and the Pacific*. UNESCAP, Bangkok.

Gilbert, J., Banik, N. (2010), Socioeconomic impacts of cross-border transport infrastructure development in South Asia. ADBI Working Paper No. 211.

Gilbert, J., Wahl, T. (2003), Labor market distortions and China's WTO accession package: an a applied general equilibrium assessment. *Journal of Comparative Economics* 31 (4), 774–794.

Hertel, T., Reimer, J. (2005), Predicting the poverty impacts of trade reform. *Journal of International Trade and Economic Development* 14 (4), 377–405.

Hertel, T., Winters, L.A. (2005), Estimating the poverty impacts of a prospective Doha Development Agenda. *World Economy* 28 (8), 1057–1071.

Hertel, T., Winters, L. A. (Eds.) (2006). *Poverty Impacts of a WTO Agreement*. World Bank, Washington, DC.

Hertel, T., Hummels, D., Ivanic, M., Keeney, R. (2007), How confident can we be of CGE-based assessments of free trade agreements? *Economic Modeling* 24 (4), 611–635.

Jones, R.W. (1965), The structure of simple general equilibrium models. *Journal of Political Economy* 73, 557–572.

Khan, H. (2008), Analyzing poverty impact of trade liberalization policies in CGE models: theory and some policy experiments in agricultural and non-agricultural sectors in South Asia. MPRA Paper No. 7609.

Mikic, M., Gilbert, J. (2009), *Trade Statistics in Policymaking: A Handbook of Commonly Used Trade Indices and Indicators*, revised ed United Nations ESCAP, New York.

Naranpanawa, R.M.A.K.B. (2005), Trade liberalization and poverty in a computable general equilibrium (CGE) model: the Sri Lankan case. PhD Dissertation, Griffith University.

OECD (2006), *Agricultural Policy and Trade Reform: Potential Effects at Global, National and Household Levels*. OECD, Paris.

Panda, M., Ganesh-Kumar, A. (2008), Trade liberalization, poverty and food security in India. Paper presented at the 11th Annual Conference on Global Economic Analysis, Helsinki, Finland.

Polaski, S., Panda, M., Ganesh-Kumar, A., McDonald, S., Robinson, S. (2008), Policy dilemmas in India: the impact of changes in agricultural prices on rural and urban poverty. Paper presented at the 11th Annual Conference on Global Economic Analysis, Helsinki, Finland.

Pradhan, B.K., Sahoo, A. (2006), The impact of trade liberalization on household welfare and poverty in India. PEP-MPIA Working Paper 2006-01.

Raihan, S. (2008), Trade liberalisation, growth employment and poverty in Bangladesh. Paper presented at the 11th Annual Conference on Global Economic Analysis, Helsinki, Finland.

Roland-Holst, D. (2008), *Social Accounting Matrix for Pakistan, 2004–2005*. University of Berkeley, Berkeley.

Saluja, M.R., Yadav, B. (2006), *Social Accounting Matrix for India 2003–2004*. India Development Foundation, Gurgaon, India.

World Bank (2007), *World Development Indicators*. World Bank, Washington, DC.

CHAPTER 10

Regional Trade Opportunities for Asian Agriculture

Shikha Jha[a], David Roland-Holst[b], Songsak Sriboonchitta[c] and Drew Behnke[d]

[a]*Economics and Research Department, Asian Development Bank, Manila, Philippines*
E-mail address: sjha@adb.org
[b]*Department of Agricultural and Resource Economics, University of California – Berkeley, Berkeley, CA, USA*
E-mail address: dwrh@berkeley.edu
[c]*Faculty of Economics, Chiang-Mai University, Chiang Mai, Thailand*
E-mail address: songsak@econ.cmu.ac.th
[d]*Department of Agricultural and Resource Economics, University of California – Berkeley, Berkeley, CA, USA*
E-mail address: drewbehnke@gmail.com

Abstract
Trade in food and other agricultural products is increasingly important across East and Southeast Asia, where high-income Asian economies have driven significant agricultural expansion, and the People's Republic of China's (PRC) momentous growth promises more stimulus to agro-food activity in the region. The PRC is expected to become a net importer of agro-food in the coming decades, which will have significant implications within the region. As its middle class continues to emerge, the resource intensity of food consumption (e.g., meat and dairy) will lead to net imports and require expansion of agricultural capacity elsewhere. Because low-income Southeast Asia is generally seen to be well below its agro-food potential, this situation suggests a significant opportunity for self-directed poverty reduction through regional agro-food market expansion. This chapter reviews the history of high-income Asia and the PRC's emergence in the region's agro-food markets. Finally, the Greater Mekong Subregion's role is analyzed for the potential of Asian agro-food trade to contribute to poverty reduction.

Keywords: Trade, Agriculture, Food, Asia

Frontiers of Economics and Globalization
Volume 7 ISSN: 1574-8715
DOI: 10.1108/S1574-8715(2010)0000007013

1. Introduction

A number of factors have improved the prospects of and the need for increased regional trade within Asia. The prospects were triggered by the loss of momentum in the latest round of multilateral trade negotiations, combined with a rise in freight costs due to higher fuel prices. This is particularly true for agriculture, a primary obstacle to the World Trade Organization (WTO) negotiations and a sector in which Asia has significant demand and supply potential. The need for enhanced regional trade has been compounded by the recession in industrial countries, which calls for rebalancing growth by creating regional demand (ADB, 2009a) and to broaden openness by expanding regional trade within Asia (ADB, 2009b). To elucidate the means by which Asia can improve its agricultural productivity and food security and promote economic growth, this study uses a multicountry general equilibrium (GE) model to assess agricultural trade growth between the People's Republic of China (PRC) and the Greater Mekong Subregion (GMS) countries. The PRC has over the past decade gone from being a small net exporter of agricultural products to become one of the world's largest importers, a trend that appears likely to continue. At the same time, the Mekong region has agricultural capacity well beyond its current production, and this subregion encompasses some of the poorest countries in Asia. Moreover, agriculture is identified as one of the priority sectors under the GMS Economic Cooperation Program to address poverty in the GMS countries, which is largely a rural phenomenon (ADB, 2007b).

As historical trends from high-income Asian (HIA) countries suggest, increased agro-food trade with the PRC could significantly contribute to growth, reduce poverty in the GMS, and contribute to two important policy objectives of the Asian Development Bank (ADB) – greater Asian cooperation and more inclusive development. By focusing on GMS engagement, the study also showcases one of ADB's most important infrastructure commitments, the two road corridors that transect the subregion. The chapter uses detailed information on the corridors' contributions to local development for regional agricultural trade.

The objective of this chapter is to demonstrate the longer-term benefits of enhanced trade extending across and between developing Asian economies. Because indirect effects can far outweigh direct or negotiated trade effects, a GE assessment gives a more complete picture of the inclusive benefits of such cooperation. More comprehensive assessment such as this implicates a much larger universe of stakeholders and represents an essential justification of both the policy agenda (integration, inclusion, etc.) and supporting investments like the GMS corridors.

2. *Motivation and background*

This chapter begins with an extensive background review of the drivers of agro-food trade in East and Southeast Asia over the past few decades. The rise of HIA economies provided an early wave of demand stimulus, accompanied by agro-food supply chain development and technology transfer around the region. This was followed by rising middle-class consumption in rapidly emerging Asian economies and, finally, with the dramatic emergence of demand from the PRC in the past two decades.

2.1. Evidence from high income Asia

Experiences of HIA countries such as Japan, Republic of Korea (Korea), and Taiwan are useful for predicting the scope of the PRC's agro-food trade patterns for two reasons. First, these countries were also densely populated before industrialization and can therefore serve as a model of what to expect as the PRC industrializes. Second, compared to western consumption preferences, these countries have similar preferences and diets, and as the PRC industrializes, its diet is likely to shift in a similar fashion to other HIA countries.

There have been clear trends in changing HIA consumption patterns over the previous decades, which have subsequently altered agro-food trade. As per-capita incomes have risen, diets have diversified away from rice and other starchy staples into a more diverse offering including meats, fresh fruits and vegetables, and dairy products. HIA countries have all seen significant reductions in rice consumption. Both Japan and Taiwan's current consumption levels are approximately half their levels in the 1950s and 1960s. Korea has seen a sharp reduction too, falling from 128.1 kg/year in 1985 to 82 kg/year in 2004 (MAFROK, 2006). Looking at data on meat consumption in HIA is another strong indicator of how tastes and preferences have changed. Compared to 1960 levels in Japan, beef consumption was 7.5 times greater by 1995, and poultry and pork consumption had increased by nearly 14 times. Korea and Taiwan show similar trends as well, although their rates of growth have not been as drastic.

These similar shifts in food consumption preferences have created profound effects on agro-food trade. Looking at Japan first, it is the world's largest importer of agricultural products and is characterized by a heavy dependence on specified countries as demonstrated by the fact that more than 60% of imported agricultural products are from just five countries, including US, PRC, and Thailand. Japan's food self-sufficiency ratio has also been falling for numerous years as it relies on imports of fruits, meats, milk and diary products, and vegetables to meet its growing demand.

Korea is also a net importer of agricultural products. The majority of Korea's imports are food crops such as corn, flour, and beans and represented 50.9% of the total share in 2003. The rest of the major agricultural imports comprises livestock products (mainly beef), forestry, and fish. Korea receives most of its agricultural imports from the United States followed by PRC, Australia, and Indonesia. Owing to the increase of livestock production to meet the growing demand for meat products, Korea's demand for wheat, soybeans, and corn as feed has also been rapidly increasing, all or most of which are served by imports.

Taiwan turned from a net exporter of agriculture products in the 1950s to a net importer by the 1990s. Owing to large inflows of foreign direct investment (FDI), agricultural products became a key part of Taiwan's export industry, representing over 90% of all exports in the 1950s. However, as the country industrialized, its share of agricultural exports decreased significantly (to 4.7% in 1996), even though the total value was increasing. The vast majority of these exports went to Japan (receiving 44.8% in 1996), which was also one of the largest donors of FDI. Concurrently, total agricultural imports began to increase rapidly as Taiwan moved into a more industrialized society. Agricultural imports increased from $75.8 million to $9,986.6 million, a 132-fold increase in a period of 36 years. The sharp rise in agricultural imports reflects the shift in Taiwan's diet, as it must import large quantities of feed grains, oilseeds, meats, fruits, and vegetables to meet changing consumer preferences. The United States is Taiwan's main supplier of agricultural imports, providing 54.5% of the total in 1996. Other sources of imports come from Malaysia (9.3%), Australia (5.5%), Indonesia (4.5%), Thailand (3.4%), and Japan (2%) (Sun *et al.*, 1998).

Clear trends emerge when looking at HIA agricultural trade patterns. Most noticeably, HIA countries have all had significant increases in meat imports as well as feed grains to fuel domestic production. Vast areas of farmland are needed to yield the grains necessary to raise cattle and other livestock, and as HIA countries are densely populated and industrialized, they cannot produce the necessary quantities. Therefore, HIA countries are dependent on agriculture imports and their self-sufficiency ratios have been in decline for numerous years. Another important trend has been the outsourcing of farmland from neighboring countries and the emergence of Southeast Asia and PRC as a food supplier for HIA. Traditionally, the Mekong region has been the rice basket for many of these countries, but more recently, meat has been playing an increasingly important role, especially poultry from Thailand. Thailand represents one of the most important trading partners in HIA and has had success that other Southeast Asian countries hope to attain as the PRC may transition into a large importer of agricultural products.

2.2. People's Republic of China

Consumption preferences in the PRC have already begun to change as the country continues to industrialize and urbanize. Much like HIA, rising incomes have increased the consumption of meats, poultry, fish, dairy products, and fruits, whereas the consumption of traditional staple grains have remained stable or declined (Chern, 1997; Guo *et al.*, 2000; Gould, 2002; Xin *et al.*, 2005). Looking first at food staples, the PRC exhibits similar characteristics to HIA countries. From 1978 to 1990, per capita consumption for rice and wheat increased at an average annual rate of 1.3% and 4.4%, respectively, which was fueled by rising incomes allowing the poor to be able to consume more. Since the early 1990s, however, per capita consumption of rice and wheat has started to decline slightly because more individuals are able to diversify their diets. Although these categories have stabilized somewhat in recent years, they can be expected to decline as the Chinese continue to diversify their diet. Meat consumption in the PRC has been steadily increasing for the past several decades. In 1978, per capita consumption of pork was 8 kg/year; beef, 0.3 kg/year; and poultry, 1.3 kg/year. However by 2004, these numbers increased to 35.9 kg/year for pork, 5.2 kg/year for beef, and 11.3 kg/year for poultry. These amounts are well within the bounds of HIA and have already begun to create massive reverberations for agricultural trade in the PRC.

However, as the PRC is a country characterized by large inequality, it is worth examining how food consumption patterns vary across income classes. The demand for quantity diminishes as income rises, and the upper-income households appear to have reached a saturation point in quantity consumed of most food items. Most additional food spending by high-income consumers is on higher quality or food in restaurants. The vast majority of households in the PRC are rural (about 60% of the population) and low-income urban households (20%) that still demand increased quantities of many foods as their income rises. These patterns suggest that the growth in the quantity of food demanded has been much slower than would be expected by the PRC's rapid economic growth. High-income households are purchasing greater value added products rather than increased quantity, which has caused much of the food expenditure growth. Low-income households have been experiencing less rapid income growth and thus growth of their food spending has been slower. This slow growth in the quantity of food demanded is one possible explanation as to how the PRC has been able to remain largely self-sufficient for many food items. However, as more and more low-income individuals' incomes continue to increase, the true test of the PRC's agricultural production will be seen (Gale and Huang, 2007).

Despite the PRC's self-sufficiency in many agricultural goods, its future growth creates uncertainty for global agro-food markets as the country has 25% of the world's population with only 7% of the world's arable land. Although many researchers have cited the rising demand for meats to lead to an increase in PRC's agricultural imports of meat and/or feed grains, the country's agricultural imports have only really begun to take off in recent years. This happened as a result of large economic growth, lower barriers to imports, higher commodity prices, and tightening domestic commodity supplies. In total terms, agricultural imports increased from less than \$11 billion in 2002 to \$25.9 billion in 2004. Soybean imports were responsible for more than 30% of this growth, increasing from \$2.5 billion in 2002 to \$7 billion in 2004. Soybeans are used for making vegetable oil and high-protein animal and fish feed. However, all these soybeans were not able to meet the PRC's demand for vegetable oil as imports of vegetable oil increased by \$2.6 billion during this time period, accounting for another 17% of agricultural import growth. Wheat was another major food commodity that was responsible for the PRC's large agricultural import growth. Wheat imports rose from \$100 million to \$1.6 billion during 2002–2004, accounting for 10% of the increase in imports. Commodities used as raw materials were also significant contributors to agricultural import growth. Cotton was the biggest sector, increasing from \$308 million in 2002 to \$3.4 billion in 2004, representing 21% of the increase of the total import growth (Gale, 2005). Imports of other food items such as meats, milk, cheese, wines, and fruits have all seen sharp increases as well, but they represent a small share of the PRC's overall agricultural imports.

Looking at future agricultural import demands, the PRC is expected to continue to rely on soybean and vegetable oils, and a sharp decline in these imports is unlikely. Meat imports are expected to grow as well, due to increasing demand. Demand for imported pork is especially strong, as domestic outbreaks of avian influenza and a ban on US beef imports have induced many consumers to substitute pork for beef and poultry products. In addition to meat imports, feed grains are also expected to rise in the coming decades, eventually reaching 25 million to 35 million tons by 2020. Although the PRC's wheat imports represent a small percentage of its total consumption, the PRC is still a very large importer of wheat in sheer quantity. In terms of global wheat markets, the PRC is responsible for nearly 15% of all wheat imports and thus predictions about world wheat markets rest heavily on the assessments of the PRC's future role. These predictions are difficult to make as the PRC's wheat markets have unique characteristics in the sense that it is the only country in East and Southeast Asia that has both a large wheat-producing and wheat-consuming rural population (Rozelle and Huang, 1998). The PRC's unique characteristics have caused many analysts to make conflicting claims. Some argue that the PRC will continue to demand large quantities of imported wheat, whereas others forecast that the country will gradually move to a position where domestic supply will meet the nation's demand. One of the most sweeping reports conducted by Rozelle and Huang in 1998, claims that the PRC's wheat imports will rise before peaking and gradually declining through 2020.

The PRC's agricultural exports have also begun to take off in recent years, although at a slower pace than imports. During 2002–2004, exports increased by $3 billion with the most important categories being processed foods, vegetables, and fruits. Japan is the largest market for the PRC's agriculture exports, accounting for approximately one-third of the total in 2004 (Huang and Gale, 2006). This is not surprising given that a large number of manufacturers from Japan have invested in the PRC. From 1985 to 2003, a total number of 310 food industry subsidiaries from Japan were set up in the PRC, and it is often remarked that the PRC has become the farm of Japan (Jin *et al.*, 2006). Most of the PRC's other major markets are neighboring countries or regions and include Hong Kong and Southeast Asia (each accounted for 12% of the PRC's exports in 2004), South Korea (7%), and Russian Federation (3%). The United States is also one of the PRC's largest agricultural export markets, representing 9% of the total share. The United States is one of the PRC's fastest growing markets with agricultural imports increasing by 43% from 2002 to 2004 (Gale, 2005).

2.3. Greater Mekong subregion

Growth in the GMS has been robust for several years, fueled in part by a very strong export sector. Exports from the GMS rose from $37 billion in 1992 to $154 billion in 2005. This corresponds to an annual rate of growth of 11.6%, which is larger than the world average of 8.4%. The vast majority of GMS trade has been in manufactured goods, although some countries have emerged as food suppliers to HIA, most notably Thailand. Various factors helped fuel the tremendous growth of trade in the GMS. Generally speaking, the dominance of state-owned enterprises was reduced, prices and trade of goods and services were liberalized, and restrictions on the private sector were eased encouraging FDI.

FDI, in particular, has been a major facilitator of growth in many of the GMS economies. Although the stories of the PRC and Thailand are particularly well known, FDI has also played important roles in less-developed countries. In Cambodia for example, FDI from HIA and the PRC helped propel its now flourishing garment export industry. This shift in production from countries with large manufacturing sectors occurred due to the eroding competitiveness of garment production with rising wages. Additionally, by shifting production to Cambodia, investors from the PRC were able to bypass the quotas in the main markets on garment imports from the PRC. FDI also played an important role in Lao PDR. Inflows in agriculture and forestry, as well mining and hydropower projects as of late, have helped contribute to export growth. In Viet Nam, FDI was originally concentrated in the extraction of crude oil and gas. However, FDI has shifted over the past decade to manufacturing. Viet Nam is becoming linked to regional production chains, which is clearly reflected in the structural shift in export composition toward assembled electrical and electronic products (ADB, 2007a).

With a relative abundance of agricultural resources, the GMS economies stand to benefit significantly from the globalization of processed food markets. Furthermore, as the PRC continues to grow and demand more food, the GMS economies can be an important supplier due to their proximity and regional ties. The agricultural sector accounts for 50–70% of jobs in Cambodia, Lao PDR, and Viet Nam, and therefore growth in production and exports from this sector will be necessary to improve incomes and reduce poverty.

The PRC's growth, along with increasing integration into world markets and reduced trade barriers with GMS, is expected to have significant effects on the structure of regional production and trade. The GMS resource-abundant economies are expected to become more intensive in natural resource-based exports and transition away from the current labor-intensive manufacturing industry. This transition is expected as a result of two parts: first, through direct bilateral trade growth as the PRC demands more natural resource-based products and, second, through direct competition with the PRC in global markets.

Indirect effects are also pushing this trend. The potential loss of revenue sources from garment manufacturing, and the lower wages that this will cause, could reduce labor costs in agricultural industries contributing directly to increased profitability, which will complement the direct effects from growth of PRC's demand of these products. Another indirect driver will be changes in FDI inflows. Although the evidence is ambiguous, decreases in FDI are expected in industries in Southeast Asia where competition with the PRC is intense. The PRC's growth and globalization is likely to cause GMS economies to experience negative terms of trade shocks for their manufacturers and positive shocks for agricultural produces (Coxhead, 2004).

Regional cooperation can provide even further opportunities to facilitate trade growth. Most notably, Thailand, PRC, and Viet Nam all provide large markets and regional knowledge from which they can continue their own strong rates of growth and from which other less-developed GMS countries can learn. One of the most positive trends has been increased flows of intra-subregional trade, investment, and technology. PRC and Thailand are especially important as private capital and technology flows to the other countries can better use the abundant land and low-cost labor to produce goods efficiently for the subregion or for export.

3. The dynamic forecasting model

The complexities of today's global economy make it very unlikely that policy makers relying on intuition or rules-of-thumb will achieve anything approaching optimality in either international or domestic arenas. Market interactions are so pervasive, and market forces so powerful in determining economic outcomes that more sophisticated empirical research tools are needed to improve visibility for both public and private sector decision makers. The preferred tool for detailed empirical analysis of economic policy is now the computable general equilibrium (CGE) model. It is ideally suited to trade analysis because it can detail structural adjustments within national economies and elucidate their interactions in international markets. The model is more extensively discussed in an appendix and the underlying methodology is fully documented elsewhere, but a few general comments will facilitate discussion and interpretation of the scenario results that follow.[1]

Technically, a CGE model is a system of simultaneous equations that simulate price-directed interactions between firms and households in commodity and factor markets. The role of government, capital markets, and other trading partners are also specified, with varying degrees of detail and passivity, to close the model and account for economy-wide resource allocation, production, and income determination.

The role of markets is to mediate exchange, usually with a flexible system of prices, the most important endogenous variables in a typical CGE model. As in a real market economy, commodity and factor price changes induce changes in the level and composition of supply and demand, production and income, and the remaining endogenous variables in the system. In CGE models, an equation system is solved for prices that correspond to equilibrium in markets and satisfy the accounting identities governing economic behavior. If such a system is precisely specified, equilibrium always exists, and such a consistent model can be calibrated to a base period data set. The resulting calibrated GE model is then used to simulate the economy-wide (and regional) effects of alternative policies or external events.

The distinguishing feature of a GE model, applied or theoretical, is its closed-form specification of all activities in the economic system under study. This can be contrasted with more traditional partial equilibrium analysis, where linkages to other domestic markets and agents are deliberately excluded from consideration. A large and growing body of evidence suggests that indirect effects (e.g., upstream and downstream production linkages) arising from policy changes are not only substantial, but may in some cases even outweigh direct effects. Only a model that consistently specifies economy-wide interactions can fully assess the implications of economic policies or business strategies. In a multicountry model like the one used in this study, indirect effects include the trade linkages between countries and regions, which themselves can have policy implications.

---

[1] The model used here is typical of modern global models and is based on the LINKAGE model developed at the World Bank (van der Mensbrugghe, 2008).

Table 1. Countries, regions, and sectors

Abbreviation	Name
PRC	China
EUR	Europe 27
HIA	High-Income Asia
CAM	Cambodia
LAC	Latin America and Caribbean
LAO	Lao PDR
ROW	Rest of the World
THA	Thailand
USA	United States
VIE	Viet Nam
ROA	Rest of Asia
XSA	South Asia
XSE	Other SE Asia
RIC	Rice
OCR	Other Crops
LVS	Livestock
FFL	Fossil Fuels
MTD	Meat and Dairy
OFD	Other Processed Food
OMF	Other Manufactures
TRD	Trade and Transport Services
PRV	Other Private Services
PUB	Public Services

This chapter uses a version of the World Bank's LINKAGE Model, a global, multiregion, multisector, dynamic applied GE model.[2] This model is implemented in the GAMS programming language, and calibrated to Version 7 of the GTAP global economic database.[3] The result is a 13-country/region, 10-sector global CGE model (concordance in Table 1), calibrated over a 16-year time path from 2005 to 2020. Apart from its traditional neoclassical roots, an important feature of this model is product differentiation, where we specify that imports are differentiated by country of origin, and exports are differentiated by country of destination. This feature allows the model to capture the pervasive phenomenon of intra-industry trade, where a country is both an importer and an exporter of similar commodities and avoids tendencies toward extreme specialization.

3.1. Scenarios

Using the model and aggregation, the dynamic CGE model is calibrated to a baseline time series reflecting a business-as-usual (BAU) scenario over

---

[2] See van der Mensbrugghe (2008) for technical documentation.
[3] See, for example, Hertel (1997) for GTAP.

2006–2020. This baseline comprises consensus forecasts for real GDP obtained from independent sources (e.g., International Monetary Fund, Data Resources International, and Cambridge Econometrics). The model is then run forward to meet these targets, making average capital productivity growth for each country and/or region endogenous. This calibration yields productivity growth that would be needed to attain the macro trajectories, and these are then held fixed in the model under other policy scenarios. Other exogenous macro forecasts could have been used and compared, but this is the standard way to calibrate these models.

As outlined in the Introduction, the main objective of the present forecasting exercise is to assess the potential for increased agro-food capacity to promote growth and reduce poverty in the GMS. To assess this potential, three primary drivers of growth and two types of risk to growth must be considered.

3.1.1. Productivity growth in agriculture and related food industries

In the first category, agricultural yields and productivity in livestock production are far below their ultimate potential in lower income GMS economies. Because of relatively small-scale land tenure patterns, it is unlikely that rural households in these countries can achieve significant livelihood improvements unless output per hectare improves, and migration trends suggest that higher output per household member will also be essential.

3.1.2. Facilitation of trade and market access

Most rural agricultural households in the GMS live behind high walls of market access barriers, including high transactions and transport costs with respect to remote markets, and these are often compounded by infrastructure and information constraints. As long as distribution margins remain high, low-income agro-food enterprises with relatively low-value products will be prevented from accessing markets. By converse reasoning, lowering market access costs and related margins enlarges the horizon of profitable trade for all, increasing commerce, capturing value added, and promoting self-directed poverty reduction.

3.1.3. Foreign direct investment

One of the defining characteristics of low-income economies everywhere is limited reserves of domestic savings, which in turn limits the progress of development by restricting investment in productive assets and enterprise expansion. The era of globalization has changed the nature of this constraint, however, with the advent of transboundary investment that permits low-income countries to leverage foreign savings for domestic investment. To help low-income GMS countries achieve their economic potential in the most timely fashion, FDI can be an essential catalyst.

3.1.4. *Persistent macroeconomic slowdown in industrial countries*

Although the Asian economies have exhibited a relatively robust recovery from the recent global economic downturn, industrial economies continue to experience serious credit constraints, extensive distressed asset challenges, and sluggish recovery of aggregate demand. To a significant extent, the demand shortfalls that have already been experienced have reset the growth path for the global economy. This will be compounded, however, if the largest markets are slower to recover. To give an indication of how this process might retard regional growth, we include a scenario where baseline growth rates for the Organisation for Economic Co-operation and Development (OECD) economies fall to zero in 2009 and return to trend linearly over the next five years.

3.1.5. *HAPI and/or other serious livestock disease outbreaks*

Since its emergence in 1996 in the PRC, the highly pathogenic avian influenza H5N1 virus has infected 61 countries, been associated with more than 260 human fatalities, and resulted in disease mortality and culling of several hundred million domestic birds. Analogously, blue-ear disease in the PRC has killed several million swine. In each case, a large-scale animal disease outbreak has caused serious regional meat shortages, threatened livelihoods, and presented threats to public health. To assess the linkage effects of such a supply chain disruption, we examine the effects of a 20% decline in livestock productivity across Asian economies. Although we do not consider human health impacts, this is admittedly a relatively extreme scenario.

The main scenarios we evaluated represent the first three of these categories. As summarized later, each of these components makes an incremental contribution to agro-food development and overall economic growth. On agricultural productivity growth, based on a review of the relevant literature and international historical data, we have experimented with 1–6% annual output growth for the three agricultural sectors in the three low-income GMS countries considered (Cambodia, Lao PDR, and Viet Nam).[4] The highest rate would double output over 2008–2020, but an upper-midrange value of 4% is probably more sustainable based on the historical evidence summarized in Table 2.

For trade facilitation, we recognize the important regional initiatives of ADB and GMS national governments to establish large transit corridors. These will significantly lower medium- and long-distance market access costs and can be expected to foster complementary infrastructure

---

[4] Unfortunately, data for Myanmar in the current version of GTAP were not deemed reliable enough to be incorporated individually in this analysis.

Table 2. Average annual growth of agricultural output

	1970–1979	1980–1989	1990–1999	2000–2006
Sub-Saharan Africa	1.31	2.6	3.1	2.2
Latin America and Caribbean	3.07	2.37	2.87	3.13
Brazil	3.83	3.73	3.29	4.41
Middle East and North Africa	2.94	3.37	2.73	2.34
NE Asia, High	2.15	1.03	−0.01	−0.01
NE Asia, Low	3.11	4.55	5.06	3.85
PRC	3.09	4.6	5.17	3.87
SE Asia	3.68	3.59	3.13	3.54
South Asia	2.56	3.39	3	2.19
India	2.69	3.52	2.94	2
North America	2.17	0.73	2.03	1.1
Oceania	1.79	1.25	2.93	−0.04
Western Europe	1.54	0.94	0.46	−0.35
Eastern Europe	1.8	0.25	−2.18	−0.19
Russian Federation	1.32	0.98	−4.62	2.7
Developing countries	2.82	3.46	3.64	3.09
Developed countries	1.88	0.86	1.21	0.39
Russian Federation and Eastern Europe	1.47	0.77	−3.88	1.81
World	2.23	2.13	2.04	2.22

Sources: United States Department of Agriculture, World Bank.
NE, northeast; SE, southeast.

for feeder road and rail access that achieves more extensive participation. For the present scenario, we chose a central case that reduces trade, transport, and transit (TTT) margins for the low-income GMS by 50%.

Finally, FDI has been a dramatic agent of growth elsewhere in the Asian region and is likely to exert significant growth leverage on the low-income GMS as new opportunities arise for agro-food development and market access increases the average profitability of regional investments by reducing costs. As our reference case, we assume that FDI in each low-income GMS country rises linearly to 4% of GDP by 2020. For reference, this would place them in the world's top quartile by this metric, including both high-income (Singapore = 12%) and low-income countries (Mongolia = 11%).

Table 3 summarizes the five core scenarios. First, around the median values used for these three primary growth components, we evaluated a distribution of alternative values. Overall, simulation results are robust with respect to these differences, and what variation they exhibit is consistent with economic intuition and the results interpretation that follows. Two additional scenarios were included to illustrate the diverse scope of potential policy application for this model.

Table 3. General scenarios

Scenario	Name	Description
1	Agro-Food Productivity	Assume that total factor productivity grows at 4% annually in agriculture and food processing sectors
2	Trade Facilitation	In addition to Scenario 1, assume trade, transport, and transit margins to and from and through low-income GMS countries are reduced by 50%
3	Foreign Direct Investment	In addition to Scenario 2, assume that FDI in the low-income GMS countries rises to 4% of GDP by 2020
4	OECD Recession	Assume OECD growth rates fall to zero in 2009 and return to baseline trends linearly in five years
5	Livestock Epidemic	Assume 2009 livestock productivity in Asia falls 20%, returning to trend five years later

GDP, gross domestic product; GMS, Greater Mekong Subregion; FDI, foreign direct investment; OECD, Organisation for Economic Co-operation and Development.

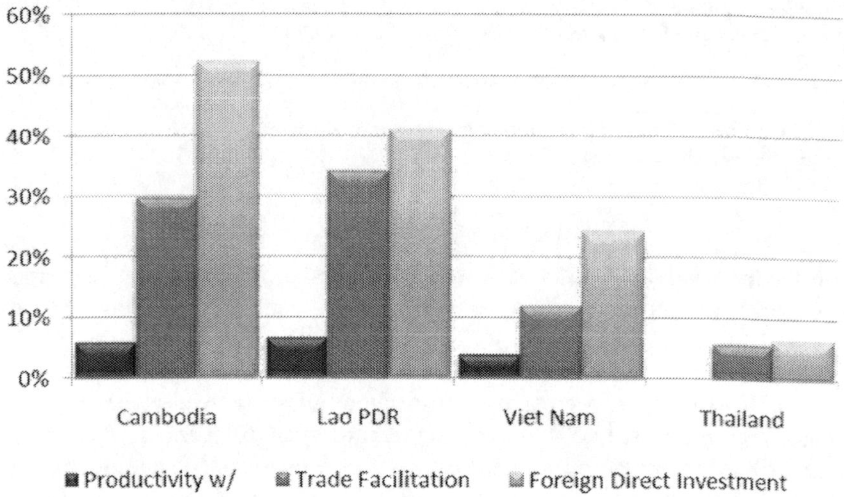

Fig. 1. Real GDP (expressed as percent change from baseline in 2020).

4. Simulation results

The macroeconomic results for the three archetype scenarios are summarized in the following tables, and Figure 1 illustrates the real GDP results for GMS economies considered. The most arresting feature of the GDP estimates is the pro-poor impact of the combined policies. When all three scenarios are considered together, Cambodia, the lowest-income country has the highest relative gain, the second lowest, Lao PDR is next, and finally Viet Nam, which would enjoy 20% higher real GDP in 2020. This finding is a logical consequence of several facts about low-income

GMS (and indeed Asian) economies, including higher initial agro-food dependence, higher initial barriers to market access, and tighter domestic saving/investment constraints.

There are also several immediate general policy lessons from these findings. First, the GMS in particular and many other poor agrarian economic regions can achieve self-directed poverty reduction with determined policies that yield higher agro-food productivity and improved market access, complemented with private agency that contributes in both these areas but also facilitates investment.

It is also clear from the same results that agro-food productivity alone will not achieve higher growth. Without the facilitating measures for market access and complementary investment, larger harvests and livestock production will simply translate into excessive inventories with falling prices and little net value added.

Another important insight comes from the fourth and fifth scenarios, suggesting that macroeconomic cycles are of much less long-term significance than sustained support for microeconomic determinants of productivity and market access. Even if livestock had a significant short-term setback, or if important OECD export markets experienced a 4–5-year recession, long-term growth potential will continue to be determined by detailed and localized economic fundamentals. For the lower income GMS countries in particular, long-term growth potential depends much more on sustained modernization and market integration than on cyclical components for individual sectors or destination markets.

Finally, it is worth noting that there can be substantial benefits for neighboring intermediary economies like Thailand, which in this case achieves over 5% higher growth in the second and third scenarios by sharing the benefits of regional trade and investment. This highlights another important characteristic of complementary policies like trade and investment facilitation. Measures like these make individual development assistance incentive compatible for neighboring countries, creating new markets and commercial partnership opportunities that promote shared – and thereby more sustained – economic growth.

Table 4 presents more detailed results for the first agro-food productivity scenario. As one would expect, the countries targeted for productivity growth are the primary beneficiaries in the macroeconomic results of Table 4. Output in the lowest income GMS countries considered, Cambodia and Lao PDR, rises by about 30% more by 2020 because of (assumed) steady improvements in the productivity of their rural sector [5% total factor productivity (TFP) growth per year]. Because both countries remain focused on primary agriculture, value added (real GDP) rises by less than the value of national agro-food output. Viet Nam, by contrast, is less reliant on primary agriculture across the economy, and this means aggregate output grows less from the same agricultural stimulus, but downstream food linkages permit more value added to be captured in

Table 4. Scenario 1 – macro results

	Cambodia	Lao PDR	Viet Nam	Thailand	Other SEA	High Asia	PRC	S. Asia	Other Asia
GDP (%)	17	23	9	6	0	0	0	0	0
Output (%)	30	29	4	6	0	0	0	0	0
Exports (%)	29	33	8	14	0	2	0	0	0
Imports (%)	41	48	24	17	0	2	0	0	0
Consumption (%)	53	55	32	10	0	1	0	0	0
CPI (%)	−6	−4	1	4	0	0	0	0	0
EV income (%)	54	57	32	10	0	1	0	0	0
GDP (USD millions)	5,194	2,717	9,704	33,130	−220	26,733	−125	588	−3
Output (USD millions)	68,497	18,128	75,135	208,710	−4,177	502,089	29,402	6,378	−13
Exports (USD millions)	26,504	4,386	51,218	148,518	−3,315	251,547	897	470	81
Imports (USD millions)	31,153	7,398	151,158	197,432	−5,035	270,927	−24,018	−226	79
Consumption (USD millions)	3,917	2,440	23,966	18,847	−294	16,787	−839	475	6
EV income (USD millions)	6,393	2,612	27,470	20,980	−278	31,395	−1,019	726	7

Source: Author estimates.

agro-food supply chains. Thus, the national GDP effect is more than double (9%) the simple output effect (4%).

In all three countries, agro-food is closely linked to export markets, and the trade impact of productivity growth strongly stimulates export competitiveness and import purchasing power (assuming small countries or low terms-of-trade effects). This new external income, combined with domestic price declines following productivity growth, supports substantial growth of equivalent variation (EV) real income and consumption for households. It is also worth noting that, via trade linkages, neighboring Thailand benefits less but still significantly. Thailand participates indirectly in low-income GMS growth through discounted imports and export demand expansions.

The sector results in Table 5 give a clearer indication of how each country adapts to higher productivity potential in the three major primary agricultural products. Recalling that our model treats crops and livestock differently, it is not surprising that different countries respond differently to uniform TFP growth. In particular, because Viet Nam has a more advance food processing sector, it is able to more completely absorb new agricultural potential, and thus we see the highest average output growth in crops and livestock. Perhaps ironically, this new potential pulls resources away from manufacturing to support dramatic expansion of the food processing sector. Given that Viet Nam's poor majority is firmly embedded in the rural sector, this resource reallocation may have greater antipoverty potential than traditional urban industrialization at this stage of the country's development.

Sector results in food processing suggest that Lao PDR is still constrained in its ability to expand agriculture with productivity. Thus, it will release resources to other sectors when marginal costs rise enough in agricultural production, even though expansion is below that of Viet Nam. Without improved market access or complementary investment, agro-food cannot take full direct advantage of productivity improvements and ends up subsidizing a shift of resources to other sectors as they are liberated by higher productivity in agriculture.

The trade implications of higher productivity are summarized in Table 6. Here we see a sector and regional breakdown of trade by origin and destination.[5] Even without complementary policies that facilitate market access and investment, agro-food productivity growth has a potent effect on trade competitiveness. The three low-income GMS countries see dramatic percentage increases in export opportunities with respect to their neighbors. To the PRC, for example, each country increases exports by more than 450%. Although in many cases this change is with respect to

---

[5] An element T_{ij} of the trade table measures annual changes from baseline in exports from country *i* (row) to country *j*, in the terminal year (2020).

Table 5. Scenario 1 – sector output results

	Cambodia	Lao PDR	Viet Nam	Thailand	Other SEA	High Asia	PRC	S. Asia	Other Asia
Rice (%)	56	51	80	−8	−2	0	0	0	2
Other crops (%)	55	93	155	−2	0	−1	0	0	0
Livestock (%)	58	72	63	2	0	0	0	0	0
Fuels (%)	32	15	9	11	0	1	0	0	0
Meat, dairy (%)	61	101	70	1	0	0	0	0	0
Other processed food (%)	74	65	113	−7	0	0	0	0	1
Manufactures (%)	24	5	−10	10	0	1	0	0	0
Trade and transport (%)	19	7	3	3	0	0	0	0	0
Private service (%)	42	21	11	6	0	1	0	0	0
Public service (%)	26	21	7	3	0	0	0	0	0
Total (%)	30	27	6	6	0	0	0	0	0
Rice ($ million)	446	549	5,736	−1,142	−758	−165	98	−1	12
Other crops ($ million)	403	445	9,252	−448	64	−1,257	−219	−214	−1
Livestock ($ million)	450	385	1,497	89	52	585	30	55	−2
Fuels ($ million)	315	54	794	4,949	409	4,748	2,232	189	−4
Meat, dairy ($ million)	280	202	3,750	123	32	−110	57	13	−3
Other processed food ($ million)	1,319	835	12,465	−2,067	92	−175	−1,053	55	118
Manufactures ($ million)	4,896	161	−19,926	23,448	−538	51,218	3,846	501	−115
Trade and transport ($ million)	1,517	139	465	2,713	−8	14,521	−1,339	191	−12
Private service ($ million)	2,355	223	5,419	6,978	−232	23,360	−218	205	−1
Public service ($ million)	1,143	629	1,841	2,158	87	2,117	322	217	2
Total ($ million)	13,125	3,621	21,294	36,801	−799	94,843	3,756	1,213	−6

Source: Author estimates.

Table 6. Scenario 1 – trade flows

	Cambodia	Lao PDR	Viet Nam	Thailand	Other SEA	PRC	High Asia	S. Asia	Other Asia
Cambodia (%)			747	446	18	459	13	4	5
Lao PDR (%)			589	547	−14	460	−13	−17	
Viet Nam (%)	51	453		699	14	798	−3	63	10
Thailand (%)	96	94	168		−7	116	−6	−7	−9
Other SEA (%)	−25	−28	−8	1	0	0	0	0	0
PRC (%)	146	133	179	203	0		0	0	0
High Asia (%)	−20	−20	−3	−1	0	0	0	0	0
S. Asia (%)	−16	−21	−5	1	0	0	0	0	0
Other Asia (%)	−16		−5	12	0	−1	0	0	0
Cambodia ($ million)	0	0	757	178	19	439	128	2	0
Lao PDR ($ million)	0	0	381	435	−2	134	−19	−2	0
Viet Nam ($ million)	1,453	269	0	2,163	574	14,931	−540	784	8
Thailand ($ million)	994	657	2,844	0	−1,542	31,613	−2,081	−340	−53
Other SEA ($ million)	−297	−6	−515	182	76	−599	233	25	3
PRC ($ million)	2,875	304	16,982	22,046	−139	0	−909	−104	−2
High Asia ($ million)	−541	−43	−849	−345	526	−2,134	653	78	21
S. Asia ($ million)	−67	−6	−147	20	16	−158	26	9	2
Other Asia ($ million)	−4	0	−7	148	−2	−36	−17	−2	1

Source: Author estimates.

a small baseline trade flow, the impetus is strong enough to suggest the potential for long-term growth leverage for the low-income exporter. Looking at level changes in the lower half of Table 6, we see that trade diversion (negative elements) plays a relatively minor role, and is far outweighed by trade creation. This is an essential characteristic of productivity-based competitiveness and is very important to multilateral promotion of this approach for regional poverty reduction. Beggar-thy-neighbor policies must be avoided as countries expand bilateral trade.

The next set of tables summarizes impacts for the intermediate scenario, including both agro-food productivity and trade facilitation. As the macroeconomic results demonstrate, the full potential of higher productivity in primary sectors cannot be realized without reducing trade and transport margins to expand eligible markets. Interestingly, output growth increases moderately, but trade in both directions and value added are nearly double that of the productivity only scenario. In other words, trade facilitation takes a similar amount of productive potential and articulates these goods into longer supply chains, including both higher exports and imports, stimulating trade as well as a broad array of intermediate services (Table 7).

This trade-driven supply chain expansion is evident in the sector results of Table 8, which shows both up and downstream increases in sectors related to agro-food production, processing, and trade. Each of these contributes to higher value added, more broad-based employment growth, and more rapidly rising incomes in these low income economies. Table 9 reveals the catalytic impact of trade facilitation. Again on relatively low initial conditions, we see very dramatic bilateral trade expansion in both directions for GMS neighbors. Again, because this trade stimulus is productivity driven, trade growth far outweighs trade diversion. This means not only that established trade relations suffer very little from the improved circumstances of lower income countries, but several of their neighbors are distinctly better off. Thailand sees 6% higher real GDP because of the improved fortunes of its neighbors, without sharing the productivity gains directly. Even HIA countries sees 1% higher GDP growth by 2020, despite the small size of the GMS economies, their increased dependence on higher tech imports from HIA, as well as access to lower cost food products, benefits the latter and provides important incentives for regional cooperation to promote self-directed, trade-oriented poverty reduction.

The third and final scenario encompasses both productivity growth and trade facilitation, but adds the FDI needed to help low-income countries overcome domestic saving insufficiency. As intuition would suggest and as the macroeconomic results of Table 10 clearly demonstrate, expanding investment opportunities in the presence of higher productivity and expanded market access yields both dramatic output growth and explosive trade expansion. Both of these responses translate into higher value added (though less dramatic because of lower rental rates under capital

Table 7. Scenario 2 – macro results

Percent	Cambodia	Lao PDR	Viet Nam	Thailand	Other SEA	High Asia	PRC	S. Asia	Other Asia
GDP (%)	30	30	14	6	0	1	0	0	0
Output (%)	50	31	12	9	0	1	0	0	0
Exports (%)	74	63	34	20	0	3	0	0	0
Imports (%)	87	82	58	31	0	4	0	0	0
Consumption (%)	68	66	48	19	0	1	0	0	0
CPI (%)	–4	4	5	7	0	1	0	0	0
EV income (%)	70	65	48	18	0	1	0	0	0
GDP ($ million)	9,046	3,524	15,125	32,395	–380	47,859	126	1,028	–13
Output ($ million)	116,570	19,742	228,670	297,902	–9,427	1,027,483	59,601	7,538	–115
Exports ($ million)	66,816	8,214	207,636	221,610	–9,319	530,824	7,795	–1,524	31
Imports ($ million)	65,878	12,698	364,527	358,554	–12,603	495,095	–45,002	–3,442	–49
Consumption ($ million)	5,101	2,896	36,152	36,467	–605	27,807	–1,363	658	–1
EV income ($ million)	8,215	2,999	40,568	40,419	–674	53,552	–1,758	810	–4

Source: Author estimates.

Table 8. Scenario 2 – sector results

Percent	Cambodia	Lao PDR	Viet Nam	Thailand	Other SEA	High Asia	PRC	S. Asia	Other Asia
Rice (%)	53	49	124	−23	−4	−1	0	0	5
Other crops (%)	61	132	204	33	1	−2	0	0	0
Livestock (%)	65	65	61	−3	0	1	0	0	0
Fuels (%)	100	24	−7	32	1	2	0	0	0
Meat, dairy (%)	54	95	71	0	0	0	0	0	0
Other processed food (%)	54	51	92	−11	0	1	0	0	2
Manufactures (%)	52	12	0	10	0	1	0	0	0
Trade and transport (%)	27	5	7	5	0	1	0	0	0
Private service (%)	61	26	18	10	0	1	0	0	0
Public service (%)	26	28	7	4	0	0	0	0	0
Total (%)	48	30	14	9	0	1	0	0	0
Rice ($ million)	425	538	8,900	−3,440	−1,137	−441	291	8	31
Other crops ($ million)	441	632	12,156	6,136	226	−4,514	−148	−127	−4
Livestock ($ million)	502	350	1,459	−161	87	1,662	114	44	−3
Fuels ($ million)	987	87	−611	14,262	679	12,971	2,844	179	−9
Meat, dairy ($ million)	249	190	3,806	−39	59	100	118	12	−6
Other processed food ($ million)	955	661	10,227	−3,051	435	3,102	−202	74	186
Manufactures ($ million)	10,781	381	−338	23,479	−1,662	106,222	7,156	396	−196
Trade and transport ($ million)	2,210	104	1,277	4,667	−96	22,338	−3,354	279	−24
Private service ($ million)	3,412	271	8,841	12,935	−394	39,805	−122	374	−7
Public service ($ million)	1,163	834	1,900	3,422	163	3,070	674	458	6
Total ($ million)	21,125	4,048	47,617	58,209	−1,640	184,315	7,372	1,697	−26

Source: Author estimates.

Table 9. Scenario 2 – trade flows

	Cambodia	Lao PDR	Viet Nam	Thailand	Other SEA	PRC	High Asia	S. Asia	Other Asia
Cambodia (%)			1255	1836	45	710	39	17	19
Lao PDR (%)			829	1246	–19	688	–9	–23	
Viet Nam (%)	876	634		1028	40	1510	11	65	37
Thailand (%)	315	185	337		–16	238	–15	–16	–21
Other SEA (%)	–37	–40	–19	0	1	0	0	0	1
PRC (%)	303	242	530	415	–1		–1	–1	0
High Asia (%)	–34	–14	–13	–3	1	0	0	0	1
S. Asia (%)	–32	–33	–14	–1	0	0	0	0	1
Other Asia (%)	–30		–8	19	0	–1	0	0	1
Cambodia ($ million)	0	0	1,272	735	48	680	372	10	1
Lao PDR ($ million)	0	0	536	992	–3	201	–14	–3	0
Viet Nam ($ million)	2,487	377	0	3,183	1,652	28,256	2,005	807	32
Thailand ($ million)	3,253	1,291	5,700	0	–3,589	65,196	–4,873	–794	–127
Other SEA ($ million)	–450	–9	–1,277	–95	175	–91	316	74	5
PRC ($ million)	5,982	553	50,390	45,050	–582	0	–3,796	–399	–28
High Asia ($ million)	–936	–30	–3,957	–1,469	1,094	1,850	1,161	162	42
S. Asia ($ million)	–133	–9	–397	–32	43	73	49	39	4
Other Asia ($ million)	–8	0	–12	226	–2	–35	–16	–3	1

Source: Author estimates.

Table 10. Scenario 3 – macro results

	Cambodia	Lao PDR	Viet Nam	Thailand	Other SEA	High Asia	PRC	High Asia	S. Asia	Other Asia
GDP (%)	52	41	24	6	0	0	1	0	0	0
Output (%)	123	60	26	10	0	0	1	0	0	0
Exports (%)	139	100	47	21	0	0	3	0	0	0
Imports (%)	160	114	74	32	0	0	4	0	0	0
Consumption (%)	121	94	57	20	0	0	1	0	0	0
CPI (%)	−7	5	5	7	0	0	1	0	0	0
EV income (%)	119	91	57	19	0	0	1	0	0	0
GDP ($ million)	15,795	4,786	26,808	35,214	−285	277	49,665	277	885	−13
Output ($ million)	284,453	38,335	509,129	312,275	−7,744	75,304	1,066,830	75,304	6,253	−52
Exports ($ million)	125,344	13,140	284,063	228,970	−8,299	18,501	552,364	18,501	−1,649	70
Imports ($ million)	120,805	17,687	466,043	368,287	−11,185	−29,972	516,988	−29,972	−3,494	−24
Consumption ($ million)	9,026	4,124	42,844	37,647	−491	−647	29,003	−647	556	0
EV income ($ million)	14,006	4,186	47,884	41,715	−554	−780	55,667	−780	675	−3

Source: Author estimates.

expansion) and much higher real domestic incomes and consumption. These effects are very dramatic for the target economies, increasing real GDP between 24% and 52% by 2020, but they also directly benefit immediate neighbors like Thailand (6% GDP and 9% real income) and the PRC (1%).

Increased access to capital, formerly severely constrained in these countries, also means that growth will be more broad-based. Sectors participating in all supply chains (i.e., both exports and imports) experience less competitive pressure for resources and can expand at lower marginal cost (Table 11). In this way, alleviating capital constraints increases the number of winners within each economy. In the previous scenarios, growth of some sectors imposed scarcity costs on others, inducing reduced average profitability and even contraction.

FDI in this way facilitates not only output expansion in the higher productivity sectors, along their supply chains, but also in sectors that would otherwise fail to capture the multiplier effects of target sector expansion. This is particularly apparent when agro-food productivity and trade facilitation combined to increase competitiveness of selected primary and tertiary sectors. Without external capital inflows, this process induced stagnation or even contraction on other sectors, whereas we see more robust and balanced growth when FDI is available.

As the macroeconomic export and import results suggest for this scenario, bilateral trade growth is explosive when policies can achieve combined productivity, market access, and external investment (Table 12). The simple leveraging of external savings can increase domestic capacity for export, along with commensurate import purchasing power, but a multiple of three or four for these small economies. This not only provides an important source of new market income, but also permits access to essential imports of higher technology capital goods, consumer products, and services. Such technology transfer can in turn be expected to generate endogenous growth benefits that will further advance the progress of these low-income countries.

Finally despite the dramatic expansion of bilateral trade across this region, trade diversion is a small fraction of trade creation. Once again, we see that constructive trade promotion policies, ones that enhance productivity, market access, and investment opportunities, can advance the welfare of more needy economies without threatening established trade or livelihoods in more advanced economies. On the contrary, all Asian economies or regions considered here are better off (or at least not worse off) in this scenario, which returns dramatic trade-induced poverty reduction in low-income GMS economies.

5. *Conclusions and policy implications*

Trade in food and other agricultural products is increasingly important across East and Southeast Asia, where HIA economies have driven

Table 11. Scenario 3 – sector results

	Cambodia	Lao PDR	Viet Nam	Thailand	Other SEA	High Asia	PRC	High Asia	S. Asia	Other Asia
Rice (%)	78	69	121	−22	−3	0	0	0	0	5
Other crops (%)	88	108	191	32	1	0	−2	0	0	0
Livestock (%)	116	93	67	−2	0	0	1	0	0	0
Fuels (%)	158	67	10	34	1	1	2	1	0	0
Meat, dairy (%)	93	115	81	1	0	0	0	0	0	−1
Other processed food (%)	120	82	109	−11	0	0	1	0	0	2
Manufactures (%)	128	53	15	10	0	0	1	0	0	0
Trade and transport (%)	104	30	20	5	0	0	1	0	0	0
Private service (%)	170	63	41	11	0	0	1	0	0	0
Public service (%)	54	42	11	4	0	0	0	0	0	0
Total (%)	120	57	28	9	0	0	1	0	0	0
Rice ($ million)	624	747	8,678	−3,363	−970	298	−353	298	27	33
Other crops ($ million)	643	517	11,355	5,993	218	−127	−4,432	−127	−98	−3
Livestock ($ million)	896	497	1,603	−92	82	124	1,636	124	36	−3
Fuels ($ million)	1,556	237	882	15,568	621	6,156	13,826	6,156	132	−11
Meat, dairy ($ million)	424	230	4,332	80	55	109	77	109	10	−6
Other processed food ($ million)	2,145	1,055	12,048	−3,079	396	−304	2,998	−304	69	198
Manufactures ($ million)	26,591	1,722	30,523	24,005	−1,469	6,469	110,216	6,469	305	−195
Trade and transport ($ million)	8,365	626	3,551	4,832	−103	−3,300	22,860	−3,300	220	−28
Private service ($ million)	9,504	658	19,693	13,353	−299	274	41,332	274	363	−8
Public service ($ million)	2,409	1,240	2,988	3,521	145	640	3,188	640	368	5
Total ($ million)	53,156	7,530	95,652	60,820	−1,324	10,340	191,350	10,340	1,432	−20

Source: Author estimates.

Table 12. Scenario 3 – trade flows

Percent	Cambodia	Lao PDR	Viet Nam	Thailand	Other SEA	PRC	High Asia	S. Asia	Other Asia
Cambodia (%)			1743	2053	88	977	83	55	66
Lao PDR (%)			1130	1277	−14	695	4	−18	
Viet Nam (%)	1425	871		1128	43	1539	20	61	43
Thailand (%)	488	238	386		−17	236	−15	−17	−21
Other SEA (%)	−14	−29	−10	0	1	0	0	0	1
PRC (%)	476	309	599	417	−1		−1	−1	0
High Asia (%)	−5	−1	−3	−3	1	0	0	0	1
S. Asia (%)	−3	−21	−4	0	0	0	0	0	1
Other Asia (%)	−1		0	20	0	0	0	−1	1
Cambodia ($ million)	0	0	1,767	821	93	936	801	32	4
Lao PDR ($ million)	0	0	730	1,017	−2	203	6	−2	0
Viet Nam ($ million)	4,047	518	0	3,492	1,768	28,801	3,698	754	38
Thailand ($ million)	5,046	1,662	6,532	0	−3,698	64,657	−5,062	−823	−131
Other SEA ($ million)	−166	−7	−686	−21	175	4	255	55	5
PRC ($ million)	9,375	704	56,960	45,240	−663	0	−4,391	−473	−37
High Asia ($ million)	−150	−2	−907	−1,314	1,091	2,136	1,052	145	41
S. Asia ($ million)	−11	−6	−129	−12	51	144	54	42	5
Other Asia ($ million)	0	0	−1	238	−2	−27	−15	−3	1

Source: Author estimates.

significant agricultural expansion and the PRC's momentous growth promises more stimulus to agro-food activity in the region. The PRC is expected to become a net importer of agro-food in the coming decades, which will have significant implications within the region. As its middle class continues to emerge, the resource intensity of food consumption (e.g., meat and dairy) will lead to net imports and require expansion of agricultural capacity elsewhere.

Because low-income Southeast Asia is generally seen to be well below its agro-food potential, this situation suggests a significant opportunity for self-directed poverty reduction through regional agro-food market expansion. This chapter reviews the history of HIA and PRC's emergence in region's agro-food markets. Finally, GMS's role is analyzed for the potential of Asian agro-food trade to contribute to poverty reduction.

After an extensive review of historical and initial conditions, we use a new dynamic simulation model to assess the prospects for rapid growth among low-income GMS economies. In particular, we examine empirically the potential contributions of agro-food productivity growth, trade facilitation, and FDI in these countries. Our results suggest that such potential is very significant, but it can only be fully realized if policies are integrated and complementary.

In particular, productivity growth alone will only generate low-value surpluses. Combining this with trade facilitation measures, including infrastructure investments like the GMS corridors, will amplify benefits but also lead to domestic resource rivalry. Finally, complementing the first two advantages with access to external investment funds achieves the highest benefit.

The estimated gains from these policies are very substantial for the low-income economies considered, and moreover, they benefit neighboring countries that do not share the direct benefits. Just as importantly, dramatic trade expansion by the beneficiaries induces significant regional trade growth, but relatively minor trade diversion. This result supports the essential argument that trade-oriented, self-directed poverty reduction policies among low-income GMS countries are incentive-compatible for their wealthier neighbors. Intuition might suggest this, but trade rivalry has a long history in this region and elsewhere. For this reason, we believe it is important to develop empirical evidence that growth dividends propagate across the region, and trade growth can be shared among regional partners without the need for intervention, trading rules, or even unrequited transfers.

Acknowledgments

For this project financial support from the Asian Development Bank is gratefully acknowledged. Douglas Brooks, the late William James, and other colleagues and seminar participants at ADB and UCB offered many helpful insights and comments. Opinions expressed remain those of the author, however, and should not be attributed to their affiliated institutions.

References

Asian Development Bank (ADB) (2007a), *Strategic Framework for Subregional Cooperation in Agriculture: 2006–2010, Greater Mekong Subregion – Economic Cooperation Program.* ADB, Manila.

Asian Development Bank (ADB) (2007b), *The Mekong Region Trade: Trends, Patterns, and Policies.* ADB, Manila.

Asian Development Bank (ADB) (2009a), *Asian Development Outlook 2009.* ADB, Manila.

Asian Development Bank (ADB) (2009b), *Asian Development Outlook Update 2009.* ADB, Manila.

Chern, W. (1997), *Estimated Elasticities of Chinese Grain Demand: Review, Assessment and New Evidence.* Institute of Economics, Academia Sinica, Beijing.

Coxhead, I. (2004), *International Trade and the Natural Resource 'Curse' in Southeast Asia: Does China's Growth Threaten Regional Development.* Department of Agricultural & Applied Economics, University of Wisconsinn, Madison.

Gale, F. (2005), *China's Agricultural Imports Boomed During 2003–04.* Economic Research Service, United States Department of Agriculture, Washington, DC.

Gale, F., Huang, K. (2007), *Demand for Food Quantity and Quality in China.* Economic Research Service, United States Department of Agriculture, Washington, DC.

Gould, B. (2002), Household composition and food expenditures in China. *Agribusiness* 18 (3), 387–407.

Guo, X., Mroz, T.A., Popkin, B.M., Zhai, F. (2000), Structural change in the impact of income on food consumption in China, 1989–1993. *Economic Development and Cultural Change* 48 (4), 737–760.

Hertel, T. W. (Ed.) (1997). *Global Trade Analysis: Modeling and Applications.* Cambridge University Press, New York.

Huang, S., Gale, F. (2006), *China's Rising Fruit and Vegetable Exports Challenge U.S. Industries.* Economic Research Service, United States Department of Agriculture, Washington, DC.

Jin, S., Tokunaga, S., Akune, Y., Kageyama, M. (2006), Agglomeration effects and Japanese food industry investment in China: evidence from the cities. International Association of Agriculture Economists' Conference, Gold Coast, Australia, August 12–18.

Ministry of Agriculture and Forestry Republic of Korea (MAFROK) (2006), *Korean Agriculture 2005.* MAFROK, Seoul.

Rozelle, S., Huang, J. (1998), *Wheat in China: Supply, Demand, and Trade in the Twenty-First Century*. Trade Research Center, Beijing.

Sun, P., Knutson, R., Lee, Y.-H. (1998), *Transition and Reform of China's Agricultural System Toward Market-Oriented Economy: Lessons from the Taiwan Experience*. Agricultural & Food Policy Center, Texas A&M University System, College Station.

van der Mensbrugghe, D. (2008), *Linkage Technical Reference Document*. Economic Policy and Prospects Group, World Bank, Washington, DC.

Xin, X., Zhou, Z., Jiang, N. (2005), Consumption of livestock products at the regional level in China. *Journal of Rural Development* 28 (2), 211–233.

CHAPTER 11

Computational Analysis of the Menu of U.S.–Japan Trade Policies☆

Drusilla K. Brown[a], Kozo Kiyota[b] and Robert M. Stern[c]

[a]*Department of Economics, Tufts University, Medford, MA, USA*
E-mail address: drusilla.brown@tufts.edu
[b]*Faculty of Business Administration, Yokohama National University, Yokohama, Japan*
E-mail address: kiyota@ynu.ac.jp
[c]*Department of Economics and Ford School of Public Policy, University of Michigan, Ann Arbor, MI, USA*
E-mail address: rmstern@umich.edu

Abstract

We have used the Michigan computable general equilibrium (CGE) model of World Production and Trade to calculate the aggregate welfare and sectoral employment effects of the menu of U.S.–Japan trade policies. The menu of policies encompasses the various preferential U.S. and Japan bilateral and regional free trade agreements (FTAs) negotiated and in process, unilateral removal of existing trade barriers by the two countries, and global (multilateral) free trade. The U.S. preferential agreements include the FTAs approved by the U.S. Congress with Chile and Singapore in 2003, those signed with Central America, Australia, and Morocco and awaiting Congressional approval in 2004, and prospective FTAs with the Southern African Customs Union (SACU), Thailand, and the Free Trade Area of the Americas (FTAA). The Japanese preferential agreements include the bilateral FTA with Singapore signed in 2002 and prospective FTAs with Chile, Indonesia, Korea, Malaysia, Mexico, Philippines, and Thailand. The welfare impacts of the FTAs on the United States and Japan are shown to be rather small in absolute and relative terms. The sectoral employment effects are also generally small in the United States and Japan, but vary across the individual sectors depending on the patterns of the bilateral liberalization. The welfare effects on the FTA partner countries are mostly positive though generally small, but there are some indications of potentially disruptive employment

---

☆This chapter has been adapted from Brown, D.K., Kiyota, K., Stern, R.M. (2006), Computational analysis of the menu of U.S.-Japan trade policies. *The World Economy* 29 (6), 805–855.

Frontiers of Economics and Globalization
Volume 7 ISSN: 1574-8715
DOI: 10.1108/S1574-8715(2010)0000007014

shifts in some partner countries. There are indications of trade diversion and detrimental welfare effects on nonmember countries for some of the FTAs analyzed. Data limitations precluded analysis of the welfare effects of the different FTA rules of origin and other discriminatory arrangements.
In comparison with the welfare gains from the U.S. and Japan bilateral FTAs, the gains from both unilateral trade liberalization by the United States, Japan, and the FTA partners and global (multilateral) free trade are shown to be rather substantial and more uniformly positive for all countries in the global trading system. The U.S. and Japan FTAs are based on "hub" and "spoke" arrangements. We show that the spokes emanate out in different and often overlapping directions, suggesting that the complex of bilateral FTAs may create distortions of the global trading system.

Keywords: Multilateral, regional, bilateral trade liberalization

JEL classifications: F10, F13, F15

1. Introduction

In this chapter, we present a computational analysis of the economic effects of the menu of U.S.–Japan trade policies. The menu encompasses the various U.S. and Japan bilateral and regional free trade agreements (FTAs) that had been negotiated and the negotiations currently in process in August 2004 when this chapter was originally written, unilateral removal of existing trade barriers by the United States, Japan, and their FTA partner countries, and global (multilateral) free trade. The analysis is based on the Michigan Model of World Production and Trade. The Michigan Model is a multicountry/multisector computable general equilibrium (CGE) model of the global trading system that has been used for more than three decades to analyze the economic effects of multilateral, regional, and bilateral trade negotiations and various other changes in trade and related policies.

In Section 2, we present a brief description of the main features and data of the Michigan Model. The results of the computational analysis of the U.S. and Japan FTAs are presented in Sections 3 and 4. In Section 5, we consider the cross-country patterns of the welfare effects of the various FTAs. In Section 6, we provide a broader perspective on the FTAs that takes into account the effects of the unilateral and multilateral removal of trade barriers by the United States and Japan, their FTA partner countries, and other countries/regions in the global trading system. Section 7 provides a summary and concluding remarks.

2. The Michigan Model of World Production and Trade

2.1. Overview of the Michigan Model

The version of the Michigan Model that we use in this chapter covers 18 economic sectors, including agriculture, manufactures, and services, in each of 22 countries/regions. The distinguishing feature of the Michigan Model is that it incorporates some aspects of trade with imperfect competition, including increasing returns to scale, monopolistic competition, and product variety. Some details follow.[1] A more complete description of the formal structure and equations of the model can be found online at www.fordschool.umich.edu/rsie/model/.

2.1.1. Sectors and market structure

As mentioned, the version of the model used consists of 18 production sectors and 22 countries/regions (plus rest-of-world). The sectoral and country/region coverage are indicated in the tables. Agriculture is modeled as perfectly competitive with product differentiation by country of origin, and all other sectors covering manufactures and services are modeled as monopolistically competitive. Each monopolistically competitive firm produces a differentiated product and sets price as a profit-maximizing mark-up of price over marginal cost. Free entry and exit of firms then guarantees zero profits.

2.1.2. Expenditure

Consumers and producers are assumed to use a two-stage procedure to allocate expenditure across differentiated products. In the first stage, expenditure is allocated across goods without regard to the country of origin or producing firm. At this stage, the utility function is Cobb–Douglas, and the production function requires intermediate inputs in fixed proportions. In the second stage, expenditure on monopolistically competitive goods is allocated across the competing varieties supplied by each firm from all countries. In the perfectly competitive agricultural sector, since individual firm supply is indeterminate, expenditure is allocated over each country's sector as a whole, with imperfect substitution between products of different countries.

The aggregation function in the second stage is a constant elasticity of substitution (CES) function. Use of the CES function and product differentiation by firm imply that consumer welfare is influenced both by any reduction in real prices brought about by trade liberalization and by increased product variety. The elasticity of substitution among different

---

[1] See also Deardorff and Stern (1990, esp. pp. 9–46) and Brown and Stern (1989a, 1989b).

varieties of a good is assumed to be 3, a value that is broadly consistent with available empirical estimates. The parameter for the sensitivity of consumers to the number of product varieties is set at 0.5.[2]

2.1.3. Production

The production function is separated into two stages. In the first stage, intermediate inputs and a primary composite of capital and labor are used in fixed proportion to output.[3] In the second stage, capital and labor are combined through a CES function to form the primary composite. In the monopolistically competitive sectors, additional fixed inputs of capital and labor are required. It is assumed that fixed capital and fixed labor are used in the same proportion as variable capital and variable labor so that production functions are homothetic. The elasticities of substitution between capital and labor vary across sectors and were derived from a literature search of empirical estimates of sectoral supply elasticities. Economies of scale are determined endogenously in the model.

2.1.4. Supply prices

To determine equilibrium prices, perfectly competitive firms operate such that price is equal to marginal cost, whereas monopolistically competitive firms maximize profits by setting price as an optimal mark-up over marginal cost. The numbers of firms in sectors under monopolistic competition are determined by the zero profits condition. The free entry condition in this context is also the basic mechanism through which new product varieties are created (or eliminated). Each of the new entrants arrives with a distinctly different product, expanding the array of goods available to consumers.

Free entry and exit are also the means through which countries are able to realize the specialization gains from trade. In this connection, it can be noted that in a model with nationally differentiated products, which relies on the Armington assumption, production of a particular variety of a good cannot move from one country to another. In such a model, there are gains from exchange but no gains from specialization. However, in the Michigan Model with differentiated products supplied by monopolistically competitive firms, production of a particular variety is internationally mobile. A decline in the number of firms in one country paired with an expansion in another essentially implies that production of one variety of a good is being relocated from the country in which the number of firms

---

[2] If the variety parameter is greater than 0.5, it means that consumers value variety more. If the parameter is 0, consumers have no preference for variety. This is the same as the Armington assumption according to which consumers view products as distinguished by country of production. Sensitivity tests of alternative parameter values are included in the Appendix.

[3] Intermediate inputs include both domestic and imported varieties.

is declining to the country in which the number of firms is expanding. Thus, we have both an exchange gain and a specialization gain from international trade.[4]

2.1.5. *Capital and labor markets*

Capital and labor are assumed to be perfectly mobile across sectors within each country. Returns to capital and labor are determined so as to equate factor demand to an exogenous supply of each factor. The aggregate supplies of capital and labor in each country are assumed to remain fixed so as to abstract from macroeconomic considerations (e.g., the determination of investment), since our microeconomic focus is on the intersectoral allocation of resources.

2.1.6. *World market and trade balance*

The world market determines equilibrium prices such that all markets clear. Total demand for each firm or sector's product must equal total supply of that product. It is also assumed that trade remains balanced for each country/region, that is, any initial trade imbalance remains constant as trade barriers are changed. This is accomplished by permitting aggregate expenditure to adjust to maintain a constant trade balance. Thus, we abstract away from the macroeconomic forces and policies that are the main determinants of trade imbalances. Furthermore, it should be noted that there are no nominal rigidities in the model. As a consequence, there is no role for a real exchange rate mechanism.

2.1.7. *Trade policies and rent/revenues*

We have incorporated into the model the import tariff rates and export taxes/subsidies as policy inputs that are applicable to the bilateral trade of the various countries/regions with respect to one another. These have been computed using the "GTAP-5.4 Database" provided in Dimaranan and McDougall (2002). This was the latest database available at the time of writing in 2006. The export barriers have been estimated as export-tax equivalents. We assume that revenues from both import tariffs and export taxes, as well as rents from non-tariff barriers on exports, are redistributed to consumers in the tariff- or tax-levying country and are spent like any other income.

---

[4] The international relocation of a particular variety of a good can be understood in the context of the ongoing outsourcing debate. Domestic firms require intermediate inputs, in addition to capital and labor. To the extent that tariff reduction leads a firm to substitute toward traded intermediate inputs, domestic firms can be thought of as outsourcing some component of production. This is particularly the case if there is a decline in the number of domestic firms in the sector from which intermediate inputs are purchased and an expansion in the supplier country.

Tariff liberalization can affect economic efficiency through three main channels. First, in the context of standard trade theory, tariff reductions reduce the cost of imports both for consumers and for producers purchasing traded intermediate inputs, thus producing an *exchange* gain. Second, tariff removal leads firms to direct resources toward those sectors that have the greatest value on the world market. That is, we have the standard *specialization* gain. Third, tariff reductions have a pro-competitive effect on sellers. Increased price pressure from imported varieties force incumbent firms to cut price. Surviving firms remain viable by expanding output, thereby moving down their average total cost (ATC) curve. The consequent lower ATC of production creates gains from the *realization of economies of scale*.

2.1.8. Model closure and implementation

We assume in the model that aggregate expenditure varies endogenously to hold aggregate employment constant. This closure is analogous to the Johansen closure rule (Deardorff and Stern, 1990, pp. 27–29). The Johansen closure rule consists of keeping the requirement of full employment while dropping the consumption function. This means that consumption can be thought of as adjusting endogenously to ensure full employment. However, in the present model, we do not distinguish consumption from other sources of final demand. That is, we assume instead that total expenditure adjusts to maintain full employment.

The model is solved using GEMPACK (Harrison and Pearson, 1996). When policy changes are introduced into the model, the method of solution yields percentage changes in sectoral employment and certain other variables of interest. Multiplying the percentage changes by the absolute levels of the pertinent variables in the database yields the absolute changes, positive or negative, which might result from the various liberalization scenarios.

2.1.9. Interpreting the modeling results

To help the reader interpret the modeling results, it is useful to review the features of the model that serve to identify the various economic effects to be reflected in the different applications of the model. Although the model includes the aforementioned features of imperfect competition, it remains the case that markets respond to trade liberalization in much the same way that they would with perfect competition. That is, when tariffs or other trade barriers are reduced in a sector, domestic buyers (both final and intermediate) substitute toward imports and the domestic competing industry contracts production while foreign exporters expand. Thus, in the case of multilateral liberalization that reduces tariffs and other trade barriers simultaneously in most sectors and countries, each country's industries share in both of these effects, expanding or contracting depending primarily on whether their protection is reduced more or less than in other sectors and countries.

Worldwide, these changes cause increased international demand for all sectors. World prices increase most for those sectors where trade barriers fall the most.[5] This in turn causes changes in countries' terms of trade that can be positive or negative. Those countries that are net exporters of goods with the greatest degree of liberalization will experience increases in their terms of trade, as the world prices of their exports rise relative to their imports. The reverse occurs for net exporters in industries where liberalization is slight – perhaps because it may already have taken place in previous trade rounds.

The effects on the welfare of countries arise from a mixture of these terms-of-trade effects, together with the standard efficiency gains from trade and also from additional benefits due to the realization of economies of scale. Thus, we expect on average that the world will gain from multilateral liberalization, as resources are reallocated to those sectors in each country where there is a comparative advantage. In the absence of terms-of-trade effects, these efficiency gains should raise national welfare measured by the equivalent variation for every country,[6] although some factor owners within a country may lose, as will be noted later. However, it is possible for a particular country whose net imports are concentrated in sectors with the greatest liberalization to lose overall, if the worsening of its terms of trade swamps these efficiency gains.

On the contrary, although trade with imperfect competition is perhaps best known for introducing reasons why countries may lose from trade, actually its greatest contribution is to expand the list of reasons for gains from trade. Thus, in the Michigan Model, trade liberalization permits all countries to expand their export sectors at the same time that all sectors compete more closely with a larger number of competing varieties from abroad. As a result, countries as a whole gain from lower costs due to increasing returns to scale, lower monopoly distortions due to greater competition, and reduced costs and/or increased utility due to greater product variety. All these effects make it more likely that countries will gain from liberalization in ways that are shared across the entire population.[7]

---

[5] The price of agricultural products supplied by the rest of the world is taken as the numeraire in the model, and there is a rest-of-world against which all other prices can rise.

[6] The equivalent variation is a measure of the amount of income that would have to be given or taken away from an economy before a change in policy to leave the economy as well off as it would be after the policy change has taken place. If the equivalent variation is positive, it is indicative of an improvement in economic welfare resulting from the policy change.

[7] In perfectly competitive trade models such as the Heckscher–Ohlin Model, one expects countries as a whole to gain from trade, but the owners of one factor – the "scarce factor" – to lose through the mechanism first explored by Stolper and Samuelson (1941). The additional sources of gain from trade due to increasing returns to scale, competition, and product variety, however, are shared across factors, and we routinely find in our CGE modeling that both labor and capital gain from multilateral trade liberalization.

The various effects just described in the context of multilateral trade liberalization will also take place when there is unilateral trade liberalization, although these effects will depend on the magnitudes of the liberalization in relation to the patterns of trade and the price and output responses involved between the liberalizing country and its trading partners. Similarly, many of the effects described will take place with the formation of bilateral or regional FTAs. But in these cases, there may be trade creation and positive effects on the economic welfare of FTA-member countries together with trade diversion and negative effects on the economic welfare of nonmember countries. The net effects on economic welfare for individual countries and globally will thus depend on the economic circumstances and policy changes implemented.[8]

In the real world, all the various effects occur over time, some of them more quickly than others. However, the Michigan Model is static in the sense that it is based on a single set of equilibrium conditions rather than relationships that vary over time.[9] The model results therefore refer to a time horizon that depends on the assumptions made about which variables do and do not adjust to changing market conditions and on the short- or long-run nature of these adjustments. Because the supply and demand elasticities used in the model reflect relatively long-run adjustments and it is assumed that markets for both labor and capital clear within countries,[10] the modeling results are appropriate for a relatively long time horizon of several years – perhaps two or three at a minimum. On the contrary, the model does not allow for the very long-run adjustments that could occur

---

[8] It may be noted that, in a model of perfect competition, bilateral trade liberalization should have the effect of contracting trade with the excluded countries, thereby improving the terms of trade for the FTA members vis-à-vis the rest of world. But in a model with scale economies, the pro-competitive effect of trade liberalization can generate a cut in price and increase in supply to excluded countries. The terms of trade of FTA members may therefore deteriorate in this event.

It should also be mentioned that rules of origin may offset some of the potential welfare benefits of FTAs insofar as they may lead to higher input costs and consequent reduction of FTA preference margins. In this connection, see Krishna (2006).

[9] As noted earlier, macroeconomic closure in the model involves the equivalent of having expenditure equal to the sum of earned incomes plus redistributed net tax revenues. However, the actual solution is attained indirectly, but equivalently, by imposing a zero change in the trade balance. Since the model allows for all net tax and tariff revenues to be redistributed to consumers, when tariffs are reduced with trade liberalization, the model implicitly imposes a nondistorting tax to recoup the loss in tariff revenues.

[10] The analysis in the model assumes throughout that the aggregate, economy-wide, level of employment is held constant in each country. The effects of trade liberalization are therefore not permitted to change any country's overall rates of employment or unemployment. This assumption is made because overall employment is determined by macroeconomic forces and policies that are not contained in the model and would not themselves be included in a negotiated trade agreement. The focus instead is on the composition of employment across sectors as determined by the microeconomic interactions of supply and demand resulting from the liberalization of trade.

through capital accumulation, population growth, and technological change. The modeling results should therefore be interpreted as being superimposed upon longer-run growth paths of the economies involved. To the extent that these growth paths themselves may be influenced by trade liberalization, therefore, the model does not capture such effects.

2.2. Benchmark data

Needless to say, the data needs of this model are immense. Apart from numerous share parameters, the model requires various types of elasticity measures. Like other CGE models, most of our data come from published sources.

As mentioned earlier, the main data source used in the model is "The GTAP-5.4 Database" of the Purdue University Center for Global Trade Analysis Project (Dimaranan and McDougall, 2002). The reference year for this GTAP database is 1997. From this source, we have extracted the following data, aggregated to our sectors and countries/regions:[11]

- Bilateral trade flows among 22 countries/regions, decomposed into 18 sectors. Trade with the rest-of-world (ROW) is included to close the model;
- Input-output tables for the 22 countries/regions, excluding ROW;
- Components of final demand along with sectoral contributions for the 22 countries/regions, excluding ROW;
- Gross value of output and value added at the sectoral level for the 22 countries/regions, excluding ROW;
- Bilateral import tariffs by sector among the 22 countries/regions;
- Elasticity of substitution between capital and labor by sector;
- Bilateral export-tax equivalents among the 22 countries/regions, decomposed into 18 sectors.

The monopolistically competitive market structure in the nonagricultural sectors of the model imposes an additional data requirement of the numbers of firms at the sectoral level, and there is need also for estimates of sectoral employment.[12] The employment data, which have been adapted from various published sources, will be noted in tables.

The GTAP-5.4 1997 database has been projected to the year 2005, which is when the Uruguay Round liberalization will have been fully implemented. In this connection, we extrapolated the labor availability in different countries/regions by an average weighted population growth rate

---

[11] Details on the sectoral and country/region aggregation are available from the authors on request.

[12] Notes on the construction of the data on the number of firms and for employment are available from the authors on request.

of 1.2% per annum. All other major variables have been projected, using an average weighted growth rate of GDP of 2.5%.[13] The 2005 data have been adjusted to take into account two major developments that have occurred in the global trading system since the mid-1990s. These include (1) implementation of the Uruguay Round negotiations that were completed in 1993–1994 and were to be phased in over the following decade; and (2) the accession of Mainland China and Taiwan to the WTO in 2001.[14] We have made allowance for the foregoing developments by readjusting the 2005 scaled-up database for benchmarking purposes to obtain an approximate picture of what the world may be expected to look like in 2005. In the computational scenarios to be presented later, we use these re-adjusted data as the starting point to carry out our liberalization scenarios for the U.S. bilateral FTAs and for the accompanying unilateral and global free trade scenarios.

The GTAP 5.4 (1997) base data for tariffs and the estimated tariff equivalents of services barriers are broken down by sector on a global basis and bilaterally for existing and prospective FTA partners of the United States and Japan in Tables 1–2. The post-Uruguay Round tariff rates on agriculture, mining, and manufactures are applied rates and are calculated in GTAP by dividing tariff revenues by the value of imports by sector.

The services barriers are based on financial data on average gross (price-cost) margins constructed initially by Hoekman (2000) and adapted for modeling purposes in Brown *et al.* (2002). The gross operating margins are calculated as the differences between total revenues and total operating costs. Some of these differences are presumably attributable to fixed costs. Given that the gross operating margins vary across countries, a portion of the margin can also be attributed to barriers to FDI. For this purpose, a benchmark is set for each sector in relation to the country with the smallest gross operating margin, on the assumption that operations in the benchmark country can be considered to be freely open to foreign firms.

---

[13] The underlying data are drawn from World Bank sources and are available on request. For a more elaborate and detailed procedure for calculating year 2005 projections, see Hertel (2000), Hertel and Martin (2000, 2001) and Hoekman and Martin (2001).

[14] The tariff data for the WTO accession of China and Taiwan have been adapted from Ianchovichina and Martin (2004). In addition to benchmarking the effects of the Uruguay Round and China/Taiwan accession to the WTO, Francois *et al.* (2003) benchmark their GTAP 5.4 dataset to take into account the enlargement of the European Union (EU) in 2004 to include 10 new member countries from Central and Eastern Europe and some changes in the EU Common Agricultural Policies that were introduced in 2000. Our EU and EFTA regional aggregate includes the 25-member EU, but the benchmark data were not adjusted to take into account the adoption of the EU common external tariffs by the new members. Because of data constraints, we have not made allowance for the Information Technology Agreement and agreements for liberalization of financial and telecommunication services following conclusion of the Uruguay Round.

Table 1. *Post-Uruguay round tariff rates by sector for the United States*

	Global (%)	Singapore (%)	Australia (%)	Morocco (%)	SACU (%)	Thailand (%)	FTAA				
							Canada	CAC	Chile	Mexico	South America
Agriculture	2.7	0.1	4.0	0.1	1.3	0.3	0.0	1.0	0.8	0.0	3.2
Mining	0.2	0.0	0.3	0.0	0.1	0.0	0.0	0.3	0.1	0.0	0.1
Food, beverages, and tobacco	3.5	1.2	3.4	2.8	2.8	1.4	0.0	3.0	1.3	0.0	1.8
Textiles	5.7	9.3	6.5	7.1	6.3	8.7	0.0	6.8	14.0	0.0	7.7
Wearing apparel	11.0	15.5	9.7	10.5	12.4	14.2	0.0	11.6	11.5	0.0	13.6
Leather products and Footwear	7.2	5.6	4.1	3.6	2.3	7.7	0.0	4.6	7.7	0.0	6.3
Wood and wood products	0.3	0.4	0.8	0.7	0.3	0.2	0.0	0.5	0.2	0.0	0.4
Chemicals	1.9	3.2	1.0	1.0	0.7	1.8	0.0	0.8	0.0	0.0	0.9
Nonmetallic mineral products	3.2	4.0	2.9	0.9	0.0	2.8	0.0	3.8	0.6	0.0	2.3
Metal products	1.4	2.3	0.2	1.4	0.6	0.9	0.0	0.5	0.5	0.0	0.6
Transportation equipment	1.2	1.0	1.5	0.3	1.7	0.1	0.0	1.3	1.4	0.0	0.2
Machinery and equipment	1.0	0.8	1.6	0.0	0.1	0.1	0.0	0.3	0.2	0.0	0.4
Other manufactures	1.3	1.3	0.9	0.0	0.4	0.4	0.0	2.2	0.1	0.0	1.5
Electricity, gas, and water	0.0	0.0	0.0	0.0	0.0	0.0	0.0	0.0	0.0	0.0	0.0
Construction	9.0	9.0	9.0	9.0	9.0	9.0	0.0	9.0	9.0	0.0	9.0
Trade and transport	27.0	27.0	27.0	27.0	27.0	27.0	0.0	27.0	27.0	0.0	27.0
Other private services	31.0	31.0	31.0	31.0	31.0	31.0	0.0	31.0	31.0	0.0	31.0
Government services	25.0	25.0	25.0	25.0	25.0	25.0	0.0	25.0	25.0	0.0	25.0

Sources: Adapted from Francois and Strutt (1999); Brown *et al.* (2002); and Dimaranan and McDougall (2002).
Note: Central America and Caribbean (CAC) members include Costa Rica, Dominican Republic, El Salvador, Guatemala, Honduras, and Nicaragua and are to be included in the FTAA.

Table 2. Post-Uruguay round tariff rates by sector for Japan

	Global (%)	Singapore (%)	Chile (%)	Korea (%)	Indonesia (%)	Malaysia (%)	Mexico (%)	Philippines (%)	Thailand (%)
Agriculture	38.1	1.3	2.9	5.3	6.7	0.3	6.1	11.5	1.7
Mining	−0.2	0.0	0.0	0.0	−0.7	−0.6	−1.7	0.0	−1.8
Food, beverages, and tobacco	25.2	20.8	4.3	18.9	3.2	2.2	44.2	4.6	17.3
Textiles	2.8	7.4	0.0	2.9	1.1	0.2	0.1	1.7	1.5
Wearing apparel	6.5	5.8	7.0	5.8	5.4	5.7	5.1	4.9	4.9
Leather products and footwear	8.9	6.1	0.0	8.4	4.5	9.1	10.3	8.0	8.4
Wood and wood products	0.4	0.3	0.1	0.2	0.0	0.3	0.5	0.0	0.0
Chemicals	1.8	0.9	0.0	0.9	1.1	0.3	0.6	0.4	0.6
Nonmetallic mineral products	1.0	0.2	0.0	0.7	1.4	0.4	0.9	0.6	1.4
Metal products	0.5	0.3	0.1	1.0	0.3	0.3	0.1	0.3	0.4
Transportation equipment	0.0	0.0	0.0	0.0	0.0	0.0	0.0	0.0	0.0
Machinery and equipment	0.0	0.0	0.3	0.1	0.2	0.0	0.1	0.1	0.1
Other manufactures	0.7	0.0	1.8	0.3	2.8	0.0	0.0	0.8	0.1
Electricity, gas, and water	0.0	0.0	0.0	0.0	0.0	0.0	0.0	0.0	0.0
Construction	3.0	3.0	3.0	3.0	0.0	3.0	3.0	3.0	3.0
Trade and transport	15.0	15.0	15.0	15.0	15.0	15.0	15.0	15.0	15.0
Other private services	12.0	12.0	12.0	12.0	12.0	12.0	12.0	12.0	12.0
Government services	28.0	28.0	28.0	28.0	28.0	28.0	28.0	28.0	28.0

Sources: Adapted from Francois and Strutt (1999); Brown *et al.* (2002); and Dimaranan and McDougall (2002).

The excess in any other country above this lowest benchmark is then taken to be due to barriers to establishment by foreign firms.

That is, the barrier is modeled as the cost-increase attributable to an increase in fixed cost borne by multinational corporations attempting to establish an enterprise locally in a host country. This abstracts from the possibility that fixed costs may differ among firms because of variations in market size, distance from headquarters, and other factors. It is further assumed that this cost increase can be interpreted as an ad valorem equivalent tariff on services transactions generally. It can be seen in Tables 1 and 2 that the constructed services barriers are considerably higher than the import barriers on manufactures. While possibly subject to overstatement, it is generally acknowledged that many services sectors are highly regulated and thus restrain international services transactions.

For the United States, the highest import tariffs for manufactures are recorded for textiles, wearing apparel, and leather products and footwear, both globally and bilaterally. For Japan, the highest import tariffs are noted in agriculture, food, beverages and tobacco, textiles, wearing apparel, and leather and leather products. The values and shares of U.S. and Japanese exports and imports are broken down by sector according to origin and destination in Tables 3–6 on a global basis as well as for FTA partners. Employment by sector is indicated for the United States and for Japan and their FTA partners in Table 7.

3. *Computational analysis of U.S. free trade agreements*

As already noted, both the United States and Japan had signed or were in the process of negotiating bilateral FTAs in 2006, at the time of writing. For the United States, these include the agreements with Chile and Singapore approved by the U.S. Congress in 2003, agreements with Central America and the Dominican Republic (CAFTA), Australia, and Morocco to be submitted for Congressional approval in 2004, and ongoing negotiations with the Southern African Customs Union (SACU), Thailand, and the Free Trade Area of the Americas (FTAA).[15] The Japanese bilateral FTAs will be analyzed later and include the agreement with Singapore signed in 2002 and subsequent and prospective agreements with Chile, Korea, Malaysia, Mexico, Philippines, and Thailand.

As we note in Brown *et al.* (2005a, 2005b, 2008) and Kiyota and Stern (2007), the United States has a myriad of objectives in pursuing FTAs, including increased market access and shaping the regulatory and political

[15] It should be noted that the FTA negotiations with the SACU and Thailand have subsequently been suspended, and FTAA negotiations have been placed on hold. FTA negotiations were being concluded with Bahrain in 2004. An FTA with Peru was approved in 2009. Negotiations have been ongoing with Colombia, Korea, and Panama and are yet to be submitted for Congressional approval. See the USTR website for more information.

Table 3. Value of U.S. sectoral exports by destination and origin, 1997 (millions of U.S. dollars)

	Global	Singapore	Australia	Morocco	SACU	Thailand	FTAA				
							Canada	CAC	Chile	Mexico	South America
Value											
Agriculture	35,176	121	109	128	65	394	2,815	1,098	47	3,242	1,547
Mining	6,421	15	22	6	38	6	1,416	26	39	214	434
Food, beverages, and tobacco	30,541	293	281	75	145	171	3,964	1,464	83	2,065	982
Textiles	11,485	113	159	11	36	56	2,538	1,362	90	2,055	565
Wearing apparel	6,847	45	35	4	8	12	423	2,428	21	1,623	213
Leather products and footwear	2,280	24	24	0	16	37	185	213	6	323	59
Wood and wood products	29,386	284	542	8	165	182	7,717	1,094	151	3,415	1,371
Chemicals	90,569	3,236	2,129	26	524	1,109	15,886	2,737	665	10,405	6,752
Nonmetallic mineral products	11,921	168	318	20	96	68	2,703	269	93	922	745
Metal products	34,238	511	312	1	97	384	10,460	712	223	5,089	1,447
Transportation equipment	102,640	1,899	1,800	89	349	1,337	33,595	953	607	8,130	3,713
Machinery and equipment	269,892	11,075	5,440	77	1,367	3,455	44,683	3,795	1,860	27,568	17,262
Other manufactures	11,322	254	210	2	55	49	1,400	273	69	794	526
Electricity, gas, and water	751	19	4	0	2	4	113	2	2	9	60
Construction	4,023	2	3	0	4	32	5	32	0	2	9
Trade and transport	81,445	879	1,675	60	549	602	2,401	514	308	744	3,069
Other private services	81,707	1,280	1,047	66	315	975	3,889	588	151	928	2,195
Government services	42,165	366	574	321	250	309	826	282	139	722	1,759
Total	852,808	20,583	14,686	894	4,080	9,183	135,019	17,843	4,554	68,250	42,708

Percent											
Agriculture	100.0	0.3	0.3	0.4	0.2	1.1	8.0	3.1	0.1	9.2	4.4
Mining	100.0	0.2	0.3	0.1	0.6	0.1	22.0	0.4	0.6	3.3	6.8
Food, beverages, and tobacco	100.0	1.0	0.9	0.2	0.5	0.6	13.0	4.8	0.3	6.8	3.2
Textiles	100.0	1.0	1.4	0.1	0.3	0.5	22.1	11.9	0.8	17.9	4.9
Wearing apparel	100.0	0.7	0.5	0.1	0.1	0.2	6.2	35.5	0.3	23.7	3.1
Leather products and footwear	100.0	1.0	1.0	0.0	0.7	1.6	8.1	9.3	0.3	14.2	2.6
Wood and wood products	100.0	1.0	1.8	0.0	0.6	0.6	26.3	3.7	0.5	11.6	4.7
Chemicals	100.0	3.6	2.4	0.0	0.6	1.2	17.5	3.0	0.7	11.5	7.5
Nonmetallic mineral products	100.0	1.4	2.7	0.2	0.8	0.6	22.7	2.3	0.8	7.7	6.3
Metal products	100.0	1.5	0.9	0.0	0.3	1.1	30.6	2.1	0.7	14.9	4.2
Transportation equipment	100.0	1.9	1.8	0.1	0.3	1.3	32.7	0.9	0.6	7.9	3.6
Machinery and equipment	100.0	4.1	2.0	0.0	0.5	1.3	16.6	1.4	0.7	10.2	6.4
Other manufactures	100.0	2.2	1.9	0.0	0.5	0.4	12.4	2.4	0.6	7.0	4.6
Electricity, gas, and water	100.0	2.5	0.6	0.0	0.2	0.5	15.1	0.3	0.2	1.3	8.0
Construction	100.0	0.1	0.1	0.0	0.1	0.8	0.1	0.8	0.0	0.0	0.2
Trade and transport	100.0	1.1	2.1	0.1	0.7	0.7	2.9	0.6	0.4	0.9	3.8
Other private services	100.0	1.6	1.3	0.1	0.4	1.2	4.8	0.7	0.2	1.1	2.7
Government services	100.0	0.9	1.4	0.8	0.6	0.7	2.0	0.7	0.3	1.7	4.2
Total	100.0	2.4	1.7	0.1	0.5	1.1	15.8	2.1	0.5	8.0	5.0

Source: GTAP 5.4 adapted from Dimaranan and McDougall (2002).

Table 4. Value of U.S. sectoral imports by destination and origin, 1997 (millions of U.S. dollars)

	Global	Singapore	Australia	Morocco	SACU	Thailand	FTAA				
							Canada	CAC	Chile	Mexico	South America
Value											
Agriculture	18,602	41	181	15	53	207	3,984	2,280	716	2,956	3,585
Mining	69,939	0	413	72	133	13	17,060	664	74	8,324	12,894
Food, beverages, and tobacco	28,813	115	898	41	138	1,672	5,553	1,421	534	1,957	2,427
Textiles	21,514	132	169	4	101	389	1,803	1,725	9	2,640	365
Wearing apparel	38,335	186	45	62	139	1,212	1,050	5,443	17	3,974	612
Leather products and footwear	21,842	9	28	5	25	782	219	438	5	607	1,572
Wood and wood products	43,785	211	85	4	81	353	25,258	165	352	2,956	1,216
Chemicals	77,142	864	302	11	259	702	15,449	879	159	2,747	4,414
Nonmetallic mineral products	14,071	17	40	2	44	161	2,572	369	18	1,365	607
Metal products	56,001	83	998	5	1,417	276	15,648	429	573	4,180	3,592
Transportation equipment	128,874	169	613	0	69	90	43,993	21	3	14,064	1,314
Machinery and equipment	307,001	17,834	549	94	117	6,053	32,119	1,128	13	38,411	1,726
Other manufactures	39,851	38	80	3	219	962	988	289	7	1,400	491
Electricity, gas, and water	2,230	2	2	1	22	2	1,445	5	0	2	117
Construction	1,268	3	3	2	3	3	4	18	0	2	7
Trade and transport	75,050	919	2,084	163	578	1,381	1,696	873	296	1,270	1,522
Other private services	59,724	1,996	1,034	77	216	642	2,111	522	94	741	1,096
Government services	18,838	125	501	222	158	115	466	335	54	144	699
Total	1,022,879	22,743	8,025	782	3,771	15,017	171,418	17,004	2,924	87,739	38,256

Percent											
Agriculture	100.0	0.2	1.0	0.1	0.3	1.1	21.4	12.3	3.9	15.9	19.3
Mining	100.0	0.0	0.6	0.1	0.2	0.0	24.4	0.9	0.1	11.9	18.4
Food, beverages, and tobacco	100.0	0.4	3.1	0.1	0.5	5.8	19.3	4.9	1.9	6.8	8.4
Textiles	100.0	0.6	0.8	0.0	0.5	1.8	8.4	8.0	0.0	12.3	1.7
Wearing apparel	100.0	0.5	0.1	0.2	0.4	3.2	2.7	14.2	0.0	10.4	1.6
Leather products and footwear	100.0	0.0	0.1	0.0	0.1	3.6	1.0	2.0	0.0	2.8	7.2
Wood and wood products	100.0	0.5	0.2	0.0	0.2	0.8	57.7	0.4	0.8	6.8	2.8
Chemicals	100.0	1.1	0.4	0.0	0.3	0.9	20.0	1.1	0.2	3.6	5.7
Nonmetallic mineral products	100.0	0.1	0.3	0.0	0.3	1.1	18.3	2.6	0.1	9.7	4.3
Metal products	100.0	0.1	1.8	0.0	2.5	0.5	27.9	0.8	1.0	7.5	6.4
Transportation equipment	100.0	0.1	0.5	0.0	0.1	0.1	34.1	0.0	0.0	10.9	1.0
Machinery and equipment	100.0	5.8	0.2	0.0	0.0	2.0	10.5	0.4	0.0	12.5	0.6
Other manufactures	100.0	0.1	0.2	0.0	0.6	2.4	2.5	0.7	0.0	3.5	1.2
Electricity, gas, and water	100.0	0.1	0.1	0.0	1.0	0.1	64.8	0.2	0.0	0.1	5.2
Construction	100.0	0.2	0.2	0.1	0.2	0.2	0.3	1.4	0.0	0.1	0.5
Trade and transport	100.0	1.2	2.8	0.2	0.8	1.8	2.3	1.2	0.4	1.7	2.0
Other private services	100.0	3.3	1.7	0.1	0.4	1.1	3.5	0.9	0.2	1.2	1.8
Government services	100.0	0.7	2.7	1.2	0.8	0.6	2.5	1.8	0.3	0.8	3.7
Total	100.0	2.2	0.8	0.1	0.4	1.5	16.8	1.7	0.3	8.6	3.7

Source: GTAP 5.4 adapted from Dimaranan and McDougall (2002).

Table 5. *Value of Japan's sectoral exports by destination and origin, 1997 (millions of U.S. dollars)*

	Global	Singapore	Chile	Indonesia	Korea	Malaysia	Mexico	Philippines	Thailand
Values									
Agriculture	493	13	1	8	49	4	3	5	14
Mining	188	2	0	13	25	7	4	3	7
Food, beverages, and tobacco	2,803	131	3	25	200	41	6	57	118
Textiles	7,581	177	2	245	543	130	22	126	186
Wearing apparel	1,054	14	1	4	50	5	5	4	7
Leather products and footwear	315	9	0	4	36	2	1	10	12
Wood and wood products	3,356	146	10	97	218	157	19	55	111
Chemicals	42,360	1,851	87	1,239	4,105	1,117	283	640	1,542
Nonmetallic mineral products	6,763	434	4	140	896	320	51	215	325
Metal products	29,106	1,638	26	1,206	3,307	1,817	296	498	2,063
Transportation equipment	92,470	1,834	390	1,961	730	1,702	666	1,156	2,001
Machinery and equipment	233,236	14,234	560	4,865	15,742	9,136	2,338	6,335	8,211
Other manufactures	7,648	228	9	74	342	161	40	34	116
Electricity, gas, and water	78	1	0	0	1	0	1	0	1
Construction	6,658	1	0	1	2	1	1	147	74
Trade and transport	33,227	356	131	171	1,045	189	287	98	205
Other private services	18,131	219	27	142	249	126	364	40	163
Government services	4,999	42	9	26	57	20	46	14	28
Total	490,466	21,329	1,260	10,219	27,597	14,936	4,430	9,438	15,184

Percent									
Agriculture	100.0	2.7	0.1	1.6	10.0	0.9	0.5	1.0	2.7
Mining	100.0	1.0	0.2	6.9	13.1	3.8	2.1	1.5	3.5
Food, beverages, and tobacco	100.0	4.7	0.1	0.9	7.1	1.5	0.2	2.0	4.2
Textiles	100.0	2.3	0.0	3.2	7.2	1.7	0.3	1.7	2.5
Wearing apparel	100.0	1.3	0.1	0.4	4.8	0.5	0.4	0.4	0.7
Leather products and footwear	100.0	2.7	0.1	1.4	11.5	0.6	0.2	3.1	3.9
Wood and wood products	100.0	4.3	0.3	2.9	6.5	4.7	0.6	1.7	3.3
Chemicals	100.0	4.4	0.2	2.9	9.7	2.6	0.7	1.5	3.6
Nonmetallic mineral products	100.0	6.4	0.1	2.1	13.3	4.7	0.8	3.2	4.8
Metal products	100.0	5.6	0.1	4.1	11.4	6.2	1.0	1.7	7.1
Transportation equipment	100.0	2.0	0.4	2.1	0.8	1.8	0.7	1.3	2.2
Machinery and equipment	100.0	6.1	0.2	2.1	6.7	3.9	1.0	2.7	3.5
Other manufactures	100.0	3.0	0.1	1.0	4.5	2.1	0.5	0.4	1.5
Electricity, gas, and water	100.0	1.5	0.2	0.6	1.7	0.6	1.0	0.5	0.9
Construction	100.0	0.0	0.0	0.0	0.0	0.0	0.0	2.2	1.1
Trade and transport	100.0	1.1	0.4	0.5	3.1	0.6	0.9	0.3	0.6
Other private services	100.0	1.2	0.1	0.8	1.4	0.7	2.0	0.2	0.9
Government services	100.0	0.8	0.2	0.5	1.1	0.4	0.9	0.3	0.6
Total	100.0	4.3	0.3	2.1	5.6	3.0	0.9	1.9	3.1

Source: GTAP 5.4 adapted from Dimaranan and McDougall (2002).

Table 6. Value of Japan's sectoral imports by destination and origin, 1997 (millions of U.S. dollars)

	Global	Singapore	Chile	Indonesia	Korea	Malaysia	Mexico	Philippines	Thailand
Values									
Agriculture	21,409	84	104	332	470	514	149	299	206
Mining	50,163	3	1,074	5,304	33	1,498	466	314	8
Food, beverages, and tobacco	31,690	166	797	1,012	1,321	387	209	257	2,161
Textiles	10,216	11	3	412	792	172	19	33	261
Wearing apparel	12,503	24	3	239	497	79	14	122	295
Leather products and footwear	5,835	17	1	214	401	3	9	22	78
Wood and wood products	19,128	121	445	2,503	188	1,386	12	137	530
Chemicals	35,097	872	40	650	2,897	634	134	146	1,005
Nonmetallic mineral products	5,436	43	2	58	289	101	38	36	236
Metal products	21,098	193	465	576	2,430	285	67	157	408
Transportation equipment	17,723	22	0	71	155	50	17	77	99
Machinery and equipment	78,030	5,413	1	944	5,064	4,049	197	2,755	3,906
Other manufactures	9,686	35	0	102	359	94	37	88	403
Electricity, gas, water	732	2	0	6	1	2	4	1	1
Construction	6,918	2	0	1	2	1	1	6	10
Trade and transport	51,819	814	180	819	559	602	1,149	296	1,048
Other private services	30,411	392	40	82	322	104	242	22	115
Government services	10,323	62	5	35	145	23	41	15	33
Total	418,217	8,275	3,161	13,358	15,926	9,985	2,807	4,782	10,805

Percent									
Agriculture	100.0	0.4	0.5	1.5	2.2	2.4	0.7	1.4	1.0
Mining	100.0	0.0	2.1	10.6	0.1	3.0	0.9	0.6	0.0
Food, beverages, and tobacco	100.0	0.5	2.5	3.2	4.2	1.2	0.7	0.8	6.8
Textiles	100.0	0.1	0.0	4.0	7.8	1.7	0.2	0.3	2.6
Wearing apparel	100.0	0.2	0.0	1.9	4.0	0.6	0.1	1.0	2.4
Leather products and footwear	100.0	0.3	0.0	3.7	6.9	0.1	0.2	0.4	1.3
Wood and wood products	100.0	0.6	2.3	13.1	1.0	7.2	0.1	0.7	2.8
Chemicals	100.0	2.5	0.1	1.9	8.3	1.8	0.4	0.4	2.9
Nonmetallic mineral products	100.0	0.8	0.0	1.1	5.3	1.9	0.7	0.7	4.3
Metal products	100.0	0.9	2.2	2.7	11.5	1.3	0.3	0.7	1.9
Transportation equipment	100.0	0.1	0.0	0.4	0.9	0.3	0.1	0.4	0.6
Machinery and equipment	100.0	6.9	0.0	1.2	6.5	5.2	0.3	3.5	5.0
Other manufactures	100.0	0.4	0.0	1.1	3.7	1.0	0.4	0.9	4.2
Electricity, gas, and water	100.0	0.2	0.1	0.8	0.1	0.3	0.5	0.1	0.2
Construction	100.0	0.0	0.0	0.0	0.0	0.0	0.0	0.1	0.1
Trade and transport	100.0	1.6	0.3	1.6	1.1	1.2	2.2	0.6	2.0
Other private services	100.0	1.3	0.1	0.3	1.1	0.3	0.8	0.1	0.4
Government services	100.0	0.6	0.0	0.3	1.4	0.2	0.4	0.1	0.3
Total	100.0	2.0	0.8	3.2	3.8	2.4	0.7	1.1	2.6

Source: GTAP 5.4 adapted from Dimaranan and McDougall (2002).

Table 7. Employment by sector, 1997: United States, Japan, and FTA partners

	United States	Japan	Korea	Singapore	Indonesia	Malaysia	Philippines	Thailand	Australia	Morocco	SACU	FTAA				
												Chile	Canada	CAC	Mexico	South America
Number of workers (1,000)																
Agriculture	3,538	3,518	2,385	5	35,850	1,481	11,262	16,696	431	552	4,686	776	1,058	4,074	9,023	18,636
Mining	634	70	26	1	897	39	124	47	75	93	308	88	365	97	108	1,021
Food, beverages, and tobacco	2,145	1,789	317	17	2,149	153	609	622	208	568	201	277	544	725	1,556	3,657
Textiles	949	630	384	2	1,683	67	190	710	41	383	68	46	143	179	495	1,119
Wearing apparel	797	460	260	9	1,050	92	459	1,241	45	653	117	40	160	513	162	1,104
Leather products and footwear	111	106	96	1	875	7	65	80	13	84	30	28	32	64	172	456
Wood and wood products	2,218	1,725	363	36	1,938	352	274	234	215	158	201	134	902	207	586	1,587
Chemicals	2,667	1,431	490	45	1,295	254	286	276	113	264	162	121	462	261	1,042	2,172
Nonmetallic mineral products	690	592	187	8	502	93	106	208	48	220	73	35	116	88	325	887
Metal products	3,054	1,760	489	42	570	152	175	363	189	140	202	107	553	118	493	1,336
Transportation equipment	2,244	1,292	543	41	354	83	75	135	97	66	84	26	534	28	583	523
Machinery and equipment	5,441	4,425	1,276	209	607	718	434	305	151	113	175	44	719	123	790	859
Other manufactures	519	287	78	4	193	31	80	119	16	3	24	4	69	34	62	169
Electricity, gas, and water	1,493	362	77	12	233	51	139	178	66	97	131	31	256	138	188	213
Construction	8,302	6,886	2,004	126	4,200	793	1,641	2,021	580	959	1,362	489	1,478	982	1,759	6,974
Trade and transport	34,466	18,968	6,967	609	21,360	2,001	5,989	5,583	2,674	2,757	3,024	1,377	8,541	3,800	9,550	23,466
Other private services	14,768	5,780	1,900	274	657	447	680	882	1,197	244	1,354	377	3,906	405	1,513	3,661
Government services	45,521	15,500	3,265	389	12,637	1,755	5,297	3,461	2,229	3,319	6,304	1,382	8,043	3,925	8,951	35,062
Total	129,557	65,580	21,106	1,831	87,050	8,569	27,888	33,162	8,387	10,675	18,508	5,380	27,880	15,761	37,360	102,901

Percent of employment																
Agriculture	2.7	5.4	11.3	0.3	41.2	17.3	40.4	50.3	5.1	5.2	25.3	14.4	3.8	25.8	24.2	18.1
Mining	0.5	0.1	0.1	0.0	1.0	0.4	0.4	0.1	0.9	0.9	1.7	1.6	1.3	0.6	0.3	1.0
Food, beverages, and tobacco	1.7	2.7	1.5	0.9	2.5	1.8	2.2	1.9	2.5	5.3	1.1	5.2	2.0	4.6	4.2	3.6
Textiles	0.7	1.0	1.8	0.1	1.9	0.8	0.7	2.1	0.5	3.6	0.4	0.8	0.5	1.1	1.3	1.1
Wearing apparel	0.6	0.7	1.2	0.5	1.2	1.1	1.6	3.7	0.5	6.1	0.6	0.7	0.6	3.3	0.4	1.1
Leather products and footwear	0.1	0.2	0.5	0.1	1.0	0.1	0.2	0.2	0.1	0.8	0.2	0.5	0.1	0.4	0.5	0.4
Wood and wood products	1.7	2.6	1.7	1.9	2.2	4.1	1.0	0.7	2.6	1.5	1.1	2.5	3.2	1.3	1.6	1.5
Chemicals	2.1	2.2	2.3	2.5	1.5	3.0	1.0	0.8	1.3	2.5	0.9	2.2	1.7	1.7	2.8	2.1
Nonmetallic mineral products	0.5	0.9	0.9	0.4	0.6	1.1	0.4	0.6	0.6	2.1	0.4	0.6	0.4	0.6	0.9	0.9
Metal products	2.4	2.7	2.3	2.3	0.7	1.8	0.6	1.1	2.3	1.3	1.1	2.0	2.0	0.7	1.3	1.3
Transportation equipment	1.7	2.0	2.6	2.2	0.4	1.0	0.3	0.4	1.2	0.6	0.5	0.5	1.9	0.2	1.6	0.5
Machinery and equipment	4.2	6.7	6.0	11.4	0.7	8.4	1.6	0.9	1.8	1.1	0.9	0.8	2.6	0.8	2.1	0.8
Other manufactures	0.4	0.4	0.4	0.2	0.2	0.4	0.3	0.4	0.2	0.0	0.1	0.1	0.2	0.2	0.2	0.2
Electricity, gas, and water	1.2	0.6	0.4	0.7	0.3	0.6	0.5	0.5	0.8	0.9	0.7	0.6	0.9	0.9	0.5	0.2
Construction	6.4	10.5	9.5	6.9	4.8	9.3	5.9	6.1	6.9	9.0	7.4	9.1	5.3	6.2	4.7	6.8
Trade and transport	26.6	28.9	33.0	33.3	24.5	23.4	21.5	16.8	31.9	25.8	16.3	25.6	30.6	24.1	25.6	22.8
Other private services	11.4	8.8	9.0	15.0	0.8	5.2	2.4	2.7	14.3	2.3	7.3	7.0	14.0	2.6	4.1	3.6
Government services	35.1	23.6	15.5	21.3	14.5	20.5	19.0	10.4	26.6	31.1	34.1	25.7	28.8	24.9	24.0	34.1
Total	100.0	100.0	100.0	100.0	100.0	100.0	100.0	100.0	100.0	100.0	100.0	100.0	100.0	100.0	100.0	100.0

Sources: ILO (2003); Taiwan Government (2002); UNIDO (2003); and World Bank (2003).

environment in FTA partner countries to conform to U.S. principles and institutions. By the same token, the FTA partners are attracted by the preferential margins for U.S. market access and opportunities to improve their economic efficiency and to design and implement more effective domestic institutions and policies. Similarly, Japan and its FTA partners are motivated by many of these objectives.

The U.S. FTAs to be analyzed are denoted as follows:

USCHFTA	U.S.–Chile FTA
USSGFTA	U.S.–Singapore FTA
USCAFTA	U.S.–Central America FTA
USAUSFTA	U.S.–Australia FTA
USMORFTA	U.S.–Morocco FTA
USSACUFTA	U.S.–Southern African Customs Union FTA
USTHFTA	U.S.–Thailand FTA
FTAA	Free Trade Area of the Americas

Our reference point is the post-Uruguay Round 2005 database together with the post-Uruguay Round tariff rates on agricultural products and manufactures and the specially constructed measures of services barriers described earlier. Four scenarios have been carried out for each FTA: (A) removal of agricultural tariffs;[16] (M) removal of manufactures tariffs; (S) removal of services barriers; and (C) combined removal of agricultural and manufactures tariffs and services barriers. Because of space constraints, we report only the results of the combined removal of agricultural and manufactures tariffs and services barriers, denoted by USCHFTA-C, etc. The results for the separate removal of the agricultural, manufactures, and services barriers and for the sectoral effects on exports, imports, and gross output are available on request.

We should emphasize that our computational analysis does not take into account other features of the various FTAs, which do not lend themselves readily to quantification. These other features cover E-commerce, intellectual property, labor and environmental standards, investment, government procurement, trade remedies, dispute settlement, and the development of new institutional and cooperative measures. By the same token, because of data constraints, we have not made allowance for rules of origin and special preferences that may be negotiated as part of each FTA and that could be designed for protectionist reasons to limit trade.

USCHFTA-C: U.S.–Chile Free Trade Agreement – The USCHFTA was approved by the U.S. Congress in 2003. The estimated global welfare

[16] The bilateral FTA scenarios in this and in the next section make no allowance for reductions in agricultural export subsidies and agricultural production subsidies, which are excluded from bilateral negotiations and fall within the scope of the multilateral negotiations.

effects are indicated in Table 8. Global welfare increases by $7.9 billion, with U.S. welfare increasing by $6.9 billion (0.1% of GNP) and Chile's welfare by $1.2 billion (1.3% of GNP).[17] The sectoral results for the United States are shown in Table 9 and indicate relatively small employment declines in U.S. agriculture, food, beverages and tobacco, wearing apparel, and leather products and footwear, and employment increases in the other sectors. The sectoral employment effects for Chile are indicated in Table 10 and show employment increases in agriculture, mining, food, beverages and tobacco, leather and leather products, metal products, and trade and transport services, and employment declines in several manufacturing sectors and other services. These employment changes for Chile suggest the extent of labor market adjustments that may occur as a result of the FTA.

USSGFTA-C: U.S.–Singapore Free Trade Agreement – The welfare effects of a USSGFTA, which was approved by the U.S. Congress in 2003, noted in Table 8, indicate an increase in global welfare of $22.5 billion, with U.S. welfare rising by $15.8 billion (0.2% of GNP) and Singapore's welfare by $2.5 billion (2.6% of GNP). In Table 9, the sectoral employment effects for the United States are relatively small, whereas in Table 10, for Singapore, there are relatively large sectoral employment increases in textiles, wearing apparel, and services, and declines in most other sectors. These sectoral changes suggest sizable employment adjustments for Singapore that may occur in the FTA with the United States.

USCAFTA-C: U.S.–Central America Free Trade Agreement – The USCAFTA was signed in December 2003 and was subsequently approved by the U.S. Congress. The estimated global welfare effects are shown in Table 8. Global welfare rises by $15.7 billion, U.S. welfare by $17.3 billion (0.2% of GNP) and the welfare of the aggregate of Central American and the Caribbean (CAC) by $5.3 (4.4% of GNP).[18,19] It can also be seen that

[17] The estimated effects on aggregate exports/imports, terms of trade, and real returns to capital and labor for this and all other FTAs to be analyzed in what follows are available from the authors on request. Changes in bilateral trade flows by country/region of origin and destination are also available.

[18] The GTAP 5.4 data refer to a CAC aggregate and do not provide separate data for the five Central American countries and the Dominican Republic that comprise the CAFTA. It is noted in Brown *et al.* (2005b) that the CAFTA countries account for a substantial proportion of CAC trade so that using CAC data may be a reasonable approximation for modeling purposes.

[19] Andriamananjara and Tsigas (2003) use the standard GTAP model to analyze the welfare effects of bilateral U.S. FTAs with 65 countries/regions. This version of the GTAP model assumes constant returns to scale, perfect competition, and product differentiation by country of origin (the so-called Armington assumption). The Armington assumption implies that countries have monopoly power in their trading relationships and that trade liberalization may thus have sizable terms-of-trade effects, depending on the structure and pattern of trade. There is reason to believe accordingly that welfare changes in this version of the GTAP model may reflect strong terms-of-trade effects. This is evident in the results of a U.S.-CAC FTA,

the CAFTA is apparently trade diverting for most of the nonmember countries/regions shown. The sectoral employment effects for the United States, noted in Table 9, indicate that the employment declines are concentrated in textiles and wearing apparel and are comparatively small as a percent of employment in these sectors, −0.6% and −1.8%, respectively. The sectoral employment changes for the CAC are shown in Table 10. The increases are quite large in textiles, wearing apparel, and leather products and footwear, and there are employment declines in all the other sectors, as the expansion of the relatively labor-intensive industries attracts workers from the rest of the economy. These results thus suggest that the CAFTA may result in significant worker displacement in the process of adjustment brought about by elimination of the import barriers.

USAUSFTA-C: U.S.–Australia Free Trade Agreement – The USAUSFTA was signed in February 2004 and was later approved by the U.S. Congress. It can be seen in Table 8 that global welfare rises by $23.1 billion, U.S. welfare by $19.4 billion (0.2% of GNP), and Australian welfare by 5.4 billion (1.1% of GNP). There are many instances of trade diversion for nonpartner countries. The sectoral effects for the United States in Table 9 and for Australia in Table 10 indicate that the U.S.–Australia FTA will have fairly small effects on the sectoral employment in the two countries.

USMORFTA-C: U.S.–Morocco Free Trade Agreement – As noted in Tables 3–4, U.S. trade in goods and services with Morocco is rather small. By far the largest proportions of Morocco's trade are with the EU and EFTA. The global welfare increase from the USMORFTA indicated in Table 8 is $7.5 billion, $6.0 billion (0.1% of GNP) for the United States, and $0.9 billion (2.0% of GNP) for Morocco.[20] The U.S. sectoral employment changes noted in Table 9 are negligible. For Morocco, in

---

which is estimated to increase U.S. economic welfare by $1.6 billion (.02% of GDP) and CAC welfare by $2.2 billion (2.4% of GDP). The decomposition of the results by the authors in their Appendix Table indicates that a substantial proportion of these welfare changes is due to changes in terms of trade. DeRosa and Gilbert (2004) also use the standard GTAP model to analyze U.S. bilateral FTAs with 13 prospective partner countries, and their results similarly suggest the predominance of terms of trade effects. In contrast, in the Michigan Model, manufactures and services products are differentiated by firm, so that countries have much less leverage over their terms of trade.

It should also be noted that, while the GTAP framework is structured to take shifts of productive resources into account and generates results for effects on real wages and the return to capital, the GTAP framework does not permit calculation of shifts in the sectoral employment of workers as is done in the Michigan Model.

[20] Andriamananjara and Tsigas (2003, p. 16) estimate that the U.S.–Morocco FTA will reduce Morocco's economic welfare by $108 million (−0.3% of GDP) and will increase U.S. welfare by $161 million (0.002% of GDP). Terms-of-trade effects are again evidently dominant, and, in any event, the overall welfare effects are much lower than the results based on the Michigan Model.

Table 8. Global welfare effects of bilateral negotiating options for the United States

	U.S.–Chile	U.S.–Singapore	U.S.–CAC	U.S.–Australia	U.S.–Morocco	U.S.–SACU	U.S.–Thailand	FTAA
Billions of dollars								
Japan	0.0	1.0	−1.4	−0.6	0.1	−0.0	−0.2	−1.6
United States	6.9	15.8	17.3	19.4	6.0	9.6	17.1	67.6
Canada	0.1	0.1	−0.2	−0.1	0.0	0.0	0.0	5.8
Australia	−0.0	0.1	−0.1	5.4	0.0	0.0	−0.0	−0.2
New Zealand	−0.0	0.0	−0.0	0.0	0.0	0.0	−0.0	−0.0
EU and EFTA	−0.2	2.3	−3.4	−0.4	0.3	−0.0	−0.3	−6.2
Hong Kong	0.0	−0.0	−0.1	−0.0	0.0	0.0	0.0	0.0
China	−0.0	0.1	−0.5	−0.1	0.0	−0.0	−0.1	−0.4
Korea	−0.0	0.2	−0.2	−0.1	0.0	−0.0	−0.0	−0.4
Singapore	0.0	2.5	−0.0	−0.0	0.0	0.0	0.0	−0.0
Taiwan	0.0	0.1	−0.2	−0.1	0.0	−0.0	−0.0	−0.2
Indonesia	0.0	0.1	−0.1	0.0	0.0	−0.0	−0.0	−0.1
Malaysia	0.0	0.1	−0.0	−0.0	0.0	−0.0	−0.0	0.0
Philippines	0.0	0.0	−0.1	−0.0	0.0	0.0	−0.0	−0.0
Thailand	0.0	0.1	−0.1	−0.0	0.0	−0.0	5.6	−0.0
Rest of Asia	0.0	0.1	−0.2	−0.1	0.0	−0.0	−0.0	−0.2
Chile	1.2	0.0	−0.0	0.0	0.0	0.0	−0.0	3.4
Mexico	−0.0	−0.0	−0.2	−0.0	0.0	0.0	−0.0	6.6
CAC	0.0	0.0	5.3	−0.0	0.0	−0.0	−0.0	7.8
South America	−0.2	0.1	−0.1	−0.0	0.0	0.0	0.0	27.6
Morocco	0.0	0.0	−0.0	−0.0	0.9	−0.0	−0.0	−0.0
SACU	−0.0	0.0	−0.0	0.0	0.0	2.2	−0.0	−0.1
Total	7.9	22.5	15.7	23.1	7.5	11.8	21.9	109.5

Table 8. *(Continued)*

	U.S.–Chile	U.S.–Singapore	U.S.–CAC	U.S.–Australia	U.S.–Morocco	U.S.–SACU	U.S.–Thailand	FTAA
Percent of GNP								
Japan	0.0	0.0	–0.0	–0.0	0.0	0.0	–0.0	–0.0
United States	0.1	0.2	0.2	0.2	0.1	0.1	0.2	0.7
Canada	0.0	0.0	–0.0	0.0	0.0	0.0	0.0	0.7
Australia	0.0	0.0	–0.0	1.1	0.0	0.0	–0.0	–0.0
New Zealand	0.0	0.0	–0.0	0.0	0.0	0.0	0.0	–0.1
EU and EFTA	0.0	0.0	–0.0	0.0	0.0	0.0	–0.0	–0.1
Hong Kong	0.0	–0.0	–0.0	–0.0	0.0	0.0	0.0	0.0
China	0.0	0.0	–0.1	–0.0	0.0	0.0	–0.0	–0.0
Korea	–0.0	0.0	–0.0	–0.0	0.0	0.0	–0.0	–0.1
Singapore	0.0	2.6	–0.0	–0.0	0.0	0.0	0.0	0.0
Taiwan	0.0	0.0	–0.1	–0.0	0.0	0.0	–0.0	–0.1
Indonesia	0.0	0.0	–0.1	0.0	0.0	0.0	–0.0	–0.1
Malaysia	0.0	0.1	0.0	–0.0	0.0	0.0	–0.0	0.0
Philippines	0.0	0.0	–0.1	–0.0	0.0	0.0	–0.0	–0.0
Thailand	0.0	0.0	–0.0	–0.0	0.0	0.0	2.8	–0.0
Rest of Asia	0.0	0.0	–0.0	–0.0	0.0	0.0	–0.0	–0.0
Chile	1.3	0.0	–0.0	0.0	0.0	0.0	–0.0	3.6
Mexico	0.0	0.0	–0.0	0.0	0.0	0.0	0.0	1.3
CAC	0.0	0.0	4.4	–0.0	0.0	0.0	–0.0	6.5
South America	–0.0	0.0	0.0	0.0	0.0	0.0	0.0	1.5
Morocco	0.0	0.0	–0.0	0.0	2.0	0.0	0.0	–0.0
SACU	–0.0	0.0	–0.0	0.0	0.0	1.2	–0.0	–0.0

Table 9. Sectoral employment effects of bilateral negotiating options for the United States

	U.S.–Chile	U.S.–Singapore	U.S.–CAC	U.S.–Australia	U.S.–Morocco	U.S.–SACU	U.S.–Thailand
Number of workers							
Agriculture	−1,427	1,335	2,173	94	1,314	973	2,458
Mining	−58	358	596	504	−44	27	129
Food, beverages, and tobacco	−548	52	495	−756	542	353	−1,077
Textiles	73	−102	−5,133	810	−32	−109	−1,230
Wearing apparel	−118	−227	−14,006	619	−129	−211	−2,530
Leather products and footwear	−28	112	1,512	207	−8	202	−395
Wood and wood products	−16	143	1,761	394	−10	163	41
Chemicals	355	617	2,667	1,555	−55	127	1,384
Nonmetallic mineral products	86	210	666	539	29	76	62
Metal products	87	1,358	2,218	1,957	−138	33	1,175
Transportation equipment	321	959	1,069	1,741	−50	369	351
Machinery and equipment	1,769	5,309	3,626	6,229	−367	1,230	2,054
Other manufactures	48	526	1,558	653	−52	77	−784
Electricity, gas, and water	−30	−56	156	15	2	13	−10
Construction	−5	−519	31	−257	−57	−13	16
Trade and transport	−849	−4,192	640	−11,719	−1,140	−2,101	−4,272
Other private services	−42	−4,255	1,362	−2,188	−194	11	932
Government services	383	−1,628	−1,390	−398	389	−1,221	1,696

Table 9. (*Continued*)

	U.S.–Chile	U.S.–Singapore	U.S.–CAC	U.S.–Australia	U.S.–Morocco	U.S.–SACU	U.S.–Thailand
Percent of employment							
Agriculture	–0.0	0.0	0.1	0.0	0.0	0.0	0.1
Mining	–0.0	0.1	0.1	0.1	–0.0	0.0	0.0
Food, beverages, and tobacco	–0.0	0.0	0.0	–0.0	0.0	0.0	–0.1
Textiles	0.0	–0.0	–0.6	0.1	0.0	–0.0	–0.1
Wearing apparel	–0.0	–0.0	–1.8	0.1	–0.0	–0.0	–0.3
Leather products and footwear	–0.0	0.1	1.5	0.2	–0.0	0.2	–0.4
Wood and wood products	0.0	0.0	0.1	0.0	0.0	0.0	0.0
Chemicals	0.0	0.0	0.1	0.1	0.0	0.0	0.1
Nonmetallic mineral products	0.0	0.0	0.1	0.1	0.0	0.0	0.0
Metal products	0.0	0.0	0.1	0.1	0.0	0.0	0.0
Transportation equipment	0.0	0.0	0.1	0.1	0.0	0.0	0.0
Machinery and equipment	0.0	0.1	0.1	0.1	–0.0	0.0	0.0
Other manufactures	0.0	0.1	0.3	0.1	–0.0	0.0	–0.2
Electricity, gas, and water	0.0	0.0	0.0	0.0	0.0	0.0	0.0
Construction	0.0	–0.0	0.0	0.0	0.0	0.0	0.0
Trade and transport	0.0	–0.0	0.0	–0.0	0.0	–0.0	–0.0
Other private services	0.0	–0.0	0.0	–0.0	0.0	0.0	0.0
Government services	0.0	0.0	0.0	0.0	0.0	0.0	0.0

Table 10. Sectoral employment effects for the U.S. FTA partner countries

	U.S.–Chile	U.S.–Singapore	U.S.–CAC	U.S.–Australia	U.S.–Morocco	U.S.–SACU	U.S.–Thailand
Number of workers							
Agriculture	9,652	−27	−23,731	−300	−3,124	−6,495	−70,515
Mining	811	−20	−12,650	−1,390	992	−961	−1,468
Food, beverages, and tobacco	1,852	29	−14,061	564	−9,562	−820	3,294
Textiles	−255	115	53,741	−244	5,431	799	23,608
Wearing apparel	−90	1,476	230,663	−145	8,580	14,668	62,579
Leather products and footwear	31	−7	9,518	−121	−376	−145	6,806
Wood and wood products	−118	−396	−18,415	−648	236	−801	−1,692
Chemicals	−1,677	−1,123	−19,202	−1,612	534	−427	−6,524
Nonmetallic mineral products	−273	−105	−6,720	−437	−995	−224	−1,545
Metal products	997	−1,178	−11,865	−2,912	889	−999	−5,548
Transportation equipment	−747	−410	−2,310	−1,196	−353	−694	−1,324
Machinery and equipment	−2,171	−6,944	−12,126	−3,490	963	−2,068	1,106
Other manufactures	−81	−64	−2,361	−390	2	−236	2,025
Electricity, gas, and water	64	34	−518	−67	113	−261	116
Construction	−528	251	−13,873	−599	−1,097	−1,185	−2,983
Trade and transport	732	4,673	−71,515	11,593	13,729	1,046	29,809
Other private services	−38	4,283	−11,273	3,160	207	−1,233	−5,628
Government services	−8,161	−588	−73,302	−1,764	−16,168	35	−32,116

Table 10. (*Continued*)

	U.S.–Chile	U.S.–Singapore	U.S.–CAC	U.S.–Australia	U.S.–Morocco	U.S.–SACU	U.S.–Thailand
Percent of employment							
Agriculture	1.2	−0.5	−0.6	−0.1	−0.6	−0.1	−0.4
Mining	1.0	−3.1	−13.6	−1.9	1.1	−0.3	−3.3
Food, beverages, and tobacco	0.6	0.2	−1.9	0.3	−1.7	−0.4	0.5
Textiles	−0.6	5.8	27.9	−0.6	1.3	1.2	3.5
Wearing apparel	−0.2	15.8	42.2	−0.4	1.2	12.8	5.2
Leather products and footwear	0.1	−0.5	14.6	−1.0	−0.5	−0.5	8.7
Wood and wood products	−0.1	−1.1	−9.0	−0.3	0.2	−0.4	−0.8
Chemicals	−1.4	−2.4	−7.3	−1.4	0.2	−0.3	−2.5
Nonmetallic mineral products	−0.8	−1.3	−7.8	−0.9	−0.5	−0.3	−0.8
Metal products	1.0	−2.8	−10.2	−1.5	0.7	−0.5	−1.7
Transportation equipment	−2.9	−1.0	−8.5	−1.3	−0.6	−0.8	−1.0
Machinery and equipment	−5.1	−3.4	−10.0	−2.3	0.9	−1.2	0.4
Other manufactures	−2.3	−1.6	−6.9	−2.4	0.1	−1.0	1.8
Electricity, gas, and water	0.2	0.3	−0.4	−0.1	0.1	−0.2	0.1
Construction	−0.1	0.2	−1.4	−0.1	−0.1	−0.1	−0.2
Trade and transport	0.1	0.8	−1.9	0.4	0.5	0.0	0.6
Other private services	−0.0	1.6	−2.8	0.3	0.1	−0.1	−0.7
Government services	−0.6	−0.2	−1.9	−0.1	−0.5	0.0	−1.0

Table 10, the largest employment increases are in trade and transport, textiles, and wearing apparel, and the largest declines in agriculture, food, beverages and tobacco, and government services. The welfare and employment effects of the U.S.–Morocco FTA are thus seen to be fairly small.

USSACUFTA-C: U.S.–Southern African Customs Union – The effects of a USSACUFTA are indicated in Table 8 and indicate an increase of $11.8 billion in global welfare, $9.6 billion (0.1% of GNP) for the United States, and $2.2 billion (1.2% of GNP) for the SACU members combined. In Table 9, there are indications of negligible sectoral employment impacts for the United States. In Table 10, the employment increases for SACU are concentrated in textiles and wearing apparel and are negative across the remaining sectors as labor is attracted toward the labor-intensive sectors.

USTHFTA-C: U.S.–Thailand FTA – In Table 8, the global welfare increase for the USTHFTA is $21.9 billion, $17.1 billion (0.2% of GNP) for the United States, and $5.6 billion (2.8% of GNP) for Thailand. There is evidence of pervasive trade diversion. The sectoral employment changes for the United States noted in Table 9 are negligible. For Thailand, in Table 10, the largest employment increases are concentrated in food, beverages and tobacco, textiles, wearing apparel, leather and leather products, other manufactures, and trade and transport, and there are employment declines especially in agriculture, mining, several capital-intensive manufactures, construction, other private services, and government services.

FTAA-C: Free Trade Area of the Americas – Discussions have been ongoing for several years to create an FTAA.[21] Since the country detail in our model does not include the individual members of the FTAA, we have chosen to approximate it by combining the United States, Canada, Mexico, and Chile with an aggregate of Central American and Caribbean (CAC) and an aggregate of other South American nations. The welfare effects of the FTAA are indicated in Table 8 and amount to $109.5 billion globally, $67.6 billion (0.7% of GNP) for the United States, $5.8 billion (0.7% of GNP) for Canada, $3.4 billion (3.6% of GNP) for Mexico, $3.4 billion (3.6% of GNP) for Chile, $7.8 billion (6.5% of GNP) for the CAC, and $27.6 billion (1.5% of GNP) for the aggregate of other South American countries. There is some evidence of trade diversion, in particular for Japan and the EU/EFTA. The sectoral employment effects for the United States, indicated in Table 11, show relatively small employment declines in agriculture, mining, food, beverages and tobacco, and other private and government services, and increases in all other

---

[21] For details on the FTAA negotiations, see the website of the Office of the United States Trade Representative (www.ustr.gov).

Table 11. Sectoral employment effects for the FTAA member countries

	United States	Canada	CAC	Chile	Mexico	South America
Number of workers						
Agriculture	−12,460	1,478	−39,042	14,744	−20,701	202,605
Mining	−3,251	−1,505	−19,685	−2,486	−553	29,499
Food, beverages, and tobacco	−3,452	−3,049	−18,987	1,953	−3,658	16,172
Textiles	−6,028	−2,060	57,999	206	−2,251	−2,133
Wearing apparel	−16,804	−2,089	244,675	−163	−3,687	818
Leather products and footwear	620	−650	11,090	301	−1,000	10,500
Wood and wood products	2,502	−166	−19,314	561	538	−6,481
Chemicals	2,883	−1,014	−16,078	−3,018	1,334	−393
Nonmetallic mineral products	957	−52	−7,194	−749	1,372	−2,081
Metal products	2,024	−151	−10,672	3,512	1,782	−3,014
Transportation equipment	2,970	5,206	−2,171	114	16,633	−7,730
Machinery and equipment	21,830	2,450	−8,320	1,611	2,489	−20,176
Other manufactures	2,148	−149	−1,828	−20	−177	−532
Electricity, gas, and water	−228	−81	−410	293	36	179
Construction	−88	−39	−14,623	−1,306	622	−11,433
Trade and transport	1,991	2,952	−62,175	−2,705	9,799	−74,080
Other private services	2,788	229	−11,146	−154	−2,190	−4,712
Government services	1,597	−1,309	−82,120	−12,693	−387	−127,009
Percent of employment						
Agriculture	−0.3	0.1	−1.0	1.9	−0.2	1.1
Mining	−0.5	−0.4	−21.2	−2.9	−0.5	2.9
Food, beverages, and tobacco	−0.2	−0.6	−2.5	0.7	−0.2	0.4
Textiles	−0.6	−1.5	30.1	0.5	−0.5	−0.2
Wearing apparel	−2.1	−1.3	44.8	−0.4	−2.3	0.1
Leather products and footwear	0.6	−2.2	17.0	1.1	−0.6	2.4
Wood and wood products	0.1	−0.0	−9.4	0.4	0.1	−0.4
Chemicals	0.1	−0.2	−6.1	−2.5	0.1	−0.0
Nonmetallic mineral products	0.1	−0.0	−8.3	−2.2	0.4	−0.2
Metal products	0.1	−0.0	−9.2	3.4	0.4	−0.2
Transportation equipment	0.1	1.0	−8.0	0.4	2.8	−1.5
Machinery and equipment	0.4	0.3	−6.8	3.8	0.3	−2.4
Other manufactures	0.4	−0.2	−5.4	−0.6	−0.3	−0.3
Electricity, gas, and water	−0.0	−0.0	−0.3	1.0	0.0	0.1
Construction	−0.0	−0.0	−1.5	−0.3	0.0	−0.2
Trade and transport	0.0	0.0	−1.6	−0.2	0.1	−0.3
Other private services	0.0	0.0	−2.8	−0.0	−0.1	−0.1
Government services	0.0	−0.0	−2.1	−0.9	−0.0	−0.4

sectors. In Table 11, the sectoral employment effects for Canada are also small, whereas the employment increases for Mexico, Chile, the CAC, and other South America are noteworthy. This suggests that the developing countries covered in the FTAA would experience more employment adjustments than the United States and Canada.

4. Computational analysis of Japan's free trade agreements

In this section, we consider the welfare and sectoral employment effects of the Japan–Singapore FTA that was concluded in 2002 and the FTAs in process with Chile, Indonesia, Korea, Malaysia, Mexico, Philippines, and Thailand.[22] These are designated as follows:

JSGFTA	Japan–Singapore FTA
JCHFTA	Japan–Chile FTA
JINDFTA	Japan–Indonesia FTA
JKFTA	Japan–Korea FTA
JMAFTA	Japan–Malaysia FTA
JMXFTA	Japan–Mexico FTA
JPHFTA	Japan–Philippines FTA
JTHFTA	Japan–Thailand FTA

As was the case for the U.S. FTAs analyzed in the previous section, we have undertaken separate computations for (A) removal of agricultural tariffs; (M) removal of manufactures tariffs; (S) removal of services barriers; and (C) combined removal of agricultural and manufactures tariffs and services barriers. In what follows, we report only the results of the combined removal of agricultural and manufactures tariffs and services barriers, denoted by JSGFTA-C, etc. The results for the separate removal of the agricultural, manufactures, and services barriers are available on request.

JSGFTA-C: Japan–Singapore Free Trade Agreement – As shown in Table 12, the combined removal of bilateral tariffs on agricultural products and manufactures and services barriers would increase global economic welfare by $6.7 billion. Japan's welfare rises by $5.0 billion (0.1% of GNP) and Singapore by $0.6 billion (0.7% of GNP). A JSGFTA appears to be trade diverting to a small extent. The other industrialized countries besides Japan show increases in welfare.[23] The sectoral results, which are shown Table 13, indicate negligible shifts in Japan's employment. For Singapore, as indicated in Table 14, there are employment

[22] It should be noted that the FTA negotiations were being concluded with Chile in 2007, Indonesia in 2008, Malaysia in 2006, Mexico in 2005, Philippines in 2008, and Thailand in 2007. FTA negotiations with Brunei, Vietnam, and Switzerland were also being concluded in 2008, 2009, and 2009, respectively.

Negotiations have been ongoing with Korea, India, Australia, and the GCC (Gulf Cooperation Council). See the METI and MOFA websites for more information.

[23] See Hertel *et al.* (2001) for a GTAP model-based analysis of the JSGFTA that takes into account the proposed bilateral tariff reductions, implementation of uniform standards for e-commerce, services liberalization, the impact of automating customs procedures in Japan, and changes in foreign direct investment. They find that customs automization plays the most important role in driving increases in merchandise trade. They estimate global welfare gains of over $9 billion, most of these gains accruing to Japan. They find no evidence of trade diversion.

Table 12. Global welfare effects of bilateral negotiating options for Japan

	Japan–Singapore	Japan–Chile	Japan–Indonesia	Japan–Korea	Japan–Malaysia	Japan–Mexico	Japan–Philippines	Japan–Thailand
Billions of dollars								
Japan	5.0	2.8	10.7	18.7	10.5	8.2	6.8	19.5
United States	0.2	−0.1	−0.2	−0.5	−0.2	−0.7	−0.1	−1.4
Canada	0.0	−0.0	−0.0	−0.0	−0.0	−0.1	−0.1	−0.1
Australia	0.0	0.0	−0.0	−0.0	0.0	0.0	0.0	−0.0
New Zealand	0.0	−0.0	−0.0	0.0	0.0	0.0	0.0	−0.0
EU and EFTA	0.5	−0.3	−0.7	−0.7	−0.3	−0.1	−0.7	−2.8
Hong Kong	−0.0	−0.0	−0.0	0.0	0.0	−0.0	0.0	−0.0
China	0.1	0.0	−0.1	0.0	0.1	−0.0	−0.1	0.1
Korea	0.0	−0.0	−0.2	2.2	−0.2	−0.0	−0.1	−0.1
Singapore	0.6	−0.0	−0.0	−0.0	−0.0	−0.0	−0.0	−0.2
Taiwan	0.0	−0.0	−0.1	−0.1	−0.1	−0.0	−0.0	−0.2
Indonesia	0.0	0.0	1.7	0.1	0.0	0.0	−0.0	0.1
Malaysia	−0.0	−0.0	−0.0	−0.0	0.3	−0.0	−0.0	−0.2
Philippines	0.0	−0.0	−0.0	0.0	−0.0	−0.0	0.9	−0.0
Thailand	0.0	−0.0	−0.0	−0.0	−0.0	−0.0	−0.0	−0.5
Rest of Asia	0.0	0.0	−0.0	0.0	0.0	0.0	−0.0	−0.1
Chile	0.0	0.9	0.0	0.0	0.0	0.0	0.0	−0.0
Mexico	0.0	−0.0	−0.0	−0.0	−0.0	3.3	−0.0	−0.1
CAC	0.0	0.0	0.0	−0.0	0.0	−0.0	0.0	0.0
South America	0.0	0.1	−0.0	0.1	0.0	−0.0	−0.0	−0.2
Morocco	0.0	−0.0	−0.0	0.0	0.0	0.0	0.0	−0.0
SACU	0.0	0.0	−0.0	−0.1	−0.0	0.0	−0.0	−0.0
Total	6.7	3.5	11.1	19.7	10.1	10.6	6.7	13.5

Percent GNP								
Japan	0.1	0.1	0.2	0.4	0.2	0.2	0.1	0.4
United States	0.0	0.0	0.0	–0.0	0.0	–0.0	–0.0	–0.0
Canada	0.0	0.0	0.0	0.0	0.0	–0.0	–0.0	–0.0
Australia	0.0	0.0	0.0	0.0	0.0	0.0	0.0	–0.0
New Zealand	0.0	0.0	0.0	0.0	0.0	0.0	0.0	–0.0
EU and EFTA	0.0	0.0	–0.0	–0.0	0.0	0.0	–0.0	–0.0
Hong Kong	–0.0	0.0	0.0	0.0	0.0	0.0	0.0	–0.0
China	0.0	0.0	0.0	0.0	0.0	0.0	–0.0	0.0
Korea	0.0	–0.0	–0.0	0.4	–0.0	0.0	–0.0	–0.0
Singapore	0.7	0.0	–0.0	–0.0	–0.0	–0.0	0.0	–0.2
Taiwan	0.0	0.0	–0.0	–0.0	–0.0	–0.0	–0.0	–0.1
Indonesia	0.0	0.0	0.7	0.0	0.0	0.0	–0.0	0.1
Malaysia	–0.0	0.0	–0.0	–0.0	0.2	–0.0	–0.0	–0.2
Philippines	0.0	0.0	–0.0	0.0	0.0	–0.0	0.9	–0.0
Thailand	0.0	0.0	–0.0	–0.0	–0.0	0.0	–0.0	–0.3
Rest of Asia	0.0	0.0	0.0	0.0	0.0	0.0	–0.0	–0.0
Chile	0.0	1.0	0.0	0.0	0.0	0.0	0.0	–0.0
Mexico	0.0	0.0	0.0	0.0	0.0	0.7	–0.0	–0.0
CAC	0.0	0.0	0.0	0.0	0.0	0.0	0.0	0.0
South America	0.0	0.0	0.0	0.0	0.0	0.0	–0.0	–0.0
Morocco	0.0	0.0	0.0	0.0	0.0	0.0	0.0	–0.0
SACU	0.0	0.0	0.0	–0.0	0.0	0.0	–0.0	–0.0

Table 13. Sectoral employment effects for Japan of bilateral negotiating options

	Japan–Singapore	Japan–Chile	Japan–Indonesia	Japan–Korea	Japan–Malaysia	Japan–Mexico	Japan–Philippines	Japan–Thailand
Number of workers								
Agriculture	−617	−4,478	−8,578	−9,008	−3,577	−3,000	−5,462	−19,994
Mining	60	188	196	−364	−228	−83	−106	−202
Food, beverages, and tobacco	−688	−4,080	−6,176	−5,893	−1,757	−1,061	−1,437	−18,178
Textiles	182	176	−29	−3,080	−634	−338	311	1,095
Wearing apparel	−2	30	−432	−1,423	−391	−86	−320	−518
Leather products and footwear	−22	33	−732	−1,317	−145	−65	−73	−183
Wood and wood products	73	117	−4,489	−825	−2,684	−116	−155	−296
Chemicals	38	373	1,186	1,132	169	−1	237	3,122
Nonmetallic mineral products	91	95	246	1,016	253	83	207	987
Metal products	460	798	2,670	2,576	1,899	512	790	4,988
Transportation equipment	500	1,214	8,079	−3,104	9,102	926	2,165	12,379
Machinery and equipment	2,390	3,049	2,723	14,480	−3,583	2,675	862	6,011
Other manufactures	22	42	7	−178	−55	7	−67	63
Electricity, gas, and water	13	31	91	88	59	41	39	184
Construction	−51	109	526	490	429	302	787	1,207
Trade and transport	−2,260	862	−515	876	−2,189	−2,329	−51	−396
Other private services	−146	409	1,485	1,376	602	1,052	621	2,375
government services	−44	1,031	3,741	3,159	2,728	1,482	1,651	7,357

Percent of employment								
Agriculture	−0.0	−0.1	−0.3	−0.3	−0.1	−0.1	−0.2	−0.6
Mining	0.1	0.3	0.3	−0.5	−0.3	−0.1	−0.2	−0.3
Food, beverages, and tobacco	−0.0	−0.2	−0.4	−0.3	−0.1	−0.1	−0.1	−1.0
Textiles	0.0	0.0	0.0	−0.5	−0.1	−0.1	0.1	0.2
Wearing apparel	0.0	0.0	−0.1	−0.3	−0.1	−0.0	−0.1	−0.1
Leather products and footwear	−0.0	0.0	−0.8	−1.4	−0.2	−0.1	−0.1	−0.2
Wood and wood products	0.0	0.0	−0.3	−0.1	−0.2	−0.0	−0.0	−0.0
Chemicals	0.0	0.0	0.1	0.1	0.0	0.0	0.0	0.2
Nonmetallic mineral products	0.0	0.0	0.0	0.2	0.0	0.0	0.0	0.2
Metal products	0.0	0.0	0.2	0.2	0.1	0.0	0.0	0.3
Transportation equipment	0.0	0.1	0.6	−0.2	0.7	0.1	0.2	0.9
Machinery and equipment	0.1	0.1	0.1	0.3	−0.1	0.1	0.0	0.1
Other manufactures	0.0	0.0	0.0	−0.1	−0.0	0.0	−0.0	0.0
Electricity, gas, and water	0.0	0.0	0.0	0.0	0.0	0.0	0.0	0.1
Construction	0.0	0.0	0.0	0.0	0.0	0.0	0.0	0.0
Trade and transport	−0.0	0.0	0.0	0.0	−0.0	−0.0	0.0	0.0
Other private services	0.0	0.0	0.0	0.0	0.0	0.0	0.0	0.0
Government services	0.0	0.0	0.0	0.0	0.0	0.0	0.0	0.1

Table 14. Sectoral employment effects for Japan FTA partner countries

	Japan–Singapore	Japan–Chile	Japan–Indonesia	Japan–Korea	Japan–Malaysia	Japan–Mexico	Japan–Philippines	Japan–Thailand
Number of workers								
Agriculture	86	23,872	373,610	46,095	14,439	17,091	111,720	1,034,564
Mining	−5	−3,378	−14,970	−44	−517	−202	−1,919	−4,884
Food, beverages, and tobacco	1,385	15,807	38,452	8,504	3,585	2,139	1,189	89,872
Textiles	−10	−768	−6,202	10,558	390	−875	1,947	−56,736
Wearing apparel	106	−376	10,027	5,818	2,913	−279	14,455	−80,148
Leather products and footwear	51	−317	28,661	5,820	−23	−123	2,169	−5,587
Wood and wood products	−145	−1,970	39,158	−868	11,665	−850	−2,565	−20,450
Chemicals	−205	−2,464	−30,953	−2,269	−4,552	−2,629	−5,869	−31,731
Nonmetallic mineral products	−48	−613	−10,341	−2,474	−1,521	−800	−3,681	−18,953
Metal products	−430	−4,750	−29,701	−4,036	−4,579	−1,282	−4,299	−57,330
Transportation equipment	−195	−1,544	−32,180	−1,251	−11,180	−2,074	−5,728	−23,004
Machinery and equipment	−2,809	−2,894	−18,322	−17,068	1,832	1,165	6,758	−19,945
Other manufactures	−18	−114	−2,901	−237	−333	−254	−70	−9,951
Electricity, gas, and water	−19	−384	−1,798	−100	−177	−101	−997	−9,851
Construction	−106	−2,293	−30,482	−5,234	−3,628	−1,506	−26,648	−120,418
Trade and transport	2,332	−10,634	−195,924	−28,848	6,096	6,602	−38,495	−430,875
Other private services	−244	−2,028	−7,742	−4,533	−3,499	−4,274	−11,163	−57,822
Government services	273	−5,153	−108,394	−9,834	−10,912	−11,749	−36,804	−176,753

Percent of employment								
Agriculture	1.6	3.0	1.0	2.0	1.0	0.2	1.0	6.0
Mining	−0.8	−4.0	−1.7	−0.2	−1.4	−0.2	−1.6	−11.0
Food, beverages, and tobacco	7.4	5.4	1.8	2.7	2.1	0.1	0.2	13.3
Textiles	−0.5	−1.7	−0.4	2.5	0.6	−0.2	1.0	−8.4
Wearing apparel	1.1	−1.0	1.0	2.2	3.1	−0.2	3.0	−6.7
Leather products and footwear	3.9	−1.2	2.7	6.0	−0.3	−0.1	3.3	−7.1
Wood and wood products	−0.4	−1.5	2.0	−0.2	3.2	−0.2	−0.9	−9.2
Chemicals	−0.4	−2.1	−2.5	−0.5	−1.9	−0.3	−2.1	−12.0
Nonmetallic mineral products	−0.6	−1.8	−2.1	−1.3	−1.7	−0.3	−3.4	−9.5
Metal products	−1.0	−4.6	−5.4	−0.8	−3.0	−0.3	−2.5	−17.0
Transportation equipment	−0.5	−6.0	−9.5	−0.2	−14.3	−0.4	−7.8	−17.9
Machinery and equipment	−1.4	−6.8	−3.1	−1.3	0.3	0.2	1.6	−7.0
Other manufactures	−0.4	−3.2	−1.5	−0.3	−1.1	−0.4	−0.1	−8.7
Electricity, gas, and water	−0.2	−1.3	−0.8	−0.1	−0.4	−0.1	−0.7	−5.7
Construction	−0.1	−0.5	−0.7	−0.3	−0.5	−0.1	−1.6	−6.2
Trade and transport	0.4	−0.8	−0.9	−0.4	0.3	0.1	−0.7	−8.1
Other private services	−0.1	−0.5	−1.2	−0.2	−0.8	−0.3	−1.7	−6.8
Government services	0.1	−0.4	−0.9	−0.3	−0.6	−0.1	−0.7	−5.2

increases especially in wearing apparel, leather and leather products, and trade and transport, and declines in many other manufacturing sectors and other private services. A JSGFTA thus appears to have relatively small effects on Japan's welfare and results in sectoral employment shifts in Singapore away from capital-intensive toward relatively more labor-intensive sectors.

JCHFTA-C: Japan–Chile Free Trade Agreement – In Table 12, a JCHFTA indicates increases in global welfare of $3.5 billion. Japan's welfare rises by $2.8 billion (0.1% of GNP), and Chile's welfare rises by $0.9 billion (1.0% of GNP). There are negative welfare effects for the United States, Canada, and several developing countries. The sectoral results for Japan, in Table 13, indicate negligible sectoral shifts. For Chile, as indicated in Table 14, there are employment increases in agriculture and food, beverages and tobacco and declines in mining and all of the manufactures and services sectors as resources are shifted away from these sectors.

JINDFTA-C: Japan–Indonesia Free Trade Agreement – As indicated in Table 12, a JINDFTA increases global welfare by $11.1 billion, Japan's welfare by $18.7 billion (0.2% of GNP), and Indonesia's welfare by $1.7 billion (0.7% of GNP). There are indications of trade diversion and negative welfare effects for most of the nonmember countries/regions. The sectoral results for Japan, in Table 13, show small negative employment effects on Japanese agriculture and labor-intensive manufactures and positive effects on most other sectors. For Indonesia, the sectoral employment effects mirror those in Japan, with employment expansion in Indonesian agriculture, food, beverages and tobacco, and labor-intensive manufactures and employment declines in all other sectors.

JKFTA-C: Japan–Korea Free Trade Agreement – In Table 12, a JKFTA increases global welfare by $19.7 billion, Japan's welfare by $18.7 billion (0.4% of GNP), and Korea's welfare increases by $2.2 billion (0.4% of GNP). There is some evidence of trade diversion for the United States, EU/EFTA, and for some developing countries. The sectoral results, shown in Table 13, indicate relatively small employment declines in Japan in agriculture and labor-intensive manufactures and increases in employment in durable manufactures and services. For Korea, as shown in Table 14, employment falls in many capital-intensive manufactures sectors and in services and rises in Korea's agriculture and labor-intensive manufactures.[24]

[24] See McKibbin *et al.* (2004) for an analysis of a JKFTA, using the Asia-Pacific G-cubed model. The G-cubed model incorporates rational expectations and forward-looking intertemporal behavior of individual agents. The model takes into account the induced changes in expected rates of return to capital by sector and consequent structural adjustments. Allowance is also made for short-term wage stickiness or adjustment costs in allocating capital. The authors conclude that Japan and Korea gain from an FTA, but there is trade diversion for the United States, Australia, and other countries. Their results also suggest greater benefits from a rapid liberalization rather than a more gradual phasing.

JMAFTA-C: Japan–Malaysia Free Trade Agreement – Global economic welfare is shown in Table 12 to increase by $10.1 billion, Japan's welfare by $10.5 billion (0.2% of GNP), and Malaysia's welfare by $0.3 billion (0.2% of GNP). In Table 13, sectoral employment declines in Japan's agriculture, food, beverages and tobacco, labor-intensive sectors, machinery and equipment, and other manufactures, and there are employment increases in the other manufactures sectors and construction, other private services, and government services. For Malaysia, in Table 14, the employment increases are concentrated in agriculture, food, beverages and tobacco, wearing apparel, wood and wood products, and trade and transport, and there are declines in capital-intensive manufactures and services except for trade and transport.

JMXFTA-C: Japan–Mexico Free Trade Agreement – As indicated in Table 12, a JMXFTA increases global welfare by $10.6 billion. Japan's welfare increases by $8.2 billion (0.2% of GNP) and Mexico's welfare by $3.4 billion (0.7% of GNP). There are indications that a JMXFTA would be trade diverting for the United States, Canada, EU/EFTA, and several developing countries. The sectoral results for Japan, shown in Table 13, indicate relatively small employment declines in agriculture, food, beverages and tobacco, and labor-intensive manufactures and increases especially in durable manufactures. For Mexico, in Table 14, the sectoral results show relatively small employment increases in agriculture, food, beverages and tobacco, and trade and transport and declines across the manufactures sectors and services.

JPHFTA-C: Japan–Philippines FTA – In Table 12, global welfare increases by $3.0 billion, Japan's welfare by $2.2 billion (0.1% of GNP), and the Philippines welfare by $0.5 billion (0.6% of GNP). The sectoral employment results for Japan, noted in Table 13, indicate declines in agriculture and food, beverages & tobacco, and labor-intensive manufactures and increases in the other manufactures sectors and services. For the Philippines, in Table 14, the employment shifts mirror those in Japan, with increases concentrated in agriculture, food, beverages and tobacco and labor-intensive manufactures and declines across other manufactures and services.

JTHFTA-C: Japan–Thailand FTA – In Table 12, a JTHFTA increases global welfare by $13.5 billion and Japan's welfare by $19.5 billion (0.4% of GNP) and reduces Thailand's welfare by $0.5 billion (−0.3% of GNP). There are indications of trade diversion across most of the other countries/regions indicated. There are sectoral employment declines in Japan, noted in Table 13, in agriculture, food, beverages and tobacco, and labor-intensive sectors and employment increases in capital-intensive manufactures and services. For Thailand, in Table 14, the employment increases are concentrated in agriculture and food, beverages and tobacco, and employment declines across the manufactures and services sectors. The reduction in Thailand's welfare stems from the shifts away from the manufactures sectors, which are modeled with increasing returns to scale, to the agricultural sector, which is modeled with constant returns to scale.

5. Hub and spoke effects of the U.S. and Japan FTAs

In the discussion of the U.S. and Japan bilateral FTAs in the preceding sections, it was noted that there were indications of negative welfare effects for a number of nonmember countries/regions. It is well known theoretically that preferential trading arrangements may result in both trade creation, which is welfare enhancing, and trade diversion, which will reduce welfare as trade is shifted from lower to higher cost sources of supply. But there is another consideration, which is that bilateral FTAs are based on the "hub-and-spoke" arrangement, with the United States or Japan representing the hub and with separate spokes connecting the bilateral FTA partners to the hub. In negotiating these bilateral FTAs, no account is taken of the effects that they may have on nonmembers, even though there may be a bilateral FTA with one or more of the nonmembers. As more and more bilateral FTAs are negotiated, the spokes of the FTAs may thus emanate out in many different and overlapping directions, with resulting distortions of global trade patterns. That is, this combination of varying preferences among different and overlapping FTAs may lead to greatly increased transactions costs for firms and the undermining of the most-favored-nation (MFN) principle of nondiscrimination that is at the heart of the multilateral trading system. These effects of the proliferation of FTAs are what Bhagwati and Panagariya (1996) refer to as "spaghetti-bowl" effects.

An indication of the trade diversion associated with the U.S. and Japan FTAs and the overlapping of the spokes involved is shown in the top half of Table 15, which has shaded cells indicating cases of positive welfare effects and white cells indicating cases of negative welfare effects. Altogether, 16 FTAs are shown, although there is some double counting insofar as the U.S.–CAC and U.S.–Chile bilateral FTAs are encompassed in the FTAA. In any event, it seems evident from Table 15 that trade diversion and negative welfare effects are pervasive. Thus, while partner-FTA countries may gain directly from their FTAs, as indicated by "X" in the table, they may be adversely affected by other FTAs that have been negotiated.

The global results of the bilateral FTAs in Tables 8 and 12 for the United States and Japan suggest that the negative welfare effects on nonmembers may be rather small in both absolute terms and as a percent of GNP. But, as mentioned in our earlier discussion, because of data limitations, our results do not reflect the potential welfare declines due to rules of origin and other discriminatory arrangements built into the bilateral FTAs. On the contrary, we do not allow for increased inflows of foreign direct investment into the partner countries or the effects of

Table 15. Welfare effects of bilateral FTAs and unilateral and global free trade

	Bilateral FTAs	United States								Japan								Number of Positive Effects
		US-CHL	US-SGP	US-CAC	US-AUS	US-MOR	US-SACU	US-THA	FTAA	JPN-SGP	JPN-CHL	JPN-IDN	JPN-KOR	JPN-MYS	JPN-MEX	JPN-PHL	JPN-THA	
		1	2	3	4	5	6	7	8	9	10	11	12	13	14	15	16	
1	Japan									X	X	X	X	X	X	X	X	11
2	US	X	X	X	X	X	X	X	X									10
3	Canada								X									8
4	Australia				X													9
5	New Zealand																	9
6	EU and EFTA																	4
7	Hong Kong																	7
8	China																	8
9	Korea												X					5
10	Singapore		X							X								7
11	Taiwan																	5
12	Indonesia											X						12
13	Malaysia													X				6
14	Philippines															X		7
15	Thailand							X									X	6
16	Rest of Asia																	9
17	Chile	X							X		X							13
18	Mexico								X						X			6
19	CAC			X					X									11
20	South America								X									10
21	Morocco					X												8
22	SACU						X											8
Number of positive effects		14	20	2	6	22	11	6	8	20	9	4	11	12	9	21	4	

Table 15. (Continued)

Unilateral and global free trade		Unilateral free trade														Global FT	Number of positive effects
		US	JPN	AUS	KOR	SGP	IDN	MYS	PHL	THA	CHL	CAC	MEX	MOR	SACU		
		1	2	3	4	5	6	7	8	9	10	11	12	13	14	15	
1	Japan		X													X	15
2	US	X														X	14
3	Canada															X	13
4	Australia			X												X	15
5	New Zealand															X	14
6	EU and EFTA															X	15
7	Hong Kong															X	14
8	China															X	13
9	Korea				X											X	15
10	Singapore					X										X	15
11	Taiwan															X	15
12	Indonesia						X									X	15
13	Malaysia							X								X	15
14	Philippines								X							X	15
15	Thailand									X						X	14
16	Rest of Asia															X	15
17	Chile										X					X	15
18	Mexico												X			X	14
19	CAC											X				X	15
20	South America															X	15
21	Morocco													X		X	15
22	SACU														X	X	14
No. of positive effects		20	19	21	21	22	22	22	22	22	22	22	20	21	22	22	

Notes: 1. Shaded cells indicate countries with positive welfare effects, whereas white cells indicate countries with negative welfare effects.
2. "X" indicates unilateral free trade countries.

improvements in productivity and increased capital formation. Unfortunately, we are not in a position to assess these potential benefits. But it seems clear from our computational results that the welfare increases from the FTA removal of trade barriers are fairly small on the whole. Pending further analysis, we therefore conclude that there is reason to be concerned about the trade diversion and overlapping spoke effects of bilateral FTAs.

6. *Welfare effects of unilateral free trade and global free trade*

In this section, we ask how the welfare of the United States, Japan, their FTA partners, and other countries/regions in the global trading system would be affected if it were feasible to adopt unilateral free trade or global free trade on a nondiscriminatory (MFN) basis as compared to the adoption of discriminatory bilateral FTAs. The results are indicated in Table 16. Unilateral free trade adopted by the United States would increase U.S. welfare by $320.2 billion (3.2% of GNP), which is about three times greater than the U.S. welfare gains from the bilateral FTAs combined. If there were global (multilateral) free trade, U.S. welfare would be increased by $401.8 billion (5.4% of GNP). Japan's welfare would increase with unilateral free trade by $200.3 billion (3.7% of GNP) and with global free trade by $542.5 billion (7.4% of GNP), as compared to the $66.9 billion to be gained from Japan's bilateral FTAs combined. There are also clear indications that the FTA partner countries would generally gain more from the adoption of unilateral free trade by the United States and Japan as compared to the partner-country gains from their bilateral FTAs. Furthermore, the FTA partner countries would generally gain even more if they adopted unilateral free trade and especially if there were global free trade.[25]

[25] In commenting on an earlier version of our chapter, Juan Carlos Hallak asked why there are larger absolute welfare gains and smaller percent changes in welfare for the large countries as compared to the small countries in our computational results. In this connection, the expectation is that, under conditions of perfect competition, a small country may appropriate a large share of the absolute gains from trade liberalization because the prices of the small country will tend to move toward the prices in the large country. Since large price changes give rise to large gains from trade, the small country may be expected therefore to realize greater gains from liberalization than the large country.

But when scale effects are present, as in the Michigan Model, the foregoing distributional logic may not hold. That is, scale gains will be substantial for countries that specialize in sectors with significant unrealized scale economies, and it may well be that large countries are in a better position to realize big-scale gains. Also, the pro-competitive effects resulting from liberalization may produce efficiency gains throughout an industry. As a consequence, the absolute gain will be proportional to the industry's/country's size. With regard to percent changes, however, there is reason to believe that a large country will exert stronger pro-competitive forces on a small country, than vice versa. We might therefore expect to observe larger percent changes in scale in small as compared to large countries. This is borne out in our calculations of scale effects for the countries/regions in the various liberalization scenarios that we have run, the results of which are available on request.

Table 16. Welfare effects of unilateral and global free trade (billions of dollars and percent of GNP)

	Unilateral free trade														Global free trade
	United States	Japan	Australia	Korea	Singapore	Indonesia	Malaysia	Philippines	Thailand	Chile	Mexico	CAC	Morocco	SACU	
Billions of dollars															
Japan	21.9	200.3	4.1	7.6	0.6	8.1	5.8	5.3	11.8	1.6	2.7	4.6	1.1	2.5	401.8
United States	320.2	10.6	2.3	11.8	1.6	7.1	2.6	9.7	8.0	2.0	−5.2	9.1	1.9	3.2	542.5
Canada	−9.7	0.9	0.3	1.7	0.2	0.9	0.3	1.4	1.0	0.2	−0.6	0.8	0.2	0.3	50.1
Australia	5.4	3.0	4.6	1.0	0.2	0.4	0.5	0.6	0.9	0.0	0.4	0.3	0.1	0.2	30.1
New Zealand	1.3	1.4	−0.2	0.3	0.1	0.1	0.1	0.1	0.2	0.0	0.2	0.1	0.1	0.1	11.5
EU and EFTA	128.9	33.4	4.0	20.8	3.4	13.6	6.7	15.1	14.9	3.1	12.2	8.3	5.3	8.5	796.2
Hong Kong	5.2	0.9	0.1	0.8	0.1	0.2	0.3	0.4	0.7	0.1	0.0	0.1	−0.0	0.2	18.1
China	5.3	−4.3	1.1	−1.0	0.1	0.7	0.4	0.5	1.5	0.2	0.3	0.3	0.1	0.4	105.0
Korea	5.0	0.5	0.8	34.9	0.1	2.3	0.4	1.1	1.1	0.3	0.6	0.5	0.1	0.8	73.2
Singapore	2.1	0.8	0.1	0.9	1.1	0.6	1.7	0.8	1.5	0.1	0.2	0.2	0.0	0.1	19.9
Taiwan	4.9	1.5	0.6	0.7	0.1	0.8	0.7	0.9	1.1	0.2	0.3	0.1	0.1	0.3	60.7
Indonesia	2.2	1.5	0.2	1.0	0.1	11.9	0.4	0.5	0.7	0.1	0.1	0.1	0.0	0.1	25.8
Malaysia	1.1	0.6	0.1	1.1	0.4	0.5	4.0	0.6	1.0	0.1	0.1	0.1	0.0	0.2	18.2
Philippines	1.6	0.6	0.1	0.7	0.1	0.4	0.2	7.5	0.4	0.1	0.0	0.0	0.0	0.1	17.0
Thailand	2.3	−0.6	0.2	0.6	0.2	0.4	0.2	0.3	14.7	0.1	0.2	0.2	0.0	0.1	27.4
Rest of Asia	3.7	1.2	0.4	1.1	0.1	0.5	0.5	0.4	0.5	0.1	0.3	0.3	0.0	0.3	40.8
Chile	0.8	0.5	0.0	0.3	0.0	0.0	0.1	0.1	0.1	5.2	0.3	0.1	0.0	0.0	10.8
Mexico	−5.6	1.1	0.1	0.7	0.1	0.3	0.0	0.2	0.2	0.3	26.4	0.4	0.1	0.3	33.6
CAC	4.0	1.3	0.0	0.5	0.0	0.2	0.1	0.1	0.2	0.1	0.2	6.2	0.0	0.1	17.7
South America	4.7	2.8	0.3	2.3	0.3	0.9	0.5	0.9	1.2	1.4	1.2	1.7	0.4	1.0	96.5
Morocco	0.5	0.4	0.0	0.1	0.0	0.0	0.0	0.0	0.0	0.0	0.0	0.0	1.6	0.0	4.8
SACU	1.1	−0.2	0.1	0.2	0.0	0.0	0.0	0.1	0.2	0.0	0.2	0.1	0.0	13.6	15.5
Total	507.0	258.0	19.3	88.0	9.0	50.0	25.6	46.8	61.9	15.2	40.0	33.7	11.3	32.3	2,417.3

Percent of GNP															
Japan	0.4	3.7	0.1	0.1	0.0	0.1	0.1	0.1	0.2	0.0	0.0	0.1	0.0	0.0	7.4
United States	3.2	0.1	0.0	0.1	0.0	0.1	0.0	0.1	0.1	0.0	−0.1	0.1	0.0	0.0	5.4
Canada	−1.2	0.1	0.0	0.2	0.0	0.1	0.0	0.2	0.1	0.0	−0.1	0.1	0.0	0.0	6.2
Australia	1.1	0.6	0.9	0.2	0.0	0.1	0.1	0.1	0.2	0.0	0.1	0.1	0.0	0.0	6.0
New Zealand	1.6	1.7	−0.3	0.3	0.1	0.1	0.1	0.2	0.2	0.0	0.2	0.2	0.1	0.1	14.0
EU and EFTA	1.2	0.3	0.0	0.2	0.0	0.1	0.1	0.1	0.1	0.0	0.1	0.1	0.0	0.1	7.3
Hong Kong	2.9	0.5	0.0	0.5	0.1	0.1	0.2	0.3	0.4	0.0	0.0	0.1	0.0	0.1	10.2
China	0.5	−0.4	0.1	−0.1	0.0	0.1	0.0	0.0	0.1	0.0	0.0	0.0	0.0	0.0	9.6
Korea	0.9	0.1	0.1	6.3	0.0	0.4	0.1	0.2	0.2	0.1	0.1	0.1	0.0	0.1	13.2
Singapore	2.3	0.9	0.1	0.9	1.2	0.6	1.8	0.8	1.6	0.1	0.2	0.2	0.0	0.1	21.0
Taiwan	1.3	0.4	0.1	0.2	0.0	0.2	0.2	0.2	0.3	0.1	0.1	0.0	0.0	0.1	15.9
Indonesia	0.8	0.6	0.1	0.4	0.0	4.5	0.2	0.2	0.3	0.0	0.1	0.0	0.0	0.0	9.7
Malaysia	0.8	0.4	0.1	0.8	0.3	0.4	3.0	0.4	0.7	0.0	0.1	0.1	0.0	0.1	13.7
Philippines	1.7	0.6	0.1	0.7	0.1	0.4	0.2	7.6	0.4	0.1	0.0	0.0	0.0	0.1	17.1
Thailand	1.2	−0.3	0.1	0.3	0.1	0.2	0.1	0.2	7.3	0.1	0.1	0.1	0.0	0.1	13.7
Rest of Asia	0.5	0.2	0.1	0.2	0.0	0.1	0.1	0.1	0.1	0.0	0.0	0.0	0.0	0.0	5.8
Chile	0.9	0.5	0.0	0.3	0.0	0.0	0.1	0.1	0.1	5.4	0.3	0.1	0.0	0.0	11.3
Mexico	−1.1	0.2	0.0	0.1	0.0	0.1	0.0	0.0	0.0	0.1	5.3	0.1	0.0	0.1	6.7
CAC	3.4	1.1	0.0	0.4	0.0	0.1	0.1	0.1	0.1	0.1	0.2	5.1	0.0	0.1	14.8
South America	0.3	0.2	0.0	0.1	0.0	0.0	0.0	0.1	0.1	0.1	0.1	0.1	0.0	0.1	5.3
Morocco	1.2	1.0	0.0	0.1	0.0	0.1	0.0	0.1	0.1	0.0	0.1	0.1	3.5	0.1	10.9
SACU	0.6	−0.1	0.0	0.1	0.0	0.0	0.0	0.1	0.1	0.0	0.1	0.1	0.0	7.4	8.5

7. *Summary and conclusions*

In this chapter, we have used the Michigan Model of World Production and Trade to calculate the aggregate welfare and sectoral employment effects of the menu of U.S.–Japan trade policies. The menu of policies encompasses the various preferential U.S. and Japan bilateral and regional FTAs negotiated and in process, unilateral removal of existing trade barriers by the United States, Japan, and the FTA partner countries, and global (multilateral) free trade. The welfare impacts of the FTAs on the United States and Japan have been shown to be rather small in absolute and relative terms. The sectoral employment effects are also generally small for both countries, but vary across the individual sectors depending on the patterns of bilateral liberalization.

The welfare effects on the FTA partner countries are shown to be mostly positive though generally small, but there are some indications of potentially disruptive employment shifts in some partner countries. The results further suggest that there would be trade diversion and detrimental welfare effects in some nonmember countries/regions. It also appears that, although FTA partners may gain from the bilateral FTAs, they may be adversely affected because of overlapping "hub-and-spoke" arrangements due to other discriminatory FTAs that have been negotiated.

The welfare gains from both unilateral trade liberalization by the United States and Japan and from global (multilateral) trade liberalization are shown to be rather substantial and more uniformly positive for all countries/regions in the global trading system as compared to the welfare gains from the bilateral FTAs analyzed.[26] The issue then is whether and when the WTO member countries will be able to overcome their divisiveness and indecisions and put the multilateral negotiations back on track. The menu choice appears to be clear.

Acknowledgments

We thank Masahiko Tsutsumi and participants in the March 2004 pre-conference meeting in Ann Arbor and the May 2004 Tokyo conference for helpful comments on earlier versions of the chapter. Kozo Kiyota was a visiting scholar at the University of Michigan, Ann Arbor, when this chapter was prepared and would like to thank the Kikawada Fellowship Program for providing financial support for the research.

---

[26] See the Appendix for sensitivity analysis of introducing alternative parameters in the model and the resulting welfare impacts of global free trade.

Appendix

A.1. Sensitivity analysis

This appendix reports on sensitivity analysis of the Michigan Model. There are three key elasticities/parameters in the model: the elasticity of substitution among varieties, which is exogenously set at 3; the parameter that measures the sensitivity that consumers have to the number of varieties, which is set at 0.5; and the elasticities of supply that are taken from the literature.

The variety parameter can take on values between 0 and 1. The larger it is, it means that consumers value variety more. If the parameter is set at 0, consumers have no preference for variety. This would correspond to the Armington assumption, according to which consumers view products depending on their place of production.

To analyze the sensitivity of our model results, we have experimented with different values of the elasticity of substitution among varieties and the consumer sensitivity to the number of varieties. The following tests were conducted: (1) increase the elasticity of substitution among varieties by 10%, holding other parameters constant; (2) decrease the elasticity of substitution by 10%, holding other parameters constant; (3) increase the consumption varieties parameter by 10%, holding other parameters constant; and (4) decrease the consumption varieties by 10%, holding other parameters constant.

The results, which are available on request, are not very sensitive to the alternative parameters of the consumption varieties. That is, a 10% increase (decrease) in these parameters yields only 2% larger (smaller) welfare effects compared to the baseline model. The sensitivity to the changes in the elasticity of substitution is large compared with the results of differences in the variety parameters. For some countries, the differences are greater than 10%.

In Brown *et al.* (2000), sensitivity tests reveal that the model may exaggerate the likely gains from economies of scale due to trade liberalization in the context of expansion of the NAFTA. But the error is small in this context because the impact of trade liberalization is small. When econometric estimates of scale economies are incorporated into the model, the welfare gains due to capital flows are shown to remain robust.

References

Andriamananjara, S., Tsigas, M. (2003), *Free Trade Agreements with the United States: What Can We Learn from 65 Simulations?* U.S. International Trade Commission, Washington, DC, (June 5).

Bhagwati, J., Panagariya, A. (1996), Preferential trading areas and multilateralism – strangers, friends, or foes? In: Bhagwati, J., Panagariya, A. (Eds.), *The Economics of Preferential Trade Agreements*. American Enterprise Institute, Washington, DC, pp. 1–78.

Brown, D.K., Stern, R.M. (1989a), Computational analysis of the U.S.-Canadian free trade agreement: the role of product differentiation and market structure. In: Feenstra, R.C. (Ed.), *Trade Policies for International Competitiveness*. University of Chicago Press, Chicago, pp. 217–245.

Brown, D.K., Stern, R.M. (1989b), Computable general equilibrium estimates of the gains from U.S.-Canadian trade liberalization. In: Greenaway, D., Hyclak, T., Thornton, R.J. (Eds.), *Economic Aspects of Regional Trading Arrangements*. Harvester Wheatsheaf, London, pp. 69–108.

Brown, D.K., Deardorff, A.V., Stern, R.M. (2000), Computational analysis of the accession of Chile to the NAFTA and Western Hemisphere integration. *The World Economy* 23 (2), 145–174.

Brown, D.K., Deardorff, A.V., Stern, R.M. (2002), CGE modeling and analysis of multilateral and regional negotiating options. In: Stern, R.M. (Ed.), *Issues and Options for U.S.-Japan Trade Policies*. University of Michigan Press, Ann Arbor, pp. 23–70.

Brown, D.K., Kiyota, K., Stern, R.M. (2005a), Computational analysis of the free trade area of the Americas (FTAA). *North American Journal of Economics and Finance* 16 (2), 153–185.

Brown, D.K., Kiyota, K., Stern, R.M. (2005b), Computational analysis of the U.S FTAs with Central America, Australia, and Morocco. *The World Economy* 28 (10), 1445–1490.

Brown, D.K., Kiyota, K., Stern, R.M. (2008), An analysis of a U.S.-SACU free trade agreement. *World Development* 36 (3), 461–484.

Deardorff, A.V., Stern, R.M. (1990), *Computational Analysis of Global Trading Arrangements*. University of Michigan Press, Ann Arbor.

DeRosa, D., Gilbert, J. (2004), Technical appendix: quantitative estimates of the economic impacts of US bilateral free trade agreements. In: Schott, J.J. (Ed.), *Free Trade Agreements: US Strategies and Priorities*. Institute for International Economics, Washington, DC, pp. 383–417.

Dimaranan, B. V., McDougall, R. A. (Eds.) (2002). *The GTAP 5 Data Base*. Center for Global Trade Analysis, Department of Agricultural Economics, Purdue University, West Lafayette, IN.

Francois, J. Strutt, A. (1999), Post Uruguay round tariff vectors for GTAP version 4. Erasmus University, manuscript.

Francois, J., Meijl, H.v., Tongeren, F.v. (2003), Trade Liberalization and Developing Countries under the Doha Round. CEPR Discussion Paper Series No. 4032 (August).

Harrison, W.J., Pearson, K. (1996), Computing solutions for large general equilibrium models using GEMPACK. *Computational Economics* 9 (2), 83–127.

Hertel, T.W. (2000), Potential gains from reducing trade barriers in manufacturing, services and agriculture. *Federal Reserve Bank of St. Louis Review* 82, 77–99.

Hertel, T.W., Martin, W. (2000), Liberalizing agriculture and manufactures in a millennium round: implications for developing countries. *The World Economy* 23 (4), 455–469.

Hertel, T.W., Martin, W. (2001), Second-best linkages and the gains from global reform of manufactures trade. *Review of International Economics* 9 (2), 215–232.

Hertel, T.W., Walmsley, T., Itakura, K. (2001), Dynamic effects of the 'new age' free trade agreement between Japan and Singapore. *Journal of Economic Integration* 16 (4), 446–484.

Hoekman, B. (2000), The next round of services negotiations: identifying priorities and options. *Federal Reserve Bank of St. Louis Review* 82, 31–47.

Hoekman, B., Martin, W. (Eds.) (2001). *Developing Countries and the WTO: A Pro-Active Agenda.* Blackwell, Oxford.

International Labor Organization (ILO) (2003), LABORSTA. Available at http://laborsta.ilo.org/cgi-bin/brokerv8.exe.

Ianchovichina, E., Martin, W. (2004), Economic impacts of China's accession to the WTO. In: Bhattasali, D., Li, S., Martin, W. (Eds.), *China and the WTO: Accession, Policy Reform, and Poverty Reduction Strategies.* Oxford University Press and the World Bank, Washington, DC, pp. 211–236.

Kiyota, K., Stern, R.M. (2007), *The Economic Effects of a Korea-U.S. Free Trade Agreement.* Korea Economic Institute, Washington, DC, (special study).

Krishna, K. (2006), Understanding rules of origin. In: Adot, O., Estevadordal, A., Suwa-Eisenmann, A., Verdier, T. (Eds.), *The Origin of Goods: Rules of Origin in Regional Trade Agreements.* Oxford University Press, New York, pp. 19–34.

McKibbin, W.J., Lee, J.-W., Cheong, I. (2004), A dynamic analysis of the Korea-Japan free trade area: simulations with the G-cubed Asia-Pacific model. *International Economic Journal* 18 (1), 3–32.

Stolper, W., Samuelson, P.A. (1941), Protection and real wages. *Review of Economic Studies* 9 (1), 58–73.

Taiwan Government (2002), Taiwan Statistical Data Book 2002. Available at www.cepd.gov.tw/encontent/m1.aspx?sNo=0001453

United Nations Industrial Development Organization (UNIDO) (2003), *UNIDO Industrial Statistics Database 2003 at the 3-digit Level of ISIC (Revision 2)* on CD-ROM. Geneva: UNIDO.

World Bank, E. (2003), *World development indicators on CD-ROM.* World Bank, Washington, DC.

CHAPTER 12

China's Growing Participation in Preferential Trade Agreements: Implications for China and Its Trading Partners

Robert Scollay[a] and John Gilbert[b]

[a]*Department of Economics, University of Auckland, Auckland 1142, New Zealand*
E-mail address: rscollay@auckland.ac.nz
[b]*Department of Economics and Finance, Jon M. Huntsman School of Business, Utah State University, Logan, UT 84322-3565, USA*
E-mail address: jgilbert@usu.edu

Abstract

Regional trading arrangements are proliferating at a rapid pace in the Asia-Pacific region, although the architecture that will eventually emerge remains uncertain. In this chapter we explore the economic implications for both China and its trading partners of the current crop of preferential arrangements and potential future developments in the Asia-Pacific region, using computable general equilibrium simulations. By doing so the chapter aims to identify factors that are likely to weigh heavily in the economic interests of the different participants in some of the alternative ways in which the trade architecture of the region might develop, and the extent of convergence or divergence in these interests.

Keywords: China, Asia-Pacific, preferential trading agreements

1. Introduction

Since the turn of the century, a decisive shift in the approach to trade liberalization has taken place in the Asia-Pacific region. A region that through much of the 1990s sought doggedly to maintain an emphasis on multilateralism and nondiscrimination has in practice largely switched its focus to preferential forms of trade liberalization, even though the rhetoric of multilateralism continues to be heard loudly at least in some parts of the region.

The "trade architecture" that will emerge in this new environment remains, however, very uncertain, with several distinct tendencies clearly discernible. The trend that has progressed most rapidly has been the

Frontiers of Economics and Globalization
Volume 7 ISSN: 1574-8715
DOI: 10.1108/S1574-8715(2010)0000007015

proliferation of bilateral free trade agreements.[1] Since 2000 some 30 bilateral FTAs have been concluded among Asia-Pacific economies, with several others under negotiation for some time, and still others at the stage of preliminary study. Asia-Pacific economies have also been actively negotiating FTAs with partners outside the Asia-Pacific region.

A second trend has been negotiation of "ASEAN Plus One" FTAs in which the ASEAN members have entered as a bloc into agreements first with the major economies of Northeast Asia and subsequently with their southern neighbors in Australasia and the emerging South Asian giant, India. The ASEAN–China FTA was the first of these agreements to be concluded, followed some time later by the ASEAN–Korea FTA (initially minus the participation of Thailand, due to a disagreement over the inclusion in the FTA of rice). Japan was the last of the three major Northeast Asian nations to conclude its FTA with the ASEAN group, after having first concluded or almost concluded bilateral FTAs with four individual ASEAN members, with bilateral FTAs with three further ASEAN members being concluded subsequently. More recently still, ASEAN has concluded an FTA with Australia and New Zealand, and an FTA with India.

These "ASEAN Plus One" initiatives reflect several important impulses. The ASEAN FTAs with Northeast Asian partners can be linked to the growing sense of East Asian regionalism, expressed in promotion of the idea of East Asia as a distinct economic bloc with its own distinct trade architecture.[2] The manifestation of this impulse in the form of these ASEAN Plus One FTAs, rather than a single East Asian FTA, reflects both the competing ambitions of the three major Northeast Asian economic powers and the ongoing difficulties in relationships between them, which have seen them each give priority to forming their own separate preferential trade links with ASEAN and other partners, rather than seeking integration among themselves as an element in wider economic integration within East Asia. More generally, the ASEAN Plus One FTAs reflect the ambition of ASEAN to place itself at the center of any economic and political architecture that develops in East Asia. The three major Northeast Asian economic powers have been content to encourage this ASEAN-centered approach to economic integration in East Asia, given that the difficulties in their own relationships with each other have so far precluded the possibility of Northeast Asian leadership, whether exercised jointly or by one of the Northeast Asian powers.

The bilateral FTA initiatives of East Asian economies on the other hand cannot be interpreted purely as manifestations of East Asian regionalism, as they are by no means limited to linkages between East Asian partners.

---

[1] See Menon (2009) for a critical analysis of the spread of bilateral trade agreements in the Asia-Pacific region.

[2] Kawai (2005) surveys the evolution of East Asian regionalism to 2005. Chia (2007) provides a later perspective, from an explicitly ASEAN perspective. See also Hufbauer and Wong (2005).

Several initiatives link East Asian partners with Australia and New Zealand in Oceania, and others establish trans-Pacific linkages with partners in the Americas. Until very recently there was a tendency for the major Northeast Asian economies to focus their trans-Pacific initiatives on FTAs with smaller economies in the Americas rather than with the United States (Japan with Mexico; Korea, China, and Japan each with Chile; China with Peru). While the conclusion in 2007 of the Korea–United States (KORUS) FTA represented an important break with this pattern, Japan and China have yet to engage in serious FTA talks with the United States.

Also in play is a proposal to create an East Asia–wide trade bloc that would subsume the existing intra–East Asian FTA initiatives: the East Asia Free Trade Area (EAFTA), encompassing the "ASEAN Plus Three Group" comprising the 10 members of ASEAN plus the three major economies of Northeast Asia. This "ASEAN Plus Three" proposal has been on the table since the late 1990s, and has been the subject of detailed investigation by an East Asian Vision Group and by two study groups, the latest of which submitted a recommendation to the "ASEAN Plus Three" leaders that steps should be taken to move this proposal to the negotiating stage. This recommendation has not, however, yet been implemented. It would require acceptance by the three major Northeast Asian economies that trade should be liberalized between them, as well as between each of them and the members of ASEAN. Agreement on economic integration within Northeast Asia remains elusive. A Northeast Asian FTA (EAFTA) between China, Japan, and Korea has in fact been discussed, and an officially commissioned study has been undertaken on an FTA between China and Korea. Negotiations for an FTA actually commenced between Japan and Korea, but have subsequently been suspended. Difficulties in the relations between the three Northeast Asian powers remain an impediment to economic integration both within Northeast Asia itself and East Asia–wide, although there have been recent indications of renewed efforts to overcome these difficulties. Another feature of the proposals for East Asian economic integration is the noninclusion of Hong Kong and Chinese Taipei (Taiwan), even though these two economies account for a significant share of East Asia's trade.

The increasing emphasis on economic integration within Asian nations could be interpreted as a threat to the original Asia-Pacific Economic Cooperation (APEC) vision of integration across the entire Asia-Pacific region. Concern to preserve the trans-Pacific dimension of regional integration lay behind the decision of four small Asia-Pacific economies – Chile, New Zealand, Singapore, and Brunei – to create the Trans-Pacific Strategic Economic Partnership (TPSEP). These countries hoped that the TPSEP could form the nucleus of a much larger trans-Pacific trade agreement, involving the major economies of the region also.

Concern was also growing over the coherence of the evolving regional trade architecture, fueled by increasing recognition that a "spaghetti bowl" of multiple overlapping and intersecting bilateral and plurilateral FTAs is most unlikely to represent an optimal way of organizing the region's trade. As the private sector began to worry about the potential for increased transaction costs resulting from the uncoordinated spread of preferential trade agreements, increasing attention began unsurprisingly to be given to ways of "rationalizing the Asia-Pacific spaghetti bowl."[3]

The proposed EAFTA clearly represented one potential avenue toward rationalization, confined of course to East Asia. In 2004 the APEC Business Advisory Council (ABAC) proposed an APEC-wide FTA, the Free Trade Area of the Asia-Pacific (FTAAP).[4] This proposal emphasized APEC-wide economic integration, encompassing the trans-Pacific dimension inherent in APEC's membership structure, as a possible alternative or complement to the East Asian economic integration represented by the EAFTA proposal. Most importantly of course, the FTAAP would include the United States, which in 2006 moved decisively to ensure that the FTAAP as a "long term prospect" was placed firmly on APEC's agenda.

A further candidate as a vehicle for region-wide trade integration emerged from the establishment of the East Asian Summit (EAS) in 2005. The EAS extends beyond the "ASEAN Plus Three" group to include India, Australia, and New Zealand, but does not include the United States or other APEC members in the Americas. Japan has proposed that a Comprehensive Partnership for East Asia (CEPEA) should be formed by the members of the EAS, and that an FTA should be an integral element in the CEPEA.[5]

Since the emergence of the CEPEA proposal, there have been three candidates for the establishment of a regional trade bloc that could serve as a vehicle for a region-wide economic integration: EAFTA, with coverage limited to East Asia alone; the FTAAP, incorporating the trans-Pacific dimension embedded in APEC, and including, crucially, the United States; and the CEPEA, excluding the United States and other APEC members in the Americas but extending southward from East Asia to include Australia and New Zealand, and westward to include India (but not the rest of South Asia).

A new development in late 2007 was the announcement by the United States, subsequently confirmed in late 2008 by the incoming Obama Administration, of its intention to join the TPSEP, henceforth known as the TPP (Trans-Pacific Partnership) or "expanded TPP." This was soon followed by announcements by Australia, Peru, and Vietnam that they too intend to join the TPP. The second round of negotiations concluded in June 2010, with further rounds scheduled.

---

[3] This growing concern is reflected, for example, in Scollay (2007).

[4] Scollay (2004) discusses at length the issues raised by the FTAAP proposal. See also Bergsten (2007).

[5] The respective merits of EAFTA and a CEPEA-based FTA are analyzed, for example, in Kawai and Wignaraja (2008).

In 2007 a further ingredient was injected into the Asia-Pacific preferential trade panorama with the launching by the European Union (EU) of a push for new preferential agreements with selected partners in the region. The EU quickly concluded negotiation of an FTA with Korea, and initiated a process intended to lead to negotiation of an FTA with ASEAN, although the EU's focus has apparently subsequently shifted to negotiation of bilateral FTAs with individual ASEAN members. The EU has pursued FTA negotiations with the Andean and Central American groups in the Americas, having already earlier completed FTAs with Mexico and Chile among the American members of APEC. As in the case of ASEAN, the emphasis in the EU approach to the Andean group subsequently shifted to negotiation of bilateral FTAs, in this case with Peru and Colombia, while negotiations with Central America have continued on a regional basis.

The evolution of Asia-Pacific preferential trade arrangements is thus at a stage where it could proceed in a number of different directions, depending on the strategies chosen by the major economies of the region in particular. China is likely to exert a powerful influence on the eventual outcome, both through the options it decides to pursue on the basis of its perception of its own economic and political interest, and also because the implications of inclusion in or exclusion from preferential arrangements involving China is likely to be an import consideration to be weighed by other economies in the region in deciding their own strategies.

The purpose of this chapter is to explore the economic implications for both China and its trading partners of the current and potential future preferential trading developments in the Asia-Pacific region, using computable general equilibrium (CGE) simulations of these developments. By doing so the chapter aims to identify factors that are likely to weigh heavily in the economic interests of the different participants in some of the alternative ways in which the trade architecture of the region might develop, and the extent of convergence or divergence in these interests.

2. *Modeling approach*

Given the magnitude of the trade liberalization measures under consideration and their broad regional and sectoral coverage, and our desire to understand both the potential economy-wide and sectoral-level impacts of the proposals, CGE analysis is an appropriate methodological choice. Trade policy changes in an economic system will often have repercussions well beyond the sector in which they occur, and by linking markets, CGE techniques are effective at capturing the complex network of feedback and flow-through effects. The CGE technique has been very widely used in the analysis of both regional trading agreements in the Asia-Pacific (see the recent surveys by Scollay and Gilbert, 2000;

Robinson and Thierfelder, 2002; Lloyd and MacLaren, 2004), and trade reforms in China (see Gilbert and Wahl, 2002).

In this chapter we adopt the Global Trade Analysis Project (GTAP) model (Hertel, 1997) for our analysis. This model has become very widely used over the last decade (see the surveys listed in the preceding paragraph), and represents a benchmark model of sorts. The structure of the model is a standard, multiregion CGE. It assumes perfectly competitive markets and constant returns to scale technology. The major departure of the model from those of standard trade theory is the assumption of product differentiation by national origin, controlled by a set of Armington substitution elasticities, serving the dual purpose of allowing two-way trade in each product category and avoiding extreme production and trade responses. Since the structure of the model is quite familiar and discussed in detail in Hertel (1997), we dispense with a detailed presentation.

The database used in these simulations is GTAP6 (Dimaranan, 2006), which has a base year of 2001. Since working with the full GTAP data is very computationally expensive, for the simulations reported in this chapter the data was aggregated into 31 sectors. We individually identify 24 economies (including 19 of the 21 APEC members) and 7 aggregate regions, each of which is an amalgamation of multiple economies (one of these being the EU-25).

In terms of data adjustments, while merchandise protection data in GTAP6 are excellent, services protection data are not available. Dee *et al.* (2000) have published their estimates of barriers to services trade, at the aggregate level. In this study we will split services into traded and nontraded categories, following the classification of Dee *et al.* (2000), and use the estimates of services barriers from that study. These barriers are implemented using several instruments (import tax equivalents, export tax equivalents, taxes on output, and taxes on domestic capital). The rates were imposed prior to the major simulations using the ALTERTAX procedure. This procedure fixes the current account balance and uses parameters such that all key shares in the model remain constant when the new taxes are imposed, while ensuring that the database remains consistent. While this allows us to capture some aspects of services protection, it should be emphasized that the approach is fairly rudimentary.

Following aggregation and data adjustments, we conduct a preliminary simulation to establish the baseline for all of our policy simulations, making a series of adjustments to the GTAP6 database to take account of accession of China to the World Trade Organization (WTO), enlargement of the EU to 25 members, phase-out of Multifiber Agreement (MFA) quotas, and implementation of the ASEAN Free Trade Agreement (AFTA). These modifications generate a "baseline" database, computed as if all of these developments had already taken place in 2001.

For simulation purposes the complex configurations of current and possible future preferential trading arrangements must be simplified, and we have chosen a series of nine scenarios outlined in Table 1. Each scenario represents a combination of FTAs that currently exist or that may exist in the future, depending on choices made by the economies of the region. The FTAs included in each scenario are assumed to be implemented simultaneously. A set of initial scenarios aims to capture features of the existing configuration of preferential arrangements. In subsequent scenarios various combinations of new preferential arrangements, representing different possible ways in which the regional trade arrangements might evolve, are superimposed on the existing arrangements.

Scenario 1 aims to capture the existing bilateral FTAs (and two plurilateral FTAs) in the Asia-Pacific region, many of which involve Japan, Singapore, and Chile. The majority of these FTAs have already entered into force. While only two of these agreements actually involve China directly, this scenario is nonetheless necessary for the simulations to account for the bilaterals that are currently or soon to be in force.

Scenario 2 adds the two early "ASEAN Plus One" FTAs and the recently concluded Korea–US FTA, thus allowing the impact of these three important FTAs, including the ASEAN–China FTA, to be isolated from the existing bilaterals, while scenario 3 adds five newer bilateral FTA initiatives that have recently been concluded or for which negotiations are continuing, two of which involve China (the completed bilateral FTA with New Zealand and the FTA still under negotiation with Australia) and scenario 4 adds two further "ASEAN Plus One" FTAs, ASEAN–Japan and ASEAN–Australia/New Zealand. This scenario essentially captures the current situation where integration in East Asia has not proceeded beyond the "ASEAN Plus One" initiatives.

In scenario 5 the "ASEAN Plus One" FTAs with China, Japan, and Korea are expanded into an EAFTA, or the "ASEAN Plus Three" FTA. This is done by supplementing scenario 4 with the removal of trade barriers between China, Japan, and Korea. Five bilateral FTA initiatives of varying status, all involving Peru and the United States, are also included in this scenario.

In scenario 6 the "ASEAN Plus Three" FTA is expanded into an "ASEAN Plus Six" FTA (the CEPEA), through the incorporation of India, Australia, and New Zealand, while scenario 7 considers the additional impact of four potential FTAs between the EU and economies in the Asia-Pacific region.

Scenario 8 incorporates the FTAAP.[6] Compared to scenario 6, this involves removing India from the CEPEA, and the removal of trade

[6] Note that the "expanded TPP" is not modeled explicitly. The greater part of the bilateral trade flows among the prospective members of the "expanded TPP" is already included within scenario 4 and two more of these bilateral flows are included within scenario 5. The remaining flows among "expanded TPP" members are incorporated into the FTAAP in scenario 8.

Table 1. Experimental design

Scenario 1	Scenario 2	Scenario 3	Scenario 4	Scenario 5	Scenario 6	Scenario 7	Scenario 8	Scenario 9
Singapore–US	Scenario 1+	Scenario 2+	Scenario 3+	Scenario 4+	Scenario 5+	Scenario 6+	Scenario 5+	Scenario 7+
Singapore–Japan								
Singapore–Australia	ASEAN–China	Australia–China	ASEAN–Japan	ASEAN+3	ASEAN+6	Korea–EU	FTAAP	FTAAP
Singapore–NZ–Chile	ASEAN–Korea	NZ–China	ASEAN–Australia	US–Thailand		ASEAN–EU		
Singapore–Korea	US–Korea	Australia–Malaysia	ASEAN–NZ	US–Malaysia		EU–Andean Group		
Japan–Mexico		NZ–Malaysia		Peru–Thailand		EU–Central America		
Japan–Malaysia		Australia–Japan		Peru–Singapore				
Japan–Philippines				Peru–Chile				
Japan–Thailand								
Japan–Chile								
Korea–Chile								
Chile–US								
Chile–China								
Chile–Canada								
Chile–Mexico								
Chile–EU								
Mexico–EU								
Australia–US								
Australia–Thailand								
NZ–Thailand								
China–Hong Kong								
Peru–USA								
Colombia–US								
Central America–US								

barriers on all remaining bilateral trade flows between APEC members as needed to complete the FTAAP. Finally, scenario 9 considers the situation if the FTAAP is introduced as a supplement to rather than as a replacement for the CEPEA. The scenario also assumes the simultaneous implementation of the same four FTAs involving the EU that were included in scenario 7.

In terms of implementing the simulations, we use a comparative static approach. No account is taken of the time path for the phasing in of liberalization commitments, either in the agreements included in the baseline or the agreements being simulated. Agreements are also simulated for simplicity as "clean" FTAs, with no account taken of any exclusion of products from each agreement. From this perspective the simulations represent the upper bounds of the liberalization that could potentially take place, since in practice agreements typically provide for the exclusion of some products (notably agricultural products), and extensive phase-in periods for the elimination of tariffs on others. The results from the simulations are not predictions of future states of the economies in the model. They should be interpreted as indicating how these economies would differ, after all adjustments have taken place, if the preferential arrangements being simulated had been implemented.

Given our interest in long-term developments in the region, a long-run closure is utilized in which all factors except natural resources are assumed to be fully mobile across economic activities. The return to capital is fixed in real terms while the stock of capital is endogenous. This closure rule, often termed a "steady-state" closure, allows us to approximate the effects of the capital accumulation that would occur in a dynamic model, at a relatively low computational cost (see Wang and Schuh, 2002; Gilbert and Wahl, 2003).

3. *Results and policy discussion*

3.1. Welfare effects

Figure 1 depicts the effects of each of the nine scenarios on China's economic welfare. The result for scenario 1 shows that China derives a small welfare gain from the existing patchwork of bilateral FTAs in the Asia-Pacific region, even though only two of the FTAs in scenario 1 actually include China as a participant. Unsurprisingly, the inclusion of the ASEAN–China FTA (ACFTA) in scenario 2 substantially increases China's welfare gain, to more than double the gain recorded for scenario 1. The addition of FTAs with Australia and New Zealand in scenario 3 further increases China's welfare gain.

The gains from scenario 3 in fact represent the peak of China's potential gains from among all the scenarios other than those that include the

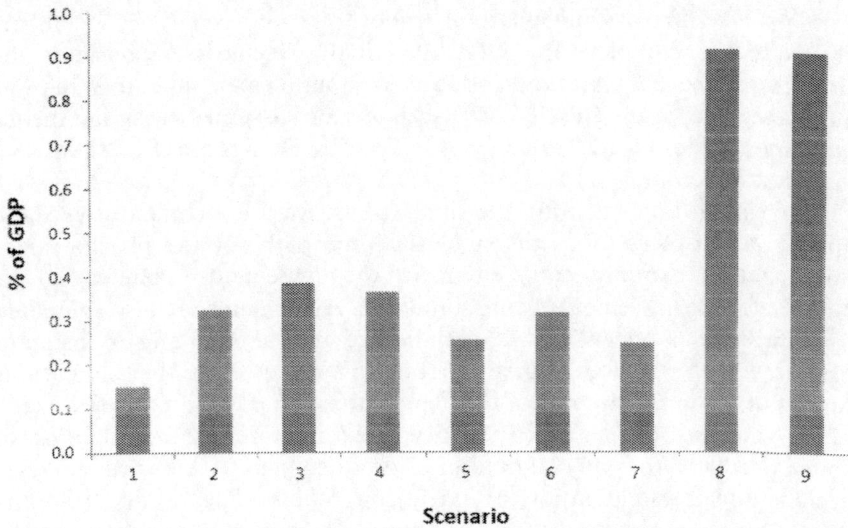

Fig. 1. Impact on China's welfare of alternative Asia-Pacific PTA scenarios.

FTAAP. Inclusion of the further "ASEAN Plus One" FTAs with Japan and Australia and New Zealand in scenario 4 results, perhaps unsurprisingly, in a slight reduction in China's welfare from the level recorded in scenario 3. The move to EAFTA in scenario 5, in combination with projected U.S. FTAs with Thailand and Malaysia, reduces China's welfare gain still further. Expansion beyond EAFTA to the "ASEAN Plus Six" configuration envisaged in the CEPEA yields a slightly improved welfare outcome in scenario 6, although still inferior to the outcome attained in scenario 3. Since China's projected FTAs with Australia and New Zealand were already included in scenario 3, the step from scenario 5 to scenario 6 for China essentially reflects the effect of the inclusion of India.

By far the largest welfare gain for China results from the introduction of the FTAAP in scenario 8. This is a clear demonstration of the potential benefit to China of liberalization of its trade flows with North America, especially the United States.

Implementation of the EU FTAs in scenario 7 simultaneously with the CEPEA results in a slight fall in China's welfare from the level associated with implementation of the CEPEA in scenario 6. On the other hand, with the FTAAP superimposed on the CEPEA in scenario 9, the implementation of the EU FTAs has minimal effect on the welfare gain for China associated with implementation of the FTAAP in scenario 8.

The next step in the analysis is to consider how far the pattern of welfare effects observed for China across the nine scenarios coincides with or diverges from the pattern observed for each of the other economies or regional groupings identified in the model. This allows an assessment to be made of how far a calculus based purely on economic welfare effects might lead to a shared view among China and its trading partners as to how the preferential trading architecture of the Asia-Pacific region should evolve. The simulated welfare effects across the nine scenarios for the other economies or regional groupings in the model are shown in Table 2.

Considering first the "non-FTAAP" scenarios, China and Hong Kong are distinctive among East Asian economies in deriving more limited welfare gains from the scenarios incorporating EAFTA ("ASEAN Plus Three") and CEPEA ("ASEAN Plus Six") than from scenario 3, where China has an "ASEAN Plus One" FTA with ASEAN and bilateral FTAs with Australia and New Zealand. Taking the step to EAFTA ("ASEAN Plus Three") also lowers the welfare gains for Singapore, the Philippines, Indonesia, and Vietnam, although for all of these other economies except Vietnam taking the next step, to the CEPEA ("ASEAN Plus Six") in scenario 6, results in welfare gains that are higher than for any of the more limited scenarios. Leaving aside Chinese Taipei, Vietnam is the only East Asian economy for which the CEPEA scenario (scenario 6) does not yield higher welfare gains than all the more limited scenarios. For Chinese Taipei (Taiwan), which is effectively excluded from all East Asian preferential trading initiatives, the picture is one of welfare losses rising as the scope of liberalization increases with each new scenario.

Thus, if economic interests were the only criterion, it might be expected that China, Hong Kong, and Vietnam should avoid moving beyond the "ASEAN Plus One" and bilateral initiatives, whereas other East Asian economies (except Chinese Taipei) would favor moving ahead to either EAFTA or the CEPEA. For all of the other East Asian economies, as well as for China and Vietnam, the welfare gains from CEPEA are greater than those from EAFTA. For the potential CEPEA participants from outside East Asia (Australia, New Zealand and India), the welfare outcome associated with CEPEA is naturally more favorable than the outcome associated with EAFTA. For New Zealand and India the welfare outcome from the CEPEA scenario is also more favorable than the outcome from the "ASEAN Plus One" and bilateral combinations in scenarios 1–4. For Australia on the other hand, moving from scenario 4 to the CEPEA in scenario 6 involves a slight reduction in economic welfare. If the East Asian region determines to advance its integration beyond the "ASEAN Plus One" and bilateral initiatives therefore, the results presented here indicate that CEPEA should deliver more favorable welfare outcomes than EAFTA for all potential members of EAFTA or CEPEA. Hong Kong and Chinese Taipei, on the other hand, which are not included in either proposed initiative, experience lower welfare gains (Hong Kong) or larger welfare losses (Chinese Taipei) under CEPEA.

There is divergence also among the East Asian economies in relation to projected welfare gains from the FTAAP, as compared with the scenarios focused on the EAFTA or CEPEA. As is the case for China and Hong Kong, for Japan, the Philippines, Indonesia, and Vietnam the FTAAP

Table 2. Welfare impacts by region of alternative preferential trade liberalization scenarios

Region	Scenario								
	1	2	3	4	5	6	7	8	9
Northeast Asia									
China	0.2	0.3	0.4	0.4	0.3	0.3	0.2	0.9	0.9
Japan	0.3	0.3	0.4	0.5	0.9	0.9	0.8	1.1	1.1
Korea	−0.2	4.4	4.5	4.4	7.5	7.8	8.6	7.8	8.8
Hong Kong	1.4	1.4	1.5	1.5	1.0	0.9	0.8	3.3	3.1
Chinese Taipei	−0.2	−0.4	−0.4	−0.4	−0.6	−0.7	−0.7	2.1	2.0
Southeast Asia									
Singapore	1.7	2.6	2.5	2.4	2.2	2.9	4.1	2.1	4.1
Malaysia	0.6	2.2	2.4	2.4	3.7	4.5	5.8	4.0	6.2
Thailand	2.1	4.1	3.6	3.5	5.6	6.0	8.4	5.9	8.7
Philippines	−0.2	0.4	0.4	0.4	0.3	0.5	1.0	2.4	3.0
Indonesia	−0.4	0.3	0.2	0.8	0.8	1.0	1.9	1.9	3.0
Vietnam	−0.1	4.3	4.2	7.3	5.6	5.8	11.0	9.0	14.5
USA	0.0	0.0	0.0	0.0	0.0	0.0	0.0	0.1	0.1
Australia	0.1	0.1	1.7	1.8	1.3	1.7	1.7	1.1	1.3
New Zealand	−0.1	−0.1	0.2	0.3	0.3	0.9	0.8	2.5	2.4
Other APEC									
Mexico	0.9	0.8	0.8	0.8	0.9	0.9	0.9	1.9	1.8
Canada	−0.1	−0.1	−0.1	−0.1	−0.1	−0.1	−0.1	0.4	0.4
Peru	1.0	0.8	0.9	0.9	1.2	1.2	1.5	1.4	1.7
Chile	1.3	1.3	1.4	1.4	1.6	1.7	1.5	1.8	1.7
Russia	0.0	0.0	0.0	0.0	0.0	0.0	−0.1	0.6	0.5
South Asia									
India	−0.1	−0.1	−0.1	−0.1	−0.1	0.9	0.9	−0.2	0.8
Rest of South Asia	−0.2	−0.3	−0.3	−0.3	−0.3	−0.3	−0.4	−0.6	−0.7
Europe									
European Union	0.0	0.0	0.0	0.0	0.0	0.0	0.1	−0.1	0.1
Latin America – other									
Brazil	−0.1	−0.1	−0.1	−0.1	−0.1	−0.1	−0.1	−0.2	−0.2
Argentina	−0.1	−0.1	−0.1	−0.1	−0.1	−0.1	−0.2	−0.2	−0.3
Uruguay	−0.1	−0.1	−0.1	−0.1	−0.2	−0.1	−0.2	−0.4	−0.4
Colombia	0.2	0.2	0.2	0.2	0.2	0.2	0.1	0.1	0.0
Rest of Andean	−0.1	−0.1	0.0	0.0	0.0	−0.4	−0.3	0.0	−0.3
Rest of South America	0.0	0.0	0.0	0.0	0.0	−0.1	−0.2	−0.2	−0.3
Central America	3.9	3.7	3.7	3.7	3.4	3.4	5.1	1.9	3.7
Rest of FTAA	−0.2	−0.3	−0.2	−0.2	−0.3	−0.3	−0.3	−0.7	−0.7
Rest of the world	−0.1	−0.1	−0.1	−0.1	0.0	−0.1	−0.1	−0.1	−0.2

Source: Authors' simulations.

yields significantly larger welfare gains than either the EAFTA-based or CEPEA-based scenarios. On the other hand, the welfare outcome from the FTAAP is significantly inferior to the welfare outcome from the EAFTA-based and CEPEA-based scenarios for Singapore, and marginally inferior for Korea, Malaysia, and Thailand. It can be hypothesized that for these latter economies the additional gains that might have been delivered by the FTAAP have already been delivered by FTAs included in the earlier scenarios, in particular the FTAs with the United States for each of the four economies.[7] Chinese Taipei, which suffers from being excluded from each of scenarios 1–7, records a substantial welfare gain from the FTAAP.

Among the additional CEPEA members, the welfare outcome delivered by the FTAAP is significantly superior to that delivered by the CEPEA for New Zealand, marginally inferior for India (which is not included in the FTAAP), and significantly inferior for Australia. The interpretation of the result for Australia may be similar to that for Singapore, namely that the majority of the incremental welfare gains that might have been delivered by the FTAAP have already been delivered by Australia's FTA with the United States, which is included in the earlier scenarios. All other APEC members naturally record more favorable welfare outcomes from the FTAAP.

Thus, if economic welfare once again were the only criterion, it might be expected that several East Asian economies would gain substantially by moving beyond EAFTA or the CEPEA to the FTAAP, with New Zealand, the United States, and other APEC members in the Americas also benefiting significantly from the move to the FTAAP. A significant drop in economic welfare as a result of moving from EAFTA or CEPEA to the FTAAP is predicted only for Australia and Singapore, while only marginal though negative changes in welfare are predicted for Korea, Malaysia, and Thailand. India's economic welfare is also affected only slightly.

3.2. Effect on exports

This section considers the effects of the preferential trade configurations in the different scenarios on China's goods exports, and offers a preliminary analysis of the impact on the exports of China's partners. It is clear that the impact of at least some of the scenarios on trade flows within the region will be substantial, to an extent not immediately evident from the analysis of welfare effects.

---

[7] Note that of the bilateral FTAs with the United States that are already included in scenario 5 (the EAFTA scenario) and scenario 6 (the CEPEA scenario); the US–Singapore FTA is operational, the US–Korea FTA negotiations have concluded but the FTA has not yet been ratified, and negotiations for the US–Thailand and US–Malaysia FTAs have stalled.

Table 3 reports the sectoral changes in China's exports under each scenario, expressed in each case as the change from the baseline scenario. Table 4 presents the same changes in a different form expressed as the change under each scenario from the preceding scenario; thus, the figures for scenario 1 indicate the changes from baseline, the figures for scenario 2 indicate the changes from scenario 1, and so on. Table 5 reports changes under each scenario in China's exports to East Asian economies, the United States, Australia and New Zealand, and India. These partners account for the overwhelming bulk of the change in China's exports under each scenario.

It is clear from Table 4 that there are three developments or potential developments in the evolution of the regional trade architecture that have the largest impact or potential impact on China's exports. The introduction of the ASEAN–China FTA in scenario 2, the EAFTA or "ASEAN Plus Three FTA in scenario 5, and the FTAAP in scenario 8 are respectively associated with increases in China's total exports of $8.4 billion, $19 billion, and $17.4 billion (all values expressed in 2001 US dollars). These values represent respectively increases of 2.4%, 5.3%, and 4.9% over the level of China's 2001 exports. The introduction of FTAs with Australia and New Zealand in scenario 3 and the move to the CEPEA or "ASEAN Plus Six" FTA in scenario 6 are responsible for smaller increases in total exports of $1.5 billion and $1.2 billion, respectively.

There are interesting differences in the sectoral composition of the increased exports in each of the above scenarios. The increase in exports in scenario 2 is largely accounted for by exports to China's ASEAN partners in the ASEAN–China FTA, and is dominated by increases in exports of electronic equipment and to a lesser extent machinery and transport equipment other than motor vehicles. There are significant offsetting falls in exports to Korea and the United States that doubtlessly reflect the impact of the KORUS FTA, and there is also a significant drop in exports to Japan.

In scenario 3 the increase in exports is primarily to Australia and New Zealand, reflecting establishment of FTAs with both those countries, and the increased exports consist almost entirely of textiles, clothing, and leather products. There is a further significant fall in exports to Japan, which may reflect the impact of a Japan–Australia FTA, and a significant fall in exports also to the United States.

When the "ASEAN Plus One" FTAs with China, Japan, and Korea are replaced by the EAFTA in scenario 5, the resulting increase in exports is predictably dominated by increased exports to Japan and Korea, which in fact exceed the increase in China's total exports. Unsurprisingly, textiles, clothing and leather products, and electronic equipment account for a little over half of the increased exports under this scenario. It is perhaps a little more unexpected that agricultural products should account for the bulk of the remainder of the increase, with substantial increases in exports of

Table 3. Value of change in China's goods exports by sector (US$2001 millions)

Sector	Scenario								
	1	2	3	4	5	6	7	8	9
Agriculture and processed foods									
Other unprocessed primary products	3	−5	−5	2	3,686	3,695	3,824	3,165	3,381
Wheat and other grains	6	−288	−262	−261	1,314	1,333	1,398	1,262	1,302
Vegetables and fruit	32	106	84	91	787	802	943	626	668
Oil seeds	8	−21	−24	−23	88	65	112	237	225
Plant-based fibers	0	10	17	18	11	11	16	3	8
Other crops	15	173	1,361	136	17	15	17	−24	−15
Other animal products	14	31	29	33	−62	−60	−53	−63	−54
Wool	2	18	62	65	2	114	87	−50	−35
Cattle meat products	−1	−1	1	0	−15	−15	−15	−12	−12
Other meat products	−461	−410	−459	−454	−259	−278	−268	−763	−765
Vegetable oils	2	−4	−4	−3	−13	−12	−12	29	29
Dairy products	4	4	7	7	34	32	32	24	25
Processed rice	134	145	101	115	3,089	3,050	3,223	2,415	2,499
Sugar	0	33	31	28	32	31	27	32	28
Other foods and beverages	−49	192	145	152	861	790	727	679	586
Resource industries									
Forestry	0	0	0	0	3	3	4	−2	−1
Fisheries	1	19	19	19	78	74	80	69	72
Energy products	68	682	721	726	1,031	1,857	1,497	659	679
Minerals and nonferrous metals	99	380	510	545	515	1,035	1,259	871	1062
Manufacturing									
Textiles, clothing, and leather	260	678	2,138	1,532	8,438	7,549	5,759	23,804	21,842
Wood and paper products	136	203	254	255	−52	−139	−52	−235	−130
Chemicals, rubber, and plastics	179	951	1,057	1,087	956	2,159	1,729	1,513	1,437
Ferrous metals	−35	47	45	37	96	96	130	27	35
Fabricated metal products	40	203	267	248	103	74	74	508	520
Motor vehicles	−28	−15	−29	−53	185	168	165	66	38
Other transport equipment	15	888	891	892	862	842	863	1,338	1,425
Electronic equipment	417	4,133	3,959	4,097	7,656	7,528	7,487	8,275	8,525
Machinery and equipment	198	1,336	1,262	1,334	1,510	1,688	1,505	2,692	2,824
Other manufactures	453	409	379	453	−881	−1283	−1261	−406	−512
Total Merchandise	1,513	9,898	11,329	11,076	30,073	31,226	29,294	46,740	45,689
Services									
Trade services	235	175	152	192	−216	−329	−174	−899	−750
Total	1,748	10,072	11,481	11,268	29,858	30,897	29,120	45,841	44,939

Source: Authors' simulations.

Table 4. Value of incremental change in China's goods exports by sector (US$2001 millions)

Sector	Scenario								
	1	2	3	4	5	6	7	8	9
Agriculture and processed foods									
Other unprocessed primary products	3	−8	0	7	3,684	9	129	−659	216
Wheat and other grains	6	−294	26	1	1,575	19	65	−136	40
Vegetables and fruit	32	74	−22	7	696	15	141	−317	42
Oil seeds	8	−29	−3	1	110	−23	47	125	−11
Plant-based fibers	0	10	τ	1	−6	0	5	−12	5
Other crops	15	158	−42	4	−119	−2	2	−40	9
Other animal products	14	17	−1	4	−95	2	7	−10	9
Wool	2	16	45	2	−62	112	−28	−136	14
Cattle meat products	−1	0	1	0	−16	0	0	4	0
Other meat products	−461	51	−49	5	195	−19	10	−495	−2
Vegetable oils	2	−6	0	0	−10	1	0	41	0
Dairy products	4	0	3	0	27	−2	0	−8	0
Processed rice	134	12	−44	13	2,975	−39	173	−808	84
Sugar	0	32	−2	−2	4	−1	−5	6	−4
Other foods and beverages	−49	241	−47	7	709	−71	−63	−48	−92
Resource industries									
Forestry	0	−1	0	0	3	0	0	−6	2
Fisheries	1	18	0	0	59	−4	6	−11	3
Energy products	68	614	39	5	305	826	−360	−838	20
Minerals and nonferrous metals	99	281	130	35	−30	520	224	−387	191
Manufacturing									
Textiles, clothing, and leather	260	418	1,459	−606	6,906	−889	−1,790	18,044	−1,962
Wood and paper products	136	68	51	1	−307	−87	87	−183	105
Chemicals, rubber, and plastics	179	773	106	29	−131	1,203	−430	−216	−76
Ferrous metals	−35	81	−2	−8	59	0	34	−103	8
Fabricated metal products	40	162	64	−19	−144	−30	0	434	12
Motor vehicles	−28	14	−14	−25	238	−17	−3	−99	−28
Other transport equipment	15	872	3	1	−30	−20	21	475	87
Electronic equipment	417	3,716	−173	138	3,559	−128	−41	788	250
Machinery and equipment	198	1,137	−73	72	175	178	−183	1,187	133
Other manufactures	453	−44	−31	74	−1,334	−402	21	856	−106
Total Merchandise	1,513	8,384	1,431	−253	18,997	1,152	−1,931	17,446	−1,051
Services									
Trade services	235	−60	−23	40	−408	−113	155	−725	149
Total	1,748	8,324	1,409	−213	18,590	1,039	−1,777	16,721	−902

Source: Authors' simulations.

Table 5. Incremental change in value of China's exports to other APEC economies and India (US$2001 millions)

Region	Scenario								
	1	2	3	4	5	6	7	8	9
Australia	−151	−11	2,782	−131	−241	−111	16	−422	−50
New Zealand	1	−4	270	−8	−30	−7	−1	−11	−10
Hong Kong	1,375	−63	−90	35	−651	−184	24	544	−151
Japan	−635	−322	−497	−421	13,402	−254	217	−3,494	−24
Korea	−60	−383	−9	2	12,564	−228	−184	−793	−380
Chinese Taipei	5	−24	−28	13	−56	−35	7	1,090	−24
Indonesia	4	1,542	−11	−159	−94	−23	0	−101	−30
Malaysia	−72	2,038	−27	9	−208	−56	−19	−223	−60
Philippines	−57	753	−13	−3	−67	−22	−14	14	−37
Singapore	109	229	−35	13	−96	26	74	−346	100
Thailand	−388	2,980	75	11	99	−29	−266	−105	−254
Vietnam	−3	1,892	−10	−106	−87	−17	179	−387	140
USA	−727	−543	−503	166	−2,100	−1,108	178	20,063	−861
India	24	−3	15	4	−72	5,399	17	−5,546	5,165

Source: Authors' simulations.

"other unprocessed primary products," processed rice, wheat and grains, "other foods and beverages," and fruit and vegetables. The implication is that China would expect to substantially increase its export of agricultural products to Japan and Korea under the EAFTA, and it can be anticipated that this prospective effect would be of concern to the governments of those two countries. It may in fact be questionable whether all agricultural products would be included in the EAFTA or whether at least some agricultural products such as rice would be excluded. The results here indicate that the implications for China's exports to Japan and Korea would be substantial. A further substantial decline in China's exports to the United States is another feature of the change in China's exports under scenario 5.

The expansion from "ASEAN Plus Three" (EAFTA) to "ASEAN Plus Six" (CEPEA) in scenario 6 predictably results in a substantial increase in China's exports to India, but this increase is largely offset by falls in exports to other partners, especially the United States, so that the net increase in exports is much smaller. On a sectoral basis the largest increases in exports under this scenario are for chemicals rubber and plastics, energy products, and minerals and nonferrous metals, while exports of textiles, clothing, and leather products register a substantial decrease.

Finally, with the introduction of the FTAAP in scenario 8, exports to the United States, which fell in all but two of the preceding scenarios, register a substantial increase of over $20 billion, slightly more than the total increase in exports under this scenario. The increase in exports under this scenario consists overwhelmingly of textiles clothing and leather products, supplemented by a much smaller increase in exports of machinery and equipment. At the same time there is a significant fall in exports to Japan and Korea, which appears to be associated with a partial reversal of the increased exports of agricultural exports that occurred under scenario 5, and which can reasonably be interpreted as the result of increased competition from the United States, especially in the Japanese market.

A further question to be addressed is the extent to which the major increase in China's exports to its partners in the various scenarios as identified above is reciprocated by an increase in exports of the same partners to China. Table 6 provides relevant information on this question. The increase in China's exports to the ASEAN countries in scenario 2, reflecting the establishment of the ASEAN–China FTA, is matched by a much larger increase in exports of the same ASEAN countries to China. Similarly, the increase in China's exports to Japan and Korea under scenario 5, reflecting the establishment of EAFTA, is matched by a very much larger increase in exports of those two countries to China. The increase in Chinese Taipei's exports to China with its inclusion in the FTAAP under scenario 8 is a multiple of China's increased exports to Chinese Taipei under the same scenario. Thus, the increases in the exports to China of its trading partners in East Asia, resulting from major steps in the evolution of the regional trade architecture, are generally much

Table 6. Incremental change in value of exports to China by other APEC economies and India (US$2001 millions)

Region	Scenario								
	1	2	3	4	5	6	7	8	9
Australia	−51	−55	1,002	−11	45	−189	−4	507	−174
New Zealand	−12	−23	515	−9	−16	−54	19	−198	14
Hong Kong	5,171	−382	−19	−32	−1,717	71	−56	−576	12
Japan	−350	−2,085	400	−170	24,154	−144	334	−2,962	114
Korea	−538	−403	−13	57	14,548	−214	−431	−500	−604
Chinese Taipei	−359	−784	−44	−2	−2,143	88	19	8,365	124
Indonesia	−50	2,139	−39	−1	−517	−159	−174	−11	−297
Malaysia	−31	4,229	16	5	−1,537	−138	−96	−230	−239
Philippines	−10	708	−12	1	−234	3	−23	−119	−18
Singapore	−240	4,285	−32	5	−1,445	−77	−93	−259	−176
Thailand	−555	4,162	512	20	−661	3	−242	147	−273
Vietnam	−5	797	−9	−124	−63	−9	−95	40	−102
USA	−176	−1,396	−79	−9	−2,334	168	36	13,563	258
India	−29	−69	−14	0	−153	1,113	13	−1,114	1,115

Source: Authors' simulations.

larger than the corresponding increases in China's exports to the same trading partners.

The results for China's trading partners outside East Asia are rather different. While their inclusion in preferential trading arrangements with China does result in a substantial increase in their exports to China, the increase in China's exports in the reverse direction is invariably larger. Thus, the increase in the exports of Australia and New Zealand under scenario 3, in which they enter into FTAs with China, is only a little more than half the increase in China's exports to them. India's inclusion in the CEPEA results in increased Indian exports to China that are little more than 20% of China's increased exports to India under the same scenario. United States' exports to China under the FTAAP in scenario 8 increase substantially, but China's increased exports to the United States under the same scenario are almost 50% higher.

Finally, simulation results (not shown here) for exports to all markets of key economies and regions among China's trading partners show exceptionally large increases in the exports of China's major Northeast Asian neighbors, Japan and Korea, arising both under the bilateral FTAs and ASEAN Plus One FTAs in Scenarios 1–4 and under the move to EAFTA in Scenario 5. These increased exports are spread across a wide range of industrial products, and also, surprisingly, include substantial increases in exports of agricultural products and processed foods mainly by Korea. The largest increases for the ASEAN group also come under these same scenarios. In the bilaterals and ASEAN Plus One FTAs ASEAN's increased exports are spread across agriculture and processed foods, textile clothing and leather products, chemical and plastic products, electronic equipment, and machinery. In scenario 5 on the other hand the increases are heavily concentrated on textile clothing and leather products.

For the United States large increases in total exports are registered only under scenario 8, heavily concentrated on agricultural products and processed foods, with significant increases also for chemicals and plastics and for machinery. For India scenario 6 generates a substantial increase in exports, with the main increases coming in agricultural products and processed foods, the resource industries, textile clothing and leather products, chemicals and plastics, and machinery. These increases, however, are largely canceled out in the move from scenario 6 to scenario 8. Further details are available from the authors.

4. Conclusions

As noted at the outset of this chapter, the "trade architecture" that will emerge in the Asia-Pacific remains very uncertain. It is clear, however, that China will play a major role in regional trading developments in the area. There are six main patterns regarding the role of China that emerge from these simulations of steps and potential steps in the evolution of the Asia-Pacific region's preferential trading architecture.

First, in terms of welfare gains, the FTAAP yields a welfare outcome for China that is far superior than that offered by any other scenario. In the absence of the FTAAP, China's highest welfare gain derives from the scenario with the ASEAN–China FTA and FTAs with Australia and New Zealand in place, stopping short of the EAFTA or the CEPEA.

Second, for the majority of China's East Asian trading partners, the FTAAP offers welfare gains that are either superior to those from any other scenario simulated, or are only very marginally inferior to the best alternative. In the absence of the FTAAP on the other hand, most of China's East Asian partners derive the greatest welfare gain from either the EAFTA or the CEPEA, indicating some divergence of economic interest between China and its partners in the sequencing of preferential trade liberalization in the region.

Third, among the scenarios simulated the largest increases in Chinese exports occur when linkages with the economies of ASEAN and Korea are established, with large increases in exports to the ASEAN countries resulting from the establishment of the ASEAN–China FTA in particular, under a possible EAFTA, resulting in large increases in exports to Japan and Korea, and under FTAAP with a large increase in exports to the United States. Smaller increases in Chinese exports are registered to Australia and New Zealand arising from the establishment of FTAs with those two countries, and to India arising from the inclusion of that country in the potential CEPEA.

Fourth, there are substantial differences in the sectoral composition of China's increased exports under each of the scenarios identified above. In the case of linkages with the economies of ASEAN, increased exports of electronic equipment and machinery predominate. The increased exports to Japan and Korea under the EAFTA include a large component of agricultural products as well as textiles clothing and leather products, and electronic equipment. Increases in exports to Australia and new Zealand under those bilateral and to the United States under FTAAP are projected to consist overwhelmingly of textiles, clothing, and leather products.

Fifth, large increases in China's exports to particular partners under given scenarios are generally matched by substantial increases in the exports of the same partners to China. In the case of East Asian partners – the ASEAN countries and Japan and Korea – the partners' increased exports to China exceed China's increased exports in the reverse direction by a substantial margin. For partners outside China, however – Australia and New Zealand, India, and the United States – the increased exports of China are much larger than the increased exports of the partner. This could conceivably exacerbate existing tensions.

Sixth, the main economies and regional groups among China's partners register very substantial increases in global exports under some scenarios.

For Japan, Korea, and ASEAN these increases come primarily under the bilateral and ASEAN Plus One FTAs and under the potential EAFTA, although smaller increases are registered under other scenarios also. For the United States the increases occur almost exclusively under FTAAP. India registers substantial increases under ASEAN Plus Six, although these increases are largely canceled out in the move to an FTAAP.

Future work in this area might usefully examine the implication of several of the newer FTA developments as they impact on China, and as the details of the agreements emerge the simulation assumptions could be finessed relative to the broad approach used here.

References

Bergsten, C.F. (2007), Toward a Free Trade Area of the Asia-Pacific. Peterson Institute for International Economics Policy Brief PB07-2.

Chia, S.Y. (2007), Whither East Asian regionalism: an ASEAN perspective. *Asian Economic Papers* 6 (3), 1–36.

Dee, P., Hanslow, K., Phamduc, T. (2000), Measuring the cost of barriers to trade in services. Paper presented at the *11th Annual NBER East Asia Seminar on Economics*.

Dimaranan, B.V. (2006), *Global Trade, Assistance, and Production: The GTAP 6 Data Base*. Center for Global Trade Analysis, West Lafayette.

Gilbert, J., Wahl, T. (2002), Applied general equilibrium assessments of trade liberalization in China. *World Economy* 25 (5), 697–731.

Gilbert, J., Wahl, T. (2003), Labor market distortions and China's WTO accession package: an a applied general equilibrium assessment. *Journal of Comparative Economics* 31 (4), 774–794.

Hertel, T. (Ed.) (1997). *Global Trade Analysis: Modeling and Applications*. Cambridge University Press, Cambridge.

Hufbauer, G.C., Wong, Y. (2005), Prospects for regional free trade in Asia. Institute for International Economics Working Paper No. 05–12, Institute for International Economics, Washington.

Kawai, M. (2005), East Asian economic regionalism: progress and challenges. *Journal of Asian Economics* 16 (1), 29–55.

Kawai, M., Wignaraja, G. (2008), EAFTA or CEPEA: which way forward? *ASEAN Economic Bulletin* 25 (2), 113–139.

Lloyd, P.J., MacLaren, D. (2004), Gains and losses from regional trading agreements: a survey. *Economic Record* 80 (251), 445–497.

Menon, J. (2009), Dealing with the proliferation of bilateral free trade agreements. *World Economy* 32 (10), 1381–1407.

Robinson, S., Thierfelder, K. (2002), Trade liberalisation and regional integration: the search for large numbers. *Australian Journal of Agricultural and Resource Economics* 46 (4), 585–604.

Scollay, R. (2004), Preliminary assessment of the proposal for a free trade area of the Asia-Pacific (FTAAP). Issues Paper for the APEC Business Advisory Council (ABAC).

Scollay, R. (2007), Prospects for linking preferential trade agreements in the Asia-Pacific region. In: Morrison, C., Pedrosa, E. (Eds.), *An APEC Trade Agenda? The Political Economy of a Free Trade Area of the Asia-Pacific*. Institute of Southeast Asian Studies, Singapore.

Scollay, R., Gilbert, J. (2000), Measuring the gains from APEC trade liberalisation: an overview of CGE assessments. *World Economy* 23 (2), 175–193.

Wang, Z., Schuh, E.G. (2002), The emergence of a greater China and its impact on world trade: a computable general equilibrium analysis. *Journal of Comparative Economics* 30 (3), 531–566.

CHAPTER 13

Ex Ante *Assessment of the Welfare Impacts of Trade Reforms with Numerical Models*☆

Joseph F. Francois[a] and Will Martin[b]

[a]*Department of Economics, Johannes Kepler University Linz, Linz, Austria*
E-mail address: joseph.francois@jku.at
[b]*Agriculture and Rural Development, Development Research Group, World Bank, Washington, DC, USA*
E-mail address: wmartin1@worldbank.org

Abstract
Most current modeling approaches identify very small gains from trade reform. In this chapter, we examine recent developments in the literature to assess whether standard modeling approaches are mis-specifying, understating, or overstating the gains from trade reform. Key areas where the impacts of trade barrier reduction appear to be understated include the measurement of barriers; the aggregation of these barriers; process productivity gains, particularly those resulting from reallocation of resources between firms; product quality improvements and expansion of product variety; factor supply; and investment of gains from trade.

Keywords: Trade policy modeling, CGE models, trade and growth

JEL codes: F17, F12, F4

1. Introduction

Trade policy reform is controversial, and information on the effects of trade reform is in great demand as a basis for policy formation. While supporters of trade liberalization generally believe that this will improve efficiency and put the economy on a path to higher growth, many others hold a less optimistic view. One of the dirty little secrets of trade policy

---

☆The expressed herein are strictly those of the authors, and are not meant to represent the views or opinions of the World Bank or any other institution with which the authors may be affiliated. Thanks are due to Alan Winters and Bernard Hoekman for helpful comments and suggestions.

Frontiers of Economics and Globalization
Volume 7 ISSN: 1574-8715
DOI: 10.1108/S1574-8715(2010)0000007016

analysis is that conventional *ex ante* measurements of welfare gains and losses from trade policy changes are consistently extremely small. However, as emphasized by Lindert and Williamson (2002) the historical experience suggests that trade actually plays a more significant role than computational models would indicate. Developing countries that have grown rapidly have also expanded their trade rapidly. Indeed, there have been no developing countries in the post–World War II era that have successfully grown without increasing their integration with the world economy. The main purpose of this chapter is to see how trade policy analysts might provide better guidance on the welfare impacts of reform.

This chapter is motivated by the perception of a broad disconnect between widely held expectations with regard to trade policy, and the estimates provided in most widely used global computational models. For example, on the basis of the measurement of comparative advantage–based efficiency gains, early studies of the impact of trade policy on economic performance in industrial countries tended to be very small. In this literature, the deadweight loss (essentially the lost income associated with producing goods that could have been obtained at lower cost through imports and reducing consumption through high prices) from trade restrictions or the potential static gain from eliminating such restrictions is estimated using information about the sensitivity of demand and supply in individual markets to changes in the price of a good. In an early study, Magee (1972) estimated that the deadweight cost of tariffs on U.S. imports of goods that were close substitutes for domestic products amounted to only 0.01% of GDP in the short run, and to 0.03% of GDP in the long run. Various other studies using similar methodologies have reported estimates in the same range. This range of results echoes the very small estimated deadweight costs of monopoly (Harberger, 1954).

The range of results from such exercises, when set next to the historical evidence, raises a fundamental problem with computational methods. Computational results seem to be inconsistent with expectations based on historical experience.[1] We expect more. One possible response to this problem might be to reduce the ambition of modeling away from estimating dollar values for economic welfare changes, and to concentrate instead on a more narrow set of objectives. One such goal might be to seek insights into the relative importance of different policy instruments – such as those sought by Anderson *et al.* (2006) in assessing the potential importance of agricultural market access relative to subsidies.

[1] There is an informal rule known as "Markusen's law," based on James Markusen's observation that with early multisector trade models (e.g., those used during the NAFTA negotiations in the 1990s), whatever the question was, the answer seemed to be 0.5% of GDP. At the same time, Markusen's law points to estimates an order of magnitude above those from even earlier studies, like Magee (1972).

However, even such a narrowing of focus need not overcome the problem. If the welfare criterion being used for the analysis is not consistently related to the true value of welfare changes, then the implied relative importance of the different measures may also be inappropriate.

The tool of choice for *ex ante* evaluation of trade reforms is generally the computable general equilibrium (CGE) model. Baldwin and Venables (1995) categorized these models into three groups: (i) first-generation models based on constant returns to scale (CRTS), perfect competition, and a fixed number of goods; (ii) second-generation models with increasing returns in at least some sectors; imperfect competition; and an endogenous number of product varieties; and (iii) third-generation models with investment and growth effects. A fourth generation of models incorporating heterogeneity of firm productivity levels along the lines of Melitz (2003) may now be starting as well. First-generation models are still widely used to analyze questions such as the implications of trade reform, since second- and third-generation models are widely regarded as more conjectural in their theoretical and empirical underpinnings, and less robust in practical simulation.

The measures of welfare gains from trade reform obtained from first-generation CGE models focus on static comparative advantage. As Rodrik (2006, p. 23) and Rutherford and Tarr (2002), have pointed out, this may be much less important than the implications of policy changes for dynamic gains in productivity – leading some to conclude that measures of static welfare gains can essentially be ignored. For the relative importance of static and dynamic effects to be examined, however, we need to ensure that the models used contain relevant potential linkages between trade reform (and other policy reforms) and gains in productivity. This is more difficult in the case of dynamic productivity gains, since there is no, as yet, agreement on the theoretical relationships involved, let alone the empirical approach to implementation. In this chapter, we consider how static and dynamic effects might, in principle, be incorporated in analytical tools used for *ex ante* policy evaluation.

Certainly, the role of trade in successful developing countries appears to have changed radically in recent decades. The traditional pattern in which developing countries supply primary commodities in return for manufactures has given way to one in which the overall exports of developing countries are dominated by manufactured exports – many of which involve relatively advanced technologies (Hertel *et al.*, 2002; World Bank, 2004). The recent emergence of global production sharing as an important mode of production, with extensive trade in parts and components (Ng and Yeats, 1999), strong links to foreign direct investment, and just-in-time inventory management, is a radically deeper form of integration than the traditional model of commodity exporting based on domestic inputs. In both manufactures and primary commodities, successful export growth seems to involve rapid expansion in the number of products produced, the export markets supplied, and in the quality of exported products (Hummels and Klenow, 2005) – all changes that offset the terms of trade concerns that underlay much of the earlier export pessimism. Adding complexity to the mix is the aggressive move of some developing countries into service exports. In the case of India, we have even seen the export of a "scarce" factor, skilled labor, through the export of software services.

However, it is also clear from the historical evidence that trade reform alone is not a panacea. Virtually all developing countries have liberalized their trade regimes enormously since the 1980s. Some have had extraordinary success in expanding their trade and in stimulating economic growth. But some others – particularly in Africa – have had only limited success (Independent Evaluation Group, 2006). A key question is what distinguishes the countries that have succeeded in using trade to promote development from those that have not had the same success. It is widely agreed that trade reform should be part of a broader package of reforms, but what are the other ingredients of this package? Is it true, in the words of Adam Smith, that "Little else is requisite to carry a state to the highest degree of opulence from the lowest barbarism but peace, easy taxes, and a tolerable administration of justice"? Or is it vital to provide missing public goods as recommended by Williamson (2000) of Washington Consensus fame? Should governments undertake growth diagnostics to identify the binding constraints as suggested by Hausmann *et al.* (2004)? Or is a more activist industrial policy to pick winners required, as advocated by Wade (2004)? Or are some economies too small and remote to succeed without international assistance (Venables, 2004; Winters and Martins, 2004)? Finally, can we provide any meaningful policy guidance by use of computational models?

The goals of this chapter are to explain the measures of the potential welfare impacts of trade reform currently provided by academia, public-sector research entities, certain NGOs, and international organizations to assess their weaknesses and limitations; and to suggest approaches by which these measures might be improved. We also try to place the exercise in the context of recent evidence on how trade may affect incomes. We focus on measures for changes in real incomes at a regional or global level. On occasion, we will also want to evaluate trade reforms taking into account other consequences of reform, including distributional impacts, government revenue impacts, and impacts on outcomes such as employment, output, and export levels for particular sectors. However, we focus on aggregate real income measures, partly to keep this survey manageable, and partly because overall real income gains are widely accepted as a necessary condition for approving a policy reform. Only reforms that increase aggregate real income meet the fundamental economic criterion that the gainers could potentially compensate the losers from the reform, and hence warrant further evaluation against other criteria.

2. *Does trade really matter?*

Before turning to how we can model correctly the interactions between trade policies and income, it makes sense to revisit the evidence on whether we should really even be doing this at all and, if so, how we might specify the linkages between trade policy and economic welfare. We try to summarize our own view of the state of play in the relevant econometric literature in this section, with the goal of using insights from this literature to guide our subsequent discussion and comparison of what we actually do model relative to what we ideally should model.

Standard theories of comparative advantage under CRTS (see, for example, Jones and Neary, 1984), taken alone, would be consistent with potentially huge costs resulting from autarchy. However, empirical investigation of one of the few observed cases of transition from something close to autarchy to something close to free trade – Japan's nineteenth century move to openness – found a welfare gain of around 9% of GDP (Bernhofen and Brown, 2005). This suggests that, even in extreme cases of reform, the static welfare gains may be smaller than would be suggested by plausible textbook examples of differences in technology or factor endowments.

In a retrospective piece written over a quarter-century ago, Johnson (1977) reviewed the post–World War II experience with economic development theory and practice and the evolution of economic thought about the relationship between world trade and development policy. Johnson's tone was at once both pessimistic and critical. By the late 1950s the economics profession, presaging the current antiglobalization movement, had managed to convince itself that lack of development was somehow a consequence of the world trading system and not of domestic policy, and that successful development therefore required careful isolation from the economic power of the industrial North. There were notable exceptions, in particular Haberler (1950) and Viner (1952). However, the first post–World War II steps toward development policy were in the direction of import substitution, in conjunction with a belief – expressed by a number of prominent economists – in the need to actively plan and manage the dynamic mechanisms required to achieve development. From where Johnson stood, he saw intellectual cycles moving between rejection and embrace of the world trading system, with a strong bias toward the former. In looking toward the future, Johnson saw development economists placing renewed emphasis on commodity price stabilization and monopoly trading schemes along the lines of OPEC. He even characterized a "belief in the righteousness of the use of monopoly power by the poor against the rich" as an intellectual constant that defines theorizing in development economics.

The next paradigm shift, the next swing in Johnson's intellectual cycles, followed the emergence of outward-oriented policies as a consensus growth prescription in the 1980s. This consensus was backed by cross-country studies of openness and growth. A pioneering attempt to classify trade regimes was conducted in an NBER study directed by Bhagwati and Krueger (Bhagwati, 1978; Krueger, 1978). The consensus from this work was that the degree of openness of the trade regime was positively correlated with not only the level of income, but also the rate of export growth, which was in turn positively correlated with real GDP growth – a link not strongly supported by conventional trade theory. A second large-scale attempt to classify countries by trade orientation was conducted by the World Bank (Choksi *et al.*, 1989), which reached the same broad conclusions. Related to this literature was parallel work pointing to the potentially high costs of rent seeking. Indeed, though empirical estimates of the static welfare costs of tariff regimes have tended to be relatively small, Krueger (1974) and Bhagwati (1982) pointed to potentially very large costs associated with actions designed to seek economic rents – either legally, as in the case of quota allocation mechanisms, or illegally as in cases where officials are bribed. These costs were simply outside the analytical box of computational estimates. They were the first evidence that other mechanisms, apart from allocative efficiency, were driving the consensus view that emerged from the World Bank's classification efforts.

What followed was a flood of cross-country empirical studies linking trade to aggregate growth rates, and broadly supporting this view. The studies by Feder (1983), Dollar (1992), and Sachs and Warner (1995) were particularly influential within this body of work, which found significant, positive effects of trade openness on output, or the growth of output. This literature focused on issues such as measuring the stance of trade policy and its impact on openness, and paid relatively little attention to the firm-level determinants of export or output growth.

The consensus view was challenged in important papers by Edwards (1993) and Rodriguez and Rodrik (2001). The criticisms went to the foundations of the immediately prior body of research, and were directed at the conclusions one can safely draw from cross-country studies. Rodriguez and Rodrik argued that we should not be comforted, but rather worried, by the apparent ability of dozens of highly disparate measures to capture the "same" relationship between openness and growth. Edwards argued that the basic approach to cross-country studies abstracts away from important factors better identified through studies of historical episodes. On the basis of such longer-term historical experience, both the Edwards and the Rodriguez and Rodrik papers concluded that the role of trade may have been overblown. However, the main result has not been a paradigm shift, but rather more careful econometrics. More recent cross-country analyses by Frankel and Romer (1999), Frankel and Rose (2002) and Noguer and Siscart (2005) have addressed these criticisms, using new specifications and statistical tests in an attempt to provide more firmly based estimates of any empirical relationship at the aggregate level.

The more recent body of work on trade growth and economic growth has internalized earlier criticisms, and emphasis is on the role of institutions and the record of experience within individual countries. Dollar and Kraay (2003) find that institutional quality is highly correlated with trade itself. They therefore focus on decadal changes in growth instrumented on changes in trade and institutions, and interpret their results as meaning that institutions and trade both matter in the long run, while trade growth offers short-term advantages over institutional improvements for fostering growth. In another paper, Dollar and Kraay (2004) examine specific episodes of liberalization, concluding that expansion of trade translates into rising incomes and falling poverty rates. Wacziarg and Welch (2003) also focus on liberalization episodes, and conclude that trade growth is linked robustly to growth and investment.

Greenaway *et al.* (2002) address a different criticism of Edwards and Rodriguez and Rodrik, linked to fundamental problems with the openness indicators used in the cross-country literature. They work with a dynamic panel and three openness indicators, concluding that the trade openness relationship is robust to the earlier criticisms. Finally, while Rodrik *et al.* (2004) do not find a direct impact of trade on incomes, they do find a more complex relationship between institutions, integration, and growth. Institutions can promote integration, while integration also has a (positive) impact on institutional quality. They find institutions important for incomes, suggesting that trade can have an indirect effect on incomes.

In our view, the consensus emerging (again) is that trade does matter, but that it is linked to the context in which it is placed. Institutions matter, as does infrastructure. Hence, the development agencies again have focused on facilitation aspects of development assistance, and emphasis is again being placed on institution building. At the World Bank, for example, Freund and Bolaky (2004) stress the importance of labor and business regulation in the trade-growth mechanism, while Chang *et al.* (2005) offer panel evidence that the broad domestic mix of policy, institutions, and infrastructure plays an important role in determining the impact of trade. Both of these studies confirm the belief that trade openness is a necessary, but not sufficient, condition for improving economic performance. The important subtext is that without reforms to other policies, such as labor market policies, trade reform may not yield the hoped-for benefits in terms of economic growth.

Recent research at the firm level has also provided important insights into the links between trade reform and growth. Firm-level studies have found that there is considerable heterogeneity in the productivity levels of different firms. A key focus of recent work has been on the potential implications of this heterogeneity for productivity growth. Aghion and Howitt (2005) emphasize the importance of Schumpeterian creative destruction for overall productivity growth. Bartelsman *et al.* (2005) show that increases in productivity are largely associated with within-firm productivity gains, but that exit of less-productive firms accounted for perhaps a quarter of the total productivity gains in a large sample of countries, with more rapid growth of more productive firms also accounting for substantial shares of overall productivity growth. Tybout (2003) finds strong evidence that trade liberalization lowers firms' markups over marginal cost, suggesting the possibility of productivity gains from firm rationalization. Another robust finding in the firm-level literature has been that exporting firms are more productive than nonexporting firms. However, the reason for these effects remains a source of controversy. Melitz (2003) offers a variety model modified to include heterogeneous firms. Baldwin (2005) shows that this model generates a number of testable hypotheses, including a range of results consistent with the empirical evidence on firm efficiency and export performance.

Yet another important element of diversity concerns the products that countries export. As noted by Hausmann and Rodrik (2003), there is a great deal of uncertainty about the specific products in which countries will have a comparative advantage and countries have to undertake a process of self-discovery that results in their exporting only a relatively small number of commodities. Dimaranan *et al.* (2006) find, for instance, that the top-25 exports of the two labor-abundant giants of Asia – India and China – contain only one product in common, and that is refined petroleum. This process of self-discovery would surely be choked off in closed economies by declining prices for the goods in which countries are able to develop a strong comparative advantage. How far would domestic prices need to fall to absorb the nonindustrial diamonds and jewelry that made up close to 20% of India's exports in 2004, or the computers, cell phones, and their parts that made up almost 30% of China's?

If trade matters, what can we then say about the mechanisms at play? Importantly for the present exercise, can we model (at least some of) these mechanisms? From the recent round of episode studies, trade liberalization does appear to lead to accelerated growth, or at least a medium-term growth dividend (Winters, 2004) in trade volumes and incomes when domestic institutions are sufficiently accommodating. However, the process is not simple. It is a function of institutional capacity and physical infrastructure. In addition, even when institutions and infrastructure are in place, the mechanics that then come into play are not well understood. Easterly and Levine (2001) argue that the evidence on income growth points to a world without diminishing returns, CRTS, or even a critical role for factor accumulation where total factor productivity (TFP) is critically important. However, empirical work in general does not distinguish well between different theoretical concepts of TFP, and work is needed to both quantify and model trade linkages to TFP.

It may be highly conjectural to summarize the mechanisms that matter, or even to rank them fully, without awaiting further econometric work.

However, we need to make some assessment, however tentative, if we are to provide any guidance for further work. From the literature on trade and growth, it appears that trade works not only through efficiency effects and investment, but also through TFP growth mechanisms in a world of scale economies, high (and increasing) degrees of factor mobility, and imperfect competition. It also works through channels (such as interactions with institutional development) that we cannot really expect to include in "real time" *ex ante* computational models. What we do draw from the trade-income econometric literature is a sense of the importance of exploring not only basic allocative efficiency mechanisms, but also effects related to economy-wide and firm-level investment, firm dynamics, international scale effects, and imperfect competition. Building on recent evidence on the role of infrastructure and institutions, computational assessment of trade facilitation measures may also provide the way to better capturing the qualitative (institutional) effects flagged in some of the econometric literature.

One surprising feature of the econometric literature on trade, incomes, and growth is that it has focused almost exclusively on the links between trade, inputs, productivity, and the volume of output – as proxied by GDP at constant prices.[2] Trade theory points to other possible linkages between trade reform and real income growth. In standard trade theory, for example, real income can rise as a result of trade reform even if the volume of output is fixed. While the resulting comparative statics income measures are frequently small, very large and sustained changes in real incomes without changes in the volume of output could arise from changes in the quality of goods or the variety of these goods available to consumers. The framework for measuring welfare changes used in this chapter must be broad enough to take these features into account.

3. *What should we measure?*

Drawing on the literature review in the previous section, we can identify five potential channels through which trade policy reform might influence economic welfare. These are

1. allocative efficiency changes;
2. process productivity changes;
3. terms-of-trade effects;
4. product variety and quality effects; and
5. investment effects.

---

[2] In the neighborhood of the initial prices, changes in GDP at constant prices can be taken as representing changes in a Divisia index of the quantity of output.

Traditional trade theory and first-generation CGE models focus on allocative efficiency and the terms-of-trade as determining the impact of trade reform on real income. In single-country trade-theoretic models, the volume of production is determined by factor endowments and is essentially fixed,[3] and the welfare effects of trade policy reform are measured only using the implications of reform for the attainable level of consumption possibilities. By contrast, the literature on the growth effects of trade (e.g., Frankel and Romer, 1999; Rodriguez and Rodrik, 2001) typically focuses solely on the effects of reform on the position of the production possibility frontier (PPF), including, in some cases, when investment effects shift the PPF. CGE models typically include the effects of changes in allocative efficiency and terms-of-trade effects, and sometimes include other elements, including product variety and quality, investment, and process productivity.

The sharp distinction between approaches focused on movements in the process productivity and those focused on allocative efficiency is highlighted in the two-good case presented in Figure 1. In the absence of trade distortions, the allocation of productive resources between the exportable good *X* and the importable, *M*, along the PPF *QQ* at point *a* is determined by the relative prices of the two goods on world markets, represented by the slope of the terms-of-trade line, *ww*. Consumption of the two goods is represented by point *b*, where the slope of the community

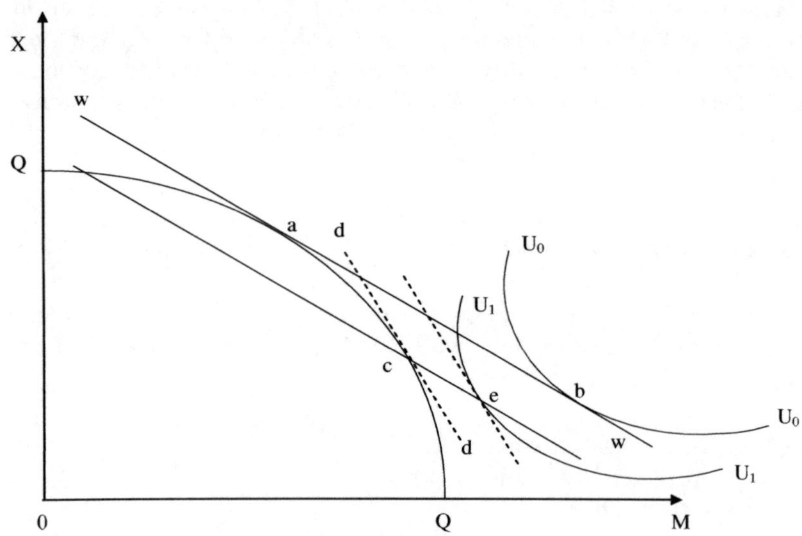

Fig. 1. ***Income gains from trade policy reform: a trade-theoretic view.***

[3] Except to the extent that it is influenced by distortions in input markets.

indifference curve, U_0U_0 is equal to the terms-of-trade line. When a tariff on good M is introduced, the price of good M rises, and is represented by the dashed line. At these prices, the production point is c and the consumption point is given by e. Approaches to evaluating the welfare effects of trade distortions based on allocative efficiency[4] measure the move inwards from U_0U_0 to U_1U_1.

Changes in productivity resulting from improvements in process efficiency can be incorporated in Figure 1 as movements in the PPF, as can effects of trade-reform-induced investment. Changes in product quality and variety that affect external demand can be represented by an outward shift in the PPF measured in effective units as perceived by the user. Changes in productivity that affect the valuation placed on goods – whether produced domestically or externally – may require adjustments in both the PPF and the external price ratio.

Macroeconomic analyses of trade and growth generally use GDP at constant prices as their indicator of output. This can be seen as a multioutput measure of shifts in the PPF. Formally, it can be thought of as a distance-function measure translating differing rates of output growth in different sectors into a single measure of the consequent shift in the PPF. It does not take into account any of the changes in allocative efficiency that are at the heart of the traditional trade-theoretic approach to measuring the welfare effects of reform. Nor does it capture any of the three other effects listed above – terms-of-trade-effects, product quality and variety effects, or induced investment effects.

3.1. Integrating the different sources of welfare gains

The balance-of-trade function approach (Lloyd and Schweinberger, 1988; Anderson and Neary, 1992) allows us to capture not just allocative efficiency and process efficiency, but all five of the links between trade reform and welfare identified above. The balance-of-trade function for a single, representative household is defined as

$$\begin{aligned} B &= e(\boldsymbol{p}, u) - r(\boldsymbol{p}, \boldsymbol{v}) - \boldsymbol{m}'(\boldsymbol{p})(\boldsymbol{p} - \boldsymbol{p}^*) - f \\ &= e(\boldsymbol{p}, u) - r(\boldsymbol{p}, \boldsymbol{v}) - \boldsymbol{m}'\tau \end{aligned} \tag{1}$$

where $\boldsymbol{p}$ is a vector of domestic prices;[5] $\boldsymbol{v}$ is a vector of resource endowments (broadly defined to include technology); $r(\boldsymbol{p},\boldsymbol{v})$ is the net revenue generated from production in the economy, $\boldsymbol{m} = (e_p - r_p)$ is a vector of net

[4] In applied models, changes in tariffs on intermediate goods influence the position of the production possibility frontier, but the highest protection, and the highest costs, are typically associated with protection to final goods.

[5] Which may need to be *effective* prices (Dixon *et al.*, 1982) to take into account the benefits of improvements in product quality or the available range of varieties.

imports; $\boldsymbol{p}^*$ is a vector of world prices; $\tau = (\boldsymbol{p}-\boldsymbol{p}^*)$ is a vector of tariff rates; and f is an exogenous financial inflow from the rest of the world. If we normalize world prices to 1, then $\tau = (\boldsymbol{p}-\boldsymbol{p}^*)$ is a proportional tariff rate. If B were held constant, then Equation (1) would be the income–expenditure condition for a behavioral model, allowing utility to be endogenously determined. If u is held constant in the expenditure function, and/or in $\boldsymbol{m}(\boldsymbol{p},\boldsymbol{v},u)$, then changes in B associated with changes in $\boldsymbol{p}$, $\boldsymbol{v}$, or $\boldsymbol{p}^*$ can be used to provide money measures of the welfare impacts of these changes.

As will be explained below, the welfare effects of changes in protection rates in a small economy can be estimated using the balance-of-trade function by comparing changes in the costs of consumer expenditure with changes in producer and government revenues. The balance-of-trade approach may also be used to measure the effects of changes in process efficiency that raise the value of output at a given level of inputs, $\boldsymbol{v}$, through the resulting changes in $r(\boldsymbol{p},\boldsymbol{v})$. The effects of changes in the terms of trade are captured by changes in $\boldsymbol{p}^*$, which again change the costs to consumers, the returns to producers, and tariff revenue changes resulting from changes in trade volumes (Martin, 1997). The effects of changes in the number of varieties or in the quality of goods can be measured using their impacts on the effective prices appearing in Equation (1). Finally, factor accumulation changes the value of $\boldsymbol{v}$ and hence can be captured using the balance-of-trade approach. The balance-of-trade approach also provides a potentially useful decomposition of a welfare change into its impact on consumer expenditure needs, producer revenues, and government tax revenues.

In the absence of distortions, two equivalent approaches may be used to measure the welfare effects of policy changes – a money metric and a compensation measure. Without distortions, there is a well-known equivalence between money-metric and compensation measures for both the equivalent variation and the compensating variation measures of welfare change. The compensation form of the equivalent variation[6] measure $\Delta B_e = e(\boldsymbol{p}^1,u^1)-e(\boldsymbol{p}^0,u^1)$ is equal to the money-metric measure of equivalent variation defined by observing the change in utility in a model and transforming the result into money terms using the expenditure function, $MM_e = e(\boldsymbol{p}^0,u^1)-e(\boldsymbol{p}^0,u^0)$ (see, e.g., Varian, 1984). The same two broad approaches to the measurement of welfare change are available in the presence of distortions but, unfortunately, they yield different results, and sometimes substantially different results (see Anderson and Martin, 1998, in press).

---

[6] For the compensating variation measures, the corresponding equivalence is $e(\boldsymbol{p}^1,u^0)-e(\boldsymbol{p}^0,u^0) = e(\boldsymbol{p}^1,u^1)-e(\boldsymbol{p}^1,u^0)$.

If we hold the level of utility constant in both the expenditure function and the import demand function, we obtain compensation measures of changes in welfare. These welfare measures focus on the transfer from outside the economy (the net transfer at world prices) required to hold utility constant at the level achieved after the reform (see Lloyd and Schweinberger, 1988; Anderson and Neary, 1992). For a change in trade policies that changes domestic prices from an initial vector $\boldsymbol{p}^0$ to a final level $\boldsymbol{p}^1$, while holding world prices and all other variables constant, a compensation-based equivalent variation measure of welfare change, ΔB_e, is given by Equation (2):

$$\Delta B_e = B(\boldsymbol{p}^1, u^1) - B(\boldsymbol{p}^0, u^1) \tag{2}$$

For a given policy-induced change in domestic prices $\boldsymbol{p}$, ΔB_e measures the changes in expenditure required to maintain a level of utility, given changes in revenues from production, plus the change in tariff revenues with utility held constant. An alternative measure, more in the spirit of compensating variation,[7] can be derived holding u constant at u^0. Applied in the context of multimarket models that contain all relevant distortions, these measures can provide definitive estimates of both the sign and the magnitude of the real income effects even in the second-best case where the merits of the reform are ambiguous from economic theory.

Compensation measures based on the balance-of-trade formulation are consistent with simpler, diagrammatic approaches to measuring the welfare impacts of trade reform. If u is held constant in both $e(\boldsymbol{p},u)$ and $\boldsymbol{m}(\boldsymbol{p},u,\boldsymbol{v})$, then a second-order Taylor series expansion about the initial price level – for a given international price, $\boldsymbol{p}^*$ – provides a diagrammatic interpretation of the potential benefit from tariff reductions (Martin, 1997). For complete abolition of a single tariff, in the absence of any other distortions, the benefit is given by the familiar shaded area in Figure 2 that depends on the size of the price reduction associated with moving to free trade, and the slope of the import demand curve. An advantage of the balance-of-trade function approach is that it is able to take into account the effects of multiple changes in tariff rates – something that is very common under reforms – without the intractable complexities that arise when attempting to use diagrammatic approaches.

The widely used money-metric measure is defined as the income transfer equivalent, at initial prices, to the policy change under consideration (Just *et al.*, 1982, p. 85). Following solution of an appropriately specified general equilibrium model, the money-metric equivalent variation for a policy change may be measured as

$$MM_e = [e(\boldsymbol{p}^0, u^1) - e(\boldsymbol{p}^0, u^0)] \tag{3}$$

[7] For small policy changes, there is essentially no difference between compensating and equivalent variation measures.

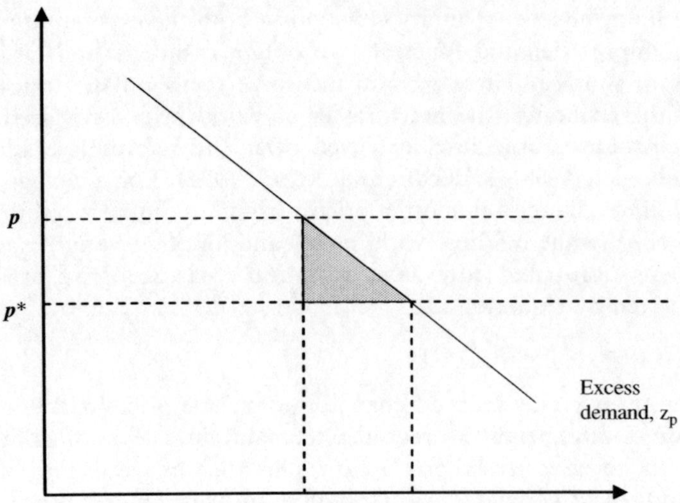

Fig. 2. Compensation measures of the benefit of removing a tariff.

where $e(\boldsymbol{p},u)$ is the expenditure needed for the representative consumer to achieve the specified level of utility, u, at prices, $\boldsymbol{p}$. A compensating-variation-type measure can be obtained by holding prices at their final, rather than their initial, level.

The money-metric measure of equivalent variation is almost invariably used in trade-oriented CGE models (Hertel, 1997) and in some public-finance studies such as Ballard and Fullerton (1992) and Dahlby (1998). It differs from the compensation measures by allowing the level of utility in the $\boldsymbol{m}$ function to vary from the initial to the final situation. The relationship between the compensation measure and the money-metric measure is given by the following derivation that takes into account the fact that $\Delta B(\boldsymbol{p}^i,u^i) = 0$ because B serves as an income-expenditure condition within the behavioral model:

$$\begin{aligned}\Delta B_e &= [B(\boldsymbol{p}^1,u^1) - B(\boldsymbol{p}^0,u^1)] = -B(\boldsymbol{p}^0,u^1)\\ &= [-e(\boldsymbol{p}^0,u^1) + r(\boldsymbol{p}^0,\boldsymbol{v}) + \boldsymbol{m}(\boldsymbol{p}^0,u^1)'(\boldsymbol{p}^0 - \boldsymbol{p}^*)]\\ &= [e(\boldsymbol{p}^0,u^1) - e(\boldsymbol{p}^0,u^0)] + [\boldsymbol{m}(\boldsymbol{p}^0,u^1) - \boldsymbol{m}(\boldsymbol{p}^0,u^0)]'(\boldsymbol{p}^0 - \boldsymbol{p}^*)\end{aligned} \tag{4}$$

or

$$MM_e = -\Delta B_e + [\boldsymbol{m}(\boldsymbol{p}^0,u^1) - \boldsymbol{m}(\boldsymbol{p}^0,u^0)]'(\boldsymbol{p}^0 - \boldsymbol{p}^*) \tag{5}$$

Recalling that MM_e is a money measure of welfare change equivalent that may be written $e_u du$, where e_u is the derivative of the expenditure function with respect to utility, and that the income effects of a small change in income can be written $\chi_I = e_{pu}/e_u$ allows us to rewrite

(5) for small changes[8] as $\Delta B = -(1-\chi_I(\boldsymbol{p}-\boldsymbol{p}^*)) \cdot MM$ or $MM = -[1/(1-\chi_I(\boldsymbol{p}-\boldsymbol{p}^*))] \cdot \Delta B$, where $[1/(1-\chi_I(\boldsymbol{p}-\boldsymbol{p}^*))]$ is a coefficient sometimes known as the foreign exchange multiplier (see Anderson and Neary, 1992), which depends on the interaction between that country's own income effects and tax/tariff distortions.

The intuition behind the foreign exchange multiplier is related to the well-known transfer problem. If a country receives a transfer from abroad that causes members of its society to spend income on taxed goods, or to reduce their supply of taxed factors such as labor, then the welfare effect of the transfer will differ from the amount of the original transfer. If, for instance, a transfer from abroad to the private sector causes citizens to increase their demand for leisure and hence reduce their supply of taxed labor, revenues will fall, and the government must raise tax rates to maintain fiscal balance, reducing economic efficiency and the welfare benefit of the original transfer.[9]

The compensation measure ΔB_e has the highly desirable feature of being comparable across countries. It is the amount paid by an external agency (perhaps such as the World Bank) that would be equivalent in welfare terms to the reform under consideration – if a transfer of $100 is required for country one and $120 for country two, then the two transfers can be added to obtain a total compensation of $220. The money-metric measures do not have this desirable feature. They differ from the compensation measure by a coefficient that depends on the specific interaction between income effects and tax rates in each individual country. The money-metric measures almost invariably used to measure welfare changes in *ex ante* evaluations of welfare change therefore cannot be added across countries to create, for instance, a measure of the global welfare gains or losses from a reform.

One potentially useful adjustment to measures of ΔB_e would be for differences in the purchasing power of income across economies. Because of Balassa–Samuelson effects and other sources of real price changes associated with development, the price of nontraded goods tends to be higher in higher-income countries than in poorer countries, causing incomes measured at market exchange rates to understate the purchasing power of incomes in poorer countries. The International Comparisons Project adjusts for this difference with the goal of calculating real incomes on a comparable basis in terms of their purchasing power. A similar adjustment might be made to estimates of welfare changes for each country, to take into account the different purchasing power of a given

---

[8] No distinction needs to be made between EV- and CV-type measures for small changes, but the distinction between money-metric and compensation measures remains.

[9] These differences can be very large, with the marginal cost of raising taxes on labor in the United States declining by a factor of four when the money metric approach is used (Fullerton, 1991).

amount of income in each country. Measures derived by adjusting nominal compensation measures for each country to the same price basis could potentially be added to obtain a relative valuation of income gains for countries at different income levels. The resulting measures of benefits would bear the same relationship to compensation measures as the measures of ICP real income do to measures of real income at market exchange rates. Thus, for any reform that benefited developed and developing countries, the measured benefits to developing countries would be more heavily weighted using ICP-type measures.

3.2. The relationship between money metric and national accounts measures

The compensation measures employed in CGE modeling are typically presented as something quite distinct from national accounts measures of real income. In fact, many modeling studies report measures of the effect of policy reform on gross domestic product, in addition to measures of welfare impacts, even in the case of a small, open economy. However, it is easy to show that there is an extremely close relationship between the money-metric measures and a conventional measure of real GDP when the expenditure function may be decomposed multiplicatively into a utility indicator and a price index, as is always assumed to be the case in national accounts measures that divide the value of output into a price and a quantity term.

To see this relationship, we first recall that revenue at producers' prices *plus* tariff revenues is precisely the definition of GDP at producers' prices (UN, 1968, p. 233). The inclusion of tariff revenues may be explicit, or a consequence of subtracting imports at cif prices (i.e., excluding the value of tariffs) from the value of total sales when estimating GDP from the demand side.

Assuming homothetic preferences, and setting B equal to zero for convenience, we may write Equation (1) as:

$$\boldsymbol{P}_1 u_1 = r(\boldsymbol{p}_1, \boldsymbol{v}) + \boldsymbol{m}'(\boldsymbol{p}_1, u_1, \boldsymbol{v})(\boldsymbol{p}_1 - \boldsymbol{p}_1^*) \tag{6}$$

so that

$$\boldsymbol{P}_0 u_1 = \left(\frac{\boldsymbol{P}_0}{\boldsymbol{P}_1}\right) \cdot (r(\boldsymbol{p}_1, \boldsymbol{v}) + \boldsymbol{m}'(\boldsymbol{p}_1, u_1, \boldsymbol{v})(\boldsymbol{p}_1 - \boldsymbol{p}_1^*))$$

This allows us to write the change in EV relative to base-period GDP as

$$\frac{\boldsymbol{P}_0 u_1 - \boldsymbol{P}_0 u_0}{r(\boldsymbol{p}_0, \boldsymbol{v}) + m(\boldsymbol{p}_0, u_0, \boldsymbol{v})} = \frac{\boldsymbol{P}_0}{\boldsymbol{P}_1} \cdot \left[\frac{r(\boldsymbol{p}_1, \boldsymbol{v}) + \boldsymbol{m}(\boldsymbol{p}_1, u_1, \boldsymbol{v})}{r(\boldsymbol{p}_0, \boldsymbol{v}) + \boldsymbol{m}(\boldsymbol{p}_0, u_0, \boldsymbol{v})}\right] \cdot -1 \tag{7}$$

which means that the change in consumption, as a share of base-period GDP, can be written for small changes as

$$G\hat{D}P - \hat{P}$$

where the circonflex superscript indicates the percentage change in each variable. The close link between EV measures and price-deflated GDP revealed in Equation (7) has several important implications for current practice. One is that the common procedure of reporting real GDP measures together with – and distinct from – money-metric measures of welfare change makes little sense. Another is that real GDP measures defined as above – rather than measures of the volume of output – are potentially more interesting as dependent variables in growth regressions than measures of the volume of output because they take into account the full range of potential sources of gain from reform, rather than merely those changes that influence the volume of output. In doing this, there is a need, however, to adjust for the impact on GDP of changes in the terms of trade, a problem addressed by Kohli (2004) in his estimate of GDP functions for Switzerland.

4. Representing different types of trade barriers

Barriers to trade take many forms (Anderson and van Wincoop, 2004) and, in principle, it is desirable to include all of these. Omitting barriers is obviously likely to reduce the estimates of potential gains from reform. Less obviously, omitting barriers may omit important second-best gains or losses resulting from changes in the quantities of trade passing over existing distortions (Harberger, 1971). A list of the key types of trade barriers to be considered is given in Table 1.

A key element of barrier assessment is the extent to which the barrier resists trade flows – something typically measured by an *ad valorem* equivalent (AVE). In addition, it is important to obtain information about the extent to which the barrier causes resources to be wasted by, for instance, creating incentives to spend real resources on the pursuit of rents.

Table 1. Key trade barriers that need to be considered

- Import tariffs
  - *Ad valorem*
  - Specific
  - Compound, mixed, and technical tariffs
  - Tariff-rate quotas
- Export taxes and subsidies
- Non tariff barriers
- Foreign exchange distortions
- Procedural barriers and trade facilitation
- Barriers to trade in services
  - Trade-restricting barriers
  - Cost-increasing policies
  - Policies that raise price–cost margins

Some policies, particularly in services, may also have features that reduce competition, and cause demand to be met by less efficient suppliers.

4.1. Tariffs

Tariffs are the simplest and most widely analyzed type of trade barrier. They are generally specified as determining the domestic price through the zero-profit condition for importers: $p_d = p_w(1+t)$, where t is the *ad valorem* tariff rate. When considering the impacts of protection, it is important to remember that there may, for a variety of reasons, be a gap between the applied tariff and the extent of protection provided – a gap frequently called water-in-the-tariff. One common situation where the tariff does not determine the price is a situation where the country is an exporter of the commodity, and the domestic price is determined by export returns, rather than by the landed price of imported goods. Another is where the tariff is prohibitive, and the domestic price matching supply and demand settles below the world price plus the tariff. For some purposes, it will be important to obtain estimates of the protection actually provided to domestic producers – as distinct from merely the protection against imports (see, e.g., Anderson and Martin, 2006).

Of the various types of tariffs, *ad valorem* tariffs are by far the simplest to analyze since the proportional tariff rate is constant over time, facilitating both observation of tariffs, tariff cutting according to nonlinear rules if required, and aggregation across commodities.[10] Even with *ad valorem* tariffs, the proliferation of preferential trade arrangements (PTAs) introduces considerable complexity relative to a situation where all trading partners pay the same tariff rate. *Ad valorem* tariffs are the predominant form of tariffs in developing countries, and in the nonagricultural sector in developed countries. Tariffs involving specific elements are, however, predominant in industrial countries' agriculture – accounting for an estimated 70% of agricultural protection in these countries, and particularly the highest agricultural tariff peaks (Jean *et al.*, 2006, p. 89).

Specific tariffs, such as \$100 per ton, present more serious problems for analysis. The protective effect of a specific tariff cannot be gauged without knowledge of the per unit value of the imported good. Unit values for many goods can be obtained from international trade data, but there is no guarantee that the value of the goods obtained from trade data will be on the same basis as those in which the tariff rates are expressed. It is desirable that unit prices be allowed to differ by supplier, because there are systematic differences in unit values of exports from different suppliers – and particularly a tendency for poorer countries to have lower-priced exports (Schott, 2004), and hence to face higher AVEs of specific tariffs.

---

[10] Subject to confronting aggregation issues to be discussed later.

One problem in dealing with this is high estimated variances in the observed unit values – a problem that has been dealt with in the CEPII/MAcMaps dataset[11] by organizing exporters into five groups on the basis of PPP-based GDP and trade openness and calculating trade-weighted median unit values (Bouët *et al.*, 2004, p. 18).

Compound tariffs, such as 5% plus $100 per ton, can be dealt with by adding the AVE of the specific part of the tariff to the pure *ad valorem* tariff. Mixed tariffs, in which the tariff is defined as the greater (or the lesser) of a specific and an *ad valorem* element, are more problematic. In the MAcMap's database, the *ad valorem* term is preferred, because of the uncertainty about the true unit values, and hence the AVE, of the specific component. Technical tariffs, based on factors such as the alcohol content of wine and spirits, are a serious problem for large-scale estimation of barriers, because trade and tariff databases contain little information of this type.

Tariff-rate quotas (TRQs), where a certain quantity of imports is allowed entry at a lower in-quota tariff and any excess must pay a higher out-of-quota tariff, are pervasive in industrial countries' agriculture. De Gorter and Kliauga (2006) point out that the products associated with these instruments account for 51% of the value of agricultural production, and 43% of the value of agricultural imports in OECD countries. These barriers pose serious challenges for research on the effects of trade reform because the tariff applied is stochastic, depending on whether the export quota is filled or not. Since the quotas are frequently allocated on a bilateral basis, the tariff applied may differ between exporters. Ideally, these mechanisms would be modeled using techniques for modeling inequalities (such as those used in Bach and Pearson, 1996), in which the regime is determined by market conditions, the size of the quota, and the level of the in-quota and out-of-quota tariffs. These approaches allow explicitly for switching between regimes depending on whether the quotas are filled or not.

One pragmatic approach to dealing with TRQs has been to focus on the marginal tariff rate applying to a particular import flow in the base period. If imports from a particular supplier equal or exceed the quota level, then the out-of-quota tariff is applied. If they fall below 90% of the quota, then the in-quota tariff is applied. If they fall between 90% and 99% of the quota, then the tariff is specified as the average of the in- and out-of-quota tariffs (Bouët *et al.*, 2004). De Gorter and Kliauga (2006, p. 137) estimate that only 36% of TRQs are filled, and the use of in-quota tariffs on many trade flows in MAcMap has contributed to a substantial gap

[11] This dataset underlies the GTAP V6 database used for most Computable General Equilibrium modeling.

(binding overhang) in industrial countries, where bound tariffs average 27% and MFN applied rates 22.1% (Jean *et al.*, 2006, p. 91).

One vitally important requirement for protection databases is that they include the preferences that are increasingly being granted, whether under preferential trade agreements, or as a form of assistance to developing countries, and particularly the least developed countries. The incorporation of these preferences on a systematic basis in the MAcMap's database is a major step forward for quantitative analysis.

4.2. Export taxes

Export taxes were once an important source of revenue for developing countries, but have diminished to a very small share of revenues, except in a few countries. However, when such taxes are used heavily, as they were in Russia and Côte d'Ivoire in 2001 when they accounted for 15% and 10% of total government revenues, they tend to be very discriminatory, as they are typically applied on a relatively small number of "traditional" exports, rather than uniformly across all exports.

4.3. Export subsidies

Subsidies specific to exports are prohibited under WTO rules, except in agriculture, where they are disciplined by Article 9 of the Uruguay Round Agreement on Agriculture (WTO, 1995). The value of export subsidies has fallen in recent years, with the European Union emerging as the only major user, and even it now makes little use of these subsidies (Hoekman and Messerlin, 2006).

In principle, export subsidies should be relatively easy to measure, with their *ad valorem* rate depending on the value of subsidies paid relative to the value of exports covered. However, these measures are typically used to support domestic prices, so their rates vary over time, often inversely with world prices. This variation makes it difficult to represent their effects adequately in comparative statics models, which are generally based largely on data for a particular year.

Export subsidies create three types of costs: they distort the domestic market for the good on which they are paid, reducing domestic consumption and increasing production; they distort world markets for the same good; and they exacerbate distortions in the market(s) in which the funds used to pay the subsidies are raised. The second and third distortions contribute to the fact that export subsidies are used much less than import tariffs – they involve potential terms-of-trade deteriorations for the country using the subsidies, where import tariffs may improve the terms of trade; and they involve costly and politically painful increases in taxes, where import duties raise revenues.

However, in a world filled with barriers to trade, export subsidies may have significant second-best welfare benefits. If, for instance, the importing country has an import duty that lowers its imports below the economically desirable level, then an export subsidy paid by its supplier can provide a double benefit to the recipient both by lowering the price paid for the import, and by increasing the volume of imports entering over the import tariff.[12] These effects are captured in any properly specified measure of welfare change of the type considered in Section 3. As a consequence of these second-best effects, Anderson and Martin (2006) found that the global welfare benefits of abolishing export subsidies would be very small, perhaps only 2% of the estimated gains from agricultural trade reform, and little over 1% of the estimated global gains from merchandise trade reform.

4.4. Nontariff measures

Nontariff measures (NTMs) take many forms, including quantitative restrictions on trade, nontariff charges, government participation in trade, customs procedures and practices, and technical barriers to trade (Dee and Ferrantino, 2005). These measures include some barriers intended to restrict trade, and some other measures – such as food quality standards – that may restrict trade as a side effect of pursuing an important social regulatory role. As suggested by Deardorff and Stern (1998) the characteristics of import-side NTMs on which it would be useful to have information include the extent to which they reduce trade; the extent to which they raise the price of imports; the extent of any change in the elasticity of demand for imports; impacts on the variability of imports; the degree of uncertainty they create; and the resource costs required to meet them. It is widely believed that standards-type barriers, including the sanitary and phytosanitary barriers applied on food products have become much more important in recent years, particularly as tariff barriers have fallen (Maskus and Wilson, 2001).

For monitoring trade policies, much use is made of simple measures such as the frequency with which different NTMs, or different types of NTMs are used (see, e.g., the IMF Trade Restrictiveness Index (IMF, 2005) or the UNCTAD TRAINS database). The problem with such measures, for analytical purposes, is that the trade-restrictive effects of different types of NTMs (or even of the same type of NTM) may vary enormously.

---

[12] If the tariff is 50% and the price of imports $100, an additional unit of imports generates a benefit valued domestically at $150 for a cost of $100. The welfare gain associated with increasing import volumes is therefore $50 per unit.

Under some circumstances, the protective effects of NTMs can be measured by price comparisons between the border prices of the good and their price in internal markets. This is the primary procedure used by the OECD (2005) in monitoring agricultural trade distortions, including tariffs, TRQs, and NTMs such as sanitary and phytosanitary measures. Unfortunately, this process is relatively costly, and is unlikely to produce satisfactory results for products that are less homogeneous than the more standardized agricultural commodities that are the focus of OECD monitoring. Even for agricultural commodities, considerable attention needs to be paid to ensure that the price comparisons match like with like. Huang *et al.* (2004) found that the results obtained for agricultural protection in China were extremely misleading unless very great care was taken – by, for instance, interviewing market participants – to ensure that the products involved were truly comparable.

An alternative, or complement, to the use of price-comparison approaches is the indirect approach to inference used by Kee *et al.* (2005, 2009) in developing measures of the restrictive effects of NTMs. In the first stage, the impacts of NTMs on import volumes are estimated by comparing import volumes with those that would be predicted by a model of the economy. Then, the impact of these deviations in import quantities on prices is inferred using estimates of the elasticities of import demand at the six-digit level of the Harmonized System – the finest level at which international comparability is feasible. Finally, the measures at the individual product level were converted into Overall Trade Restrictiveness Index (OTRI) measures that show the uniform tariff that would be equivalent, in terms of its effect on export market opportunities, to the observed NTMs.

Kee *et al.* (2005, 2009) find that the AVEs of NTMs are generally higher than the tariffs on the same products. They also find that these AVEs have a tendency to rise with income. Using this methodology, the World Bank (2005, p. 128) concluded that the protective effect of NTMs in industrial-country agriculture was roughly twice the tariff, making the overall OTRI three times as high as the component due to tariff protection. In manufacturing, the trade restrictiveness of NTMs was close to four times as large as the corresponding tariffs, making the overall OTRI roughly five times as high as the tariff.

Bearing in mind that the cost of a trade barrier goes up with the square of its tariff equivalent, the OTRI measures in World Bank (2005) would imply increasing the costs of protection in agriculture by a factor of 9 and the costs of protection in manufacturing by a factor of 25. For a quick back-of-the-envelope indicator, these ratios could be applied to the estimated gains of $169 billion from abolition of agricultural tariffs, and $105 billion from nonagricultural tariff elimination (Anderson *et al.*, 2006, p. 349). The resulting estimate of the gains from elimination of tariffs and NTMs would be $4.1 trillion rather than the $274 billion estimated using tariffs alone.

4.5. Foreign exchange distortions

Foreign exchange distortions can impose substantial trade barriers that bring about large changes in the relative prices of different traded goods.[13] This is most clear in the case of a two-tier exchange rate system where exporters must surrender their foreign exchange earnings at an official exchange rate, while importers must meet their marginal needs for foreign exchange on a secondary market. In this case, the gap between the official and the secondary market rate is a tax on trade equivalent in effect to a uniform import or export tax (Anderson and Martin, 2006). Frequently, however, these regimes involve multiple rates, or administrative allocation, which adds both to their economic costs and to the complexity of their evaluation.

Controlled exchange rate regimes that generated exchange rate distortions of this type were very common until the 1990s (Bhagwati, 1978). The black market premia that they created have played an extremely important role in the econometric literature on trade and growth, and particularly in the influential Sachs and Warner (1995) analysis. Their welfare impacts have been analyzed in a number of CGE studies, including Dervis *et al.* (1981), Tarr (1990), and Martin (1993). These studies point out, that when administered efficiently, exchange rate distortions act as a – frequently very substantial – tax on trade. When, as is frequently the case, they involve rationing and quantitative allocation of foreign exchange, the costs associated with trade taxes are compounded with the efficiency costs associated with rent dissipation and those resulting from differences in the valuation of foreign exchange between different recipients. Jensen and Tarr (2003) found abolition of the exchange rate distortion to account for potential of gains of around 7% of GDP in Iran, out of total potential gains in the order of 50%.

4.6. Procedural barriers

The procedures used to regulate trade can, of themselves, generate substantial trade barriers. Some of these costs arise from the time involved in procedures, some from actual compliance costs and others from the incentives for corruption created by complex and time-consuming procedures. Recent research such as Hummels (2001) has highlighted the potentially large costs associated with even apparently small increases in the time taken to transport goods. These costs are potentially more serious

---

13 Real exchange rate changes that change the relative price of all traded goods relative to non-traded goods change the incentives facing producers, but are endogenous responses to factors such as changes in trade policies, or changes in savings-investment balances, rather than trade distortions.

than the costs associated with tariffs, since supply and demand are balanced by incurring real costs. Investment climate surveys (www.worldbank.org) and other international surveys provide information on key issues such as customs delays and perceptions of corruption. Wilson *et al.* (2005, p. 869) argue that more than half of the estimated potential trade expansion of $377 billion, resulting from improvements in trade facilitation, would come from improvements in the administration of trade.

4.7. Services trade barriers

Barriers to trade in services are particularly difficult to analyze. This is partly because of the range of different modes by which trade in services can be conducted – partly because barriers to trade in services normally take the form of regulations, rather than of price-based measures such as tariffs; and partly because barriers to trade in services may affect trade flows, the price–cost margin, or costs and productivity.

There are indications that the costs of barriers to trade in services may be very substantial, and potentially larger than the barriers presented by conventional trade measures such as tariffs and subsidies (Department of Foreign Affairs and Trade, 1999; Dee *et al.*, 2000; Francois, 2001; Francois and Hoekman, in press). This finding arises even when barriers to trade in services are treated as taxes on trade and production.

Konan and Maskus (2006) point out that the costs of services protection are likely to be larger than those on merchandise trade because they typically involve restrictions not only on cross-border trade (Mode 1 of GATS) but also on supply by establishing enterprises in the country or by the movement of service suppliers (Modes 3 and 4 of GATS). They estimate the extent to which barriers to establishment trade create costs through adverse impacts on the competitive environment and through lower efficiency of producing firms.

Characterization of services barriers in CGE assessment is important. For example, representing them as deadweight costs has been important in CGE-based assessments of potential WTO liberalization and regional integration. An implication for empirical efforts to determine the effects of policy is that it is not enough to focus on price–cost margins as that does not allow one to disentangle the two effects of deadweight costs and efficiency effects. Better econometrically based decomposition of the various price and cost margins linked to international service transactions is an important and sorely needed building block in guiding policy formation. When barriers to trade in services are represented as reducing productivity in producing sectors, the measured benefits of reforming trade in services are even larger. Jensen *et al.* (2004) find that the benefits of reform in services trade completely dominate as a source of benefits from likely reforms following Russia's accession to the WTO.

There has been substantial progress in the development of models that include the dimensions of trade in services not included in standard CGE models – particularly trade through establishment of foreign subsidiaries and through movement of service providers (Dee *et al.*, 2000). For example, Konan and Maskus (2006) argue that increasing international competition on service markets will reduce the "cartel effect" – the markup of price over marginal cost that incumbents are able to charge due to restricted entry, and attenuate what they term the "cost inefficiency effect" – the fact that in an environment with limited competition marginal costs of incumbents are likely to be higher than if entry were allowed. The latter is most important as inefficiency imposes a cost on all sectors and households that consume the services involved.

The credence that should be placed in the numbers generated by CGE analyses depends very much on the validity of the modeling assumptions made and the data that are used. While the accuracy of the specific numbers generated is certainly open to question, the conclusion that services liberalization can generate much larger welfare effects than goods liberalization is probably robust. Clearly, to be more informative, CGE analyses need to be able to draw on empirical research that determines the effects of policies on markups and costs.

4.8. Specification of the counterfactual level of protection

For all of the different types of protection considered above, the choice of counterfactual is important. The usual approach is to use the level of protection in some base period as the level of protection that would apply in the absence of the reform under consideration. This is likely to be seriously misleading in a number of situations. The first is where the expected level of protection is changing over time, and the second is where protection is stochastic, either in response to changes in the determinants of the political support function determining the level of protection, or as a consequence of random shocks.

If we have no information on the evolution of protection in the absence of reform, then the assumption that the initial level of protection would prevail is a defensible assumption. If, however, research has provided alternative insights into the likely future path of protection, then we may be able to do better. Research on the political economy of protection has highlighted a number of determinants of protection that change systematically over time. In agriculture, for instance, protection tends to be relatively low in poor countries but to rise with economic growth, as farmers become less numerous, easier to organize, and more market oriented, while consumers become more numerous, harder to organize, and less concerned about the price of staple foods (Anderson and Hayami, 1986; Lindert, 1991).

Even in the absence of secular trends in protection, the assumption of a fixed, deterministic tariff rate may be misleading when protection varies over time – as it manifestly does in agriculture. As shown by Francois and Martin (2004), the marginal effect of a constraint, such as a WTO tariff commitment on a stochastic tariff, depends on the probability that the applied tariff would have exceeded the commitment, rather than on a discrete choice of whether the commitment is below the initial binding. Since these commitments rule out the highest, and hence the most costly, incidents of protection, they can potentially cause substantial reductions in the cost of protection. Francois and Martin found that some tariff commitments above the average level of pre-Uruguay Round protection substantially reduced the cost of protection. Had the standard approach been followed, these would have appeared to have no impact on the cost of protection. By contrast, a stochastic approach to specifying the counterfactual implies that commitments to reduce protection below its initial level have a smaller cost impact than would be indicated using the deterministic counterfactual.

5. *Problems in measuring welfare change*

Even under the standard assumptions of CRTS in production and a fixed number of goods, there are some serious problems involved in measuring welfare change within the conceptual framework, and with the measures of protection, identified above. Many of these problems can, if not properly dealt with, result in seriously biased estimates. Key examples of these problems include

1. aggregation of distortions;
2. utilization and dissipation of government revenues;
3. labor market linkages; and
4. bias in parameter estimates.

5.1. Aggregation of distortions

Trade barriers frequently vary enormously across commodities, and frequently also across suppliers. This variation in rates of protection increases the cost of any given "average" level of protection, since the cost of protection increases with the square of the rate of protection. Unfortunately, some degree of aggregation is essential if the available information on the structure of production and consumption is at a higher level of aggregation than information on tariffs and trade. Further aggregation is typically employed for computational reasons. Other problems are introduced by the typical approach to aggregation of trade barriers – the use of averages weighted by external trade. As protection weights rise, the weights associated with these measures decline, so that a tariff that completely blocks trade has the same measured impact as a zero tariff.

The modern approach to tariff aggregation pioneered by Anderson and Neary (1992) provides an indication of a possible means of dealing with the aggregation problem. Anderson and Neary develop a single tariff aggregator that captures the welfare impacts of a nonuniform tariff. Building on this approach, Bach and Martin (2001) used a tariff aggregator to capture the impacts of changes in the tariff regime on the expenditure required to achieve a given level of utility, and another to capture the impact on tariff revenues. Manole and Martin (2005) provided closed-form measures of these aggregators for the widely used constant-elasticity-of-substitution functional form. Applying these procedures to a sample of seven developing countries, they found that appropriate aggregation increased the estimated cost of protection on average 20-fold relative to the cost estimated using the weighted average tariff. Anderson (2009) proposed a similar approach combining an expenditure aggregator and the average tariff for tariff revenues, and found that proper aggregation of tariffs increased the estimated cost of protection in India (a country with a relatively low coefficient of variation in its tariff schedule) by a factor of three. Laborde, Martin and van der Mensbrugghe (2010) find that using appropriate aggregators roughly doubles the gains from global trade liberalization.

5.2. Revenue utilization and dissipation

It is routine in quantitative analysis of trade reform to assume that the government revenues associated with trade barriers are redistributed in lump-sum fashion to consumers. There are two broad questions that must be considered. The first is whether the trade barriers, in fact, generate revenues to the country concerned. The second is how government budget balance will be restored – whether through adjustments in transfers, in government spending, or through the imposition of replacement taxes.

Krueger (1974) and Bhagwati (1982) examined how tariff revenues or quota rents may be dissipated in wasteful economic activity. In some cases, such as when quota rents are allocated on the basis of costly activities such as the construction of production capacity, it seems likely that the rent-seeking activities would roughly dissipate the expected quota rents. In other cases, the degree of dissipation of the revenues could be higher or lower. Anderson and Neary (1992, 2003) point to another possibility with measures such as quotas or TRQs, where the rents are shared between importers and exporters. Both of these phenomena can readily be incorporated into the balance-of-trade framework simply by adding rent dissipation or rent-sharing coefficients to the tariff revenue term in

Equation (1). As Krueger (1974) has shown, these terms may be very large relative to the conventional measured losses of economic efficiency.

The conventional treatment of changes in tariff revenues as lump-sum transfers has been criticized by Ackerman (2005) and others for assuming that lost revenues are either replaced by a lump-sum tax, or accommodated by reducing a lump-sum transfer. While this is a valid criticism of the usual presentation of results, the lump-sum approach has the advantage of neutrality given that we do not, in general, know what choices governments will make in replacing these revenues. The choices include raising alternative taxes and reducing government expenditures. Once the choices are known, the costs of raising government revenues, or of government expenditures foregone, can be combined with the estimated gains from trade reform to make an overall assessment of the overall implications. If a specific choice about how revenues are to be replaced is made, and a single net estimate of benefits or costs is provided, there will not be enough information to allow analysis of alternative choices.

One plausible approach to dealing with this problem is to assume that the government will raise any lost revenues through adjustments to the rates of an alternative tax. This effectively augments the income–expenditure condition for the economy with a government budget constraint. A more general framework would incorporate the benefits to the economy of the goods provided by governments as well as the budget constraint (see, e.g., Martin and Anderson, 2005). This broader approach allows for a wider range of adjustments to the change in revenues.

Harrison *et al.* (2002) show that incorporating tariff revenue replacement can make a large difference to the results. While, in principle, a value-added tax (VAT) should be uniform across sectors, and hence much less distorting than a typical tariff regime, they found that the Chilean VAT varied considerably across sectors. They found that the marginal cost of funds for the existing VAT was 7.6%, as against 18.5% for the customs tariff – suggesting that replacing tariff revenues by a VAT increase would reduce the measured welfare gains from trade reform by roughly 40%.

Current, conventional CGE models typically assume that governments collect tariff revenues on all imports – whether for consumption, for production of domestic outputs, or for production of exports. Some economies, however, have much lower duty collections because of exemptions and/or duty drawbacks of various kinds. One response to these exemptions is to use the average rate of duty collections in place of the statutory rate. However, the statutory rate typically does apply to some categories of transactions, such as "ordinary" trade in China, while a lower (and frequently zero) rate applies to other categories of transactions. A better way to deal with this problem is the approach used by Ianchovichina and Martin (2004) or Warlters and Auriol (2005), under which the flows subject to reduced rates of taxation are differentiated from those subject to taxation at the statutory rates. Proper incorporation of these measures will generally reduce the measured welfare benefits of reform – since the duty exemption/drawback arrangements are a partial reform – they may also have important impacts on key quantity and price outcomes. Martin *et al.* (2003) found that failing to account for the presence of duty exemptions on intermediate inputs used in the production of exports resulted in substantially overstated estimates of the effects of trade reform on China's exports.

5.3. Labor markets

The most common specification in model-based studies focusing on trade reform is a relatively neutral one such as assuming that employment, or total unemployment, is unchanged as a consequence of trade reforms. This approach has been challenged by authors such as Ackerman (2005), who have argued for approaches such as determining employment endogenously in the presence of a fixed real consumer wage. Given the prevalence of distortions in world labor markets, it would be desirable to do much better than the simple assumption of fixed employment or unemployment. However, adequately capturing the many different distortions prevailing in global labor markets is difficult, and some simple alternative assumptions may have unintended consequences.

The specification of a fixed real consumer wage has been widely used in some trade-focused applications, and particularly in many applications of the ORANI model in Australia (Dixon *et al.*, 1982). This approach made considerable sense in the Australian institutional environment, where informal employment was relatively uncommon, wages tended to be indexed for movements in the consumer price index, and unemployment benefits were readily available to those unable to find employment at institutionally determined wages. There seems little evident justification for adopting such a specification in economy-wide models of developing countries, where none of these conditions are satisfied.

One feature of this specification is that trade liberalizations tend to be strongly favorable for employment and for real income. This is due to the fact that wages are linked to the consumer price index, which is a weighted average of the price of imported and nontraded goods. When trade barriers are lowered, the CPI tends to fall more than the producer price index, which is a weighted average of the same nontraded goods prices and the prices of exported goods. Under this specification, trade liberalization reduces the producer real wage – the wage relative to the average price of producers' output – and this reduction in the producer real wage stimulates employment. If there is surplus labor earning no return, the estimated welfare gains from trade reform are likely to be much larger than using conventional measures, since every unit of additional labor employed generates a social welfare gain equal to its wage.

This contributed to Polaski (2006) finding welfare gains from trade reform comparable with those of Anderson *et al.* (2006) even though smaller estimates would have been expected given the much smaller trade elasticities in the Carnegie model.

Ideally, modeling of labor market behavior would be based more closely on the institutional features of each country, in order to capture the impacts of trade reform and other shocks on the labor market outcomes. For developing countries, this is likely to require careful analysis of both formal and informal labor markets, and of the links between them. When there is substantial reported unemployment in the formal sector, the inadequacies of social safety nets in most developing countries typically force workers excluded from the formal-sector workforce to participate in informal labor markets.

Even with an ideal specification of labor markets, considerable care needs to be given to the interpretation of the results. Is it appropriate to identify the welfare effects of trade reform in the presence of labor market distortions with the trade reforms themselves? If one follows standard rules on policy assignment (see Mundell, 1962), then responsibility for trade policy would be assigned to one set of actors, and labor market policy to another, such as the labor ministry. If changes in trade policies require adjustments in the labor market, the responsibility for making the adjustments needed to restore balance in that market would fall on the labor ministry. Under this assignment, only the direct costs associated with trade distortions need to be attributed to trade policy – any adverse outcomes in the labor market are the responsibility of the labor ministry and require adjustments in labor market policies.

One surprising feature of the specification of labor markets in most studies of global trade reform is that the supply of labor is exogenous. While the *uncompensated* labor supply elasticity of prime-working-age males is widely thought to be close to zero, the *compensated* supply of most categories of labor, including prime-working-age males, is generally thought to be quite price responsive. If, as we propose, compensated measures of welfare change are used, it is the compensated, rather than the uncompensated, labor supply elasticity that is relevant.

Adding labor supply responsiveness would introduce an additional channel of response to the change in tax rates. If labor market distortions were also introduced, it might be expected to introduce substantial welfare changes, since the distortions prevailing in labor markets – including taxes on earnings, and wage interventions such as minimum wages – are frequently very large relative to average tariff rates. If, for instance, trade reform reduced the disincentive to supply effort associated with a 50% income tax rate, the welfare benefits could be substantial.

If wage-responsive labor supply is introduced, however, considerable thought needs to be given to the welfare measures to be used. As noted in Section 2, the money metric measures take into account the impacts of income changes on spending on taxed goods. If tariffs generated substantial welfare costs, then the measured impact of these costs would be offset by a stimulus to labor supply resulting from the consequent reduction in the demand for leisure. As argued in Martin and Anderson (2005), it makes no sense to count this as a reduction in the costs of the tariff, since the provision of public goods, or of redistributive transfers, would offset the income effect of the tax on labor supply.

Harrison and Leamer (1997) provide evidence that the impact of trade reforms on aggregate employment might be smaller than many have suspected. Their country studies for Morocco and Mexico suggested that the effects of trade reform on overall employment, and even on sectoral employment, were quite modest. They also point out that fixed minimum wages, even where they exist, do not typically determine total employment. If minimum wages become binding, their effect is typically to transfer employment from the formal labor market to informal labor markets, where wages are lower and more flexible.

5.4. Parameter estimates

One of the major influences on standard estimates of the welfare impacts of trade reform is the parameters used. Even in the standard case of comparative statics analysis of trade reform – where the conceptual framework is based on agreed economic theory – the estimated results for trade reform are extremely sensitive to the key elasticity parameters. In most cases, the crucial parameters are the so-called Armington elasticities that characterize the ease of substitution between domestic and imported goods.

As Krugman (1989) pointed out, the estimated trade elasticities obtained from econometric procedures are frequently unrealistic as indicators of the consequences of sustained export expansion. In Krugman's analysis, elasticities of export demand were generally found to be very low, while the estimated income elasticities of demand were high for rapidly growing exporters and low for slower-growing exporters. Krugman suggested that this might reflect a rapid expansion in the range of products produced by rapidly growing exporters – an expansion that was wrongly attributed to high-income elasticities for exports from these countries. Feenstra (1994) confirmed this hypothesis.

In a recent paper, Ruhl (2005) has built on this explanation by emphasizing the increase in the number of varieties exported following trade reform. Drawing on the evidence that sustained reductions in trade barriers result in new entry by exporters, he distinguishes between high-frequency estimates of trade parameters, such as those routinely estimated from time-series data, and those estimated on the basis of long-run changes in policies, such as changes in tariff rates. His econometric estimation yields elasticities between 0.2 and 3.5 from high-frequency data analysis, and from 6 to 15 when the long-run effects of plants entering export markets in response to trade liberalization are taken into account.

6. *Productivity and competition effects*

In the first generation of CGE models, production structure was based strictly on CRTS technology, with competitive markets and unchanging levels of factor productivity. Important departures from this approach include changes in firm- and industry-level efficiency for a variety of reasons. Firm effects range from learning-by-doing to a Schumpeterian process of creative destruction, where competition from trade drives out less efficient firms. Industry effects involve imperfect competition, leading to various industry-level effects known, collectively, as "procompetitive effects" (Markusen *et al.*, 1995). Recent models of firm-level efficiency effects are embedded in models of monopolistic competition, so that firm and industry effects both part of the same complex analytical mix.

6.1. Variety with identical firms

An important move away from the CRTS, perfect competition approach began in the 1980s. It was inspired by the Dixit–Stiglitz (1977) formulation of preferences, which takes into account the number of different varieties available to purchasers of intermediate inputs of goods and/or services (see Harris, 1984; Brown, 1994; Francois and Roland-Holst, 1997; Jensen *et al.*, 2004). Important path-breaking work in this area involved the Michigan model (Brown, 1994). The more recent trade and geography literature explores, theoretically and numerically, the equilibrium properties of this class of CGE model (Fujita *et al.*, 1999; Puga and Venables, 1999).

This approach has been applied in assessments of the Uruguay Round, and can be traced to earlier CGE work on United States–Canada trade in the 1980s (see, for example, Roland-Holst *et al.*, 1994) and the literature on deeper integration in the European Community (see, e.g., Smith and Venables, 1988). These models integrate firm-level differentiation of intermediate and final goods with intermediate good linkages and input-output linkages.

Typically, in this homogenous firm type of variety models, it is assumed that the individual varieties are symmetric in terms of selling at the same price and quantity, but that increases in the number of varieties yield benefits because they are perceived to be different by their purchasers. Under these circumstances, the cost of an input, i, supplied by n different firms is given by:

$$E = (np^{1-\sigma})^{1/(1-\sigma)}q \quad (8)$$

where E is expenditure on the good, n is the number of different varieties of the good available, σ is the elasticity of substitution between varieties of the good or service, and q is effective volume of the input required. With this formulation, the cost of the required volume of input diminishes with the number of available inputs, since $E = n^{1/(1-\sigma)}pq$ Given the condition of this model, that σ is positive and greater than one, it is clear that the expenditure required to obtain the volume q of the good declines with the number of available varieties.

The use of Dixit–Stiglitz preferences for intermediate and final goods can result in larger estimates of the overall welfare benefits of trade reform by expanding the range of varieties available to consumers who prefer variety. Broadly speaking, in this class of models, effects are much larger with firm-based variety effects than with models based on the Armington (1969) specification.[14] The love-of-variety specification is widely used for nonagricultural sectors, but rarely used for agriculture, and this difference in specification can bring about large differences in the measured welfare implications of reform from different sectors, with the Michigan Model, in particular, generating much larger gains from reform of the manufacturing sector relative to the agricultural sector. (Brown, 1994; Brown *et al.*, 1999).

An important question about this class of models has been raised by Hummels and Klenow (2005), who note that the pure Dixit–Stiglitz model attributes all export expansion to increases in varieties exported. However, they find that only around 60% of the increase in exports in growing economies comes from increases in product variety, with the remainder coming from increases in both the quantity and quality of goods exported. Ardelean (2006) estimates a model of export expansion that nests the conventional, Armington model and the Dixit–Stiglitz model and finds that consumers' love of variety is roughly 40% less than would be suggested by a pure Dixit–Stiglitz model. Fan (2006) found in a simulation model context that full love-of-variety resulted in an apparently excessive preference for variety and obtained more plausible results in a model that was intermediated between the Armington and Dixit–Stiglitz type models.

6.2. Variety, heterogeneous firms, and firm efficiency

Early work on firm-level efficiency effects of trade typically assumed that the process of exporting created productivity differences through learning-by-doing – exporting firms might, for instance, learn about new techniques and products from their foreign buyers in the manner suggested by Arrow (1962). However, a number of influential firm-level studies, including

[14] Francois and Roland-Holst (1997) provide a comparison of results based on CRTS models, Cournot competition with and without scale, and monopolistic competition involving intermediate and final goods.

Clerides *et al.* (1998) and Bernard and Jensen (1999), concluded that the changes in productivity following entry into export markets arise primarily because higher-productivity firms self-select into exports. Basically, one strand of the literature has tested for and failed to find evidence of learning-by-doing following entry into export markets. However, this conclusion remains controversial.

A number of more recent studies contradict the result of no learning-by-doing with findings of empirically important increases in productivity after firms enter export markets. Blalock and Gertler (2004) find evidence of an increase in firm productivity of between 2% and 5% after Indonesian firms enter export markets. Fernandes and Isgut (2006) find evidence of an increase in productivity from learning-by-exporting when Colombian firms entered export markets. van Biesebrock (2005) finds that African exporting firms had higher productivity before entering export markets, but that their productivity levels, and their subsequent rates of productivity growth, grew after entering export markets. Girma *et al.* (2004) found both higher initial levels of productivity and higher productivity growth rates after entry into exporting. Moreover, these sources of productivity gain from improvements in production processes are additional to any resulting from improvements in product variety or product quality.

As noted in section 2, recent research at the firm level has also provided important insights into key aspects of the growth process. Melitz (2003) has developed an influential theoretical version of the variety model, replacing homogenous firms with heterogeneous firms. The model is consistent with the observed tendency for higher-productivity firms to enter export markets, many intermediate-productivity firms to continue servicing the domestic market, and less-efficient firms to exit following trade liberalization. Baldwin (2005) shows that this model generates many important testable hypotheses, including that greater openness raises productivity, and that policy reforms that lower marginal costs of trade may have different implications from those that lower, fixed beachhead costs. Melitz and Ottaviano (2005) extend this model to allow for endogenous markups that respond to the strength of competition – something observed in firm-level analyses. Bernard, Redding and Schott (2006) extend these models in the direction of (re-)incorporating differences in factor intensities across industries.

In an empirical study building on the Melitz model, Falvey *et al.* (2004) find that reallocation effects predicted by this model, and particularly firm entry, account for 45% of annual productivity growth in Sweden. An empirical evaluation of the consequences of European integration by Gatto *et al.* (2006) concludes that introducing prohibitive trade barriers within Europe would have reduced national income by roughly 13%.

6.3. Oligopoly

Specifying oligopolistic competition in sectors where this appears to be appropriate can substantially affect the estimated static welfare implications of trade reform and related measures such as the productivity implications of trade reform (Harrison, 1994). Reductions in trade barriers can reduce price–cost margins in oligopolistic industries, and result in gains to national income resulting from output expansion and greater exploitation of scale economies as well as those from increased imports (Devarajan and Rodrik, 1991). The Devarajan and Rodrik study, in which the outputs of domestic firms were assumed to be perfect substitutes, found that expansion of firm output in the presence of scale economies was an important source of gain from trade reform in Cameroon, with the benefits increasing from around 1% of GDP to 2% when this component of adjustment was included. By contrast, the Harrison *et al.* (1995) study with national monopolistically competitive firms producing a composite good that substituted imperfectly for imported goods found little benefit from firm rationalization.

For identical multilateral experiments involving global rather than local competition between firms (an approach more in keeping with the theoretical and broader CGE literature), the benefits (and costs) of liberalization tend to be substantially larger than under a hybrid Dixit–Stiglitz–Armington assumption. (Francois *et al.*, 1996a, 1996b). This is because such models exhibit reduced-form scale effects, and because the base for scale is global and regional rather than national. Firm-level product differentiation models without an over-arching Armington structure therefore yield much larger effects (positive and negative) than do static models with perfect competition and models with nationally monopolistically competitive industries producing Armington composites. In addition, when combined with investment mechanisms, these effects can be significantly greater, again either in a positive or negative direction. We will return to this issue in the numerical simulations section of the chapter.

The Eastman–Stykolt specification of collusive behavior, under which firms are assumed to set their prices on the basis of a limit determined by the landed price of imports, results in larger potential welfare gains because it brings about greater rationalization of firm output than alternative assumptions. In Cox and Harris (1985), this assumption contributed to much larger estimated welfare gains from trade reform than monopolistic competition because Eastman–Stykolt resulted in much greater rationalization of firm output. However, the assumptions of the Eastman–Stykolt assumption appear not to have been borne out in subsequent analysis (Baggs *et al.*, 2002).

6.4. New products and new markets

A recent body of research focuses on the "missing flows" in trade data. In particular, bilateral trade data are populated by zero flows between individual partners, and within certain product categories. Trade growth involves not just the same products to the same markets. It also involves a mix of new products and new markets. This may reflect beachhead effects and fixed costs for entering new markets, defined over country or product space. Hummels and Klenow (2005) show that over 60% of export growth resulting from income growth generally comes about not through increases in the volume of products already exported, but through their extensive margin – expansion in the range of products exported to that market. Within their intensive margin – exporting increased values of the same goods – a 1% increase in GDP per worker tended to raise export prices by 0.09% because of improvements in quality, while increasing volumes by 0.34%. The increase in product variety will, assuming a preference for variety by consumers, increase the demand for exports, offsetting to some degree the terms of trade deterioration built into conventional Armington-type models such GTAP (Hertel, 1997). Evenett and Venables (2002) estimated that almost a third of the expansion in developing-country exports since 1970 arose from shipments of existing products to new markets. Kehoe and Ruhl (2003) emphasize the emergence of new products as part of the adjustment to trade reform, and particularly the reduction of trade barriers.

7. *Quantifying investment effects*

The relationship between trade and growth is of critical importance for long-term poverty reduction and the importance of these links is widely understood by policy makers. As Romer (1994) has observed, even a small impetus to sustained growth can have an enormous impact on living standards over time – and certainly a greater impact than the relatively small static income gains typically measured. However, the link between trade reform and growth is highly controversial, in part because of difficulties in distinguishing the causal relationship between trade reform and growth.

There are two fundamental types of linkage between trade policy reform and growth. The first is impacts of trade reform on the transition path from one equilibrium to another, which may occur over an extended period. The second is impacts on the long-term rate of technical change in the economy – impacts that, in the presence of continued growth, may provide an infinitely lived stimulus to growth. Scale economies can greatly magnify the income distance covered on the transitional growth path, even when we are not in the presence of permanent growth effects.

The empirical literature on the macroeconomic impact of openness stresses dynamics, while static CGE models stress allocative efficiency effects. Though some trade models now include investment-based dynamics, there is still a substantive gap between what CGE models typically examine, and what the theoretical and econometric literature suggests they should examine. Investment-based dynamic effects do feature prominently in a number of numerical studies of trade liberalization and regional integration. This includes models of the Uruguay Round (surveyed in Francois, McDonald, and Nordström, 1995), EU Enlargement (Baldwin *et al.*, 1997), and the Doha Round (Francois *et al.*, 2005; Anderson and Martin, 2006). Recent approaches vary, including recursive dynamics, overlapping generation models, and Ramsey-type models with intertemporal optimization [examples]. Often, the numerical policy literature focuses on steady-state dynamics in a competitive setting, either in the form of comparative steady states or in the calculation of transition paths starting from initial steady states. However, recent work with stylized fully dynamic models suggests that, for small countries, combining accumulation effects with variety effects may lead to far greater gains than in the competitive case (see Rutherford and Tarr, 2002).

We will start with our GDP function as defined above, and denote GDP as Y.

$$Y = g(\boldsymbol{p}, \boldsymbol{v}, \boldsymbol{p}^*), \quad \text{where } \boldsymbol{v} = (v_k = \lambda\alpha_k K, \; v_L = \lambda\alpha_L L) \tag{9}$$

In specifying Equation (9), we have assumed that our endowment vector $\boldsymbol{v}$ includes both capital K and labor L. Furthermore, we have included a coefficient for Hicks-neutral technical change (λ) and also coefficients for factor augmenting change α.

Consider the impact of a policy reform on steady-state incomes. To simplify things, we will represent policy reform as a boost to the efficiency of our GDP function (9) as represented by a change in our technical efficiency coefficients. If we assume fixed savings rates, the capital accumulation following from the growth in income and savings implies that our GDP values will be higher in steady state, and that indeed the steady-state increase will be higher than the initial static boost to efficiency. In steady state, we have the additional condition that

$$K = sY \tag{10}$$

where s is the savings rate. Differentiating Equations (9) and (10) with respect to technical change parameters α and making substitutions, the boost to income in steady state can be shown to be as follows (Francois *et al.*, 1999):

$$\hat{Y} = (1 - \theta_{v_k})^{-1}[\theta_{v_k}\hat{\alpha}_k + \theta_{v_L}\hat{\alpha}_L] \tag{11}$$

In Equation (11), the term θ represents the factor income shares of GDP, and α is defined in Equation (9). Alternatively, if we assume forward-looking households and intertemporal optimization in a Ramsey model, then instead of Equation (10), the following equation will hold, as rates of return are fixed by the rate of time discount.

$$\frac{\partial g}{\partial k} = \rho + \delta \tag{12}$$

where ρ and δ are the rates of time discount and depreciation. After differentiation of (9) and (12) with respect to the technical change terms α, and some manipulation, the steady-state change in income can be shown to be as follows:

$$\hat{Y} = [\theta_{v_k}\hat{\alpha}_k + \theta_{v_L}\hat{\alpha}_k] - \left[\frac{\theta_{v_k}}{v_k}\left(\frac{\partial^2 g}{\partial v_k \partial v_k}\right)^{-1}\left(\frac{\partial g}{\partial v_k}\right)\hat{\alpha}_{v_k}\right] \times \left[\frac{\theta_{v_k}}{v_k}\left(\frac{\partial^2 g}{\partial v_k \partial v_k}\right)^{-1}\left(\frac{\partial g}{\partial v_L}\right)\hat{\alpha}_{v_L}\right] \tag{13}$$

In the special case where we have a Cobb–Douglas GDP function and where the efficiency gains are Hicks neutral, representing the efficiency gains through λ, both Equations (10) and (11) collapse to Equation (12):

$$\hat{Y} = \left(1 + \frac{\theta_{v_k}}{1 - \theta_{v_k}}\right)\hat{\lambda} \tag{14}$$

In Equation (14), the term $\theta_{v_k}/(1 - \theta_{v_k})$ is known as the Baldwin multiplier (Baldwin, 1992). It provides one indication of the gap between policy-induced changes in long-run GDP, and the effects captured in static models.

Variations in (11) and (13) have served as a relatively standard shortcut for estimating the medium-term investment-based impact of trade policy reforms (Francois *et al.*, 1997). Unfortunately, such an approach can be quite misleading. To be valid, such comparative statics between steady states assume that the starting point is itself a steady state. This may be a reasonable assumption for OECD countries. It certainly is not for many developing economies.

To illustrate the importance of this point, we turn now to the impact on income along the transition path, assuming a country is growing outside of the steady state. Francois *et al.* (1999) show that while Equation (14) holds in the steady state with a Cobb–Douglas GDP function, along the transition path we will have the following impact on incomes:

$$\hat{Y}(t) = h(k^* - k(0), t)\hat{\lambda}, \text{ where } h_1 > 0,\ h_2 > 0 \tag{15}$$

The critical component of Equation (15) is the $h(\cdot)$ function.[15] This is an increasing function of the gap between steady-state capital stocks per capita, k^*, and capital stocks at the time we experienced the policy reform $k(0)$. If we compare our original income at any point along the old growth path, $Y(t)$, and along the new growth path following the policy reform, then the proportional difference $\hat{Y}(t)$ is an increasing function of our distance from steady state. In other words, the poorer a country is, the greater is the income benefit at each point in time from a given policy shock. A consequence is that the impact on growth rates is also higher for faster growing countries than for countries closer to their long-run income levels.

Our discussion of the benefits of policy-induced investment does not support the more general claim that policy should target investment. Indeed, if we have no policy distortions to begin with, then a policy-induced increase in investment provides no benefit. This is because savers are then acting optimally, and are indifferent between current and future consumption. However, by its nature, policy reform is motivated by distortions that mean that the private and social returns to investment are not equal. In such cases, the welfare effects, such as the effect on income paths, can be quite substantial. What all of this suggests is that proper, intertemporal, multisector modeling should yield larger income gains for developing countries than frameworks that focus on steady-state comparisons would suggest.

There can be other reasons, apart from policy distortions, for a gap between private and social returns. This can follow, for example, from scale economies and related agglomeration effects, from labor market distortions, or from market power that varies across sectors (see Rutherford and Tarr, 2002, for a numerical example). All such cases point to potential welfare gains greater than static analysis would suggest, as long as investment levels increase, and as long as social returns exceed private returns. For small countries, they can be particularly large.

7.1. Adjustment costs

The absence of adjustment costs from most trade-focused CGE models has received a great deal of criticism (see, e.g., Ackerman, 2005). These can

[15] This is a much abbreviated version of the more elegant per-capita expression below from Francois *et al.* (1999), where a is the Cobb–Douglas coefficient for capital and k is the capital–labor ratio, n is population growth, and g is exogenous technical change.

$$\hat{y} = \left(1 - a\frac{(k(0)/k^*)^{(1-a)}e^{-(1-a)(n+g+\delta)t}}{[(k(0)/k^*)^{(1-a)} - 1]e^{-(1-a)(n+g+\delta)t} + 1}\right)\hat{\lambda}$$

be added to the dynamic framework outlined above by incorporating increasing costs of adjusting stock variables such as sectoral capital stocks, as is done by McKibbin and Sachs (1991) and McKibbin and Wilcoxen (1999). The presence of adjustment costs raises the costs of achieving the benefits associated with reforms, and delays the full receipt of these benefits. Along the adjustment path from the initial equilibrium, agents are seeking to minimize not just adjustment costs but also the combined costs of adjustment and being out of equilibrium, so that minimization of adjustment costs alone is an inadequate guide to policy formulation.

The presence of adjustment costs raises three important questions: (i) How large are these costs?; (ii) What influence do they have on the timing of reform?; and (iii) What policies might be used to reduce them? Matusz and Tarr (2000) examine the first question, using several case studies, and conclude that the social costs are generally very small relative to the benefits obtainable from trade reform, even when the benefits are measured using conventional procedures that generate small benefits. They also note that the private costs to individuals may frequently be greater than the social costs as, for example, when people are earning rents in employment from which they are displaced by trade reform.

Mussa (1984) analyzes the question of the optimal timing of policy reforms. He concludes that the presence of adjustment costs does not affect the optimal timing of reform unless there are distortions. If it is optimal to change from current trade policy to a better trade policy (which need not be free trade), without any distortions, the best approach is to make the policy change immediately. Delaying merely delays the receipt of the benefits from reform. Adjustment will reduce the benefits from reform, and will delay the full response to reform, but as long as agents are trading off accurately between the costs of adjustment (which increase with the rate of adjustment) and the costs of being out of equilibrium, markets, or an omniscient planner, will adjust efficiently.

Mussa (1984), however, notes that the presence of distortions can change this recommendation in many ways. If, for instance, labor markets are distorted, the optimal policy might involve either delay in implementation of reforms, or even subsidies to accelerate the rate of adjustment. Mussa's fundamental principle that adjustment costs are not policy-relevant in the absence of distortions, but potentially relevant in their presence, is an important organizing principle – allowing narrowing down of the situations in which adjustment costs are relevant, and better identification of appropriate policies in cases where they are. Models such as those of McKibbin and Wilcoxen (1999) that incorporate both adjustment costs and distortions in particular markets could potentially provide a framework for devising optimal policies for dealing with adjustment costs in the presence of distortions.

The speed at which the economy manages to redirect resources in response to liberalization is a direct reflection of the magnitude of adjustment costs. Adjustment costs depend on a wide number of factors.[16] However, the flexibility of labor and credit markets is of particular importance. If firms in sectors with potential for expansion do not have strong incentives to hire new employees, for instance because of administrative regulations or externally imposed labor market contract requirements, the adjustment will be more costly than otherwise. Likewise, firms will need to invest in order to exploit new opportunities, and this requires access to credit. The possibility of smooth adjustment also depends on the functioning of other markets. For example, the speed at which workers find alternative employment may depend on the flexibility of the housing market. Schaffner (2000) makes an important point in arguing that the focus should be shifted from the presence and size of adjustment costs to the need to design or reform institutions in ways that will reduce these costs.

Another reason why adjustment costs may be important involves political economy. Private adjustment costs are significant determinants, together with the long-run effects of trade liberalization, of the identity of winners and losers from trade liberalization. They influence the lineup of interests that might oppose trade liberalization, despite any aggregate gains it may bring. There is a fair amount of empirical evidence that trade liberalization may entail significant losses for some groups. For instance, several studies report that replaced workers may earn substantially less in their new occupations, even several years after replacement.[17]

8. *Exploring relative magnitudes*

So far, we have inventoried in a somewhat disparate fashion an extensive list of mechanisms from the literature that appear to link trade to performance. To repeat just a subset, economic welfare may rise in response to increased efficiency, increased availability of varieties, and increased quality of the available goods. Indeed these effects may interact. It seems reasonable to ask if these effects make a difference to current practice. In other words – should we care? We would answer this question "Yes!" and in this section provide some numeric examples to make

[16] The question of the appropriate design of government measures to ease adjustment has been the focus of a recent analytical economic literature (see e.g. *Journal of International Economics* 36, 1994, which contains several contributions). There is also an empirical literature that considers the efficiency of adjustment programs. A common finding is that the resources spent on these programs do not reach the intended targets, but are appropriated by others (see, e.g., Richardson, 1982).

[17] Jacobson *et al.* (1993a, 1993b) provide examples of the former case for the United States, while a more positive picture is painted in Mills and Sahn's (1995) study of Guinea.

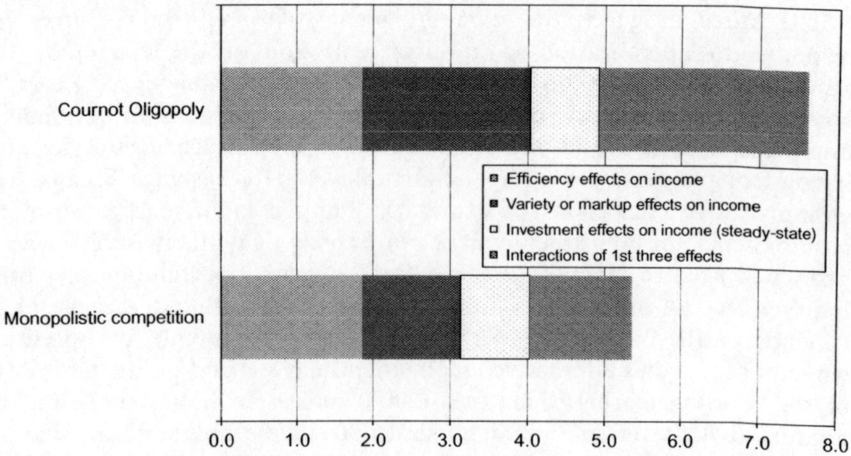

Fig. 3. Interaction of market structure and investment dynamics: real income effects of global free trade for Japan (percentage change). Source: Our own calculations.

our point. We focus on interactions between market structure (including variety) and investment.[18]

We work with a simple free trade experiment involving a two-region (Japan and the rest of the world), three-sector (primary, manufacturing, and services) model. Our application of this maquette model updates earlier estimates to combine both the GTAP model extensions for investment provided by Francois *et al.* (1996) and market structure features from Francois (1998). Figures 3 and 4 illustrate why it is important that we get the mechanisms right. The figures compare the impact on incomes, production, and trade that follow from a simple free trade experiment. While the experiment is identical in all cases, the model is not. On the basis of variations in models structure, Figure 3 provides a decomposition of real income effects from static efficiency gains, procompetitive effects (changes either if product varieties or markups), induced investment, and the interaction of all three. While all effects are, in isolation, important to total effects, it is also clear that they interact with each other, such that we have income effects that follow from the complex interaction of variety/markup, efficiency, and scale effects.

---

[18] Some work has been done to incorporate a love-of-variety in multiregion models in the behavior of consumers (Brown *et al.*, 1999), producers (Jensen *et al.*, 2004), and both (Francois *et al.*, 1996b; Francois and Roland-Holst, 1997). Little appears to have been done to allow for Grossman-Helpman (1992) type quality upgrading of producer and consumer goods, although Hummels and Klenow (2005) provide estimates that suggest it is important as a source of income gains. Hummels and Lugovskyy (2005) suggest that the benefits of increases in variety alone may be important in poor countries, but diminish in higher-income countries, where the range of available varieties is typically much wider.

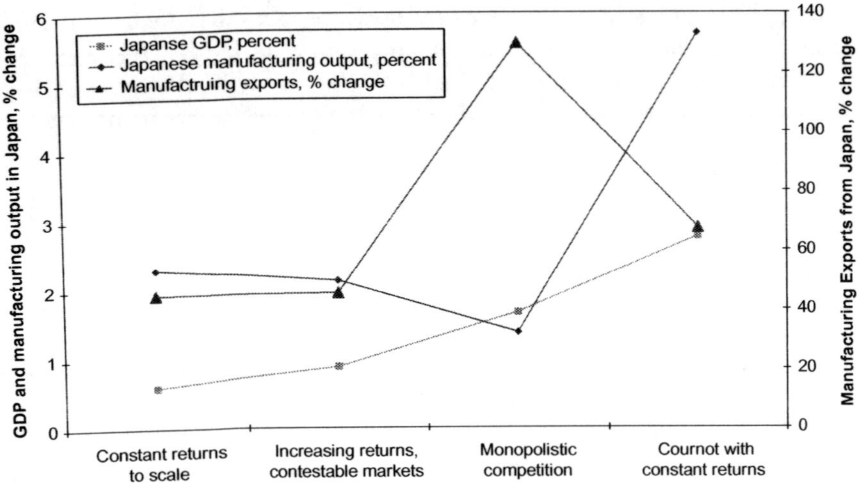

Fig. 4. Market structure and global free trade: effects on Japan. Source: Our own calculations.

In Figure 4, we have a different illustration of the same basic point. Figure 4 illustrates changes in income, manufacturing output, and manufacturing exports as we vary model structure. In addition to variations of degree, effects also vary in sign as a function of the underlying specification of market structure. These examples only reflect a subset of the structural issues raised here – variety, markup, and induced investment. The addition of quality upgrading and extensive margin trade growth would reinforce the basic point.

Indeed, casual evidence suggests that quality upgrading may be an important element of response to trade reform, and yet this appears to have been ignored both in the literature on trade and growth, and in the CGE literature. Unfortunately, the literature on the response of both product and process technology to trade reform is not widely used in the development of empirical models. One of the few things on which proponents and sceptics of trade reform in developing countries appear to agree is that such technological advances are potentially much more important than the static gains from greater exploitation of comparative advantage. Yet, little serious effort appears to be made to incorporate such linkages in a rigorous fashion.

9. Conclusions and recommendations

This (overly long) survey of welfare measurement in models of trade reform has identified a number of key areas in which further work seems to be needed to better understand the consequences of trade reform for welfare. Our discussion of the welfare measures actually used highlighted a stark difference between econometric models of the trade–growth relationship and CGE models. Econometric models typically focus entirely on advances in productivity resulting from improvements in production processes, a set of developments that is typically ignored or ruled out in CGE models (e.g., Anderson *et al.*, 2006). We show that these measures potentially omit a large amount of the gains from trade, including all of the potential gains in welfare at a given level of the PPF – the benefits that are the focus of trade theory and most CGE model applications.

The measures of welfare change used in CGE models are potentially a source of confusion. The money-metric version of equivalent variation that is almost universally used is potentially misleading for individual countries – if the current account is not closed, welfare can be raised in individual countries simply by raising spending relative to income. The estimates of welfare gains that it provides are not comparable across countries, and would lead to potentially serious over-estimation of welfare gains if labor supply were specified to be endogenous. Use of a compensation-based measure overcomes these problems by specifying welfare gains in terms of the international transfers of income that would be equivalent to the policy reforms considered. It also provides a potential basis for adjustments, reflecting differences in the purchasing power of these transfers to recipients living in different countries or regions.

The quality of the measures of trade policy distortions is another area where considerably more work appears to be needed. The standard procedures includes only tariffs, aggregates these tariffs using external trade weights, and ignores barriers to trade in services. In fact, recent World Bank (2005) research suggests that the tariff equivalents of nontariff barriers are generally higher than the tariffs on the same products, and that they tend to rise with income levels. If correct, applying a simple rule of thumb that the costs of distortions rises with the square of their level suggests that proper accounting for these distortions would raise the static welfare benefits of trade reform from the $278 billion annually estimated by Anderson *et al.* (2006) to $4.1 trillion per year.

The use of external trade weights to aggregate trade barriers is known to be flawed, since this weighting procedure leads to weights that decrease with the severity of the trade barrier, to the point where prohibitive trade barriers receive a zero weight. Careful work is needed to improve the procedures by which trade barriers are aggregated. While progress has been made with the development of the Trade Restrictiveness Index and the Mercantilist Trade Index (Anderson and Neary, 1992, 2003) and indexes for use in CGE models (Manole and Martin, 2005), more work is needed to integrate these measures in a form that allows their use in empirical studies of trade reform. Initial indications are that use of proper aggregation procedures would multiply the size of the measured, static gains from trade several fold.

The data on estimates of the barriers to trade in services – and on the volumes of trade themselves – are woefully inadequate. While theoretical frameworks that categorize the barriers to trade in services into measures affecting market access and those affecting flows of trade in services have been developed, we lack the information to routinely assign the available information on barriers to trade flows or production costs. As a consequence, the available estimates of the benefits of trade reform vary enormously across studies. Clearly, more work is needed to develop the analytical framework, and the data, needed as a basis for reliable, large-scale estimation of the consequences of reform.

Most CGE models use the Armington specification under which each country's exports are differentiated from those of other countries. Further, the available econometric estimates of these elasticities tend to be low (Krugman, 1989), making terms-of-trade impacts an important contributing factor to the overall welfare outcome even for small countries producing relatively homogenous products. Under this specification, countries never change either the range of products they produce, or the range of countries to which they export.

Increased attention to changes in the range and quality of products produced and exported is another important priority. The recent work of Hummels and Klenow (2005) makes an important point. The majority of export expansion associated with income growth seems to come at the extensive margin – through exports of new products. In addition, they find evidence of substantial improvements in the quality of exports from growing economies – a source of benefits ignored in previous work. Initial simulations that incorporate these effects in an analysis of export growth from China and India (Dimaranan *et al.*, 2006) indicate that they can substantially increase the gains to growing economies, and to the rest of the world. The work of Krugman (1989) and Feenstra (1994) suggests that failure to account for increases in the range of products exported may also be resulting in serious downward bias in the export demand elasticities used in quantitative analysis.

More work is clearly needed on the linkages between trade reform and productivity growth. The outpouring of work based on models such as Melitz (2003) that incorporate heterogeneity of firm productivity has identified an additional source of potential dynamic gains from trade reform. Firm rationalization by entry of more efficient firms into exporting, and the exit of less productive firms, appears to provide an important additional channel from trade reform to productivity and income. Recent empirical research also seems to suggest that the widespread rejection of Arrow-type learning-by-doing from exporting was perhaps premature.

Another key area is wider accounting for investment responses to reforms. Rutherford and Tarr (2002) have shown that accounting for increases in variety and the cumulative gains associated with investment may lead to order of magnitude increases in the measured gains from welfare reforms. Whether these gains can be realized or not depends heavily on the policy framework governing investment in the country.

It seems desirable to allow for responses of factor supply, and particularly labor supply, to changes resulting from reform. However, a move from the currently typical approach of specifying labor supply as fixed requires more than a simplistic specification such as a fixed consumer real wage. The supply of different types of labor needs to respond endogenously to wage rates, while wage and employment outcomes should depend on the specific institutions applying in the country.

Particularly if labor supply is made endogenous, welfare measurement should be moved to a compensation basis, rather than the almost ubiquitous money-metric basis. This avoids underestimation of the costs of raising tariffs associated with income effects operating on the supply of labor. It also allows comparability and addition of the measures across countries, and potentially their adjustment on to a PPP basis.

Clearly, despite many years of progress, much remains to be done before our economic models will be equal to the task of adequately capturing the consequences of trade reform. Current approaches focused on static comparative advantage are probably only measuring the tip of the iceberg, but way too little is known about the size or nature of the remainder of the iceberg.

References

Ackerman, F. (2005), The shrinking gains from trade: a critical assessment of Doha Round projections. Global Development and Environment Institute Working Paper No. 05-01, Tufts University, Medford, MA.

Aghion, P., Howitt, P. (2005), Appropriate growth policy: a unifying framework. Joseph Schumpeter Lecture delivered to the 20th Annual Congress of the European Economic Association, Amsterdam.

Anderson, J.E. (2009), Consistent policy aggregation. *International Economic Review* 50 (3), 903–927.

Anderson, K., Hayami, Y. (1986), *The Political Economy of Agricultural Protection East Asia in International Perspective*. Allen and Unwin, London.

Anderson, J.E., Martin, W. (1998), Evaluating public expenditures when governments must rely on distortionary taxation. World Bank Policy Research Working Paper No. 1981, World Bank.

Anderson, K., Martin, W. (Eds.) (2006). *Agricultural Trade Reform and the Doha Development Agenda*. Palgrave Macmillan and the World Bank, Basingstoke and Washington, DC.

Anderson, J.E., Martin, W. (in press), Costs of taxation and benefits of public goods with multiple taxes and goods. *Journal of Public Economic Theory*.

Anderson, J., Neary, J.P. (1992), Trade reform with quotas, partial rent retention, and tariffs. *Econometrica* 60 (1), 57–76.

Anderson, J., Neary, J.P. (2003), The mercantilist index of trade policy. *International Economic Review* 44 (2), 627–649.

Anderson, J.E., van Wincoop, E. (2004), Trade costs. *Journal of Economic Literature* 42 (September), 691–751.

Anderson, K., Martin, W., van der Mensbrugghe, D. (2006), Doha merchandise trade reform: what's at stake for developing countries? World Bank Policy Research Working Paper 3418. Available at http://www.worldbank.org/trade/wtowww.worldbank.org/trade/wto. Submitted to *World Bank Economic Review*.

Ardelean, A. (2006), How strong is the love of variety? Paper presented to the European Trade Study Group Conference, Vienna, September. Available at www.etsg.org

Armington, P. (1969), A theory of demand for products distinguished by place of production. *IMF Staff Papers* 16 (1), 159–178.

Arrow, K. (1962), The economic implications of learning by doing. *Review of Economic Studies* 29 (3), 155–173.

Bach, C., Martin, W. (2001), Would the right tariff aggregator for policy analysis please stand up? *Journal of Policy Modeling* 23, 621–635.

Bach, C., Pearson, K. (1996), Implementing quotas in GEMPACK or how to linearize an inequality. GTAP Technical Paper No. 4, Global Trade Analysis Project, Purdue University. Available at www.gtap.org

Baggs, J., Head, K., Ries, J. (2002), Free trade, firm heterogeneity and Canadian productivity. Mimeo, University of British Columbia. Available at www.sauder.ubc.ca. Accessed on January 15, 2006.

Baldwin, R.E. (1992), Measurable dynamic gains from trade. *Journal of Political Economy* 100 (1), 162–174.

Baldwin, R.E. (2005), Heterogeneous firms and trade: testable and untestable properties of the Melitz model. NBER Working Paper No. 11471, National Bureau of Economic Research, Cambridge, MA.

Baldwin, R.E., Venables, A.J. (1995), Regional economic integration. In: Grossman, G., Rogoff, K. (Eds.), *Handbook of International Economics* (Vol. III). North Holland, Amsterdam.

Baldwin, R.E., Francois, J., Portes, R. (1997), Costs and benefits of eastern enlargement: the impact on the EU and central Europe. *Economic Policy* 12 (24), 125–170.

Ballard, C., Fullerton, D. (1992), Distortionary taxes and the provision of public goods. *Journal of Economic Perspectives* 6 (3), 117–131.

Bartelsman, E., Haltiwanger, J., Scarpetta, S. (2005), Measuring and analyzing cross-country differences in productivity. Mimeo. Available at http://www.euklems.net/meetings/CM_Helsinki/Bartelsman,_Haltiwanger_&_Scarpetta_(2005).pdf

Bernard, A.B, Redding, S.J., Schott, P.K. (2006), Multi-product firms and trade liberalization. NBER Working Paper No. 12782, National Bureau of Economic Research, Cambridge, MA.

Bernard, A., Jensen, J. (1999), Exceptional exporter performance: cause, effect, or both? *Journal of International Economics* 47, 1–25.

Bernhofen, D., Brown, J. (2005), An empirical assessment of the comparative advantage gains from trade: evidence from Japan. *American Economic Review* 95 (1), 208–222.

Bhagwati, J. (1978), Anatomy and consequences of exchange control regimes. In: *Foreign Trade Regimes and Economic Development* (Vol. 11). Ballinger Publishing Co. (for the National Bureau of Economic Research), Cambridge, MA.

Bhagwati, J. (1982), Directly unproductive, profit-seeking (DUP) activities. *Journal of Political Economy* 90 (5), 988–1002.

Blalock, G., Gertler, P. (2004), Learning from exporting revisited in a less developed setting. *Journal of Development Economics* 75, 397–416.

Bouët, A., Decreux, Y., Fontagné, L., Jean, S., Laborde, D. (2004), A consistent, *ad valorem* equivalent measure of applied protection across the world: the MAcMaps-HS6 database. CEPII Working Paper No. 2004-22, CEPII, Paris.

Brown, D. (1994), Properties of applied general equilibrium trade models with monopolistic competition and foreign direct investment. In: Francois, J., Shiells, C. (Eds.), *Modeling Trade Policy: Applied General Equilibrium Assessments of North American Free Trade*. Cambridge University Press, Cambridge, UK.

Brown, D., Deardorff, A., Stern, R. (1999), *The Michigan Model of World Production and Trade*. The MIT Press, Cambridge, MA. http://www.fordschool.umich.edu/rsie/model/. Accessed on January 15 2006.

Chang, R., Kaltani, L., Loayza, N. (2005), Openness can be good for growth: the role of policy complementarities. World Bank Policy Research Working Paper No. 3763, September.

Choksi, A., Michaely, M., Papageorgiou, D. (Eds.) (1989). *Liberalizing Foreign Trade*. Oxford University Press, Oxford.

Clerides, S., Lach, S., Tybout, J. (1998), Is learning by exporting important? Micro-dynamic evidence from Colombia, Mexico and Morocco. *Quarterly Journal of Economics* 113 (3), 903–947.

Cox, D., Harris, R. (1985), Trade liberalization and industrial organization: some estimates for Canada. *Journal of Political Economy* 93 (1), 115–145.

Dahlby, B. (1998), Progressive taxation and the social marginal cost of public funds. *Journal of Public Economics* 67, 105–122.

Deardorff, A., Stern, R. (1998), *Measurement of Nontariff Barriers*. University of Michigan Press, Ann Arbor, MI.

Dee, P., Ferrantino, M. (2005), *Quantitative Methods for Assessing the Effects of Non-Tariff Measures and Trade Facilitation*. World Scientific

Publishing and the Asia-Pacific Economic Cooperation Committee on Trade and Investment, Singapore.

Dee, P., Hanslow, K., Phamduc, T. (2000), Measuring the cost of barriers to trade in services. Paper presented to the Eleventh Annual NBER East Asian Seminar, 22–24 June, Seoul.

De Gorter, H., Kliauga, E. (2006), Reducing tariffs versus expanding tariff rate quotas. In: Anderson, K., Martin, W. (Eds.), *Agricultural Trade Reform and the Doha Development Agenda*. Palgrave Macmillan and the World Bank, Basingstoke and Washington, DC.

Department of Foreign Affairs and Trade (1999), *Global Trade Reform: Maintaining Momentum*. Australian Department of Foreign Affairs and Trade, Canberrawww.thecie.com.au

Dervis, K., de Melo, J., Robinson, S. (1981), A general equilibrium analysis of foreign exchange shortages in a developing economy. *Economic Journal* 91, 891–906.

Devarajan, S., Rodrik, D. (1991), Pro-competitive effects of trade reform: results from a CGE model of Cameroon. *European Economic Review* 35 (July), 1157–1184.

Dimaranan, B., Ianchovichina, E., Martin, W. (2006), Competing with giants: who wins, who loses? In: Winters, L.A., Yusuf, S. (Eds.), *Dancing with Giants*. World Bank, Washington, DC.

Dixit, P., Stiglitz, J. (1977), Monopolistic competition and optimum product diversity. *American Economic Review* 67, 297–308.

Dixon, P., Parmenter, B., Sutton, J., Vincent, D. (1982), *ORANI: a multi-sectoral model of the Australian economy*. North Holland, Amsterdam.

Dollar, D. (1992), Outward-oriented developing economies really do grow more rapidly: evidence from 95 LDCs, 1976–1985. *Economic Development and Cultural Change* 40 (3), 523–544.

Dollar, D., Kraay, A. (2003), Institutions, trade, and growth. *Journal of Monetary Economics* 50, 133–162.

Dollar, D., Kraay, A. (2004), Trade, growth, and poverty. *Economic Journal* 114, F22–F49.

Easterly, W., Levine, R. (2001), It's not factor accumulation: stylized facts and growth models. *World Bank Economic Review* 15 (2), 177–219.

Edwards, S. (1993), Openness, trade liberalization, and growth in developing countries. *Journal of Economic Literature* 31 (3), 1358–1393.

Evenett, S., Venables, A. (2002), *Export Growth in Developing Countries: Market Entry and Bilateral Trade Flows*. Available at www.alexandria.unisg.ch/Publikationen/22177

Falvey, R., Greenaway, D., Yu, Z., Gullstrand, E. (2004), Exports, restructuring and industry productivity growth. Research Paper No. 2004/40, University of Nottingham.

Fan, Z. (2006). Preferential trade agreements in Asia: alternative scenarios of hub and spoke. Paper presented at the Conference on Global Economic Analysis, Addis Ababa, June. Available at www.gtap.org

Feder, G. (1983), On exports and economic growth. *Journal of Development Economics* 12, 59–73.

Feenstra, R. (1994), New product varieties and the measurement of international prices. *American Economic Review* 84 (1), 157–177.

Fernandes, A., Isgut, A. (2006), Learning-by-exporting effects: are they for real? Mimeo, World Bank.

Francois, J.F. (1998), Scale economies and imperfect competition in the GTAP model. GTAP consortium Technical Paper No. 14. Available at http://www.gtap.agecon.purdue.edu/resources/res_display.asp?RecordID=317

Francois, J.F. (2001), *The Next WTO Round: North-South Stakes in New Market Access Negotiations*. CIES, University of Adelaide, and the Tinbergen Institute, Adelaide.

Francois, J.F., Hoekman, B. (in press), Services trade and policy. *Journal of Economic Literature*.

Francois, J., Martin, W. (2004), Commercial policy, bindings and market access. *European Economic Review* 48 (June), 665–679.

Francois, J.F., Roland-Holst, D.W. (1997), Scale economies and imperfect competition. In: Francois, J.F., Reinert, K.A. (Eds.), *Applied Methods for Trade Policy Analysis: A Handbook*. Cambridge University Press, New York.

Francois, J.F., McDonald, B., Nordstrom, H. (1995), Assessing the Uruguay round. In: Martin, W., Winters, L.A. (Eds.), *The Uruguay Round and the Developing Economies*. World Bank, Washington, DC.

Francois, J.F., McDonald, B., Nordstrom, H. (1996), Trade liberalization and the capital stock in the GTAP model. GTAP Consortium Technical Paper No. 07. Available at http://www.gtap.agecon.purdue.edu/resources/res_display.asp?RecordID=310

Francois, J., McDonald, B., Nordström, H. (1996a), A user's guide to Uruguay round assessments. CEPR Discussion Paper No. 1410, Centre for Economic Policy Research, London.

Francois, J., McDonald, B., Nordström, H. (1996b), The Uruguay round: a numerically based qualitative assessment. In: Martin, W., Winters, A. (Eds.), *The Uruguay Round and Developing Countries*. Cambridge University Press, Cambridge, UK.

Francois, J.F., McDonald, B.J., Nordstrom, H. (1997), Capital accumulation in applied trade models. In: Francois, J.F., Reinert, K.A. (Eds.), *Applied Methods for Trade Policy Analysis: A Handbook*. Cambridge University Press, New York.

Francois, J., Nordström, H., Shiells, C. (1999), Transition dynamics and trade policy reform in developing countries. In: Baldwin, R.E., Francois, J.F. (Eds.), *Dynamic Issues in Applied Commercial Policy Analysis*. Cambridge University Press, Cambridge, UK.

Francois, J.F., van Meijl, H., van Tongeren, F. (2005), Trade liberalization in the Doha development round. *Economic Policy* 20 (42), 349–391.

Frankel, J.A., Romer, D. (1999), Does trade cause growth? *American Economic Review* 89 (3), 379–399.

Frankel, J., Rose, A.K. (2002), An estimate of the effect of common currencies on trade and growth. *Quarterly Journal of Economics* 117 (469), 437–466.

Freund, C., Bolaky, B. (2004), Trade, regulations, and growth. World Bank Policy Research Working Paper No. 3255, November.

Fujita, M., Krugman, P., Venables, A. (1999), *The Spatial Economy: Cities, Regions and International Trade*. MIT Press, Cambridge, MA.

Fullerton, D. (1991), Reconciling recent estimates of the marginal welfare cost of taxation. *American Economic Review* 81 (1), 302–308.

Gatto, M., Mion, G., Ottaviano, G. (2006), Trade integration, firm selection and the costs of non-Europe. CEPR Discussion Paper No. 5730, Center for Economic Policy Research, London, June.

Girma, S., Greenaway, D., Kneller, R. (2004), Does exporting increase productivity? A microeconometric analysis of matched firms. *Review of International Economics* 12 (5), 855–866.

Greenaway, D., Morgan, W., Wright, P. (2002), Trade liberalization and growth in developing countries. *Journal of Development Economics* 67, 229–244.

Grossman, G., Helpman, E. (1992), *Innovation and Growth in the Global Economy*. MIT Press, Cambridge, MA.

Haberler, G. (1950), *International Trade and Economic Development*. National Bank of Egypt, Cairo.

Harberger, A. (1954), Monopoly and resource allocation. *American Economic Review* 44 (2), 77–87.

Harberger, A. (1971), Three basic postulates for applied welfare economics: an interpretative essay. *Journal of Economic Literature* 9, 785–797.

Harris, R.G. (1984), Applied general equilibrium analysis of small open economies with scale economies and imperfect competition. *American Economic Review* 74 (5), 1016–1032.

Harrison, A. (1994), Productivity, imperfect competition and trade reform. *Journal of International Economics* 36, 53–76.

Harrison, A., Leamer, E. (1997), Labor markets in developing countries: an agenda for research. *Journal of Labor Economics* 15 (July), S1–S19.

Harrison, G., Rutherford, T., Tarr, D. (1995), Quantifying the Uruguay round. In: Martin, W., Winters, L.A. (Eds.), *The Uruguay Round and the Developing Countries*. Cambridge University Press, Cambridge.

Harrison, G., Rutherford, T., Tarr, D. (2002), Trade policy options for Chile: the importance of market access. *World Bank Economic Review* 16 (1), 49–79.

Hausmann, R., Rodrik, D. (2003), Economic development as self-discovery. *Journal of Development Economics* 72, 603–633.

Hausmann, R., Rodrik, D., Velasco, A. (2004), Growth diagnostics. Mimeo, Kennedy School of Government, Harvard University.

Hertel, T. (Ed.) (1997). *Global Trade Analysis: Modeling and Applications.* Cambridge University Press, New York.

Hertel, T., Hoekman, B., Martin, W. (2002), Developing countries and a new round of WTO negotiations. *World Bank Research Observer* 17 (1), 113–140.

Hoekman, B., Messerlin, P. (2006), Removing the exception of agricultural export subsidies. In: Anderson, K., Martin, W. (Eds.), *Agricultural Trade Reform and the Doha Development Agenda.* Palgrave Macmillan and the World Bank, Basingstoke and Washington, DC.

Huang, J., Rozelle, S., Chang, M. (2004), The nature of distortions to agricultural incentives in China and implications of WTO accession. In: Bhattasali, D., Li, S., Martin, W. (Eds.), *China and the WTO: Accession, Policy Reform and Poverty Reduction Strategies.* Oxford University Press and the World Bank.

Hummels, D. (2001), Time as a trade barrier. Mimeo, Purdue University.

Hummels, D., Klenow, P. (2005), The variety and quality of a nation's exports. *American Economic Review* 95 (3), 704–723.

Hummels, D., Lugovsky, V. (2005), *Trade in Ideal Varieties: Theory and Evidence.* NBER Working Paper Number 11828.

Ianchovichina, E., Martin, W. (2004), Economic impacts of China's accession to the world trade organization. *World Bank Economic Review* 18 (1), 3–28.

IMF (2005), Review of the IMF's trade restrictiveness index. International Monetary Fund, February 14. Available at www.imf.org

Independent Evaluation Group (IEG) (2006), *Assessing World Bank Support for Trade, 1987–2004.* World Bank, Washington, DC.

Jacobson, L.S., LaLonde, R.J., Sullivan, D.G. (1993a), Earnings losses of displaced workers. *American Economic Review* 83 (4), 685–709.

Jacobson, L.S., LaLonde, R.J., Sullivan, D.G. (1993b), Long-term earnings losses of high-seniority displaced workers. *Federal Reserve Bank of Chicago Economic Perspectives* 17 (6), 2–20.

Jean, S., Laborde, D., Martin, W. (2006), Consequences of alternative formulas for agricultural tariff cuts. In: Anderson, K., Martin, W. (Eds.), *Agricultural Trade Reform and the Doha Development Agenda.* Palgrave Macmillan and the World Bank, Basingstoke and Washington, DC.

Jensen, J., Tarr, D. (2003), Trade, exchange rate and energy pricing reform in Iran: potentially large efficiency effects and gains to the poor. *Review of Development Economics* 7 (4), 543–562.

Jensen, J., Rutherford, T., Tarr, D. (2004), The impact of liberalizing barriers to foreign direct investment in services: the case of Russian accession to the World Trade Organization. *Review of Development Economics* 11 (3), 482–506.

Johnson, H.G. (1977), Changing views on trade and development: some reflections. *Economic Development and Cultural Change* 25 (Supplement), 363–375.

Jones, R., Neary, J.P. (1984), The positive theory of international trade. In: Jones, R., Kenen, P. (Eds.), *Handbook of International Economics* (Vol. 1). North-Holland, Amsterdam.

Just, R., Hueth, D., Schmitz, A. (1982), *Applied Welfare Economics and Public Policy*. Prentice-Hall, Englewood Cliffs, NJ.

Kee, H.L., Nicita, A., Olarreaga, M. (2005), Import demand elasticities and trade distortions. CEPR Discussion Paper No. 4669, and World Bank Policy Research Working Paper No. 3452.

Kee, H.L., Nicita, A., Olarreaga, M. (2009), Estimating trade restrictiveness indices. *Economic Journal* 119 (534), 172–199.

Kehoe, T., Ruhl, K. (2003), How important is the new goods margin in international trade? Federal Reserve Bank of Minneapolis Staff Report No. 324.

Kohli, U. (2004), Real GDP, real domestic income, and terms-of-trade changes. *Journal of International Economics* 62, 83–106.

Konan, D., Maskus, K. (2006), Quantifying the impact of services liberalization in a developing country. *Journal of Development Economics* 81, 142–162.

Krueger, A. (1974), The political economy of the rent-seeking society. *American Economic Review* 64 (3), 291–303.

Krueger, A. (1978), Liberalization attempts and consequences. In: *Foreign Trade Regimes and Economic Development* (Vol. 11). Ballinger Publishing Co. (for the National Bureau of Economic Research), Cambridge, MA.

Krugman, P. (1989), Differences in income elasticities and trends in real exchange rates. *European Economic Review* 33 (5), 1031–1046.

Laborde, D., Martin, W., van der Mensbrugghe (2010), Measuring the benefits of global trade reform with consistent aggregators of distortions. Policy Research Working Paper, World Bank, Washington, DC.

Lindert, P. (1991), Historical patterns of agricultural protection. In: Timmer, P. (Ed.), *Agriculture and the State*. Cornell University Press, Ithaca, NY.

Lindert, P., Williamson, G. (2002), Does globalization make the world more unequal? NBER Working Paper No. 8228, National Bureau of Economic Research, Cambridge.

Lloyd, P., Schweinberger, A. (1988), Trade expenditure functions and the gains from trade. *Journal of International Economics* 24 (May), 275–297.

Magee, S. (1972), The welfare effects of restrictions on U.S. trade. *Brookings Papers on Economic Activity* 1972 (3), 645–701.

Manole, V., Martin, W. (2005), Keeping the devil in the details: a feasible approach to aggregating trade distortions. Paper presented at the European Trade Study Group Meetings, Dublin, September.

Markusen, J.R., Melvin, J.R., Kaempfer, W.H., Maskus, K.E. (1995), *International Trade: Theory and Evidence*. McGraw-Hill, New York.

Martin, W. (1993), Modelling the post-reform Chinese economy. *Journal of Policy Modeling* 15 (5 and 6), 549–579.

Martin, W. (1997), Measuring welfare changes with distortions. In: Francois, K., Reinert, K. (Eds.), *Applied Methods for Trade Policy Analysis*. Cambridge University Press, Cambridge.

Martin, W., Anderson, J. (2005), Costs of taxation and the benefits of public goods: the role of income effects. World Bank Policy Research Working Paper No. 3700.

Martin, W., Dimaranan, B., Hertel, T., Ianchovichina, E. (2003), Trade policy, structural change, and China's trade growth. In: Hope, N., Yang, D.T., Li, M.Y. (Eds.), *How Far Across the River? Chinese Policy Reform at the Millennium*. University of Chicago Press, Chicago.

Maskus, K., Wilson, J. S. (Eds.) (2001). *Quantifying the Impact of Technical Barriers to Trade: Can it be Done?* University of Michigan Press, Ann Arbor.

Matusz, S., Tarr, D. (2000), Adjusting to trade policy reform. In: Krueger, A. (Ed.), *Economic Policy Reform: The Second Stage*. University of Chicago Press, Chicago, Also available as World Bank Policy Research Working Paper No. 2142, 1999. www.worldbank.org

McKibbin, W., Sachs, J. (1991), *Global Linkages: Macroeconomic Interdependence and Cooperation in the Global Economy*. The Brookings Institution, Washington, DC.

McKibbin, W., Wilcoxen, P. (1999), The theoretical and empirical structure of the G-cubed model. *Economic Modelling* 16, 123–148, Also, Brookings Discussion Papers in International Economics No. 118, December 1995.

Melitz, M. (2003), The impact of trade on intra-industry reallocations and aggregate industry productivity. *Econometrica* 71 (6), 1695–1725.

Mills, B.F., Sahn, D.E. (1995), Reducing the size of the public sector workforce: institutional constraints and human consequences in Guinea. *Journal of Development Studies* 31 (4), 505–528.

Melitz, M., Ottaviano, G. (2005), Market size, trade and productivity. NBER Working Paper No. 11393, National Bureau of Economic Research, Cambridge, MA.

Mussa, M. (1984), The adjustment process and the timing of trade liberalization. NBER Working Paper No. 1458, National Bureau of Economic Research, Cambridge, MA.

Mundell, R. (1962), The appropriate use of monetary and fiscal policy for internal and external stability. *IMF Staff Papers* 9, 70–79.

Ng, F., Yeats, A. (1999), Production sharing in East Asia: who does what for whom and why? World Bank Policy Research Working Paper No. 2197.

Noguer, M., Siscart, M. (2005), Trade raises income: a precise and robust result. *Journal of International Economics* 65, 447–460.

OECD (2005), *Agricultural Policies in OECD Countries: Monitoring and Outlook*. OECD, Paris.

Puga, D., Venables, A.J. (1999), Agglomeration and economic development: import substitution vs. trade liberalisation. *Economic Journal* 109 (455), 292–311.

Polaski, S. (2006), *Winners and Losers: Impact of the Doha Round on Developing Countries*. Carnegie Endowment for International Peace, Washington, DC.

Richardson, D. (1982), Trade adjustment assistance under the United States trade act of 1974: an analytical examination and worker survey. In: Bhagwati, J. (Ed.), *Import Competition and Response*. University of Chicago Press, Chicago.

Rodriguez, F., Rodrik, D. (2001), Trade policy and economic growth: a Skeptic's guide to the cross-national evidence. In: Bernanke, B., Rogoff, K.S. (Eds.), *Macroeconomics Annual 2000*. MIT Press (for the National Bureau of Economic Research), Cambridge, MA, pp. 261–324.

Rodrik, D. (2006), What's so special about China's exports? CEPR Discussion Paper No. 5484, Center for Economic Policy Research, London.

Rodrik, D., Subramanian, A., Trebbi, F. (2004), Institutions rule: the primacy of institutions over geography and integration in economic development. *Journal of Economic Growth* 9, 131–165.

Roland-Holst, D.W., Reinert, K.A., Shiells, C.R. (1994), A general equilibrium analysis of North American economics integration. In: Francois, J.F., Shiells, C.R. (Eds.), *Modeling Trade Policy: Applied General Equilibrium Assessments of North American Free Trade*. Cambridge University Press, New York, pp. 47–82.

Romer, P. (1994), New goods, old theory and the welfare costs of trade restrictions. *Journal of Development Economics* 43, 5–38.

Ruhl, K. (2005), Solving the elasticity puzzle in international economics. Unpublished paper, University of Texas at Austin. Available at http://www.eco.utexas.edu

Rutherford, T., Tarr, D. (2002), Trade liberalization, product variety and growth in a small open economy: a quantitative assessment. *Journal of International Economics* 56, 247–272.

Sachs, J.D., Warner, A.M. (1995), Economic convergence and economic policies. *Brookings Papers in Economic Activity* (1), 1–95.

Schaffner, J. (2000), Comment on the paper by Matusz and Tarr. In: Krueger, A. (Ed.), *Economic Policy Reform: The Second Stage*. University of Chicago Press, Chicago.

Schott, P. (2004), Across-product versus within-product specialization in international trade. *Quarterly Journal of Economics* 119 (2), 647–678.

Smith, A., Venables, A. (1988), Completing the internal market in the European community. *European Economic Review* 32, 1501–1525.

Tarr, D. (1990), Second-best foreign exchange policy in the presence of domestic price controls and export subsidies. *World Bank Economic Review* 4 (2), 175–193.

Tybout, J. (2003), Plant and firm-level evidence on new trade theories. In: Choi, K., Harrigan, J. (Eds.), *Handbook of International Trade*. Blackwell, Malden, MA.

UN (1968), *A System of National Accounts*. United Nations, New York.

van Biesebrock, J. (2005), Exporting raises productivity in sub-Saharan African manufacturing firms. *Journal of International Economics* 67, 373–391.

Varian, H. (1984), *Microeconomic Analysis*. Norton, New York.

Venables, A. (2004), Small, remote and poor? *World Trade Review* 3, 453–457.

Viner, J. (1952), *International Trade and Economic Development*. Free Press, Glencoe, IL.

Wacziarg, R., Welch, K.H. (2003), Trade liberalization and growth: new evidence. NBER Working Paper No. 10152, December.

Wade, R. (2004), *Governing the Market: Economic Theory and the Role of Government in East Asian Industrialization*, second paperback ed. Princeton University Press, Princeton.

Warlters, M., Auriol, E. (2005), The marginal cost of public funds in Africa. Policy Research Working Paper No. 3679, World Bank, Washington, DC.

Williamson, J. (2000), What should the World Bank think about the Washington consensus? *The World Bank Research Observer* 15 (2), 251–264.

Wilson, J., Mann, C., Otsuki, T. (2005), Assessing the global benefits of trade facilitation: a global perspective. *The World Economy* 28 (6), 841–871.

Winters, L.A. (2004), Trade liberalization and economic performance: an overview. *Economic Journal* 114 (February), F4–F21.

Winters, L.A., Martins, P. (2004), When comparative advantage is not enough: business costs in small, remote economies. *World Trade Review* 3, 347–383.

World Bank (2004), *Global Economic Prospects 2004: Realizing the Development Promise of the Doha Agenda*. World Bank, Washington, DC.

World Bank (2005), *Global Monitoring Report 2005*. World Bank, Washington, DC.

WTO (1995), *The Results of the Uruguay Round of Multilateral Trade Agreements: The Legal Texts*. World Trade Organization, Geneva.